ENCYCLOPEDIA OF
EVALUATION

Encyclopedia of Evaluation
Editorial Board

ENCYCLOPEDIA OF
EVALUATION

─○─

EDITOR
SANDRA MATHISON
UNIVERSITY OF BRITISH COLUMBIA

DISCARDED

Sponsored by the American Evaluation Association
www.eval.org

A SAGE Reference Publication

SAGE Publications
Thousand Oaks ■ London ■ New Delhi

For my parents
Mildred and George Mathison
who have quietly supported me in so many ways

For information:

Sage Publications, Inc.
2455 Teller Road
Thousand Oaks, California 91320
E-mail: order@sagepub.com

Sage Publications Ltd.
1 Oliver's Yard
55 City Road
London EC1Y 1SP
United Kingdom

Sage Publications India Pvt. Ltd.
B-42, Panchsheel Enclave
Post Box 4109
New Delhi 110 017 India

Printed in the United States of America

Library of Congress Cataloging-in-Publication Data

Mathison, Sandra.
Encyclopedia of evaluation / Sandra Mathison.
    p. cm.
Includes bibliographical references and index.
ISBN 0-7619-2609-7 (cloth)
  1. Evaluation research (Social action programs)—Encyclopedias. I. Title.
H62.M312 2005
001.4′03—dc22

                            2004009988

04   05   06   07   10 9 8 7 6 5 4 3 2 1

Acquisitions Editor:	Lisa Cuevas Shaw
Editorial Assistant:	Margo Beth Crouppen
Production Editor:	Melanie Birdsall
Copy Editor:	Catherine M. Chilton
Typesetter:	C&M Digitals (P) Ltd.
Proofreader:	Kris Bergstad
Indexer:	Molly Hall
Cover Designer:	Michelle Kenny

Contents

List of Entries

Reader's Guide

CONCEPTS, EVALUATION

Advocacy in Evaluation
Evaluand
Evaluation
Evaluator
Evaluator Roles
External Evaluation
Formative Evaluation
Goal
Grading
Independence
Internal Evaluation
Judgment
Logic of Evaluation
Merit
Metaevaluation
Objectives
Personnel Evaluation
Process Evaluation
Product Evaluation
Program Evaluation
Quality
Ranking
Standard Setting
Standards
Summative Evaluation
Synthesis
Value Judgment
Values
Worth

CONCEPTS, METHODOLOGICAL

Accountability
Achievement
Affect
Analysis
Applied Research

Appraisal
Appropriateness
Assessment
Audience
Best Practices
Black Box
Capacity Building
Client
Client Satisfaction
Consumer
Consumer Satisfaction
Control Conditions
Cost
Cost Effectiveness
Criterion-Referenced Test
Critique
Cut Score
Description
Design Effects
Dissemination
Effectiveness
Efficiency
Feasibility
Hypothesis
Impact Assessment
Implementation
Improvement
Indicators
Inputs
Inspection
Interpretation
Intervention
Interviewing
Literature Review
Longitudinal Studies
Measurement
Modus Operandi
Most Significant
    Change Technique
Norm-Referenced Tests
Opportunity Costs
Outcomes

Outputs
Peer Review
Performance Indicator
Performance Program
Personalizing Evaluation
Rapport
Reactivity
Reliability
Sampling
Score Card
Secondary Analysis
Services
Setting
Significance
Situational Responsiveness
Social Indicators
Sponsor
Stakeholder Involvement
360-Degree Evaluation
Treatments
Triangulation

CONCEPTS, PHILOSOPHICAL

Aesthetics
Ambiguity
Amelioration
Argument
Authenticity
Authority of Evaluation
Bias
Conclusions, Evaluative
Consequential Validity
Construct Validity
Context
Credibility
Criteria
Difference Principle
Empiricism

EVALUATION THEORY

Activity Theory
Evaluation Theory
Program Logic
Program Theory
Theory in Action
Theory-Driven Evaluation
Transdiscipline

LAWS AND LEGISLATION

Aid to Families With
    Dependent Children (AFDC)
Elementary and Secondary
    Education Act (ESEA)
Goals 2000
Government and Evaluation
Government Performance
    and Results Act (GPRA)
Legislative Monitoring
A Nation at Risk
No Child Left Behind (NCLB)

ORGANIZATIONS

Abt Associates
Active Learning Network for
    Accountability and Performance
    in Humanitarian Action (ALNAP)
American Institutes for Research (AIR)
American Evaluation Association (AEA)
Buros Institute
Centers for Disease
    Control and Prevention (CDC)
Center for the Study of Evaluation (CSE)
Center for Instructional Research and
    Curriculum Evaluation (CIRCE)
Center for Research on
    Evaluation, Standards,
    and Student Testing (CRESST)
Centre for Applied Research
    in Education (CARE)
ERIC Clearinghouse on
    Assessment and Evaluation
Evaluation Center, The
Evaluation Research Society (ERS)
Evaluators' Institute™, The
General Accounting Office (GAO)
International Development
    Evaluation Association (IDEAS)
International Development
    Research Center (IDRC)
International Organization for
    Cooperation in Evaluation (IOCE)

International Program in Development
    Evaluation Training (IPDET)
Joint Committee on Standards for
    Educational Evaluation
Mathematica Policy Research
MDRC
National Assessment of
    Educational Progress (NAEP)
National Institutes of Health (NIH)
National Science Foundation (NSF)
Organisation for Economic Co-operation
    and Development (OECD)
Performance Assessment
    Resource Centre (PARC)
Philanthropic Evaluation
RAND Corporation
Research Triangle Institute (RTI)
United States Agency of International
    Development (USAID)
Urban Institute
Westat
WestEd
World Bank
World Conservation Union (IUCN)

PEOPLE

Abma, Tineke A.
Adelman, Clem
Albæk, Erik
Alkin, Marvin C.
Altschuld, James W.
Bamberger, Michael J.
Barrington, Gail V.
Bhola, H. S.
Bickel, William E.
Bickman, Leonard
Bonnet, Deborah G.
Boruch, Robert
Brisolara, Sharon
Campbell, Donald T.
Campos, Jennie
Chalmers, Thomas
Chelimsky, Eleanor
Chen, Huey-Tsyh
Conner, Ross
Cook, Thomas D.
Cooksy, Leslie
Cordray, David
Cousins, J. Bradley
Cronbach, Lee J.
Dahler-Larsen, Peter
Datta, Lois-ellin
Denny, Terry
Eisner, Elliot
Engle, Molly
Farrington, David

Fetterman, David M.
Fitzpatrick, Jody L.
Forss, Kim
Fournier, Deborah M.
Freeman, Howard E.
Frierson, Henry T.
Funnell, Sue
Georghiou, Luke
Glass, Gene V
Grasso, Patrick G.
Greene, Jennifer C.
Guba, Egon G.
Hall, Budd L.
Hastings, J. Thomas
Haug, Peder
Henry, Gary T.
Hood, Stafford L.
Hopson, Rodney
House, Ernest R.
Hughes, Gerunda B.
Ingle, Robert
Jackson, Edward T.
Julnes, George
King, Jean A.
Kirkhart, Karen
Konrad, Ellen L.
Kushner, Saville
Leeuw, Frans L.
Levin, Henry M.
Leviton, Laura
Light, Richard J.
Lincoln, Yvonna S.
Lipsey, Mark W.
Lundgren, Ulf P.
Mabry, Linda
MacDonald, Barry
Madison, Anna Marie
Mark, Melvin M.
Mathison, Sandra
Mertens, Donna M.
Millet, Ricardo A.
Moos, Rudolf H.
Morell, Jonathan A.
Morris, Michael
Mosteller, Frederick
Narayan, Deepa
Nathan, Richard
Nevo, David
Newcomer, Kathryn
Newman, Dianna L.
O'Sullivan, Rita
Owen, John M.
Patel, Mahesh
Patton, Michael Quinn
Pawson, Ray
Pollitt, Christopher
Porteous, Nancy L.
Posavac, Emil J.

Preskill, Hallie
Reichardt, Charles S. (Chip)
Rist, Ray C.
Rog, Debra J.
Rogers, Patricia J.
Rossi, Peter H.
Rugh, Jim
Russon, Craig W.
Ryan, Katherine E.
Sanders, James R.
Scheirer, Mary Ann
Schwandt, Thomas A.
Scriven, Michael
Shadish, William R.
Shulha, Lyn M.
Simons, Helen
Smith, M. F.
Smith, Nick L.
Stake, Robert E.
Stanfield, John II
Stanley, Julian C.
Stufflebeam, Daniel L.
Tilley, Nick
Torres, Rosalie T.
Toulemonde, Jacques
Trochim, William
Tyler, Ralph W.
VanderPlaat, Madine
Wadsworth, Yoland
Walberg, Herbert J.
Walker, Rob
Weiss, Carol Hirschon
Whitmore, Elizabeth
Wholey, Joseph S.
Wildavsky, Aaron B.
Worthen, Blaine R.
Wye, Christopher G.

PUBLICATIONS

American Journal of Evaluation
EvalTalk
Evaluation and Program Planning
Evaluation & the Health Professions
*Evaluation Review: A Journal of
    Applied Social Research*
*Evaluation: The International Journal
    of Theory, Research and Practice*
Guiding Principles for Evaluators
New Directions for Evaluation (NDE)
The Personnel Evaluation Standards
*Practical Assessment, Research on
    Evaluation (PARE)*
The Program Evaluation Standards

QUALITATIVE METHODS

Archives
Checklists

Comparative Analysis
Constant Comparative Method
Content Analysis
Cross-Case Analysis
Deliberative Forums
Delphi Technique
Document Analysis
Emergent Design
Emic Perspective
Ethnography
Etic Perspective
Fieldwork
Focus Group
Gendered Evaluation
Grounded Theory
Group Interview
Key Informants
Mixed Methods
Narrative Analysis
Natural Experiments
Negative Cases
Observation
Participant Observation
Phenomenography
Portfolio
Portrayal
Qualitative Data
Rapid Rural Appraisal
Reflexivity
Rival Interpretations
Thick Description
Think-Aloud Protocol
Unique-Case Analysis
Unobtrusive Measures

QUANTITATIVE METHODS

Aggregate Matching
Backward Mapping
Benchmarking
Concept Mapping
Correlation
Cross-Sectional Design
Errors of Measurement
Fault Tree Analysis
Field Experiment
Matrix Sampling
Meta-analysis
Multitrait-Multimethod Analysis
Panel Studies
Pre-Post Design
Quantitative Data
Quantitative Weight and Sum
Regression Analysis
Standardized Test
Statistics
Surveys
Time Series Analysis

REPRESENTATION, REPORTING, COMMUNICATING

Cartooning
Executive Summary
Metaphor
Narrative
Narrative Representation
Photography
Poetry
Recommendations
Reporting
Representation
Storytelling
Voice

SYSTEMS

Change
Complex Adaptive Systems
Incremental Change
Learning Organization
Organizational Change
Organizational Culture
Quality Assurance
Quality Circles
Quality Control
Strategic Planning
Syndemic
Systems and Systems Thinking

TECHNOLOGY

Alpha Test
Beta Test
Electronic Surveys
Instructional Technology, Evaluation of

UTILIZATION

Conceptual Use
Evaluation Use
Intended Users
Intended Uses
Misuse of Evaluations
Process Use
Utility Tests
Utilization of Evaluation
Utilization-Focused Evaluation

List of Contributors

Tineke A. Abma
University of Maastricht, The Netherlands

Clem Adelman
Freelance Writer

Marvin C. Alkin
University of California, Los Angeles

James W. Altschuld
The Ohio State University

James T. Austin
The Ohio State University

Michael Baizerman
University of Minnesota

Robert L. Bangert-Drowns
University at Albany, SUNY

Gail V. Barrington
Barrington Research Group, Inc.

Reid Bates
Louisiana State University

Leonard Bickman
Peabody College and Vanderbilt University

Robert O. Brinkerhoff
Western Michigan University

Denice A. Cassaro
Cornell University

Huey-Tsyh Chen
University of Alabama, Birmingham

Chin Mei Chin
Ministry of Education, Malaysia

Christina A. Christie
Claremont Graduate University

Poh-Pheng Chua
Pennsylvania State University

Jean Clarke
Waterford Institute of Technology, Ireland

Anne Coghlan
ATC Consulting

Donald W. Compton
ECB Services

Ross Conner
University of California, Irvine

Jessica Dart
Victorian Department of Primary Industries, Australia

Lois-ellin Datta
Consultant, Hawaii

Jane Davidson
Western Michigan University

Robert Donmoyer
University of San Diego

John Elliott
University of East Anglia

David M. Fetterman
Stanford University

Jody L. Fitzpatrick
University of Colorado, Denver

Deborah M. Fournier
Boston University

Melissa Freeman
University at Albany, SUNY

Leslie K. Goodyear
Education Development Center

Jennifer C. Greene
University of Illinois, Urbana-Champaign

David Hamilton
University of Umeå

Alison Harrow
University of Dundee

Karin Haubrich
German Youth Institute

Mark Hawkes
Dakota State University

Gary T. Henry
Georgia State University

Stafford L. Hood
Arizona State University

Ernest R. House
University of Colorado, Boulder

Malcolm Hughes
University of the West of England

Rosalind Hurworth
University of Melbourne

Edward T. Jackson
Carleton University, Canada

Janice M. Jackson
Independent Consultant

Steve Jacob
Free University of Brussels

Conrad G. Katzenmeyer
National Science Foundation

Jean A. King
University of Minnesota

Richard A. Krueger
University of Minnesota

David D. Kumar
Florida Atlantic University

Jody Zall Kusek
World Bank

Saville Kushner
University of the West of England

Stephan Laske
University of Innsbruck

Henry M. Levin
Teachers College, Columbia University

Miri Levin-Rozalis
Ben Gurion University of the Negev

Yvonna S. Lincoln
Texas A&M University

Arnold Love
Consultant, Toronto

Jason K. Luellen
University of Memphis

Linda Mabry
Washington State University, Vancouver

Barry MacDonald
University of East Anglia

Cheryl MacNeil
Evaluation Consultant

Melvin M. Mark
Pennsylvania State University

John Mayne
Office of the Auditor General, Canada

Donna M. Mertens
Gallaudet University, Washington, DC

Bobby Milstein
Centers for Disease Control and Prevention

Jonathan A. Morell
Altarum Institute

Michael Morris
University of New Haven

Marco A. Muñoz
Jefferson County Public Schools

Nigel Norris
University of East Anglia

John M. Owen
University of Melbourne

Michael Quinn Patton
Union Institute and University

Ray Pawson
University of Leeds

Joseph M. Petrosko
University of Louisville

Hallie Preskill
University of New Mexico

Stephanie Reich
Vanderbilt University

Charles S. Reichardt
University of Denver

Valéry Ridde
Laval University, Canada

Ray C. Rist
World Bank

Debra J. Rog
Vanderbilt University

Patricia J. Rogers
*Royal Melbourne
Institute of Technology*

Vera Roos
University of Pretoria

Barbara Rosenstein
Ben Gurion University

Darlene F. Russ-Eft
Oregon State University

Craig Russon
W. K. Kellogg Foundation

D. Royce Sadler
Griffith University, Australia

Maria José Sáez Brezmes
Valladolid University

Rolf Sandahl
*National Financial
Management Authority, Sweden*

Thomas A. Schwandt
University of Illinois, Urbana-Champaign

Michael Scriven
Western Michigan University

Marco Segone
UNICEF Brazil

Denise Seigart
Mansfield University

William R. Shadish
University of California, Merced

Cathy Shutt
*Asia Disaster Preparedness Centre,
Thailand*

Hendrik J. Smith
*Agricultural Research
Council, South Africa*

M. F. Smith
The Evaluators' Institute

Robert E. Stake
University of Illinois, Urbana-Champaign

Stacey Hueftle Stockdill
EnSearch, Inc.

Daniel L. Stufflebeam
Western Michigan University

Hazel Symonette
University of Wisconsin

Markus Themessl-Huber
University of Dundee

Charles L. Thomas
George Mason University

Nick Tilley
*Nottingham Trent University and
University College London*

Rosalie T. Torres
Developmental Studies Center

William Trochim
Cornell University

Jeffrey G. Tucker
Evaluation Works

Lori Tucker
Grantmakers for Effective Organizations

Frédéric Varone
Catholic University of Louvain

Dimitris Vergidis
University of Patras

Elizabeth Whitmore
Carleton University, Canada

Bob Williams
Consultant, New Zealand

David D. Williams
Brigham Young University

About the Editor

Sandra Mathison is Professor of Education at the University of British Columbia. She has been conducting evaluations, primarily in educational settings, for more than 25 years. She began her career as an internal evaluator in a Canadian community college and has subsequently conducted dozens of external evaluations; she served as Director of Evaluation for the University of Chicago School Mathematics Project for 3 years. Over these many years, and through these many opportunities to do and study evaluation, she has developed an interest in and made contributions to the field of evaluation through her emphasis on democratic principles and possibilities. Throughout her work runs a deep concern for the limitations and limiting nature of evaluation in schools. Now more than ever, the nature of evaluation within schools constrains what it means to adequately determine what is good and bad in schools, thus constraining the possibilities for improvement. Her current research focuses on these limits of evaluation in schools. With funding from the National Science Foundation, she is conducting research on the effects of high-stakes testing on teaching and learning in elementary and middle schools. Mathison has written extensively about this topic, for the popular press as well as for the academic community, in an effort to encourage a more informed public discourse about the value of schools and schooling. She chaired the American Evaluation Association task force that created a policy statement (the association's first-ever policy statement) on high-stakes testing in K-12 schooling. She is Coeditor, with E. Wayne Ross, of *Defending Public Schools: The Nature and Limits of Standards Based Reform and Assessment*.

About the Contributors

Tineke A. Abma is Senior Researcher at the Institute for Health Care Ethics, University of Maastricht, The Netherlands. Her scholarly work focuses on responsive approaches to evaluation and related ideas in other disciplinary fields.

Clem Adelman has evaluated curricula, pedagogic innovation, higher education, health-care provision, creative arts, interethnic relationships in schools, and bilingual education, among other work. Adelman's concluding professorship was at the Norwegian University of Science and Technology. He is now a freelance writer and musician in quite good condition for his mileage.

Marvin C. Alkin is Professor and Chair of the Social Research Methods Division, Graduate School of Education and Information Studies, University of California, Los Angeles. He has written extensively on evaluation utilization and comparative evaluation theory. Alkin founded and directed the UCLA Center for the Study of Evaluation. He is a winner of the AEA's Lazarsfeld Award for Evaluation Theory.

James W. Altschuld is Professor of Educational Research, Evaluation, and Measurement, The Ohio State University. His publications include two books about needs assessment, one on the evaluation of science and technology education, and articles regarding the professional training of evaluators.

James T. Austin is Research Specialist at The Ohio State University. His research interests include methodology, job performance measurement, and goal striving.

Michael Baizerman, Ph.D., is Professor, School of Social Work, University of Minnesota, where he specializes in Youth Studies. He has worked in program evaluation since the early 1970s, first on hotlines and youth crisis centers, then on educational evaluations, and most recently at the American Cancer Society.

Robert L. Bangert-Drowns is Associate Professor in the Department of Educational Theory and Practice and Associate Dean of the School of Education at the University at Albany, SUNY. He has published many meta-analyses and articles on meta-analytic method. His work focuses on instructional design issues in instructional technology and educational programs for the prevention of social problems.

Gail V. Barrington established Barrington Research Group, Inc., in 1985, an independent consulting firm that specializes in program evaluation and applied social science research and training in Canada and the United States. She has conducted or managed more than 100 evaluation studies. In 1994, she was nominated for the Canadian Woman Entrepreneur of the Year Award.

Reid Bates is Associate Professor in the Human Resource Development at Louisiana State University, where he teaches undergraduate and graduate courses in human resource development. His research interests include employee development; learning transfer; the role of values, ethics, and culture in human resource development; and global and international human resource development.

Leonard Bickman is Professor of Psychology, Psychiatry and Public Policy; Associate Dean for Research at Peabody College; Director of the Center for Mental Health Policy at the Vanderbilt Institute for Public Policy; and Director of the National Institutes of Mental Health–supported training program in child and adolescent mental health services research.

Robert O. Brinkerhoff is Professor at Western Michigan University. He is the author of 11 books and

CEO for The Learning Alliance, a firm providing consultation in training effectiveness. Brinkerhoff has been a U.S. Navy officer, a carpenter, a charter-boat mate in the West Indies, a grocery salesman in Puerto Rico, and a factory laborer in Birmingham, England.

Denice A. Cassaro is Assistant Director for Community Center Programs at Cornell University and also a doctoral candidate in the Department of Policy Analysis and Management at Cornell University. She is a Certified Social Worker.

Huey-Tsyh Chen is Professor at the University of Alabama at Birmingham. He has contributed to the development of evaluation theory and methodology and is one of the leading scholars to propose the use of theory in designing and conducting an evaluation.

Chin Mei Chin is an education officer at the Ministry of Education, Malaysia. Prior to her work in evaluation, she was an English language and history teacher in Malaysia.

Christina A. Christie is Assistant Professor and Associate Director of the Institute of Organizational and Program Evaluation Research at Claremont Graduate University. She is Chair of the Theories of Evaluation Topical Interest Group of the American Evaluation Association and recently founded the Southern California Evaluation Association, Inc.

Poh-Pheng Chua is a doctoral student at Pennsylvania State University. Her interests include the evaluation of education and health programs that target ethnic minority populations and, more generally, the utilization of evaluation results in policy making and in improving existing programs.

Jean Clarke is Head of Nursing and Health Sciences at Waterford Institute of Technology, Ireland. She is a former public health nurse and has worked in nursing education for 15 years. She has published in the areas of public health nursing and the gendered role of nursing within health-care organizations.

Anne Coghlan is Evaluation Specialist at the Peace Corps, based in Washington, DC. Previously, she was Director of Evaluation and Research at Innovation Network and a participatory evaluation consultant for community-based AIDS programs in eastern and southern Africa.

Donald W. Compton has many years' experience designing, conducting, and managing practical, usable, low-cost evaluations to meet the needs of funders and organizations' planning, policy-making and management needs. He has received AEA's Myrdal Award for outstanding contributions to evaluation practice and the Hamline University Making the World a Better Place Award. He is President of ECB Services.

Ross Conner is Director, Center for Community Health Research, University of California, Irvine, and Associate Professor, Department of Planning, Policy and Design. His research focuses on community health promotion and disease prevention. He is currently studying a program involving cancer control with Korean and Chinese communities and another involving HIV prevention with Latino men. He is Past President of the American Evaluation Association.

Jessica Dart works in Australia with the Evaluation Support Team of the Victorian Department of Primary Industries. Her professional interests are in qualitative evaluation methods, evaluation theory, participatory approaches, and action research. She has adapted and tested a dialogical story-based evaluation tool, the Most Significant Change technique.

Lois-ellin Datta served as National Director of Research and Evaluation for Project Head Start, Director of the National Institute of Education's Teaching and Learning Division, and Director of the U.S. General Accounting Office's Program Evaluation, Human Service Area. Now living in Hawaii, she continues consulting, teaching, working in theory and practice in evaluation, and is learning to be a coffee farmer.

Jane Davidson is Associate Director of The Evaluation Center at Western Michigan University and Program Director of the interdisciplinary Ph.D. in Evaluation. Her main areas of specialization are in organizational learning, theory-based evaluation, causation, needs assessment, evaluation logic and methodology, personnel evaluation and performance management, and the evaluation of organizational change.

Robert Donmoyer is Professor at the University of San Diego; previously, he worked for 20 years as Professor and Administrator at The Ohio State University. His scholarship has focused on issues related to research and evaluation utilization in policy making.

John Elliott is Professorial Fellow of Education within the Centre for Applied Research in Education, which he directed from 1996 to 1999, at the University of East Anglia. He is internationally known for his role in developing the theory and practice of action research in the contexts of curriculum and teacher development.

David M. Fetterman is Professor and Director of the Policy Analysis and Evaluation Program at Stanford University. He was formerly Professor and Research Director at the California Institute of Integral Studies, Principal Research Scientist at the American Institutes for Research, and a Senior Associate at RMC Research Corporation.

Jody L. Fitzpatrick is Associate Professor with the Graduate School of Public Affairs at the University of Colorado–Denver. She has been a practicing evaluator for more than 25 years, has served as Chair of the Ethics Committee for the American Evaluation Association, and has worked to increase evaluators' knowledge and use of ethical codes in their practice.

Deborah M. Fournier is Assistant Professor and Director of Educational Research and Evaluation, School of Dental Medicine, Boston University. Since 1996, she has served on an annual site visit team as Curriculum Consultant to the National Council on Dental Accreditation.

Melissa Freeman is interested in methodological and theoretical issues in interpretive research, discursive practices in schools, and critical cultural theories. She is currently Project Manager for a National Science Foundation–funded longitudinal, interpretive study exploring the impact of mandated high-stakes testing on the practice of teaching and learning in several New York State school districts.

Leslie K. Goodyear is Senior Research Associate at the Education Development Center and was the Director of Evaluation for City Year, a nonprofit organization. Her interests include new and different approaches to presenting evaluation findings; participatory, interpretivist, and mixed-method evaluation designs; and building innovative evaluation systems that support multisite organizations.

Jennifer C. Greene has been an evaluation scholar-practitioner for more than 25 years. She has held academic appointments at the University of Rhode Island, Cornell University, and (currently) the University of Illinois. Her evaluation scholarship has broadly focused on probing the intersections of social science method and political discourse and has specifically advanced qualitative, mixed-method, and participatory approaches to evaluation.

David Hamilton is Professor of Education at the University of Umeå, Sweden. His evaluation experiences reach back to the 1970s when, as a research student, he realized that curriculum evaluation was an uncharted field. He was, and still is, greatly influenced by the epistemological upheavals of that period, otherwise known as the Kuhnian, qualitative, or postpositivist turns.

Alison Harrow is Research Nurse, School of Nursing and Midwifery, University of Dundee. She has particular interests in the care of women with breast cancer and the development of nurse-led interventions. This has brought her to focus on gaining an understanding of the impact of women's breast cancer from the male partners' perspectives.

Karin Haubrich is a researcher at the German Youth Institute. Her work focuses on transition from school to work, cooperation between youth services and schools, vocational aid for disadvantaged young people, social outreach and street work, vocational and social integration of young migrants, networking among regional youth services, and intercultural approaches to social services.

Mark Hawkes is Coordinator of Graduate Studies in Educational Technology in the College of Education at Dakota State University. He has led and participated in a number of district and statewide evaluations of educational technology, fueling his research interests in the outcomes of educational technology application on student learning and teacher professional development.

Gary T. Henry is Professor in the Andrew Young School of Policy Studies at Georgia State University. He previously served as Director of Evaluation and Learning Services for the David and Lucile Packard Foundation. He has published extensively in the field of evaluation and policy analysis.

Stafford L. Hood is Associate Professor, Division of Psychology in Education at Arizona State University, where he teaches graduate courses in psychological testing, program evaluation, and multicultural counseling. He is the founding Codirector of the annual Relevance of Assessment and Culture in Evaluation national conference.

Ernest R. House is Emeritus Professor, University of Colorado, Boulder; a long-time faculty member at the University of Illinois, Urbana-Champaign; and a member of the Center for Instructional Research and Curriculum Evaluation. He has contributed substantially to a growing discussion on the role of values, ethics, and social justice in evaluation, as well as to metaevaluation, evaluative reasoning, and the philosophical basis of evaluation.

Malcolm Hughes is Program Leader for Continuing Professional Development at the University of the West of England, United Kingdom. He manages the accreditation of experiential learning program of the Faculty of Education and lectures in mathematics and educational technology.

Rosalind Hurworth is Director of the Centre for Program Evaluation at the University of Melbourne, Australia. She has done numerous national, state, and local evaluations, particularly in the health, education, and welfare sectors. She has particular expertise in the use of qualitative methods.

Edward T. Jackson is Associate Professor of Public Administration and International Affairs at Carleton University, Canada. He is President of E. T. Jackson and Associates Ltd. and has served as evaluation consultant to the Canadian International Development Agency, World Bank, and governments and nongovernmental organizations in more than 30 developing countries.

Janice M. Jackson is an independent consultant and former Senior Lecturer of the University of Guyana who currently works in the areas of gender analysis, social development, poverty analysis, and participatory processes. Her specific interests lie in the areas of individual and collective self-evaluation.

Steve Jacob is Researcher at the Free University of Brussels (Belgium). He has published several articles and reports on policy evaluation and public administration in Belgium. His research deals with the institutionalization of policy evaluation.

Conrad G. Katzenmeyer is Senior Program Director in the Division of Research, Evaluation and Communication of the National Science Foundation, where he designs and oversees evaluation contracts and grants and coordinates evaluation activities with other parts of NSF and other federal agencies.

Jean A. King currently teaches in the Department of Educational Policy and Administration, University of Minnesota, where she serves as Coordinator of Evaluation Studies. King is the author of numerous articles, chapters, and reviews and, with Laurie Stevahn, is currently writing a book on interactive evaluation practice.

Richard A. Krueger is a professor and extension evaluation leader for the University of Minnesota. He has written extensively about focus group interviewing, including six books and numerous chapters in edited books. His areas of specialization include program evaluation, applied research methodology, and qualitative research.

David D. Kumar is Professor of Science Education at Florida Atlantic University and a Fellow of the American Institute of Chemists. His research involves evaluation and policy in science and technology education.

Jody Zall Kusek is a Senior Evaluation Officer at the World Bank. She is currently involved in supporting the efforts of seven governments to move to a focus of performance-based management. She has spent many years in the area of public sector reform, serving the Vice President of the United States, the U.S. Secretary of the Interior, and the U.S. Secretary of Energy in the areas of strategic planning and performance management.

Saville Kushner is Professor of Applied Research and Director of the Centre for Research in Education and Democracy at the University of the West of England, United Kingdom. He is a specialist in case study evaluation and the author of the approach known as *personalized evaluation.*

Stephan Laske is Professor of Business Management and Management Education and Head of the Institute for Organization and Learning, University of Innsbruck.

Henry M. Levin is the William Heard Kilpatrick Professor of Economics and Education at Teachers College, Columbia University, and the David Jacks Professor of Higher Education and Economics, Emeritus, at Stanford University. He specializes in the areas of cost effectiveness and cost-benefit analyses and is a former President of the Evaluation Research Society and a recipient of its Myrdal Award.

Miri Levin-Rozalis, sociologist and psychologist, is a faculty member and Head of the evaluation unit of the Department of Education at Ben Gurion University of the Negev. She is one of the founders and a former chairperson of the Israeli Association for Program Evaluation; currently she is a member of its executive board.

Yvonna S. Lincoln holds the Ruth Harrington Chair of Educational Leadership and is University Distinguished Professor of Higher Education at Texas A&M University. She is a former President of the

American Evaluation Association and has been an evaluation practitioner and consultant for more than 25 years. Her interests lie in democratic, inclusionary, participative, and social justice issues in evaluation and public policy formulation.

Arnold Love is a consultant based in Toronto, with more than 20 years experience in evaluation. He served as President of the Canadian Evaluation Society and has received its National Award for Distinguished Contribution to Evaluation. He has been recognized for his contributions to building a worldwide evaluation community, especially development of the International Organization for Cooperation in Evaluation.

Jason K. Luellen is a graduate student in Research Design and Statistics at the University of Memphis. His general interests are in experimental and quasiexperimental design, and his current research concerns finding ways to use propensity scores to improve estimates from quasiexperiments.

Linda Mabry is Professor of Education at Washington State University, Vancouver. She specializes in program evaluation, the assessment of K-12 student achievement, and qualitative research methodology, with special interests in ethics and postmodernism in research and evaluation and in performance assessment, consequential validity, and high-stakes testing for educational accountability.

Barry MacDonald was Director of the Centre for Applied Research in Education at the University of East Anglia. One of the founders of CARE, he was also the director of the Ford Success and Failure and Recent Innovation project and a guiding light of the Cambridge Conferences.

Cheryl MacNeil is a community activist and a believer in the capacities of people. As an evaluation consultant, she weaves her value for the wisdom of communities into her practices. Her evaluations are designed to provide people with opportunities to talk about their beliefs and examine their responsibilities to one another.

Melvin M. Mark is Professor of Psychology and Senior Scientist at the Institute for Policy Research and Evaluation at Pennsylvania State University. He is Editor of the *American Journal of Evaluation.* His interests include the theory, methodology, practice, and profession of program and policy evaluation, as well as the development of evaluation training.

John Mayne was Director, Evaluation Policy in the Office of the Comptroller General in Canada and in 1995 joined the Office of the Auditor General. He was instrumental in developing the federal government's approach to evaluating program performance. He was President of the Canadian Evaluation Society and was awarded the CES Award for Contribution to Evaluation in Canada.

Donna M. Mertens is Professor in the Department of Educational Foundations and Research at Gallaudet University in Washington, DC. Her research focuses on the transformative paradigm in evaluation and the development of the inclusive approach to evaluation. She has been the President of the American Evaluation Association's Board of Directors and a board member.

Bobby Milstein is an evaluation coordinator at the Centers for Disease Control and Prevention. He helped launch the CDC Evaluation Working Group, which established CDC's policy on program evaluation. He now leads the Syndemics Prevention Network and specializes in the evaluation of complex initiatives to ensure conditions in which people can be healthy.

Jonathan A. Morell does research and evaluation at the intersection of business process and information technology. He is Editor-in-Chief of *Evaluation and Program Planning* and winner of the American Evaluation Association's Distinguished Service Award. Presently he is Senior Policy Analyst at the Altarum Institute.

Michael Morris is Professor of Psychology and Director of Graduate Field Training in Community Psychology at the University of New Haven. His major research interest is ethical issues in evaluation, and he served as the first Editor of the Ethical Challenges section in the *American Journal of Evaluation.*

Marco A. Muñoz is an evaluation specialist with the Jefferson County Public Schools in Louisville, Kentucky, and is Adjunct Faculty, University of Louisville, where he teaches research methods and statistics. He received the American Evaluation Association's Marcia Guttentag Award for his contribution in the area of school district evaluation research.

Nigel Norris is Professor of Education in the Centre for Applied Research in Education, University of East Anglia. He teaches applied research methodology and the history, theory, and practice of evaluation. He specializes in conducting program and policy evaluations, primarily in educational settings.

John M. Owen is interested in evaluation as knowledge creation for use in organizational decision making. He has been a contributor to theory related to these issues in journals and conferences in Australasia and overseas for more than a decade. He is currently Principal Fellow at the Centre for Program Evaluation, University of Melbourne.

Michael Quinn Patton serves on the graduate faculty of Union Institute and University and is an independent program evaluation consultant. He is former President of the American Evaluation Association and recipient of the Myrdal Award for Outstanding Contributions to Useful and Practical Evaluation Practice from the Evaluation Research Society and the Lazarsfeld Award for Lifelong Contributions to Evaluation Theory from the American Evaluation Association.

Ray Pawson is a sociologist at the University of Leeds and has been active in the United Kingdom and European Evaluation Societies. He entered evaluation quite by accident when he was asked to research the effectiveness of a prisoner education program.

Joseph M. Petrosko is Professor of Education in the Department of Leadership, Foundations, and Human Resource Education at the University of Louisville. He teaches courses in statistics, evaluation, and research. His professional interests include studying school reform and teacher preparation programs.

Hallie Preskill is Professor of Organizational Learning and Instructional Technologies at the University of New Mexico, Albuquerque. She teaches graduate-level courses in program evaluation; organizational learning; and training design, development, and delivery. She received the American Evaluation Association's Alva and Gunnar Myrdal Award for Outstanding Professional Practice in 2002.

Stephanie Reich is a doctoral student in Community Psychology and Program Evaluation at Vanderbilt University in Nashville, Tennessee. Her research focuses on prevention programs for children from newborns to 5 years old, with an emphasis on home and school environments.

Charles S. Reichardt is Professor of Psychology at the University of Denver, where he has been for the past 24 years. He is interested in the logic of research methods and statistics. His focus is on the use of experimental and quasiexperimental designs for assessing program effectiveness.

Valéry Ridde ran humanitarian emergency and development program for medical NGOs in several countries, including Afghanistan, Mali, Niger, Iraq, Haiti, and East Timor. He is now a consultant in program evaluation in Canada and in developing countries. He is also a doctoral student in community health at Laval University (Québec).

Ray C. Rist is a senior evaluation officer in the Operations Evaluation Department of the World Bank. His work focuses on building evaluation capacity in developing countries. He has held senior government positions in both the executive and legislative branches of the U.S. Government and professorships at Cornell, Johns Hopkins, and George Washington Universities.

Debra J. Rog is Senior Research Associate in Vanderbilt University's Institute for Public Policy Studies and Director of the Center for Mental Health Policy in Washington, DC. She continues to reflect on the practice of evaluation, especially with respect to conducting multisite evaluations and conducting research with hard-to-reach, vulnerable populations. Since 1980, she has been coediting the Applied Social Research Methods series of textbooks.

Patricia J. Rogers is an evaluation practitioner, researcher, and educator and the founder of the Collaborative Institute for Research, Consulting and Learning in Evaluation at the Royal Melbourne Institute of Technology, Australia. Her focus is on building the evaluation capability of public sector organizations, particularly through the use of program theory, and the integration of qualitative and quantitative monitoring and evaluation.

Vera Roos' interests lie in community and developmental psychology. Currently, she is involved in the facilitation of learning in primary, community-based interventions.

Barbara Rosenstein was introduced to the field of evaluation through work with the Bernard van Leer Foundation and has studied, taught, and practiced evaluation ever since. Her main focus has been on community-based programs concerned with education, empowerment, and coexistence.

Darlene F. Russ-Eft is Assistant Professor in the Community College Leadership Program and in the

Adult Education Program within the School of Education at Oregon State University. She has managed evaluations of training products and services and directed evaluations of federal programs, such as the Adult Education Program and VISTA.

Craig Russon is an Evaluation Manager for the Food Systems/Rural Development program area of the W. K. Kellogg Foundation. He founded the International and Cross-Cultural Evaluation TIG Silent Auction, AEA Travel Grants, and the AEA Book Exchange. He also created a listserv for persons interested in international and cross-cultural evaluation issues.

D. Royce Sadler is Professor of Higher Education at Griffith University in Brisbane, Australia, where he is also Director of the Griffith Institute for Higher Education. His recent publications and current research interests lie in the areas of grading, achievement standards, and the formative and summative assessment of academic learning.

Maria José Sáez Brezmes is Professor in the Faculty of Education in Valladolid University, Spain, and Vice Rector of International Affairs at Valladolid University. Her research interests focus on educational evaluation.

Rolf Sandahl works as an expert advisor on evaluation and performance management at the National Financial Management Authority in Sweden. He has been working for both the Swedish government and parliament and is the author of many books and articles in the areas of policy instrument, evaluation, and management by results.

Thomas A. Schwandt is Professor of Education in the Department of Educational Psychology and affiliated faculty in the Unit for Criticism and Interpretive Theory at the University of Illinois, Urbana-Champaign. He has lectured and taught extensively throughout Norway, Sweden, and Denmark.

Michael Scriven has taught at several colleges in the United States of America, including 12 years at the University of California, Berkeley, in departments of philosophy, psychology, and education, as well as at the University of Western Australia and the University of Auckland, and is currently Professor of Evaluation and Philosophy at Western Michigan University. His 330 publications include nearly 100 in evaluation, and he has received various awards for his work on faculty evaluation, evaluation theory, policy studies, and educational research.

Marco Segone worked in Bangladesh, Pakistan, Thailand, Uganda, and Albania in integrated development projects. He worked for the Regional UNICEF Office for Latin America and the Caribbean and as Monitoring and Evaluation Officer for UNICEF Niger, where he founded and coordinated the Niger Monitoring and Evaluation Network. Since 2002, he has been working for UNICEF Brazil.

Denise Seigart is Associate Professor in the Department of Health Sciences at Mansfield University, Pennsylvania. She is currently pursuing research and publications that contribute to an increasing body of knowledge concerning feminist theory and its applicability to evaluation.

William R. Shadish is Professor and Founding Faculty at the University of California, Merced, and was previously a clinical psychologist and Professor at the University of Memphis. He has been AEA President and the winner of the 1994 AEA Lazarsfeld Award for Evaluation Theory, the 2000 Ingle Award for service to the AEA, and the 2002 Donald T. Campbell Award for Innovations in Methodology from the Policy Studies Organization.

Cathy Shutt spent 7 years in the Philippines working with the International Institute of Rural Reconstruction, a learning NGO dedicated to participatory development. She then moved to Cambodia and worked as a consultant undertaking evaluations. She currently works as a Monitoring and Evaluation Manager for the Asia Disaster Preparedness Centre in Thailand.

Hendrik J. Smith is a senior researcher of ARC-ISCW, involved in the South African Landcare Program and other rural development initiatives. His experience lies in the fields of soil science, sustainable land management, land-use planning, land degradation, rural development, and monitoring and evaluation.

M. F. Smith is Director of The Evaluators' Institute and Professor Emeritus, University of Maryland. She previously held positions in education, agriculture, medical centers, cooperative extension services, and vocational and special education.

Robert E. Stake (Emeritus) is Director of the Center for Instructional Research and Curriculum Evaluation at the University of Illinois. Since 1965, he has been a specialist in the evaluation of educational programs. Recently he led a multiyear evaluation study of the Chicago Teachers Academy for Mathematics and Science. For his evaluation work, he received the Lazarsfeld Award from the American Evaluation Association and an honorary doctorate from the University of Uppsala.

Stacey Hueftle Stockdill is CEO of EnSearch, Inc. She has designed and conducted evaluations since 1980. She is a recipient of the American Evaluation Association's Myrdal Award for Evaluation Practice.

Daniel L. Stufflebeam is Distinguished University Professor, the McKee Professor of Education, and founder and former Director of The Evaluation Center at Western Michigan University. He developed the CIPP Model for Evaluation and led the development of the Joint Committee's professional standards for program and personnel evaluations.

Hazel Symonette is Senior Policy and Planning Analyst at the University of Wisconsin–Madison. She is committed to creating and sustaining authentically inclusive and vibrantly responsive teaching, learning, and working communities that are conducive to success for all.

Markus Themessl-Huber is Research Fellow for the Scottish School of Primary Care based in the School of Nursing and Midwifery and the Tayside Centre of General Practice at the University of Dundee, United Kingdom. His current research interests are the evaluation of service developments in health and social care and the application of action research approaches to evaluation.

Charles L. Thomas is Associate Professor of educational psychology in the Graduate School of Education, George Mason University. His current research interests include problems related to the assessment of minority groups and the evaluation of community-based health programs.

Nick Tilley is Professor of Sociology at Nottingham Trent University and Visiting Professor at the Jill Dando Institute of Crime Science, University College London. He was seconded as a research consultant to the British Home Office Research, Development and Statistics Directorate from 1992 to 2003.

Rosalie T. Torres, Ph.D., is Director of Research, Evaluation, and Organizational Learning at the Developmental Studies Center in Oakland, California, where she practices an organizational learning approach to evaluation.

William Trochim is Professor, Department of Policy Analysis and Management, Cornell University, and Director of the Office for the Management of Not-for-Profit Institutions at Cornell. His research is broadly in the area of applied social research methodology, with an emphasis on program planning and evaluation methods.

Jeffrey G. Tucker is a doctoral student in evaluation at the University of Louisville. He recently left his position as Director of Research at the National Center for Family Literacy to establish Evaluation Works, an independent consulting firm. Primary areas of research include the evaluation of reading strategies for at-risk readers, the intergenerational transmission of literacy, and adult and workplace literacy.

Lori Tucker is Program Manager at Grantmakers for Effective Organizations. She is responsible for overseeing program activities such as communications, the Web site, conference planning, research, and publications.

Frédéric Varone is Professor of Political Science at the Catholic University of Louvain in Belgium and Codirector of the Association Universitaire de Recherche sur L'action Publique. His research fields include comparative policy analysis, program evaluation, and reform of public services.

Dimitris Vergidis teaches at the Department of Education at the University of Patras, Greece. He has published papers in Greece and abroad (in French and in English) about adult education, illiteracy, and evaluation in education.

Elizabeth Whitmore is Professor at Carleton University, Canada, and has found participatory action research to be a natural fit in her research and evaluation work. She has translated this into participatory approaches to evaluation and has conducted a number of evaluations based on the principles and practices of PAR.

Bob Williams is based in New Zealand and divides his time among evaluation, strategy development, facilitating large-group processes, and systemic organizational change projects. He is a qualified windsurfing instructor and, invariably, the oldest snowboarder on the field.

David D. Williams is an Associate Professor, Department of Instructional Psychology and Technology, David O. McKay School of Education, Brigham Young University. His research interests include cross-cultural evaluation issues; evaluation in schools and universities; evaluation of technology-based teaching and learning; and philosophical, cultural, and moral foundations of evaluation.

Preface

The *Encyclopedia of Evaluation* is a who, what, where, how, and why of evaluation. Evaluation is a profession, a practice, a discipline—and it has developed and continues to develop through the ideas and work of evaluators and evaluation theorists working in real places with high hopes for social improvement. Each individual entry in this book gives a glimpse of a particular aspect of this development, and taken as a whole, the encyclopedia captures the history of evaluation in all these many ways.

In conceptualizing what this book would include, my intention was to capture the components that make evaluation a *practice,* a *profession,* and a *discipline.* Evaluation is an ancient practice and, indeed, probably the most common form of reasoning used by all people virtually all the time. All humans are nascent evaluators. The more formal practice of evaluation has moved from the margins to the center of many organizations and agencies. Once it was work primarily practiced under other names and as a part-time activity. Evaluation practice has become institutionalized, it is common practice, and indeed, it is an important commodity in social and political life. Evaluation practice is not institutionalized in the same way around the world, but the reaches of development organizations and globalization have meant that evaluation, like many commodities, is traded worldwide.

Also, the practice of evaluation has grown, expanding to include much more than the earliest notions, which borrowed heavily from traditional social science approaches to research. Although the methods of psychology and psychometrics continue to be a mainstay, evaluation practice has expanded, drawing on many more disciplines, such as anthropology, ethics, political science, literary criticism, systems theory, and others, for inspiration. It is a complex and varied practice, sometimes even incoherent. This encyclopedia covers all of these areas, providing the reader with information on the many perspectives in evaluation.

As the practice of evaluation has grown worldwide, evaluation has become increasingly professionalized. Evaluation has grown into its professional posture as it has developed into a group of people recognized as having special knowledge and skills that serve a useful purpose. Formal educational programs, associations, journals, and codes of professional and ethical conduct are a central part of the profession of evaluation.

This profession is tied together by the discipline of evaluation. Although narrow conceptions of "discipline" might not apply to evaluation, there are basic concepts that underlie and inform the practice of evaluation. Granted, there is much lively discussion, debate, and critique of these concepts, another indicator of evaluation's arrival as a discipline. A good example is the basic concept of *stakeholder involvement* in the discipline of evaluation. This is a core idea with which every evaluator and evaluation theorist agrees, although, of course, the details of what it means to different evaluators are different. Another example is the essential understanding that what distinguishes evaluation is that it is about value, not truth (although naturally there are lively discussions about the relationship between value and truth).

The entries in this encyclopedia capture this sense of evaluation as a practice (methods, techniques, roles, people), as a profession (professional obligations, shared knowledge, ethical imperatives, events, places), and as a discipline (theories and models of evaluation, ontological and epistemological issues).

An attempt has been made to convey a global, international view of evaluation. Although it is the case that much of the evaluation literature is from the United States, and the history of strong American governmental support for evaluation has had a profound impact on the nature of evaluation, so has the U.S. export of evaluation had an impact on the proliferation and development of evaluation around the world. Indeed, evaluation in other parts of the world has exploded, as indicated by the creation of professional evaluation associations on every continent. Development agencies have played a key role in spreading evaluation because of the accountability side of assistance to developing countries.

The encyclopedia will be useful to evaluation practitioners, theorists, and the public—people who may simply want to understand the terms and concepts of evaluation that are a part of everyday life.

ORGANIZATION AND USER SUGGESTIONS

The key word list for the encyclopedia was created through content analyses of frequently used texts in evaluation, evaluation journals around the world, and in collaboration with the Editorial Board. That key word list includes concepts, models, techniques, applications, theories, events, places, people, and things, and the book began with a much longer list than those that found their way into the finished volume. The final choice of what was included or excluded rests entirely with me as the Editor. There were entries and contributors I would have liked to include, but for a multitude of different reasons that was not possible. A special comment about the inclusion of people in the encyclopedia is necessary—the list of *who* to include was created in the same way as other terms. Some people chose not to be included, and others we were unable to contact. The book is, in that sense, incomplete. It does not exhaustively cover each and every element of evaluation or every person or event that has contributed to evaluation. It is, however, a single reference source that captures the essence of evaluation, one that provides definitions, covers the complexity of approaches to evaluation, and illustrates the central issues being addressed by the field.

The book is organized alphabetically. There is a Reader's Guide, organized into 18 thematic categories, that provides a quick overview of the almost 600 entries. Most entries provide suggestions for further reading that will take the reader into greater depth and detail related to the entry, and where useful, cross-referencing to other entries in the encyclopedia has been provided, with the occasional use of blind entries to redirect the reader when more than one term might be used for a given topic.

In an effort to provide a more global picture of evaluation, the contributors are from around the world, representing most regions. In addition, there are a number of stories about evaluation practice around the world that are set off as sidebars in the text. These stories provide a glimpse into the nature of evaluation practice in a diverse set of circumstances, delineate the common and uncommon issues for evaluators around the world, and point to the complexities of importing evaluation from one culture to another. These stories appear in the encyclopedia contiguous to an entry related to the substance of the story.

In all cases, the entry author's name appears at the end of the entry, and in the absence of a name, the reader should assume that the Editor is the author of that entry.

ACKNOWLEDGMENTS

A project of this magnitude is possible only with the help of many, many people. C. Deborah Laughton had the idea for this book, and without her initiative, support, and commitment to evaluation, it would not have happened. I continue to benefit from her commitment to the field and to creating good books. The people at Sage Publications who were instrumental to its completion are Rolf Janke, Lisa Cuevas-Shaw, Yvette Pollastrini, Margo Crouppen, and Melanie Birdsall, and I appreciate all they have done. The American Evaluation Association Board of Directors endorsed this project as worthwhile and me as a worthy editor.

Obviously, this encyclopedia would not be were it not for the more than 100 contributing authors, evaluators from around the world. I feel privileged to have worked with this international, diverse, committed group of individuals. I hope they forgive my nagging to get the entries completed and share a sense of pride in what we have created together.

Then there are those who agreed to serve on the Editorial Board, all of whom read long lists of terms, gave thought to what should be included and what should not, volunteered to write entries (sometimes on very short notice), reviewed entries, and provided ongoing collegial support. I want especially to thank Michael Patton, Hallie Preskill, and Tom Schwandt for their incredible responsiveness and willingness to help me out whenever I asked. Also, thanks to Saville Kushner for his commitment and good ideas; Lois-ellin Datta for her affirmational messages, which reminded me of the importance and value of this project when it seemed especially onerous, and Melissa Freeman and Cheryl MacNeil for helping me to do the research for the biographical entries—but most especially, for their friendship.

Everything I do in my life, personal and professional, is done with the support and love of Wayne and Colin. I write this preface on a day when Colin gets his report card and we discuss the meaning of evaluation—the relationship between judging and improving, the pain and the glory of good and bad. My codification of this set of evaluation words and meanings was, in part, inspired by Colin's joy in the discovery of words and meaning. And always there for me is Wayne, providing encouragement and giving joy to my life, in every way and every day.

—Sandra Mathison
Editor

◾ ABMA, TINEKE A.

(b. 1964, Joure, Holland). Ph.D. Institute for Health Care Policy and Management, Erasmus University of Rotterdam; M.A. Health Care Administration, Erasmus University, Rotterdam; B.Sc. Nursing, Health Care Academy of Groningen.

Since 1990, Abma has worked at the Institute for Health Care Policy and Management, Erasmus University, Rotterdam, and is affiliated with the Institute for Health Ethics, University of Maastricht. She has been involved in numerous evaluations, including responsive evaluations of palliative care programs for cancer patients, rehabilitation programs for psychiatric patients, quality of care improvement in coercion and constraint in psychiatry, and injury prevention programs for students in the performing arts.

Her primary contribution to the field of evaluation is the exploration of how narrative and dialogue can create responsive evaluation approaches that strengthen stakeholders' contribution to policy making in transformational health-care programs. Social constructionist and postmodern thought, hermeneutics, and the ethics of care inform her evaluation practice. Primary influences on her evaluation work include Robert Stake, Egon Guba, Yvonna Lincoln, Thomas Schwandt, Jennifer Greene, Zygmunt Bauman, Rosi Braidotti, Kenneth Gergen, Sheila McNammee, Dian Hosking, Hans-Georg Gadamer, Guy Widdershoven, Joan Tronto, and Margret Walker.

Abma edited the books *Telling Tales, On Evaluation and Narrative, Dialogue in Evaluation,* a special issue of the journal *Evaluation,* and

"Responsive Evaluation," an issue of *New Directions in Evaluation.* Her dissertation was nominated for the Van Poelje Prize by the Dutch Association for Public Administration.

◾ ABT ASSOCIATES

Founded by Clark Abt in 1965, Abt Associates is one of the world's largest for-profit research firms, with over 1000 employees located in nine corporate and 25 project offices around the world. Abt Associates applies rigorous research techniques to investigate a wide range of issues relating to social and economic policy formulation, international development, and business research. Abt clients are found in all levels of government, business, and industry, as well as nonprofit organizations and foundations. Abt Associates is one of the 100 largest employee-owned companies in the United States, with gross revenues exceeding $184 million in fiscal year 2002.

—*Jeffrey G. Tucker*

◾ ACCESSIBILITY

Accessibility is a common criterion in evaluation, especially of programs, services, products, and information, when the target audience (such as disabled individuals) or the intervention (such as online teaching or Web pages) is presumed to present special challenges of access. These two factors often coincide in evaluations, as for example in evaluating Web-based teaching for persons with disabilities. Many

1

government agencies have developed guidelines for determining accessibility of a range of services.

▛ ACCOUNTABILITY

Accountability is a state of, or a process for, holding someone to account to someone else for something— that is, being required to justify or explain what has been done. Although accountability is frequently given as a rationale for doing evaluation, there is considerable variation in who is required to answer to whom, concerning what, through what means, and with what consequences. More important, within this range of options, the ways in which evaluation is used for accountability are frequently so poorly conceived and executed that they are likely to be dysfunctional for programs and organizations.

In its narrowest and most common form, accountability focuses on simple justification by requiring program managers to report back to funders (either separate organizations or the decision makers within their own organization) on their performance compared to agreed plans and targets.

In theory, this sounds attractive. It seems likely that such a system will contribute to good outcomes for programs and organizations through providing an incentive system that encourages managers and staff to focus on and achieve better performance and through providing information for decision makers that will enable them to reward and maintain good performance and intervene in cases of poor performance. In practice, as has been repeatedly found, many systems of accountability of this type are subject to several forms of corruption and hence are likely to reduce the sense of responsibility for and quality of performance.

The most common problem is a too-narrow focus on justification through meeting agreed targets for service delivery outputs. In organizations in which this is the case, and in which, additionally, rewards and sanctions for individuals and organizations are tightly tied to the achievement of pre-established targets, goal displacement is highly likely (in goal displacement, people seek to achieve the target even at the expense of no longer achieving the objective). The most notorious example comes from the Vietnam War, during which the emphasis on body counts, used as a proxy for success in battles, led to increased killing of civilians in one-sided and strategically unimportant battles. Public sector examples of this sort of problem abound, but there are also many private sector examples in which senior managers have been rewarded handsomely for achieving specific targets at the cost of the long-term viability of the company.

Another common effect is that what gets measured gets done, as intended, but what is not measured is no longer valued or encouraged. A program may turn to "creaming": selecting easier clients so that targets of throughput or outcomes can be achieved, at the cost of reduced access for those who most need the service. Other important values for the organization, such as cooperation across different units of the organization, may no longer be encouraged because of the emphasis on achieving one's own targets. Finally, there are many reported cases in which such a system encourages data corruption: Reported outcomes are exaggerated or modified to match targets.

Disquiet about the effects of this sort of evaluation is at the heart of concerns about high-stakes testing of children in schools, in which case serious sanctions for children, teachers, and schools follow poor performance in standardized tests.

Even if rewards and sanctions are not tightly tied to these forms of accountability—that is, there are few consequences built into the accountability system— other problems arise: cynicism about the value of monitoring and evaluation and the commitment of decision makers to reasonable decision-making processes.

What are the alternatives? It is not necessary to abandon the notion of being accountable for what has been done but to return to the meaning and focus on systems that both justify and explain what has been done. This requires careful consideration of who is being held accountable, to whom, for what, how, and with what consequences. More thoughtful and comprehensive approaches to accountability should demonstrably support good performance and encourage responsibility. Some have referred to this as *smart accountability*.

The first issue to consider is who is being held accountable. Those being held accountable are most often program managers but could and possibly should include staff, senior managers, and politicians. Politicians often claim that their accountability is enacted through elections, but these are clearly imperfect because they are infrequent, involve multiple issues, and often reflect party allegiances rather than responses to specific issues.

The second issue is to whom these parties are being held accountable and how. They are most often held accountable to those making funding decisions but could and possibly should be accountable to the community, citizens, service users, consumer advocacy groups, taxpayers, relevant professions, and international organizations for compliance with international agreements and conventions. These different audiences for accountability have been labeled *upwards accountability* and *outwards accountability,* respectively. Parties are most often held accountable through performance indicators shown in regular reports to funders, but may also be held accountable through diverse methods such as annual reports, spot inspections, detailed commentaries on performance indicators, or public meetings and reporting.

Real accountability to citizens would involve making appropriate information accessible to citizens, together with some process for feedback and consequences. Annual reports from government departments, corporate entities, and projects are one method for providing this information but are usually used instead as a public relations exercise, highlighting the positive and downplaying problems. The information availability that has been produced by the Internet has created many more opportunities for reporting information to citizens who have ready access to the Internet if there is a central agency willing to provide the information. So, for example, in Massachusetts, parents seeking to choose a residential neighborhood, and hence a schooling system, can access detailed performance indicators comparing resources spent on education, demographic characteristics, activities undertaken, and test scores in different neighborhoods to help inform their decision. However, there remain difficulties for parents in synthesizing, interpreting, and applying this information to decisions about what would be best for their particular children. Without appropriate analysis and interpretation, there are risks that clients and taxpayers will draw dangerously wrong conclusions. For example, some senior bureaucrats have advocated making surgeons accountable to the public by publishing their rates for complication and death. The obvious problem is that without suitable adjustment for various factors, those surgeons would appear less effective who treated the most severe cases or patients with the poorest health.

The third aspect that needs to be addressed is that for which people are being held accountable. Given the concerns outlined so far, it is clear that consideration must be given to more than simply meeting targets. Other aspects of performance that may need to be included are coverage (matching actual clients with intended target groups), treatment (providing services in the agreed way and in the agreed amount), fiscal management (spending the money on the agreed inputs, proper controls against fraud), and legal compliance (ensuring procedural adherence to laws, policies, and regulations). It is not reasonable, of course, to expect programs to be able to simultaneously meet unilaterally set targets for all of these. An example would be schools or hospitals that are expected to meet standards for open access to all cases, legal requirements about curriculum or standards of care, and fiscal targets linked to reduced budgets and are punished for not meeting the same outcomes for students or patients as organizations with fewer competing accountabilities.

Accountability needs to be understood not just in terms of reporting compliance and meeting targets but in terms of explaining and justifying legitimate variations, including necessary trade-offs between competing imperatives and accountability. Easy achievement of a timid target can easily be reported. Understandable and legitimate differences between the target and actual performance will require space and a sympathetic audience for a more detailed explanation.

Accountability also needs to go beyond those outcomes that are directly under the control of those who are being held accountable—for example, employment outcomes of school students or long-term family outcomes for children in foster care. Although it is not reasonable to suggest that the performance of these programs and managers should be assessed only by these long-term outcomes, it is also unreasonable to base it only on the completion of units of service that they can totally control. A better form of accountability expects them to be aware of the subsequent causal chain and to be actively seeking to have a beneficial effect on it or to be redeveloping the program so that it is more likely to do so.

The final and most important aspect of an accountability system is the consequences for those providing the reports. Reputational accountability and market accountability, where adverse performance can affect credibility and market pressures, respectively, depend on evidence of performance being available to be scrutinized by relevant parties. More usually, accountability systems focus on reporting discrepancies between targets and performance to funders, the assumption being that they will use this information in future funding and policy decisions. However, accountability systems rarely provide sufficient information to make it possible for funders to decide if such discrepancies should be followed by decreased funding (as a sanction), increased funding (to improve the quality or quantity of services being provided), or termination of the function.

Accountability requires a much more comprehensive explanation of performance, an incentive system that encourages improvement of performance rather than misreport and distortion of it, and a commitment to address learning as well as accountability. In other words, accountability systems need to be a tool for informed judgment and management rather than a substitute. This is the smart accountability that has been increasingly advocated.

Smart accountability includes demonstrating responsible, informed management; including appropriate risk management, such as cautious trials of difficult or new approaches; and a commitment to identify and learn from both successes and mistakes. The incentive system for accountability needs to reward *intelligent failure* (competent implementation of something that has since been found not to work), discourage setting easy targets, discourage simply reporting compliance with processes or targets, and encourage seeking out tough criticism.

The acid test of a good accountability system is that it encourages responsibility and promotes better performance.

—*Patricia J. Rogers*

Further Reading

American Evaluation Association. (2002). *American Evaluation Association position statement on high stakes testing in preK-12 education*. Retrieved April 23, 2004, from http://www.eval.org/hst3.htm

Mayne, J. (2001). *Science, research, & development: Evaluation workshops. Seminar 1: Performance measurement.* Retrieved April 23, 2004, from http://www.dpi.vic.gov.au/dpi/nrensr.nsf/FID/-341A311BA4C565A7CA256C090017CA16? Open Document#1

Perrin, B. (1999). Performance measurement: Does the reality match the rhetoric? *American Journal of Evaluation, 20*(1), 101-114.

ACCREDITATION

Accreditation is a process and an outcome, and it exists in two main forms. First, there is accreditation offered by an institution or awarding body to individuals on the basis of academic or training credit already gained within the institution or as a direct result of prior or current learning. Second, there is accreditation sought by an institution from an outside awarding body through some form of formal professional review.

The processes of accreditation make credible the autonomous privilege of an organization or body to confer academic or training awards. Furthermore, accreditation is commonly used to form new programs or to open opportunities for a wider adoption of courses leading to the confirmation of awards. In the context of wider participation in education and training, it is not unusual to hear questions about whether academic standards are the same across a nation or state or comparable between institutions capable of awarding academic or training credit. The idea here is not to point the finger at any single phase of education or the quality assurance process but to address difficult questions openly. The reality is a raft of issues concerned with comparing and formally evaluating standards of attainment.

STANDARDS AND PHILOSOPHY

The process of accreditation is a complex course of action that attempts to evaluate standards of attainment. Indeed, the definition and evaluation of attainable, objective standards relevant to the discipline or domain are often part of the expressed goals for accreditation. This argument may appear to ascribe greater worth to evaluating the outcomes of a training process rather than understanding the kinds of personal change and development expected during the training. However, whether we are outcome or process driven, it is important to know what principles and ideals drive accreditation.

As suggested in the foregoing argument, a philosophy of accreditation is more often determined by the definition of the concerns and principles underpinning the process. Focusing on such principles should diminish any undue reliance on evaluation of course outcomes as a single focus of assessment. Indeed, confidence in a single overriding criterion for assessment can create a negative model of noncompliance. For example, close matching of prior experiential learning-to-learning outcomes of particular modules within a program can capture some evidence of equivalence of experience, but it is less robust as evidence of corresponding learning. This approach can result in the accreditation of the matching process rather than learning and leads us to ask the question, "Are we measuring the comparability of standards, the quality of learning, or the similarity of experience?"

ACCREDITED LEARNING

Accreditation of students' or trainees' learning can apply where awards are credit rated, with all program and award routes leading to awards offered within the institution, calibrated for credit as an integral part of the validation process. The outcome of this accreditation process is credit, a recognizable educational "currency" that students can seek to transfer from one award to another, from one program to another, and from one institution to another. Although credit can be transferred, the marks achieved by the student are not usually transferable.

Accredited learning is defined as formal learning, including learning assessed and credit rated or certificated by the institution or an external institution or similar awarding body and learning that has not been assessed but that is capable of assessment for the purpose of awarding credit.

Credit gained in the context of a named award may be transferred to another named award. However, credit transfer across named awards is not automatic. Transfer of credit from one award route to another is dependent on the learning outcomes being deemed by the institution as valid for the new award. To be recognized as contributing credit to an award, the evidence of the accredited learning must be capable of demonstrating the following:

- Authenticity, by evidence that the applicant completed what was claimed
- Direct comparison, by evidence of a matching of the learning outcomes with those expected of comparable specified modules approved by the university for the award sought
- Currency, by evidence that the learning achieved is in keeping with expectations of knowledge current in the area of expertise required
- Accreditation of experiential learning

Experiential learning is defined as learning achieved through experience gained by an individual outside formalized learning arrangements. An applicant may apply for the award of credit on the evidence of experiential

learning. Such evidence must be capable of assessment and of being matched against the learning outcomes of the program for which the applicant is seeking credit.

The normal forms of assessment for the accreditation of experiential learning include the following:

- A structured portfolio with written commentary and supporting evidence
- A structured interview plus corroborating evidence
- Work-based observation plus a portfolio or other record
- Assignments or examinations set for relevant, approved modules or units

FORMAL PROFESSIONAL REVIEW

Institutions that are intent on gaining accreditation must freely and autonomously request a formal evaluation from an awarding organization or body. Accreditation involves an external audit of the institution's ability to provide a service of high quality by comparing outcomes to a defined standard of practice, which is confirmed by peer review.

Current accreditation arrangements rely on the assumption that only bona fide members of a profession should judge the activities of their peers, and by criteria largely or wholly defined by members of the profession. Historically, there are some interesting examples of nonexpert examination of the professional practices of institutions (for example, Flexner's examination of medical schools in the United States and Canada in the early 1900s), but this form of lay review is not at all typical of the way modern forms of formal review for accreditation have grown up.

Rather, accreditation of an institution has largely become a formal process of program evaluation by peers, which, if successful, testifies that an institution or awarding body:

- has a purpose appropriate to the phase of education or domain of training
- has physical and human resources, teaching schemes, assessment structures, and support services sufficient to realize that purpose on a continuing basis
- maintains clearly specified educational objectives that are consistent with its mission
- is successful in achieving its stated objectives
- is able to provide evidence that it is accomplishing its mission

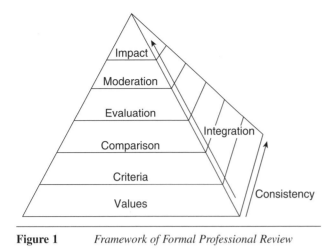

Figure 1   *Framework of Formal Professional Review*

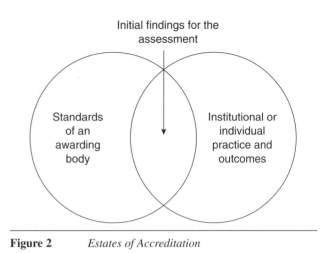

Figure 2   *Estates of Accreditation*

The requirements, policies, processes, procedures, and decisions of accreditation are predicated on a full commitment to integrity and on institutions dedicating themselves to being learning societies, capable of inclusive and democratic activity. The existence of a single accreditation process in a variety of learning contexts requires adherence to agreed-on evaluation criteria within a common framework of formal program evaluation, and this may not always be possible or desirable. Indeed, it is the development of an adequate accreditation design that is the single most important activity in matching the accreditation process to the context to which it is being applied.

FRAMEWORK OF FORMAL PROFESSIONAL REVIEW

The development of an adequate accreditation design is best placed within a conceptual framework of formal professional review underpinned by a common value system and an agreed-on set of criteria. A model of formal professional review is shown in Figure 1.

Values

Underpinning the review process is an agreed-on set of fundamental principles and values relevant to the awarding body and the institution under review, and these principles and values are shared by all. For example, one of the values might be that the highest duty of all concerned is to preserve life and to labor to improve the quality of life. This is a foundation from which the right to award accreditation is offered and sought.

Without such foundations, the review process might well become a somewhat arid inspection of organizational structures, course content, and assessment practices.

Criteria

The formal review is structured around a set of requirements made specific in the form of observable criteria that are grouped in appropriate ways and listed in a convenient form for reference and substantiation. These criteria are embedded in the structure of the value system underpinning the common concern and exist wholly within the parameters of the shared principles. The formulation of criteria affects the organization of the review and the nature of how accordance is recorded.

Comparison

A comparison is made (Figure 2) between two *estates of accreditation:* institutional or individual practice and the standards of the awarding body. Comparisons are made by observation of practice, scrutiny of documentation, and engagement in professional discourse. These processes lie fully within the agreed-on criteria, so when contextual and other interesting matters arise, these are not carried forward into the next stage. The extent to which there is an overlap between the two estates provides initial findings for the assessment.

Evaluation

Reviewers consider the nature and content of the overlap between the two estates and how that might affect their overall judgment. Value is ascribed and evidence is reviewed to discriminate between discernment, opinion, and critique. Some elements of the comparison may be eliminated from the evaluation process as not pertinent in this context (whether accreditation should be awarded). An argument could be made that evaluation is best carried out by peer professionals, who bring expert experience, knowledge, and understanding to the process, and that this expertise goes beyond commonsense approaches.

Moderation

In this part of the process, the reviewers affirm their judgments and authenticate their findings by grounding them back into the evidence base, verifying the sources of their evidence, and ensuring the rigor of the process that has taken place. If thought necessary or made necessary by some sampling arrangement, alternative opinions are sought and compared with the substantive findings and outcomes. Perceptions are sought of the extent to which practice in assessment and evaluation has been informed by an agreed-on set of fundamental principles and values.

Before the final part of the framework of formal professional review is considered, two dimensions of the framework should be examined that not only form the glue that binds the framework together but make the importance of the impact phase more apparent when they are defined.

Consistency

The consistency dimension is one in which judgments can be made about the extent to which what appears on the face of the institution can be consistently found throughout its structures and organization. At a time when institutions are increasingly positioning themselves as "student facing" or "business facing," it is becoming vital to take a metaphorical slice across the organization to see to what extent attempts to create a compliant façade are supported with scaffolding by the remainder of the organization. Toward the top of the Framework of Formal Professional Review (Figure 1), there is less depth to the organization, and thus approaches to assessment, moderation, and the student experience should be more transparent.

Integration

The division of any process into sections inevitably raises questions about the extent to which judgments

about an institution should contain an element of gestalt. Indeed, the extent to which an organized whole is greater than the sum of its parts is a judgment that needs to be made. The successful integration of the structures, provision, programs, and procedures of any institution is a significant part of its ability to provide evidence that it is accomplishing its mission.

Impact

At the apex of Figure 1 is *Impact*. The impact is often on the individual learner, whose experience is difficult to capture but whose story of personal change and development is pivotal to full understanding of the nature of what takes place in the overlap between the two estates of accreditation. What has happened to this individual and to all the other individuals in the impact section of the framework is of momentous importance to making things better in classrooms, in hospital wards and theaters, in workplaces and homes. It could be argued that securing intelligence of what happens to individual learners and how they are changed by their learning experiences remains an unconquered acme of accreditation.

—Malcolm Hughes and
Saville Kushner

Further Reading

Evans, N. (1992). *Experiential learning: Its assessment and accreditation.* New York: Routledge.

Council for National Academic Awards. (1990). *Accreditation: The American experience.* London: Author.

Fretwell, D. (2003). A framework for evaluating vocational education and training (VET). *European Journal of Education, 38*(2), 177-190.

Stufflebeam, D. L. (2001). The metaevaluation imperative. *American Journal of Evaluation, 22*(2), 183-209.

ACCURACY. *See* BIAS, OBJECTIVITY, RELIABILITY, VALIDITY

ACHIEVEMENT

In education, *achievement* is the construct of understanding student learning and educational effectiveness. Because what a student knows and can do cannot be measured directly but must be inferred, determining the nature and level of a student's achievement—identifying achievement in real-life cases—is necessarily problematic. Apparent precision in achievement test scores belies the elusiveness of achievement and maintains public confidence that test scores accurately indicate achievement. Although increasingly prominent since the mid-19th century, standardized high-stakes achievement testing has generated concern and opposition. Thus, as achievement has become ever more crucial in educational accountability and evaluation, determining achievement has become correspondingly controversial.

—Linda Mabry

■■ ACTION RESEARCH

The main features of action research are as follows:

- It includes a developmental aim that embodies a professional ideal and that all those who participate are committed to realizing in practice.
- It focuses on changing practice to make it more consistent with the developmental aim.
- In identifying and explaining inconsistencies between aspiration and practice (such explanation may lie in the broader institutional, social, and political context), it problematizes the assumptions and beliefs (theories) that tacitly underpin professional practice.
- It involves professional practitioners in a process of generating and testing new forms of action for realizing their aspirations and thereby enables them to reconstruct the theories that guide their practice.
- It is a developmental process characterized by reflexivity on the part of the practitioner.

From an action research perspective, professional practice is a form of research and vice versa.

Good action research is informed by the values practitioners want to realize in their practice. In social work, for example, it is defined by the professional values (e.g., client empowerment, antioppressive practice) social workers want to realize. Professional values are ideas about what constitutes a professionally worthwhile process of working with clients and colleagues. Such values specify criteria for identifying appropriate modes of interaction. In other words, they define the relationship between the content of professional work, practitioners, and their various clients.

Terms such as *care, education, empowerment, autonomy, independence, quality, justice,* and *effectiveness* all specify qualities of that relationship. Good action research is developmental; namely, it is a form of reflective inquiry that enables practitioners to better realize such qualities in their practice. The tests for good action research are very pragmatic ones. Will the research improve the professional quality of the transactions between practitioners and clients or colleagues? Good action research might fail this particular test if it generates evidence to explain why improvement is impossible under the circumstances, in which case it justifies a temporary tolerance of the status quo. In each case, action research provides a basis for wise and intelligent decision making. A decision to wait awhile with patience until the time is ripe and circumstances open new windows of opportunity is sometimes wiser than repeated attempts to initiate change.

These are not extrinsic tests but ones that are continuously conducted by practitioners within the process of the research itself. If practitioners have no idea whether their research is improving their practice, then its status as action research is very dubious indeed. It follows from this that action research is not a different process from that of professional practice. Rather, action research is a form of practice and vice versa. It fuses practice and research into a single activity. Those who claim they have no time for research because they are too busy working with clients and colleagues misunderstand the relationship. They are saying they have no time to change their practice in any fundamental sense. When practice strategies are viewed as hypothetical probes into ways of actualizing professional values, they constitute the core activities of a research process, a process that must always be distinguished from research on practice by outsiders.

Action research aims to realize values in practice. Practitioner action research may use outsider research, but it always subordinates the generation of propositional knowledge to the pursuit of practical situational understanding.

ACTION RESEARCH DEVELOPS THE CURRICULUM

Good action research always implies practice development. Practice is never simply a set of statements about the content of activities. It always specifies a mode of interaction. If it is specified in terms of specific behavioral objectives, then the message to clients and colleagues is that the objectives of professional work define them in terms of deficits and that remedies for these deficits may be found only within a dependency relationship. The question then is whether such practices enable professional workers to represent their work in a form that is consistent with the nature of facilitative, caring, or educational relationships.

Professional practice embodies psychological, sociological, political, and ethical theories. It is through action research that the potential of these theories can be assessed. Through action research, practices are deconstructed and reconstructed in both content and form. Practice designs (plans, guidelines, etc.) need not simply determine practice; rather, by means of action research, they themselves can be shaped through practice. Good practice planning will not only specify the content of action but articulate general principles governing the form in which it is to be enacted. In other words, it should specify action hypotheses in the form of strategies for realizing such principles, which practitioners in general can explore in their particular professional contexts. Such strategies need not be confined to immediate interpersonal processes but can refer to the wider organizational practices that shape social relationships and the amount of time available to various participants for working on certain kinds of tasks. A good practice design not only specifies good professional practice but also provides guidance on how to realize it. The outcome of good action research is not simply improvement in the quality of professional work for those engaged in it but the systematic articulation of what this involves and how others might achieve it. Good action research does not generate private knowledge for an elite core of staff. It renders what they have achieved public and open to professional scrutiny.

ACTION RESEARCH IMPLIES *REFLEXIVE* PRACTICE, NOT SIMPLY *REFLECTIVE* PRACTICE

Good action research generates evidence to support judgments about the quality of practice. The evidence is always about the mode of interaction. Practitioner research that focuses on everything other than the interpersonal conditions established by practitioners is not good action research. Good action research is always reflexive, not merely reflective. One can

reflect about all manner of things other than one's own actions. Evidence of client outcomes does not, in isolation, constitute evidence of practice quality. Outcomes need to be explained. The quality of immediate practice activities is only one possible explanation for success or failure. Other kinds of evidence need to be collected before the contribution of the individual practitioner's decision making to client outcomes can be judged. Outcome data may provide a basis for hypothesizing about the nature of this contribution, but the hypotheses will need to be tested against other evidence concerning the professional process. Outcome data are very indirect evidence of quality. Judging the quality of outcomes and the quality of practice are different enterprises.

ACTION RESEARCH INVOLVES GATHERING DATA ABOUT PRACTICE FROM DIFFERENT POINTS OF VIEW

Evidence about the quality of practice can be gathered from a number of sources: practitioners' own accounts of their practice, clients' and colleagues' accounts, peer observations of each others' practice, "outsiders'" observational accounts, and video and audio recordings of professional transactions. This process of gathering data from a multiplicity of sources is called *triangulation*. There are three fundamental sources of evidence: from observers and from the major participants, that is, the practitioner and her or his clients and colleagues. In a fully developed action research process, practitioners will be comparing and contrasting the accounts of observers and clients or colleagues with their own.

ACTION RESEARCH DEFINES RATHER THAN APPLIES QUALITY INDICATORS

These are the sources of evidence, but how do practitioners make sense of this evidence? How do they know what to look for? Do they need a precoded checklist of quality indicators—specific behaviors that are indicative of the qualities they want to realize in their practice? The problem with suggesting that they do is that it preempts and distorts what is involved in doing action research. Quality indicators cannot be predefined because it is the task of action research to define them. When practitioners choose certain courses of action as a possible means of realizing their educational values in practice, they are exploring the question, "What actions are indicative of those values?" Evidence then has to be collected to determine whether the means selected are indicative of the professional values the practitioner espouses. Practitioners may select a course of action in the belief that it will facilitate the empowerment of clients or colleagues and, in the light of triangulation data, discover this belief to be problematic. Clients may, for example, report that they experience the actions as constraints, and such reports may appear to be consistent with observational accounts. The evidence thus renders the practitioners' actions problematic as quality indicators and challenges practitioners to redefine what constitutes good practice in the circumstances they confront.

Professional quality indicators are determined through action research, not in advance of it. Pre-specifications of quality indicators prescribe what practitioners must do to realize professional values. By standardizing responses, they render the responses insensitive to context and substitute standardized assessments of performance in the place of action research. Good action research acknowledges the fact that what constitutes quality in professional practice cannot be defined independently of the particular set of circumstances a practitioner confronts. It can only be defined *in situ* through action research. Practitioners may, through action research, generalize indicators across a range of contexts, but this outcome provides a source of hypotheses to be tested and not a prescriptive straitjacket that preempts practitioners from ultimately judging what actions are indicative of quality in particular circumstances. Good action research involves grounding such judgments in triangulated case data.

—*John Elliott*

Further Reading

Argyris, C., Putnam, R., & Smith, D. M. (1985). *Action science: Concepts, methods and skills for research and intervention.* San Francisco: Jossey-Bass.

Carr, W., & Kemmis, S. (1986). *Becoming critical: Education knowledge and action research.* London: Falmer.

Elliott, J. (1991). *Action research for educational change.* Milton Keynes, PA: Open University Press.

Kemmis, S., & McTaggart, R. (1988). *The action research planner* (3rd ed.). Geelong, Victoria, Australia: Deakin University Press.

ACTIVE LEARNING NETWORK FOR ACCOUNTABILITY AND PERFORMANCE IN HUMANITARIAN ACTION (ALNAP)

Established in 1997, the Active Learning Network for Accountability and Performance in Humanitarian Action (ALNAP) is an international interagency forum dedicated to improving the quality and accountability of humanitarian action by sharing lessons; identifying common problems; and, where appropriate, building consensus on approaches. ALNAP consists of 51 full members and approximately 300 observer members. Member representatives are drawn from the policy, operations, evaluation, and monitoring sections of organizations involved in humanitarian action.

ACTIVITY THEORY

Activity theory is an approach to psychology based on Marx's dialectical materialism that was developed by revolutionary Russian psychologists Vygotsky, Leont'ev, and Luria in the 1920s and 1930s. The focus of analysis is the activity undertaken by a person (subject) with a purpose (object) that is mediated by psychological tools (systems of numbers, language) and often performed in collaboration with others. An activity occurs in a cultural context that includes conventions, such as cultural rules, and forms of relationships, such as a division of labor.

See also Systems and Systems Thinking

Further Reading

Nardi, B. (1996). (Ed.). *Context and consciousness: Activity theory and human-computer interaction.* Cambridge: MIT Press.

ADELMAN, CLEM

(b. 1942, Tring, England). Ph.D. Science Education, London University; B.Sc. Education, London University.

Adelman began teaching about and doing research and evaluation in 1964. Since 1972 he has worked at the Center for Applied Research in Education (CARE), University of East Anglia, United Kingdom, and has also held appointments at the University of Reading and the University of Trondheim in Norway.

At CARE, Adelman initially worked on the Ford Foundation Teaching Project, which promoted self-evaluation and classroom action research, and then on an ethnographic study of 3- to 5-year-old children in schools. He became increasingly involved in evaluation problems arising from fieldwork and case studies, especially those in which the evaluators aspired to be democratic in their principles and conduct. He has worked on various evaluations, including those concerning arts education; bilingual schooling in Boston, MA; assessment of oral English; school-industry links; and residential care for the handicapped.

His work on the feasibility of institutional self-evaluation has contributed to a broad understanding of how and why educational organizations engage in evaluation. His book (with Robin Alexander) *Self-Evaluating Institution: Practice and Principles in the Management of Educational Change* reflects these contributions. Some of his other books include *The Politics and Ethics of Evaluation; Guide to Classroom Observation* (with Rob Walker); and the edited volume *Uttering, Muttering: Collecting, Using and Reporting Talk for Social and Educational Research.*

Adelman's work has been influenced by fellow evaluators Bob Stake, Barry McDonald, Ernie House, and Gene Glass, as well Bela Bartok, H. S. Becker, Ernest Gellner, Stephen J. Gould, Nat Hentoff, Georg Simmel, and Spinoza.

Adelman has lived and worked in the south of France, Norway, northwest China, and Hungary. He is an accomplished saxophone player.

ADVERSARIAL EVALUATION.
See JUDICIAL MODEL OF EVALUATION

■■ ADVOCACY IN EVALUATION

Advocacy, defined in many of the debates as taking sides, is seen as one of the more intractable matters in contemporary evaluation. For example, Linda Mabry notes, "Whether reports should be advocative and whether they can avoid advocacy is an issue which has exercised the evaluation community in recent years. The inescapability [from a constructionist stance] of an evaluator's personal values as a fundamental undegirding for reports has been noted but resisted by objectivist evaluators [who have] focused on bias management through design elements and critical analysis. At issue is whether evaluation should be proactive or merely instrumental." M. F. Smith, considering the future of evaluation, writes, "The issue (of independence/objectivity versus involvement/ advocacy) is what gives me the most worry about the ability of our field to be a profession."

Mabry's and Smith's concerns seem well justified. Granted, the issue of advocacy in evaluation is *complex* in that examining one aspect (for example, the nature of objectivity in social science) leads to another aspect (such as methods of bias control), then another (such as the role of the evaluator as an honest broker, a voice for the disenfranchised, or something else), then another as quickly. The issue is *high stakes* in that the approach taken may lead to different evaluation processes, designs, measures, analyses, conclusions, and, probably, consequences. With a few exceptions, there appears to be little systematic comparative study on this point. The issue of advocacy is *divisive* in our field in that beliefs about advocacy seem deeply and sometimes rancorously held. Last, despite the development of evaluation standards and guidelines, in practice, there is no more than chance agreement and *considerable unpredictability* on what experienced evaluators would do in quite a few ethical situations involving advocacy.

Often, advocacy issues are posed as questions: What is the role of the evaluator? Is impartiality a delusion? In particular, do the Guiding Principles of the American Evaluation Association place a priority on Principle E (Responsibilities for General and Public Welfare) before Principles A through D, if all cannot be satisfied equally? Does credibility require objectivity? These questions were prominent in the 1994 examination of the future of evaluation, based on statements of more than 25 leading evaluators, and they became even more so in the 2000 statements.

PART OF THE CONTEXT

Relatively powerful groups largely fund evaluations— foundations; large philanthropies such as the United Way; local, state, and federal governments; boards and directors of organizations. The questions the evaluator is to help answer are specified initially by the organizations funding the evaluation. In some instances, so are the evaluation designs (for example, use of randomized control groups to help rule out alternative explanations of results); so are the constructs to be measured (for example, reading readiness); and, at times, so are the measures themselves, particularly the performance indicators.

Speculatively, all might have been well, if, in the early decades of evaluation, most studies showed reasonably positive effects, leading to more services for more people in need. Evaluations, however, often have yielded macronegative results: no measurable evidence of program benefits. Lacking evidence of benefits, programs may be closed down or revised and underlying policies discredited. If one believes in the evaluation results, this is good utilization of evaluation. Truly ineffective programs waste funds and, worse, deprive service recipients of possibly much more effective assistance if something different were tried: If it doesn't work, programmatically, try another approach.

Many of the programs under fairly constant review, revision, or sometimes closure, however, affected low-income people, minorities, and persons of color; many public expenditures benefiting relatively wealthier persons or groups never got evaluated. Evaluations of such programs tended to focus on service delivery, efficiency, and costs rather than effectiveness. In addition, being perceived as an unfriendly critic or executioner is painful. Understandably, evaluators—particularly those at the local level but also many distinguished evaluation theorists—looked carefully at the adequacy of the evaluation frameworks, designs, measures, analyses, and processes. Could the results derived through evaluation approaches seen as biased toward the most privileged groups be trusted? If not, as a matter of social justice and practicality, another approach should be tried, one more likely to "level the playing field." Thus around the mid-1970s and early 1980s, evaluation began to split along the fault line of the possibility or impossibility of objectivity.

THE POSSIBILITY OF OBJECTIVITY

Some evaluators conclude that evaluator neutrality is at the heart of evaluation; that it is necessary for credibility; that meaningful, reliable, valid information about a situation usually is available; and that frameworks offering objective, trustworthy answers are possible. Recognizing (a) the need and benefits of listening to stakeholders; (b) the value of including, where appropriate, extensive study of process and context that can help explain how observed outcomes came about; and (c) the value of mixed methods, theorists such as Rossi and Freeman, Boruch, Chelimsky, Scriven, and Stufflebeam have emphasized methodologies they see as offering the most certain, least equivocal answers to client questions.

In this view, social good means spending money on programs that work by criteria seen as their raison d'etre by the funders and by others, backed by strong evidence to rule out alternative explanations or rule in plausible causes. One tries to understand the hopes and the fears for the program, to look for unintended as well as intended consequences, to study the program as it actually happens as well as the program as intended. Pragmatically, because stakeholder involvement can make for better evaluations and better utilization, it is an important part of the evaluation process. Also, in this view, evaluators try to understand, explain, and show what was happening, including context, that best accounts for the findings. They should not, however, take the side of any stakeholder group but strive to be impartial sources of reliable information. Theory-driven evaluation and its application in program logic models (Chen); realist evaluation (Henry, Mark, Julnes); frameworks connecting context, input, processes, and results (Stufflebeam); integrative meta-analyses (Shadish, Lipsey, Light); and contemporary experimental designs (Boruch) evolved from these concerns.

THE IMPOSSIBILITY OF OBJECTIVITY

Other evaluators, such as Lincoln and Guba, Mertens, and House and Howe, conclude that evaluations in which the more powerful have an exclusive or primary say in all aspects of the evaluation are inherently flawed, both as a matter of social justice and because of the impossibility of objectivity. Evaluators should be open and up-front in acknowledging their own value stances about programs; should accept that all sources of information about programs will reflect the value stances of the people with whom they are interacting; and, as a matter of responsible evaluation, should give extra weight to the most disenfranchised. Approaches such as Fourth Generation Evaluation

(Lincoln and Guba), Utilization Focused Evaluation (Patton), and Empowerment Evaluation (Fetterman) emphasize meaning as a social construct; place strongest emphasis on diverse stakeholder involvement and control, particularly the participation of service deliverers and service recipients; and see the evaluator role as "friendly critic" or consultant in helping the learning organization examine itself.

In one variant of this general approach, the evaluator becomes an open advocate for social justice as she or he perceives social justice in each case, for the most disenfranchised and the least powerful. This could mean, for example, making the best possible case for the continuation of a program offering what the evaluator saw as social benefits, such as employment of low-income persons as program staff. It could mean that negative evidence potentially leading to loss of jobs or services for low-income persons might not be reported. It could mean that evidence of what the evaluator perceives as a social injustice (an interviewee tells of an instance of sexual harassment) is reported and the program director threatened, when the line of inquiry was not part of the original study. In other words, the evaluator takes sides for or against the interests of certain, primarily less powerful groups before, during, and after the evaluation.

Ahn offers some information on evaluators' "program entanglements" as they affect practice decisions. Based on interviews of a range of evaluators, Ahn reports,

> Many evaluators considered and identified "the least powerful or marginalized group" in the program, whose voices are rarely heard, as crucial in their work. And their allegiance to this group was addressed in a variety of ways in their program. DM, who viewed "emancipation" as the role of her evaluation, for example, spoke of the importance of evaluators being attentive to the needs of "people who could be hurt the most," giving voices to them and promoting their participation. R was also concerned with questions of power. For example, in reporting her evaluation findings, she devoted the largest section in her report to presenting the perspectives of the least powerful who had the most to lose.

Where the voices of contrasting evaluators can be heard on same evaluation situation, as in Michael Morris' ethics in evaluation series in the *American Journal of Evaluation,* the powerful urge to administer on-the-spot social justice (as an advocate for an individual, program, or principle) is perhaps startlingly clear in ways the theorists probably had not intended.

TOWARD COMMON GROUND

Both broad approaches can be caricatured. No constructionist, for example, advocates making up imaginary data to make a program look good. Most would present negative findings but in ways they believed would be appropriate and constructive, such as informally and verbally. And no "neopositivist" ignores human and contextual factors in an evaluation or mindlessly gets meaningless information from flawed instruments to an obviously biased question.

There is much common ground. The leading proponents of advocacy in evaluation indicate that they mean advocacy for the voices of all stakeholders, not only the most powerful, and advocacy for the quality of the evaluation itself. They are concerned with fairness to all stakeholders in questions, designs, measures, decision making, and process, not with taking sides before an evaluation begins. And so are leading proponents of more positivist approaches.

Nonetheless, too little is known about actual decisions in evaluation practice. Recently, some evaluation organizations have been making all aspects of their studies transparent, even crystalline, from raw data to final reports (for example, the Urban Institute's New Federalism evaluation series). Articles focused on specific evaluations and specific evaluators, such as the *American Journal of Evaluation's* interviews with Len Bickman and with Stewart Donaldson, are showing how some evaluators work through practice choices. This kind of clarity should help us sort out conflicts among standards and principles and establish some agreed-on instances, in a sort of clinical practice, case-law sense.

There seems to be considerable agreement that as evaluators, our common ground is fairness. Our warrant is our knowledge of many ways of fairly representing diverse interests, understanding complexity and context, and wisely presenting what can be learned from a systematic, data-based inquiry. Our need is to anchor our debates on neutrality and advocacy in analysis of specific practice decisions so all can understand what constitutes nobly seeking fairness and what, notoriously exceeding our warrant.

—Lois-ellin Datta

Further Reading

Ahn, J. (2001, November). *Evaluators' program entanglements: How they related to practice decisions.* Paper presented at the annual meeting of the American Evaluation Association, St. Louis.

Datta, L.-e. (1999). The ethics of evaluation neutrality and advocacy. In J. L. Fitzpatrick & M. Morris (Eds.), Current and emerging ethical issues in evaluation. *New Directions for Evaluation, 82,* 77-88.

House, E. R., & Howe, K. R. (1998). The issue of advocacy in evaluations. *American Journal of Evaluation, 19*(2), 233-236.

Mabry, L. (2002). In living color: Qualitative methods in educational evaluation. In T. Kelleghan & D. L. Stufflebeam (Eds.), *International handbook of educational evaluation* (pp. 167-185). Dordrecht, The Netherlands: Kluwer Academic.

Scriven, M. (1997). Truth and objectivity in evaluation. In E. Chelimsky & W. Shadish (Eds.), *Evaluation for the 21st century: A handbook* (pp. 477-500). Thousand Oaks, CA: Sage.

Smith, M. F. (2002). The future of the evaluation profession. In T. Kelleghan & D. L. Stufflebeam (Eds.), *International handbook of educational evaluation* (pp. 373-386). Dordrecht, The Netherlands: Kluwer Academic.

◼◼ AESTHETICS

Aesthetics is a field of study within the discipline of philosophy that, at least currently and during much of the 20th century, has addressed questions about the nature and function of art. Aesthetic theory became part of the discourse within the evaluation field primarily through the work of Elliot Eisner. Eisner used aesthetic theory from a number of philosophers (such as Susanne Langer and John Dewey) to conceptualize and create a justifying rationale for an approach to evaluation based on art criticism. Among other things, Eisner's connoisseurship-criticism model emphasized the use of literary techniques to capture and communicate the aesthetic dimensions of the phenomena being evaluated.

—*Robert Donmoyer*

See also CONNOISSEURSHIP

Further Reading

Dewey, J. (1980). *Art as experience.* New York: Perigee Books.

Langer, S. (1957). *Problems of art.* New York: Scribner.

◼◼ AFFECT

Affect refers to observable behavior or self-reports that express a subjectively experienced feeling or emotion. *Affect* and *attitude* are sometimes used interchangeably. Whether affect is independent of cognition is a debated topic. On the one hand is the assertion that people can have a purely emotional reaction to something without having processed any information about it. On the other hand is the assertion that at least some cognitive (albeit not always conscious) processing is necessary to evoke an emotional response. Affective measures are used in evaluation. Self-reports of affect provide information on preferences, although indirect measures of affect are sometimes considered more robust; that is, there is likely to be more stability shown in what people are observed to do than in what they say they do. Because interventions may focus specifically on changing people's affect (for example, emotional responses to gender, race, environmentalism, and so on), it is important for evaluators to establish valid indicators of affect.

◼◼ AGGREGATE MATCHING

In conditions where participants cannot be randomly assigned to program and control groups, the use of proper nonrandomized control groups is recommended to more accurately assess the effects of the independent variable under study. *Aggregate matching* is a procedure for devising matched controls in quasiexperimental evaluation research. Individuals are not matched, but the overall distributions in the experimental and control groups on each matching variable are made to correspond. For example, as a result of this procedure, similar proportions of characteristics such as gender and race would be found in both the program and comparison groups.

—*Marco A. Muñoz*

◼◼ AID TO FAMILIES WITH DEPENDENT CHILDREN (AFDC)

Building on the Depression-era Aid to Dependent Children program, Aid to Families with Dependent Children (AFDC) provided financial assistance to needy families from the 1970s to 1996. The federal government provided broad guidelines and program requirements, and states were responsible for program formulation, benefit determinations, and administration. Eligibility for benefits was based on a state's standard of need as well as the income and resources available to the recipient. In 1996, the Personal Responsibility and Work Opportunity Reconciliation Act replaced the AFDC program with the Temporary Assistance for Needy Families program.

—*Jeffrey G. Tucker*

■■ ALBÆK, ERIK

(b. 1955, Denmark). Ph.D. and M.A. in Political Science, University of Aarhus, Denmark.

Albæk is Professor of Public Administration, Department of Economics, Politics and Public Administration, Aalborg University, Denmark. Previous appointments include Eurofaculty Professor of Public Administration, Institute of International Relations and Political Science, University of Vilnius, Lithuania, and Associate Professor of Public Administration, University of Aarhus, Denmark. He has been an American Council of Learned Societies Fellow and Visiting Scholar in Administration, Planning, and Social Policy, Graduate School of Education, Harvard University, and in the Science, Technology, and Society program at Massachusetts Institute of Technology. Currently, he is Editor of *Scandinavian Political Studies* and previously was Editor of *GRUS*. Since 1989, he has participated in a variety of cross-national research projects with colleagues throughout Europe and the United States.

His primary contributions to evaluation focus on the history, utilization, and functions of evaluation, as well as decision theory, and his primary intellectual influences are to be found in the works of Herbert Simon, Charles Lindbloom, James March, and Carol Weiss. He wrote *HIV, Blood and the Politics of "Scandal" in Denmark,* cowrote *Nordic Local Government: Developmental Trends and Reform Activities in the Postwar Period,* and coedited *Crisis, Miracles, and Beyond: Negotiated Adaptation of the Danish Welfare State.* In addition, he has authored numerous articles and book chapters in both English and Danish.

■■ ALKIN, MARVIN C.

(b. 1934, New York). Ed.D. Stanford University; M.A.Education, and B.A. Mathematics, San Jose State College.

Alkin was instrumental in helping to shape the field of evaluation through his work on evaluation utilization and comparative evaluation theory. He drew attention to ways of categorizing evaluation theories and provided the discipline with a systematic analysis of the way in which evaluation theories develop. As a professor, Alkin developed novel ways of teaching graduate-level evaluation courses, including the use of simulation and role-playing.

His interest in systems analysis was cultivated through his association with Professor Fred MacDonald in the Educational Psychology Department at Stanford University. His thinking and early writings on cost-benefit and cost-effective analysis were fostered by Professor H. Thomas James, also at Stanford University. He was also influenced by his collegial relationships with other evaluators, such as Dan Stufflebeam, Bob Stake, and Michael Quinn Patton.

Alkin founded and served as the Director of the Center for the Study of Evaluation at the University of California, Los Angeles (UCLA), which gave him the opportunity to expand his thinking about issues related to evaluation theory. He was Editor-in-Chief for the *Encyclopedia of Educational Research* (6th edition) and Editor of *Educational Evaluation and Policy Analysis* (1995-1997). He is also a Founding Editor of *Studies in Educational Evaluation.* He received the American Paul F. Lazarsfeld Award from the American Evaluation Association for his contributions to the theories of evaluation.

He is a grandfather of five grandchildren and a dedicated UCLA basketball fan, having attended the full season every year since 1965.

■■ ALPHA TEST

A term used frequently in software development, *alpha test* refers to the first phase of testing in the development process. This phase includes unit, component, and system testing of the product. The term *alpha* derives from the first letter of the Greek alphabet.

■■ ALTSCHULD, JAMES W.

(b. 1939, Cleveland, Ohio). Ph.D. Educational Research and Development, M.S. Organic Chemistry, The Ohio State University; B.A. Chemistry, Case Western Reserve University.

A professor of education at The Ohio State University, Altschuld has contributed to the field of evaluation, especially in the areas of needs assessment and the evaluation of science education and technology, and has coauthored influential books on both topics. He has worked collaboratively with Ruth Witkin on an approach to needs assessment, a central construct in evaluation practice. Together they have written two books on needs assessment: *Planning and Conducting Needs Assessment: A Practical Guide* and *From Needs Assessment to Action: Transforming Needs Into Solution Strategies.* Along with collaborator David Kumar, Altschuld has developed a model of the evaluation of science education programs, reflected in his edited volume *Evaluation of Science and Technology Education at the Dawn of a New Millennium.* Altschuld has contributed substantially to evaluation as a profession through his position papers on certification of evaluators and in *The Directory of Evaluation Training Programs,* published in 1995.

He considers Ruth Altschuld, his wife, and Belle Ruth Witkin, a colleague, to be the major intellectual influences in his life.

Altschuld received the American Evaluation Association Alva and Gunnar Myrdal Evaluation Practice Award in 2002; in 2000, The Ohio State University College of Education Award for Research and Scholarship; in 1997, the Best Program Evaluation Research Award (with Kumar) from the Society for Information Technology and Teacher Evaluation; in 1990, the Evaluation Recognition Award from the Ohio Program Evaluators' Group; and in 1988, The Ohio State University Distinguished Teaching Award.

Altschuld is a reluctant but regular jogger and a devoted grandfather to Andrew and Lindsay.

■■ AMBIGUITY

Ambiguity refers to the absence of an overall framework to interpret situations. Multiple meanings can exist side by side, and this often causes confusion and conflict. Ambiguity differs from uncertainty. Whereas uncertainty—a shortage of information—can be reduced by facts, new and more objective information will not reduce ambiguity because facts do not have an inherent meaning. Ambiguity poses particular problems for evaluators: How is one to evaluate a policy or program if the underlying concept has no

clear meaning? A possible way out is to conduct a responsive approach that takes ambiguity as a departure point for reflexive dialogues on the evaluated practice.

—*Tineke A. Abma*

Further Reading

Abma, T. A. (2002). Evaluating palliative care: Facilitating reflexive dialogues about an ambiguous concept. *Medicine, Health Care and Philosophy, 4*(3), 259-276.

Weick, K. (1995). *Sensemaking in organizations.* Thousand Oaks, CA: Sage.

■■ AMELIORATION

To engage in evaluation is to engage in an activity that has the potential to improve the evaluand, or the human condition, more generally. Logically speaking, no evaluation in and of itself must necessarily purport to be helpful, and making a value judgment does not entail providing prescriptions, remediation, or amelioration. Michael Scriven has clearly delineated the distinction between doing evaluation, making a value judgment, and making a recommendation. In a theory of evaluation, this is an important distinction. In evaluation practice, however, the making of value judgments and the provision of recommendations becomes blurred because we have come to expect the work of evaluators and the purpose of evaluation to be more than simple rendering of value judgments: The purpose of evaluation is also *to make things better.* Acknowledging the serious logical and conceptual problems of moving from evaluative to prescriptive claims or actions, evaluation is meant to be helpful.

The assertion that evaluation should lead to improvement is in most senses self-evident. What is less evident is how evaluation is expected to contribute to making things better. Indeed, different approaches to evaluation conceptualize *helpfulness* and *improvement* differently. Speaking broadly, amelioration takes the form of progress either through science or through democratic processes. The first sort of amelioration is typical of quasiexperimental, decision-making, and systems analysis approaches to evaluation. The second sort of help is typical of participatory, collaborative, and deliberative approaches to evaluation.

Evaluations that are based on amelioration through science focus on the methods used (quasiexperimental or at least controlled) because these methods permit the examination of causal hypotheses. It is these causal relationships that are the key to amelioration— if one knows what causes what (e.g., whole-language teaching causes higher reading achievement), then this causal claim can be used to improve programs or services by choices that reflect the causal claim (e.g., adopting whole-language pedagogy). These causal claims might be reflected in their contribution to a general theory (of, say, academic achievement) or program theory (of, say, reading programs).

Evaluations that are based on amelioration through democratic processes assume that the meanings of good and right are socially constructed rather than scientifically discovered. This view suggests that truth claims are not natural causal laws but rather informed, sophisticated interpretations that are tentatively held. These interpretations depend on deliberation and dialogue, and it is this emphasis on evaluation process that flags this perspective of amelioration. Participatory, deliberative, and democratic approaches to evaluation reflect the ameliorative assumption based on faith in inclusiveness, participation, public dialogue, and constructivism as the means to improving or helping. Programs, services, and communities will be better as a result of an evaluation that includes stakeholders in genuine ways, thus enabling self-determination in problem definitions and solutions.

Further Reading

Scriven, M. (1995). The logic of evaluation and evaluation practice. In D. Fournier (Ed.), Reasoning in evaluation. *New Directions for Program Evaluation, 68.*

AMERICAN EVALUATION ASSOCIATION (AEA)

The American Evaluation Association (AEA) is an international professional association of evaluators devoted to the application and exploration of program evaluation, personnel evaluation, technology evaluation, and many other forms of evaluation. The association was formed in 1986 with the merger of the Evaluation Network and the Evaluation Research Society. AEA's mission is to improve evaluation practices and methods, increase evaluation use, promote evaluation as a profession, and support the contribution of evaluation to the generation of theory and knowledge about effective human action. AEA has

approximately 3000 members, representing all 50 states in the United States, as well as many other countries.

AMERICAN INSTITUTES FOR RESEARCH (AIR)

Founded in 1946, the American Institutes for Research (AIR) is a not-for-profit research corporation with a long history of research, evaluation, and policy analysis. AIR's staff of some 800 professionals performs basic and applied research, provides technical support, and conducts analyses using established methods from the behavioral and social sciences. Program areas focus on education, health, individual and organizational performance, and quality of life issues.

—*Jeffrey G. Tucker*

AMERICAN JOURNAL OF EVALUATION

The *American Journal of Evaluation* (*AJE*) is an official, peer-reviewed journal sponsored by AEA. Between 1986 and 1997, the journal was published under the title *Evaluation Practice.* Prior to 1986, a predecessor publication, *Evaluation News,* was sponsored by the Evaluation Network, one of the two organizations that merged to create AEA. *AJE*'s mission is to publish original papers about the methods, theory, practice, and findings of evaluation. The general goal of *AJE* is to publish the best work in and about evaluation. Blaine Worthen was Editor during the transition from *Evaluation Practice* to *AJE,* and Melvin M. Mark succeeded him in 1999. M. F. Smith and Tony Eichelberger previously served as editors of *Evaluation Practice.*

—*Melvin M. Mark*

ANALYSIS

Analysis may be defined as the separation of an intellectual or material whole into its constituent parts and the study of the constituent parts and their interrelationships in making up a whole. Analysis has both a qualitative dimension (what something is) and a quantitative dimension (how much of that something there is). In logic, analysis also refers to the tracing of things to their source, the search for original principles. In evaluation, judging evaluands requires an analysis by identifying important aspects of the evaluand and discerning how much of those aspects is present. The opposite of analysis is synthesis.

APPLIED RESEARCH

Applied research refers to the use of social science inquiry methods in situations where generalizability may be limited. Such research provides answers to questions dealing with a delimited group of persons, behaviors, or outcomes. Applied research contrasts with basic research, which has the purpose of addressing fundamental questions with wide generalizability; for example, testing a hypothesis derived from a theory in economics. Both applied and basic researchers can use any of the social science research methods, such as the survey, experimental, and qualitative methods. Differences between the research roles do not relate to methods of inquiry; they relate to the purposes of the investigation. Applied researchers focus on concrete and practical problems; basic researchers focus on problems that are more abstract and less likely to have immediate application.

Evaluation provides many avenues for applied research. For example, an evaluator might perform a needs assessment to determine whether a program aimed at a particular group of clients should be planned and implemented. A community psychologist who surveys directors of homeless shelters to assess the need for a substance abuse counseling program is performing applied research. The range of generalizability is limited to the community being surveyed. The problem being addressed is practical, not theoretical. Formative evaluation activities involve applied research almost exclusively. For example, a director of corporate training might use methods such as surveys, interviews, observations, and focus groups to revise and refine instructional materials. The purpose of the research is to obtain feedback about which aspects of the material should be changed for specific users.

An evaluation can sometimes have dimensions of both applied and basic research. For example, a summative evaluation can have both practical uses and implications for theory. A demonstration project on preschool education could simultaneously reveal the merit of the project and test a theory about the impact of instructional activities on the school readiness of 4-year-olds. Although evaluation is associated more with applied research than with basic research, the latter has strongly influenced some evaluation frameworks. A prime example is theory-driven evaluation, which focuses on structuring the evaluation to test whether predicted relationships among variables are verified by the program. An evaluator using this approach might employ statistical models, such as path analysis, that require a set of hypothesized relationships to be tested with empirical data derived from program participants.

—*Joseph M. Petrosko*

APPRAISAL

Appraisal, sometimes used as a synonym for *evaluation,* refers most specifically to estimating the market or dollar value of an object, such as a property or a piece of art or jewelry. The term is also used in valuing intangibles, such as investments; business and industry value, solvency, and liability; and even psychological traits such as motivation.

APPRECIATIVE INQUIRY

Appreciative inquiry is a method and approach to inquiry that seeks to understand what is best about a program, organization, or system, to create a better future. The underlying assumptions of appreciative inquiry suggest that what we focus on becomes our reality, that there are multiple realities and values that need to be acknowledged and included, that the very act of asking questions influences our thinking and behavior, and that people will have more enthusiasm and motivation to change if they see possibilities and opportunities for the future. Appreciative inquiry is based on five principles:

1. Knowledge about an organization and the destiny of that organization are interwoven.

2. Inquiry and change are not separate but are simultaneous. Inquiry is intervention.

3. The most important resources we have for generating constructive organizational change or improvement are our collective imagination and our discourse about the future.

4. Human organizations are unfinished books. An organization's story is continually being written by the people within the organization, as well as by those outside who interact with it.

5. Momentum for change requires large amounts of both positive affect and social bonding—things such as hope, inspiration, and sheer joy in creating with one another.

Appreciative inquiry is often implemented as a "summit" that lasts from 2 to 5 days and includes 20 to 2500 people. During their time together, participants engage in a four-stage process of discovery, dream, design, and destiny, during which they respond to a series of questions that seek to uncover what is working well, what they want more of, and how the ideal might become reality. Appreciative inquiry questions might include, "As you reflect on your experience with the program, what was a high point?" "When did you feel most successful in terms of your contributions to the project?" "What are the most outstanding moments or stories from this organization's past that make you most proud to be a member of this organization?" "What are the things that give life to the organization when it is most alive, most effective, most in tune with the overarching vision?"

Appreciative inquiry and participatory, collaborative, and learning-oriented approaches to evaluation share several similarities. For the most part, they are catalysts for change; emphasize the importance of dialogue and, through questioning, seek to identify values, beliefs, and assumptions throughout the process; are based on the social construction of reality; stress the importance of stakeholder involvement; embrace a systems orientation; and reflect an action orientation and the use of results.

Appreciative inquiry is being used to evaluate a wide variety of programs and services around the world. While some evaluators use appreciative inquiry as an overarching framework (as with utilization-focused or empowerment frameworks), others are adopting appreciative inquiry principles to construct interview protocols and procedures. Using appreciative inquiry for evaluation may be particularly useful (a) for framing and implementing developmental and formative evaluations, (b) as a method to focus an evaluation study, (c) as an interviewing technique, and (d) as a means to increase an organization's commitment to engaging in evaluation work.

—*Hallie Preskill*

Further Reading

Hammond, S. A. (1996). *The thin book of appreciative inquiry.* Plano, TX: CSS.

Watkins, J. M., & Cooperrider, D. (2000). Appreciative inquiry: A transformative paradigm. *OD Practitioner, 32*(1), 6-12.

Watkins, J. M., & Mohr, B. J. (2001). *Appreciative inquiry: Change at the speed of imagination.* San Francisco: Jossey-Bass.

■■ APPROPRIATENESS

In the focus on effectiveness, efficiency, and economy, the appropriateness of programs, projects, policies, and products is often ignored—to the detriment of sound judgments about worth. To evaluate appropriateness, one of two comparisons is made. The program may be compared to the needs of the intended clients, using any of the techniques of needs analysis. Alternatively, the program can be evaluated in terms of its compliance with process. In health, for example, some evaluations focus on appropriate care, including treatment of conditions (heart disease) or events (childbirth). Appropriateness can be determined through expert review of individual cases.

—*Patricia J. Rogers*

■■ ARCHIVES

An *archive* is a place in which past and current records and artifacts of ongoing value are protected and made available to people such as evaluators. Such material often forms part of historic memory and can enhance understandings of cultures, organizations, and programs. Archives may contain primary or secondary sources such as memorabilia (e.g., photographs, documents, letters), equipment, newspaper articles, rare books, minutes of meetings, and records. Locations of archives vary: They can be found in government departments, libraries, museums, newspaper offices, universities, private companies, and religious organizations.

From archives, evaluators may gain valuable insights into organizations and programs that may not have been apparent before and that could not have been discovered in any other way. Frequently, evaluators must go to the archival site, although some archives are now being made available through microfiche and the Internet.

—*Rosalind Hurworth*

ARGUMENT

In an evaluation context, *argument* is the framework, or methodological reasoning, used to persuade an audience of the worth or value of something. Rarely do evaluations find definitive answers or compelling conclusions; most often, evaluations appeal to an audience's reason and understanding to persuade people that the findings of an evaluation are plausible and actionable. Different audiences want different information from an evaluation and will find different constructions of that information compelling. Evaluators use information and data collected during the evaluation process to make different arguments to different audiences or stakeholders of the evaluation. Evaluation is a process of deriving criteria for what counts as important in the evaluation (either as an expert, in concert with program managers or staff, or through participatory processes for deriving these criteria); collecting, analyzing, and interpreting data; and presenting those analyses and interpretations to audiences of interested parties.

Argumentation (methodological reasoning) is an inherent element of designing and carrying out an evaluation; the points of decision that confront evaluators as they work to understand a program or policy and put together the most compelling description possible of their findings are similar to the decision points necessary to construct a valid argument. Evaluators buttress their arguments with data from the evaluation process. However, persuasion comes into play when presenting those facts to audiences: For example, school boards and parents may find measures of student achievement most compelling; educators and school administrators may find evidence of heightened interest in learning, gathered through student interviews, most compelling. An evaluator's job is to present the information in as unbiased a fashion as possible and make the most credible, persuasive argument to the right audiences. Rather than convince and demonstrate, an evaluator persuades and argues; rather than amass and present evidence that is compelling and certain, an evaluator strives to present evidence that is widely accepted as credible.

—*Leslie K. Goodyear*

Further Reading

House, E. R. (1980). *Evaluating with validity.* Beverly Hills, CA: Sage.

ARTISTIC EVALUATION

Artistic evaluation is a general term that could be used to refer to a number of ideas and activities within the evaluation field. Three possible meanings are discussed here.

EISNER'S ARTISTIC EVALUATION MODEL

Possibly the most obvious referent would be the approach to educational evaluation that Elliot Eisner has fashioned using art criticism as a model. Eisner's connoisseurship-criticism model can be considered an artistic approach to evaluation for at least four reasons.

First, Eisner draws on a number of aesthetic theories, including those of John Dewey and Susanne Langer, to conceptualize and justify his educational connoisseurship and criticism model. Second, the model emphasizes the use of artistic and literary forms of discourse to describe the program that is being evaluated. (Only evocative, somewhat poetic language can capture the aesthetic dimensions of what is being studied, Eisner argues.) Third, the model emphasizes the eclectic use of social science theory to interpret the phenomena being evaluated, and this eclectic use of theory can be thought of as being artistic, at least in a metaphorical sense, because it is not rule governed or systematized. Finally, Eisner argues that social phenomena are like works of art in a number of respects, including their complexity, and he applies John Dewey's dictum about evaluating works of art to evaluating educational and other social phenomena: The worth of complex phenomena cannot be assessed by applying a predetermined standard; rather, the evaluator's judgment must be employed.

ARTISTIC FORMS OF DISPLAYING EVALUATION DATA AND RESULTS

The term *artistic evaluation* might also be used to reference the growing use of art forms and artistic techniques to display evaluation findings. Evaluators' use of alternative forms of data display—including forms that are rooted in the arts—normally is motivated by a desire to communicate more effectively with different evaluation audiences, including audiences that are unlikely to respond positively to (or, for that matter, even to read) traditional social science–sounding evaluation reports.

An example of an artistic data display technique that has been used to communicate evaluation findings in contracted evaluation studies is readers' theater. Readers' theater is a stylized, nonrealistic form of theater in which actors hold scripts and audience members are asked to use their imaginations to visualize details that, in realistic theater, would be provided for them by the scenery and costume designers. In this respect, readers' theater productions are like radio plays; the difference, of course, is that, in a readers' theater production, the actors are visible to the audience and may engage in some visually observable behavior to symbolize certain significant activities (e.g., an actor might turn his back to the audience to symbolize that he or she has left the scene).

Robert Donmoyer and Fred Galloway used readers' theater in an evaluation project funded by the Ball Foundation. The project assessed the foundation's educational reform project in a Southern California school district. Specifically, the readers' theater data display technique was used to communicate evaluation findings to an audience of teachers and administrators involved with the reform. Teachers and administrators in the district also served as readers and actors in the production of the readers' theater script.

The readers' theater script titled *Voices in Our Heads: A Montage of Ideas Encountered During the Evaluation of the Ball Foundation's Community of Schools Project in the Chula Vista Elementary School District* was constructed from quotations excerpted from interview transcripts. The script frequently juxtaposed different and, at times, antithetical points of view about the foundation-funded reform initiative in the district.

Those present judged the presentation to be both an enjoyable and an effective way to communicate important ideas emerging from the evaluation to an audience that was unlikely to read the rather lengthy written report that the two evaluators had produced. Foundation officials, in fact, were so pleased with this artistic approach to reporting evaluation findings that they contracted with the two evaluators to evaluate the annual conference the foundation sponsored for the schools and school districts it funded and to report the results of that evaluation in another readers' theater production.

Before proceeding, it should be noted that the use of alternative modes of displaying data—including modes rooted in the arts—is hardly a novel idea. Both Robert Stake, in his discussions of his "responsive" approach to evaluation, and Elliot Eisner, in discussing his educational connoisseurship and criticism model of evaluation, endorsed the use of artistic modes of data display in evaluation work as early as the mid-1970s.

THE PROCESS MEANING OF ARTISTIC EVALUATION

There is at least one other meaning that could be associated with the term *artistic evaluation.* The term might refer to the fact that all forms of evaluation have a serendipitous, unplanned element. Even when an evaluator is intent on rigidly following predetermined and prespecified standard operating procedures and making the evaluation process systematized and rule governed, things do not always turn out as planned, and, consequently, an improvisational element always creeps into evaluation work. To state this point another way: Effective evaluation work inevitably requires a degree of artistry, metaphorically speaking.

For some, the artistic dimension of evaluation work is not seen as a necessary evil. Indeed, at times, the artistic element of evaluation work is lauded and brought front and center in discussions about the designs to be employed in evaluation studies. A positive view of the use of artistry in designing and conducting evaluation studies is on display in Michael Quinn Patton's book *Creative Evaluation,* for example. Whether or not one decides to embrace and cultivate the serendipitous aspects of evaluation work as Patton clearly does, these dimensions will be present in some form and to some degree in all evaluation work. In this respect, all evaluations can be considered to be, to a greater or lesser extent, artistic evaluation.

—*Robert Donmoyer*

See also CONNOISSEURSHIP

Further Reading

Donmoyer, R., & Yennie-Donmoyer, J. (1995). Data as drama: Reflections on the use of readers' theater as a mode of qualitative data display. *Qualitative Inquiry, 1,* 397-408.

Patton, M. Q. (1988). *Creative evaluation.* Thousand Oaks, CA: Sage.

■■ ASSESSMENT

From the Greek, "to sit with," *assessment* means an evaluative determination. Roughly synonymous with *testing* and *evaluation* in lay terms, *assessment* has become the term of choice in education for determining the quality of student work for purposes of identifying the student's level of achievement. A more important distinction is between the terms *assessment* and *measurement* because educational constructs such as *achievement,* like most social phenomena, cannot be directly measured but can be assessed.

—*Linda Mabry*

■■ ASSOCIATIONS, EVALUATION

A hierarchy of evaluation organizations is slowly emerging. At the global level are organizations such as the International Organization for Cooperation in Evaluation (IOCE) and the International Development Evaluation Association (IDEAS). The IOCE is a loose coalition of some 50 regional and national evaluation organizations from around the world. The mission of the IOCE is to legitimate and strengthen evaluation societies and associations by promoting the systematic use of evaluation in civil society. Its intent is to build evaluation capacity, develop principles and procedures in evaluation, encourage the development of new societies and associations, procure resources for cooperative activity, and be a forum for the exchange of good practice and theory in evaluation.

The initiative to establish IDEAS arose from the lack of an international organization representing the professional interests and intellectual needs of development evaluators, particularly in transition economies and the developing world. IDEAS seeks to fulfill that need by creating a strong body of committed voluntary members worldwide, particularly from developing countries and transition economies, that will support essential, creative, and innovative development evaluation activities; enhance capacity; nurture partnerships; and advance learning and sharing of knowledge with a view to improving the quality of people's lives.

The regional level of the hierarchy is made up of evaluation organizations that have a geographical focus that spans two or more countries. The regional

evaluation organizations registered to attend the IOCE inaugural assembly include the African Evaluation Association, the Australasian Evaluation Society (AES), the European Evaluation Society, the International Program Evaluation Network (IPEN) of Russia and the Independent States, and the Program for Strengthening the Regional Capacity for Evaluation of Rural Poverty Alleviation Projects in Latin America and the Caribbean. Most, if not all, regional evaluation organizations are based on individual memberships. To a lesser extent they serve as umbrella organizations for the national evaluation organizations that lie within their geographical focus. Like their national counterparts, regional evaluation organizations offer many benefits to their memberships.

The national level of the hierarchy is made up of evaluation organizations that operate throughout a single country. The national evaluation organizations registered to attend the IOCE inaugural assembly include the American Evaluation Association (AEA), Associazione Italiana di Valutazione, Canadian Evaluation Society (CES), Egyptian Evaluation Society, Eritrean National Evaluation Association, Ghana Evaluators Association, Israeli Association for Program Evaluation, IPEN-Georgia, IPEN-Ukraine, IPEN-Russia, Kenya Evaluation Association, Malawi Network of Evaluators, Malaysian Evaluation Society, Rede Brasileira de Monitoramento e Avaliaçao, Réseau nigérien de Suivi Evaluation (ReNSE), Réseau de Suivi et Evaluation du Rwanda, Sociedad Española de Evaluación, Société Française de l'Evaluation, South African Evaluation Network, Sri Lankan Evaluation Association, United Kingdom Evaluation Society, and Zimbabwe Evaluation Society.

The structure of regional and national evaluation organizations arises organically in response to contextual variables that are unique to their respective areas of geographic focus. In democratic countries, a common structure is the association or society. (A notable exception is Utvärderarna, a very loose evaluation network in Sweden.) In nondemocratic countries, informal networks whose memberships are not registered with the government have often been found to be preferable. There also appears to be a natural progression to the development of regional and national evaluation organization structure. National organizations often begin as informal networks. As the organizations mature and contextual variables change, oftentimes the networks begin to formalize. Eventually, some networks take the step of becoming legal organizations that are formally recognized by their governments.

Regional and national evaluation organizations provide many benefits to their members. Conferences are a common benefit. These meetings provide an opportunity for professional development and networking. Some organizations seek to connect members who have common interests. The American Evaluation Association does this by grouping members into 32 interest groups that deal with a wide variety of evaluation topics. Journals are another common benefit. Journals provide members with news of the profession as well as information about the latest approaches and methods. Some regional and national evaluation organizations (e.g., AEA, AES, CES, IPEN, etc.) have defined ethical codes to guide the conduct of their members. Finally, several regional and national evaluation organizations (e.g., Swiss Evaluation Society, German Evaluation Association, African Evaluation Society, Australasian Evaluation Society) are in various stages of publishing program evaluation standards. In many cases, these standards are based on the Joint Committee for Educational Evaluation's Program Evaluation Standards.

The subnational level of the hierarchy is made up of evaluation organizations that operate within a region, state, or province of a country. Examples of these types of organizations include the Société québécoise d'évaluation de programme, the Societe Wallonne de l'Evaluation et de la Prospective, the province chapters of the CES, and the local affiliates of the American Evaluation Association. The IOCE has created an enabling environment that permits international cooperation at the subnational level. For example, the Michigan Association for Evaluation (one of AEA's local affiliates) and the Ontario Province Chapter of CES have been exploring opportunities for cooperation such as joint workshops and conferences, professional exchanges, shared publications, and so on. It may be at the subnational level that individuals most directly experience the benefits of international cooperation.

—*Craig Russon*

Further Reading

International Organization for Cooperation in Evaluation. (2002). [Home page]. Retrieved April 27, 2004, from http://home. wmis.net/~russon/ioce/

ATTITUDES

Attitude is a predisposition to classify objects, people, ideas, and events and to react to them with some degree of evaluative consistency. Inherent in an attitude is a judgment about the goodness or rightness of a person, thing, or state. Attitudes are mental constructs that are inferred and are manifest in conscious experience of an inner state, in speech, in behavior, and in physiological symptoms. Measurements of attitudes are often evaluation data, as they may reflect responses to an evaluand.

See also AFFECT

AUDIENCE

An *audience* is the identified receiver of the findings or knowledge products (evidence, conclusions, judgments, or recommendations) from the evaluative investigation. One can think of a hierarchy of audiences—primary, secondary, and so on. The primary audience is an individual or group to which the findings are directed during the evaluation. Early identification of a key individual who has influence in an organization can significantly affect the utilization of evaluation findings in that organization, and there is evidence that influential groups can be similarly influential.

—*John M. Owen*

AUDITING

Broadly defined, *auditing* is a procedure in which an independent third party systematically examines the evidence of adherence of some practice to a set of norms or standards for that practice and issues a professional opinion. For several years, this general idea has informed the process of metaevaluation—a third-party evaluator examines the quality of a completed evaluation against some set of standards for evaluation. In addition to this generic way of thinking about the nature of auditing and its relevance for evaluation, more specifically, one can examine the relations between the practices of program evaluation and program and performance auditing at state and national levels. For many years, these activities have existed side by side as distinct practices with different professional cultures, literatures, and academic preparation (e.g., training in financial and performance auditing or in disciplines of social science research). During the last several decades, each practice has gone through substantial changes that have influenced the dialogue between the two practices on issues of purpose and methodology. As defined by the Comptroller General of the United States, a performance audit is "an objective and systematic examination of evidence of the performance of a government organization, program, activity, or function in order to provide information to improve public accountability and facilitate decision-making." A program audit is a subcategory of performance auditing, in which a key objective is to determine whether program results or benefits established by the legislature or other authorizing bodies are being achieved.

Both evaluation and performance auditing share an interest in establishing their independence and in warranting the credibility of their professional judgments. Furthermore, both practices are broadly concerned with assessing performance. However, some observers have argued that evaluation and performance auditing differ in the ways they conceive of and accomplish that aim. Some of the differences between the two practices include the following: Auditors address normative questions (questions of what is, in light of what should be), and evaluators are more concerned with descriptive and impact questions. Auditors work more independently of the auditee than evaluators do with their clients. Auditors are more exclusively focused on management objectives, performance, and controls than are evaluators. Auditors work with techniques for generating evidence and analyzing data that make it possible to provide quick feedback to auditees; evaluations often (though not always) have a longer time frame. Although both auditors and evaluators base their judgments on evidence, not on impressions, and both rely on an extensive kit of tools and techniques for generating evidence, they often make use of those tools in different ways. For example, auditors plan the steps in an audit, but an evaluator is more likely to establish a study design that may well take into account examining related evaluation studies and their results. Both study designs and reporting in evaluation are likely to include great detail on methods; for example, interview schedules, the process of selecting interviewees, and the conditions of interviewing. Evaluators also often draw on multiple methods of generating and analyzing data, moreso than auditors. Finally, auditors operate under statutory authority; evaluators work as fee-for-service consultants or as university-based researchers. Other observers have argued that the practices of auditing and evaluation, although they often exist independently of one another, are being blended together as a resource pool for decision makers responsible for public programs. In this circumstance, an amalgamated picture is emerging of professional objectives (e.g., placing high value on independence, strict attention to documentation of evidence), purpose (e.g., combining normative, descriptive, and impact questions), and methodologies (e.g., making use of a wide range of techniques).

—*Thomas A. Schwandt*

Further Reading

Chelimsky, E. (1985). Comparing and contrasting auditing and evaluation: Some notes on their relationship. *Evaluation Review, 9,* 485-503.

Wisler, C. (Ed.). (1996). Evaluation and auditing: Prospects for convergence. *New Directions for Evaluation, 71.*

■ AUTHENTICITY

Authenticity is defined as a report writer's attempt to present the voices of the evaluands integrated with the context of the action in a way that seems to correspond with and represent the lived experience of the evaluands. Claims of authenticity are best corroborated by the evaluand's supportive feedback on the report, perhaps as part of the pursuit of construct validity. Criteria to be satisfied include whether the report is accurate, has appropriate coverage, and is balanced and fair. Audio and visual recordings of the action do not in themselves provide authenticity when transcribed and otherwise interpreted by the evaluator, for they lack the experiential accounts and are, for all their detail, partial, like all other data. Evaluators who have employed the concept of authenticity in their work include Elliot Eisner, Rob Walker, Terry Denny, and Saville Kushner. The origins of the concept of authenticity can be found in *The Confessions* of J. J. Rousseau and also in the works of Camus and Heidegger.

—*Clem Adelman*

See also CONTEXT

AUTHORITY OF EVALUATION

Authority in evaluation is contingent on myriad reciprocal and overlapping considerations, some obvious and some subtle, as well as on starkly different perspectives as to what constitutes evaluation as a professional practice.

WITHIN THE PROFESSIONAL COMMUNITY

Broad distinctions between stakeholder-oriented and expert-oriented evaluation approaches have implications for authority. Expert-oriented evaluation approaches invest authority in a professional evaluator (e.g., Stufflebeam's context-input-process-product, or CIPP, model), a connoisseur (i.e., Eisner's connoisseurship approach), or a group of professionals or technical experts (e.g., evaluation or accreditation teams, advisory and blue-ribbon panels). In contrast, stakeholder-oriented approaches may confer authority on program personnel, participants, and relevant others or may involve shared authority. Less explicitly, a stakeholder-oriented evaluator may retain authority as well as closely attend to stakeholder aims, priorities, and criteria.

An important consideration in the first half of the 20th century has been the variety of approaches to evaluation, roughly corresponding (but not limited) to the so-called models of evaluation, of which there are about a dozen, depending on categorization schemes. Even the question of whether the evaluator is obliged to render an evaluative judgment regarding the quality, worth, merit, shortcoming, or effectiveness of a program depends, in part, on his or her approach. According to some, the evaluator's basic responsibility is to define foci and questions, determine data collection methods, establish analytic criteria and strategies, and report evaluative conclusions (e.g., Scriven's approach). In other approaches, such decisions and activities are undertaken collaboratively with clients. In articulating the continuum (controversially), Scriven has decried as "not quite evaluation" approaches in which the evaluator leaves authority for final judgment to program participants (e.g., Stake's responsive evaluation) and as "more than evaluation" (i.e., consultation) those approaches in which the evaluator continues to work with clients after an evaluation report to ensure its useful implementation (e.g., Patton's utilization-focused evaluation) and approaches in which overarching goals include improved working relationships among program personnel (e.g., Greene's participatory evaluation) or their improved political efficacy (e.g., Fetterman's empowerment evaluation).

In any approach—perhaps appropriately, perhaps inevitably—some stakeholder aims, priorities, and criteria will be emphasized over others. For example, all approaches are vulnerable to threats of managerialism, the prioritizing of managers' interests and concerns, because managers are often the contracting agents. All approaches are also susceptible to clientism (attempts to ensure future contracts by giving clients what they want) and, to varying degrees, to the emergence of relationships between evaluators and stakeholders. The day-by-day conduct and internal politics of an evaluation demonstrate that authority in evaluation both varies and fluctuates.

Locus of authority is also affected by evaluation purpose. With its general intent to assess program accomplishment at a specific point in time (e.g., the end of a granting agency's designated funding period), summative evaluation may tend toward the investment of authority in an evaluator. By comparison, formative evaluation (monitoring to improve program implementation) may tend toward shared authority, as ongoing use of evaluation findings by program personnel is the aim. Purposes more specific than these broad strokes also shade evaluation authority.

Authority in an evaluation is influenced by the nature of the evaluator's position vis-à-vis the program itself or the organization of which the program is a part. External evaluation by an outside professional contracted for the purpose of conducting a specific evaluation is often considered more credible than internal evaluation conducted by program personnel or by an organization's internal evaluation unit because of the external evaluator's presumed independence and lack of investment in the program. Independence suggests that external evaluation may tend toward locating authority in the evaluator. Internal evaluators may be subject to particularly intense encroachments on their authority. Even where there is formal provision for independence, they must report findings to their superiors and colleagues who, if threatened or dissatisfied, may actively undermine their credibility or status. Internal evaluators may find themselves caught between reporting fully and accurately, expected in competent practice, and keeping their jobs. This complication of independence suggests that authority may tend to be more diffuse in internal evaluation.

Calls for metaevaluation (e.g., by Scriven and Stufflebeam), especially in large-scale, high-impact, and expensive projects, imply that even well-placed and well-exercised authority in evaluation guarantees neither competent practice nor credibility to clients. Metalevel review of evaluation projects further disperses authority in evaluation, signifying that even the most autocratic evaluator may not be the final authority regarding his or her own evaluation studies.

BEYOND THE PROFESSIONAL COMMUNITY

Clients may feel that authority should be theirs regarding the focus of an evaluation, dissemination of results, and perhaps other matters, such as identifying key contacts and informants and selecting methods (e.g., specifying an interview study or a population to be surveyed). Having commissioned evaluation for their own reasons, clients may insist, blatantly or subtly, on their authority, as they would with other types of outsourced services. Wrangles may ensue over how an evaluation should be conducted and over publication of findings, even after good-faith contract negotiations. Difficulty may be unavoidable when evaluators believe they have an ethical responsibility to report publicly or to right-to-know or need-to-know audiences but clients fear that broad dissemination may damage their programs by revealing hurtful deficiency. In this way, ethical consideration of the public interest may give the public an authoritative influence in evaluation.

Funding agencies frequently require evaluations of the programs they support and constitute important audiences for evaluation reports. Consequently, they may exercise real authority over some aspects of an evaluation, as when their review panels accept or reject proposals on the basis of whether they conform to the funding agency's interests (e.g., the World Bank's interest in economic aspects of educational projects). Even an applicant's awareness of the evaluation designs of successful prior proposals may give funding agencies oblique authority over evaluations.

Where program managers and program funders are distinct entities rather than one and the same and where the interests of program managers and funders clash, their struggles for authority over evaluations are predictable. For example, formative first-year evaluation reporting may be expected to serve program managers' interests in improving the program and simultaneously serve funders' decisions about funding continuation or termination. Full reporting of early program difficulties may be opposed by program managers because of the risks to personnel but be demanded by funders, each tugging for authority over reporting.

AUTHORITY IN MEANING MAKING

Who should determine the criteria or standards of quality against which a program will be judged, and whether the criteria for determining the quality, worth, merit, shortcomings, or effectiveness of a program should be preordinate or explicit, are issues of authority regarding meaning making, framing the interpretation of data and the development of findings. These issues have been debated in the professional community, sometimes as a matter of criteriality. Partly reflecting evaluators' models or approaches to evaluation, the responsibility to identify or devise criteria is seen by some as an obligatory part of the evaluator's role. Alternatively, clients may justifiably feel that the authority to determine criteria of quality should be the responsibility of professional organizations in their respective fields (e.g., early childhood education standards, rehabilitation standards) or should be shared, giving them a right to comment on whether the standards are sufficiently sensitive for their programs or appropriate for programs of their kind.

Other evaluators consider that useful, sensitive criteria are not well captured in formal, explicit statements, even standards promulgated within the program or within its field of endeavor. Ill-advised criteria, as preordinate criteria determined at the start of an evaluation when relatively little is known about the program may be, could mislead an evaluation, most seriously if taken as guideposts from the outset, exercising authority over all aspects of the study from initial focus to final analysis. From this perspective, emergent criteria intuited by the evaluator during the conduct of the evaluation as the program becomes familiar may seem more nuanced, more appropriate, and more useful. However, explicit, preordinate criteria can foster client awareness and encourage client input in ways not available to unstated intuitive criteria, rendering claims about the greater sensitivity of intuitive criteria vulnerable to challenge.

Audiences may unknowingly exercise authority regarding evaluation results as evaluators strive to achieve accessibility in reporting and to encourage appropriate use. Evaluators often try to be conscious of prospective audiences as they design and conduct their studies, considering what types of data may be meaningful to readers and hearers, for example, and, as they analyze data, considering what types of interpretations may be useful and how to present them comprehensibly. Audiences take what they can and what they will from an evaluation report. Their background (educational level, cultural values, personal experiences, socioeconomic status, and the like) will affect what they glean from anything they read. Audiences' varied agendas also affect their understanding and use of information. Accordingly, evaluators are commonly admonished to consider accessible report formats and styles and to try to predict likely uses and misuses of reports.

Ultimately, those empowered to make decisions affecting programs assume authority for the implementation of evaluation-stimulated program changes. Such decisions can occur at many program levels, with one group of stakeholders citing an evaluation report to press for changes opposed by another group of stakeholders citing the same report. For example, from their reading of a report, program managers may move to expand intake of information about their clients' backgrounds to fine-tune service delivery, and beneficiaries may better understand their rights from reading the same report and resist deeper incursions into their privacy. Stakeholders' common failures to implement evaluation findings, failures to implement them appropriately, and attempts to suppress reports and discredit evaluators have raised enduring issues of utility and responsibility. They also raise issues of authority because a stakeholder might know better than an evaluator what would constitute appropriate interpretations of data, appropriate report dissemination, and appropriate implementation of findings. An evaluator, however conscientious regarding appropriate distribution of authority, cannot claim omniscience or prevent error.

POSTMODERN CONCERN ABOUT AUTHORITY

One way to think about these issues is to see them as leading inexorably to troubling postmodern perspectives regarding authority. Postmodernism is characterized by doubt and denial of the legitimacy of the understandings and cultural practices underlying modern societies and their institutions—including evaluation. Postmodernism views science as error prone, methods as value laden, logic and rationality as hopelessly discontinuous with reality, and strategies for social improvement as the beginnings of new failures and oppressions by new authorities.

In its implacable skepticism about truth and knowledge, postmodernism implies that all evaluators abuse their authority, misrepresenting to greater or lesser degree the programs they intend to document. Postmodernists view evaluators (and others) as unable to escape their personal or professional ways of knowing and unable to compel language, if meanings vary across contexts and persons, to convey fully what they think they know. Falling especially on outsiders such as external evaluators, postmodern opposition to metanarratives and to the hidden presence of authors (and their values and agendas) in their texts implies that evaluation reports are necessarily insensitive to insiders, diminishing real persons, who are reconfigured as mere stakeholders. Postmodernism implies condemnation of evaluators' presumptions of authority, as authors whose claims of expertise regarding the quality of the program override and overwrite program participants' understandings, which are based on lived experience. Postmodernism also recognizes that authorizing evaluation is an exercise of power, with evaluators both assuming power and serving the powerful, contributing to a status quo that undeniably privileges some and oppresses others.

In this dark recognition, it is not clear how evaluators, heirs of the 18th-century Enlightenment, might revise their professional practices so as to promote appropriate and legitimate authority in evaluation. Encouraging clients and stakeholders to demand a share or a balance of authority would not necessarily better protect the accuracy, sensitivity, or utility of an evaluation or report. Fuller negotiation or sharing of authority implies the possibility of consensus, but clarifying or redrawing boundaries and expectations might promote dissensus instead. If, for example, the criteria for judging program quality were open to input by various interested parties, the many values dear to the many stakeholders might prove so diverse that standards could not be selected or devised without neglecting or offending some.

Similarly, favoring readerly texts, which explicitly leave interpretive options open to readers for their own meaning making, over writerly texts, disparaged by postmodernists as improper usurpations of authority by authors, might engender stakeholder confusion and professional reproach, especially from colleagues who hold that provision of evaluative interpretations or findings is requisite to competent practice. When authority for conducting evaluation is dispersed beyond reclamation and divisiveness becomes entrenched, the evaluation of a program can be thwarted. It is not clear that absence of authority would serve stakeholders or society better than modernist evaluation does.

THE RELATIONSHIP BETWEEN AUTHORITY AND RESPONSIBILITY IN EVALUATION

Has the evaluator the authority or the responsibility to decide the focus, methods, findings, and audiences for an evaluation? The considerations offered here regarding this question imply new questions: Has the evaluator the authority or the responsibility to advocate for a particular focus, methods, interpretation, audience, or stakeholder group? Has the evaluator the authority or the responsibility to advocate for evaluation as a profession, for evaluation's professional codes of conduct, or for social science generally? Has the evaluator the authority or the responsibility to advocate for his or her personal views of social improvement or equity?

If the credibility and social utility of the profession are to be preserved, being a good professional may very well require something like professional disinterest rather than advocacy for any group or value. However, if being a good professional requires professional disinterest rather than advocacy for any group or value, then evaluators foreclose on their obligations as citizens by restricting their participation in the democratic fray within programs or within the political contexts in which programs exist. If being a good professional requires professional disinterest rather than advocacy for any group or value, then evaluators similarly foreclose on their obligations as human beings by restricting challenges to inequity they might otherwise take up.

Appropriate exercise of authority in evaluation is not a simple matter but is contingent on methodological views, interpersonal politics, contextual exigencies, and philosophical perspectives, none of which are absolute, unequivocally clear, or static. In a given situation, either an exercise of authority or a refusal to exercise unilateral authority might be justified on similar grounds. Appropriate exercise of authority is ultimately a judgment call in an environment where different judgments can be made and defended—and must be.

—*Linda Mabry*

■■ BACKWARD MAPPING

Evaluation and policy analysis are fields concerned with cause-and-effect relationships implicit in policies. The traditional approach to policy analysis is the top-down process of forward mapping, which assumes a straightforward relationship between policy creation and outcomes and assumes that a clear delineation of goals from policy makers will lead to well-organized support, effective implementation, and greater success. The policy maker's power to affect local implementation processes is uncertain. Backward mapping (BM) starts with a specification of the desired endpoint and then works backwards to determine what must be done to answer evaluation policy questions. BM is not limited to determining success or failure based on measurement objectives; it seeks to understand why and under what conditions policies are adopted locally. An argument can be made for studying policy using both the traditional forward perspective (from design to local implementation) and a backward point of view (from implementation to original intent). Forward mapping, however, does not consider the local actor, the characteristics of the organizations, or the local environment beyond the obvious focus of study. BM considers internal and external aspects of the local environment, as well as local discretion of the local actors. BM completes the analysis by looking back at what was originally intended. In a recent BM study related to school-to-work policy, organizational characteristics of a school district were considered to help explain why policies fail and succeed. Policy makers cannot always foresee the impact of environmental influences (e.g., organizational, political, and technical conditions) on implementation.

BM challenges some of the most basic assumptions of the top-down approach. It does not assume that all organizations are the same. Each school district, for example, has varying environments that affect its decision making in relation to addressing local problems. Furthermore, BM does not assume that all organizations are even interested in implementation. BM places value on the role of the local actor and organization that is focusing on resolution of the problem. The process determines if the organization does not identify itself as having the problem, or has the problem but is not concerned about it. In either event, BM sets the stage for further analysis to determine why either case occurred. Evaluation and policy analysis involve not only the measurement of outcomes based on policy goals but also an understanding of the environment in which the problem resides and within which the implementation takes place. Furthermore, the comparison of intent and actual implementation is only one step in BM; it is also useful for analyzing why the implementation did or did not take place. Answering this question requires a process to examine the conditions surrounding the policy. BM is an effective tool in explaining the relationship between the original policy, the implementing locality, and the actual implementation. The use of BM is universal in its application to evaluations associated with policy studies by providing for a more global understanding of how policy implementation works and what affects its success.

—*Marco A. Muñoz*

Further Reading

Elmore, R. F. (1979). Backward mapping: Implementation research and policy decisions. *Political Science Quarterly, 94*(4), 601-616.

Recesso, A. M. (1999, March 31). First year implementation of the School to Work Opportunities Act policy: An effort at backward mapping. *Education Policy Analysis Archive, 7*(11). Retrieved April 28, 2004, from http://epaa.asu.edu/epaa/v7n11.html

■■ BAMBERGER, MICHAEL J.

(b. 1939, England). Ph.D. and B.S. Sociology, London School of Economics.

Since retiring from the World Bank in 2001, Bamberger has continued to work as a consultant on international evaluation and development. During his 23 years with the World Bank, his assignments included Senior Sociologist in the Gender and Development Unit; Training Coordinator for Asia for the Economic Development Institute; and Advisor on Monitoring and Evaluation for the Urban Development Department, which included coordination of a 5-year, four-country evaluation of the social and economic impacts of low-cost housing programs. Prior to working at the World Bank, he lived in Latin America for 13 years, working with a number of nongovernmental organizations (NGOs) and involved in community development and social research in low-income urban areas throughout the continent.

His primary contributions to the field of evaluation have flowed directly from his experiences working with government agencies and NGOs in more than 60 developing countries. His work has involved integrating qualitative and quantitative evaluation methods in international evaluation; developing gender-inclusive evaluation methods, with particular attention to their application to poverty reduction strategies; helping design, analyze, and disseminate project and program evaluations in more than 30 countries in Africa, Asia, Latin America, and the Middle East; and organizing training programs on monitoring and evaluation in more than 20 countries. He has been involved in developing "shoestring evaluation" methods to provide guidelines for conducting methodologically sound impact evaluations when operating with budget, time, or data constraints. His edited volume *Integrating Quantitative and Qualitative Research in Development Projects* addresses these concerns.

His publications include *Monitoring and Evaluating Social Programs in Developing Countries: A Handbook for Policymakers, Managers, and Researchers* (with Joseph Valadez); two chapters in *Policy Evaluation;* a chapter in *Evaluation for the 21st Century: A Handbook;* a chapter (with Donna R. Podems) titled "Gender Issues in International Evaluation" in the *Feminist Evaluation* volume of *New Directions in Evaluation;* a chapter on gender for the *World Bank Sourcebook for Poverty Reduction Strategies* (with Mark Blackden, Lucia Fort, and Violetta Manoukian); and *Impact Evaluation of Development Assistance: A Practical Handbook for Designing Methodologically Sound Impact Evaluations Under Budget, Time and Data Constraints* (with Nobuko Fujita).

Bamberger has been actively involved with the American Evaluation Association's International and Cross-Cultural Topical Interest Group, and he has arranged for the participation of teams of evaluators from Brazil, Bangladesh, and Tunisia in AEA conferences. He was a member of the AEA Board from 1998 to 1999 and has also served on the editorial advisory boards of the *American Journal of Evaluation, New Directions for Evaluation,* and *Sustainable Development.*

■■ BARRINGTON, GAIL V.

(b. 1945, Montreal, Quebec, Canada). Ph.D. Educational Administration, University of Alberta, Canada; M.A. English Literature, Carleton University, Canada; B.A. English Literature, McGill University, Canada.

Barrington has owned and managed Barrington Research Group, Inc., since 1985, shepherding it from a sole proprietorship to an incorporated company with more than 20 employees. She has managed or conducted more than 100 program evaluation studies, many in the areas of education and health promotion. Key studies include the midterm evaluation of the Hepatitis C Prevention, Support & Research Program (Health Canada 2002); the evaluation of the HIV/AIDS Initiative for Young Adults (Alberta Health 1993-1998); the Evaluation of the Peer Counseling Program; Alberta Safe House (The Muttart Foundation, 1993-1996); and the Integrated Services Review, Yellowhead School Division No. 12 (The Premier's Council on the Status of Persons with

Disabilities and Alberta Education, 1991). This latter study won the 1992 Annual Evaluation Report Awards Competition, Division H, American Educational Research Association.

Since 1995, Barrington has been the national evaluator for the Canada Prenatal Nutrition Program, a holistic, community-based program for high-risk pregnant women that is offered by approximately 350 community-based agencies and funded by the Population and Public Health Branch of Health Canada. This study has been described in the *Canadian Journal of Program Evaluation* as an exemplary evaluation that demonstrates that an empowerment approach can be successful in the evaluation of important large-scale innovative programs intended to lead systemwide change. She manages a companion evaluation for a similar program offered for Inuit projects and funded by the First Nations and Inuit Health Branch of Health Canada.

Key characters from literature and a fondness for mystery and detective novels have fuelled Barrington's curiosity about the human condition and what makes organizations tick. Being a teacher and adult educator has also helped to frame her approach to working with clients, as every project becomes a teaching opportunity. When she opened her independent consulting firm, which specializes in program evaluation, role models were few, and she credits the panel presentation on independent consulting by Deborah Bonnet, Tara Knott Davis, and Michael Hendriks at the 1985 joint AEA/CES conference in Toronto with encouraging her to pursue this goal. Barrington's popular annual workshop on consulting skills stems from this event; with it, she hopes to inspire others as they inspired her.

In 2001, she cochaired the Canadian Evaluation Society annual conference in Banff, Alberta. She is currently a Certified Management Consultant and a member of the Canadian Evaluation Society, the American Evaluation Association (and a member of the AEA Ethics Committee), Phi Delta Kappa, the Professional Market Research Association, and the Calgary Chamber of Commerce.

▚ BENCHMARKING

Benchmarking is a method used by organizations to compare their performance, processes, or practices with peer organizations or those in other business sectors. This method can focus on performance, in which case one identifies the most important indicators of success and then compares one's own performance with that of other organizations. The focus can also be a particular process, such as billing or information technology. This method is common in business and industry, and it has seen growing acceptance in the public sector, where it is most associated with the identification of best practices. Often, benchmarking is a collaboration among like organizations that attempts both to identify important indicators of success and to provide data to the collaborating organizations about performance.

One example of benchmarking is the Malcolm Baldrige National Quality Award. The Baldrige award is administered by the U.S. Commerce Department's National Institute of Standards and Technology and is awarded by the president of the United States to businesses, education, and healthcare organizations that are judged to be outstanding in seven areas: leadership, strategic planning, customer and market focus, information and analysis, human resource focus, process management, and business results.

See also BEST PRACTICES

Further Reading

Spendolini, M. J. (2003). *The benchmarking book* (2nd ed.). New York: Amacon.

BENEFICENCE. *See* AMELIORATION

▚ BEST PRACTICES

The concept of best practices captures the hope that systematic comparative evaluation of different programs, or program components, will yield conclusions about which are most effective and therefore "best." Once identified, information about such best practices would be disseminated so that others could adopt them. Philanthropic foundations and government agencies have been especially interested in supporting identification and dissemination of best practices.

Although the idea is attractive, substantial difficulties exist in identifying a practice as "best." Comparisons can be difficult when programs have different goals, serve populations with varying degrees of need, and include different elements in implementation. Thus, it is important to be quite specific in asserting a "best practice": best for whom, under what conditions, for what purposes, in what context, with what level of evidence, using what criteria, and compared to what alternatives?

The issue of generalizability is at the heart of the concept of best practices. Comparative evaluations have shown that what works effectively in one setting may not transfer to new settings. A program that works on a small scale may not work as well when attempted on a large scale. From a systems point of view, something that works effectively in one system may not work at all in a different system. Suppose automobile engineers identified the best fuel injection system, the best transmission, the best engine cooling system, and so on. Now suppose, as is likely, that these best components come from different car models (Lexus, Audi, Mercedes, etc.). Once all the "best" components from different cars were brought together, it would not be possible to assemble them into a working car. The components are not interchangeable. Moreover, it has proven especially challenging in evaluations to isolate the effective components of complex programs to determine best practices. Even when an intervention works effectively in one context at one point in time, the question of the temporal validity of "best practices" concerns generalizability to the same local population or in the same setting at later points in time.

Having a technique labeled a best practice is such a powerful magnet for support and attention that the idea has been politicized, with ideological adherents of some unsubstantiated or poorly evaluated practices asserting that a practice is best because it conforms to a group's value preferences. In general, it has proven easier to identify practices that are ineffective than to identify practices that work in different settings, with different staff or target populations. Indeed, so many things are problematic about the notion that a particular practice is "best" that many evaluators prefer more modest and confirmable phrases, such as "evidence-based practices" (meaning that the practice has been subjected to at least some significant empirical validation), "promising practices" (meaning that the practice has been shown to work in some settings and is worth experimentation and evaluation in other settings), "better practices" (suggesting that more effective practices have been separated from those less

effective without asserting that the more effective is also best), or simply "effective practices" (meaning that there is at least credible evidence of effectiveness).

—*Michael Quinn Patton*

Further Reading

Patton, M. Q. (2001). Evaluation, knowledge management, best practices, and high quality lessons learned. *American Journal of Evaluation, 22,* 329-326.

■ BETA TEST

A term used most frequently in software development, a *beta test* is the second phase of testing in which a sample of intended users tries out the product. Beta testing is often considered prerelease testing of a product. Beta versions of software are now distributed widely via the Internet to give the product a real-world test, as well as providing a preview of the release of a new or updated product. The term *beta* derives from the second letter of the Greek alphabet.

■ BHOLA, H. S.

(b. 1932, Lahore, Undivided India). Ph.D. Education, The Ohio State University; M.A. History and English Literature, B.A. Hons. Physics and Mathematics, Punjab University, India.

Bhola is Professor of International and Comparative Education at Indiana University and teaches courses in comparative education, education policy, social change, and evaluation. He is a former employee of and consultant to the United Nations Educational, Scientific, and Cultural Organization (UNESCO) and has been a consultant to several national governments, including China and Tanzania. He has been invited to speak, conduct evaluation training, and perform evaluations in numerous countries, including Tanzania, Kenya, Malawi, Zambia, Zimbabwe, South Africa, Namibia, and several Asian countries. He has gained international recognition for his research in educational systems evaluation and adult literacy, with a focus on the interconnections of planned change and systematic evaluation.

His career in evaluation began with a perceived need for systematic feedback from behavioral and social interventions within programs of adult literacy (and adult education) for community development in India during the 1950s and early 1960s. From 1963 to 1965, as a graduate student at The Ohio State University, Bhola was influenced by Egon G. Guba, who, with others at the time, was shaping and promoting the development of educational evaluation theory and practice. As a UNESCO senior literacy field expert in Tanzania, East Africa (1968-1970), Bhola introduced the concept of internal evaluation to the field workers and supervisors engaged in UNESCO-UNDP (UNESCO–United Nations Development Program) work-oriented adult literacy programs. Bhola's paper "Making Evaluation Operational Within Literacy Programs" attracted considerable attention within the multinational UNESCO-UNDP project, and it was later published. His recent work has been related to constructivist approaches to evaluation, the special structures of policy evaluation, and the need to focus on evaluative accounts rather than stand-alone evaluation studies. Another important theme of his recent work is the globalization of evaluation models and approaches around the world and, concomitantly, the necessity for careful and self-conscious contextualization of evaluation practice in each culture and community.

Bhola's *Evaluating "Literacy for Development": Projects, Programs and Campaigns,* published by UNESCO, is available in English, French, Spanish, Arabic, and Persian. In 2003, he was awarded the American Evaluation Association Myrdal Award for outstanding contributions to evaluation practice.

⊞ BIAS

Bias, which typically means prejudice or preference, is characterized as a negative condition that inhibits evaluators or evaluations from finding true, pure, and genuine knowledge. *Bias* is considered synonymous with *subjective, unfair, partial,* and *prejudiced* and is defined as errors based on beliefs or emotions that are wrong or irrelevant and that may adversely affect people and programs. Bias is sometimes erroneously equated with prior knowledge; impartiality is thus mistakenly equated with ignorance. An example of this mistake is the expectation that a judge's prior knowledge will bias her or his ruling rather than informing and enriching the ruling. An individual with strong views will have prejudgments (the literal meaning of prejudice), but the critical issue with regard to bias is whether those views are justified.

Whether based on rationality or some other foundation, the possession of strong views, about, for example, child abuse or abortion, may not necessarily demonstrate bias.

Bias is based on the assumption that there is an objective (and single) fact or truth and that humans have a natural tendency to see things in a prejudiced way. Particular methods (sampling, randomization, statistical controls, triangulation, and so on) are usually the means for overcoming this natural tendency. Alternatively, the hermeneutic tradition also accepts this natural and inevitable tendency but employs reflection on bias and prejudice as a key element in understanding and knowledge creation. The control of bias is a key issue in designing and conducting an evaluation and should be understood less as an attempt to eliminate bias and more as an attempt to limit unjustified views and to provide opportunities for examining preferences and prejudices in the evaluation context.

Bias can be a feature of a person, practice, or organization. Evaluators may be biased, other stakeholders may be biased, but so too can practices and activities be biased. Often, evaluations examine the biases of practices or activities in social contexts. For example, differential performance by males and females on standardized tests of achievement is appropriately examined in evaluations of the quality of schools.

See also OBJECTIVITY, SUBJECTIVITY

Further Reading

Scriven, M. (1976). Evaluation bias and its control. In G. V Glass (Ed.), *Evaluation studies review annual* (Vol. 1). Newbury Park, CA: Sage.

⊞ BICKEL, WILLIAM E.

(b. 1946). Ph.D. Foundations of Education, M.A.T. Elementary Education, University of Pittsburgh; B.A. U.S. History, Oberlin College.

Bickel is Professor of Administrative Policy Studies in the School of Education and a Senior Scientist at the Learning Research and Development Center, University of Pittsburgh. His research interests include evaluation methodology and research on evaluation utilization in various organizational and policy contexts and educational reform policy studies. Bickel's evaluation work is focused on investigating how evaluation processes in educational systems and related organizational and policy settings can contribute to improved practice. He addresses this question in part by conducting evaluation studies for policy and decision makers in a variety of reform and community settings. His recent work has emphasized investigations of the role evaluation plays in private foundations in the United States. He currently directs an evaluation partnership with the Heinz Endowments for its regional educational initiatives focused on comprehensive, school-based reform; preservice education policy and practice; and technology dissemination in urban school systems.

He was the Director of an institutional evaluation partnership between the University of Pittsburgh and the Lilly Endowment (1990-1997). The 7-year partnership assisted program officers in the Lilly Endowment's Education Division with the design and implementation of evaluation activities related to a wide range of policy and educational reform initiatives in both basic and higher education settings. In the past several years, Bickel has been a consultant to a number of foundations (e.g., the California Endowment, Robert Wood Johnson Foundation, Kellogg Foundation, Pew Charitable Trusts, Packard Foundation, DeWitt-Wallace Funds) on matters concerning the effective use of evaluation-related processes to support organizational learning. He has coauthored a book on research methodology, *Decision-Oriented Educational Research* (with W. W. Cooley), and is the author of numerous book chapters, monographs, journal articles, and technical reports.

▊ BICKMAN, LEONARD

(b. 1941, Bronx, New York). Ph.D. City University of New York; M.A. Columbia University; B.S. City College of New York.

Bickman was among the first evaluators to recognize the importance of not doing "black box" evaluations in which only inputs and outputs were measured. He stressed the significance of understanding how a program was supposed to produce a predicted outcome. His alternative approach provided a different way of understanding program success and failure. Bickman also led several award-winning evaluations that demonstrated how to use program theory and how to conduct large-scale cost-effectiveness evaluations that had significant policy impact.

His professional undertakings have been most influenced by people early in his career, such as Stanley Milgram and Harold Proshansky, professors of Bickman's at the City University of New York who taught him to ask creative research questions outside the mainstream. Evaluator colleagues Donald Campbell and Tom Cook helped him to understand the finer points of experimental design. His friend Will Shadish exposed him to the breadth of program evaluation theories.

After more than a decade of conducting large-scale evaluations of child and adolescent mental health services, in which he found that systems changes resulted in increased costs but not better clinical outcomes, Bickman turned his attention to attempting to develop an effective intervention. In his current career endeavors, he is combining his background in social psychology with his contributions in program theory and logic modeling to produce a theory of change. His theory under study combines attribution theory, cognitive dissonance theory, and self-regulation theory to better understand the conditions under which new programs or interventions will be implemented and maintained. His theory is currently being evaluated for the determination of whether and how the behavior of pediatricians can be changed as they diagnose and treat attention deficit hyperactivity disorder.

Bickman is Past President and Board Member of the American Evaluation Association. He is Coeditor, along with his colleague Debra Rog, of the Sage series on applied social research and *The Handbook of Applied Social Research.* He has been designated among the top 5% in productivity nationally among faculty in Developmental Sciences 2001 and carries an extensive history of accolades, including his most recent honors: Vanderbilt University Benefactors of the Commons Designation Award 1999-2001; American Evaluation Association Award for the Outstanding Evaluation of 2000; 1998/1999 American Psychological Association Public Interest Award for Distinguished Contribution to Research in Public Policy; 1998 Distinguished Paper Award for Systems of Care, Florida Mental Health Institute; and 1998 Distinguished Faculty Award, Vanderbilt University.

▊ BLACK BOX

A *black box* is an evaluation of program outcomes without the benefit of an articulated program theory to provide insight into what is presumed to be causing those outcomes and why. Black box evaluation refers to those evaluations that examine the outputs of a program without examining its internal operation and processes. Black box evaluations serve well when consumers evaluate manufactured objects such as cars or TVs; consumers need to know which cars perform better than others, not why. This type of evaluation does not serve well when social programs are being evaluated and the evaluation is expected to lead to continuous program quality improvement.

—*Marco A. Muñoz*

■ BONNET, DEBORAH G.

(b. 1951, Billings, Montana). M.B.A. Indiana University; M.S. Industrial Engineering and Operations Research, B.S. Psychology, Virginia Polytechnic and State University.

Bonnet is Vice President for Evaluation at the Lumina Foundation for Education, where she designs and manages the evaluations of the foundation's grants and research work. Before joining Lumina Foundation, she headed the Indianapolis-based virtual firm DBonnet Associates, where she specialized in evaluation services for private foundations and nonprofit organizations. Over the course of 27 years of evaluation consulting, she has conducted more than 100 evaluation studies in a variety of fields, including education, health, human services, community development, leadership, and the arts. She is a pioneer in independent evaluation consulting. Her work has been influenced by Don Campbell, from whom she gained the vision of an experimenting society; Michael Scriven, the quest for correct answers; and Michael Patton, permission to settle for the doable. She is currently working on a model framework for foundation-level evaluation.

She has been an active conference presenter and member of the American Evaluation Association since 1981 and has served as Board Member, Secretary-Treasurer, Chair of the Independent Consulting TIG, and Chair of the Ethics Committee. She served on the Advisory Board of AEA's *New Directions in Evaluation* and has authored several articles on evaluation, as well as a chapter in *Applied Strategies for Curriculum Evaluation.*

■ BORUCH, ROBERT

(b. 1942, New Jersey). Ph.D. Psychology and Statistics, Iowa State University; B.E. Metallurgical Engineering, Stevens Institute of Technology.

Boruch is University Trustee Chair Professor of Education in the Graduate School of Education and of Statistics in the Wharton School of Business at the University of Pennsylvania; Director, Center for Research and Evaluation of Social Policy; and Director, Policy Research, Evaluation and Measurement Program. He serves on the Board of Trustees for the W.T. Grant Foundation; the Board of Directors for the American Institute for Research; and advisory committees for the U.S. Department of Education, National Center on Education Statistics, and other federal agencies.

Previously, he was a member of the faculty at Northwestern University. Boruch is a Fellow of the American Academy of Arts and Sciences and of the American Statistical Association.

Boruch's research involves determining the severity and scope of problems, implementing programs and policies, and estimating the effects and effectiveness of innovations. He contributes to work on randomized trials in education and training programs, welfare reform, health services, housing, and crime and justice, with a particular interest in the assessment or improvement of programs sponsored by federal governments in the United States and abroad and by private foundations. He is interested in the design of randomized controlled field trials for planning and evaluation, survey methods, and developing methods for assuring individual privacy in research settings. He has worked on a range of high-profile projects, such as the Third International Science and Mathematics Study and the International Campbell Collaboration on Systematic Reviews.

He is the author of *Randomized Experiments for Planning and Evaluation,* "The Honestly Experimental Society" in *Validity and Social Experimentation: The Campbell Legacy,* and *Evidence Matters: Randomized Trials in Education Research* (edited with Frederick Mosteller). He also contributed to the National Academy of Science's publication *Scientific Research in Education: Report of the Committee on Scientific Principles in Education Research.*

■ BRISOLARA, SHARON

(b.1963, New Orleans, Louisiana). Ph.D. Program Evaluation and Planning, M.S. Human Service Studies, Cornell University, Ithaca, New York; B.A. Louisiana State University.

Brisolara's primary contributions to the theory, practice, and profession of evaluation include writings on participatory and feminist evaluation. She is currently involved in evaluation capacity building in rural California. She is interested in exploring the links between participatory, mixed-method evaluations of rural-based programs and capacity building.

Her work has been energized and guided through her involvement with grassroots community groups. She has been most inspired by the writings and works of Jennifer Greene and Michael Quinn Patton. The poetry of Sharon Olds, Louise Gluck, Adrienne Rich, David Lehman, and R. M. Rilke has encouraged her to take a profound look at the workings of things and the relationships between people and events.

■■ BUDGETING

Budgeting involves identifying probable areas of expense for an evaluation and determining the costs associated with those expense areas. A budget for an evaluation typically includes the following: salaries or compensation for the evaluator(s), the clerical staff, and any consultant(s); materials, supplies, and equipment; communications, printing, and reproduction; travel and associated expenses; facilities; overhead and general administrative costs; and miscellaneous or contingency costs. Table 1 shows an example of such a budget.

Beyond creating the budget, the evaluator should review the proposed budget, comparing it against the actual expenditures, on a regular basis and make needed adjustments to avoid overrunning the budget. If adjustments cannot be made, the evaluator should immediately notify the client and important stakeholders. Furthermore, in some evaluations, information on the budget, to-date expenditures, and remaining funds must be communicated to the client on a regular basis. Such requirements are typically presented in the contract for the evaluation.

—Darlene F. Russ-Eft

Table 1   Illustration of an Evaluation Budget

Budget Categories	Costs
Evaluators' salaries	$50,000
Clerical staff salaries	$20,000
Travel for data collection	$4500
Airfare (5 trips @ $500/trip)	$2500
Hotel (10 days @ $100/day)	$1000
Auto or taxi costs ($100/trip)	$500
Per diem expenses ($50/day)	$500
Communications	$1000
Phone interviews	$500
Postage for surveys	$200
Focus group invitations and thank-you letters	$200
Overnight mailing costs	$100
Materials, supplies, and equipment	$1000
Focus group refreshments	$700
Tapes and batteries	$100
Printing and duplication	$200
Total Costs	**$56,500**

■■ BUROS INSTITUTE

Named for Oscar Buros and in existence for more than 70 years, the institute is best known for publishing *The Mental Measurements Yearbook* and *Test in Print* series. Introduced in 1938, these series have become the standard for reviews of commercially available tests. In 1977, the Buros Institute moved to the University of Nebraska, and in 1994, with a grant from Luella Buros, a center was created there that combined the role of test evaluation with a consultation and outreach service.

CAMBRIDGE CONFERENCES

Four meetings of U.K. and U.S. qualitative evaluators, initiated by CARE, sponsored by the Nuffield Foundation, and held in Cambridge, England, are referred to as the *Cambridge Conferences*. The first, in 1974, focused on methodological issues in qualitative evaluation. Key papers and articles were published as *Beyond the Numbers Game*. The participants were those who had devised and developed illuminative, democratic, responsive, and naturalistic evaluation. The second conference was devoted to case study, and most of the papers were published in *Toward a Science of the Singular*. The conferences gave a significant voice and impetus to qualitative evaluation and to case study.

—*Clem Adelman*

CAMPBELL, DONALD T.

(b. 1917, d. May 6, 1996). Ph.D. Psychology, A.B. Psychology, University of California, Berkeley.

Donald Campbell was University Professor of Social Relations, Psychology, and Education at Lehigh University until he retired in 1994. Previously, he held faculty positions at Northwestern University, Syracuse University, University of Chicago, and The Ohio State University, as well as lecturing at Oxford, Harvard, and Yale Universities. He also served in the U.S. Naval Reserve during World War II.

Campbell's intellectual concerns were broad and covered psychological theory, methods, sociology of science, and descriptive epistemology. He is most widely known for his work on experimental and quasi-experimental research design, which greatly influenced the entire field of research and evaluation designs. His development of a basic taxonomy that distinguishes between "true" (randomized) experiments, quasiexperiments, and nonexperimental designs has dramatically shaped inquiry discussions to date. He was particularly interested in improving the ways in which scientists learn about the real world and in the identification and control of sources of bias that preclude that knowledge.

He is the author of more than 235 journal articles in the areas of social psychology, sociology, anthropology, education, and philosophy, covering a broad scope of topics. He is most widely known, however, for the articles "Convergent and Discriminant Validation by the Multitrait-Multimethod Matrix" (with Donald W. Fiske, 1959), "Experimentation and Quasi-Experimental Designs for Research" (with Julian C. Stanley, 1973), and for *Quasi-Experimentation: Design and Analysis Issues for Field Settings* (with Thomas D. Cook, 1979). He was the recipient of numerous honorary degrees and awards, including the 1977 Alva and Gunnar Myrdal Science Award from the American Evaluation Association, the American Psychological Association's Distinguished Scientific Contribution Award, and the Distinguished Contribution to Research in Education Award from the American Educational Research Association. He also served as president of the American Psychological Association and was a member of the National Academy of Sciences.

■ CAMPOS, JENNIE

(b. 1946, Globe, Arizona). Ed.D. International Education and Development, University of Massachusetts, Amherst; M.Ed. Educational Foundations, University of Hawaii; B.A. Elementary Education, Arizona State University.

Campos has worked as a participatory evaluator and educator in more than 30 developing countries, most recently in postwar settings, including the Sudan, Cambodia, and the Balkans. She has educated more than 800 foreign nationals about basic education and girls' education. Campos uses a common participatory approach in working with highly educated government officials, as well as semiliterate or illiterate parents and community members. Her focus is on using straightforward tools and techniques of participatory learning and action in linking policy makers with program stakeholders to ensure that program planning fits the needs and interests of grassroots constituents. Campos continues to work as a participatory development practitioner abroad and in the United States and with groups to confront social injustice. The Brazilian educator-philosopher Paulo Freire, her mentor during her doctoral fieldwork in Guatemala, has largely influenced her work.

Campos' work promotes the idea of marginalized groups as active "question makers" as opposed to being passive "question answerers." This concept is elaborated in a handbook she coauthored for the United Nations, *Who Are the Question-Makers? A Handbook for Participatory Evaluation.* She is credited with influencing evaluation strategies for several nongovernmental organizations and many major donor agencies.

■ CAPACITY BUILDING

Capacity building in the context of evaluation is evaluation capacity building (ECB). ECB was defined conceptually by Compton, Baizerman, and Stockdill (2002) as "a context-dependent, intentional action system of guided processes and practices for bringing about and sustaining a state of affairs in which quality program evaluation and its appropriate uses are ordinary and ongoing practices within and/or between one or more organizations/programs/sites."

ECB is understood as professional practice related to but distinct from professional evaluation practice. ECB is oriented toward the organization and its structure, social and cultural practices, and personnel,

with the goal of making regular and ordinary in that context professional evaluation studies and their use. In contrast, professional evaluation is oriented toward managing or performing quality evaluation studies and using the data provided by such evaluations, although it too may focus on organizational change and development. These Weberian, ideal-type distinctions are crucial theoretically and practically because no number of discrete evaluation studies can be cumulated to result in ongoing ECB: Evaluation studies are distinct, although related, orientations and practices. ECB is more like an infinite game of ongoing, emergent rules, procedures, practices, and politics, and evaluation practice is more like a finite game of clear, normative, professional approaches and methods. ECB and evaluation practice can also be distinguished in their orienting perspectives and in related practitioner roles with ECB focused on the infrastructures and practices necessary to create and sustain in an organization an evaluation presence and the performance and use of quality studies. In contrast, the evaluator's perspective and related practitioner roles are oriented to performing the discrete, quality studies that are used.

From the program evaluation practitioner's perspective, developing and sustaining an evaluation unit within an organization focuses primarily on the finite task at hand. Typically, this means responding to the next request to conduct a study, standardizing data-collection instruments for use by multiple clients, and ensuring clients' use of the evaluation findings. In this way, developing and sustaining the unit is seen as responding to the demand for evaluation in the moment. Less attention is given to the larger goal of systematically creating ways for evaluation and its uses to be seen as regular practices throughout the organization.

For the ECB practitioner, however, the focus is on responding to requests for evaluation services and being mindful of how today's work will contribute to sustaining the unit in the longer term. This dual role might be thought of as "wearing bifocals" that allow a given situation to be assessed differently by the program evaluation practitioner and the ECB practitioner. Put differently, in interactions with a client, the evaluation practitioner asks the question, "How will this contribute to making the study better, making use of the results more likely, and making another quality study possible?" The ECB practitioner asks, "How will this moment in this particular evaluation contribute to the organization's learning and development such that the next study will be asked for and the results used?" In this way, the ECB practitioner

Program Level	Agency Level
Designate coordinators and staff	Designate organizational leader or champion
Dedicate resources	Develop evaluation consultation corps
Create logic models with linked evaluation plans and information systems	Coordinate policies and activities
Conduct evaluations	Train staff
Create technical assistance directories	Produce materials
Create incentives	Sustain leadership

considers how each study is connected to the development of the organization and to meeting the organization's goals and mission.

ECB case examples strongly suggest that actual ECB work is site specific and highly contingent on context and situation in its goals and actual practices. For example, King's work in a school district attempted to achieve four ECB goals within the everyday realities of declining resources, changing personnel, personalities, and politics:

- To develop staff commitment and skills in program evaluation and its use
- To build an infrastructure for data collection, analysis, and presentation that would support program evaluation and its use within the school district
- To facilitate the existing school improvement process
- To create a network of people across the district that would assist in making classroom- or school-based inquiry routine

ECB is seen in the work of Bobby Milstein and others at the federal Centers for Disease Control, who narrate a 3-year story of capacity building at that research and program agency. Their recommendations to promote program evaluation at the CDC were as shown the table above.

At the World Bank, Mackay shows that ECB is synergistic with other capacity-building work in countries where the focus is on governance, including service delivery. Here, context is a country's "circumstances"; ECB goals are similar across the three cases, and the scale of work moves from a single school district to a federal agency and its relationships with state and local health departments to national and cross-national efforts at capacity building.

Compton, Baizerman, and Stockdill (2002) offer a beginning framework for ECB and an initial practical ECB checklist. The framework suggests core ECB

themes, basic concepts, relevant knowledge and basic skill competencies and is a first attempt at building an ECB research agenda. More case studies are needed to document the range of practices within and across programmatic domains; organizational types and levels; funding sources; and practitioner background, experience, and responsibilities. Participant observation and focused, in-depth interviews of ECB practitioners are also necessary. Without such data, it will be impossible to strengthen those ECB elements and practices that are science, craft, and art. Pending such research, an initial practical checklist of ECB indicators usable for assessing a site was constructed from the case studies, informal interviews, and professional practice: It is far more craft and art than science. This checklist, also, awaits use and evaluation.

ECB is an emergent frame for understanding the established practice of working intentionally and continuously "to create and sustain overall organizational processes that make quality evaluation and its uses routine."

—*Michael Baizerman, Donald W. Compton, and Stacey Hueftle Stockdill*

Further Reading

Boyle, R., & Lemaire, D. (Eds.). (1999). *Building effective evaluation capacity: Lessons from practice.* New Brunswick, NJ: Transaction.

Carse, J. (1986). *Finite and infinite games: A vision of life and play as possibility.* New York: Ballentine Books.

Compton, D., Baizerman, M., & Stockdill, S. H. (Eds.). (2002, Spring). The art, craft and science of evaluation building. *New Directions for Evaluation, 93.*

Preskill, H., & Torres, R. J. (1999). *Evaluation inquiry for learning in organizations.* Thousand Oaks, CA: Sage.

Reason, P., & Bradbury, H. (Eds.). (2001). *Handbook of action research.* Thousand Oaks, CA: Sage.

Schön, D. (1983). *The reflective practitioner: How professionals think in action.* New York: Basic Books.

Evaluation Practice Around the World

Niger

The Nigerien Way of Monitoring and Evaluation Capacity Development:
The Case of the Nigerien Monitoring and Evaluation Network (ReNSE)

THE AFRICAN SELF-EMPOWERMENT PROCESS TOWARD MONITORING AND EVALUATION CAPACITY DEVELOPMENT

A high-level seminar held in 1998 in Abidjan, Cote d'Ivoire, and in 2001 in Johannesburg, South Africa, brought together teams of senior officials from 12 African countries and 21 international development agencies. Their task was to look at the current status of monitoring and evaluation (M&E) capacity development in Africa. Participants acknowledged that M&E was once seen as primarily a donor activity, but no longer. A number of African countries are seeking to build national M&E capacity to realize its benefits within their own development agendas. In response to this evolving movement, in 1999, the African Evaluation Association was launched during a conference held in Nairobi, and a second conference took place in June 2002. These conferences accelerated the formation of national evaluation groups in Africa. Kenya formed its own national association, and national networks were formed in: the Comoro Islands, Eritrea, Ethiopia, Madagascar, Malawi, Niger, and Rwanda. After the conference, focal points for constituting national networks were identified in Benin, Botswana, Burkina Faso, Burundi, Cape Verde, Ghana, Malawi, Nigeria, Senegal, South Africa, Tanzania, and Uganda.

The Nigerien Monitoring and Evaluation Network (ReNSE–Reseau Nigerien de Suivi et Evaluation) was created in August 1999. Its creation was in response to two processes:

- At the national level, the growing demand for M&E and the unorganized potential offer stimulated the necessity of a sustainable local organization to coordinate, facilitate, and advocate M&E culture and function.
- At the global level, the necessity for Niger to fit into the African process of constituting national networks and the global process of constituting a world M&E community was indicated if Niger were to benefit from and contribute to the exchange of experiences and competency at international level.

ReNSE is an informal group of monitoring and evaluation professionals. Its members are M&E specialists working in public administration, in the United Nations system, in international and national NGOs and bilateral projects, at Niger's university, and in the private sector. The members of the network adopted objectives, a plan of action, and a calendar of events.

During the inaugural meeting in August 1999, participants discussed and adopted the following objectives.

Global Objectives

- Support a national sustainable process of monitoring and evaluation capacity development (M&ECD) through the implementation of a forum that will contribute to the definition of norms, methodologies, and professional practices in Niger.

Specific Objectives

- Facilitate informal learning by sharing experiences and skills in the field of monitoring and evaluation.
- Organize formal training sessions.
- Facilitate information sharing (meetings, training sessions, scholarships, grants, books and manuals, newsletters, international electronic networks, etc.).
- Bring purchasers and providers of monitoring and evaluation services together to promote a mutual understanding of evaluation needs.
- Create and maintain a database of evaluators containing information on areas of expertise, experience, and recent publications.
- Facilitate the definition of professional norms and practices.

The strategies that follow have been used to create and develop the network or, in other words, to build national evaluation capacity.

Inclusiveness and Empowerment Approach. The network's meetings are open to every person and organization interested in M&E, regardless of position covered, institutional affiliation, seniority, or experience. Every member is asked to volunteer his or her time, competency, and technical skills to the network's activities. Internal working groups have been organized to widen the possibility of active participation in the network's life and to optimize the potential of each member.

Transparency. The members, during general meetings, make all major decisions. A coordination committee was elected during the inaugural meeting for a 2-year mandate. In 2001, a second committee was elected to cover the period from 2002 to 2004. A Web site was created so that all major decisions and activities related to the network could be posted, disseminated, and made freely and openly available. It is regularly updated.

Nigerien Led and Owned. The network is based in Niger and its objectives and activities are relevant to, and implemented in, Niger. Almost the totality of the network's members are Nigerien monitoring and evaluation specialists.

Broad Representation. One of the major added values of the network is its capacity to represent the perspectives, needs, and priorities of different stakeholders. This capacity is assured by the fact that the coordination committee members were chosen to represent different categories connected to monitoring and evaluation, notably public administration, the United Nations system, NGOs and bilateral projects, the university, and the private sector.

Valorization of Local Capacities. In Niger, there is important potential for local capacities. For this reason, the network is based in local experience and knowledge, and its focus is on national M&E capacity development. At each bimonthly meeting, local institutions or specialists are invited to present their own experiences and systems. A database with curriculum vitae of national evaluators was created, and the network's Web site hosts calls for African evaluators from development agencies.

Knowledge Acquisition, Construction, and Dissemination. To efficiently share and disseminate technical knowledge, the network organizes bimonthly meetings in which technical issues are presented and discussed. Moreover, the network's Web site hosts almost 30 manuals, methodological documents, and newsletters that can be downloaded free of charge, as well as several links to national M&E organizations and to the evaluation offices of several development agencies.

Coordination and Networking. The network facilitates the creation and development of contacts and relationships among different institutions, ministries, and agencies. A list of the network's members (complete with telephone, e-mail, and postal addresses) was created and is updated every 2 months, and e-mail is used to disseminate day-to-day messages.

Common Understanding. Evaluation, whatever its ultimate and appropriate nature may be for a given developing country, must have a clear set of concepts to which all can agree in principle. Achieving this should be considered an essential early step for an M&ECD effort. For this reason, one of the network's first priorities was the organization of a meeting to discuss and reach clear terminology and a common understanding of M&E.

Even though the network has been active for only 4 years, important lessons have been learned.

Focus on Technical Issues and Not on Internal Organizational Issues. M&E specialists are more interested in M&ECD than in internal organizational issues. ReNSE was able to organize itself during the first two meetings (adoption of objectives, adoption of a plan of action, themes to be discussed at the next meetings, election of the coordination committee). From the third meeting on, the core themes presented and discussed were technical, and organizational issues have been kept to a minimum.

Keep the Structure as Light as Possible. The network is based on the voluntary work of members and has no budget. For this reason, the bureaucratic structure of the network has been kept at a minimum level. The secretariat was supported by the United Nations Children's Fund (UNICEF) from 1999 to 2001 and by the Uniteed Nations Development Program (UNDP) from 2002 to 2004.

The Coordination Committee Has a Central Role to Play. The coordination committee is extremely important in assuring the network's function and development. It proposes new strategies and activities, facilitates their discussion and adoption, monitors their implementation, and reports to the general assemblies.

Be Open and Transparent. The network is based on trust among the members and credit with external institutions. To ensure personal commitment to the network's objectives and activities, every major decision is taken openly and transparently.

Keep Focused on the Openly Discussed and Adopted Objectives. Members are experts interested in M&ECD. To ensure that use of the limited resources available is optimized and interest is kept high, the coordination committee ensures that the network's activities are relevant to openly discussed and adopted objectives.

Look for Strategic Alliances With Similar Institutions. The network, being representative of different stakeholders, has a huge potential to advocate and mobilize strategic alliances to strengthen M&E within the country. The real value of the network is its capacity to coordinate and facilitate synergies and potentialities already existing in Niger.

—Marco Segone

◨ CAPITALISM

Capitalism is an economic system characterized by private property ownership and private ownership of the means of production. Both individuals and companies compete for their own economic gain through the acquisition of capital and the employment of labor. Capitalism is based on the premise that government intervention in the economy should be minimized and that free enterprise, the forces of supply and demand, should determine the prices of goods and services and will ultimately maximize consumer satisfaction. The role of the state is to regulate and protect the public from the potential abuses of capitalism, which have historically ranged from slavery and apartheid to more contemporary monopolies, cartels, and financial fraud.

The principles of capitalism can be found in Adam Smith's *The Wealth of Nations*. Its modern importance began in the 18th century when the bourgeoisie (bankers, merchants, industrialists) began to displace landowners. However, the seeds of capitalism date from much earlier times and can be found in the writing of Aristotle, especially in the assertion that people pay most attention to their own private property and less to what is communally owned. In the 13th century, St. Thomas Aquinas believed in the naturalism of private property ownership, albeit with a humanist expectation that private ownership would permit access by those in greatest need. Mercantilism, or the expansion of nation-state wealth through exporting finished products for the accumulation of gold and silver, was the prevailing perspective that Smith rejected in *The Wealth of Nations*. Smith argued that mercantilism created an oversupply of money and, consequently, rampant inflation. The opposing force to mercantilism was the doctrine of laissez-faire, the idea that economic systems function best when there is no interference by governments. It is also based on the idea that there is a natural economic order that, when undisturbed, will lead to maximum well-being for the individual and therefore for the community as a whole. Smith, under the influence of David Hume, believed that in a laissez-faire economy, self-interest would bring about public welfare.

In contemporary evaluation, the idea of capitalism as more a political and moral system of belief than an economic one of private ownership is deeply embedded. Evaluation is a commodity of which the nature, availability, and cost are largely controlled by demand (by the government agencies and philanthropic foundations that fund most evaluation). In one sense, evaluation is seen as a rationalizing mechanism for determining what works in the best interest of the many; for example, in determining which antipoverty program leads to the greatest reduction in poverty. Evaluation works within the perceived role of governments in advanced capitalism and is presumed to aid in the amelioration of its ills. In addition, evaluation plays a key role in globalization, the expansion of capitalism across nation-states, through the examination of the quality and quantity of services and goods in developing nations receiving international aid.

CARE. *See* CENTRE FOR APPLIED RESEARCH IN EDUCATION

◨ CARTOONING

Cartooning has been used as a tool to communicate findings in oral or written evaluation reports. Cartoons afford evaluators an opportunity to present findings in an illustrative and succinct way to attract the attention and interest of readers to an evaluation report. As pictorial representations, cartoons can reach out to audiences who may not be especially literate or familiar with the technical language in evaluation reporting. In this regard, cartoons are particularly useful for readers of an evaluation report who are visual learners.

The versatility of cartoons as a representational form can be seen in their ability to depict various kinds of ideas—humorous or grim; political, economic, or social; theological, philosophical, or psychological. The idea for a cartoon in an evaluation report can be derived in different ways. It can be perceived by an evaluator based on his or her interpretation of the data in an evaluation study. It can also be grounded in the data itself when evaluation participants provide information about humorous situations that highlight certain issues within an evaluand. An example of this is *cartoon transcreation,* a process of producing cartoon illustrations (from data and other sources pertinent to an evaluation study) that incorporate findings that constitute humor, findings that needed to be conveyed gently, or findings that are deemed important to create awareness among readers of the report.

Figure 1   *An Example of a Cartoon Representation Produced From the Cartoon Transcreation Process*

Once the idea has been conceived, an evaluator or a freelance cartoonist can draw the cartoon. Besides human figures, nonhuman figures can also be used to represent an evaluation finding. Cartoons using nonhuman figures are known as anthropomorphic cartoons: Animals or objects portray the behavior of humans. Along with technical credibility, it is important to ensure content credibility through feedback from evaluation participants whose information is depicted in the cartoons.

As an art form, cartoons are subject to multiple interpretations by readers of a report. The awareness of multiple interpretations can help readers realize and confront multiple realities and the complexity of the program being evaluated. Cartoons can also serve as a data collection tool if new pertinent information is gathered from multiple interpretations of the primary program stakeholders. This situation challenges current ontological and epistemological assumptions in conventional representational forms (graphs, tables, quotations, etc.) that reflect *subject-object dualism,* whereby a reader remains detached from a finding and excludes any value considerations from influencing it.

As an alternative form of representation, cartoons require audience assessment to ascertain if there is any cultural or social objection to cartooning before the decision is made to adopt cartoons to represent evaluation findings. In the context of an evaluation study in which the confidentiality of evaluation participants is upheld, caricatures may not be suitable in a cartoon representing findings. Used judiciously, a cartoon may very well help increase the repertoire of representational forms in an evaluator's toolbox.

The cartoon shown in Figure 1 depicts a finding about a child's motivation to read, based on data provided by an evaluation participant (parent) of an elementary school reading program in Florida known as SRA. It also illustrates a finding concerning the importance of home support for the child's motivation to read.

—Chin Mei Chin

Further Reading

Chin, M. C. (2003). *An investigation into the impact of using poetry and cartoons as alternative representational forms in evaluation reporting.* Unpublished doctoral dissertation, Florida State University, Tallahassee.

■■ CAUSATION

This concept has had a stormy history, from which it has not yet emerged. Today the "causal wars" (the controversy about what counts as evidence for causation) are raging as never before. Because almost every evaluation involves some claims about causation—for example, that the program being evaluated had certain outcomes—this issue is of crucial importance in evaluation. This entry briefly covers the present state of the search for a definition of cause and then focuses at greater length on outlining a compromise position on the required methodology, as this is a work aimed to assist evaluation rather than a purely logical exploration.

THE LOGIC OF CAUSE

In the history of the analysis of this crucial notion, Aristotle laid down a four-part analysis that was widely treated as dominant in the Western tradition until Hume undertook to reanalyze the concept. Hume identified three requirements of a cause: It should be prior to its effect, contiguous to it, and constantly correlated with it. None of these conditions are correct if what we are seeking to analyze is the common notion of cause because causes frequently occur simultaneously with their effects (a vertical air jet keeps a ball in the air), are frequently remote from their effects (the earth's mass causes the moon to hold its orbit), and are frequently erratic in their effects (heart attacks often, but not always, occur without fatal results). John Stuart Mill improved the Humean analysis, retaining precedence but adding theory connectedness and the elimination of alternative causes, both still widely supported. However, that left some loose ends (more details of the history may be found in Cook & Campbell, 1979). The current best version of this approach is set out in the following paragraph.

When we flip the light switch to turn the lights on, that is, to cause the lights to come on, there is a sense in which our action is necessary to produce the intended effect and a sense in which it is sufficient. However, that sense is not as simple as people have sometimes thought. In particular, our action is not categorically necessary: There are other events that can bring about the same effect, including a similar action by others and a short circuit in the wiring. Similarly, flipping the switch is not categorically sufficient because its effectiveness depends on the proper functioning of the switch, the wiring, and the light bulbs. It is possible to reconstruct the conditions required as follows: (a) What is commonly, though implicitly, meant by *cause* is that our action is one of a set of conditions, not all of which we can spell out, which are jointly sufficient to bring about the effect; hence, given the presence of the other conditions, it is *sufficient* to add this one factor. (b) This factor, the flipping of the switch, is, moreover, not a redundant member of the set of conditions—that is, the rest of the set is

not sufficient in and of itself to produce the effect in the absence of this factor—so this factor is in that sense *necessary* to bring about the effect.

Although this refinement of the early attempts to define cause avoids many of the early confusions and limitations, it is not adequate mainly because of its failure to handle tricky cases of overdetermination. Cases of overdetermination can be constructed where two potential causes meet the given definition but only one of them does in fact cause the effect; however, if it had not, the other would have brought about the identical effect at the identical time (e.g., two warriors fight for the honor of carrying the king's message to a distant general; the survivor takes the message, but if he had not won, it would have gotten there at the same time). In such cases, we have not the slightest difficulty identifying the actual cause, because the chain of events through which it operated, and only that chain, was completed: the causal chain of the lurking, unrealized, but overdetermining alternative possible cause was intercepted and terminated at some point by the chain of the cause that won the race. Such cases are not purely imaginary. In complex open systems, common in the social and biological sciences, lurking overdetermination factors are often present. They represent considerable problems for experimental investigations that do not follow the causal chains in detail, a well-known characteristic of many quantitative designs in practice. The logical significance of such cases is far reaching, for they are cases in which we do not have the slightest difficulty in applying the notion of cause, although our most sophisticated analysis of it cannot match the discriminations we so easily make.

What does that tell us about the concept? It tells us that we must accept a conclusion of a kind that is always unwelcome to analysts. We must agree that cause is an epistemological primitive, well understood by humans but not entirely reducible to other logical notions such as necessity and sufficiency. This conclusion from the logical investigation has extensive consequences for the methodological considerations to which we now turn.

THE METHODOLOGY OF CAUSE

In scientific searches for—or attempts to support—causal claims, the current controversy centers around the status that should be accorded to a particular, highly sophisticated experimental design, the use of randomized control trials; that is, trials in which subjects are allocated between an experimental and a control group by a strictly (not informally) random procedure. On the one hand, a group of distinguished researchers argues that only this design (referred to as the RCT design) can provide legitimate support for causal claims in the educational, social, and medical sciences. On the other side, a large number of researchers argues that many alternative designs can do this. The latter group varies considerably in the other claims they wish to add: Some of them would merely argue that one or a few quasiexperimental designs are also satisfactory, others would add the claim that even some qualitative studies can suffice, and yet others would argue that RCTs are often unable to do the trick themselves. The RCT group includes many but not all researchers who would describe themselves as in the quantitative camp on other research design issues; the opposition, similarly, includes many but not all individuals who would usually support qualitative approaches. Hence we do not use the more general labels here, referring instead to the RCT and non-RCT camps. Politics has no place here, but the importance of this issue does, and so this one comment is included: Under the reign of the President George W. Bush, the RCT group has received so much support that at the time of writing they have complete control of all federal educational research funds in the United States, totaling about $500 million per annum, and are now moving to obtain similar control in the social science area and in countries other than the United States.

The debate is so important to research practice today, and to the intellectual scene, that an effort was made in preparing this entry to review most of the considerable literature again and to consult with Tom Cook, perhaps the most widely respected of all those in the RCT group. In the light of that survey, several conclusions were reached that supported each side in this controversy, conclusions that are stated here without using inflammatory language in the hope that we can proceed toward some reconciliation and progress. (That hope is somewhat tempered by the realization that each side is also said by the other side to be at fault in some of the following conclusions.) Brief elaborations of the reasoning behind the more controversial of these propositions will be provided later in this entry.

1. The RCT design, if properly executed, is an extremely powerful and, in many cases, optimal tool for causal investigations. However, it is, as no one denies, a tool requiring considerable sophistication and experience to use well.

2. The RCT design has often been bypassed for poor reasons, especially in educational research, when it should have been used, and it has often been attacked on general grounds for failings that it does not have, such as the inability to provide explanations of individual cases.

3. Much research that has been undertaken in the education and social science areas has been of very poor quality, including much that was wrongly said to have established causal claims. Although plenty of this is education research, several texts are full of recent examples of invalid research published in refereed psychology journals.

4. A considerable amount of RCT research has been done, often at great expense, with zero useful results because of bad design, bad implementation, inadequate monitoring, or bad analysis. Restricting all funding to RCT (as is now de facto the case in the United States) is likely to increase this amount dramatically because investigators with less of the relevant experience or expertise are converting to RCT designs.

5. The RCT design is often referred to as the "gold standard" for causal investigations, but this is certainly inappropriate, both because the RCT design is all too often imperfectly implemented (a point stressed by Tom Cook) and because it is a much weaker design than one that might more plausibly be so labeled, the double-blind design. Double-blind designs, like RCT designs, can and should be used more often than they have been, although their use requires ingenious experimenters.

6. It is widely accepted, not just by RCT supporters, that quasiexperimental designs are weaker than RCT designs, essentially on the grounds that there are more threats to their validity. However, that does not, contrary to the common assumption, show that they are incapable of establishing conclusions *beyond reasonable doubt* (BRD). BRD is the top category of evidential quality for all scientific (by contrast with mathematical) conclusions, as it is for legal, technological, and commercial conclusions. It seems more appropriate to think of gold-standard designs in causal research as those that meet the BRD standard rather than as those that have certain design features, thereby avoiding the weakness connoted by the term *quasiexperimental* (which Campbell and Stanley clearly

intended). The existence of more threats to internal or external validity in quasiexperimental designs does not entail a reduction of validity for *well-done* studies below the RCT level of validity protection.

7.   Note that "well done," when applied to RCTs or quasiexperimental designs, is a very tough standard to meet. In Tom Cook's words,

> Interpreting [RCT] results depends on many other things—an unbiased assignment process, adequate statistical power, a consent process that does not distort the populations to which results can be generalized, and the absence of treatment-correlated attrition, resentful demoralization, treatment seepage and other unintended products of comparing treatments. Dealing with these matters requires observation, analysis, and argumentation. (Cook, 2004)

Note that the last sentence in particular is a pretty fair summary of the principal instruments of qualitative inquiry.

8.   Some official RCT announcements have identified one and only one particular quasiexperimental design, the regression discontinuity (RD) design, as an acceptable "next best" approach when an RCT design cannot be done. Since there are many occasions when RCT designs are ethically and legally unusable, in some of which the RD design is feasible and useful, this reduces, although it does not eliminate, the number of cases where the RCT group is unable to support any research at all.

9.   It seems clear that there are a number of other quasiexperimental designs that can, if carefully applied, easily qualify as establishing causal conclusions BRD and hence meet a realistic gold standard. These certainly include interrupted time series experiments, especially when these are done at many locations or with random interrupts.

10.   In what might be regarded as the quantitative "Parthenon," there are thus a number of research designs that meet the gold standard: these include, at least, double-blind studies, single-blind studies, zero-blind studies (RCTs), regression discontinuity studies, strong interrupted time series studies, and, for some research questions, identical twin studies.

11.   In the *scientific* Parthenon, however, it can be argued that we should recognize two other groups of studies that establish causal claims to the satisfaction of scientists. One of these groups includes studies that are experimental in the usual sense but not quasi-experimental even in the Campbell and Stanley sense.

These include the usual laboratory experiments used in forensic studies (in an autopsy) to determine the cause of death and in engineering studies the cause of a structural failure (in, e.g., a bridge, a building, or a jet airliner), as well as much of criminalistics and medical lab testing.

12.   A second group of scientifically accepted causal claims are theory based but not experimental in any sense: These include, for example, the astrophysicist's conclusions about supernovas as the cause of certain astronomical configurations and Darwin's conclusions about the cause of speciation in the Galapagos finches. It is therefore hard to justify recent claims that the only *scientific* basis for causal claims is the RCT design. Also, although one may not wish to call history a science, it should be noted that all historical claims about causation fall into this group and should surely not *all* be dismissed as ill founded or merely speculative.

13.   Finally, after these suggestions, which simply create a more realistic perspective for the claims about RCT (by identifying it as just one of a group of at least eight scientifically acceptable approaches), we come to a conclusion that turns the RCT approach on its head. This is the absolutely inescapable conclusion that the most important and reliable source of causal claims is observation. To substantiate it, it is time to move away from the list format.

To understand this more radical claim, we need to consider the cognitive ontogenesis of the concept of cause. Its really distinctive feature, from this point of view, is its foundation as a sensorimotor concept. Although it is as fundamental as the primitive but merely sensory concepts of color, sound, smell, motion, and touch, it is special in its connection to the concept of the self as agent, as a proactive and not a merely reactive element in the world. As the very young child develops the grasp reflex and then the ability to rattle things and to move things and eventually to throw things, it is acquiring the sense of itself as a cause. Not long after that, the child extrapolates the notion to the point where it understands that others can also be causes, can turn off lights that are out of the reach of its own hands and produce goodies it cannot access. Somewhat later, it extrapolates the same notion to nature, as it comes to see that strong winds can close doors and knock down trees, that great waves can destroy sandcastles and boats. Causation is a core notion of the self-concept and of the world concept for every human being. A great wonder—and no wonder that it is irreducible to logical primitives.

Our experience of the world and our part in it is not only well understood by us but is pervasively, essentially, perpetually a causal experience. A thousand times a day we observe causation, directly and validly, accurately and sometimes precisely. We see people riding bicycles, driving trucks, carrying boxes up stairs, turning the pages of books, picking goods off shelves, calling names, and so on. Thus the basic kind of causal data, vast quantities of highly reliable and checkable causal data, come from observation, not from elaborate experiments. Experiments, especially RCTs, are a marvelously ingenious extension of our observational skills, enabling us to infer causal conclusions where observation alone cannot take us. However, it is surely reversing reality to suppose that experiments are the primary or only source of reliable causal claims: They are, rather, the realm of flight for such claims, where the causal claims of our everyday lives are the ground traffic of them.

Interestingly enough, a reread of Cook and Campbell (1979, p. 33) uncovered a remarkable passage in which this view appears to be conceded, although its huge implications for causal methodology were never developed: "We do not find it useful to assert that causes are 'unreal' and are only inferences drawn by humans from observations that do not themselves directly demonstrate causation."

The implications for the causal wars of the position provided earlier in proposition 12 are profound. Not only are such field sciences as biology and anthropology liberated from second-class citizen status for their frequent claims to have observed causal connections; the entire universe of case study methodology must be recognized as capable in principle of extensive causal analysis—for example, the recently elaborated version called the Success Case Method (Brinkerhoff, 2003). Stress must be placed on the qualification "in principle," however, because extremely careful application of rigorous requirements must be observed if we are to observe more than anecdotes masquerading as scientific findings. This means, specifically but not only, that we must seek and normally require (a) independent confirmation of observational causal claims or extremely strong documentation of "expert witness" status where valid triangulation is impossible and (b) extremely careful elimination of alternative possible causes, the constant companion to (a) in the armory of scientific causal confirmation.

It is worth stressing that the elimination of alternative explanations has a key role even in RCT designs because much of the work of controlling threats to their validity involves careful observation aimed at picking up the intrusion of confounding variables (alternative possible causes). This does suggest that RCTs are perhaps best seen as hybrid qualitative-quantitative designs in themselves. Similarly, untangling cases of overdetermination and forensic causation typically involves essentially qualitative analysis of causal chains and patterns.

In conclusion, then, it seems clear that the implications of a careful analysis of causation support the policy of a pluralistic (but not an "open admissions") approach to funding, coupled with severe standards of rigor for each of the several defensible approaches. This will not only make it possible to answer many important questions that cannot be answered by using any one method; it is likely to increase the kind of hybrid vigor that results from attacking problems from more than one methodological platform.

—*Michael Scriven*

Further Reading

Brinkerhoff, R. O. (2003). *The success case method.* San Francisco: Berrett-Koehler.

Cook, T. D. (2004). *Beyond advocacy: Putting history and research on research into debates about the merits of social experiments* (Social Policy Report No. 12). Ann Arbor, MI: Society for Research in Child Development.

Cook, T. D., & Campbell, D. T. (1979). *Quasi-experimentation: Design and analysis issues.* Boston: Houghton Mifflin.

CDC. *See* CENTERS FOR DISEASE CONTROL AND PREVENTION

CENTER FOR APPLIED RESEARCH IN EDUCATION. *See* CENTRE FOR APPLIED RESEARCH IN EDUCATION

CENTER FOR INSTRUCTIONAL RESEARCH AND CURRICULUM EVALUATION (CIRCE)

The Center for Instructional Research and Curriculum Evaluation was organized in 1964 within the College of Education, University of Illinois at Urbana-Champaign. It was created to continue the Illinois Office of Statewide Testing (until 1969) and to provide evaluation services to curriculum development activities on campus and elsewhere. It was created in response to U.S. Office of Education interest in locating a research and development center on campus specializing in measurement and evaluation. Tom Hastings, Lee Cronbach, and Jack Easley authored the proposal, but Cronbach left, and the university created the center without federal funding. Hastings was first Director, and Bob Stake succeeded him in 1975. Across the years, the staff has included Claire Brown, Mary Ann Bunda, Rita Davis, Judy Dawson, Terry Denny, Gene Glass, Tom Kerins, Dennis Gooler, Arden Grotelueschen, Mel Hall, Stafford Hood, Terry Hopkins, Ernie House, Gordon Hoke, Stephen Kemmis, Steve Lapin, Bob Linn, Linda Mabry, Tom Maguire, Sandra Mathison, Duncan McQuarrie, Jim Pearsol, Oli Proppe, Jim Raths, Doug Sjogren, Nick Smith, Terry Souchet, Joe Steele, Peter Taylor, Jim Wardrop, and many others.

—*Robert E. Stake*

■■ CENTER FOR RESEARCH ON EVALUATION, STANDARDS, AND STUDENT TESTING (CRESST)

Located within UCLA's Graduate School of Education and Information Studies, the Center for Research on Evaluation, Standards, and Student Testing (CRESST) endeavors to improve the quality of education and learning in America. CRESST is a pioneer in the development of scientifically based evaluation and testing techniques and a leading proponent of the accurate use of data, test scores, and technology for improved accountability and decision making. CRESST researchers, along with CRESST's many partners, explore the impact of different approaches to assessment and accountability on instruction and the impact of variations in system design on the validity of inferences, with a special emphasis on the challenges and requirements of the No Child Left Behind legislation.

—*Jeffrey G. Tucker*

■■ CENTER FOR THE STUDY OF EVALUATION (CSE)

The UCLA Center for the Study of Evaluation (CSE) was established in 1966 based on a national competition and was designated the national center for research in educational evaluation. The center has been continuously funded by the research office of the U.S. Department of Education and other federal and state agencies and has employed more than 150 people. Many seminal ideas in evaluation, methodology, and measurement originated and were first published at CSE: Scriven's *Goal Free Evaluation,* Bloom's *Mastery Learning,* Alkin's work on evaluation utilization, House's *Logic of Evaluation Argument,* and Herman's *CSE Evaluation Kit* (for these and other publications, see the National Center for Research on Evaluation, Standards, and Student Testing's Web site at http://www.cse.ucla.edu).

—*Marvin C. Alkin*

■■ CENTERS FOR DISEASE CONTROL AND PREVENTION (CDC)

Part of the U.S. Public Health Service, the CDC is a scientific agency dedicated to protecting people's health and safety. Created as a malaria control unit in 1946, the CDC has developed into 12 centers housing experts in a vast array of topics (e.g., chronic disease, injury, infectious disease, environmental hazards), all guided by the vision of "healthy people in a healthy world, through prevention." A distinguished track record, including global smallpox eradication, established the CDC's reputation for excellence in responding to widespread, deadly, and mysterious health threats. The information that the CDC releases is widely regarded as trustworthy, and its recommendations are often accepted as definitive standards for public health practice.

—*Bobby Milstein*

Further Reading

Centers for Disease Control and Prevention. (2003). *About CDC.* Retrieved May 3, 2004, from http://www.cdc.gov/aboutcdc.htm.

Etheridge, E. W. (1992). *Sentinel for health: A history of the Centers for Disease Control.* Berkeley: University of California Press.

CENTRE FOR APPLIED RESEARCH IN EDUCATION (CARE)

CARE is based at the University of East Anglia, England, and is first cousin to the Center for Instructional Research and Curriculum Evaluation (CIRCE) at Urbana, Illinois. These two centers formed, in the 1970s and 1980s, a transatlantic axis for the advancement of case study approaches to evaluation. CARE was founded in 1970 by Lawrence Stenhouse, with the impetus of the Humanities Curriculum Project. Some key curriculum principles from that project (pedagogical neutrality, values pluralism, information brokerage) found an easy match to, and to some extent fueled, democratic evaluation discourse. Barry MacDonald was Project Evaluator for the Humanities Curriculum Project and became Director of CARE at Stenhouse's death in 1982.

CARE promoted political, ethical, and methodological principles of applied educational research; specifically, research responsive to the dilemmas of educational practice, interacting with those dilemmas in situ, aiming to generate theory from experience and which subjects itself to the judgment of those it serves. Promoting these principles and elaborating them through funded research and evaluation projects, CARE became an engine for the development of case-based methodologies. It was here that Stenhouse, John Elliott, and Clem Adelman developed classroom action research; Rob Walker, Adelman, MacDonald, Stephen Kemmis, Helen Simons, and others developed educational case study; MacDonald developed democratic evaluation; and Kushner developed personalized evaluation. CARE published early, influential methodological texts dealing with case study and case-based evaluation. CARE has been one of the few sites for the training of evaluation methodologists rather than for training in method.

—Saville Kushner

CERTIFICATION

Certification in evaluation is a process leading to a formal statement (document) that specifies what a person knows about evaluation principles, what evaluation skills they possess, and that they are able to conduct evaluations. Generally, certification is based on an individual's having passed a standardized test soon after having completed an educational program in a field or specialty. It might also require successfully taking multiple examinations throughout a program of study, as in medicine and actuarial science.

Determining the content of the certification examination is usually the purview of professional groups (e.g., the American Evaluation Association, the Canadian Evaluation Society, the Japanese Evaluation Society). Maintaining certification is an individual responsibility, but most fields mandate what is needed for certificate renewal, such as participating in continuing education courses (or workshops), producing examples of one's work, and, less frequently, being retested at regular intervals.

Certification is distinct from licensing and credentialing, with the distinctions often blurred. A license is granted by an official governmental entity that not only legally controls licenses to practice in a field but also the removal of same for cause. For the vast majority of fields, the license is based on performance in the certification examination, with responsibility for the content of the test and the standards to be achieved residing in the professional society. These standards are accepted by the government entity, which assumes the role of a regulator.

To illustrate the distinction between certification and licensing: A physician could be certified, but not licensed (have the legal right to engage in the practice of medicine) because he or she was known to have abused drugs or committed a felony. Each year in the United States, physicians, lawyers, pharmacists, and others who are certified in their respective disciplines lose their licenses through the actions of state-sanctioned boards of professional conduct and practice. Under due process, practitioners may legally challenge a decision to revoke or suspend their license in their chosen field of practice.

Credentialing refers to the completion of certain requirements (approved courses, applied field internships, apprenticeships, on-the-job training) for which one would be given a credential.

A professional group, such as the American Chemical Society, may give credentials, and to some extent, a university degree could be considered a credential. The passage of a certification examination (or examinations) may not be mandatory for a credential. Attestation to an individual's level of skill or performance by a professional group or a government body is neither present nor implied. Credentialing simply shows that a person has had exposure to certain information and has been involved in specified experiences. Credentialing is less rigorous than certification.

Certification is predicated on the concept of a profession as characterized by (a) a specialized body of literature and skills that must be acquired, (b) work that requires using those specialized skills and knowledge, (c) a common set of interests that set apart members of the profession from other individuals and groups, (d) the formation of professional societies, (e) a sense of calling (a strong desire to engage in the work), (f) full-time practitioners, (g) formal training based on content determined by the professional society, (h) standards determined by the society that guide the conduct of work in the field, and (i) controlled entry. Entry, as noted previously, is via matriculation through established training programs, testing at or near the completion of training, and, in some instances, supervised participation in work in the field under an appropriately qualified individual.

Rationales for certification (and licensing) are numerous; a few reasons are given here. One is the protection of the general public or consumers from those who do not have the qualifications to offer the services at a minimum level of competency or who would be unscrupulous, that is, who would not subscribe to or follow professional standards. The intent is that organizations hiring evaluators would be more confident that quality work up to the level proposed by the profession would be performed. A second reason is that certified individuals periodically update their skills and knowledge in accord with new developments and changes in the field so that practices are as current as possible. A third, perhaps less noble, reason is that certification enables a profession to limit how many are admitted to practice and is, in essence, a way of enhancing the financial base for a profession.

The description of three issues will demonstrate the difficulties inherent in certification for the field of evaluation. First, the training of evaluators is highly varied and not similar across disciplines, universities, or other venues. Evaluators receive their training in education, psychology, sociology, public policy and management, social work, and business. Curricula may overlap, but they can be quite different, with organizational climate and structure emphasized in one, evaluation models in another, and qualitative or quantitative approaches to evaluation dominating yet

a third. Without fairly clear consensus about content and skills, as in other fields (medicine, dentistry, pharmacy, and actuarial science), the development of one examination in the United States or across the globe would be highly problematic and contentious. Those who teach evaluation, especially in universities, may have different foci in their programs and therefore be unwilling to standardize or come to agreement on what should be taught and how it should be taught.

Second, some feel that by establishing a certification system, sufficient and in-depth training will be delivered only by larger and well-funded universities. This will tend to undermine, over time, the more limited instruction now available in smaller institutions and their participation in the evaluation enterprise.

Third, protection of the consumer is subtler in evaluation than it is in other fields. Most consumers are not equipped to judge the quality of an evaluation—how it was carried out and whether it was done in accord with evaluation standards. Furthermore, evaluations can be conducted in many equally acceptable and unique ways, with stress on altogether diverse parts of projects. In so doing, there could be divergent, yet valid, findings from these multiple perspectives, making it even harder for consumers to make an overall assessment or judgment. Therefore "protection of the consumer" may be a somewhat tenuous argument for the certification of evaluators.

—*James W. Altschuld and James T. Austin*

Further Reading

Altschuld, J. W. (1999). The case for a voluntary system for credentialing evaluators. *American Journal of Evaluation, 20*(3), 507-517.

Browning, A. H., Bugbee, A. C., Jr., & Mullins, M. A. (Eds.). (1996). *Certification: NOCA handbook.* Washington, DC: National Organization for Competency Assurance.

Impara, J. C. (Ed.). (1995). *Licensure testing: Purposes, procedures, and practices.* Lincoln, NE: Buros Institute.

▓ CHALMERS, THOMAS

(b. 1917, d. 1995). Graduate 1939, Yale University; M.D., Columbia College of Physicians and Surgeons.

Chalmers worked as a physician, studying liver disease at Harvard University and Tufts University Medical School from 1947 to 1968. He also worked with the Veterans Administration in Washington, DC, and served as director of the Clinical Center at the

National Institutes of Health. From 1973 to 1983, Chalmers was President of Mount Sinai Medical Center and Dean of Mount Sinai School of Medicine, where he founded the Department of Biostatistics.

Chalmers' primary contribution to the field of evaluation was in the application of randomized field trials and meta-analysis in clinical settings and in medical schools. One of his last efforts was to incorporate more evidence and probability theory and general statistics into the curriculum of the first years of medical school. A profound influence on Chalmers' career was the work and lecture series of Sir Austin Bradford Hill, which introduced Chalmers to randomization.

He published over 300 papers during his lifetime, 200 of which were influenced by meta-analysis and randomized trials. In one such paper, considered to be a landmark work, he revealed the serious inconsistencies in existing evidence among authoritative medical textbooks. Among other honors, Chalmers was asked to travel to Japan to study an outbreak of hepatitis among Korean-based American soldiers, and in 1982, he received the American Evaluation Association's Paul F. Lazarsfeld Award for evaluation theory.

▪▪ CHANGE

Social scientists have created a comprehensive body of theoretical knowledge about change. Havelock's seminal work includes a taxonomy of change models that provides a basis for ideological and political debates about how best to implement change in organizational settings.

These debates revolve around the locus of the change initiative. Proponents of the use of science evidence maintain that research-based knowledge should be the critical force in the development of rationally based social interventions. An alternative view, encapsulated in the community development movement, is based on the primacy of locally produced knowledge due to the perceived relevance of local conditions to decisions about effective interventions. A key element of the debate is about control: Who should control decisions—an external authority or those who are close to the action?

It is within this context that the role of evaluation on change must be considered. There are parallels between the evolution of evaluation practice and what has been discussed here. Although there was an emphasis in early evaluation practice on the use of evaluation to solve problems on a large scale if not on a national basis, there are now a large number of evaluators who work to support programs that are more localized and in the hands of the community.

Links between evaluation and change involve an acknowledgment that evaluation findings should affect individuals and organizations. Changes in individuals are often associated with learning, knowing, and understanding information about the program that was previously not known. With regard to the utilization of research and evaluation findings, this has been labeled as *conceptual use*. Achieving conceptual understanding of findings is now regarded as the minimum desired outcome in an evaluation study, and evaluators should employ strategies to achieve this outcome. In the context of policy research and evaluation, three phases of individual change have been identified.

Phase 1: Reception. Utilization takes place when policy makers receive policy-relevant information. When the communication comes to rest in the "in basket," so that the findings reach the policy maker rather than remaining with the evaluator, reception has occurred.

Phase 2: Cognition. The policy maker must read, digest, and understand the findings for cognition to occur.

Phase 3: Reference. If frame of reference is the criterion, the evaluation findings must change the way the policy maker sees the world. If information changes her or his preferences or understandings, change is a reality. Altering frames of reference is important because, in the long run, the policy maker's new vision will emerge in new policy priorities.

This final phase points to a second level of change: the use of findings as a basis for action, which has been described as *instrumental use*. Examples of changes of an instrumental nature include developing a new program or modifying an existing one, clarifying an existing program plan or design, and refining the delivery of a program that is already being implemented.

Such changes imply an organizational perspective because programs are rarely the responsibilities of individuals acting outside an organizational context. It is likely that groups rather than individuals would be engaged in programmatic activities such as policy planning, developing program logic, and implementing new procedures that directly affect the clients concerned in the intervention.

In addition, evaluations can affect changes in more fundamental ways. This could be through modifying the rules of an organization, changing its structure, or influencing its underlying mission or philosophy. Changes of such a radical nature are rare, however.

This discussion has emphasized that the findings of an evaluation are fundamental to utilization and change. Still, some theorists suggest that the act of evaluation can in itself stimulate thinking and lead to instrumental changes in organizations. This is likely to happen when the evaluator is an insider or where the evaluation works closely and cooperatively with organizational groups who participate in the evaluation process. The knowledge that accrues is known as *process use*.

Process use refers to cognitive and behavioral changes that result from users' engagement in the evaluation process. Process use occurs when those involved learn from the evaluation process—as, for example, when those involved in the evaluation later believe that the impact on their program came not so much from the findings as from going through the thinking process that the evaluation required.

One of the more interesting conceptual developments has been to link utilization theory and change theory. Kotter suggests eight critical steps that need to be taken to successfully manage a major change effort.

1. *Building a case for change.* Key stakeholders, such as managers and staff, need to understand why change is necessary. The evidence for change must be collated and articulated to those who are affected by the change. Change is about risk, so the risk of not changing needs to be perceived as greater than the risk of going ahead with the change.

2. *Forming a powerful coalition.* This involves molding a group of individuals into an effective team and providing them with enough power to lead the change effort.

3. *Creating a vision.* What is initially required is a sense of direction, not myriad plans. There is a need for those involved in the change effort to share the vision.

4. *Communicating the vision.* There is a need for those involved in the change to share the vision that could be promoted by a charismatic leader.

5. *Empowering others to act on the vision.* Structures need to be set up that will support the vision and remove potential obstacles.

6. *Planning for and creating short-term wins.* This is about ensuring that there are short-term wins and opportunities to celebrate successes.

7. *Consolidating improvements.* This involves incorporating change into the fabric of the organization and requires person-intensive and resource support from the administration.

8. *Institutionalizing the change.* This involves making sure that those in the organization understand the change and how it affects organizational outcomes.

It is possible to view different kinds of evaluation as a support to these change efforts. As indicated earlier, there are different evaluation models with different purposes and uses. An up-front or proactive evaluation could support a case for change. An evaluation that has a clarifying purpose could assist in creating the visions. An improvement or process-focused evaluation could show the nature and extent of short-term wins. Finally, a more traditional impact evaluation should provide evidence about institutionalizing the change.

This discussion implies that decisions about organizational change and improvement can be more effective if there is a commitment to the use of evaluation findings. It is doubtful whether this is the modal situation across the public and private sectors in Western societies, let alone across the world stage. A commitment to the use of evaluation implies an evidence-based perspective on organizational management, a notion that is foreign in many organizational contexts.

Nevertheless, recent research shows that an increasing number of decision makers value the findings of social and educational research. There is a reason to be optimistic about the future impact of evaluation on change if the professional evaluation community makes a commitment to ensuring that its work is usable.

—*John M. Owen*

Further Reading

Havelock, R. G. (1971). *Planning for innovation through dissemination and utilization of knowledge.* Ann Arbor MI: Center for Research on Utilization of Scientific Knowledge.

Kotter, J. P. (1995, March-April). Leading change: Why transformation effects fail. *Harvard Business Review*, pp. 59-67.

Owen, J. M., & Rogers, P. (1999). *Program evaluation: Forms and approaches* (2nd ed.). London: Sage.

Senge, P. M. (1990). *The fifth discipline: The art and practice of the learning organization.* Garden City, NY: Doubleday.

CHANGE PROCESS. *See* CHANGE

■■ CHAOS THEORY

A theory based on the mathematical notion that small changes in nonlinear systems can produce large and unpredictable results. Nonlinear systems react in complex ways to feedback. This extreme sensitivity to initial conditions is known as the *butterfly effect* (the idea that the flapping of a butterfly's wings in Asia may eventually alter the course of a hurricane in Florida). Chaos theory provides a theoretical framework for evaluators interested in holistic or systems analysis. Complex feedback processes take the place of linear cause-effect chains of events, emphasizing the examination of dynamic interrelationships among stakeholders and practices within social systems.

—*Melissa Freeman*

Further Reading

Lorenz, E. (1993). *The essence of chaos.* Seattle: University of Washington Press.

■■ CHECKLISTS

Procedures for the use of the humble checklist, although no one would deny their utility in evaluation and elsewhere, are usually thought to fall somewhat below the entry level of what we call a methodology, let alone a theory. However, many checklists used in evaluation incorporate a quite complex theory, which we are well advised to uncover—and the process of validating an evaluative checklist is a task calling for considerable sophistication. It is interesting that although this theory is less ambitious than the kind

that we normally call program theory, it is often all the theory we need for an evaluation. This entry covers some of the basic features of checklists and their application in evaluation, but it does not claim to exhaust their logic or methodology.

BASIC CONCEPTS

A checklist is defined here as a list of factors, properties, aspects, components, criteria, tasks, or dimensions, the presence or amount of which are to be separately considered in the performance of a certain task. There are many different types of checklist, although all have at least one nondefinitional function in common—that of being a mnemonic device. This function alone makes them useful in evaluation, as the nature of evaluation calls for a systematic approach to determining the merit, worth, and so on, of what are often complex entities. Hence, a list of the many components or dimensions of performance of such entities is frequently valuable.

Checklists are of various kinds: At the bottom of the checklist pecking order is the eponymous laundry list, which is almost entirely a mnemonic device and nonetheless useful for that. Notice that the order in which one calls on the items in a laundry list does not affect the validity of the list: We can start by entering on the list whatever items are at the top of the laundry pile. However, the entry of entities into the right place on the list is crucial to avoid the equivalent of keyboarding errors in empirical data entry. Also, the grouping of items as the list is being constructed is often quite important: For example, shirts with colors that may bleed need to be kept separate from white shirts. Note that a real laundry list is not an evaluative list, but plenty of "laundry lists" are used in evaluation, and one of these is discussed later.

Next is the sequential checklist, where the order does matter. The first kind of these is what we might call the strongly sequential kind, wherein the sequencing (of some or all checkpoints) must be followed to get valid results. One example of this is the preflight checklist, whose use is compulsory, not merely recommended, for the flight crews on aircraft carrying hundreds of thousands of passengers a day. It is sequential because, for example, the accuracy of the reading of instrument A depends on whether or not the setting on instrument A has been zeroed, so one must do the setting before the reading. The use of the preflight checklist is evaluative because it is designed to provide support for the evaluative conclusion that the plane is in good enough condition to fly safely. Many sequential checklists, however, are not intrinsically evaluative, although they might nevertheless be used in the course of an evaluation. Flowcharts often imply one or more sequential checklists, but they are often a better way to represent inference chains that involve extensive conditionals (i.e., "if-then" statements), as well as sequences.

A weakly sequential checklist is one where the order is important, but for psychological or efficiency reasons rather than from logical or physical necessity. Example: In the early days of the development of the Program Evaluation Standards, Dan Stufflebeam recalls Lee Cronbach making a strong argument that the first group of these standards should not contain the Accuracy standards that were the obvious candidates but the Utility standards, because—as Cronbach saw it—people were getting sick of evaluations that might be accurate but showed every sign of being, and usually turned out to be, useless. Convince them that evaluations were going to be useful, he argued, and you would get their attention when you turned to matters such as accuracy.

Efficiency considerations can also suggest a certain ordering of a checklist. For example, if experience reveals that a required level of performance on a particular dimension of merit—perhaps a certain minimum productivity figure—is the one most commonly failed by candidates in a recurrent competition, efficiency suggests putting it first in the order because that will eliminate the need to spend time checking out the performance on other criteria of those candidates that flunk this requirement. Again, this will be a weakly ordered (sequential) checklist.

An iterative checklist is sequential, in whole or part, but requires—or may require—multiple passes to reach a stable reading on each checkpoint. The Key Evaluation Checklist, one of those provided at the University of Western Michigan's Evaluation Checklist Project Web site, is iterative. Used for evaluating a program, it places the Cost checkpoint ahead of the Comparisons checkpoint because until one has determined the cost of something, it is hard to determine what alternatives to it should be considered. After going farther down the checklist, however, one may be led to think of still further alternatives for the comparison group. This does no harm, by contrast with the situation in

the strongly sequential preflight checklist—one can still correct the tentative conclusions on the Comparisons checkpoint. Hence, the Key Evaluation Checklist is not strongly sequential, but weakly.

Another type of checklist, one that is sometimes but not always sequential, is based on flowcharts. This is the diagnostic checklist that is used by—for example—mechanics, taxonomists, and toxicologists. It typically supports a classificatory kind of conclusion—one that is descriptive, not evaluative—but the conclusion is sometimes evaluative. This may be because the checklist is explicitly evaluative; for example, a troubleshooting list in which the conclusions must necessarily be faultfinding and hence evaluative (e.g., "The problem with this engine seems to be that the fuel injector nozzles are seriously worn"; "The culprit in this death seems to be overexertion"). If the checklist itself is not be evaluative, the context of use may still justify certain types of evaluative conclusions; for example, "This specimen is too badly damaged to make a final classification possible." It is worth noting that the diagnostic checklist, although it may not itself be couched in theoretical terms, often leads us to causal conclusions because it is often theory based under the surface (e.g., based on a limited theory about the modus operandi of a poison).

Probably the most important kind of checklist for evaluation purposes is the criteria of merit checklist (hence, COMlist or, here, comlist). This is what judges use when rating entries in a skating or barbecue or farm produce competition; it is what evaluators use—or should be using—for evaluating teachers or researchers or colleges or funding requests and what teachers or researchers use when evaluating evaluations and evaluators. At "the Royal"—the crown of the competitive barbecue season in Kansas City, which only winners of the major regionals are eligible to enter—the judges use one of the simplest examples of a decision-controlling comlist. All entries (called "Qs") are rated on (a) appearance, (b) tenderness, and (c) taste, with equal weight to each.

Comlists are widely used as the basis for a particular scoring procedure: The criteria are given weights (e.g., on a 1-5 scale), the candidates are given performance scores on a standard scale (e.g., 1-10), and the sum of the products of the weights (of each criterion by the performance on that dimension) for each candidate is used as the measure of merit. However, comlists can be used with benefit without using this particular scoring procedure (the numerical weight and sum, or NWS, procedure), so their value is not dependent on the known invalidity of that scoring procedure. The comlist is often a tough item to develop and validate: It has to meet some stringent requirements that do not apply to the simpler types of checklists discussed so far. For example, it is essential that it be complete, or very close to it, meaning that it must include every significant criterion of merit. Otherwise, something that scores well on the comlist may be quite inferior because of its poor performance on some missing but crucial dimension of merit. Again, the criteria in a comlist should not overlap if the list is to be used as a basis for scoring, to avoid "double counting" in the overlap area.

By now enough examples have been covered to support some general conclusions on the pragmatic side, worth mentioning before the hard work starts.

THE VALUE OF CHECKLISTS

1. Checklists are mnemonic devices; that is, they reduce the chances of forgetting to check something important, and they reduce errors of omission.

2. Checklists in general are easier for the lay stakeholder to understand and validate than most theories or statistical analyses. Because evaluation is often required to be credible to stakeholders as well as valid by technical standards, this feature is often useful for evaluators.

3. Checklists in general, and particularly comlists, reduce the influence of the "halo effect" (the tendency to allow the presence of some highly valued feature to overinfluence one's judgment of merit). Checklists do this by forcing the evaluator to consider separately and allocate appropriate merit to each of the relevant dimensions of possible merit. Note that checklists do not eliminate the use of holistic considerations, which can be listed as separate criteria of merit.

4. Comlists reduce the influence of the Rorschach effect (the tendency to see what one wants to see) in a mass of data. They do this by forcing a separate judgment of each separate dimension and a conclusion based on these judgments.

5. The use of a valid comlist eliminates the problem of double weighting.

6. Checklists often incorporate huge amounts of specific knowledge about the particular evaluands

for which they have been developed. Look at the checklist for evaluation contracts, for example: It is based on, and manifests, a huge amount of experience. Roughly speaking, this amount is inversely proportional to the level of abstraction of the items in the checklist. (Example: The preflight checklist for any aircraft is highly type specific.) Hence, checklists are a form of knowledge about a domain, organized so as to facilitate certain tasks, such as diagnosis and evaluation.

7. In general, evaluative checklists can be developed more easily than what are normally described as theories about the domain of the evaluand; hence we can often evaluate (or diagnose, etc.) where we cannot explain. (Example: yellow eyes and jaundice.) This is analogous to the situations where we can predict from a correlational relationship, although we cannot explain the occurrence of what we predict (e.g., aspirin as analgesic).

For these and some other reasons to be developed later, checklists can contribute substantially to (a) the improvement of validity, reliability, and credibility of an evaluation and (b) our useful knowledge about a domain. Now we return to some further development of the logic of the comlist.

REQUIREMENTS FOR COMLISTS

Most of the following are self-explanatory and refer to the criteria or checkpoints that make up a comlist:

1. Criterial status (not mere indicators; see the following)

2. Complete (no significant omissions)

3. Nonoverlapping (if list is used for scoring)

4. Commensurable (explained later)

Also, of course:

5. Clear

6. Concise (mnemonic devices that can themselves be easily remembered score double points)

7. Confirmable (e.g., measurable or reliably inferable)

The first of these requirements is crucial and needs the most explanation. Suppose you are evaluating wristwatches with a view to buying one for yourself or a friend. Depending on your knowledge of this slice of technology, you might elect to go in one of two directions. (a) You could use indirect indicators of merit, such as the brand name or the recommendations of a knowledgeable friend, or (b) you could use criteria of merit, which essentially define the merit of this entity. Such criteria are sometimes called *direct indicators of merit* or *primary indicators of merit*. Their epistemological status is superior; but practically, they are less convenient because they refer to characteristics that are both more numerous and less accessible than indirect or secondary indicators.

For example, many people think that the brand name Rolex is a strong indicator of merit in watches. If you do believe that (or if you care only how the gift is perceived, not how good it is in fact), you just need a guarantee that a certain watch is a genuine Rolex to have settled the merit issue. That guarantee is easily obtained from reputable dealers, leaving you with only aesthetic considerations to get you to a purchase decision. However, if you want to get to the real truth of the matter without making assumptions, you will need to have (a) a comlist, (b) good access to evidence about the performance of several brands of watch on each checkpoint in the comlist, and (c) a valid way to combine the evidence on the several checkpoints into an overall rating. None of these are easy to get.

Conscientious evaluators can hardly rely on secondary indicators of merit with respect to their principal evaluands. They are obliged to use criteria of merit, so they typically need to be good at developing (or finding and validating) comlists. This approach has its own rewards: For example, it quickly uncovers the fact that Rolex makes poor watches by contemporary standards and charges several hundred to 1000% more for them than a competitive brand in terms of merit. What you pay for in a Rolex is a massive advertising campaign and the snob value. Apart from the waste of money in buying one, in terms of true merit there is also the fact that you considerably increase the chance of being robbed or carjacked.

A comlist for wristwatches, or anything else you are thinking of buying, begins with what we can call the core comlist, defining the general notion of merit in wristwatches, to which we can add, as a guide to purchase, any personal or special-group preferences such as affordability, aesthetic, or snob-value considerations—the personal criteria of merit. In evaluating programs for some agency, the professional evaluator's typical task, the personal criteria have no place (you are not going to buy the program), and hence we focus on the core comlist. When *Consumer Reports* is evaluating wristwatches or other consumer products, they similarly deal only with the core comlist, leaving the rest up to the reader. Now, what does a core comlist look like for wristwatches?

1. *Accuracy.* Roughly speaking, this can be taken to require, at a minimum, accuracy within less than a minute a month; most busy people will prefer to cut this by at least 50%, which reduces the resets to about three a year. Idiosyncratically, others will demand something considerably better: As an accuracy of better than a second a century is now available at under $100 (watches radio controlled by the National Bureau of Standards), a minute a year may be considered to be the maximum allowable inaccuracy. The Rolex is certified as a chronometer, an out-of-date standard that is worse than any of those just mentioned.

2. *Readable dials.* Some of Rolex's "jewelry watches" for women are very hard to read.

3. *Durability of watch and fittings.* The watch should be able to survive being dropped onto a wooden floor from 4 feet. The band should survive more than 2 years (leather usually does not).

4. *Comfortable to wear.* Gold is usually too heavy. A titanium bracelet is best.

5. *Flexibility of fit.* The band should be easily adjustable, without help from a jeweler. (Fit depends on temperature, diet, etc.)

6. *Low maintenance.* Batteries should last several years, routine servicing the same. Rolex does not use batteries, and recommended cleaning and servicing is frequent and very expensive.

Each of these claims requires some data gathering, some of it quite difficult to arrange. (To these criteria of merit, we would, for personal use, add idiosyncratic requirements about appearance and features, e.g., luminous hands, stopwatch or alarm functions, waterproofing, and cost.)

By contrast, an indicator list could be used, like this:

1. Made by Rolex

Evidence for this, easy to get, would be that it was sold by an authorized Rolex dealer, who guaranteed it in writing and by serial number. The validity of this indicator, as of any secondary indicator, is (roughly) the correlation between it and the cluster defined by the first set of six indicators. The hints provided make it clear that this correlation is low.

CRITERIA VERSUS INDICATORS

Given that the path of righteousness for evaluators is the path of criteria, not indicators, how do we identify true criteria for an evaluand X?

The key question to ask is this: What properties are parts of the concept (the meaning) of "a good X"? Note: In general, you will not get good results if you start by identifying the defining criteria for X itself and try to go from there to the criteria for "good X." Thus, in our example, to call something a good watch is to say that it tells the time accurately, is easy to read, is durable, is comfortable to wear, and so on.

Is this to say that a watch that misses on one of these criteria is by definition not a good watch? Not quite. A watch that is rather fragile, for example—enough so that one would not call it durable—but excels on the other criteria would probably be called "good but not great." Still, that failing raises some doubt about whether we should really call it a good watch, and any more shortcomings would make us hesitate even more. A criterion of merit is one that bears on the issue of merit, sometimes very heavily (so that a failure on that criterion is fatal), but often just in the sense of being one of several that are highly relevant to merit although not in themselves absolutely essential.

How does one validate a checklist of criteria of merit? Essentially, by trying to construct hypothetical cases in which an entity has the properties in the proposed comlist but still lacks something that would be required or important to justify an assignment of merit. Looking at the provided checklist for a watch, for example, one might say, "Well, all that would get you a watch that ran well if you stayed home all the time, but suppose you have to fly from one part of the country to another. That will require you to reset the time, and there are watches where that is a virtually impossible task unless you carry an instruction book with you (e.g., the Timex Triathlon series). Surely that flaw would lead you to withhold the assignment of merit?" That is a pretty good argument, and clearly another criterion of merit is needed. So we now have

the following (can you see other loopholes? There is at least one minor one):

1. Accurate
2. Easily readable
3. Durable
4. Comfortable
5. Easily adjustable
6. Inexpensively maintainable (batteries, cleaning, repair)
7. Easily settable

Some things are taken for granted in these lists. For example, we could add the requirements that the watch does not emit evil radiation, does not induce blood poisoning or skin eruptions, and so on. We simply put those into the general background for all consumer products, not thereby belittling them—there are documented cases of radiation damage from the early days of luminous dials. But these possibilities (and there are many more) would extend comlists beyond necessity. We can deal with such cases as and when they arise.

There are other interesting issues, which we pass over here: For example, should luminous dials be taken as an extension of readability, as an idiosyncratic preference, or as an entry under an additional heading (Versatility)?

EVALUATIVE THEORIES

The informational content of checklists has already been stressed. For example, the watch checklist exhibits knowledge of the components of watches; the contracting checklist exhibits considerable knowledge of the process whereby organizations approve contracts. Now, what theory underlies the watch comlist? It is not a theory about how watches work but about what they need to do well to perform their defining function well. That may be just the kind of theory that we need for evaluation purposes.

These "evaluative theories" are not as ambitious as an explanatory theory of the total operation of the evaluand, something that is more than anyone can manage with many complex evaluands, such as large educational institutions. However, it is not so hard to say what such an institution has to do to be regarded as meritorious—it is not a trivial task, but it is at least much easier. One attraction of an evaluative theory is thus that it is much easier to demonstrate its truth than it is to demonstrate the truth of an explanatory theory.

Those who favor an outcome approach to program evaluation will perhaps be particularly attracted to this kind of theory because of the emphasis on performance. However, it can easily include process variables, such as comfort in wearing a watch.

It is true that evaluative theories—the underpinnings of comlists—are not particularly adept at generating explanations and recommendations; program theories are supposed to excel at exactly this, if you are lucky enough to have a valid one. Evaluative theories do have a trick up their sleeves, however: They are outstandingly good at one valuable aspect of formative evaluation—identifying the areas of performance that need attention.

CRITERIA, SUBCRITERIA, AND EXPLANATORY TEXT

The richness and value of a comlist is often greatly increased when some of the criteria are unpacked. In particular, the value in formative evaluation can be greatly improved by this procedure. Here are the main headings from the comlist for evaluating teachers, which can be found at the Western Michigan University Evaluation Center site:

1. Knowledge of subject matter

2. Instructional competence

3. Assessment competence

4. Professionalism

5. Nonstandard but contractual duties to school or community (e.g., chapel supervision)

Not too controversial, but also not too useful. It is still a long way from the trenches. The following demonstrates how the second entry here might be expanded so that the comlist could really make distinctions between better and weaker teachers.

Instructional Competence

1. Communication skills (use of age-appropriate vocabulary, examples, inflection, body language)

2. Management skills

   a. Management of (classroom) process, including discipline
   b. Management of (individual students' educational) progress
   c. Management of emergencies (fire, tornado, earthquake, flood, stroke, violent attack)

3. Course construction and improvement skills

   a. Course planning
   b. Selection and creation of materials
   c. Use of special resources
      (1) Local sites
      (2) Media
      (3) Specialists

4. Evaluation of the course, teaching, materials, and curriculum

Now what is being included is much clearer, and we are much closer to being able to apply the checklist. However, in the publication where the original list appeared, experience led the authors to add 8000 words of more specific detail, some for each subcriterion, to complete a working checklist. This points up one feature of the use of checklists that has to be kept in mind: the balance between ease of understanding and length. Brevity is desirable, but clarity is essential—especially, of course, when people's careers or other highly important matters are at stake.

The second matter that can be illuminated from this example is the criterion (for checklists) of commensurability. What this means is that headings at one level of a checklist have to be of roughly the same level of generality. In the present example, there are four levels of headings. Looking at any one set in its location under a higher level heading, one can see that all items in the set are of the same level of specificity. The other side of the commensurability coin is that one must pay some attention to the function of the checklist in grouping and naming subheadings. For example, in the laundry list, if the function is to control the actions of the laundry person, colored articles need to be listed separately from white ones. If, however, the function is simply to make a record of what went to the laundry, the color of the shirts is irrelevant.

Another matter that requires close attention when building checklists into one's methodology is thoughtfulness in the application of checklists. Daniel

Stufflebeam reports on a pilot whose considered judgment was that some pilots he had flown with focused on covering the preflight checklist in the sense of checking items off on it, but not on the meaning of the checkpoints, thereby creating serious risks.

THE USE OF COMLISTS FOR PROFILING AND SCORING PURPOSES

Possibly the most important use of checklists in evaluation involves using them as the basis for assessing and representing the overall merit, worth, or importance of something. In rating decathletes, for example, we can simply set up a graph in which each of the 10 merit-defining events is allocated half an inch of the horizontal axis, and the decathlete's best score in each event is represented by a normalized score in the range 1 to 10 on 5 inches of the vertical axis. Using this kind of bar graph is called profiling, and it is a very useful way to display achievement or merit, especially for formative evaluation purposes. However, it will not (in general) provide a ranking of several candidates; for that, we need to amalgamate the subscores into an overall index of some kind. In the decathlete case, this is easily done: Equal weight is allotted to each performance (as that is how the decathlon is scored) and the normalized performance scores are added up. The athlete with the top score is the best selection, the second highest score identifies the runner-up, and so on.

But in program evaluation and most personnel evaluation, matters are not so easy. One often feels that different criteria of merit deserve different weights, but it is very hard to make a case for a quantitative measure of that difference. Worse, the use of a single weight for each criterion of merit is an oversimplification. It is often the case that a certain level of performance in criterion N is much more important than a certain level of performance in criterion M, but increments above that level in N are no more important than increments in M. In other words, the value or utility function is not a linear function of performance. If that is so, what kind of function is it? Evaluators might begin to feel out of their depth at this point. The following remarks may be helpful.

1. Do not abandon equal weighting without overwhelming evidence. In the first place, it may not be exactly right, but it may be the best approximation. In the second place, even if it is not the best approximation, results based on this assumption may be highly correlated with results based on the correct function or weighting, and you cannot determine the latter, so it is this way or no way.

2. If you are certain that N is more important, throughout its range, than M, make a simple intuitive estimate of the difference as the basis for a trial exploration of its effect. Do this very cautiously: At first, consider whether to use 1.5 as the factor rather than 2, and almost never go beyond that ratio. It is extremely hard to justify a higher ratio than 2, to others: "If 3, why not 4?" is hard to refute.

3. If the ratio you pick seems not to apply constantly across the whole range of performance on a particular criterion, try varying it for a certain interval.

4. Testing your attempts to set differential weights requires some judgment about whether the results show it to have been a success or failure. Do this by inventing and considering a range of hypothetical cases, to see whether they lead to implausible results. You are likely to find out quickly that large differences in weights allow for the easy creation of counterexamples.

5. A procedure that combines qualitative weighting with minimalist quantitative procedures is set out in the fourth edition of the *Evaluation Thesaurus*.

CONCLUSION

Laundry lists, sequential checklists, and comlists all serve important roles in evaluation. A basic logic covering only some of their properties has been set out here in the hope that it may lead to increased attention to and the improved utility of checklists.

—*Michael Scriven*

Further Reading

Evaluation Checklist Project, Evaluation Center, Western Michigan University. (2004). *Evaluation checklists.* Retrieved May 4, 2004, from http://www.wmich.edu/ evalctr/checklists/

Scriven, M. (1959). The logic of criteria. *Journal of Philosophy, 56,* 857-868.

Scriven, M. (1991). *Evaluation thesaurus* (4th ed.). Newbury Park, CA: Sage.

CHELIMSKY, ELEANOR

Chelimsky is an independent evaluation consultant. She has more than 30 years of experience conducting evaluations and consulting for national and international organizations on evaluation practice and policy. From 1966 to 1970, she was an economic analyst for the U.S. Mission to NATO, charged with statistical, demographic, and cost-benefit studies. From 1970 to 1980, she worked at MITRE Corporation, where she directed work in evaluation planning and policy analysis, criminal justice, and research management. Between 1980 and 1994, she was Assistant Comptroller General for Program Evaluation and directed the U.S. General Accounting Office's Program Evaluation and Methodology Division, whose mission was to serve the U.S. Congress through evaluations of government policies and programs and through the development and demonstration of methods for evaluating those policies and programs. She has also assisted many other countries—Canada, China, Columbia, France, Germany, Malaysia, Pakistan, Poland, Sweden, and the United Kingdom—in instituting their own evaluation organizations.

Chelimsky's contributions to the theory and practice of evaluation are substantial. She is Coeditor of *Evaluation for the 21st Century: A Handbook* (with William R. Shadish), a member of the editorial board for the Sage Research Series in Evaluation, and serves on the editorial boards of *Policy Studies Review, Policy Studies Review Annual, New Directions for Program Evaluation*, and the new international journal *Evaluation*. She was President (1980) of the Evaluation Research Society and President (1994) of the American Evaluation Association and was elected a Fellow of the National Academy of Public Administration in 1994. She is a member of the advisory boards for the University of Chicago's School of Social Service Administration and Carnegie Mellon's John Heinz School of Public Policy. She received the 1982 Alva and Gunnar Myrdal Award for Government Service from the Evaluation Research Society, the 1985 GAO Distinguished Service Award, the 1987 GAO Meritorious Executive Award, the 1991 Comptroller General's Award (GAO's top honor), and a 1994 National Public Service Award.

CHEN, HUEY-TSYH

Currently Professor at the School of Public Health at the University of Alabama at Birmingham, Chen previously worked at the University of Akron until 1997, and joined the Centers for Disease Control and Prevention (CDC) as Chief of an evaluation branch. Chen had taken a leadership role in designing and implementing a national evaluation system for evaluating the CDC-funded HIV prevention programs based in health departments and community-based organizations. His evaluation vision and interests have been expanded and enriched by such practical experiences.

Chen has contributed in the development of evaluation theory and methodology, especially in the areas of program theory, theory-driven evaluation, and evaluation taxonomy. He has published extensively on this topic, including *Theory-Driven Evaluations* and *Using Theory to Improve Programs and Policies,* co-edited with Peter H. Rossi. His most recent text, *Practical Program Evaluation: Assessing and Improving Planning, Implementation, and Effectiveness,* provides a systematic conceptual framework and strategies that benefit evaluation practitioners by systematically identifying stakeholder needs, selecting evaluation options best suited for particular needs and reconciling trade-offs among these options, and putting the selected approaches into action.

In 2001, he received the Award for Dedication and Scientific Direction in the Development and Implementation of Program Evaluation Research Branch from CDC; in 1998, the Senior Biomedical Research Service Award also from CDC; and in 1993, the Paul F. Lazarsfeld Award for contributions to evaluation theory from the American Evaluation Association.

CIPP MODEL (CONTEXT, INPUT, PROCESS, PRODUCT)

The CIPP Model for evaluation is a comprehensive framework for guiding formative and summative evaluations of programs, projects, personnel, products, institutions, and systems. This model was introduced by Daniel Stufflebeam in 1966 to guide mandated evaluations of U.S. federally funded projects because these emergent projects could not meet requirements for controlled, variable-manipulating experiments, which then were considered the gold standard for program evaluations. Since then, the model has been widely applied and further developed. Those applying or contracting others to apply the model have included government officials, foundation officers, program and project staffs, international assistance personnel, school administrators, physicians, military leaders, and evaluators. The model is configured for use in internal evaluations conducted by an organization's evaluators, in self-evaluations conducted by project teams or individual service providers, and in contracted external evaluations. It has been employed throughout the United States and around the world and applies to short-term and long-term investigations in the full range of disciplines and service areas.

CONTEXT, INPUT, PROCESS, AND PRODUCT EVALUATIONS

The model's core features are denoted by the acronym CIPP, which stands for evaluations of an entity's context, inputs, processes, and products. *Context* evaluations assess needs, problems, assets, and opportunities as bases for defining goals and priorities and judging outcomes. *Input* evaluations assess alternative approaches, competing action proposals, and associated budgets for meeting targeted needs and achieving objectives. They are used in planning programs, writing funding proposals, allocating resources, and, ultimately, judging the adopted approach and budget. *Process* evaluations assess the implementation of plans to guide activities and later judge program performance and help explain outcomes. *Product* evaluations identify intended and unintended outcomes, both to help keep an enterprise on track and, ultimately, to gauge its success in meeting targeted needs.

In the formative case—where evaluation helps guide an effort—context, input, process, and product evaluations respectively ask: What needs to be done? How should it be done? Is it being done? Is it succeeding? The evaluator submits interim reports addressing these questions to keep stakeholders informed about findings and to help guide decision making and improvement. In preparing the final summative report, the evaluator refers to the store of context, input, process, and product information and gathers additionally needed information to address the following retrospective questions: Were important needs addressed? Was the effort guided by a defensible design and budget? Was the service design executed correctly and modified as needed? Did the effort succeed?

In summing up long-term evaluations, the product evaluation component may be divided into assessments of impact, effectiveness, sustainability, and transportability. These product evaluation subparts ask: Were the right beneficiaries reached? Were their pertinent needs met? Were the gains for beneficiaries sustained? Did the processes that produced the gains prove transportable and adaptable for effective use elsewhere?

Beyond context, input, process, and product evaluations, the CIPP Model includes several other essential features.

EVALUATION DEFINITIONS AND STANDARDS

The CIPP Model's *operational definition of evaluation* is the process of delineating, obtaining, reporting, and applying descriptive and judgmental information about some object's merit, worth, probity, and significance to guide decision making, support accountability, disseminate effective practices, and increase understanding of the involved phenomena. The bases for judging CIPP evaluations are pertinent standards, including especially the Joint Committee for Educational Evaluation's standards for evaluation of programs, personnel, and students, which require evaluations to meet conditions of utility, feasibility, propriety, and accuracy. Moreover, the CIPP Model stipulates that evaluations themselves should be rigorously evaluated, a process referred to as metaevaluation.

INVOLVEMENT OF STAKEHOLDERS

Another of the CIPP Model's key features is its orientation to involve and serve an enterprise's stakeholders. First and foremost, evaluators are charged to identify and communicate with the effort's rightful beneficiaries, assess their needs for services, obtain information needed to design responsive programs or other services, assess and provide feedback of use in guiding implementation of services, and ultimately assess and report the enterprise's strengths, weaknesses, and accomplishments. Moreover, CIPP evaluations accord beneficiaries and other stakeholders more than a passive recipient role. Evaluators must control the evaluation process to assure its integrity, but they are advised to keep stakeholders informed and provide them with opportunities to contribute. Consistent with the Joint Committee's *Program Evaluation Standards* and the writings of many evaluators, evaluators are expected to search out all relevant stakeholder groups and engage them in communication and consensus-building processes to help define evaluation questions; clarify evaluative criteria; contribute needed information; and reach firm, defensible conclusions. Involving all levels of stakeholders is considered ethically responsible because it equitably empowers the disadvantaged as well as the advantaged to help define the appropriate evaluation questions and criteria, provide evaluative input, and receive and use evaluation findings. Involving all stakeholder groups is also seen as an intelligent thing to do because sustained, consequential involvement positions stakeholders to contribute valuable insights and inclines them to study, accept, value, and act on evaluation reports.

FOCUS ON IMPROVEMENT

The CIPP Model emphasizes that evaluation's *most important purpose* is not to prove but to improve. Evaluation is thus conceived of as a functional activity oriented in the long run toward stimulating, aiding, and abetting efforts to strengthen and improve enterprises. However, the model does not discount the likelihood that some programs or other services are unworthy of attempts to improve them and instead should be terminated. By helping to stop unneeded or hopelessly flawed efforts, evaluations serve an improvement function through assisting organizations to free resources and time for use in more worthy enterprises. Also, consistent with its quest for improvement, the model stresses that evaluation should capture and report valuable lessons from both successful and failed efforts.

OBJECTIVIST ORIENTATION

The CIPP Model's orientation is objectivist, not relativist. Objectivist evaluations are based on the theory that moral good is objective and independent of personal or human feelings. Such evaluations are firmly grounded in ethical principles, such as the U.N.'s Universal Declaration of Human Rights; strive to control bias, prejudice, and conflicts of interest in conducting assessments and reaching conclusions; invoke and justify appropriate and (where they exist) established technical standards of merit; obtain and validate findings from multiple sources; search for best answers, although these may be difficult to find; set forth and justify best available conclusions about the evaluand; report findings honestly, fairly, and as circumspectly as necessary to all right-to-know audiences; subject the evaluation process and findings to independent assessments against pertinent standards; and identify needs for further investigation. Fundamentally, objectivist evaluations are intended, over time, to lead to conclusions that are correct—not correct or incorrect relative to an evaluator's or other party's predilections, position, preferences, standing, or point of view. The model contends that when different objectivist evaluations are focused on the same object in a given setting, when they are keyed to fundamental principles of a free society and agreed-on criteria, when they meaningfully engage all stakeholder groups in the quest for answers, and when they conform to the evaluation field's standards, different evaluators will arrive at fundamentally equivalent, defensible conclusions.

PROSPECTIVE AND RETROSPECTIVE APPLICATIONS OF THE CIPP MODEL

Originally, the CIPP Model was developed as an evaluative aid to planning and successfully implementing special projects. The intent was to supply decision makers—such as school boards, project directors, school principals, teachers, and counselors—with timely, valid information of use in identifying an appropriate project area; formulating sound goals and activity plans; successfully carrying out work plans; periodically deciding whether to repeat or expand an effort and, if so, how; and meeting the sponsors' accountability requirements. Essentially, the orientation was formative—toward helping groups mount and operate special projects—and placed less emphasis on summative evaluation of completed efforts.

However, if evaluators effectively conduct, report, and document formative evaluations, they will have much of the information needed to produce a

Table 1   The Relevance of Four Evaluation Types to Formative and Summative Evaluation Roles

Evaluation Roles	Context	Input	Process	Product
Formative evaluation: Prospective application of CIPP information to serve decision making and quality assurance	Guidance for identifying needed interventions and choosing and ranking goals (based on assessing needs, problems, assets, and opportunities)	Guidance for choosing a program or other strategy (based on assessing alternative strategies and resource allocation plans); examination of the work plan	Guidance for implementing the operational plan (based on monitoring and judging activities and periodic evaluative feedback)	Guidance for continuing, modifying, adopting, or terminating the effort (based on assessing outcomes and side effects)
Summative evaluation: Retrospective use of CIPP information to sum up the program's merit, worth, probity, and significance and meet accountability requirements	Comparison of objectives and priorities to assessed needs, problems, assets, and opportunities	Comparison of the program's strategy, design, and budget to those of critical competitors and to the targeted needs of beneficiaries	Full description of the actual process and record of costs; comparison of the designed and actual processes and costs	Comparison of outcomes and side effects to targeted needs and, as feasible, to competitive programs; interpretation of results against the effort's assessed context, inputs, and processes

defensible summative evaluation report. The key is to establish and maintain a functional information storage and retrieval system within which to record context, input, process, and product evaluation information. Table 1 summarizes uses of the CIPP Model for both formative and summative evaluations. The matrix's cells encompass much of the evaluative information required to guide enterprises and produce summative evaluation reports.

USE OF MULTIPLE METHODS

As a comprehensive approach to evaluation geared to use in development, the CIPP Model requires engagement of multiple perspectives, use of a wide range of qualitative and quantitative methods, and triangulation procedures to assess and interpret a multiplicity of information. Given the emergent nature and dynamic environments of many of the evaluands assessed by CIPP evaluations, common laboratory controls usually are not feasible; pertinent, validated data-gathering instruments often do not exist; and typically there is too little time to thoroughly design, pilot test, and validate the needed instruments. In such situations, the evaluator has to be resourceful in pulling together much reasonably good information that in the aggregate

tells a consistent, truthful story. The model advocates engaging multiple observers and informants with different perspectives, constructing "homemade" instruments as needed, and addressing each evaluation question in a timely manner, using multiple procedures. In following this advice, evaluators are expected to search out and investigate both convergence and contradictions in findings and be appropriately circumspect in generating conclusions.

Table 2 illustrates the variety of methods of use in evaluations of context, input, process, and product (with product divided into the subparts of impact, effectiveness, sustainability, and transportability). Almost all the methods listed down the table's vertical axis apply to more than one type of evaluation. As indicated by multiple checkmarks in each column, use of multiple methods for each type of evaluation provides needed cross-checks on findings.

SUMMING UP AND REPORTING EVALUATION RESULTS

At an enterprise's attainment of maturity or end, the CIPP Model sees evaluators compiling all relevant information in a comprehensive summative evaluation report. Consistent with its objectivist orientation, the model

Table 2   Illustration of Methods of Potential Use in CIPP Evaluations

Methods	Context	Input	Process	Impact	Effectiveness	Sustainability	Transportability
Survey	✓		✓	✓	✓	✓	
Literature review	✓	✓					
Document review	✓	✓	✓	✓	✓		
Visits to other programs		✓		✓	✓		✓
Advocate teams		✓					
Delphi technique	✓	✓					
Program profile or database		✓	✓	✓	✓	✓	
On-site observer			✓	✓	✓	✓	
Case studies			✓	✓	✓	✓	
Stakeholder interviews	✓		✓	✓	✓	✓	✓
Focus groups	✓	✓	✓	✓	✓	✓	✓
Hearings	✓	✓			✓		
Cost analysis		✓	✓		✓	✓	
Secondary data	✓				✓		
Goal-free evaluation			✓	✓	✓	✓	✓
Photographic record	✓		✓	✓	✓	✓	✓
Task reports and feedback meetings	✓	✓	✓	✓	✓	✓	✓
Synthesis or final report	✓	✓	✓	✓	✓	✓	✓

seeks convergence on conclusions about an enterprise's value plus identification of lessons learned. To address the full range of audiences, the summative report should provide information including and reaching beyond context, input, process, and product evaluation. An illustrative outline for a summative report is as follows:

Part 1:   Program Background

   The operating organization

   Genesis of the program

   Program environment

Part 2:   Program Implementation

   Program beneficiaries

   Program financing

   Program staff

   Program operations

Part 3:   Program Results

   Evaluation design

   Findings

      Context

      Inputs

      Process

      Impact

      Effectiveness

      Sustainability

      Transportability

   Conclusions

      Judgments of merit, worth, probity, and significance

      Lessons learned

In this example, Part 1 is descriptive and targeted to persons lacking information on the operating organization, why it started the program, and the program's locale. The mainly descriptive Part 2 is directed to those who might be interested in replicating all or part of the program. Part 3 presents a comprehensive appraisal of the enterprise and its outcomes and is targeted to all members of the audience.

CONCLUSION

The CIPP Model for evaluation treats evaluation as an essential concomitant of improvement and accountability. Moreover, it responds to the reality that evaluations of innovative efforts typically cannot employ experimental designs or work from published evaluation instruments—both of which yield far too little information anyway.

The model contends that society and its agents cannot make their programs, services, and products better unless they learn where they are weak and where they are strong. They cannot be sure program goals are worthy unless they are compared to beneficiaries' needs. They cannot plan effectively and invest time and resources wisely if options are not identified and assessed. They cannot earn continued respect and support if programs cannot show that commitments have been fulfilled and beneficial results have been produced. They cannot build on past experiences if lessons from both failed and successful efforts are not studied and preserved.

The CIPP Model was developed to enable and guide comprehensive, systematic examination of efforts that occur in the dynamic, septic conditions of the real world. It is designed to help service providers sort out good from bad, point the way to needed improvements, be accountable to sponsors and clients, make informed institutionalization and dissemination decisions, and learn from experiences. The model's present version is based on a wide range of applications, is keyed to professional standards for evaluations, and is supported by an extensive literature. The model affords evaluators and their clients a comprehensive, realistic, practical, and philosophically grounded approach to conducting transparent, defensible, and effective evaluations.

—Daniel L. Stufflebeam

Further Reading

Guba, E. G., & Stufflebeam, D. L. (1968). Evaluation: The process of stimulating, aiding, and abetting insightful action. In R. Ingle & W. Gephart (Eds.), *Problems in the training of educational researchers.* Bloomington, IN: Phi Delta Kappa.

Reinhard, D. (1972). *Methodology development for input evaluation using advocate and design teams.* Unpublished doctoral dissertation, The Ohio State University, Columbus.

Stufflebeam, D. L. (1966). A depth study of the evaluation requirement. *Theory Into Practice, 5*(3), 121-133.

Stufflebeam, D. L. (1969). Evaluation as enlightenment for decision making. In A. Walcott (Ed.), *Improving educational assessment and an inventory of measures of affective behavior.* Washington, DC: Association for Supervision and Curriculum Development.

Stufflebeam, D. L. (1971, Fall). The relevance of the CIPP evaluation model for educational accountability. *Journal of Research and Development in Education.*

Stufflebeam, D. L. (1985). Stufflebeam's improvement-oriented evaluation. In D. L. Stufflebeam & A. J. Shinkfield (Eds.), *Systematic evaluation* (pp. 151-207). Boston: Kluwer-Nijhoff.

Stufflebeam, D. L. (1997). *Strategies for institutionalizing evaluation: Revisited* (Occasional Paper Series, No. 18). Kalamazoo: Western Michigan University Evaluation Center.

Stufflebeam, D. L. (2000). The CIPP model for evaluation. In D. L. Stufflebeam, G. F. Madaus, & T. Kellaghan (Eds.), *Evaluation models* (2nd ed., pp. 279-317). Boston: Kluwer.

Stufflebeam, D. L. (2002). *CIPP evaluation model checklist.* Retrieved May 4, 2004, from http://www.wmich.edu/evalctr/checklists/cippchecklist.htm

Stufflebeam, D. L. (2003). The CIPP model for evaluation. In T. Kellaghan & D. L. Stufflebeam (Eds.), *The international handbook of educational evaluation* (chap. 3). Boston: Kluwer.

Stufflebeam, D. L., Foley, W. J., Gephart, W. J., Guba, E. G., Hammond, R. L., Merriman, H. O., et al. (1971). *Educational evaluation and decision making.* Itasca, IL: Peacock.

Stufflebeam, D. L., & Webster, W. J. (1988). Evaluation as an administrative function. In N. Boyan (Ed.), *Handbook of research on educational administration* (pp. 569-601). White Plains, NY: Longman.

CLASS. *See* SOCIAL CLASS

▚ CLIENT

This is the person, group, or organization that pays for the evaluation. The client can be external to the evaluator's organization, resulting in an external evaluation. The client can be a person or group within the same organization as the evaluator, resulting in an internal evaluation. That person, group, or organization may or may not be one of the major stakeholders in the evaluation but should be considered part of the stakeholder group.

—Darlene F. Russ-Eft

▋▋ CLIENT SATISFACTION

This implies that the client is satisfied with the conduct and results of the evaluation. An evaluator is obligated to satisfy the client with the conduct of the evaluation but not necessarily with the outcomes or the findings. Thus there may be occasions when the findings of an evaluation are not welcomed by the client and other stakeholders. Following *Program Evaluation Standards'* Accuracy Standards, the evaluation should have used defensible information sources and systematic and well-described procedures, and should have justified all conclusions.

—Darlene F. Russ-Eft

▋▋ CLUSTER EVALUATION

The term *cluster evaluation* was coined in 1988 by W. K. Kellogg Foundation staff in an evaluation of a foundation-funded initiative; the concept was further developed and the technique practiced by Kellogg Foundation evaluation consultants and other practitioners in the evaluation community. A *cluster* is defined as a strategic collection of grants exploring or developing new approaches to an issue related to program area issues or strategy, with moderate focus on sustainability. Although there is probably not a single, comprehensive definition of cluster evaluation that is agreed on by all who are familiar with this type of evaluation, various evaluators have pointed out several basic characteristics:

1. It seeks to determine impact through aggregating outcomes from multiple sites or projects, whereas multisite evaluation seeks to determine outcomes through aggregating indicators from multiple sites.

2. It looks across a group of projects to identify common threads and themes that, having cross-project confirmation, take on greater significance.

3. It seeks not only to learn *what* happened with respect to a group of projects but also *why* those things happened by discovering factors that contribute to or constrain success within the environment of the projects and the strategies employed.

4. It occurs in a collaborative way that allows all players—projects, foundation, and cluster evaluators—to contribute to and participate in the process so that what is learned is of value to everyone.

5. It helps to strengthen the evaluation efforts of all who are involved, and it supports the work of foundation program officers, who have limited time to interact with the projects because of the numerous other demands on their time.

6. Cluster evaluators receive most of their data from the project or grantee evaluators, although some primary data are also collected.

In practice, a group of projects, usually five or more, is designated as a cluster because they are alike in strategy or targeted population group. They may be at different stages in their funding cycle, but, to the extent possible, they should be within the first half of the grant term. This allows projects adequate time to adapt and modify their activities as appropriate as they participate in the cluster evaluation and networking with other projects.

The projects are brought together to share evaluation plans for each individual project and to discuss important questions that may be common to all projects and that may form the basis for a cluster evaluation. At the W. K. Kellogg Foundation, the practice has been that external evaluators be invited by the foundation to sit in on the discussions so that they may familiarize themselves with the projects and with the foundation's goals in having funded this group of projects. The evaluators then prepare plans for seeking out answers to the important questions through evaluation activities across the cluster. This may involve a variety of methodologies.

Cluster evaluations typically are funded for upwards of 4 years. During that time, a series of networking meetings will be held at which all projects in the cluster convene. These meetings generally include updates on individual projects and on the cluster evaluation, but they also revolve around concerns of broad interest to that cluster; specifically, legislation in the subject area, management questions, and the use of computer technology. In some networking meetings, cluster evaluators engage in some form of data collection.

The W. K. Kellogg Foundation uses the information collected through cluster evaluation to enhance the effectiveness of grant-making efforts, clarify the strategies of major programming initiatives, and inform public policy debates. Cluster evaluation is not a substitute for project-level evaluation, nor do cluster evaluators evaluate individual projects. Cluster evaluation focuses on progress made toward achieving the broad goals of a programming initiative. Cluster evaluators provide feedback on commonalties in program design, as well as innovative methodologies used by projects during the life of the initiative. In addition, cluster evaluators are available to provide technical assistance in evaluation to projects that request it. Cluster evaluation is not metaevaluation and should not be viewed that way. It focuses on the impact and high-level learning across projects within the realm of the initiative.

A number of contemporary challenges that face cluster evaluation have been identified. These include the following:

- *Multiple stakeholders.* Cluster evaluation can have many audiences (e.g., board of directors, programming staff, grantees) who want information for different purposes. This requires the cluster evaluator to address multiple needs and requires more complex evaluation designs and skills in managing interpersonal relationships.

- *Evaluation as intervention.* Part of a project's intervention may include data collection or the provision of technical assistance, in which case cluster evaluators may find themselves in the dual role of programmer and evaluator. Clarity of roles and responsibilities is required at the early stage of programming development if conflict of interest is to be avoided.

- *Evaluator as interpreter.* When providing technical assistance, the cluster evaluator may interpret the funder's intent to grantees. When conducting evaluation, the cluster evaluator needs to interpret local outcomes in the context of overall strategic intent. This may require different skills and maybe even multiple evaluators.

- *Evaluating sustainability.* Sustainability has many definitions. The W. K. Kellogg Foundation emphasizes sustaining capability to address local concerns. Better ways are required of assessing the adaptability of community systems.

—Craig Russon, with assistance from the W. K. Kellogg Foundation staff

Further Reading

Millet, R. (1995). *W. K. Kellogg Foundation cluster evaluation model of evolving practices.* Battle Creek, MI: W. K. Kellogg Foundation.

Sanders, J. R. (1997). Cluster evaluation. In E. Chelimsky & W. R. Shadish (Eds.), *Evaluation for the 21st century: A handbook* (pp. 396-404). Thousand Oaks, CA: Sage.

Evaluation Practice Around the World

Germany

Transferring Cluster Evaluation to Model Programs in Germany

Cluster evaluation is still an emerging approach that has not yet been comprehensively discussed in the evaluation literature. Nevertheless, it had already been transferred to the evaluation of model programs run by the German federal government in the field of child and youth services just a few years after its elaboration within the framework of programming initiatives by the W. K. Kellogg Foundation. Progress of this kind is often triggered by minor events. When the German Youth Institute was looking for a suitable way to evaluate a federal model program and had discussed and discarded different current multiple site evaluation approaches, Michael Quinn Patton held a workshop in Cologne in July 1998. During a break, I told him about our "thorny" evaluand and the problems we were facing in trying to deal with contradictory demands in a single evaluation approach. His response was that there was a rather new approach that might be useful for us: cluster evaluation. This hint, followed by an intensive search for information on this approach, brought cluster evaluation to Germany. It quickly proved to be an excellent answer to the multiple challenges presented by evaluating multisite federal model programs in the field of child and youth services in that it not only permits the development of heterogeneous, experimental, innovative, and locally adapted project implementations based on a general program vision but also allows for statements on the overall impact of the program and the transferability of successful strategies.

However, transferring cluster evaluation to a political context and an evaluand that differs, in some aspects, from the programming initiatives of the W. K. Kellogg Foundation for which it was developed in the early 1990s has required some adaptations and changes. These constituted the main challenge in the transfer because the literature published on cluster evaluation so far has not made any clear distinction between the indispensable methodological core elements of cluster evaluations and the specificities of their application in the W. K. Kellogg Foundation initiatives.

The differences between the use of cluster evaluation in the North American and German contexts mainly relate to the accompanying scientific structure, the funding agency's role in directing the program, the traditions governing evaluation practices that prevail among politicians and field practitioners, and the content and objectives of the evaluation.

Doing program evaluation in conjunction with additional project evaluations is not necessarily a typical trait of federal model programs in Germany. In contrast, cluster evaluations in the United States are based on a two-level approach. In Germany, project-related formative evaluation—a valuable element in the development of projects—is thus either skipped or carried out by the project organizers on a voluntary basis, in the form of self-evaluation or external evaluation. Although project-related evaluations are not a prerequisite for cluster evaluation, they constitute a useful supplement: They help to take into account the specific information required by individual projects. Moreover, local evaluations may support data collection for cluster evaluation.

In the United States, cluster evaluation was developed for a philanthropic foundation with a strong interest in accompanying, directing, and learning from programming initiatives. However, these conditions are not necessarily typical in other contexts. If the funding agency's directing functions are rather limited (as in our case), we must find ways and means to create a central program responsibility conducive to maintaining and nourishing a common program vision. In cluster evaluations, minimal consensus on key program dimensions that constitute the framework for discussing and analyzing project activities is a must.

Tried-and-tested strategies are to appoint an independent coordinator based at either the research institution carrying out the evaluation or at another organization. A third possibility involves directing the program via regular meetings of important stakeholders. The problem is to find a balance between an independent evaluation that does not take on directive tasks and the concerted work of the two parties.

Another key characteristic of cluster evaluations is the collaboration of evaluators and stakeholders. This enables all players to participate in the evaluation process, making the results both usable and valuable for everybody. On the part of the stakeholders, this requires a professional identity that makes them actively contribute to the process as the future users of the evaluation results. In Germany, both the political and the professional actors in the social service sector are gradually developing such an identity, but it definitely cannot be taken for granted. The question arises, to what extent is it the evaluation's task to foster this professionalism; for example, by adult education?

Transferring the content of questions typical of cluster evaluations in the United States to another evaluand is also difficult. Sustainability is a key issue in cluster evaluations in the United States, but in Germany, the evaluation of model programs focuses on the time-limited model testing of professional strategies and their transferability to other locations. Elaborating knowledge that is both usable and valuable beyond the program for public policy makers and practitioners in the respective field is definitely the main purpose of such a cluster evaluation. Compared to this goal, formative elements at the project level are of minor importance.

Transferring cluster evaluation to another national context and to another evaluand has widened the range of its application. At the same time, this transfer has shown which organizational settings and professional skills of those participating in the program constitute a prerequisite for the successful application of a cluster evaluation. It has also shed light on methodological key elements, on elements that may be changed, and on how the changes affect the planning of a cluster evaluation.

—*Karin Haubrich*

COLLABORATIVE EVALUATION.
See PARTICIPATORY EVALUATION

■■ COMMUNICATIONS

Communication with others is the means through which evaluation occurs—through which it is designed and carried out and through which findings are reported. Communications that initiate and conclude an evaluation (its design and reporting of findings) tend to be more formal, involve a wider range of audiences, and may be more interactive than communications necessary to conduct the evaluation. Reporting of findings is the primary objective of most evaluations and is addressed in the separate entry on reporting. This entry discusses communications about evaluation activities that take place prior to reporting.

Communications necessary to carry out an evaluation include those undertaken as a very first step to identify stakeholders' concerns and conceptualize the evaluation problem. Further communications among stakeholders and evaluators usually take place when decisions are made about data collection methods and other evaluation activities, and then finally when data are collected. Evaluations that are explicitly designated as collaborative or participatory will involve more communication during the evaluation than other evaluation approaches. Communications during an evaluation usually involve its most immediate stakeholders—those for whom the evaluation is being conducted and those most directly involved in the program or entity being evaluated. Evaluation communications typically take place via meetings or working sessions, individual discussions (formally planned or impromptu), letters, memos, postcards, e-mail, written plans, and other documents that describe aspects of the evaluation.

Meetings and working sessions between evaluators and stakeholders during the evaluation are often the most productive forms of communication, during which significant input and decision making about evaluation questions, design, methods, and implementation can take place. Planned and impromptu discussions can also inform any of these topics and may take place when individuals are not available to participate in a meeting (whether it be held in person, via teleconference, or via videoconference).

Once an evaluation's design and methods are established, the evaluators and key stakeholders are familiar with each other, and other stakeholders are identified, communications tend to take place on an as-needed and less formal basis. Formats for shorter, more informal communications include telephone conversations, individual meetings, or memos sent via e-mail, fax, or postcard.

Short communications are vital tools for establishing and maintaining ongoing contact among evaluators, clients, and other stakeholders. Brief, sometimes frequent communications about the evaluation are useful for reaching a wide group of stakeholders. Short communications can be used during all phases of the evaluation for quick and timely communication that keeps pace with evolving evaluation processes. Further, if written, short communications provide a record of events, activities, and decisions about a program, evaluation, or both. The focused content of short communications makes for easy reading and assimilation of information. Flexible formats can heighten visual attraction and attention through the use of color and interesting layouts with varied headings and graphics. Information clearly and succinctly presented in these ways is more likely to be remembered.

Initial meetings and subsequent short communications often lead to the development of longer, more formal documents that are shared with stakeholders. These may describe the evaluation plan, logistics and schedules, or instruments, or they may be progress reports on evaluation activities.

—Rosalie T. Torres

See also REPORTING

■■ COMMUNITIES OF PRACTICE (CoPs)

A *community of practice* is a small group of people who work together over a period of time. People in CoPs can perform the same job, collaborate on a shared task, or work together on a product. They are peers in the execution of real work and share a common sense of purpose. There are communities of practice within a single company but also in a profession, and most people belong to more than one. Evaluators participate in communities of practice with other professionals and evaluators in performing evaluations and in promoting evaluation as a profession, such as through evaluation associations.

■■ COMMUNITY-BASED EVALUATION

Community-based evaluation, also known as *community evaluation*, is evaluation focused on communities and conducted in partnership with the community. It involves project-level or community-level evaluation questions, community-sensitive evaluation methods and measures, and community-focused evaluation reporting and dissemination.

The community itself defines the "community" that is the focus of the evaluation. This community can be geographically based, such as a town or a neighborhood, or it can be spatially spread but linked by a similar characteristic, such as ethnicity, interest, or ideology. The community must be identifiable and organized to the extent that representatives from it can work as partners with the evaluation team.

Because communities generally think holistically about themselves and act on several aspects of the community at once, their evaluation questions tend to be both about the community as a whole and about specific projects. Consequently, the evaluation team's task in community-based evaluation is to address both kinds of questions in its evaluation. This often means that there is not a single evaluation but, instead, a series of evaluations, over time, that together provide a picture of community changes. Communities also are dynamic, with planned and unexpected but regularly occurring "interventions" separate from those that are the initial focuses of the evaluation.

Community-based evaluation, therefore, is lengthier, less controllable, and more complex than single-project–based evaluation. Most of the tools of the evaluation field are focused on assessing relatively stable single projects (e.g., a math enrichment program), not initiatives consisting of multiple, loosely related projects with both project-level and community-level outcomes. Each community initiative is unique and occurs in a dynamic context, and therefore it requires the development, implementation, and ongoing adjustment of a tailored, flexible evaluation.

Because of these unique evaluation demands, the key to successful community-based evaluation is the development and maintenance of a partnership between the evaluation team and the community. Both sets of partners bring and share their expertise to plan and implement, and adjust when necessary, a community-sensitive evaluation. Community-based evaluation, therefore, is not simply evaluating one or more community projects; instead, it is evaluation performed *with* a community *of* that community.

If the community has community-level evaluation questions, the evaluation will include community-level evaluation designs and measures. Community-level designs are typically limited to comparisons with other, similar communities or other communities relevant to the target community (for example, other communities in the state). Community-level measures typically involve indicator sets or indices that allow periodic tracking of changes in general dimensions related to community aspects (for example, employment, education, safety, and social cohesion). Several measures typically make up each dimension and tap different aspects of a dimension. Jacksonville, Florida, has used such a set of indicators to track its

community's progress for more than a decade. Other communities around the world are also using and disseminating indicator sets, although sometimes without any explicit association with the evaluation of community projects and initiatives.

Community-based evaluation has another distinguishing characteristic: It facilitates evaluation use. This is a consequence of the ongoing partnership between the evaluation team and the community. The community is involved in the evaluation throughout, including the dissemination and use of the evaluation results. This use includes formative changes over the course of the evaluation and also summative ones at the conclusion.

Community-based evaluation has limitations that relate to the open and changing nature of the community initiatives that are its focus, in contrast to the project-specific focus of traditional evaluation. In community-based evaluation, it is difficult to develop a comprehensive, static logic model or theory of change to guide the evaluation; evaluation designs do not exist for definitive causal attribution; and community-sensitive and -appropriate measures are not usually available and must be created. When these limitations can be mitigated, however, community-based evaluation contributes to greater understanding of the community by that community and to more effective action on the part of a community, using the evaluation information.

—Ross Conner

■■ COMPARATIVE ANALYSIS

This is a general term for all sorts of comparisons of data. Each segment of data should have similar components if comparisons are to be made. Each segment of the data has usually been thoroughly analyzed before similarities and differences with other like data are sought. The comparison takes into account the context of the data, when it was collected, and from which sites. The comparative analysis seeks discrepancies between like data in context, and the apparent discrepancies are examined to see if they are structural or peculiar. Structural discrepancies become the source of fresh understandings of the data, usually leading to higher order conceptual organization of the overall data. Peculiar discrepancies are retained to see if and how they subsequently relate. The comparative method was devised by mid-19th–century linguists, taken up by historians, and, in the early 20th century, pioneered in sociology. Multisite evaluations often use comparative analysis, as do sets of case studies.

—*Clem Adelman*

Further Reading

Thomas, W. I., & Znaniecki, F. (1996). *The Polish peasant in Europe and America.* New York: Knopf.

Turpin, R. S., & Sinacore, J. M. (Eds.). (1990). Multisite evaluations. *New Directions for Program Evaluation, 50.*

▪▪ COMPLEX ADAPTIVE SYSTEMS

Complex adaptive systems (CAS) are characterized by four key elements. First, they are made up of units that are able to sense and react to their environment. In CAS terms, these units are called *agents.* Second, CAS agents are autonomous; that is, each agent acts on a set of internal decision rules, without purposive collaboration with other agents. Third, a CAS is made up of a large number of interacting agents, usually with rich opportunity for the action of any given agent to affect others. Finally, agents can vary in their level of internal complexity. For instance, in a large company, the agents may be the company's subsidiaries, divisions within the subsidiaries, departments within the divisions, work groups within the departments, or people who make up the work groups. The implications of CAS extend to evaluation theory, methodology, and measurement. This is so because such systems exhibit behaviors, including patterns and causal relationships, that differ markedly from those normally considered by evaluators. Examples of these behaviors include emergence, stability or chaos, adaptation, and attraction.

Emergence. A condition in which large-scale, ordered behavior appears as a function of the independent action of many agents. Beehives are one good example: Very complex patterns emerge from the interaction of many bees, each of which is wired to follow only a few simple rules about movement, eating, depositing material, and so forth. Adam Smith's "invisible hand" is another well-known example: A system (the economy) succeeds in allocating resources efficiently in the absence of central control and only as a result of the collective action of individuals who are seeking to maximize their own returns.

Stability, Chaos, and Their Border Regions. Complex adaptive systems can be highly stable in the face of very powerful environmental perturbations. They can also, however (for short periods of time, before they disappear or change radically), be so unstable as to be unpredictable and uncontrollable. Finally, systems can exist on the "edge of chaos," where they remain stable for long periods of time in the face of great turbulence and then change at a very rapid rate. Frequently, these large changes are precipitated by seemingly small stimuli. This is the characteristic of a CAS that gives rise to the phenomena of "sensitive reliance on initial conditions" (the butterfly effect) and "phase shifts."

Adaptation. Complex adaptive systems can be seen as entities that follow the evolutionary imperative to adapt to their environment, or, in other words, to fill their ecological niche. Depending on the structure of that environment, a CAS may fare better or worse by changing in small, incremental ways, or in radical jumps from its present state to a new state.

Basins of Attraction and Strange Attraction. A *basin of attraction* is a "space" in which movement of a variable is confined. A common form of these attractors is a *point attractor*, that is, a case in which a variable's movement eventually settles down to a fixed value. Thus the attractor is defined both by the boundaries of the basin and by its "resting point." A *strange attractor* might be thought of as having boundaries but no resting point. In such cases, the value of a variable is predictably confined and specifiable, but the actual value of the variable at any given time never repeats, or if it does, it does so only by coincidence. As an illustration, consider the difference between disturbing a classroom and the actions of quality improvement teams. In the classroom case (assuming not too major a disturbance and a reasonably competent teacher), the behavior of the students will eventually settle down to the predisturbance level. With quality improvement teams, one might predict that all their actions will be within the basin of "improved efficiency," but no team will do exactly the same thing as the others, nor will any given team do the same thing twice.

These phenomena are by no means a complete list of the behavior of CAS, but they do provide a sense that systems exhibiting CAS behavior may be difficult to evaluate using the traditional tactics of evaluation. Some of the more prominent problems include the following:

1. Traditional logic modeling may not be applicable because the reasons systems change, and the nature of the change, are emergent, rather than the consequence of specifiable relationships among higher level variables.

2. System behavior is dependent on multiple choices the system has in adjusting to its environment, thus making it difficult to hypothesize the direction of change.

3. Similar systems, in similar circumstances, may "choose" different paths of adaptation, thus leading to very different behavior in systems that might have been expected to change in similar ways. Consequently, it is difficult to specify outcome variables in advance.

4. An understanding of how a program works is required because of the frequent use of evaluation to explain not only outcome but the reasons for a program's behavior. That understanding entails hypotheses about program dynamics that are blind to emergence, as a function of freely interacting agents, as the explanation for program behavior.

5. If a program's impact is best explained in terms of strange attraction within a defined basin, intermediate measures of outcome do not reliably explain overall impact. To continue the quality improvement case, "cost" may define the boundaries of impact for all the innovations, but local changes affecting cost will differ from local innovation to local innovation.

All of the implications of CAS for evaluation are familiar to experienced evaluators. Examples include unintended consequences, irreproducible effects, difficulty in assessing the fidelity of a program to its intention, multiple paths to the same set of outcomes, slippery program requirements, and difficulty in specifying treatments. One major contribution of the CAS perspective is that it sets all of these evaluation problems within a common explanatory framework.

—*Jonathan A. Morrell*

See also Chaos Theory, Logic Model, Systems and Systems Thinking

Further Reading

Marion, R. (1999). *The edge of organization: Chaos and complexity theories of formal organizations.* Thousand Oaks, CA: Sage.

■■ CONCEPT MAPPING

The term *concept mapping* refers to any methodology that is used to produce a picture or map of the ideas or concepts of an individual or group. There are a wide variety of such methodologies and analogous approaches that go by such labels as "idea mapping," "mind maps," "causal mapping," or "cognitive mapping." All forms of concept mapping are at least tangentially related to evaluation in that they encourage people to give greater thought to the ideas that underlie what they do. However, two very distinct forms of concept mapping have particular relevance in evaluation.

The first is individual-based concept mapping, championed by Joe Novak and Robert Gowin at Cornell University. Their approach, based on Ausubelian learning theory in education, is used by an individual to draw a picture of key ideas relative to a problem area. Central ideas are typically drawn in the center of the map, with more peripheral concepts connected outward from these by lines that include appropriate, linking, conjunctive terms. The approach has been used primarily in education, as a process that encourages more effective thinking on the part of the student. Simple scoring procedures have been adopted that enable an individual's map to be scored with respect to the complexity and accuracy of his or her thinking. The primary use of this methodology in evaluation has been in the evaluation of student learning.

The second approach to concept mapping of relevance to evaluation is based on the work of William Trochim, also of Cornell University. This approach, referred to more technically as *structured conceptualization*, although usable by individuals under some circumstances, is primarily a mixed-methods, group idea-mapping methodology based on the integration of familiar group processes such as brainstorming and idea sorting with the multivariate statistical methods of multidimensional scaling and hierarchical cluster analysis. The process involves six steps: *preparation* (identification of focus, participants, and schedule); *generation* of ideas (usually, but not necessarily, through brainstorming); *organization* of the ideas through sorting and rating them; *representation* of the ideas in maps based on the sequence of multivariate analyses; *interpretation* of the maps by the participants;

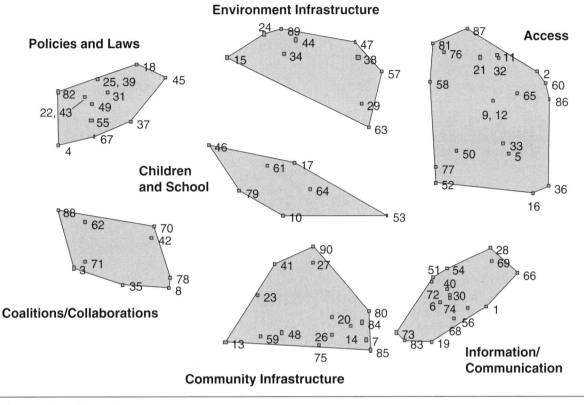

Figure 1   *Point Cluster Map*

NOTE: The map shows 90 ideas grouped into seven clusters. Used to help in statewide planning for public health spending of tobacco settlement money in Hawaii, this map provided a framework for subsequent follow-up evaluation.

and *utilization* of the maps in planning, evaluation, or both. The maps that result are often accompanied by a unique graphic and statistical analysis called "pattern matching" that assesses consensus across subgroups, patterns over time, or the relationship of expected to observed outcomes.

This multivariate group-based concept mapping has been used in both formative, ex ante and in more summative, ex post evaluation contexts. For example, Figure 1 shows a concept map used in ex ante public health planning for use of tobacco settlement funds in Hawaii. The map was developed collaboratively by a statewide group of stakeholders and by a national panel of public health experts. Figure 2 shows a pattern match from the same project that assesses the correspondence between the cluster-level average importance (left axis) and average feasibility (right axis) ratings of the ideas.

Concept mapping is potentially useful in evaluation for a variety of purposes, including: as a form of

stakeholder needs assessment; as an alternative to focus groups or Delphi methodology; for building outcome logic models; for developing conceptual frameworks for programs or measures; and for assessing construct validity.

—William Trochim

Further Reading

Davison, M. L. (1983). *Multidimensional scaling.* New York: John Wiley.

Everitt, B. (1980). *Cluster analysis* (2nd ed.). New York: Halsted Press.

Kruskal, J. B., & Wish, M. (1978). *Multidimensional scaling.* Beverly Hills, CA: Sage.

Novak, J. (1998). *Learning, creating and using knowledge: Concept maps as facilitative tools in schools and corporations.* Mahwah, NJ: Lawrence Erlbaum.

Trochim, W. (1989). An introduction to concept mapping for planning and evaluation. *Evaluation and Program Planning, 12*(1), 1-16.

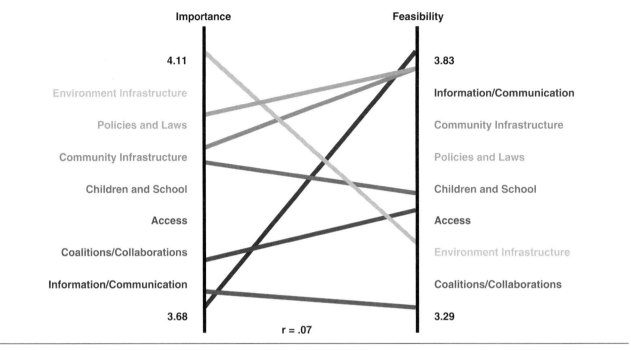

Figure 2   *Pattern Match*

NOTE: Based on the map in Figure 1, this figure demonstrates the relationship between stakeholder estimates of the average relative importance and feasibility of the ideas in clusters on the map.

◼ CONCEPTUAL USE

Although instrumental use of evaluation refers to direct, attributable use of the evaluation results or process to inform decisions, conceptual use refers to the ways in which evaluation can have an impact on the way people think about the evaluand, on the issues it is designed to address (needs or problems), or on the way the evaluation should be conducted. Conceptual use of the evaluation process is particularly common when it involves development of a logic model. Conceptual use of the evaluation results is enhanced with a public archive of evaluation reports.

—*Patricia J. Rogers*

CONCLUSIONS, EVALUATIVE. *See* LOGIC OF EVALUATION

◼ CONFIDENTIALITY

Confidentiality is part of the ethics repertoire of the evaluator—a procedural device in which the privacy of respondents is assured pending negotiations over the use of their data. Confidentiality procedures emerged with case study evaluation in the 1970s and from the principle that people "own" the data concerning their own lives—that attributable data is only available to the evaluator on a negotiated basis. In democratic evaluation, for example, the evaluator balances the individual's right to privacy with the public's right to know. Treating data as confidential and negotiable is the trade-off for final release. Confidential does not mean off the record, beyond the reach of the evaluation. Rather, it is assumed that the data is available to be used but only once it has been reviewed by the respondent for its fairness, relevance, and accuracy. Confidentiality must also not be confused with anonymity, wherein the respondent's identity is concealed and the data are freely available. Confidentiality assumes that data may be attributed to the respondent.

—*Saville Kushner*

See also ETHICS

Further Reading

Jenkins, D. (1986). An adversary's account of SAFARI's ethics of case study. In M. Hammersley (Ed.), *Controversies in classroom research*. Milton Keynes, PA: Open University Press.

Simons, H. (1987). *Getting to know schools in a democracy*. London: Falmer.

◼◼ CONFLICT OF INTEREST

Conflicts of interests occur when evaluators' personal or financial relationships have the potential to influence the design, conduct, or reporting of an evaluation. Evaluators are hired because they are perceived to be independent and free from bias and thus able to provide an objective assessment of the value of a program or policy. Although no one is entirely free from bias, evaluators should be sensitive to the potential conflicts of interest that occur in many evaluations and be prepared to deal with these conflicts in a way that maintains the integrity of the evaluation.

Conflicts of interest are often defined in financial terms. For example, if an elected official awards a contract to a firm in which she or he holds a financial interest, the decision is seen as a conflict. The elected official's interest in the company prevents an unbiased or objective choice being made of the best firm to perform the task. Financial conflicts of interest also occur in evaluation. Internal evaluators should not be involved in evaluations that affect the financial viability of their organization because such decisions affect their own livelihood. External evaluators should avoid the temptation to shape evaluations or their results to help them secure future contracts with either the current client or related clients.

Conflicts of interest extend beyond the financial. Often, in evaluation, conflicts of interest concern personal or organizational relationships or even personal beliefs. Evaluators often have relationships with people in the organizations that they evaluate or relationships with competing organizations, and these relationships can pose a conflict. Evaluators would not want to be in the position of judging a program managed by a close friend. Similarly, evaluators may have personal beliefs that influence their approach to a program. For example, an evaluator who has been a victim of a violent crime is more likely to have strong beliefs about victims' rights programs. Evaluators who have knowledge of the organization or the program under consideration or who have personal experience with the problems clients confront are often hired because their knowledge and experience can improve their ability to make useful recommendations. However, this familiarity also provides the potential for conflict of interest.

Both the American Evaluation Association Guiding Principles and the *Program Evaluation Standards* address conflicts of interest. The *Program Evaluation Standards* state: "Conflict of interest should be dealt with openly and honestly, so that it does not compromise the evaluation processes and results." Disclosure may not be sufficient. In some cases, the conflict may be sufficiently great that either the client or the evaluator may choose to decline the evaluation. In other cases, where the conflict is not so extreme, the evaluation may proceed. The *Program Evaluation Standards* note that it is a mistake to avoid hiring a well-qualified evaluator solely because of fear of potential conflicts. Instead, care should be taken to disclose potential conflicts and to consider processes to avoid bias. The evaluator should seek input from others with different perspectives on the evaluation approaches and methods, interpretations of findings, recommendations, and ultimate judgments.

—*Jody L. Fitzpatrick*

Further Reading

Joint Committee on Standards for Educational Evaluation. (1994). *The program evaluation standards: How to assess evaluations of educational programs* (2nd ed.). Thousand Oaks, CA: Sage.

Fitzpatrick, J. L., Sanders, J. R., & Worthen, B. R. (2003). *Program evaluation: Alternative approaches and practical guidelines.* New York: Longman.

◼◼ CONNER, ROSS

(b. 1946, Denver, Colorado). Ph.D. and M.A. Northwestern University; B.A. Johns Hopkins University.

Conner is Professor, School of Social Ecology, Department of Urban and Regional Planning, University of California, Irvine, and is Acting Director of an initiative to establish a multischool, campus-community center for community health research.

Conner has contributed to the evaluation profession through his works on community-based evaluation, evaluation in international and cross-cultural settings, and collaborative approaches to evaluation. He has extensive evaluation experience, having worked on diverse topics (e.g., community-based planning, AIDS prevention, leadership, education, criminal justice, and rural development) and with a variety of stakeholders (e.g., Korean and Chinese community coalitions, Mexican farm workers, urban Latino men, agriculture leaders, and teen youth). His early experience as a Peace Corps volunteer in Tunisia set the stage for his work in international evaluation.

He was mentored by Donald Campbell at Northwestern University and was influenced by his ideas about reforms as experiments.

He is the author, coauthor, editor, or coeditor of nine books, including *International Innovations in Evaluation Methodology; Advancing Public Policy Evaluation: Learning From International Experience;* and the *Evaluation Studies Review Annual* (Vol. 9).

As President of the American Evaluation Association, he elected to explore the theme of international and cross-cultural evaluation during the annual meeting in San Francisco. Despite disruption of the annual meeting due to an earthquake just before its start, the theme took root in the association and has grown into a topic of special interest. He currently serves on the AEA President's Special Committee on International Evaluation. In 2002, he received the Outstanding Evaluation Award from the American Evaluation Association for a set of studies conducted over 8 years on the Colorado Healthy Communities Initiative. Conner is a Fellow of the American Psychological Association and the American Psychological Society and was a W. K. Kellogg Foundation National Fellow (1984-1987).

◼◼ CONNOISSEURSHIP

Connoisseurship is a term that traditionally has been associated with phenomena such as wine tasting and art appreciation rather than the supposedly scientific and technical enterprise of formal evaluation. Similarly, the notion of criticism traditionally has been associated with the assessment of literary or artistic works and not with the assessment of education or other sorts of social programs. During the 1970s, however, the terms *connoisseurship* and *criticism* became part of the discourse within the evaluation field, primarily through the writings of Elliot Eisner.

THE HISTORICAL CONTEXT

Eisner's introduction of the ideas of connoisseurship and criticism into the discourse of the field of evaluation was part of a more general movement within the evaluation field in the United States and Europe (especially Great Britain) during the 1970s. During that time, there was a growing recognition that quasi-experimental design and other standard operating procedures of science might be inappropriate—or, at the very least, inadequate—for evaluating education and

other social programs. Such procedures, critics charged, had difficulty accommodating the complexity of social phenomena and addressing the multiple values of different stakeholders.

The growing skepticism about traditional scientific approaches to evaluation encouraged a number of evaluation scholars to rethink the form and function of formal evaluation. These scholars were influenced by a wide variety of academic disciplines and fields, including anthropology, journalism, philosophy, and law, and they produced a number of evaluation models, including the naturalistic-constructivist approach, responsive evaluation, goal-free evaluation, and the adversary-advocate strategy. Elliot Eisner's rethinking of the evaluation process was influenced by the arts and aesthetics. He suggested that we could think of evaluators of educational programs as educational connoisseurs and the evaluation process as being analogous to art criticism.

THE COMPONENTS OF EDUCATIONAL CRITICISM AND THEIR JUSTIFICATION

According to Eisner, educational criticism (a term that Eisner used to refer both to a process and to the written product produced through that process) should have three components: description, interpretation, and evaluation.

The Descriptive Component. The descriptive component of educational criticism, according to Eisner, is different from the descriptive component of most other forms of qualitative inquiry, including those adapted from ethnography. As in art criticism, the emphasis in educational criticism is on using literary language and metaphor to capture the aesthetic (or "feeling") dimensions of the phenomenon being evaluated. The goal is for the reader of educational criticism to be able to vicariously experience the phenomenon that is being evaluated at a visceral, not just an intellectual, level.

Eisner's thinking about the descriptive component of educational criticism was informed by the work of aesthetician Susanne Langer. Langer distinguished between two kinds of symbols that she labeled *representational* and *presentational*. Nonpoetic language and numbers are examples of representational symbols. Such symbols have no inherent meaning; rather, they receive their meaning through conventional association. As a result, representational symbols can only point to (represent) the phenomena they are referencing. Works of art, by contrast, are presentational symbols. In such symbols, meaning is inherent in the symbol itself. Even a Martian who had just arrived on earth would be able to "read" the colors, shapes, textures, and so on of a Picasso painting (assuming, of course, the Martian had the same sensory apparatus that we have).

Langer emphasizes that only presentational symbols can "give form to feeling" and, consequently, that such forms of symbolization are essential for thinking about and reflecting on the aesthetic aspects of life. Eisner seized on this idea to help make the case that his connoisseurship-criticism model was a necessary complement to other forms of evaluation. He argued that traditional approaches to evaluation, and even alternative approaches, such as ethnography, used only one form of symbolization and, hence, had a built-in bias: They could not adequately encode the aesthetic or feeling dimensions of the phenomena being studied.

To be sure, Eisner emphasized that traditional approaches could be useful: If one wants to know what size rug to buy, for instance, one needs to measure the room in which the rug will be placed and have numerical information about the rug under consideration. However, if one wants to know about the aesthetic properties of a rug that may be ordered from, say, a catalog, a different sort of symbolization is required. A color photograph of the rug must be viewed or an evocative description read of the rug's qualities. Eisner argued that this different sort of description was also important in understanding educational programs and, consequently, that viewing evaluation as a process analogous to art criticism was a necessary complement to both traditional, statistically based forms of evaluation and the qualitative forms of evaluation emerging out of social science fields such as anthropology and sociology that employed traditional social science forms of discourse to describe the programs studied.

The Interpretive Component. It is important to note that Eisner did not totally eliminate the social sciences from the evaluation process when his educational criticism approach was being employed. Rather, Eisner emphasized that social science theory was to be employed in the interpretive component of the educational criticism process and the written products produced by that process.

Indeed, according to Eisner, a knowledge of a wide range of social science theories is a defining characteristic of an educational connoisseur, just as knowledge of art history and of different artistic genres (and the criteria appropriate for assessing these genres) is an essential tool for the art connoisseur or critic. Social science theory helps the education connoisseur both to see things as significant that nonconnoisseurs would be likely to miss and to make sense of why things occurred as they did in the program being evaluated. Social science theory also provides language that can be used to help others see and make sense of the phenomena being studied in more sophisticated ways than they would have at their disposal if left to their own devices. This sense-making process is the essence of the interpretive component of educational criticism; the expectation is that educational connoisseurs will use social science constructs and theories eclectically to aid them and their readers in interpreting the phenomena that have been observed and described.

The connoisseur's or critic's eclectic use of social science theory to make sense of social phenomena in the interpretive component of educational criticism could also be cited as part of a justifying rationale for Eisner's approach to evaluation (although Eisner himself does not tend to emphasize this point). As noted, one reason that traditional approaches to evaluation design were judged to be inadequate involves their inability to address the many different values that multiple stakeholders might legitimately employ to assess a program's worth.

The philosopher Stephen Toulmin clarifies this point when he notes that policy makers will not necessarily build a dam where a group of civil engineers hired to evaluate the situation recommends that the dam be built. Policy makers cannot totally ignore the advice of the civil engineers and build the dam in a place where it will collapse, of course, but they might decide to build the dam in a less optimal spot because they must balance the engineers' technical criteria with other concerns (e.g., the economic impact of building the dam in certain places, the political impact—including the impact on the policy makers' reelection, etc.). The connoisseurs who write educational criticism can use a wide range of theories and, consequently, address a wide range of criteria in helping the readers of their criticisms to better understand the different criteria that need to be considered and possibly accommodated in making decisions about the educational or social program being evaluated.

The Evaluative Component. The final component of educational criticism, according to Eisner, is the evaluative component. Eisner uses this component to (a) distinguish his educational criticism approach from certain other alternative approaches to traditional quantitative forms of evaluation that emerged during the 1970s (most notably Robert Stakes' description-oriented responsive approach and approaches inspired by ethnography, which also tended to emphasize description and, occasionally, some interpretation) and (b) make the case for the comparative worth of the educational connoisseurship and criticism model. His argument is a simple one: Education is a normative enterprise and, consequently, evaluation models that merely describe or interpret what is happening are inadequate. According to Eisner, evaluators in a normative field such as education need to assess the worth of what they describe and interpret.

As was the case with the descriptive component of educational criticism, Eisner's thinking about the evaluative component of educational criticism was influenced by aesthetic theory. Here, the theory was John Dewey's. In his masterwork on aesthetics, *Art as Experience,* Dewey distinguished between two different approaches to assessing the worth of something: One approach involves applying predefined, clearly articulated standards; the other involves making judgments.

Dewey had argued that works of art are too complex and idiosyncratic to have their worth assessed by predetermined standards. Rather, art critics, according to Dewey, had to make judgments in critiquing a work of art. Because good critics are connoisseurs, their judgments are informed by a wide array of knowledge of different artistic genres and an array of criteria that are appropriate for assessing work in different genres. This knowledge, along with extensive prior experience viewing works of art, helps critics see things in a work of art that ordinary viewers would be likely to miss. The connoisseur's knowledge also helps him or her make a sophisticated judgment about the worth of a piece of art, a judgment that employs criteria appropriate for the genre in which the artist had worked or, in the case of truly idiosyncratic, genre-breaking work, is not bounded by established criteria.

Eisner argued that educational phenomena were no less complex than works of art and, consequently, that they, too, did not lend themselves to being assessed by applying a predefined standard or set of standards. Rather, according to Eisner, the judgment of connoisseurs is required to do justice to the complexity of educational phenomena (and also, as noted earlier, to the multitude of values and criteria that should be taken into account in assessing the worth of an educational program).

Eisner's position on the standards and judgment issue is probably best understood when seen in the context of his earlier work on curricula. In a 1967 monograph titled *Instructional and Expressive Educational Objectives: Their Formulation and Use in Curriculum,* for instance, Eisner made the case for what he referred to at the time as *expressive objectives* (later renamed, at one point, *expressive activities* and, more recently, *expressive outcomes*) as a necessary complement to behavioral objectives in designing curricula. Although instructional or behavioral objectives precisely specify in advance what students will learn (and be able to do) after a particular section of a curriculum is delivered, an expressive activity is a rich educational encounter (e.g., a school trip to the zoo, a student production of *Romeo and Juliet,* a Web site established and run by the class) that can produce quite different and often unexpected outcomes because different students bring different sets of experiences to the encounter.

Clearly, because expressive outcomes cannot be specified in advance, it would be impossible to assess the worth of an expressive activity by applying a predetermined standard or set of standards to it. Thus, a commitment to rooting evaluation, at least in part, in the judgment of a sophisticated evaluator (a connoisseur, in Eisner's terms) rather than in predetermined metrics associated with preformed standards is a logical—and, in fact, necessary—extension of Eisner's work on curriculum design.

OTHER CONTRIBUTORS TO THE CONNOISSEURSHIP-CRITICISM TRADITION

Although Eisner first articulated the notions of connoisseurship and criticism in the context of evaluation and remains the best-known spokesperson for the tradition, many other evaluators and researchers (most of whom were Eisner's students) have also written about and provided examples of work in the educational criticism "genre." Heading the list of other contributors, most certainly in terms of the quantity and arguably also in terms of the quality of his contributions, would be Thomas Barone. Barone, in fact, has done what Eisner generally did not do: In addition to writing about educational criticism, Barone also has provided a number of examples of educational criticism. His criticism "Things of Use and Things of Beauty," which appeared in a 1983 issue of *Daedalus* focusing on the arts and humanities in American schools, remains one of the best examples of the criticism genre. The list of others who have provided excellent examples of different forms of educational criticism includes David Flinders, Gail McCutcheon, Bruce Urmacher, and Elizabeth Vallance.

CRITICISMS OF CRITICISM AS AN EVALUATION DESIGN

It is of interest that the work alluded to was not produced in actual evaluation projects. In fact, there is little evidence that the connoisseurship-criticism approach has been used in actual evaluation work (as opposed to doctoral dissertations or more general research projects).

An article by Robert Donmoyer titled "The Evaluator as Artist," which appeared in a 1980 issue of the *Journal of Curriculum Theorizing* and was later reprinted in Giroux, Penna, and Pinar's *Curriculum and Instruction: Alternatives in Education,* describes an exception to this statement. The article contains excerpts from two educational criticisms that were written as part of a contracted evaluation project of an innovative middle school program. The article, however, also calls into question the viability of using the criticism approach in evaluation contexts.

Among the issues raised is the elitism implicit in the notion of connoisseurship. Even if it is the case that connoisseurs can view educational programs from a greater number of vantage points than ordinary citizens can and are aware of a greater number of criteria by which a program can be judged, it is not necessarily the case that the connoisseur's preferred criteria and, consequently, his or her ultimate judgment about a program's worth and the recommendations that follow from this judgment are inherently superior to the ideas and preferences of others.

Thus, criticism appears to be defensible only if it is seen as a formative enterprise or, possibly, as an initial phase of a multiphase summative process, a phase designed to expand thinking about the things that should be considered in evaluating the phenomena being studied. Even then, it would seem as if one would be required to employ multiple connoisseurs

who would tend to think about educational issues in radically different ways.

Eisner, of course, did not conceptualize his connoisseurship-criticism model as the first stage in a multistage process. Donmoyer, however, did later go on to develop, experiment with, and write about what he referred to as a deliberative strategy that attempted to accommodate the problems with the criticism model articulated in "The Evaluator as Artist." The strategy is discussed in an article titled "Postpositivist Evaluation: Give Me a For Instance" that appeared in a 1991 issue of *Educational Administration Quarterly.*

It is not surprising that Eisner himself has written little about connoisseurship and criticism in recent years; rather, he has focused on what he refers to as arts-based research. In other words, although Eisner originally conceptualized his artistic approach to inquiry as functioning in evaluation contexts, in recent years he has resituated it in the context of research projects that are not explicitly evaluative in nature.

THE CONTRIBUTIONS OF THE CONNOISSEURSHIP-CRITICISM TRADITION

Even though discussions of connoisseurship and criticism have not produced an extensively used approach to evaluation, such discussions have made at least three contributions. First, they have provided a healthy critique of both traditional and other alternative approaches to evaluation and, in the process, provided a better sense of what other, more widely used evaluation strategies can and cannot do. For instance, Eisner's appropriation of Dewey's distinction between applying a standard and making a judgment certainly exposes the bias of certain evaluation designs against more emergent and improvisational approaches to teaching and curriculum design and, consequently, makes it less likely that the evaluation tail will wag the curriculum dog without people being aware that this is happening. Similarly, Eisner's use of Langer's discussion of presentational and representational forms of symbolizing experience alerts us to the fact that supposedly objective forms of reporting also have a built-in bias and that, consequently, they are not as objective as they initially appear to be.

Second, the work of Eisner and others associated with the connoisseurship-criticism tradition has helped open the door to using a wide variety of qualitative data techniques in evaluation work. For instance, although one would be hard pressed to find examples of educational criticism per se being used in evaluation work today, one might see more literary and narrative elements in the descriptive component of research reports. Even innovative data display techniques such as readers' theater have begun to be used to communicate evaluation findings to selected audiences.

Finally, discussions of connoisseurship and criticism have helped open the door for a wide variety of more artistic approaches to doing and reporting research in general. The list would include, for instance, Lightfoot's portraiture approach and also various forms of narrative research. Although most of this work could not be narrowly defined as evaluation research, it could be seen as having an evaluative dimension. Carol Weiss' work on research and evaluation utilization, after all, suggests that even in designated evaluation studies, the impact of findings is often indirect, long-term, and has more to do with problem framing than problem solving. If Weiss' analysis is at all on target, in other words, the line between research and evaluation may be a bit fuzzier than many believe.

—*Robert Donmoyer*

Further Reading

Eisner, E. (1976). Educational connoisseurship and criticism: Their forms and function in educational evaluation. *Journal of Aesthetic Education, 10*(3/4), 135-150.

Eisner, E. (1991). *The enlightened eye: Qualitative inquiry and the enhancement of educational practice.* New York: Macmillan.

■■ CONSEQUENTIAL VALIDITY

The consequential basis of test validity originally addressed the value implications of test interpretations and the social consequences of test use in specific situations. In the context of program evaluation, consequential validity refers to the value implications and social consequences associated with evaluation conclusions and utility. For example, a program evaluation of the impact of expanded social services that ignores the insights of program users or implements culturally insensitive data collection procedures is likely to produce conclusions and recommendations that misrepresent the object of the evaluation and the misappropriation of subsequent social service resources.

—*Charles L. Thomas*

Further Reading

Messick, S. (1980). Test validity and the ethics of assessment. *American Psychologist, 35,* 1012-1027.

■■ CONSTANT COMPARATIVE METHOD

The *constant comparative method* is an inductive data coding process used for categorizing and comparing qualitative data for analysis purposes. Developed by sociologists Barney Glaser and Anselm Strauss in 1965, it is usually associated with the methodology of grounded theory, although it is widely used with other research and evaluation frameworks as well. Theory developed using the constant comparison method is considered "grounded" because it is derived from everyday experience as constituted by the data. True to its roots in symbolic interactionism, inductive analysis enables the investigator to build an understanding of the phenomena under investigation through the lives, relations, actions, and words of the participants themselves.

The constant comparative method is an ideal analytic tool for evaluators using qualitative or mixed methods. Because different stakeholders often support different values, understandings, and perceptions of programs and policies, this approach provides a basis for systematically organizing, comparing, and understanding the similarities and differences between those perceptions. A unit of data (e.g., interview transcript, observation, document) is analyzed and broken into codes based on emerging themes and concepts, which are then organized into categories that reflect an analytic understanding of the coded entities, not the entities themselves. The essential feature of this method is that each unit of data is analyzed and systematically compared with previously collected and analyzed data prior to any further data collection. Purposeful sampling is consistently employed in this iterative process to solicit data variations that exhaust all angles of a topic.

Although this method focuses on the subjective experiences of individuals and is considered to be qualitative, it is not bound to any one paradigmatic orientation. Glaser and Strauss assumed a correspondence between generated explanatory propositions and real-life incidents, although others who use this method do not. For example, *Fourth Generation Evaluation,* developed by Egon Guba and Yvonna

Lincoln, uses the constant comparative method within a radical constructivist framework. In their model, the constant comparative method is reenvisioned as a hermeneutic dialectic process: a dynamic tool for gathering and generating participants' constructions of the practice being evaluated. Much as in the constant comparative method, a respondent is interviewed and asked to describe the nature of her or his perceptions of the evaluand. Immediate analysis follows, for the purpose of grasping the respondent's point of view and to acquire material to include in subsequent interviews. The second respondent is interviewed first for his or her personal viewpoint and then for comments on the first respondent's characterizations. This process is repeated as long as new perspectives are brought into the dialogic process. The aim is not to develop explanatory theories but to enable a group of divergent stakeholders to jointly construct a deeper level of understanding of the practice or program being evaluated.

—Melissa Freeman

See also FOURTH-GENERATION EVALUATION

Further Reading

Glaser, B. G., & Strauss, A. L. (1965). *Awareness of dying.* Chicago: Aldine.

Glaser, B. G., & Strauss, A. L. (1967). *The discovery of grounded theory.* Chicago: Aldine.

Guba, E. G., & Lincoln, Y. S. (1989). *Fourth generation evaluation.* Newbury Park, CA: Sage.

■■ CONSTRUCT VALIDITY

Construct validity refers to the degree to which inferences can legitimately be made from the theoretical constructs on which operationalizations within the study are based. Simplistically, construct validity is about naming something (a program, an attribute) accurately. For example, when an evaluator measures student achievement, the issue of construct validity entails a judgment about whether the measures or the operationalization of achievement are really measuring student achievement, as opposed to, for example, social capital. Methods for establishing construct validity include correlating test scores with scores on measures that do and do not measure the same trait (convergent and discriminant validity), conducting a factor analysis, determining if changes in test scores

reflect expected developmental changes, and seeing if experimental manipulations have the expected impact on test scores. Cronbach and Meehl's classic discussion of the construct validity of psychological tests grounds subsequent understanding and use of the term. In addition to asking whether a particular measure is what we think it is, they also considered questions about the degree to which a test is embedded in a culture and whether the different ways in which individuals score differently are indeed relevant for construct validity.

Further Reading

Cronbach, L. J., & Meehl, P. E. (1955). Construct validity in psychological tests. *Psychological Bulletin, 52,* 281-302.

■■ CONSTRUCTIVISM

Constructivism is a philosophical perspective that posits that knowledge is mediated by cognition and that humans construct meaning of their experiences and situations. In this perspective, humans are considered to be active organisms seeking meaning. The mind produces mental models that explain what has been perceived. An assumption is that all humans conceive of external reality somewhat differently, based on each individual's unique set of experiences with the world and beliefs about those experiences, but that there is substantial overlap in individual meaning making, which is the essence of socially constructed knowledge. This perspective is indebted to the work of Jean Piaget in developmental psychology and to Berger and Luckmann in their classic work *The Social Construction of Reality.* In evaluation, this philosophical orientation is most closely associated with fourth-generation evaluation and other qualitative approaches, such as empowerment evaluation and participatory evaluation.

■■ CONSULTANTS, EVALUATION

Consultants provide independent, objective information and advice to clients in a variety of organizational settings to assist them in achieving their objectives. In an evaluation context, consultants conduct research studies to assess program effectiveness and efficiency, collect and synthesize information, identify problems, and recommend solutions to improve organizational performance and implement change. Consultants provide their professional expertise on a temporary basis and have no authority to implement the changes they recommend. They have both academic and practical experience as well as strong communication and instructional skills. In their independent capacity, it is critical that they model ethical business and research practice.

—Gail V. Barrington

■ CONSUMER

An actual or potential recipient, user, or impactee of a program, policy, product, service, system, or other evaluand. Consumers are the individuals, families, organizations, or communities whose needs are (or should be) met or to whom some effects may occur as a result of the program or policy. These effects may be immediate, short or long term, intended or unintended (the latter are called side effects). In product, service, and personnel evaluation, the term *internal customer* is used to refer to recipients of goods or services within the organization, and the term *external customer* refers to recipients outside the organization.

—Jane Davidson

■ CONSUMER SATISFACTION

Consumer satisfaction reflects the extent to which a consumer's conscious desires or expectations are fulfilled. It is generally unwise to place too much emphasis on satisfaction because (a) conscious desires overlap only partially with true needs, which are more important and may be unconscious; (b) expectations may be unreasonably high or low, and are limited by what the consumer thought was possible; and (c) desires and expectations fluctuate over time more erratically than true needs, making them a less reliable indicator of true quality or value. However, satisfaction is a useful outcome to complement other (qualitative and quantitative) information about quality or value.

—Jane Davidson

■ CONTENT ANALYSIS

Content analysis is a research strategy that examines the presence of concepts in texts, such as interviews, discussions, newspaper headlines and articles, historical documents, speeches, conversations, advertisements, theater, informal conversations, performances, drawings, or images. Evaluators analyze the presence, meanings, and relationships of words and concepts and make inferences about the messages within the texts, the writers, the audience, the program, the organization, and even the larger culture.

This type of analysis may be qualitative or quantitative and involves breaking the text into manageable categories that are labeled, or "coded." These categories may be words, phrases, sentences, or themes. A content analysis requires decisions about sampling (what will be included), the unit of analysis (the size and boundaries of the unit of text), and the goals of the analysis. A content analysis may be conceptual or relational. Conceptual analysis establishes the existence and frequency of concepts (perhaps by examination of the most frequently used words, phrases, metaphors, or concepts), and relational analysis examines the relationship among concepts in the text (perhaps by looking at the co-occurrence of particular concepts).

Content analysis is useful for directly and unobtrusively analyzing language use, meaning, relationships, and changes over time. It can, however, be time consuming, can be open to multiple interpretations, may be simplistic if the focus is primarily on word counts, and may take texts out of context. The use of qualitative data analysis software has increased the feasibility and quality of content analysis tremendously.

Further Reading

Haney, W., Russell, M., Gulek, C., & Fierros, E. (1998, January-February). Drawing on education: Using student drawings to promote middle school improvement. *Schools in the Middle, 7*(3), 38-43.

Krippendorff, K. (2003). *Content analysis: An introduction to its methodology* (2nd ed.). Thousand Oaks, CA: Sage.

Neuendorf, K. A. (2002). *The content analysis guidebook.* Thousand Oaks, CA: Sage.

■ CONTEXT

The concept of *context* figures centrally in all evaluation theories, and the challenges of context are inescapably present in all evaluation practice. Yet, the meanings of context, what dimensions of it are most important, and its role in practice vary substantially across different genres of evaluation. Moreover, the idea of just what context is—how it is conceptualized in various evaluation theories and how it is engaged in diverse evaluation practices—fundamentally differentiates one evaluation approach from another.

Broadly speaking, context refers to the setting within which the evaluand (the program, policy, or product being evaluated) and thus the evaluation are situated. Context is the site, location, environment, or milieu for a given evaluand. It is an enormously complex phenomenon. Many evaluands are implemented in multiple contexts; for example, in multiple sites, which always differ in some important ways. Most contexts have multiple layers or levels, as in classrooms within schools within districts within communities within states. Perhaps most challengingly, contexts have multiple strands or dimensions, all of which can be intertwined in important ways with the character and quality of an evaluand. These dimensions include (a) the descriptive and demographic character of a setting, in terms of the numbers, characteristics, and diversity of people who inhabit it; (b) the material and economic features of a setting, in terms of the quantity and quality of its physical features (buildings, gathering spaces, resources such as books and technology), along with other indicators of material wealth or scarcity; (c) the institutional and organizational climate in a setting, in terms of the character of the organization (agency, public institution, private business) that is administering or implementing the evaluand—its norms, decision-making structures, climate features, and so forth; (d) the interpersonal dimensions of a setting, in terms of the nature of interactions that take place and the norms that frame and guide relationships; and (e) the political dynamics of a setting, particularly in terms of contested issues and interests and in terms of power, influence, and privilege.

Context, in all of its complexity, is variously engaged in evaluation theory and practice. In experimentalist evaluation, which seeks primarily to address the causal effects of a treatment on desired outcomes, context is viewed as a source of influence to be controlled. Randomization and matched comparison groups are strategies expressly designed to hold constant the contextual influences on outcomes so that observed influences can be more confidently attributed to the treatment alone. To illustrate, in an experimental evaluation of a teen pregnancy program implemented in four northeastern cities, site variations such as the demographic diversity of program participants, the organizational characteristics of the implementing agencies, and the political history of adolescent sexuality policies in each city would be viewed as potentially important influences on desired program outcomes and, therefore, influences to be controlled. If such contextual characteristics are similar in the experimental and control or comparison groups, then observed differences in outcomes can be more confidently attributed to the treatment program.

In realist and some theory-oriented approaches to evaluation, context is viewed as an inevitable and thus a rich source of explanatory influences on desired program or performance outcomes. These evaluation approaches seek causal explanations of how observed changes in outcomes are accomplished or understandings of the contextualized mechanisms that underlie such changes. In these approaches, context is thus an inextricable part of causal explanation. An evaluation of a problem-focused middle school science education program, for example, would intentionally assess teacher, school, and community characteristics in all program sites, expecting program-site interactions, some of which could hold important explanatory value. Exceptionally strong outcomes in one district might be explained, in part, by the district's recent adoption of problem-based learning throughout its elementary schools, causing its children to bring some proficiency in real-world problem solving to the problem-focused science they encountered in middle school.

In many qualitative approaches to evaluation, context is not considered a separable influence on program experiences and outcomes but rather is viewed as an important constitutent of them. From this perspective, human experience is embedded in and thereby meaningful only in context. Decontextualized information loses its meaning, yet the express intention of qualitative inquiry is the understanding of meaningfulness. Thus qualitative evaluators aim for rich, detailed, elaborated descriptions of multiple dimensions of context, often with particular attention to norms of action and interaction. To illustrate, in a qualitative evaluation of the health benefits of a Tai Chi exercise program for elders, the interactional norms of the program and its organizational setting would probably be significant parts of an intricate contextual description, as these norms would be viewed as constitutive of the elders' program experiences and meaningfulness thereof.

In participatory and democratizing approaches to evaluation, context is viewed as the site or arena for political change. The purpose of evaluation in these approaches is to effect social change in the form of greater equity or justice in the context being evaluated—from the microcontext of a specific program site to the macrocontext of the organization or the socioeconomic policies being shaped. These politically engaged evaluators thus attend most closely to the political dimensions of evaluation contexts. In the work of such evaluators, participatory and democratic processes are designed and implemented in the political spaces of the evaluation contexts to change those spaces. A participatory evaluation of a statewide energy conservation program, for example, could use participatory processes in an effort to reconstitute the state's energy board to include more ordinary citizens and members of politically marginalized groups.

All evaluators agree that context matters, for the programs, policies, and products we evaluate and for the conduct and probable effectiveness of our work as evaluators. All evaluators also agree that good evaluation is responsive to, respectful of, and tailored to its contexts in important ways. A more sophisticated conceptualization and study of just how context matters in evaluation is a strong candidate for future theoretical study in the field, as such a conceptualization would be likely to improve evaluation practice across its many genres.

—*Jennifer C. Greene*

CONTEXT-MECHANISM-OUTCOME CONFIGURATION. *See* REALISTIC EVALUATION

▪ CONTRACT, EVALUATION

The contract for an evaluation is an agreement between the evaluator and the client in which both have certain roles and responsibilities. The client agrees to participate in the evaluation, approve the evaluation plan, review and approve the evaluation report, and provide the agreed-on funding. The evaluator, in turn, agrees to complete certain work within a specified time period and budget; follow human subject protection guidelines; collect, store, and retrieve data; and edit and disseminate reports.

According to the *Program Evaluation Standards,* the following are components of this agreement: evaluation purpose, evaluation questions, listing of stakeholders, deliverables, data collection procedures, data analysis procedures, management plan, reporting plan, quality control procedures, timelines, budget, provisions for periodic review, contract amendment, and contract termination. In some evaluations, there may also be the need for specifying subcontracts and subcontractors. The subcontract, then, would be an agreement between the evaluator and another person or organization that consents to undertake certain work on behalf of the evaluator and to further the evaluation effort. Such a subcontracting situation may arise with a large-scale or complex evaluation that requires certain expertise beyond the scope of the evaluator.

In most but not all cases, and particularly with an external evaluation or a subcontract, the contract is a written agreement. With a written contract or subcontract, the client and the evaluator or the evaluator and the subcontractor sign the contract. This written contract serves as a legal document binding both parties. Note that either party can break a contract or subcontract. If a contract is broken, there may, however, be legal or financial ramifications.

Even with an internal evaluation, the evaluator should provide a memorandum of agreement indicating the work, the personnel, the procedures, the deliverables, and the timelines. A well-designed evaluation plan that contains statements about the background and rationale, the evaluation purpose, the stakeholders and audiences, and the key questions can provide the critical information needed to negotiate the basic evaluation work for either the contract or the memorandum of agreement.

—*Darlene F. Russ-Eft*

Further Reading

Joint Committee on Standards for Educational Evaluation. (1994). *The program evaluation standards: How to assess evaluations of educational programs* (2nd ed.). Thousand Oaks, CA: Sage.

Russ-Eft, D., & Preskill, H. (2001). *Evaluation in organizations: A systematic approach to enhancing learning, performance, and change.* Cambridge, MA: Perseus Press.

▪ CONTROL CONDITIONS

Control conditions refers to the setting or circumstances experienced by persons who are not of primary interest to the researcher or evaluator. For example, a summative evaluator might use a quasiexperiment to contrast the outcomes of program participants with subjects in control conditions. These should be as similar as possible to program conditions, with the exception of those critical components (treatments, interventions, experiences) that uniquely define the program. Thus, if the program participants display superior outcomes to control subjects, the finding can plausibly be attributed to the program, not to irrelevant factors in the environment of participants.

—*Joseph M. Petrosko*

See also EXPERIMENTAL DESIGN, QUASIEXPERIMENTAL DESIGN

Further Reading

Shadish, W. R., Cook, T. D., & Campbell, D. T. (2002). *Experimental and quasi-experimental designs for generalized causal inference.* New York: Houghton Mifflin.

⊞ COOK, THOMAS D.

Ph.D. Communication Research, Stanford University; B.A. German and French, Oxford University.

Cook is John Evans Professor of Sociology at Northwestern University, where he is also Professor of Psychology and of Education and Social Policy and a Faculty Fellow of the Institute for Policy Research. He was a member of the MacArthur Foundation Network on Successful Adolescence in High Risk Settings and is a trustee of the Russell Sage Foundation and a member of its Committee on the Future of Work.

Cook has contributed to evaluation through exploring methods for inferring causation and for probing the generalization of causal hypotheses. He is substantively interested in educational evaluation, especially as it concerns preschool programs (*Sesame Street*), whole-school reform initiatives (James Comer's School Development Program), and understanding why experimentation has been so rare in educational evaluation.

Cook has numerous publications, including two recent books: *Managing to Make It: Urban Families in High-Risk Neighborhoods* and *Experimental and Quasi-Experimental Designs for Generalized Causal Inference* (with Shadish and Campbell). Cook was the recipient of the Gunnar and Alva Myrdal Prize for Science from the Evaluation Research Society in 1982, the Donald Campbell Prize for Innovative Methodology from the Policy Sciences Organization in 1988, and the Distinguished Scientist Award of Division 5 of the American Psychological Association in 1997. He was elected to the American Academy of Arts and Sciences in 2000 and was named a Margaret Mead Fellow of the American Academy of Political and Social Science in 2003.

⊞ COOKSY, LESLIE

(b. 1958, Eureka, California). Ph.D. Program Evaluation and Public Policy, Human Service Studies, M.S. Rural Sociology, Cornell University; B.S. Applied Behavioral Sciences, University of California, Davis.

Cooksy is Director of the Center for Community Research and Service and Associate Professor, University of Delaware. Previously, she was Assistant Professor in the Department of Educational Psychology at Florida State University; Senior Social Science Analyst for the U.S. General Accounting Office's Program Evaluation and Methodology Division in Washington, DC; and served for 2 years in the U.S. Peace Corps in Sierra Leone as an Agricultural Workshop Instructor.

She brings a "multilingual" perspective to her work, which incorporates both qualitative and quantitative approaches and a wide variety of disciplines. Her evaluation work extends across public and mental health services, family and youth programs, welfare benefits, and international agricultural programs. Influences on her work include Jennifer Greene, William M. K. Trochim, Joe Wholey, and Eleanor Chelimsky. Her work has added to the growing literature about program theory, logic models, and metaevaluation.

She has served as a member of AEA's Board of Directors, during which time she chaired the publications committee. She was also Program Chair of AEA's topical interest group (TIG) on the Teaching of Evaluation. She is currently Associate Editor of the *American Journal of Evaluation* and a member of the Editorial Boards of *New Directions for Evaluation* and *Evaluation & the Health Professions*. She received the 2001 Certificate of Appreciation from the University of Delaware Graduates of the Master of Arts Program in Urban Affairs and Public Policy for commitment and excellence in teaching and putting the needs of students first. She is the 1993 recipient of the American Evaluation Association's Marcia Guttentag Award for promising young evaluators and the 1994 recipient for the U.S. General Accounting Office's Meritorious Service Award.

◼◼ CORDRAY, DAVID

Ph.D., Claremont Graduate School, Claremont, California.

Cordray is Professor of Public Policy and Professor of Psychology at Vanderbilt University. He is a past president of the American Evaluation Association and served on AEA's Board of Directors. He also served on the Evaluation Review Panel of the U.S. Department of Education, in the National Academy of Public Administration, on the Panel on the Status of Education in the Federal Government, the National Research Council/Institute of Medicine Panel of Needle Exchange and Bleach Distribution Programs, the National Research Council, and the Steering Committee for the Workshop on Work-Related Musculoskeletal Injuries.

His research focuses on estimating the numerical effects of social interventions directed at at-risk populations (e.g., homeless, substance abusers). In addition to conducting multisite evaluations of intervention programs, he has contributed to the development of methodological refinements of quasiexperimental designs, meta-analysis, and nontraditional forms of causal inquiry.

Cordray has served on the Editorial Boards of *New Directions for Program Evaluation, Evaluation Review,* and *Evaluation and Program Planning.* As President of the American Evaluation Association in 1972, Cordray appointed an ad hoc committee to examine the need for written principles of conduct for evaluators, and from that work the *AEA Guiding Principles of Evaluators* were developed. Cordray's publications include *Meta-analysis for Explanation: A Casebook* (with Cook, Cooper, Hartman, Hedges, Louis, Light, and Mosteller) and *Psychosocial Rehabilitation Assessment: A Broader Perspective* (with Pion).

◼◼ CORRELATION

Correlation is a measure of the degree or strength of relationship between two or more variables. It does not prove causation because we may not know which variable came first or whether alternative explanations for the presumed effect exist. For example, earnings and schooling are correlated, but it is unknown which one goes first. Correlations also do little to rule out alternative explanations for a relationship between two variables such as education and income. That

relationship may not be causal at all but rather due to a confounding variable, such as family socioeconomic status, that causes both earning and schooling.

—Marco A. Muñoz

Further Reading

Shadish, W. R., Cook, T. D., & Campbell, D. T. (2002). *Experimental and quasi-experimental designs for generalized causal inference.* Boston: Houghton Mifflin.

◼◼ COST

Cost refers to the value of all resources required to obtain a specific evaluation outcome, whether the resources are purchased, donated, or borrowed. The usual procedure for estimating costs is to specify, in detail, the resources that are required and to estimate their market values. In some cases, the lack of a market for a resource means that other methods of costing are applied. Total costs can also be subdivided among the various stakeholders to identify their particular cost burdens. Identification of costs is necessary to determine the feasibility and cost effectiveness of alternatives.

—Henry M. Levin

Further Reading

Levin, H. M., & McEwan, P. J. (2001). *Cost-effectiveness analysis: Methods and applications* (2nd ed.). Thousand Oaks, CA: Sage.

◼◼ COST-BENEFIT ANALYSIS

Cost-benefit analysis and cost-effectiveness analysis represent the principal tools for evaluating alternatives when economic constraints and limited resources are considered. Both tools embrace the usual methods of evaluating outcomes, but they also consider results in the light of the resource investments required to obtain them. In this way it is possible to identify and choose those intervention policies that will maximize desired results for any resource constraint.

Cost-benefit and cost-effectiveness analyses differ in a fundamental way. Cost-effectiveness analysis focuses on the costs for outcomes restricted to the measurable goals of an intervention, such as mortality rates, reading scores, and criminal recidivism. In contrast, cost-benefit analysis evaluates alternatives in terms of the monetary value of their goals or benefits in comparison to their costs. That is, cost-benefit analysis represents an attempt to establish the cost of alternatives in monetary units such as dollars and the value of the benefits in such units so that costs and benefits for each alternative and among alternatives can be compared directly.

Cost-benefit analysis provides answers to two questions that link evaluation to policy consideration. First, is the intervention "worth it" in the sense that its benefits will exceed its costs? Second, among those alternatives that meet the first criterion, which have the greatest benefits relative to costs? In answering the first question, one would wish to limit policy considerations to only interventions that yield at least a dollar of benefit for each dollar of cost. However, many potential options may meet that minimal standard. Accordingly, overall benefits are maximized when resources are devoted to those alternatives that yield the greatest benefits relative to costs. Some options in education and health, for example, show benefits of $6 or more for each dollar of resource investment. It is these high-yield alternatives that should have priority in the use of scarce resources.

Cost-effectiveness analysis is limited to evaluating the efficiency of resource use among alternatives with similar goals and measures of outcome, but cost-benefit analysis has no such limitation. From a societal perspective, it is possible to compare cost-benefit results for potential projects both within and among different service domains. Thus, one can evaluate the cost-benefit performance of alternatives among areas as diverse as public transportation, health, education, economic development, and recreation, as well as of interventions within each area. In contract, cost-effectiveness evaluations can provide only comparability among alternatives for interventions with precisely the same goals and measures of effectiveness.

Cost-benefit analysis has a major limitation, in that it can be used only to evaluate those interventions with outcomes that can be measured directly in or converted to benefits in monetary units. This means that interventions must have results that can be assessed according to market valuations. For example, many education and training projects can be placed in a cost-benefit framework because their outcomes can be assessed in terms of increased productivity and income. Health interventions resulting in societal savings for health care or greater productivity or fewer days absent from work can also be measured in monetary terms. Benefits of reduced criminal recidivism can be assessed by considering the savings in resources that would otherwise be devoted to criminal justice. Improved transportation systems such as airports, highways, port facilities, and public transit can be evaluated according to the value of improved efficiency in moving people and goods to desired destinations. Water resource projects such as hydroelectric plants can be evaluated according to the value of electricity, potable water, recreation, and flood control that they produce. All of these have market outcomes that enable monetary estimates of their benefits to be calculated and used for comparison with the costs of the interventions and cost-benefit calculations among the various options.

COST-ESTIMATION

Obviously, both costs and benefits must be measured for a cost-benefit evaluation. Conceptually, the costs of an intervention are viewed as the value of all the resources that are given up by society to undertake an activity. These resources are referred to as the ingredients of the intervention, and it is their social value that determines the overall cost. The premise for this economic definition of cost is the concept of *opportunity cost*, in which the value of resources in their best alternative use is the appropriate measure of the cost of an endeavor. Accounting practices that report costs have typically been developed for other purposes and do not necessarily reflect accurate cost measurement for purposes of cost-benefit studies.

The first step in estimating the cost of an alternative is to specify the ingredients that are required for the particular intervention. These will include personnel, facilities, materials, and other resources that are needed to achieve the benefits that will be ascertained. Ingredients should be specified as precisely as possible in terms of quantities and characteristics. Thus, full-time and part-time personnel should be distinguished by function, with detail about the educational, skill, and experience requirements for each position. Likewise, facilities should be described in terms of the amount of space, construction features, amenities, and location. All ingredients must be listed, whether they are paid for by the project directly or by others or provided in kind. That is, no matter who bears the cost of an ingredient, there is a cost entailed. Later, one can divide costs according to who pays them.

Once the ingredients are specified, it is possible to place a cost value on them. Typically this is done by using their market value, where the market value of personnel includes not only required salaries but other benefits that must be provided. A variety of techniques is used to determine the costs of those ingredients that are not obtained through competitive markets. Costs are summed over all of the ingredients to obtain the total cost of the intervention.

BENEFIT ESTIMATION

Benefits are estimated using conventional evaluation methods, such as randomized experiments, quasi-experiments, or statistical studies. Clearly, the more rigorous the evaluation design and its implementation, the more accurate will be the measures of outcome. What are thought of as results or effectiveness of the particular interventions being assessed must be converted into benefits in terms of their monetary value. In the case of some market outcomes, such as higher earnings from training or from an additional level of education, the benefits may be readily measured in monetary terms. However, in other cases, the results will be measured in their own terms, such as the number of days of attendance gained in the workplace by virtue of healthier lifestyles. In those cases, the measures of effectiveness are converted into an estimate of their monetary values or benefits. For example, additional days of healthy activity from smoking cessation might be valued according to potential wages or workplace productivity, as well as savings in health resources that would otherwise be needed to treat illness.

A variety of approaches exist for converting measures of effectiveness into monetary benefits. To the degree that a competitive market exists for the outcomes of an intervention (e.g., better-trained workers), market values can be used to estimate the benefits. In some cases, the additional supply created by an intervention such as a large hydroelectric dam will change the market dynamics. In this case, one might have to make adjustments to existing price structures in estimating benefits, on the basis that a large increase in the supply of electricity will reduce its market price. The estimation of benefits for outcomes that lack competitive markets is done through techniques that generate "shadow prices" that emulate what markets might produce.

COMBINING COSTS AND BENEFITS

Costs and benefits can be combined in several ways for a cost-benefit analysis. The first step is to compare the costs and benefits of each alternative to gauge whether the benefits exceed the costs. Any option for which the estimated benefits are less than the estimated costs is usually eliminated from consideration. The most common forms of cost-benefit comparison among alternatives are rate of return, cost-benefit ratios, and net present values. Internal rates of return represent estimates of annual percentage returns on investment that can be compared among alternative interventions as well as to returns in financial markets.

Cost-benefit ratios represent a comparison in which costs are compared with the monetary value of benefits. Those alternatives with the highest ratio of benefits to costs are viewed as most attractive. In performing these calculations, it is necessary to adjust benefit and cost streams of projects that have multi-year lifetimes by discounting or penalizing costs and benefits in the future to make them comparable with outlays or benefits received at present. That is, for multiyear projects it is necessary to calculate the benefits and costs in terms of their present values, for which a standard discounting technique is available.

Another approach is to calculate the net present value of the overall investment for each alternative by subtracting present values of benefits from present values of costs. The necessary condition for consideration of an alternative is that its net present value should be positive. The most attractive alternative is the one for which the net present value is largest for any investment level.

It is important to note that one should not be seduced by the apparent precision of cost-benefit estimates into believing that differences in results among alternatives are always strict guides for policy. As with all forms of evaluation, cost-benefit analysis often requires assumptions and judgments on the treatment of data. Differences in judgments among reasonable analysts can lead to differences in results. For this reason, a good cost-benefit analysis should attempt to do a "sensitivity analysis" in which a range of reasonable assumptions is used in the calculations to see if the findings are robust. It is also important to note that very small differences in cost-benefit results should not be used too strictly to rank alternatives. When differences are small, other considerations, such as ease of implementation, should be used in selecting options.

COST-BENEFIT STUDIES

These techniques can be demonstrated for specific studies. Probably the most prominent cost-benefit study of preschool education is Barnett's analysis of the Perry Preschool Program, a program designed to provide preschool services of high quality to children in at-risk situations. It embraced low student-teacher ratios, weekly home visits by qualified teachers, and 2-hour weekday classes with well-developed curricula. In the early 1960s, 128 African American students between 3 and 4 years old and from low-income families were randomly assigned to the preschool treatment or to a control group. Attrition was relatively low, and follow-up surveys were done periodically on the status of members of the two groups to see if differences emerged, with the most recent data collected when the subjects were 27 years old. Comparisons showed consistent and statistically significant advantages for the treatment group for a wide range of outcome variables, including test scores, earnings, arrest rates, and welfare participation.

Costs were estimated using the ingredients method in 1992 dollars (to control for changes in the price level). Benefits were estimated for the treatment students for the value of child care, reductions in special educational services and in retention in grade at the elementary and secondary levels, higher earnings, reduced involvement in the criminal justice system, and reduced public assistance. The net present value of the social investment per program participant—the difference between the present value of benefits and costs—was estimated at almost $100,000. The benefit-cost ratio for society for such an investment was between 6 and 8, meaning that for every dollar of investment there was a return of about $7.

This return on investment is considerable and argues for greater societal investments in preschool services for children who are at risk educationally. With returns this high, it is unlikely that alternative assumptions or errors in the estimates would obviate the conclusion of high benefits to costs. However, this evaluation also shows how outcomes from evaluations, when measured in their own terms (e.g., test scores, educational attainments, crime), can be converted into monetary measures that can be compared with costs.

In a different context, the use of cost-benefit analysis was applied to nutritional programs for reduction of anemia in developing countries. Such countries have very limited resources to apply to issues of public health and must choose among strategies on the basis of those that have a maximal impact relative to social investments. Iron deficiency anemia is very widespread among developing societies, resulting in physical weakness and listlessness and impairment of work capacity, as well as greater susceptibility to infection and poor learning consequences in school. Although this type of anemia is exacerbated by intestinal parasites that cause bleeding, the major concern is dietary: the provision of sufficient iron in bioabsorbable forms. This can be done through dietary supplementation, with injections or pills or iron fortification of food staples such as salt and sugar.

The concentration of hemoglobin in the blood is the standard measure for ascertaining iron sufficiency. A large range of studies found that for every 1% improvement in hemoglobin within anemic populations, there is an improvement in work capacity and output of between 1% and 2%. This consistent finding was used to calculate the monetary benefits of greater work output in three countries: Indonesia, Kenya, and Mexico. Adjustments were made for the fact that some of the additional output might displace the employment of workers in societies with high unemployment and underemployment.

Costs were estimated by using the ingredients method for both iron supplementation (using community health workers) and iron fortification of the food supply. Other costs were associated with the higher caloric needs of iron-satiated workers expending more energy. Benefit-cost ratios for investing in iron fortification or supplementation for the three countries were found to be extraordinarily high and very robust under different assumptions. For dietary fortification, the benefits exceeded the costs in a range from 7 to 70, depending on the country; for dietary supplementation, the range was from 4 to 38. All estimates showed considerable benefits relative to costs. Even these investment returns are understated because they are limited to the improvements in work output and do not incorporate improvements in overall health, learning, and feelings of well-being.

SUMMARY

Cost-benefit analysis represents an evaluation tool that takes into account both the relative effectiveness of alternatives and their costs in a form that allows consideration of how to maximize results for any resource constraint. It adds a policy dimension to standard evaluation studies by taking the costs of alternatives into account. Although not widely used at present among evaluators (in comparison with economists), it has the potential to provide additional information when choosing among alternative policies where resources are limited.

—Henry M. Levin

Further Reading

Barnett, W. S. (1996). *Lives in the balance: Age-27 benefit-cost analysis of the High/Scope Perry Preschool Program.* Ypsilanti, MI: High/Scope Press.

Levin, H. M. (1986). A benefit-cost analysis of nutritional programs for anemia reduction. *World Bank Research Observer, 1*(2), 219-245.

Levin, H. M., & McEwan, P. J. (2001). *Cost-effectiveness analysis: Methods and applications* (2nd ed.). Thousand Oaks, CA: Sage.

▪▪ COST EFFECTIVENESS

Cost effectiveness is the defining element of a method for comparing both the costs and results of different alternatives for addressing particular goals. Criteria for measuring effectiveness must be similar among alternatives for a cost-effectiveness comparison. Effectiveness estimates are based on the usual experimental, quasiexperimental, or statistical designs. Cost estimates are based on a careful specification of required resources and their market values. Selection of alternatives with the greatest effectiveness per unit of cost will generally provide the largest overall impact for a given resource constraint. In performing a cost-effectiveness analysis, adequate scrutiny must be given to both cost measurement and estimation of outcomes.

—Henry M. Levin

▪▪ COUNTENANCE MODEL OF EVALUATION

In publishing the now classic article "The Countenance of Educational Evaluation," Robert E. Stake did not mean to create an evaluation model, and to this day, he would assert that it is not a model. Nonetheless, a brief review of the evaluation literature since its publication illustrates its characterization as such. What has captured the imagination of evaluators

since the article's 1967 publication in *Teachers College Record* is Stake's clear distinction between description and judgment (although uses of his work focus more on the description aspect of evaluation), his clarity in dealing with the kinds and sources of data in evaluation, and his discussion of the complexity of any evaluand.

Stake's description of the then-current countenance of evaluation and a suggested fuller, more rounded countenance for educators and evaluators hint at issues relevant in evaluation theory and practice up to this day. For example, both description and judgment are necessary in evaluation, although Stake sees a greater emphasis on description—still true for many evaluators today. He described judgments as data, foreshadowing the contemporary emphasis on values as data. The complexity of education (and programs and evaluation) is reflected in Stake's attention to the connections among antecedents (prior conditions), transactions (processes), and outcomes, which he called contingencies, and between intentions and observations, which he called congruence. He also highlights the typical emphasis on outcomes but enjoins evaluators to consider antecedents and transactions, a suggestion no less relevant today, especially in education.

Although the standards and judgment part of the Countenance article is less frequently mentioned, Stake outlined how the descriptive data matrix was itself the basis for a judgment that could result from a relative comparison of one program to another or an absolute comparison of a program to standards of excellence.

The ideas in the Countenance article are similar to contemporary ideas of Stufflebeam and Provus, and in the article, Stake seriously engaged Scriven's ideas of the role of evaluators, especially with regard to making judgments, and formative and summative evaluation, as well as Cronbach's ideas on generalization.

Further Reading

Stake, R. E. (1967). The countenance of educational evaluation. *Teachers College Record, 68*(7), 523-530.

▪▪ COUSINS, J. BRADLEY

(b. 1955, Toronto, Ontario, Canada). Ph.D. Educational Theory: Educational Measurement and Evaluation, Ontario Institute for Studies in Education, University of Toronto, Canada; M.A. Psychology, Lakehead University, Canada; B.A. Psychology, Trent University, Canada.

Cousins is Professor of Educational Administration in the Faculty of Education, University of Ottawa, Canada. He was previously on the faculty at the Ontario Institute for Studies in Education, University of Toronto.

His primary contributions to the field of evaluation have been the empirical study of evaluation and the development of evaluation theory, especially regarding evaluation utilization and participatory and collaborative forms of evaluation and applied research. Other areas of interest include evaluation utilization, knowledge utilization, organizational learning, and the implementation of innovative programs. Main intellectual influences on his work include Kenneth Stanley, Kenneth Leithwood, John Ross, Marvin Alkin, and Michael Huberman.

He is the author of many journal articles, evaluation reports, and chapters, including a chapter in the *International Handbook of Educational Evaluation.* He is the author of *Participatory Evaluation Up Close* and Coeditor of *Participatory Evaluation in Education: Studies in Evaluation Use and Organizational Learning* (with Lorna M. Earl). He is also Coauthor of *Classroom Assessment: Changing the Face; Facing the Change* (with L. Earl); and *Developing Leaders for Future Schools* (with K. Leithwood and P. Begely). He is currently Editor-in-Chief of the *Canadian Journal of Program Evaluation* and ex-officio member of the Canadian Evaluation Society National Council. He is the recipient of the Doctoral Dissertation Award from the Canadian Association for Studies in Educational Administration and the 1999 Contributions to Evaluation in Canada Award from the Canadian Evaluation Society.

CREDIBILITY

In evaluation, evaluators and evaluations themselves must not only be valid but also must be seen to be valid, which denotes *credibility*. Indeed, in naturalistic and participatory models of evaluation, credibility is an attribute of validity itself. In qualitative evaluation, trustworthiness is a criterion for judging the quality of the evaluation. To be trustworthy, or credible, the evaluation should make sense to stakeholders, be authentic, provide sufficient data and detail to make transfer of knowledge possible or from which to make generalizations, and explicate the process for arriving at conclusions. Any number of

strategies may enhance the credibility of an evaluation, such as triangulation, peer debriefing, and member checking.

CRESST. *See* CENTER FOR RESEARCH ON EVALUATION, STANDARDS, AND STUDENT TESTING

CRITERIA

The aspects, qualities, or dimensions that distinguish a more meritorious or valuable evaluand from one that is less meritorious or valuable constitute *criteria*. Criteria are central to any evaluation, whether they are determined at the beginning of the evaluation or emerge during the evaluation process. In most cases, it is possible, using a needs assessment and an analysis of other relevant values, to identify many criteria. However, the open-ended elements of an evaluation often uncover other criteria that should also be considered when drawing conclusions. Performance or attributes are evaluated on each criterion, and the results are then synthesized to draw evaluative conclusions.

—Jane Davidson

CRITERION-REFERENCED TESTS

Criterion-referenced tests are designed to yield test scores whose interpretations are linked to specified performance criteria. To attain such meaning, the original responses on the test (raw scores) must be transformed into a scale-score system that provides for interpretations directly related to the criterion domain. For achievement tests, the criterion may represent operational definitions of established standards of achievement, and the scale scores reflect ordered levels of proficiency, each level specifically defined in terms of the skills students should be able to exhibit. For psychological tests, the scale scores may yield classifications related to such areas as personality and psychopathology.

—Charles L. Thomas

Further Reading

American Educational Association, American Psychological Association, & National Council on Measurement in Education. (1999). *Standards for educational and psychological testing.* Washington, DC: American Educational Research Association.

Hopkins, K. D. (1998). *Educational and psychological measurement and evaluation* (8th ed.). Needham Heights, MA: Allyn & Bacon.

CRITICAL INCIDENTS

The concept of *critical incidents* is derived mainly from work in psychology that suggests there are events that occur in the life of a person, program, organization, or culture that substantially alter or direct subsequent events. The Critical Incident Technique (CIT), developed by John C. Flanagan during World War II, is based on studies conducted for the Aviation Psychology Program of the U.S. Army and Air Force. Common critical incidents for individuals are trauma, illness, divorce, moving, and so on. In health care, critical incidents are especially those that induce stress and may lead to undesirable consequences. Depending on the field, critical incidents are variously associated with crises (e.g., law enforcement, health care) or classic and recurring problems (e.g., teaching, management). An analysis of critical incidents is intended to systematically identify actions or events that contribute to the success or failure of individuals or organizations. This technique may underestimate the importance of routine practices or events, and there is a danger of stereotyping in the identification and characterization of critical incidents.

See also SUCCESS CASE METHOD

CRITICAL THEORY EVALUATION

Critical theory evaluation is an activity concerned with the unveiling of false culture and determination of the merit, worth, or value of something, or the product of that process. Critical theory evaluation aspires to push praxis into motion through the conduct of inquiry. In positioning evaluation stakeholders as reflective and dialogic agents in discerning what is needed, what is good, and why this is so, critical theory evaluation seeks to change the way things are by challenging the way we make sense of things.

Building from the philosophies of critical social science, critical theory evaluation is conducted from a standpoint of questioning how we live our lives in the midst of false constructions about our social, political, and economic circumstances. The evaluation is influenced by an explicit value position that we operate beneath layers of false consciousness contributing to our own and others' exploitation and oppression. False ways of knowing and understanding have been shaped through unrecognized patterns of dominant discourses. As a response, critical theory evaluation seeks to engage evaluation participants in a dialectic process of questioning the history of their ideas and thinking about how privileged narratives of the past and present will influence future value judgments.

Recognizing how power presents itself and the situated position of power during an evaluation is a central characteristic of critical theory evaluation. The critical theory evaluator experiences the context of an evaluation as an arena of competing hegemonic interests. An economy of power is presumed to be inherent to the production of knowledge: People who have power over others have the resources to create the kind of information they need to maintain their privileged position. The fashioning of evaluative information can serve to reinforce the imbalanced status quo or ameliorate disparities in power distributions.

The power of whose ideas are represented throughout the evaluation is a value-laden activity mediated through critical theory evaluation. Evaluations conducted from feminist, deliberative democratic, or emancipatory perspectives reflect varying modes of critical theory evaluation. The amelioration of oppressive circumstances derives from the ability to regain new positions in and belief systems about power relationships. Therefore, the politics of weighting values and opinions (including the evaluator's) during a critical theory evaluation is not viewed as a liability but a responsibility.

The critical theory evaluator recognizes how power is structured through narrative and often cloaked by the language surrounding an evaluand. The organization is regarded as a socially constructed entity acting through a hierarchy of narratives, as Donald Campbell put it. To unmask the historical constructedness of dominant narratives, the evaluation processes attend to the politics of narrative within the organization and the influences of larger social, political, and economic factors that shape a master narrative. Evaluators make explicit their value position from the point of entry and work with evaluation participants to raise consciousness about how narratives shape the "house paradigm."

The primary roles of the critical theory evaluator are that of educator and change agent. The evaluator views the organization as a collection of learners who may or may not be aware of the oppression in their lives but are intelligent and capable of coming to new understandings. As an educator, the evaluator adopts a Frierian problem-posing stance toward education. Working through the dialogue of the evaluation, learners are positioned to question the genesis of past knowledge and its influence on present ways of being. The current state of affairs is open to transformation through a process of critical reflection. This requires creating opportunities for genuine discourse free of systematic distortion and building commitments toward collective action.

As a change agent, the evaluator holds the learners responsible for active participation in the process of exploring narrative, engaging in political conversations, collectively reauthoring narrative, and accounting for the next edition of their story. The evaluator acts as a steward of deliberation, elucidating the personal, programmatic, and systematic impacts of competing narratives and cultivating a renewed relational responsibility for dialogue among organizational participants. Creating a deliberative process of public critique, the evaluation aims to build a narrative community.

For example, when designing an evaluation of a social services organization, the critical theory evaluator solicits ideas from different stakeholders. The administration of the organization might think it important to generate information about service utilization. The program managers might believe it useful to examine program processes and operations. The people who access the services are likely to suggest that looking at consumer choice and input is a priority. All of these standpoints will generate information about the program and, if investigated independent of each other, would produce different kinds of stories. The privileging of one narrative over another could strengthen or balance the power distribution in the organization, depending on how the different points of view are integrated into the design of the evaluation.

If the evaluator emphasizes storylines of the administration and program managers, with little input from the people using the services, the information produced might create narratives about the kinds of services being used, the demographics of the people served, how many units of services were delivered, and so forth. The evaluation might conclude that many services were used and being delivered in an efficient manner (from an organizational perspective) and that therefore things are good and satisfactory. However, this evaluation would tell us little about whether the services are the kinds of things the people using them really want or need or find helpful. Given the opportunity to be included, the people using the services might talk about wanting fewer services in their lives, creating different kinds of supports outside of the service system, and basic quality of life issues. An evaluation conducted from the point of view of people using social services would be likely to produce a very different kind of story than an evaluation conducted from the point of view of the administration.

The critical theory evaluator would bring the program administration, the program managers, and the people using services together in the design phase of the evaluation to discuss their different ideas about what should be evaluated, giving them an opportunity to discuss their different narratives and to explore how present and future service practices are related to larger sociopolitical and economic narratives. The conversations might include administrators talking about how accountability to the narratives of insurance companies shape their information needs; program managers offering stories about responding to the narratives of medical practitioners, licensing bodies, and an undereducated community; and the people using the services sharing narratives of what it is like to live with a disability and to be on the receiving end of care that is managed. Bringing the different perspectives to the forefront offers the potential to move the conversations beyond the case at hand and to share insights into higher social, economic, moral, and political issues about the ways we provide help in our culture.

The beginning of a new organizational story rests in the design stage of the evaluation. In crafting a hermeneutic dialectic process among diverse organizational participants, the evaluator hopes to create shared understandings and negotiate and coconstruct the authorship of the questions to be investigated. The evaluation is intended to be a transformative process. Engaging participants in democratic dialogue about what should be investigated, why, who should be involved, and how to go about unfolding the process is a significant first step for emancipating the community from its master narratives. The reauthoring process is best supported when the expectations for a dialogic community are established at the very earliest stages of the evaluation and are cultivated through continuing a critical, hermeneutic, and reflexive accounting of narratives throughout the study.

The dialectic processes of the critical theory evaluation are fashioned to engender empowering circumstances for evaluation participants; however, empowerment is something one does for oneself, not something done to or for someone else. Evaluation participants must come into their own sense of power through the questioning, analysis, and recognition of dominant narratives. Participants must develop a self-awareness that changes their relationship to others and the organizational context. As the words that disguise oppressive circumstances are made opaque and situated in their origins, evaluation participants experience an emancipation that will allow them to rewrite and act on a new organizational script. This is the ultimate goal of the critical theory evaluator: to catalyze praxis during the evaluation.

Critical theory evaluations are concerned with issues of social justice. Praxis is a transformative vehicle toward a more just society. Beyond the standards and guidelines of the professional evaluation community, critical theory evaluators will judge their evaluation efforts by the "degree to which the evaluation reorients, focuses and energizes participants toward knowing reality in order to transform it," or the catalytic validity of the study, in the words of Patti Lather. The evaluator is concerned with the degrees of systematic reflexivity embedded throughout the study. The dialectic activity is carried into the final stages of the inquiry process as the evaluator sets about scripting the story for the evaluation report.

Critical theory evaluations are likely to include experimentation with different kinds of reporting formats, including visual, poetic, performance, storytelling, and other arts-based forms of representation. Alternative forms of data representation acknowledge the variety of ways in which experience is coded. The process of evaluation reporting is an opportunity to be creative in communicating different experiences. Multiple forms of data representation cater to multiple audiences and are a means by which to include people of different thinking and privilege in the reporting process. Whatever format is negotiated to best suit the information needs of the organizational community, the

report is considered another medium for forwarding ongoing dialogue, reflection, and transformation.

—*Cheryl MacNeil*

Further Reading

Banks, K. C., & Marshall, J. M. (1999). *The company of neighbours.* Toronto, ON: University of Toronto Press.

Campbell, D. (2000). *The socially constructed organization.* New York: Karnac.

Fay, B. (1987). *Critical social science.* Ithaca, NY: Cornell University Press.

Friere, P. (1997). *Pedagogy of the oppressed.* New York: Continuum.

Habermas, J. (1970). On systematically distorted communication. *Inquiry, 13*(4), 205-218.

Lather, P. (1991). *Getting smart: Feminist research and pedagogy within the postmodern.* New York: Routledge & Kegan Paul.

MacNeil, C. (2002a). Evaluator as steward of citizen deliberation. *American Journal of Evaluation, 23*, 45-53.

MacNeil, C. (2002b, November). *The politics of narrative.* Paper presented at the annual meeting of the American Evaluation Association, Washington, DC.

Mertens, D. M. (1998). *Research methods in education and psychology: Integrating diversity with quantitative and qualitative approaches.* Thousand Oaks, CA: Sage.

Seigart, D., & Brisolara, S. (Eds.). (2002). Feminist evaluation explorations and experiences. *New Directions for Evaluation, 96.*

▊▊ CRITIQUE

Critique is a synonym for evaluation. A critique is a critical analysis or evaluation of a subject, situation, literary work, or other type of evaluand. It is critical in the sense of being characterized by careful analysis and judgment and analytic in the sense of a separating or breaking up of a whole into its parts, especially for examination of these parts to find their nature, proportion, function, interrelationship, and so on. A common fallacy is equating *critique* with *critical* or *negative*, neither of which is implied.

▊▊ CRONBACH, LEE J.

(b. 1916, Fresno, California; d. 2001, Palo Alto, California). Ph.D. Educational Psychology, University of Chicago, Illinois; M.A. University of California, Berkeley; BA, Fresno State College.

Cronbach took the Stanford Binet IQ test at age 5 and reportedly scored a 200, and he was then placed in

Lewis Terman's landmark study of the intellectually gifted. He finished high school when he was 14 years old and college when he was 18. Thurstone's work on attitude measurement provided early influence on Cronbach's lifelong engagement with educational and psychological measurement. However, Cronbach refused to narrowly specialize. "Weaving strands into a tapestry was what I enjoyed, not spinning the thread."

His life's work spanned three major domains: (a) measurement—where he invented the most widely used reliability coefficient today, the Cronbach alpha; developed a seminal work in generalizability theory; and developed a significant exposition of the core meanings of construct validity; (b) his interactionist approach to instruction and to educational research, in the pursuit of which he argued convincingly for the complementarity of experimental and correlational approaches to inquiry and in which he contributed significantly to ensuring that complex human phenomena were not studied via simple main effects but rather via interactionist approaches, labeled by Cronbach and his colleague Dick Snow as aptitude-treatment interactions. Cronbach later abandoned his pursuit of stable interactions, but he retained his commitment to honoring complexity. This commitment is evident in his third domain of contribution, (c) his work in program evaluation work.

Cronbach envisioned and championed a major educative role for evaluation and legitimized the formative, program improvement purpose for evaluation. He brought a conceptualization of who the audience for evaluation should be—the policy-shaping community, which included not only decision makers but advocacy groups; educators; the media; and interested citizens. Cronbach envisioned evaluation's primary role as educating the policy-shaping community about the nature and contours of persistent educational and social problems and how best to address them. He understood evaluation as fundamentally political, largely because it is conducted in politicized settings, often with high stakes.

Instead of one massive experiment or quasiexperiment (the "horse race" model of evaluation, said Cronbach), he favored an eclectic, broad-based, open methodological approach to evaluation; a fleet of smaller studies, each pursuing an important case or component of the policy or program under study. Cronbach encouraged evaluators to design evaluations to understand in some depth the nature of each context and the quality of the intervention in that context. Over time, then, with many such studies, the policy-shaping community could learn in some depth about that social problem and how best to address it. In addition, Cronbach encouraged evaluators to involve members of the setting in the evaluation study and to provide feedback throughout the course of the study (for program improvement purposes) rather than just at the end.

Cronbach theorized his approach in his 1982 *Designing Evaluations of Educational and Social Programs* as the units, treatments, observations, and settings (UTOS) framework. This framework championed the importance of external validity in evaluation—will this intervention repeat its successes in a different context characterized by A, B, C? This was in marked opposition to Campbell's continuing privileging of internal validity in evaluation studies.

Cronbach's professional honors were numerous. He was President of the American Educational Research Association, the American Psychological Association, and the Psychometric Society and a member of the National Academy of Sciences, the National Academy of Education, the American Philosophical Society, and the American Academy of Arts and Sciences. He received many honorary degrees, including ones from Yeshiva University; the University of Gothenburg, Sweden; and the University of Chicago.

■■ CROSS-CASE ANALYSIS

An analysis that examines themes, similarities, and differences across cases is referred to as a *cross-case analysis*. Cross-case analysis is used when the unit of analysis is a *case*, which is any bounded unit, such as an individual, group, artifact, place, organization, or interaction. Cross-case analysis is often the second level of analysis associated with a case study approach. This type of analysis is used in quantitative, statistical analysis, such as in hierarchical modeling, and in qualitative analysis, such as in the constant comparative method of Glaser and Strauss' grounded theory approach. A cross-case analysis is both a way of aggregating across cases and the means for making generalizations. In evaluation, the focus of a cross-case analysis is often particular common outcomes for a number of cases. For example, an evaluation of a mathematics curriculum may have classrooms as the

		School Number					
		1	2	3	4	5	6
Supports:	Administration	✓	✓	✓	✓	✓	✓
	Staff	✓	✓	✓		✓	✓
	Parents and community	✓	✓	✓	✓	✓	
	Welcoming atmosphere	✓	✓	✓	✓	✓	✓
	Appreciation	✓	✓		✓	✓	✓
	Consideration of parent's needs	✓	✓	✓	✓	✓	
	Communication	✓			✓	✓	✓
	Church-school connection	✓			✓		
	Unifying issues			✓	✓		

Figure 1   *Illustration of a Visual Representation of Cross-Case Analysis (Factors most commonly identified as contributing to successful parent involvement with schools)*

unit of analysis, or case, and the cross-case analysis might look at teacher satisfaction and student achievement across all classrooms.

Cross-case analysis often includes visual displays of similarities and differences across cases, particularly in qualitative approaches (see Figure 1).

See also COMPARATIVE ANALYSIS

Further Reading

Miles, M. B., & Huberman, A. M. (1994). *Qualitative data analysis: An expanded sourcebook* (2nd ed.). Thousand Oaks, CA: Sage.

CROSS-SECTIONAL DESIGN

Cross-sectional design is a research method in which data are collected on more than two categories or variables at the same time and analyzed for their association. For example, a study of adult development might measure 25-, 35-, 45-, 55-, and 65-year-olds on such variables as life satisfaction, relationships, and goal attainment. The analysis involves a baseline from one value of the first variable—for example, 25-year-olds or 65-year-olds—and the measures of the other variables, to which all other groups are compared. This type of design is cost effective but weak in establishing causality.

—*Jeffrey G. Tucker*

CULTURALLY RESPONSIVE EVALUATION

Culturally responsive evaluation, a recent addition in the development of educational evaluation, calls for changes in the traditional ways of practicing educational evaluation. Culturally responsive evaluation is not the new phenomenon that some might think, but its practice has been limited to practitioners serving clients of similar backgrounds.

HISTORY

About 60 years ago, an African American evaluator, Aaron Brown, sounded the call for cultural responsiveness in educational evaluation, but his plea went unheeded. Brown persuasively argued that African Americans had special and critical needs due to their unique experiences in American society. He appropriately raised the question in the 1940s of whether there should be special considerations given when evaluating schools for African Americans.

Issues devolving from the consideration of multiple stakeholders have been around for a long time, as well. During the 1950s, Leander Boykin prophetically saw the importance of including the perspectives of multiple program stakeholders in conducting an evaluation. Boykin was the first African American to receive a Ph.D. in Education from Stanford University (1948), and he did postdoctoral work at Harvard University in 1957 and 1958. In one of several works on evaluation, Boykin provided a set of 10 guiding principles, characteristics, and functions of effective evaluation. One principle asserted that evaluation should be a cooperative effort that involved not only students, parents, teachers, and principals as important stakeholders in the school community but also others who played important roles but were typically overlooked, such as custodial and lunchroom personnel. He saw the need to involve custodial workers if one wanted to understand deeply the cultural context of a school being evaluated.

It would be an exaggeration to say that Ralph Tyler alone invented modern-day educational evaluation, but his name stands tall in the history of the field. Tyler challenged evaluation practitioners to move beyond mere achievement testing to reveal the merit and worth of classroom programs, curricular influence, and student growth. The enormity of Tyler's influence is undeniable.

Similarly, one can point to the seminal vision of Robert Stake in his early articulation of the parameters of a responsive evaluation in 1973. Stake argued persuasively for the inclusion of contextual issues beyond student achievement, teacher behavior, administrator leadership, and community descriptors. He maintained that the complete educational evaluation should be responsive to a host of influences that fall outside the ken of traditional approaches to educational evaluation. Stake's influence resulted in a broadening of evaluators' view of their task and a diminution of their reliance on quantification as the principal indicator of worth. Recent work by Stafford Hood has sought a further extension of the work of Tyler and Stake by positing an approach that embraces considerations of culture in evaluation designs.

THE CURRENT STATE OF CULTURALLY RESPONSIVE EVALUATION

Educational evaluation must address issues relating to the influence of cultural context if practitioners are to be responsive to the settings in which their evaluations occur. Many evaluators (including Hood, Hopson, Greene, Kirkhart, Frierson, Senese, Hall, and LaFrance) assert that it is difficult, if not impossible, for evaluators to see, hear, and understand cultural

nuance that differs from their lived experience. However, they do not see culturally responsive evaluation as being a matter of race or ethnicity having exclusive rights or insights because of their families of origin. Rather, they advocate a broad-scale, multidimensional, and multidisciplinary view of the issues relating to culturally responsive evaluation and call for a positive and helpful response from the field. It is a matter of acknowledging who knows what and how the field can use its collective talent, skills, and insight to make educational evaluation as effective as possible.

Culturally responsive evaluations require practitioners with clear understandings of crucial aspects of the culture of the youngsters and teachers within the programs being evaluated. Supporters of culturally responsive evaluations condemn the practice of assigning culturally illiterate evaluators to projects that serve the least-served children of our society (i.e., children of color and poverty). They see the universal educational evaluator—"one size fits all"—as a wrong-headed idea and plead the case for more evaluators to be recruited from the cultural milieu of the learners being evaluated.

ISSUES RELATED TO CULTURALLY RESPONSIVE EVALUATION

Practitioners of responsive evaluation aver that the cultural milieu deeply influences educational activities, as well as evaluators' attempts to describe those influences. However, proponents of culturally responsive evaluation call for educational evaluators to broaden their view beyond mere responsiveness to the cultural contexts being examined, and merely espousing a strategy of cultural responsiveness may be insufficient for the task. Descriptions of cultural contexts written by evaluators who do not possess the requisite understanding of the behavior and nuances unique to the cultures being observed may introduce errors of oversight and misinterpretation.

Issues Confronting Those Who Seek to Design and Implement Culturally Responsive Evaluations

How one begins the evaluation process may forecast its results. Culturally responsive evaluations often seek inclusiveness by employing multiethnic evaluation teams to increase the chances in the early stages of an evaluation of hearing the voices of underrepresented students, their parents, and other members of the community. Although evaluators usually listen to what stakeholders say when they collect on-site data from students, teachers, parents, and others, they often cannot hear what has been said. They may lack the cultural references that underpin commentary. Subtleties of language are an example. In language, the African tradition, for example, often aims at circumlocution rather than at exact definition. The direct statement is considered crude and unimaginative; the veiling of meaning in ever-changing paraphrases is considered the criterion of intelligence and personality. Similar intercultural differences can be seen in arenas of humor, clothing, and body language. In a word, the evaluation team has to have the appropriate cultural talent on hand to do the job, and they have to be perceived by their clients as being the right people for the job.

The issue of evaluator credibility lies at the heart of culturally responsive evaluations. The Joint Committee on Standards for Educational Evaluation's standard on evaluator credibility supports the argument for designing and implementing culturally responsive evaluations. Its second utility standard requires not only that evaluators be competent and trustworthy but also that they understand the impact of social and political forces on less powerful stakeholders. Consequently, the plan and the evaluation team should be responsive to key stakeholders, including the least powerful ones. Stakeholders in the least powerful positions can be the most affected by the results of an educational evaluation—students, for example, or their parents or caregivers. When focusing an evaluation on program improvement and decision-makers' needs, it is easy to overlook the roles that students and parents might play in the early stages of issue identification.

Evaluators capable of being responsive to the cultural context of the project increase the likelihood that accurate perspectives of participants will be recorded, particularly when qualitative data are collected through interviews and focus groups. Culturally responsive evaluators are willing to trade some threat of impartiality for the possibility of more fully understanding stakeholders' positions by engaging in extensive dialogue with stakeholders. The questions and issues that will guide an educational evaluation are crucial to the undertaking and ultimately to the success of the venture. Evaluation questions should not appear to the stakeholders to be counterintuitive. Culturally responsive evaluators spend a good deal of time crafting the wording of evaluative

questions so that they are understandable and seen as important by their clients. Framing the right questions is not easily accomplished. In a culturally responsive evaluation, the questions will have been considered not only by the evaluators but by the stakeholders. Moreover, the evaluation should focus on the needs related to the environment or context in which the project is located. It is also of critical importance that the evaluation results should be presented so that the intended audiences can understand the evaluation (but this is typically ignored). Again, the culturally responsive evaluator has to know the culture of the audience.

DIFFICULTIES

Being responsive to the cultural context often complicates rather than simplifies the role of evaluators. For example, culturally responsive evaluations attempt to involve key community individuals in the planning of the evaluation. This may prove to be difficult and contentious. The evaluator may find that a particular group of stakeholders does not see the value of equitable participation in the evaluation by other stakeholders. One cannot minimize the importance of reaching agreement on the need for communication with diverse groups of stakeholders early in the evaluation planning.

Questions about what constitutes acceptable evidence for groups of stakeholders should be discussed before conducting the evaluation. An evaluator without sufficient knowledge of the cultural context of the program under evaluation may experience great difficulty with this task. Discussions of what is important and how we will know if we have acceptable evidence are often messy and contentious. Such democratic discussions are necessary, and the culturally responsive evaluator will be surprised neither by the style and content of the local oral discourse nor by the nonverbal communication attendant on the oral discourse. A democratic approach to evaluation increases the need for competent, culturally responsive evaluators who have a shared lived experience with the stakeholders and who can take the heat.

CONDUCTING THE EVALUATION

The cultural competence and responsiveness of a person collecting student test papers in the classrooms may not matter a great deal, but cultural responsiveness does matter in other forms of data collection. In truth, it may indeed matter how the test papers are handed out to the students and how the test is introduced; the atmosphere at the site where the students are being tested may also be of importance. The situation becomes far more complex in the collection of evaluative information through observation and interview. The need for training data collectors (e.g., observers, interviewers) in evaluation studies is great and, unfortunately, goes largely unaddressed in most evaluations.

How the stakeholders perceive the evaluator may be problematic. C. A. Grace noted in 1992 that the age, race, and sex of evaluators, with their credentials, hold considerable weight with some cultures. She uses the example that in the African American community, it is not unusual for older African American evaluators with recognized academic credentials and expertise to be the more influential and respected members of the evaluation team.

Nonverbal behaviors can be difficult to recognize among culturally diverse populations. For example, African American children may express themselves through considerable body language; adopt a system of nuances of intonation and body language, such as eye movement and position; and be highly sensitive to others' nonverbal cues of communication. The culturally responsive evaluator will use this as evaluative information. Too often, nonverbal behaviors are treated as "error variance" in the observation and ignored. The same considerations prevail when interviewing an African American program participant and stakeholder.

Clearly, evaluation team members cannot do anything about their age, gender, race, or general appearance, but to deny that such factors influence the amount and quality of the data they collect is folly. One thing that can be done to increase the probability of gathering evaluative information in a culturally responsive manner is to ensure that the principal evaluator and team members involved in the data collection understand the cultural context in which they are working and are seen as credible by their clients.

Culturally uninformed evaluators who collect interview data in inner city schools populated by professionals and students of color soon become aware of their inability to get the real story from their informants. As a consequence, they are limited to interpreting the inadequate data they were able to collect. Further, cultural nuances are missed on a regular basis by evaluators who have not shared a lived experience with those whose efforts they are evaluating. Evaluators who are culturally ignorant of disenfranchised racial minority groups are prone to interpret lack of parental participation in school programs as a lack of interest in the well-being of their children. Uninformed evaluators may find the noise level of students in transition between classes, or while waiting for a class to start, to be unacceptable. They may just not "get" why a child from a particular culture is not participating in class discussion. The list of possible pitfalls in data collection that await the culturally informed evaluator is a long one.

How one reports the results of a culturally responsive evaluation is yet another issue to explore. Oral reports can be more effective than written reports in certain cultural contexts when presented to interested audiences of stakeholders. Oral reports may be presented to selected audiences, advisory or executive groups, or key decision makers, at designated meetings or in public forums. Informality can be a key to increasing receptivity for certain audiences. Individuals in such audiences are more likely to have read the summary or abstract or even the executive summary rather than the full evaluation report. Question-and-answer sessions are often at the heart of the oral presentation. Culturally responsive and responsible evaluators are sensitive to the oral traditions of the community in which they find themselves.

To this end, supporters of culturally responsive evaluation often create review panels comprising stakeholder groups, for the purpose of examining the evaluative findings gathered by the principal evaluator or an evaluation team. When stakeholder groups comprising separate panels of parents, students, and community representatives review evaluative findings, the meaning of evaluative data is frequently given fresh, is unanticipated, and does not always confirm interpretations to which the culturally responsive evaluator must respond.

WHAT LIES AHEAD?

Professional organizations have begun to address the issues surrounding culturally responsive educational evaluations. At the 1994 annual meeting of the AEA, Karen Kirkhart's presidential address proposed what may have been one of the most radical demands concerning the relevance of culture in program evaluation that has been issued by an AEA president. Kirkhart forcefully asserted that multicultural validity must be a central dimension and focus in evaluation theory, methodology, practice, and metaevaluation.

The culturally responsive evaluator orchestrates an evaluation that culminates in a presentation of findings that comes closest to the audience being able to see, hear, and touch the essence of the program and how it is functioning. Evaluators of color are more likely to have had direct experiences with their own racial or cultural group that may inform their evaluation of programs serving this group, thereby enhancing their ability to provide the audience with a vicarious experience that comes closest to the direct experience.

In sum, advocates of culturally responsive evaluations call for a much larger cadre of evaluators who are culturally informed and committed to designing, conducting, and reporting culturally responsive educational evaluations. A major contributor to the field of cultural understanding, Edmund Gordon, has consistently called for educational researchers to be vigilant that the knowledge they generate is not counterintuitive to culturally diverse stakeholders and makes little contribution to understanding the people. Culturally responsive evaluation seeks to provide that

safeguard. Evaluators of color, largely absent in the evaluation community until recently, constitute unsuspected reservoirs for enriching the future of evaluation. The democratization of program evaluation will occur when the field becomes truly pluralistic by involving individuals who have been historically and traditionally underrepresented. Program evaluators who embrace cultural responsiveness at the heart of their work produce evaluations with broadened and enriched findings that are perceived as useful by their clients.

It is the culturally responsive thing to do.

—*Stafford L. Hood*

Further Reading

Frierson, H., Hood, S., & Hughes, G. (2002). Strategies that address culturally responsive evaluation. In J. Frechtling (Ed.), *The 2002 user-friendly handbook for project evaluation*. Arlington, VA: National Science Foundation.

Grace, C. A. (1992). Practical considerations for program professionals and educators working with African-American communities. In M. Orlandi (Ed.), *Cultural competence for evaluators: A guide for alcohol and other drug abuse prevention practitioners working with ethnic/racial communities* (DHHS Pub. No. [ADM] 92-1884). Washington, DC: Government Printing Office.

Evaluation Practice Around the World

Israel

Diversity and Evaluation in Israel

My career as an evaluator began in a development town in the northwest Negev of Israel in 1984. Development towns were established in the 1950s in an effort to settle waves of emigration from North African and Middle Eastern countries in the sparsely populated periphery of the newly established State of Israel. Often neglected by higher government priorities, these development towns "developed" slowly. Hence, by the 1980s, a large number and variety of educational and community projects proliferated. Among such projects was Early Childhood Education in Communities in the Negev, supported by the Bernard van Leer Foundation. The project planners, operators, and participants inaugurated me into the world of evaluation.

We worked in a spirit of participation, reflection on process development, and community empowerment at the time that these concepts began to appear in evaluation journals. Most of the work was carried out by young mothers who were born in Israel but whose parents were born in Morocco, Iraq, Iran, and other countries in the Middle East and around the Mediterranean. My job as evaluator was to monitor activities, join in weekly deliberations concerning the progress of the project, interview participants, and report to the foundation in Holland.

The project branched out to other development towns. In one town, where much of the population came from the Jewish communities in Southern India, a door opened to an entire world in one short home visit. I had arranged to interview a participant in a home-visiting program for new mothers. By the time I found the apartment in a maze of four-story buildings, it was around 5:00 in the evening. The mother apologized for having to cut the interview short because her masseuse was arriving at 6:00 p.m. She said that whenever an Indian woman gives birth, the "Auntie" comes to show her how to massage her baby and to massage the new mother. I asked if she would explain the procedures to the early childhood coordinator of the project, and she agreed, although surprised at my interest. As a result, the project started giving baby massage workshops to all the new mothers in the programs. Many mothers remembered other massage styles that their mothers used in the "old country." The images were so strong that I photo- and video-documented the workshops and discussions. The learning generated by the photographs and videos set me on a path of image-based research for evaluation purposes, a path I followed in my evaluations of other projects around the country.

Working on small projects entails work on several projects at once. One such project involved folklore exchanges between Arab and Jewish children. Located in Ramle, the project paired Arab and Jewish schools with the goal of encouraging positive interaction based on an exchange of folklore. The project staff worked with sixth-grade classes, including teachers, children, and parents. Children were to ask their parents and grandparents about specific traditions (food, games, toys, stories, etc.). In joint sessions, they shared, discussed, and documented the traditions against a background of mutual respect and discovery. Through extensive use of videotape as a means of collecting data and giving feedback, the evaluation helped the project focus on realistic goals. One mother, who had low expectations of the program, claimed that the children "don't want to be friends" and "aren't interested." Upon viewing a video clip of a joint session, however, she realized that she had been mistaken in her low assessment of the activity. She exclaimed in amazement, "Something is going on!" and became a staunch project supporter. A focus group composed of parents from both schools facilitated the process of reflection that followed viewing the video clip. The parents gained a greater understanding of the goal of the program and of the distinction between interaction and friendship. The project developers adjusted their own expectations and concentrated on more feasible goals. The project expanded to work with schools in Jerusalem and continued conducting its own internal evaluation.

At the same time, I was the internal evaluator for a project in Beer Sheva, the destination of many waves of immigration. One such wave was Operation Solomon, the large emigration from Ethiopia in the late 1980s. The Association for the Advancement of the Ethiopian Family and Child in Israel had developed early childhood and community programs for the Ethiopian immigrants who came to Israel at the end of the 1970s and in the early 1980s. The association readjusted its goals to include the newly arrived population. The challenge of working with this new population was fascinating. Fellow Ethiopians who came in other "operations" spoke a different language and had already adjusted to Israeli life. Programs had to deal with a plethora of unforeseen difficulties such as sense of time, change in family hierarchy, and adaptation to a new culture. On one of my first visits to the caravan parks where the newly arrived immigrants were temporarily housed, I sat on a bench and talked at length to a young girl about 10 years old. During our conversation in broken Hebrew, she kept looking from my polished fingernails to my face and back again. Finally I asked her if something was wrong. She said that in her country, Ethiopia, only prostitutes (using slang she had heard on the street) wore nail polish. Not evaluators! My role as evaluator was to assist the project in defining goals, implementing programs, and following up participant progress.

The projects I have described here illustrate only one aspect of evaluation in Israel. Generally, the Ministries of Education, Labor and Social Services, Health, and Project Renewal sponsor mainstream projects that work across the board with all segments of the population and include standard large-scale evaluations using external evaluators. My professional choice has been to work with small, local projects that consider it part of their goal to address the diversity of the populations they serve. This commitment calls for diversified approaches to problem solving so doors can open and reveal otherwise hidden perceptions of the common reality. It is the role of evaluation to help make sense of such perceptions.

These are the three projects referred to:

1. *Early Childhood Education in Communities in the Negev, Sderot.* Eventually, when financial support ended after the designated time, local institutions and organizations incorporated some of the project's programs.

2. *The Center for Creativity in Education and Cultural Heritage, Jerusalem.* This program is still in operation and is currently being evaluated by Rivanna Miller.

3. *The Association for the Advancement of the Ethiopian Family and Child in Israel, Beer Sheva.* No longer in operation under the same name and auspices.

—Barbara Rosenstein

■ CUT SCORE

The cut, or critical, score is determined by those values in the sampling distribution that represent the beginning of the region of rejection. It is at this point on the distribution that, if the level is exceeded, the null hypothesis is rejected. Cutoff scores also are used in regression discontinuity designs. In this type of design, the experimenter assigns units to condition on the basis of a cut score. The assignment variable can be any measure taken prior to treatment in which the units scoring on one side of the cut score are assigned to the treatment group and those on the other side to the control group.

—*Marco A. Muñoz*

Further Reading

Trochim, W.M.K. (1984). *Research design for program evaluation: The regression-discontinuity approach.* Beverly Hills, CA: Sage.

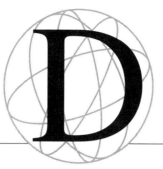

◼ DAHLER-LARSEN, PETER

(b. 1961, Nørre Lyndelse, Denmark). Ph.D. Organizational Studies, M.A. Social Science, M.A. Economics, Odense University (now the University of Southern Denmark).

Dahler-Larsen is Professor, Department of Political Science and Public Management, University of Southern Denmark. He has been a visiting scholar at the Center for Organizational Research at Stanford University and, for 10 years, an evaluation consultant to various international organizations. He currently serves as a board member of the European Evaluation Society.

His primary contribution to the field of evaluation has been in terms of studying evaluation as a cultural and institutional phenomenon, exploring how evaluation is shaped by modern organizations and how evaluative thinking affects cultural practices. His primary intellectual influences in this scholarship include neoinstitutional organizational theory; the phenomenological sociology of Alfred Schutz, Peter Berger, and Thomas Luckmann; and the contemporary macrosociology of Cornelius Castoriadis and Ulrich Beck. His favorite quotation is from Castoriadis: "The ultimate finality of the living creature is enveloped in a dense fog of mystery." He is the author of *At Fremstilling af kvalitative data* (The "making" of qualitative data), *Den rituelle reflection: Om evaluering i organisationer* (The ritual of reflection: On evaluation in organizations), *Social Bonds to City Hall,* and (with H. Krogstrup) *Tendenser i Evaluering* (Trends in evaluation).

◼ DATTA, LOIS-ELLIN

(b. 1932, Paterson, New Jersey). Ph.D. Comparative and Physiological Psychology, M.A. Social Psychology, Bryn Mawr College; M.A. Sociology, B.A. Psychology, West Virginia University.

Datta is president of Datta Analysis, consulting in statistics, evaluation, and policy analysis. She worked for 30 years in Washington, DC, in the U.S. Department of Education as Director of the Teaching and Learning Program and in the U.S. General Accounting Office (GAO) as Director of Program Evaluation in Human Services.

Datta has consistently been interested in mixed methods approaches to evaluation, and her contribution to thoughtful evaluation design is substantial. For example, as Director of the National Evaluation for Head Start (she was responsible for one of the first Head Start contracts), she brought qualitative researchers into Head Start centers to observe individual child development. From her point of view, monomethods often are appropriate for evaluation questions and situations, but many of the evaluations in which she has been involved have used multiple approaches in the quest for both rich understanding and reasonable generalizability. Datta's *Case Study Evaluations* and *The Prospective Evaluation Synthesis,* both published in 1990 by the U.S. GAO, are influential, frequently cited works that have contributed to understandings about the complexity of evaluation and the need for thoughtful design decisions.

The title of Datta's doctoral dissertation, *Maze Learning in the Earthworm, Lumbricus Terrestris,* illustrates the breadth of her knowledge and interests.

A significant influence on her evaluation theory and practice is the discovery of the variety of approaches to learning, from anthropology to physics to zoology. Her undergraduate and graduate research provided the opportunity to explore the theoretical and practical characteristics of learning in these various fields. Her views and work in evaluation have been greatly influenced by the work of Edward Suchman, Don Campbell, Marcia Guttentag, Michael Scriven, Michael Quinn Patton, and Eleanor Chelimsky.

Datta has played a large role in bringing together those interested in doing and studying evaluation. She was instrumental in the merger of the Society for Applied Social Research and the Evaluation Research Society. Also, during her terms as President of the Evaluation Research Society, Datta worked to merge that organization with Evaluation Network (ENet), a merger that occurred in 1986 to form the American Evaluation Association. As editor of *New Directions for Program Evaluation,* Datta promoted an emphasis on multiple perspectives on evaluation methods, both through topics chosen and in grooming Jennifer C. Greene and Gary Henry as the next editors. She is Senior Contributing Editor for *Science Communication.*

A recipient of both the American Evaluation Association's Myrdal Evaluation Practice Award in 1981 and the Robert Ingle Service Award in 1990, Datta retired to Hawaii, where she has served on numerous local boards and committees, including the Hualalai Academy, Girl Scouts, Kona and Waikoloa Outdoor Circles, Kona Krafts, and Hawaii Island United Way; she also served as Chair of the state's Goals 2000 Panel on Assessment. She enjoys spending time with her family, sailing, and growing organic coffee.

DECISION-MAKING MODEL.
See CIPP Model

■■ DECONSTRUCTION

An analytic strategy most closely associated with poststructuralism and postmodernism and popularized by the work of Jacques Derrida, *deconstruction* grew out of the hermeneutic tradition (especially of Heidegger) of analysis of texts and is based on the assumption that language is ambiguous, indeterminant, and replete with taken-for-granted meanings. Deconstruction is the demystification of language by examining what is said, what is not said, what is obscured or hidden, and by considering oppositional positions (often defined as binary opposites such as good-evil, right-wrong, male-female) in their broader context. Take, for example, a common cultural claim, such as "the book is always better than the movie," then consider the claim that Disney's Winnie the Pooh movies are better than the book. Deconstruction would examine this statement in light of the fact that our assessment of A. A. Milne's original Pooh stories is based on Disney's Pooh movies. Research on evaluation may involve deconstruction through examinations of language as a signifier used in an evaluation and for talking about evaluation.

See also Metaphor

DEDUCTION. *See* Inference

■■ DELIBERATIVE DEMOCRATIC EVALUATION

Deliberative democratic evaluation is an approach to evaluation that uses concepts and procedures from democracy to arrive at justifiable evaluative conclusions. It aspires to arrive at unbiased conclusions by considering all relevant interests, values, and perspectives; by engaging in extended dialogue with major stakeholders; and by promoting extensive deliberation about the study's conclusions—in addition to employing traditional evaluation methodologies. Deliberative democratic evaluation aspires to studies that are unbiased (impartial) regarding fact and value claims. Of course, biases can never be fully eliminated, but there are ways of reducing them.

The justification is that evaluation is a societal institution vital to the realization of democratic societies beyond the conduct of studies by individual evaluators. Amid the claims of the mass media, public relations, and advertising, evaluation can be an institution noted for the accuracy and integrity of its claims. To do so, it needs principles to guide its practices. The three principles of deliberative democratic evaluation are inclusion, dialogue, and deliberation.

INCLUSION

The first principle of deliberative democratic evaluation is the inclusion of all relevant interests in the study. It would not be right for evaluators to provide evaluations to only the most powerful or sell them to the highest bidders, thus biasing the evaluation toward some particular interests. It would also not be right to let sponsors revise findings so they could delete parts they did not like or enhance findings with self-serving additions. These are conditions of use that evaluators should not condone.

The basic tenet of democracy is that all legitimate, relevant interests should be included in decisions that affect those interests. This principle separates democracy from other forms of government. When only a few people decide social policy, then an aristocracy, plutocracy, or technocracy exists, depending on whether talent, money, or expertise is the source of authority. Evaluation in democratic societies should be explicitly democratic, and evaluative expertise has an important role to play.

Evaluation studies should aspire to accurate representations of states of affairs, not rhetorical devices for furthering the interests of some over others. The interests of all stakeholders are central, and the interests of all relevant parties should be considered. If relevant interests are not included, we have a biased evaluation in which some voices have been excluded.

Among the main threats to democratic decisions are those of power imbalances. Power imbalances are endemic, and it is easy to see how they can distort evaluations. The powerful may dominate the discussions, or those without power may not be represented. There must be some minimal balance and equality of power for proper deliberation to occur in democracies, and this is true in evaluations as well. Evaluators should design evaluations so that relevant interests are represented and so that there is some balance of power among them, which sometimes may mean representing the interests of those who have been excluded in the discussions, as those interests are most likely to be overlooked. Deliberation should be based on discussion of merits, not on the social status or political power of participants.

Of course, determining and weighing interests is complex. Not all interests have the same moral force. Interests attached to genuine needs are morally weightier. An interest might be defined as anything conducive to the achievement of an agent's wants, needs, or purposes. A need is anything (contingently or absolutely) necessary to the survival or well-being of an agent, whether the agent currently possesses it or not. Satisfaction of a need, in contrast to fulfillment of a want or purpose or desire, cannot ever per se make an individual or group worse off. Needs are associated with a level of urgency or importance not possessed by wants or market preferences. Hence, needs take precedence over mere wants.

DIALOGUE

The second principle of deliberative democratic evaluation is that it be dialogical. Determining interests is particularly difficult because individuals and groups are not always able to determine their own interests when left to their own devices. They can be misled by the media or interest groups "spinning" evidence or by not having opportunities to obtain information.

The real interests of an individual or group are not necessarily the same as perceived interests. Real interests might be defined this way: Policy X is in A's interests. If A were to experience the results of X and Policy Y, A would choose the result of Policy X rather than that of Policy Y. Identifying "real" interests is critical. Choice alone is not necessarily determinative of real interests. It must be choice exercised under the right conditions.

Discovering real interests is a major task of dialogical interaction in evaluation. Evaluators cannot assume automatically that they know what the interests of the various parties are. Perhaps the evaluators are mistaken. It is better to engage participants through dialogues of various kinds to be sure. It may be that through dialogue and deliberation, stakeholders will change their minds as to what their real interests are. After they examine findings and engage in argument and discussions, they may see their interests as different from those with which they began. Participants and evaluators must identify the real issues and even formulate them in many cases. Evaluation findings are emergent from these processes. They are not waiting to be discovered, necessarily, but are forged in the evaluation and the discussions of findings.

Of course, there is a danger here that the evaluators may be unduly influenced through extensive dialogue with various stakeholder groups. Although this threat to impartiality is significant—evaluators might lose their impartiality by identifying too closely with stakeholders—the greater danger is of evaluators not understanding the position, views, and interests of stakeholder groups or of unintentionally misrepresenting those groups in the evaluation. It makes sense to balance some threat to impartiality for the possibility of fully understanding stakeholder positions by engaging in extensive dialogue with stakeholders. Threats to impartiality are also blunted by including all relevant interests in the dialogue. In certain situations, it may be that there is little danger of misunderstanding stakeholder views. Perhaps in product evaluations, evaluators can posit or determine the interests of typical consumers with a minimum of interaction because the context of the study may be precisely defined in advance. For example, perhaps *Consumer Reports* can capture accurately the views of typical consumers through long practice and interaction with its readers, in a sense, presuming what they want.

However, in evaluations of complex programs and policies, understanding stakeholders and their positions is not easy or to be taken for granted. There may be several stakeholders and issues, and the interests of various groups may conflict. The more complex the situation, the more dialogue is needed to sort it out. In this sense, product evaluations are a special case of evaluations rather than the paradigm case. Dialogue is not only desirable but necessary in most cases.

DELIBERATION

The third principle of deliberative democratic evaluation is that it be deliberative. Deliberation is a cognitive process, grounded in reasons, evidence, and valid argument, prominently including the methodological canons of evaluation. In many instances, the expertise of evaluators plays a critical role. By contrast, in some views of democracy, the preferences, values, tastes, and interests of citizens are taken as given, and the point is to find ways to maximize those interests. Evaluators cannot question those preferences. In such views, facts lend themselves to specialist determination, but values are chosen and cannot be dealt with rationally. Hence, the best one can do is to satisfy preferences, regardless of what the preferences are. Such reasoning leads to a conception of democracy in which preferences and values are unexamined.

The deliberative democratic view is one in which values are subject to examination through rational processes, rather than taken as given. Evaluation is a procedure for determining values, which are emergent and transformed through deliberative processes into evaluation findings. Evaluation thus serves a deliberative

democracy in which interests and values are rationally determined. Discussion and determination require the expertise of evaluators acting as experts with special knowledge.

To be sure, evaluation should not take the place of voting and other decision procedures in a democracy. Rather, evaluation produces evaluation findings that can be used in democratic processes. Evaluation informs voting and other authoritative decision procedures in democratic societies; it does not preempt them.

After all, evaluation is linked to the notion of choice: what choices are to be made, who makes choices, and on what basis. Evaluation of public programs, policies, and personnel is based on the notion of collective choice and on some sense of drawing conclusions on the basis of merit. By contrast, one can imagine individuals weighing various factors and arriving at conclusions solely as individuals based on their own personal interests. This is a model of consumer choice, essentially a market model, with many individuals making choices based on available information and in which collective choice is simply the sum of individual choices.

Most evaluations of public programs are not like this. The relevant interests have to be determined as part of the evaluation. Consumer choice, also, is not the same as collective choice derived from collective deliberation. Collective deliberation requires reciprocity of consciousness among participants and a rough equality of power if participants are to reach a state in which they deliberate effectively about their collective ends.

In thinking about the evaluator's authority in these situations, it is useful to distinguish between power and authority. Evaluators should accept roles of authority but not power. For example, A has power over B when A can affect B's behavior contrary to B's interests. By contrast, A has authority over B when B complies because A has influenced B through good reasons attached to B's own interest. Democratic deliberation exists when deliberations are discussions of merit that involve the interests of A and B or their collective interests. Evaluators should have authority in the sense that people are persuaded by the evaluation for good reasons.

The principles of inclusion, dialogue, and deliberation overlap. For example, the quality of deliberation is not separable from the quality of dialogue, which, in turn, affects whether inclusion (as opposed to tokenism) is achieved. In general, the three principles of inclusion, dialogue, and deliberation cannot be completely distinguished from each other. They affect and reinforce each other. If the inclusion and dialogue principles are met but the deliberative principle is not, we might have all relevant interests represented (provisionally) but have them inadequately considered, thus resulting in erroneous conclusions. If the inclusion and deliberative principles are met but the dialogical principle is missing, we might misrepresent interests, resulting in inauthentic evaluations based on false interests and dominated by those with the most power. Finally, if the dialogue and deliberative principles are met but not all stakeholders are included, the evaluation may be biased toward particular interests.

IMPLEMENTATION

Evaluators conduct their studies in the real social world, and deliberative democratic evaluation is too ideal to be implemented fully in the world as it exists. An uncompromising commitment to such an ideal would be impractical. However, because the ideal cannot be fully attained does not mean that it cannot be a guide to practice.

Evaluators should not ignore imbalances of power or pretend that dialogue about evaluation is open when it is not. To do so is to endorse the existing social and power arrangements implicitly. It may be that the existing arrangements are acceptable, but evaluators should consider the issue explicitly. The solution is to face the issue and adopt a position of democratic deliberation as an ideal for handling value claims. In this conception, the evaluator is not a passive bystander, an innocent facilitator, or a philosopher king who makes decisions for others, but rather a conscientious professional who adheres to carefully considered principles for enhancing inclusion, dialogue, and deliberation.

The following 10 questions about evaluation studies reflect the deliberative democratic view.

1. *Whose interests are represented?* The interests of all relevant parties should be considered in the evaluation. Normally, this means the views and interests of all those who have a significant stake in the program or policy under review.

2. *Are major stakeholders represented?* Of course, not every single, individual stakeholder can be involved.

Usually, evaluators must settle for representatives of stakeholder groups, imperfect though this might be. No doubt there are occasions when not all stakeholders can be represented. Representation may mean that evaluators must bring the interests of some stakeholders to the study in their absence.

3. *Are any stakeholders excluded?* Sometimes, important groups will be excluded, and often these will be those groups without power or voice; that is, the poor, powerless, and minorities. It is a task of evaluators to represent these interests as best they can.

4. *Are there serious power imbalances?* When the evaluation is surveyed, it is often the case that particular interests are far too powerful and threaten the impartiality of the findings. Often these are the clients or some powerful stakeholders who dominate the terms of the study or the views represented in the study.

5. *Are there procedures to control the imbalances?* It must fall within the evaluator's purview to control power imbalances. Just as teachers must be responsible for creating conditions for effective discussion in classes, evaluators must establish conditions for successful data collection, dialogue, and deliberation. Admittedly, this requires refined judgment.

6. *How do people participate in the evaluation?* The mode of participation is often critical. Direct involvement is expensive and time consuming. It is also potentially biasing. Still, getting the correct information requires serious participation from stakeholder groups.

7. *How authentic is people's participation?* For example, respondents are used to filling out surveys they care little about. As respondents become swamped with accountability demands, they become careless about their answers. This tendency seems to be a problem, as cosmetic uses of evaluation result in inauthentic findings.

8. *How involved is stakeholder interaction?* Again, although interaction is critical, perhaps there can be too much. Should stakeholders be involved in highly technical data analyses? This could bias the findings. On the other hand, superficial involvement and interaction may be just as bad.

9. *Is there reflective deliberation?* Typically, evaluators finish studies behind schedule, rushing to

meet a deadline. The findings are not mulled over as long as they should be, nor is sufficient deliberation built into the study. There is a temptation to cut short the involvement of others at this stage of the study.

10. *How considered and extended is the deliberation?* In general, the more extensive the deliberation, the better the findings. For the most part, there is not enough deliberation in evaluation. The deliberative democratic view is demanding.

—Ernest R. House

See also PARTICIPATORY EVALUATION,
RESPONSIVE EVALUATION

Further Reading

House, E. R., & Howe, K. R. (1999). *Values in evaluation and social research.* Thousand Oaks, CA: Sage.

House, E. R., & Howe, K. R. (2000, October). *Deliberative democratic evaluation checklist.* Retrieved May 11, 2004, from http://www.wmich.edu/evalctr/checklists/dd_checklist.htm

▓ DELIBERATIVE FORUMS

Deliberative forums consist of facilitated, democratic conversations during evaluative inquiry. Deliberative forums reinforce principles of democratic pluralism by consciously positioning people with different opinions and authority in evaluative discourse. The methodology of the deliberative forum is an instrumental tool for bringing the theory of deliberative democratic evaluation into practice.

Deliberative forums are most useful when crafted into the unfolding dialogue during the design phase of an evaluation; they can be reformulated throughout the inquiry. Differences of perception among evaluation stakeholders are the focus of the deliberative forum. For example, when designing an evaluation for a social service program, the funders of the program might propose examining the frequency of service utilization. The providers of the services might want to examine program processes and operations. The clients of the services might suggest that consumer satisfaction be the primary focus for the evaluation. The deliberative forums provide an opportunity for the diverse stakeholders to talk with one another about their different points of view. By consciously balancing the representation of administrators, program managers, and clients in discussions about the design of the evaluation, the evaluator hopes to create a degree

of mutuality of understanding among the participants. Questions for the evaluation study can then be cocreated so that they are inclusive of the different points of view.

Evaluations that integrate deliberative forums into the inquiry process are attentive to the overt and tacit power distributions surrounding the evaluand. It is assumed that power differentials exist and that there will be degrees of risk associated with deliberations among people who have more authority than others. Attention is granted to weighting the representation of the typically disenfranchised stakeholders in the deliberative forums. The evaluator is careful to craft opportunities that will elicit the inclusion of those with lesser authority into the deliberations. Incorporating deliberative forums into the inquiry process is more successful when the evaluator has established a partnership within an organization that promotes a culture of learning. Evaluators often serve as community builders and educators as they attempt to create safe spaces for dissonance among participants who might be struggling with each other's different points of view.

Evaluators choosing to integrate deliberative forums into their practices tend to be concerned with the role of evaluation as it relates to issues of social justice. Deliberative forums provide opportunities for evaluation participants to widen their awareness of how their circumstances are linked. In creating an equal values exchange among participants of different authority and opinion during evaluative inquiry, deliberative forums offer evaluation participants the opportunity to think together about *what is important to know* and *how to go about the knowing.*

—Cheryl MacNeil

Further Reading

House, E. R., & Howe, K. R. (1999). *Values in evaluation and social research.* Thousand Oaks, CA: Sage.

MacNeil, C. (2000). Surfacing the realpolitik: Democratic evaluation in an anti-democratic climate. In K. Ryan & L. DeStefano (Eds.), Evaluation as a democratic practice: Inclusion, dialogue and deliberation. *New Directions for Evaluation, 85,* 51-62.

▓ DELPHI TECHNIQUE

The *Delphi technique* is a group method used in evaluation to reach consensus for future action. It is a predictive technique (hence the name, which is derived from the ancient Oracle at Delphi) and ascertains the views of a number of experts on a question or questions over several rounds. Answers to the first round are analyzed and categorized, and then a second round of questioning takes place. For example, in an evaluation of training needs, 230 emergency managers around Australia were e-mailed and asked the question, "What training is needed for Emergency Managers like yourselves in the next five years?" Hundreds of varied answers were returned and analyzed so that a list of the top 20 items could be produced. In the second round, the 20 items were listed randomly, and the managers were asked to pick 10 and rank these in order of importance. In this way, consensus was reached about training priorities in the near future.

To undertake the technique it is necessary to follow these steps:

1. Develop a specific question or questions likely to produce a great variety of responses (it is important to note here that participants must be genuinely interested in the questions posed or the approach will not work)

2. Select a sample of potential respondents consisting of any type of stakeholder who has the necessary knowledge to answer the questions (the number of participants in the exercise may be a few or more than 100)

3. Send questions by e-mail or ordinary mail

4. Receive replies

5. Carry out a first round of analysis to draw out categories

6. Send out a second time so participants can see new categories and rank or review them

7. Repeat as necessary until the necessary level of consensus is approached or achieved

Theoretically, there can be any number of rounds, but two or three are usually enough.

Some advantages to this approach include the following:

- The task is focused.
- When e-mail is used, there is usually a very quick turnaround time.

- Participants do not have to come together or be known to one another.
- It can link people who are apart or who are very busy.
- Geographical barriers can be overcome.
- It enables large groups of people to be contacted cheaply.
- Participants remain anonymous to one another.
- All participants have equal status and have a chance to contribute.
- It avoids group pressure.
- There is some time for reflection.
- It generally requires less time than other group techniques.

Disadvantages are that if ordinary mail is used, considerable time is required for surveys to go back and forth between the evaluator and the participants. In addition, participants are not able to discuss issues, so the technique will not produce the depth and rich quotes that, for example, focus groups are able to produce. There is also some debate among evaluators concerning the validity of the method: Some argue that it fails to meet the standards set for other forms of data collection.

—Rosalind Hurworth

Further Reading

Linstone, H. A., & Turoff, M. (1975). *The Delphi method: Techniques and applications.* Reading, MA: Addison-Wesley.

▪▪ DEMOCRATIC EVALUATION

Thirty years have passed since Barry MacDonald published "Evaluation and the Control of Education," in which he set out an ideal classification of evaluation studies in terms of their political assumptions. There were three categories, two of which were based on his knowledge of existing early practices. The first and most prevalent he called "Bureaucratic Evaluation," defined as an unconditional service to government agencies that accepted their values and helped them to accomplish their policy objectives. The second he called "Autocratic Evaluation," defined as a conditional service that offered external validation of policy in exchange for compliance with its recommendations.

But neither of these approaches, the first justified by the reality of power and the second by the responsibility of office, offered a solution to the imminent certainty that the control of education was about to pass out of the hands of professional educators and into those of politicians and civil servants. Although no one could have predicted the extent to which that transfer of power would be accompanied by an intensive project to control the products of government-funded research and evaluation, the signs were ominous enough to provoke MacDonald into fashioning an alternative approach. Here is how he described it in 1974:

> Democratic evaluation is an information service to the whole community about the characteristics of an educational program. Sponsorship of the evaluation study does not in itself confer a special claim upon this service. The democratic evaluator recognizes value pluralism and seeks to represent a range of interests in his issues formulation. The basic value is an informed citizenry, and the evaluator acts as a broker in exchanges of information between groups who want knowledge of each other. [The democratic evaluator's] techniques of data gathering and presentation must be accessible to non-specialist audiences. [The evaluator's] main activity is the collection of definitions of, and reactions to, the program. [The evaluator] offers confidentiality to informants and gives them control over his use of the information they provide. The report is non-recommendatory, and the evaluator has no concept of information misuse. The evaluator engages in periodic negotiation of his relationship with sponsors and program participants. The criterion of success is the range of audiences served. The report aspires to "best-seller" status. The key concepts of democratic evaluation are "confidentiality," "negotiation" and "accessibility." The key justificatory concept is "the right to know."

Clearly, the main issue addressed by this set of propositions is the relationship among power, accountability, and the transmission of knowledge. It could be summed up by the question, "Who gets to know what about whom?" MacDonald's response has several strands. The sine qua non is that the evaluation must be independent of its sponsors, otherwise its credibility will be suspect and its focus confined. Independence should be used to establish rights for those whose activities are under scrutiny, yielding to them some control over how their work is represented. This creates a buffer between the knowledge generated and the knowledge transmitted, with the evaluator in a brokerage role. In this sense, the right to know is tempered by the right to be discrete. Evaluators will always know more than they can tell. What this amounts to is a strategy that builds in checks and balances that go some way toward reducing power differentials between the major players, including the evaluator.

What about the public right to know and the opportunity to judge? This is where the methodological strand comes in. The democratic model demands a reemphasis on aspects from psychometry to literacy, from numbers to narrative, from quantitative to qualitative criteria of judgment. The fundamental issue is the impact of evaluation on the distribution of power, and this may come down to a choice of discourse—a question of language. Evaluators who choose the discourse of technocratic management will empower the managers. Evaluators who choose the language of social science will empower themselves and their sector. Evaluators who choose a widely shared language may empower all of us.

MacDonald (with his colleague Rob Walker) followed up his "control" article with another, "Case Study and the Social Philosophy of Educational Research," in which the "social and ethical inadequacy" of the case study tradition in the social sciences was attacked. Taking democratic evaluation as their starting point, MacDonald and Walker listed a number of issues as a basis for questioning the tradition:

- To the needs and interest of whom does the research respond?
- Who owns the data (the researcher, the subject, the sponsor)?
- What is the status of the researcher's interpretation of events vis-à-vis the interpretations of others? (Who decides who tells the truth?)
- What obligations does the researcher owe to subjects, sponsors, fellow professionals, others?
- For whom is the research intended?

Although MacDonald had, in his previous article, made clear distinctions between evaluation and research, he was well aware that future evaluators were likely to be recruited from the research community, and he hoped to gain support for at least some of the principles of the democratic model. For him, if not for Walker, the most important of the issues listed was also the most contentious—who owns the data? If he could get support for the notion of an ownership shared with informants, this would undermine political claims to official ownership of data. In the event, this proposition, when put to the 1975 assembly of the British Educational Research Association, was met with an uproar of hostility. Nevertheless, the two articles were widely read and triggered a decade-long debate in the research and evaluation community about the ethics and politics of educational investigation.

In those early years of modern ("new wave") evaluation, MacDonald could be seen to play a pivotal role in the development of U.K. theory and practice. Based at the Centre for Applied Research in Education at the University of East Anglia, he assembled a group of evaluation theorists and practitioners with whom he further developed democratic approaches to methodology. CARE, under the Directorship of Lawrence Stenhouse, had become a hotspot for curriculum research and, under John Elliott, for the leadership of the action research movement. These developments, along with that of democratic evaluation, drew from a common educational and political ethic.

The work of CARE paralleled and was articulated by the work of CIRCE at the University of Illinois. Both centers sought to respond to the perceived transnational failure of policy to make a significant impact on the problems and promises of schooling and the growing realization of the limitations of existing methodologies to understand the complexities of change and the contested nature of program ambitions and experiences. One response emanating from CIRCE was Stake's responsive evaluation; one response from CARE was democratic evaluation.

From the early 1970s, CARE attracted sponsorship of its ideas from prominent sources—the Ford and Nuffield Foundations, the English Social Sciences Research Council, and the British government. Concern with policy and methodology failures was widespread, and many were engaged in the search for and sponsorship of alternative ways of understanding change.

One result was a 3-year funding by Ford of a case study evaluation of the medium-term impact of the British curriculum reform movement. This evaluation (titled Success and Failure and Recent Innovation, or SAFARI) produced a book about changing the curriculum, but perhaps more important were two monographs that elaborated thinking and experience around the development of democratic methodologies.

A CASE OF DEMOCRATIC EVALUATION

In December 1972, the first Cambridge Evaluation Conference was convened, drawing together these transatlantic groups of democratic theorists and producing a manifesto for action. It was attended, in an observation capacity, by Richard Hooper, the director of a new U.K.-wide 5-year program in computer-assisted learning. Hooper was looking for an educational evaluator and was drawn to the school case study that MacDonald had brought with him to the conference. This program was unprecedented in many ways. It was funded and managed by seven different government departments, each of them represented on a program committee. They included the three branches of the military and the Department of Trade and Industry. The committee was about 40 strong, with the England and Wales Department of Education in the chair. The program bypassed existing official structures for curriculum reform and development. This was not only the first postwar example of interdepartmental collaboration on such a scale but the first example of direct executive control of educational development. Funding was "categorical" to ensure that the interests of all the participating departments were equitably covered. Stepped funding, no more than 2 years in the first instance, was introduced, achievement being subject to external evaluation. Matched funding was another inclusion, designed to secure installation.

MacDonald's subsequent evaluation bore the title Understanding Computer Assisted Learning. One could hardly imagine a better test for his evolving formulation of democratic evaluation than this, and he framed the evaluation as such, although the implications of his proposal were not entirely clear to the program committee sponsors, as yet unrehearsed in the politics of evaluation. For example, here is his introduction to the proposal:

> The everyday meaning of the word "evaluate" is unambiguous. It means quite simply to judge the worth of something. This is a long established usage, and it is hardly surprising that many people assume that the task of the educational evaluator is to judge the worth of educational program. Some evaluators do, in fact, share that assumption, and a few would even argue that the evaluator has a right to expect that his judgments would be suitably reflected in subsequent policy. But there are others, including the present writer, who believes [sic] that the proper locus of judgments of worth and the responsibility for taking them into account in the determination of policy, lie elsewhere. In a society such as ours, educational power and accountability are widely dispersed, and situational diversity is a significant factor in educational action. It is also quite clear that our society contains

groups and individuals who entertain different, even conflicting, notions of what constitutes educational excellence. The evaluator therefore has many audiences who will bring a variety of perspectives, concerns and values to bear upon his presentations. In a pluralist society, he has no right to use his position to promote his personal values, or to choose which particular educational ideologies he shall regard as legitimate. His job is to identify those who will have to make judgments and decisions about the program, and to lay before them those facts of the case that are recognized by them as relevant to their concerns.

The nuances of this democratic rhetoric were, at that time, with sponsors lacking experience, hard to grasp, and many subsequent interactions with MacDonald and his team produced tensions and surprises. Over the following years of sustained conflict with the program committee, this was the piece to which MacDonald turned to justify his actions. Looking back on these 4 years, this is how he summarized the main issues in contention:

1. They wanted an aims/achievement evaluation. The projects were required to state their objectives. They wanted a focus on whether those objectives were achieved.

We said no—that was unfair. None of the projects would achieve all their objectives. We would portray their efforts to achieve those objectives so that the Committee could judge whether they were engaged in worthwhile activities, given their constraints and opportunities.

2. They wanted us to make recommendations about which projects should be supported, and which terminated.

We said no—it was their task and responsibility to make such judgments, not ours. They would have to read our reports and make up their minds. We are just brokers of information.

3. They wanted us to add to the written reports, to tell them things about the projects we could not put in the reports.

We said no—no secret reporting. Our reports were negotiated with the projects, and not given to the Committee until those people agreed that they were accurate, relevant and fair. We could not add to them.

4. They said the reports were too long and complex for a busy committee to deal with. Could we not summarize them?

We said they were as brief as we could make them and still negotiate them with the people whose work [was] being evaluated. We serve the judgment, not the judge.

5. They said, but we cannot handle all this complexity. Are you saying we should not be making these decisions?

We said, that is for you to say, and for others who read the evaluation report on the work of this Committee.

6. They said, what do you mean, the evaluation of this Committee? We don't want you to evaluate us, just the projects.

We said, we must. It would not be fair only to gather information about the projects. They want to know how you do your work, whether you reach your objectives, whether you are doing a good job.

7. They said, who do you think you are? We are paying you to do as we say.

We said, we are your independent democratic evaluators. Simply because you pay for the evaluation does not mean you have any special claim on its services, or exemption from its focus. You cannot buy such an evaluation, you can only sponsor one. Anyone has the right to raise questions and issues for inclusion on the agenda of the evaluation, and no-one has the right to ask for information without being prepared to give it.

It is not difficult to see how important the preamble was in defending the evaluation's stance in relation to these issues. As for the inclusion of the management within the program case, this was signaled from the start. The very first report to the committee was concerned exclusively with the issues, options, and problems facing the committee, set in the context of government policy. The report took the form of a fictional conversation between two people, using an advocate-adversary model. In fact, the two people were MacDonald and Robert Stake (who was on sabbatical at CARE). The committee was furious, but that fury was directed entirely at the form of the report rather than at its substance or focus, although those may well have been its underlying concern. On another matter, the case study approach to the evaluation of the projects was undoubtedly a success. In a competitive funding environment, applicants have an understandable tendency to promise more than they can realistically deliver. More problematically, proposals are written on the assumption that no one falls ill or has an accident or a divorce or leaves the project for more attractive employment. It is as if the project is cocooned from the everyday realities of social life, which it most certainly is not. "We don't want to know who is sleeping with whom," grumbled one committee member. MacDonald's response was, "How can you make a fair judgment unless you take the unpredictable into account?"

In fact, the first evaluation reports on the progress of the projects were welcomed by the committee as "a refreshing change from the reports we are used to getting." But over time, as more and more projects were launched, their attitude changed, as noted in MacDonald's summary. At the end of the program, over a pint of beer in the nearest pub, one of the committee members, who had been hostile to the evaluation throughout, said to MacDonald, "You know, the last four years have been a better in-service course in evaluation for administrators than anyone could ever have designed."

That was some comfort, but MacDonald was resigned to the certainty that he would never get another commission from a government department for democratic evaluation. A few months later, to his astonishment, he was offered the second of a number of government contracts. When he enquired of an insider why he was chosen, he was told something like this. "There are two contracts, one large and one somewhat smaller. It was decided that you were too big a risk to trust with the large one, but worth the risk with the other. They said your politics were naïve, but professionally, you were capable and could be relied on to deliver. That's important; we have problems with the Treasury about evaluations that have not delivered or have not been delivered on time."

That was in 1978. From then up to his recent retirement, MacDonald was never out of evaluation work—in education and other social services, and in many countries. As to the impact of democratic evaluation on the world of evaluation, it is impossible to say. In recent years, the conjunction of the two words has appeared in many publications, in a number of countries, and in at least one worldwide organization, but whether these outcrops are consistent with Macdonald's interpretation or enhancements of it or, indeed, rhetorical distortions of it is not at this point clear. The test is empirical. More recently, in the context of a debate about evaluation and democracy, Bob Stake asked MacDonald to send him a brief clarification of his approach. MacDonald replied as follows.

1. The purpose of program evaluation is to promote knowledge of the program on the part of those who have the right to know, or the duty to advise, or the obligation to provide, or the power to stipulate. Priority of audiences depends on context and opportunity variables.

2. Democratic evaluation is most appropriate in contexts where there is widespread concern about new developments in the management and control of education (e.g., Thatcher's New Right). It is also appropriate in circumstances where institutions are trying to establish new organizational forms that are less hierarchical, more collective. In these circumstances, highly participative approaches may be appropriate.

3. Promoting knowledge should stop short of advocating courses of action. Our job is to inform debate, not preclude it. Modesty is called for.

4. We see power in action. In most if not all programs we see injustices in how power is exercised. In all the cases I can think of, the misuse of power is detrimental to the realization of the program's stated aims. In drawing attention to malpractices of various kinds, it is difficult to separate democratic values from concerns for program effectiveness.

5. Most of the evaluations I do offer some opportunities to invite significant participants to think again about how they discharge their responsibilities. Evaluation should be educative in intent, and this should be evident in its processes. Micro impact is as important as macro, may be more so.

6. I do not seek confrontation with the powers that be, but challenge is sometimes unavoidable. Mine is a hundred year project, not a quick fix.

—*Barry MacDonald and Saville Kushner*

Further Reading

Simons, H. (1987). *Getting to know schools in a democracy: The politics and process of evaluation.* London: Falmer.

Norris, N. (1990). *Understanding educational evaluation.* London: Kogan Page.

■■ DEMONSTRATION PROJECT

Demonstration projects are designed to explore innovative approaches for the delivery of social assistance programs, build capacity to develop and administer such programs, and identify barriers to effective, efficient delivery. Such projects are often built on the findings of a pilot project, and developers are typically required to develop frameworks to evaluate projects so that the lessons learned from the individual projects can be used in the development of a redesigned social assistance policy framework.

—*Jeffrey G. Tucker*

DENNY, TERRY

(b. 1930, Detroit, Michigan). Ed.D. Educational Psychology, University of Illinois; M.A. Developmental Psychology, University of Michigan; B.A. Political Science and Russian, Wayne State University.

Denny has been a teacher and mentor in the evaluation world for 40 years. He spent 20 years working with Robert Stake, J. Thomas Hastings, and other notables in and near the Center for Instructional Research and Curriculum Evaluation (CIRCE) at the University of Illinois, Urbana-Champaign. Although he wrote about educational evaluation and taught courses in educational evaluation, he claims he never conducted an educational evaluation. He wrote stories and advocated storytelling as a necessary precursor to research and evaluation. His students suffered a strict regimen of gathering stories from the field and learning how to write them.

His message to the evaluation community was a simple one: no story, no evaluation. He thought most educational evaluators did not sufficiently understand the enterprise or the cultural context and because of this, did not know what or how to evaluate properly. He felt similarly about educational research. Denny argued further that even when evaluators and researchers did understand the story, they rarely had the ability to tell it to others. Illustrative of his claim that the story is central to our understanding of what goes on in schooling is his question: "When a parent, teacher, or student wants to learn about the quality of a school in a neighboring district, do they turn to a school board document or a state department report or an evaluation journal? Or do they ask a parent, teacher, or student from that district for their stories about what is going on?"

DESCRIPTION

Description uses ordinary vocabulary to convey deep and rich meanings about people, places, and programs and is a device that is expected particularly in evaluations that use case studies, participant observation, and other qualitative approaches. Description is needed by evaluators to portray what is happening, what a setting looks like, and what the people involved are thinking and doing. Providing such description can help to evoke emotions and to convey implicit values and judgments so that an audience can be persuaded by the arguments presented. It is also important to recognize that description is the basis for more abstract interpretations of

data, and without it, coding, categorization, theory, and hypothesis development could not occur.

—Rosalind Hurworth

DESIGN EFFECTS

Design effects stem from the evaluation itself and confound the study results. Design effects can stem from any aspect of the research process, including the measures selected and their reliability or consistency, the validity of each measure (i.e., its ability to measure what it intends to measure), the relevance of each measure to the program's goals, and the feasibility of using the measures as designed within existing evaluation constraints. Stochastic (chance differences) between treatment and control groups will also produce design effects, as will biased study samples in the treatment or control groups that result from refusals, dropouts, and inaccessibility; nonrandom missing data; and reactivity to being in an evaluation.

—Debra J. Rog

Further Reading

Rossi, P., Lipsey, M., & Freeman, H. (2003). *Evaluation: A systematic approach.* Thousand Oaks, CA: Sage.

DESIGN, EVALUATION

The *design* is the methodological blueprint of an evaluation. It outlines the overall approach and plan for conducting the evaluation. The major elements of an evaluation design include the following:

- The units of analysis that will be involved in the study and how they will be selected. This refers to the participants or entities involved in the evaluation. In program evaluation, the most common unit of analysis is the program participant. For some evaluations, however, the unit may be entities such as states, hospitals, classrooms, and so forth.

- The parameters or aspects of a program that will be evaluated. Will it be all components of a program or selected components (e.g., just the science workshops in the academic series)? Will it be all projects sites or a sample?

- The comparisons needed, if any. Depending on the type of evaluation question being addressed, it may be important to have a basis of comparison for understanding the significance of the results. The comparison could be what occurs in the absence of a program (e.g., services as usual compared to a new mental health intervention), what occurs in an alternative program (e.g., school curriculum A compared to school curriculum B), what occurs prior to the program, and so forth.

- Variables and concepts to be measured, including concrete descriptions of what effectiveness or success would look like, the schedule on which data will be collected, and the methods that will be used to collect the data. Selection of variables and concepts should be guided by the theory underlying the program. Determining the operationalization and measurement of variables is a process that strives to produce data that will be reliable, useful, and valid. Reliable data are those that can be collected consistently across units and over time. Useful data are those that meet the interests and needs of the stakeholders. Data that have high construct validity measure what they are intended to measure.

- Boundaries of the study (time, population, geographic). Decisions on the boundaries of a study affect the generalizability or external validity of the results. In some instances, the research question directs the selection process (e.g., the interest in an education program is on just seniors participating in the program this year, rather than on all high school students in the program over the past 3 years). When an evaluator cannot include all people or entities within a program, all program locations, or all relevant time periods, some form of sampling is typically used. In situations in which the population is small or political considerations are important to take into account (e.g., a nationwide program in which all governors have a vested interest), it may be imperative to the credibility and usefulness of the results to include the entire relevant population, time periods, and geographic areas.

- Level of precision needed to produce useful and credible results. Knowing how precise the results need to be affects the rigor of the design, the sampling strategies chosen, the sample size, and the nature of the data collection methods. For example, how big a difference in the reduction of homelessness is considered practically significant? Is there interest in detecting smaller differences?

Decisions on these design elements are guided by the purpose of the evaluation and the nature of the

primary evaluation questions. Two broad purposes of evaluation include (a) examining the process of a program and its implementation and (b) assessing the outcomes and impact of a program.

For process and implementation evaluations, the designs generally are of a descriptive nature, involving case studies, needs assessments, and surveys. The purpose of a descriptive design is to provide a picture of the program as it occurs. The key design elements for these studies typically include selecting the program parameters; determining the data collection plan, including the key variables to study; and deciding on the boundaries to draw for the study.

For evaluations that are intended to provide information on a program's effectiveness or outcomes, the evaluator has the same design elements to consider as the evaluator designing a process or implementation evaluation, as well as additional concerns about the unit of analysis, the comparisons to be made, and the level of precision of the results. The unit of analysis is generally determined by the level of outcomes the program is intended to affect and is often focused on the program participant. The level of precision of the results is affected by how the units are sampled and the number that is sampled but also by the choice of comparisons.

Experimental and quasiexperimental designs are used in helping to address these considerations. An experimental design tests the effectiveness of a program by randomly assigning the units in a study to the conditions in the study (generally the treatment program and a comparison program or group). Quasiexperimental designs also are intended to estimate a program's effects and attempt to approximate the true experiment by substituting other design features for the randomization process. The features include adding either nonequivalent comparison groups or pre- and posttreatment measurements for the treatment group or both groups. Experimental designs are considered the most rigorous of the outcome designs, as they provide the most control over threats to internal validity (i.e., the extent to which a program's effects can be isolated to the program). Quasiexperiments have greater vulnerability to threats to internal validity but can often be constructed to provide support for causal inferences about the program's effects on the outcomes.

Although the nature of the evaluation questions provides the initial direction for the design, other factors that help to shape it include the resources that are available for the evaluation, feasibility concerns, and the audience and potential uses of the information from the evaluation. Resources include availability of data sources (including extant data such as administrative records); time required to conduct the study; type and number of evaluation personnel needed, including the skills needed (e.g., clinical interviewing skills); and money needed to plan and implement the evaluation. Feasibility concerns include whether the initial approach can be implemented with integrity given the resources available, the current program context, and the greater context in which the program is set. For example, new immigrant laws that focus on undocumented individuals may hamper conducting an evaluation of a health program for indigent workers. Various adjustments to the design elements may be needed to ensure that the design can be implemented. Finally, how the information is likely to be used and by whom also influences the design decisions, such as the level of precision of the data, the variables of interest, and the boundaries of the study, especially decisions about the geographic and population scope of the evaluation. How all these factors (resources, feasibility, and potential uses) are addressed affects the quality and credibility of the data; the strength of the conclusions; and the cost, timeliness, and usefulness of the evaluation.

—*Debra J. Rog*

Further Reading

Hedrick, T. E., Bickman, L., & Rog, D. J. (1993). *Applied research design: A practical approach.* Thousand Oaks, CA: Sage.

Rossi, P. H., Lipsey, M. W., & Freeman, H. E. (2003). *Evaluation: A systematic approach.* Thousand Oaks, CA: Sage.

■■ DEVELOPMENTAL EVALUATION

The purpose of a developmental evaluation is to help develop the intervention or program. In developmental evaluation, evaluators become part of the program design team or an organization's management team. They are not apart from the team or merely reporting to the team but are fully participating in decisions and facilitating discussion about how to evaluate whatever happens. All team members, together, interpret evaluation findings, analyze implications, and apply results to the next stage of development. Evaluators become involved in improving the intervention and use evaluative approaches to facilitate ongoing program, project, product, staff, and organizational development. The evaluator's primary function in the team is to facilitate

and elucidate team discussions by infusing evaluative questions, data, and logic and to support data-based decision making in the developmental process. In this regard, developmental evaluation is analogous to research and development (R&D) units in which the evaluative perspective is internalized in and integrated into the operating unit. In playing the role of developmental evaluator, the evaluator helps make the program's development an R&D activity.

Developmental evaluation changes the role of the evaluator from that of a facilitator of evaluation only, adding to it the tasks of facilitating program or organizational development. There are sound arguments for defining evaluation narrowly to distinguish genuinely evaluative efforts from other kinds of organizational engagement. However, on a comprehensive menu of possible evaluation uses, organizational development is a legitimate use of evaluation processes. What is lost in conceptual clarity and purity with regard to a narrow definition of evaluation that focuses only on judging merit or worth is made up for with a gain in appreciation for evaluation expertise. When evaluation theorists caution against crossing the line from rendering judgments to offering advice, they may underestimate the valuable role evaluators can play in design and program improvement based on cumulative knowledge. Part of the value of an evaluator to a design team is the evaluator's reservoir of knowledge (based on many years of practice and having read a great many evaluation reports) about what kinds of things tend to work and where to anticipate problems. Young and novice evaluators may be well advised to stick fairly close to the data. However, experienced evaluators have typically accumulated a great deal of knowledge and wisdom about what works and what does not work. More generally, as a profession, the field of evaluation has generated a great deal of knowledge about patterns of effectiveness. That knowledge makes evaluators valuable partners in the design process. Crossing that line, however, can reduce independence of judgment. The costs and benefits of such a role change must be openly acknowledged and carefully assessed with primary intended users.

—*Michael Quinn Patton*

Further Reading

Patton, M. Q. (1994). Developmental evaluation. *Evaluation Practice, 15*(3), 311-320.

Patton, M. Q. (1997). *Utilization-focused evaluation.* Thousand Oaks, CA: Sage.

DIALOGUE

Dialogue is the interaction between people with different perspectives and interests who are intent on learning from one another. Dialogue can be conceptualized in a number of ways—as a conversation, a debate, a discussion, a critique, a lesson, and so on. It also presumes a certain respect for others (especially among those who may be different from each other), mutuality, honesty, and the ability to engage in critical thinking. Engaging in dialogue creates the opportunity for new understandings—the focus is on exploring others' and ones' own perspective or viewpoint. There is less agreement about whether dialogue should result in consensus or mutual deep understanding, whether of similarities or differences.

Dialogues can occur between a few or many people, and although they are typically face-to-face interactions, modern technology allows for many other forums for dialogue, such as listservs or online collaborative journaling, as in "blogs" (Web logs).

Dialogue is a key element in a number of approaches to evaluation, including the democratic deliberative, empowerment, participatory, and critical approaches to evaluation. Dialogue in evaluation is intended to promote inclusion and understanding of stakeholders' interests. It is also understood to be an essential step in identifying issues and opportunities within a program, organization, or community that can ultimately lead to a better quality of life.

Successfully incorporating dialogue into evaluation is inextricably linked with stakeholder identification and involvement, which requires sensitivity and planning for the differential power and authority of stakeholder groups. An evaluator cannot assume that stakeholders will always be aware of their interests and able to represent them or that all stakeholders will participate genuinely and respectfully in the dialogue. Some will seek to use authority, intimidation, or charisma to thwart the intentions of the dialogue.

See also DELIBERATIVE DEMOCRATIC EVALUATION, DELIBERATIVE FORUMS

Further Reading

Government Services of Canada. (2001). *Canadian Rural Partnership community dialogue toolkit: Supporting local solutions to local challe*nges. Ottawa, ON: Minister of Public Works and Government Services of Canada. Retrieved May 13, 2004, from http://www.rural.gc.ca/dialogue/ tool/index_ e.phtml

Ryan, K. E., & DeStefano, L. (2000). Disentangling dialogue. In K. E. Ryan & L. DeStefano (Eds.), Evaluation as a democratic process: Promoting inclusion, dialogue, and deliberation. *New Directions for Evaluation, 85,* 63-76.

DIFFERENCE PRINCIPLE

A principle in Rawls' theory of justice-as-fairness that states that social and economic inequalities are to be arranged so they are to the greatest benefit of the least advantaged. Rawls' theory focuses on both liberty (the opportunity for individuals to make choices) and equality, which is the focus of the difference principle. Rawls' principle is based on the premise that people deserve neither their natural abilities nor their place in the social hierarchy, and he contends that it would be unfair to allow distribution of benefits, resources, and so on to be influenced by such factors that are arbitrary from a moral point of view. This is a key principle in Ernest R. House's work on justice and evaluation.

See also SOCIAL JUSTICE

DISCREPANCY EVALUATION

A model or approach to evaluation associated with Malcolm Provus, which had its beginnings in his evaluation of Title I reading programs in Pittsburgh public schools in the late 1960s. This approach is an elaboration of the sometimes more simplistic goals-based evaluation, and it focuses on the gaps between stated objectives and the results from performance measures of those objectives. The value of the discrepancy model of evaluation is that it makes explicit what may otherwise be implied; that is, it clearly and explicitly states what the objectives are, what the expected outcomes are, and measures the distance between the two.

Discrepancy evaluation entails establishing performance standards, collecting evidence of compliance with these standards, identifying discrepancies between standards and actual performance, and taking corrective actions. In most applications and discussions of discrepancy evaluation, the focus is on the formative purpose of evaluation. The steps are as follows:

1. Develop a list of standards that specify the characteristics of ideal implementation of the evaluand.

2. Determine the information required to compare actual implementation with the defined standards.

3. Design methods to obtain the required information.

4. Identify the discrepancies between the standards and the actual learning program.

5. Determine reasons for the discrepancies.

6. Eliminate discrepancies by making changes to the implementation of the learning program.

Discrepancies are determined by examining three program aspects (inputs, processes, outputs) at different stages of program development. Provus identified four such stages: (a) program definition, which focuses on the design and nature of the project, including objectives, students, staff, activities, and so on; (b) program implementation; (c) program process, conceived of as a formative stage in which evaluators serve in a formative role, focusing on the extent to which interim objectives are being achieved; and (d) program product, or the final comparison of outcomes to standards or objectives, noting, of course, any discrepancies.

In general, the discrepancy evaluation model assigns the task of identifying objectives and acceptable performance to program managers or consumers—the evaluator assists in operationalizing the dimensions of the stated objectives and identifying evidence that will satisfy the program managers' needs. The evaluator, therefore, is a facilitator of the client's judgment of the worth of an evaluand.

This model shares much in common with others developed during the late 1960s and early 1970s, such as Stake's countenance model, objectives-based approaches, and Stufflebeam's CIPP model.

See also CIPP MODEL, OBJECTIVES-BASED EVALUATION

Further Reading

Provus, M. (1971). *Discrepancy evaluation.* Berkeley, CA: McCutcheon.

■■ DISENFRANCHISED

Disenfranchised refers to an individual or a group of individuals deprived of political or legal rights or some privilege. Its most common usage is in regard to people who have been deprived of the right to vote because of their status as felons or as possessors of an emotional or cognitive disability. However, the term is also used in a broader sense to describe those who are deprived of, for example, access to

health care, Internet technology, or academic programs that are instructionally and culturally relevant to marginalized groups, such as people with disabilities or members of racial or ethnic minority groups. It is frequently used together with the term *disadvantaged.*

—*Donna M. Mertens*

■■ DISSEMINATION

Dissemination is the process of distributing a specific product; for example, the findings from an evaluation or evaluations. Foundations, government agencies, and corporations often collect the findings of the evaluations of many initiatives and programs as products to be disseminated, such as information about all funded HIV/AIDS programs (see http:// www. themeasurementgroup.com/edc.htm). Dissemination of a program, product, or intervention may also be an evaluand and thus the object of an evaluation.

—*Jeffrey G. Tucker*

See also REPORTING

DISTAL OUTCOMES. *See* OUTCOMES

■■ DOCUMENT ANALYSIS

Document analysis is required to inform all types of evaluation. However, even though document analysis is a common task, only a meager amount of literature has been written about this form of data collection in relation to evaluation.

The analysis of documents is useful to evaluators for a number of reasons:

- Analysis allows the gathering of new facts about a program, to understand why a program is the way it is.
- It is useful for determining the purpose or rationale of a program.
- It may help in determining the major stakeholders involved.
- It can assist in determining the history and other retrospective information about a program (and this may be the only way that such information is available).
- It can help the evaluator to see what data still need to be collected.

The definition of *document* is wide ranging; a document may comprise existing or elicited material and be public or private. For example, one can use existing records, maps, plans, diagrams, minutes of meetings, correspondence, journals, biographies, annual reports, handbooks, guidelines, artifacts, articles, files, policies, legal documents, and prior evaluation reports. On the other hand, it may be appropriate to elicit new diaries, artifacts, records, submissions, and so on.

Most people associate "document" with textual material, but other formats can be useful, such as visual media (including existing or elicited audiotapes, photographs, films, and videotapes) and, most recently, electronic data. Consequently, evaluators are now using e-mail, multimedia, and Internet chat rooms and forums as new forms of documentation to be scrutinized or promoted for evaluation purposes.

The length of time it takes to find and analyze documents can vary from a few hours to (in the case of submissions) a few months. If time and financial resources are limited, documents may have to be sampled.

Advantages of carrying out document analysis include the following:

- The evaluator is provided with information about events prior to an evaluation.
- Document analysis may be superior to interviewing for collecting some kinds of retrospective data. For instance, dates may be more reliable from past records than from personal recall, and often those responsible for instigating a program may no longer be available.
- Documents appear more credible than other forms of data, as there is less evaluator bias in the production of such data.

- Document analysis can save time and money by providing information that would otherwise have to be discovered through original data collection and analysis.
- Documents may be available free or at little cost.
- Documents may be convenient to use.
- Documents are nonreactive.

Documents must, however, be used with caution. Problems can arise because documents can be written to make programs appear better than they are (as in the glossy brochure or company report) and so can be misleading; documents may not be clear or detailed enough; sections may be missing; inappropriate selections may have been made; there may be typographical errors, biases, or outright deception; the documents available may be quite unrepresentative; and there may be confidentiality issues. Other major problems can be associated with inaccurate record keeping, variable quality between program sites, material that is out of date, and time lag if agencies are behind with entries. Particular challenges for analysis also lie in comprehending how and why the documents were produced, determining the degree of accuracy, and understanding internal organizational texts.

Reporting from document analysis can take various forms, ranging from a literature synthesis to graphing the number of articles produced over a certain time period on a particular topic.

—*Rosalind Hurworth*

Further Reading
Caulley, D. (1983). Document analysis in program evaluation. *Evaluation and Program Planning, 6,* 19-29.

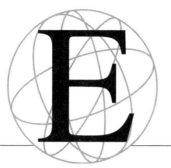

■ EDUCATION, EVALUATION OF

The evaluation of education is a broad domain that encompasses six types of evaluative work: teacher evaluation, a form of personnel evaluation focused on instructors; curriculum evaluation, which examines the effects and effectiveness of specific courses of study; education and training program evaluation, a specialty within the general field of program evaluation; educational context evaluation, which studies the differential effects of educational settings on achievement; student evaluation, which addresses questions of learning and other instructional outcomes; and school accreditation, which measures school functioning against a set of predetermined standards. Educational evaluation takes place in varied arenas, including formal school settings, informal educational settings for students of all ages, and adult learning and training contexts within and outside the workplace. Numerous antecedents exist to current practice in educational evaluation (e.g., the 19th-century work of British royal commissions and Massachusetts educator Horace Mann). Broadly speaking, however, the roots of evaluation of education in the United States may be found in two distinct activities: school accreditation and standardized testing, the use of which expanded during the early decades of the 20th century.

The evaluation of educational programs played a critical role in the development of program evaluation as a field in the United States. First, the celebrated Eight Year Study, directed by Ralph Tyler, led ultimately to the development of Tyler's objectives-oriented approach, which connects educational outcomes with educators' intentions prior to instruction, an approach that dominated the field for many years. Second, the rise of federally funded education programs that both mandated and funded evaluation from the late 1950s to the late 1970s, especially the Elementary and Secondary Education Act of 1965, created an expanded need for evaluation, one that led evaluation practitioners, primarily from university settings, to develop numerous models and approaches.

The evolution of educational evaluation in recent years documents an expanded set of venues (including business and industry and informal settings outside of schools); an increasing awareness of the complexity of teaching and learning; and, simultaneously, an increased sophistication in approaches to documentation. For example, teacher evaluation has moved from examining general characteristics of effective teachers toward explicit attention on the actions of teachers in different contexts that result in valued types of student achievement. Curriculum evaluation has moved beyond so-called curricular horse races—pitting two versions of a curriculum against each other to see which "wins"—and seeks instead to understand the results associated with a given course of study in a given context with specific types of students. Education and training program evaluation has moved beyond a black box, input-output model focusing on objectives to an approach that carefully examines activities, program theory, and outcomes. School accreditation now goes well beyond counting existing resources to supporting data-based school improvement efforts, and the evaluation of student learning has broadened to include alternative ways to measure achievement, including performance assessments. The educational accountability movement and President George W. Bush's proposed national testing requirements for public schools, however, have placed new emphasis on the results of standardized achievement tests.

—*Jean A. King*

EDUCATIONAL EVALUATION AND POLICY ANALYSIS (EEPA)

A house journal of the American Educational Research Association (AERA), *Educational Evaluation and Policy Analysis (EEPA)* publishes articles concerned with issues in the formulation, implementation, and evaluation of education policy. *EEPA* is open to all of the diverse methodologies and theoretical orientations and focuses primarily on policy analysis.

EFFECTIVENESS

Effectiveness is the extent to which an evaluand produces desired or intended outcomes. Effectiveness alone provides a poor assessment of overall evaluand merit or worth: It is possible for something to be "effective" (i.e., produce desirable intended outcomes) but at the same time produce serious detrimental, if unintended, effects. It is also possible for an evaluand to be highly effective but extremely inefficient or overly costly. Claims of effectiveness require the demonstration of a causal link between the evaluand and the desired changes to show that they are, in fact, outcomes caused by the evaluand and are not coincidental changes.

—*Jane Davidson*

EFFICIENCY

Efficiency is the extent to which an evaluand produces outputs and outcomes without wastage of time, effort, money, space, or other resources. Efficiency alone is insufficient to determine merit or worth—an evaluand could be highly efficient but produce outcomes of insufficient value (e.g., too small an effect), or it could still be excessively costly even though it used as few resources as possible (i.e., it exceeded budgetary or time constraints, even in its most efficient form).

—*Jane Davidson*

EISNER, ELLIOT

(b. 1933, Chicago, Illinois). Ph.D. and M.A. Education, University of Chicago; M.S. Art Education, Illinois Institute of Technology; B.A. Art and Education, Roosevelt University.

Eisner is Lee Jacks Professor of Education and Art at Stanford University. He has been a faculty member at the University of Chicago and The Ohio State University and a high school art teacher in Chicago.

Eisner has contributed to the field of evaluation through promoting and furthering arts education and developing the role of artistic thinking in the conduct of social science research. He has influenced the field through his use of the arts in framing educational goals and curriculum development, and he developed the connoisseurship approach for educational evaluation. His seminal work *The Educational Imagination: On the Design and Evaluation of School Programs* made possible a new expert approach to evaluation, one based on the capacity of artistically rendered forms to illuminate complex and subtle educational practices and, as a result, to provide opportunities for more useful evaluation. Eisner's development of educational connoisseurship and educational criticism made way for the articulation of the concept *forms of representation*, through which he illustrated the uses and limits of representation as a form of communication.

He is the author of many publications that have influenced evaluation theory and practice, as well as art education, qualitative research, and curriculum theory, including *The Educational Imagination, The Enlightened Eye, Cognition and Representation,* and *Do American Schools Need Standards?* Eisner is on the advisory board of the J. Paul Getty Center for Education in the Arts and the editorial advisory board of *Kappan* and is the consulting editor of *Curriculum Perspectives.* He is a member of the editorial board of *Critical Inquiry into Curriculum and Instruction* and the editorial advisory board of *Just and Caring Education* and is the former president of the John Dewey Society, the American Educational Research Association, the International Society for Education Through Art, and the National Art Education

Association. Eisner has been awarded five honorary doctorates.

ELECTRONIC SURVEYS

Electronic surveys have revolutionized the way evaluators and researchers collect information. The growth of Internet service providers has made electronic mail communication and the World Wide Web broadly accessible. The ubiquity of desktop and portable computing and Internet connectivity has prompted many evaluators to turn to these communication forms for data collection.

Electronic surveys appear on a computer screen just as they would in hand. Distributed as Web forms on the Internet, a unique location gives all respondents access the survey. Web-based surveys are developed with design tools and can accommodate any range of item types, including dichotomous answer questions (yes-no, true-false), multiple-choice, ranking and scaled response options, and open-ended questions. When the survey is complete, the respondent hits a "submit" button and the raw data are loaded into an active server page for later export or to database software (SPSS, Excel, Access, etc.) for manipulation or analysis. When electronic surveys are distributed as electronic mail messages, the preformatted document is completed and returned by the respondent as an e-mail message, with or without an attachment. In terms of convenience for the respondent and data collection and analysis compatibility for the evaluator, Web-based surveys are preferable.

Currently, vendors can produce Web-based survey software that does not require evaluators to also be Web-page designers. These products range from free Web-based shareware to packages costing several thousand dollars or more (i.e., Perseus, Remark, Questionmark, WebSurveyor, Super Collect). Higher end products have premium features that allow for branching, multisided table questions, and tabular display. Where survey data are heavily used in evaluation and no local expertise is available to develop customized software, some evaluation groups have made useful investments in Web-based survey software.

Key advantages to the use of electronic surveys include ease of survey editing and analysis, faster transmission and response time, and higher response rates. With an identifiable survey sample or parameter, tracking and follow-up is easier and less expensive.

Research has also shown that electronic survey respondents may answer more candidly and provide more detailed responses to open-ended questions than respondents in paper surveys or interviews. There is some concern that due to the open nature of most online networks, it is difficult to guarantee the confidentiality of electronic surveys. However, many information assurance and security features make electronic surveying more reliable than postal mail surveying.

Respondents are limited to those with computer and online network access. This is especially problematic when working with low socioeconomic status or international populations. Also, constructing the format of a computer questionnaire can be difficult, leaving some evaluators to wish they had computer programming experience. Electronic surveys also usually require more respondent instruction and orientation.

Some electronic surveys, depending on system operation (server versus client based) can be very difficult to navigate. For example, a respondent may not be able to log off and then back on with answers intact. Using the back button on the toolbar or changing a previous answer may wipe out all previous answers. Occasionally, the print capability of electronic surveys may not function. As it is with technology in general, it is true with electronic surveys that there is a greater likelihood of glitches than with oral or written forms of communication.

—*Mark Hawkes*

ELEMENTARY AND SECONDARY EDUCATION ACT (ESEA)

ESEA was passed in 1965 and replaced the previous National Defense Education Act as the federal legislation that authorizes expenditures for elementary and secondary schools. This legislation was at the center of Lyndon Johnson's Great Society programs and was targeted specifically at providing educational opportunity to economically disadvantaged children, with Title I being the cornerstone of the legislation. It is worth noting that ESEA was passed at a time when pressure from counterculture groups was high (especially concerning the War in Vietnam), and the legislation reflected this cultural context of populist democracy. ESEA was reauthorized about every

5 years, each time being amended and broadened in scope. Over time, ESEA was elaborated to expand target populations and topics and include bilingual education, migrant education, American Indian education, native Hawaiians, native Alaskans, neglected and delinquent youth, education in corrections facilities, technology, math and science, libraries and media, violence prevention, safe and drug-free schools, Even Start, women's equity, magnet schools, foreign language in elementary schools, the gifted and talented, arts education, charter schools, education improvement activities (from training to innovation grants to model demonstration grants to higher education), midnight basketball, gun-free schools, tobacco smoke–free environments, and provisions for everything from improving materials and textbooks to maintenance and construction of school buildings.

One of the provisions of ESEA, an amendment demanded by Senator Robert Kennedy, was evaluation of Title I programs, and with this legislation the opportunity for large-scale, well-funded educational evaluation expanded dramatically. In many cases, local educators were underprepared to conduct the evaluations demanded by ESEA, and the demand for evaluation expertise was a direct impetus for the development of many extant models of evaluation. For example, The Ohio State University Evaluation Center staff, in collaboration with the Columbus, Ohio, public school district, developed the original version of the CIPP model to meet the evaluation demands of ESEA.

In 2001, ESEA was reauthorized as the No Child Left Behind Act (NCLB), and its federal reach into local education dramatically expanded.

See also NO CHILD LEFT BEHIND

Further Reading

McLaughlin, M. W. (1975). *Evaluation and reform: The Elementary and Secondary Education Act of 1965.* Cambridge, MA: Ballinger.

■ EMERGENT DESIGN

The term *emergent design* is particularly associated with qualitative, inductive approaches to evaluation and so occurs frequently when participant observation or case study methods are used. It means that during fieldwork, the original evaluation plan may need to be adjusted or altered considerably. For example, one may have to change the number of program sites to be examined, introduce extra data collection methods, reduce the number of interviews, or increase the number of evaluators. Such actions may be required to be responsive to unanticipated positive or negative circumstances. This contrasts with deductive, hypothesis-driven evaluations in which the design is worked out in advance and does not change for the duration of the evaluation.

—*Rosalind Hurworth*

■ EMIC PERSPECTIVE

An *emic perspective* is the insider's or native's perspective of reality. It is at the heart of good ethnographic research. Native perceptions may not conform to an "objective" reality, but they help the fieldworker understand why members of the social group do what they do. In contrast to a priori assumptions about how systems work from a simple, linear, logical perspective—which might be completely off target—ethnography typically takes a phenomenological approach to research. An emic perspective compels the recognition of multiple realities. Documenting multiple perspectives of reality in a given study is crucial to an understanding of why people think and act in different ways.

—*David M. Fetterman*

■ EMPIRICISM

Empiricism is an epistemological position that acknowledges only sensory knowledge as legitimate and can be contrasted with rationality, in which knowledge is based on reasoning and idealism, and the mind, rather than the senses, is the legitimate source of knowledge. The modern conception of empiricism, which dominates social science research, holds that experiments and observation are superior to reasoning and reflection. All evaluation is empirical in the sense that evaluation includes information about experiences, but in general, evaluation does not fall within the dominant view of empiricism in the social sciences. This is so because empiricism rejects much of the data used in making evaluative judgments and in doing evaluations, namely unobservable processes, beliefs, needs, and wants that can be inferred through observation but cannot be directly observed.

EMPOWERMENT EVALUATION

Empowerment evaluation is the use of evaluation concepts, techniques, and findings to foster improvement and self-determination. It is guided by a commitment to truth and honesty. It is designed to help people help themselves and improve their programs using a form of self-evaluation and reflection. Program participants—including clients, consumers, and staff members—conduct their own evaluations; an outside evaluator often serves as a coach or additional facilitator, depending on internal program capabilities. Internalizing and institutionalizing self-evaluation processes and practices can develop a dynamic and responsive approach to evaluation.

There are three steps involved in helping others learn to evaluate their own programs: (a) developing a mission, vision, or unifying purpose; (b) taking stock, or determining where the program stands, including strengths and weaknesses; and (c) planning for the future by establishing goals and helping participants determine their own strategies to accomplish program goals and objectives. In addition, empowerment evaluators help program staff members and participants determine the type of evidence required to document and monitor progress credibly toward their goals. These steps, combined, help to create a *communicative space* to facilitate emancipatory and communicative *action*.

MISSION

The first step in an empowerment evaluation is to ask program staff members and participants to define their mission. This step can be accomplished in a few hours. An empowerment evaluator facilitates an open session with as many staff members and participants as possible.

Participants are asked to generate key phrases that capture the mission of the program or project. This is done even when an existing mission statement exists, because there are typically many new participants, and the initial document may or may not have been generated in a democratic, open forum. Proceeding in this fashion allows fresh new ideas to become a part of the mission; it also allows participants an opportunity to voice their vision of the program. During this process, it is common for groups to learn how divergent their participants' views are about the program, even when they have been working together for years. The evaluator records these phrases, typically on a poster sheet.

A workshop participant is then asked to volunteer to write these telescopic phrases into a paragraph or two. This document is shared with the group, revisions and corrections are made in the process, and the group is then asked to accept the document on a consensus basis: that is, they do not have to be in favor of 100% of the document; they just have to be willing to live with it. This mission statement represents the values of the group and, as such, represents the foundation for the next step, taking stock.

TAKING STOCK

The second step in an empowerment evaluation is taking stock. This step can also be conducted in a few hours, and it has two sections. The first involves generating a list of key activities that are crucial to the functioning of the program. Once again, the empowerment evaluator serves as a facilitator, asking program staff members and participants to list the most significant features and activities associated with the program. A list of 10 to 20 activities is sufficient. After generating this list, it is time to prioritize and determine which are the most important activities meriting evaluation at this time.

One tool used to minimize the time associated with prioritizing activities involves voting with dots. The empowerment evaluator gives each participant five dot stickers and asks the participants to place them by the activity on which the participant wants to focus. The participant can distribute them across five different activities or place all five on one activity. Counting the dots easily identifies the top 10 activities. The 10 activities with the most dots become the prioritized list of activities meriting evaluation at that time (see Figure 1 for an example). (This process avoids long arguments about why one activity is valued more than another when both activities are included in the list of the top 10 program activities anyway.)

The second phase of taking stock involves rating the activities (see Figure 2 for an example). Program staff members and participants are asked to rate how well they are doing concerning each activity on a 1 to 10 scale, with 10 as the highest level and 1 as the lowest. The staff members and participants have only minimal definitions of the components or activities at

Taking Stock
Part I

- List activities
- Prioritize (dots)

Activities	Prioritization With Dots
Communication	● ● ● ●
Product development	● ● ● ● ● ● ● ●
Fundraising	● ● ● ● ● ●

Figure 1   *Taking Stock, Part 1*

this point. Additional clarification can be pursued as needed; however, detailed definition and clarification become a significant part of the later dialogue process. (The group will never reach the rating stage if each activity is perfectly defined at this point. The rating process then sets the stage for dialogue, clarification, and communication.)

Typically, participants rate each of the activities as they are in their seats, using their own piece of paper. They are then asked to come up to the front of the room and record their ratings on a sheet of poster paper. This allows for some degree of independence in rating. In addition, it minimizes a long stream of second guessing and checking to see how others are rating the same activities.

At the same time, there is nothing confidential about the process. Program staff members and participants place their initials at the top of the matrix and then record their ratings for each activity. Contrary to most research designs, this system is designed to ensure that everyone knows and is influenced by everyone else's ratings (*after* they are recorded on the poster sheet). This is part of the socialization process that takes place in an empowerment evaluation, opening up the discussion and stepping toward more open disclosure–speaking one's truth.

The taking-stock phase of an empowerment evaluation is conducted in an open setting for three reasons: (a) it creates a democratic flow and exchange of information, (b) it makes it more difficult for managers to retaliate because it is in an open forum, and (c) it

increases the probability that the disclosures will be diplomatic because program staff members and participants must remain in that environment. Open discussions in a vacuum, without regard for workplace norms, are not productive. They are often unrealistic and can be counterproductive.

Staff members and participants are more likely to give their program a higher rating if they are asked to give only an overall or gestalt rating about the program. Consequently, it is important that program staff members and participants be asked to begin by assessing individual program activities. They are more likely to give some activities low ratings if they are given an equal opportunity to speak positively about, or rate, other activities highly. The ratings can be totaled and averaged by person and by activity. This provides some insight into routinely optimistic and pessimistic participants. It allows participants to see where they stand in relation to their peers, which helps them calibrate their own assessments in the future. The more important rating, of course, is across the matrix or spreadsheet by activity. Each activity receives a total and average. Combining the individual activity averages generates a total program rating that is often lower than an external assessment rating. This represents the first baseline data concerning that specific program activity. These data can be used to compare change over time.

All of this work sets the tone for one of the most important parts of the empowerment evaluation process: dialogue. The empowerment evaluator facilitates a discussion about the ratings. A survey would have accomplished the same task up to this point. However, the facilitator probes and asks why one person rated communication a 6, whereas two others rated it a 3 on the matrix. Participants are asked to explain their rating and provide evidence or documentation to support the rating. This plants the seeds for the next stage of empowerment evaluation, planning for the future, during which they will need to specify the evidence they plan to use to document that their activities are helping them accomplish their goals. The empowerment evaluator serves as a critical friend during this stage, facilitating discussion and making sure everyone is heard, and at the same time being critical and asking, "What do you mean by that?" or asking for additional clarification and substantiation about a particular rating or viewpoint.

Participants are asked for both the positive and negative basis for their ratings. For example, if they give communication a 3, they are asked why. The typical response is because there is poor communication, and they proceed to list reasons for this problem. The empowerment evaluator listens and helps record the information and then asks the question again, focusing on why it was a 3 instead of a 1. In other words, there must be something positive to report as well. An important part of empowerment evaluation involves building on strengths; even in weak areas, there is typically something positive that can be used to strengthen that activity or other activities. If the effort becomes exclusively problem focused, all participants see are difficulties instead of strengths and opportunities to build and improve on practice.

Some participants give their programs or specific activities unrealistically high ratings. The absence of appropriate documentation, peer ratings, and a reminder about the realities of their environment—such as a high drop-out rate, students bringing guns to school, and racial violence in a high school—help participants recalibrate their ratings. Participants are reminded that they can change their ratings throughout the dialogue and exchange stage of the workshop, based on what they hear and learn from their peers. The ratings are not carved in stone. However, in some cases, ratings stay higher than peers consider appropriate. The significance of this process, however, is not the actual rating so much as it is, as noted earlier, the creation of a baseline from which future progress can be measured. In addition, the process sensitizes program participants to the necessity of collecting data to support assessments or appraisals.

After examining four or five examples, beginning with divergent and ending with similar ratings (to determine if there are totally different reasons for the same or similar ratings), this phase of the workshop is generally complete. The group, or a designated subcommittee, continues to discuss the ratings, and the group is asked to return to the next workshop (planning for the future) with the final ratings and a brief description or explanation of what the ratings mean. (This is normally shared with the group for review, at a time in which ratings can still be changed, and then a consensus is sought concerning the document.) This process is superior to surveys because it generally has a higher response rate—close to 100%, depending on how many staff members and participants are present—and it allows participants to discuss what they meant by their ratings and to recalibrate and revise their ratings based on what they learn, thus minimizing "talking past each other" about certain issues or other miscommunications, such as defining terms differently and using radically different rating systems. Participants learn what a 3 and an

Taking Stock Part II

- Rating 1 (low) 10 (high)
- Dialogue

Activities	[Initials of Participant]	[Initials of Participant]	[Initials of Participant]	Average
Communication	3	6	3	4.00
Teaching	4	5	9	6.00
Funding	5	2	1	2.67
Product development	1	8	4	4.33
Average	3.25	5.25	4.25	4.25

Figure 2   *Taking Stock, Part II*

8 mean to individuals in the group in the process of discussing and arguing about these ratings. This is a form of norming, helping create shared meanings and interpretations within a group.

PLANNING FOR THE FUTURE

After rating their program's performance and providing documentation to support that rating, program participants are asked, "Where do you want to go from here?" They are asked how they would like to improve on what they do well and not so well. The empowerment evaluator asks the group to use the taking-stock list of activities as the basis for their plans for the future so that their mission guides their taking-stock phase and the results of their taking stock shape their planning for the future. This creates a thread of coherence and an audit trail for each step of their evaluation and action plans.

Goals

Program staff members and participants are asked to list their goals based on the results of their taking-stock exercise. They set specific goals associated with each activity. The empowerment evaluator then asks members of the group for strategies to accomplish each goal. They are also asked to generate forms of evidence to monitor progress toward specified goals. Program staff members and participants supply all of this information.

Empowerment evaluators are not superior or inferior in this process. They are equals. They add ideas, as deemed appropriate, without dominating discussions. Their primary role is to serve as coach, facilitator, and critical evaluative friend. Empowerment evaluators must be able to serve as facilitators, helping program members and participants process and be heard. Evaluators must also be analytical and critical, asking or prompting participants to clarify, document, and evaluate what they are doing, to ensure that specific goals are achieved. If evaluators are only critical and analytical, the group will walk away from the endeavor. Empowerment evaluators must maintain a balance of these talents or team up with other coaches from within the group or outside the group who can help them maintain this balance.

The selected goals should be established in conjunction with supervisors and clients to ensure relevance from both perspectives. In addition, goals should be realistic, taking into consideration such factors as initial conditions, motivation, resources, and program dynamics. They should also take into consideration external standards, such as accreditation agency standards, a superintendent's 5-year plan, board of trustee dictates, board standards, and so on.

In addition, it is important that goals be related to the program's activities, talents, resources, and scope of capability. One problem with traditional external evaluation is that programs have been given grandiose goals or long-term goals that participants could only contribute to in some indirect manner. There is no link between an individual's daily activities and ultimate long-term program outcomes in terms of these goals. In empowerment evaluation, program participants are encouraged to select intermediate goals that are directly linked to their daily activities. These activities can then be linked to larger, more diffuse goals, creating a clear chain of reasoning and outcomes.

Program participants are encouraged to be creative in establishing their goals. A brainstorming approach is often used to generate a new set of goals. In such a process, individuals are asked to state what they think the program should be doing. The list generated from this activity is refined, reduced, and made realistic after the brainstorming phase, through a critical review and consensual agreement process.

There is a bewildering number of goals to strive for at any given time. As a group begins to establish goals based on this initial review of their program, it realizes quickly that a consensus is required to determine the most significant issues on which to focus. These are chosen according to (a) significance to the operation of the program, such as teaching in an educational setting; (b) timing or urgency, such as recruitment or budget issues; and (c) vision, including community building and learning processes.

Goal setting can be a slow process when program participants have a heavy work schedule. Sensitivity to the pacing of this effort is essential. Additional tasks of any kind and for any purpose may be perceived as simply another burden when everyone is fighting to keep their heads above water. However, individuals interested in specific goals should be asked to volunteer to be responsible for them, possibly as team leaders, to ensure follow-through and internal accountability.

Developing Strategies

Program participants are also responsible for selecting and developing strategies with which to accomplish program objectives. The same process of brainstorming, critical review, and consensual agreement is used to establish a set of strategies that is routinely reviewed to determine effectiveness and appropriateness. Determining appropriate strategies in consultation with sponsors and clients is an essential part of the empowering process. Program participants are typically the most knowledgeable about their own jobs, and this approach acknowledges and uses that expertise—and in the process, puts them back in the driver's seat.

Documenting Progress

Program staff members and participants are asked what type of documentation or evidence is required to monitor progress toward their goals. This is a critical step. Each form of documentation is scrutinized for relevance to avoid devoting time to collecting information that will not be useful or pertinent. Program participants are asked to explain how a given form of documentation is related to specific program goals. This review process is difficult and time consuming but prevents wasted time and disillusionment at the end of the process. In addition, documentation must be credible and rigorous if it is to withstand the criticism that this evaluation is self-serving.

The entire process of establishing a mission, taking stock, and planning for the future creates an implicit logic model or program theory, demonstrating that there is nothing as practical as a good theory of action, especially one grounded in participants' own experiences.

—*David M. Fetterman*

Further Reading

Connell, J. P., Kubisch, A. C., Schorr, L. B., & Weiss, C. H. (Eds.). (1995). *New approaches to evaluating community initiatives: Concepts, methods, and contexts.* Washington, DC: Aspen Institute.

Dugan, M. (1996). Participatory and empowerment evaluation: Lessons learned in training and technical assistance. In D. M. Fetterman, S. Kaftarian, & A. Wandersman (Eds.), *Empowerment evaluation: Knowledge and tools for self-assessment and accountability.* Thousand Oaks, CA: Sage.

Fetterman, D. M. (1993). *Speaking the language of power: Communication, collaboration, and advocacy.* London: Falmer.

Fetterman, D. M. (1994). Steps of empowerment evaluation: From California to Cape Town. *Evaluation and Program Planning, 17*(3), 305-313.

Fetterman, D. M. (1998). Empowerment evaluation and accreditation in higher education. In E. Chelimsky & W. Shadish (Eds.), *Evaluation for the 21st century: A handbook.* Thousand Oaks, CA: Sage.

Fetterman, D. M., Kaftarian, S., & Wandersman, A. (Eds.). (2001). *Empowerment evaluation: Knowledge and tools for self-assessment and accountability.* Thousand Oaks, CA: Sage.

Patton, M. (1997). Toward distinguishing empowerment evaluation and placing it in a larger context. *Evaluation Practice, 18*(2), 147-163. Retrieved May 14, 2004, from http://www.stanford.edu/~davidf/patton.html

Vanderplaat, M. (1995). Beyond technique: Issues in evaluating for empowerment. *Evaluation, 1*(1): 81-96.

■ ENGLE, MOLLY

(b. 1947, Fort Leavenworth, Kansas). Ph.D. Program Evaluation/Research Design, M.S. Psychiatric-Mental Health Nursing, B.S.N., University of Arizona.

Engle is Associate Professor, Department of Public Health, College of Health and Human Sciences, Oregon State University, Corvallis. She is also Evaluation and Grant Specialist, Extension Staff Development, Oregon State University. Previously, she held faculty and research and evaluation positions at the University of Alabama School of Medicine in Birmingham.

Her interest in the field of evaluation focuses on the role and scope that evaluation training has both nationally and internationally. Her work in this area is highlighted in Volume 62 of *New Directions for Program Evaluation,* "The Preparation of Professional Evaluators: Issues, Perspectives, and Programs." She has produced and directed more than a dozen informational

and prevention-oriented videotapes for Medical Television, such as *Preventing Falls and Other Injuries in the Elderly; No Easy Answers: Ethical Dilemmas in Health Care for the Elderly;* and *Substance Abuse and the Pregnant Woman: A Series.* She is also interested in the impact on and connection of evaluative thinking to systems thinking. Her work has been influenced by Phyllis Adele Germann, Keith Meredith, Sarah Dinham, Ruth Krall, Yvonna Lincoln, and Jennifer Greene.

She is a member of several organizations, including the American Evaluation Association, the American Society on Aging, and the Society for Prevention Research. She has served on numerous committees for the American Evaluation Association and has been President (2001-2003) and Board Member (1992 1994). She is also listed in *Who's Who of American Women* (2002-2003).

■ EPISTEMOLOGY

Epistemology is one of the core areas of philosophy (along with metaphysics and ethics) and is concerned with the nature, sources, and limits of knowledge. There is a vast array of views on those topics, but a central question in epistemology is: What constitutes knowledge?

Further Reading

Klein, P. D. (1998). Epistemology. In E. Craig (Ed.), *Routledge encyclopedia of philosophy.* London: Routledge.

EPP. See EVALUATION AND PROGRAM PLANNING

■ EQUITY

In assessment, *equity* refers to issues of test score interpretation (*test bias*) and test use (*test fairness*) for specific groups. Examples include differential reliability of tests across specified groups, differential item functioning, and inequality of the predictive utility of tests across age, gender, and disability, and racial, ethnic, cultural, and linguistic groups. In program evaluation, equity applies to the balanced focus and equality of treatment of all stakeholders. It may also relate to values such as respect for individuals' self-worth, dignity, and security during the evaluation process and the differences among stakeholders that are based in race, ethnicity, culture, gender, disability, religion, and sexual orientation.

—*Charles L. Thomas*

Further Reading

Rogers, T. B. (1995). *The psychological testing enterprise: An introduction.* Pacific Grove, CA: Brooks/Cole.

Shadish, W. R., Newman, D. L., Scheirer, M. A., & Wye, C. (Eds.). (1995). Guiding principles for evaluators. *New Directions for Program Evaluation, 66,* 24-26.

ERIC CLEARINGHOUSE ON ASSESSMENT AND EVALUATION

Housed at the University of Maryland, the ERIC Clearinghouse on Assessment and Evaluation is one of 16 subject-oriented clearinghouses operated by the U.S. Department of Education, Office of Educational Research and Improvement. Since its inception in 1966, the Educational Resources Information Center (ERIC) has become one of the major bibliographic databases in the world. ERIC has acquired, reviewed, and processed more than one million citations that policy makers, program planners, researchers, and other users can readily identify and obtain. ERIC as a system is now widely recognized as the central source in the education and social science fields. The Clearinghouse on Assessment and Evaluation collects information of particular interest to evaluation practitioners and researchers.

ERRORS OF MEASUREMENT

Evaluators using instruments such as questionnaires and tests should recognize that scores on measures in the affective and cognitive domains are assumed to have errors of measurement. A person's obtained score (e.g., 52 on an algebra test) is likely to be higher or lower than the person's true score (e.g., 55.25). The higher the reliability of an instrument, the closer the obtained score will be to the true score. Highly reliable instruments have a relatively low standard error of measurement, which is a mathematical index of both the reliability and the size of measurement error.

—*Joseph M. Petrosko*

Further Reading

Nunnally, J. C., & Bernstein, I. H. (1994). *Psychometric theory* (3rd ed.). New York: McGraw-Hill.

ETHICAL AGREEMENTS

One difference between evaluators and researchers is that evaluators are hired by clients. Many clients are new to evaluation or may have inappropriate views of the evaluator's role and the nature of evaluation work. For this reason and many others, the evaluator-client relationship is fraught with potential ethical conflicts.

The Program Evaluation Standards and the *Guiding Principles for Evaluators* both speak to agreements between clients and evaluators. The standards give particular attention to formal agreements. In practice, however, evaluation contracts often focus on the evaluation plan and budget. Written agreements specifying the roles and responsibilities of the evaluator, the client, and other stakeholders can be useful in clarifying expectations and avoiding some, though certainly not all, future ethical dilemmas.

Ethical agreements may address the responsibilities of the evaluator; the roles of clients, program staff and participants, and other stakeholders; methodological issues; and interpretation and use of results. Many evaluators choose to share the *Guiding Principles* or *Program Evaluation Standards* with clients to educate them about evaluators' ethical obligations. Although the specific content of ethical agreements will differ with the nature of the evaluation, a few common areas will be discussed here.

Evaluators are ethically bound to include different stakeholders and to consider the public interest. Clients new to evaluation may consider themselves to be the sole audience for the study and may be unaware of evaluators' broader obligations. Although evaluators' actions in regard to the public good may be difficult to anticipate, the role of the client and other stakeholder groups at each stage of the evaluation can be delineated as a first step in raising the client's awareness of the evaluator's active role in involving other groups.

The collection and management of data have important ethical implications. The evaluator and client must agree on the use of informed consent and confidentiality and the means for maintaining promised confidentiality. Who will manage, store, and keep the data? Under what circumstances, if any, will the client and other stakeholders be provided access to raw data? How will confidentiality of these data be maintained?

The interpretation and reporting of results is another thorny area. In many cases, evaluators seek input from clients and other stakeholders on draft reports, but the final report is the evaluator's domain. Evaluators have responsibilities for ensuring that results are disseminated in appropriate ways to different stakeholders. Who will write or present results to various audiences? What role will clients and stakeholders have in presenting and disseminating results? In making choices about the information presented to each audience?

Written agreements cannot incorporate all potential ethical conflicts because al possibilities cannot be foreseen at the time the agreement is written. Contractualism, or blindly following the contract, can also lead to ethical mistakes. Nevertheless, the evaluator has a responsibility to educate clients about ethical issues that arise in evaluation and about the evaluator's ethical obligations. Ethical agreements provide the means for opening this discussion and clarifying responsibilities so that the rights of the client, program participants, other stakeholders, and the public, as well as the integrity of the evaluation, are preserved.

—*Jody L. Fitzpatrick*

Further Reading

House, E. R., & Care, N. (1979). Fair evaluation agreement. *Educational Theory, 29,* 159-169.

Joint Committee on Standards for Educational Evaluation. (1994). *The program evaluation standards* (2nd ed.). Thousand Oaks, CA: Sage.

▊▊ ETHICS

At a general level, the domain of *ethics* deals with issues of moral duty and obligation, involving actions that are subject to being judged as good or bad, right or wrong. It is not surprising that the nature of evaluation generates many circumstances in which practitioners, in the course of their work, can encounter challenges, conflicts, or dilemmas that are deemed to be ethical. As is the case in other professions, various groups of evaluators have developed standards and guidelines to provide guidance to practitioners in preventing or coping with ethical problems. *The Program Evaluation Standards* and the *Guiding Principles for Evaluators* are the two most well known of these efforts.

THE LENS OF ETHICS

Although research indicates that most evaluators report that they have faced ethical conflicts in their careers, a significant minority of evaluators maintains that they have not. In part, this latter finding appears to be due to differences among evaluators in how they categorize similar or identical events. What one evaluator may view as an ethical challenge, another may see as "simply" a political, philosophical, or methodological dispute. For example, Evaluator A might believe that an evaluator who fails to thoroughly involve stakeholders in designing and monitoring an evaluation is behaving unethically. Evaluator B might regard this neglect of stakeholder involvement as methodologically or philosophically regrettable, but not as morally blameworthy. Thus Evaluator A perceives the situation through an ethical lens, but Evaluator B does not.

The factors responsible for these differences in perspective are not well understood. There is research evidence suggesting that internal evaluators are less likely than external evaluators to see problems through an ethical lens. This may be due to role pressures that internal evaluators experience as members of the setting they are evaluating, pressures that can lead to co-optation and decreased ethical sensitivity. In this context, it is important to note that viewing a situation in ethical terms typically raises issues of personal responsibility and accountability for the perceiver. The perceiver often feels compelled to take action of some sort, an action that may put him or her at professional or personal risk. Thus, in many circumstances, the perceiver may have much to gain from not viewing a problem through an ethical lens. This is a fertile area for future research.

THE NATURE OF ETHICAL CHALLENGES

Ethical conflicts can arise during any stage of an evaluation: entry or contracting, design of the study, data collection, data analysis and interpretation, communication of findings, and utilization of findings. According to evaluators' self-reports, ethical difficulties are most likely to arise in the entry or contracting stage and toward the end of the evaluation (i.e., communication and utilization of results). The following challenges are the ones most frequently described for the entry or contracting stage:

- A stakeholder has already decided what the evaluation findings "should be" or plans to use the findings in an ethically questionable fashion.
- A stakeholder declares certain research questions off limits in the evaluation, despite their substantive relevance.

- Legitimate stakeholders are omitted from the planning process.
- Various stakeholders have conflicting expectations, purposes, or desires for the evaluation.
- The evaluator has difficulty identifying key stakeholders.

From the evaluator's vantage point, this list depicts a truism that is all too familiar to practitioners: An effective working relationship with an appropriate set of stakeholders who operate in good faith regarding the evaluation is much easier to seek than to achieve. However, failing to achieve it is seen by many evaluators as ethically problematic.

The fact that different stakeholders can bring very different perspectives to an evaluation raises a key ethical, and practical, question: Where stakeholders are concerned, to whom is the evaluator most accountable? Evaluation theorists do not speak with one voice on this issue. For example, those who emphasize the social justice functions of evaluation tend to explicitly or implicitly assign high priority to the needs of disenfranchised, disadvantaged, and marginalized stakeholders. Those with a preference for utilization-oriented models of evaluation are more likely to attend to the views of organizational decision makers and program implementers. Thus, how one answers ethical questions dealing with accountability to stakeholders is linked to the overall vision of evaluation that guides one's practice.

The ethical conflicts most commonly identified by evaluators during the communication-of-results phase include the following:

- The evaluator is pressured by a stakeholder to alter presentation of the findings.
- The evaluator is unsure of his or her ability to be objective or fair in presenting findings.
- The evaluator is pressured by a stakeholder to violate confidentiality.
- Although not pressured to violate confidentiality, the evaluator is concerned that reporting certain findings could—or would—represent such a violation.

On the basis of existing research, it appears that being pressured by stakeholders to alter the presentation of findings is, by far, the most frequent ethical challenge faced by evaluators. This pressure usually consists of a stakeholder (typically the primary client) urging the evaluator to portray the program in a more positive light than the evaluator believes is warranted by the data. Occasionally, however, the influence may be in the opposite direction, with a stakeholder desiring a more negative report than the program deserves. This can occur when a stakeholder wishes to discredit a program or the administration or staff associated with it. It is also possible for stakeholders and evaluators to disagree over the meaning and substantive significance of certain results, apart from their positive or negative quality, and these disputes can lead to attempts by stakeholders to influence results or their presentation, which evaluators would see as inappropriate.

The various ways in which confidentiality can be threatened are also highlighted by the conflicts that evaluators report during the communication-of-findings phase. Stakeholders sometime directly ask evaluators to identify specific respondents, or they may request data in a form (e.g., descriptions of small subgroups of respondents) that would allow individuals to be identified. Even when not pressured to violate confidentiality, evaluators can encounter situations in which confidentiality is at risk. For example, quotations from respondents can add richness and depth to a written report, but they can also lead to intensive—and sometimes accurate—speculation about the identity of the source of the quote. There is also the classic dilemma of an evaluator discovering evidence during an evaluation of illegal, dangerous, or unethical behavior on the part of a program's stakeholders (e.g., sexual harassment, fraud, substance abuse). In these situations, the evaluator can be faced with a choice between honoring individual confidentiality and promoting the wider public interest, a choice that may be complicated by the legal mandates (e.g., required reporting policies).

The final cluster of frequently encountered ethical conflicts pertains to the utilization of findings. Here the challenges include the following:

- A stakeholder suppresses or ignores findings.
- Disputes or uncertainties exist concerning ownership or distribution of the final report, raw data, or other items.
- A stakeholder misuses the findings; for example, to punish another stakeholder.
- A stakeholder deliberately modifies findings prior to releasing them.
- A stakeholder misinterprets the findings.
- A stakeholder engages in plagiarism or misrepresentation of authorship.

The nature of these conflicts is fairly self-evident and reinforces the notion that, in the minds of evaluators, the ethical history of an evaluation does not end with the submission of the final report; a number of things can go wrong after that point. Unfortunately, the precise actions an evaluator should take to deal with these developments are not always as self-evident. In part, this reflects the fact that the evaluator's power and influence customarily diminish in the utilization-of-findings phase, unless explicit agreements have been reached during entry or contracting that ensure the evaluator's involvement in follow-up activities and are responsive to the types of problems characteristic of the utilization stage. Even under the best of entry or contracting circumstances, however, it may be difficult to develop effective strategies for addressing certain end-stage problems, such as suppression or ignoring of findings by key stakeholders.

The ethical challenges discussed thus far do not, of course, represent the only ethical problems that can affect an evaluation. Rather, they are the ones that evaluators claim they encounter most frequently. Ethical conflicts that stem from the behavior of the evaluator are likely to be underreported due to the operation of self-serving biases. Thus, issues such as failure to provide informed consent; conflicts of interest; and incompetent or disputed evaluator performance in study design, data collection, or data analysis are less likely to be highlighted than if descriptions of ethical problems were obtained from other evaluation stakeholders. Indeed, the limited research that has focused on these stakeholders (e.g., program administrators, staff, and clients) suggests that their views of ethical violations only partially overlap with those of evaluators. For example, program staff may believe that the use of randomization to generate control groups in an evaluation is unethical or, more fundamentally, may object to the use of any control group. The withholding of potentially beneficial interventions from needy individuals is regarded as a serious matter by virtually all ethicists, and evaluators should be well grounded in arguments justifying the ethicality of such procedures. The greater the understanding evaluators have of ethical objections to various aspects of research design, the more effective they can be in responding to them. Against this background, a major task for future ethics researchers is to assess more systematically the perspectives of the full range of evaluation stakeholders on ethical issues.

STRATEGIES FOR ETHICAL PRACTICE

Evaluators can take a variety of steps to prevent ethical problems and to handle them effectively if they do arise. These include the following:

1. Proactively Manage the Evaluation's Entry or Contracting Stage

The entry or contacting stage is where evaluators and key stakeholders develop, share, and negotiate their expectations for the evaluation. This stage represents a prime opportunity for the evaluator to solicit the ethical concerns of stakeholders, as well as to bring up ethical issues that the evaluator believes need to be addressed. It can be helpful here if the evaluator introduces an overall set of professional standards or principles to frame the discussion (e.g., *The Guiding Principles for Evaluators*), to impress upon stakeholders the responsibilities that the evaluator must uphold throughout the evaluation. The more time and thought the evaluator puts into the entry or contracting phase, the greater the benefits for all aspects of the study, not just for those of ethical significance.

2. Conduct an Ethics Cost-Benefit Analysis

In an ethics cost-benefit analysis (ECBA), one compares the ethical risks of an evaluation with the social good that the evaluation is likely to produce. The analysis typically focuses on the welfare of current and future program clients and addresses concerns such as informed consent, assurances of confidentiality and anonymity, respect for privacy, quality of data monitoring, and the strength or coerciveness of incentives for participation in the study. A thorough ECBA should help the evaluator answer two crucial questions about the research: Are risks (costs) being minimized, and will benefits significantly exceed the study's risks? Ethicists generally agree that affirmative answers to both questions are needed if the study is to be deemed ethical.

Exploring these questions can be a challenging endeavor, given that program clients are not the only stakeholders who experience risks and benefits in an evaluation. Program staff and administrators, as well as clients' significant others, represent just three examples of constituencies whose welfare might deserve attention in a particular ECBA. Guidelines for performing ECBAs are available from organizations such as the U.S. Department of Health and Human Services.

3. Review Relevant Professional Guidelines

Guidelines such as *The Program Evaluation Standards* and the *Guiding Principles for Evaluators* provide an overall framework for ethical decision making on the part of the evaluator. Although there may be instances in which professional guidelines can provide a straightforward answer to a specific ethical problem in an evaluation, the general and abstract nature of professional guidelines makes them much more useful as an orienting device, alerting evaluators to issues that should be considered when entering a particular stage of the evaluation or responding to an ethical challenge. It is also the case that circumstances can arise in which adhering to one professional guideline can result in the violation of another guideline contained in the same set of standards, with the standards themselves providing little help with respect to how to resolve the conflict. In these situations, evaluators must identify criteria (e.g., an ECBA, a legal requirement, or a personal value) other than the guidelines themselves as the ultimate basis for making a decision.

4. Consulting With Colleagues

Seeking input from experienced colleagues will almost always broaden the perspective that an evaluator brings to an ethical challenge, providing him or her with a wider range of potential responses than would otherwise have been the case. It is true, of course, that evaluators will often disagree in their recommendations concerning such matters, but therein lies much of the value of seeking their input in the first place. Diversity of input can enhance the quality of the decisions that are reached. In this context, it is important that evaluators fully grasp the ethical reasoning underlying their colleagues' recommendations, rather than just the recommendations themselves. This will generate a heightened appreciation for the judgments and trade-offs that are factored into ethical action and enhance future ethical decision making.

5. Review One's Own Value System

The utility of professional guidelines, cost-benefit analyses, and the perspectives of colleagues is greatest when evaluators can incorporate this input into their own well-articulated sets of personal values. These values become especially meaningful when other sources of ethical guidance appear to offer conflicting recommendations. One characteristic of personal value systems is that they tend to be prioritized. Some values are more deeply held than others and thus become the basis for decision making when conflicts occur. For example, the ethical principle of *do no harm* (non-maleficence) is judged by many ethicists to be the core (i.e., highest priority) principle that applies to professional practice, taking precedence over principles such as respecting others' autonomy, beneficence (doing good), justice (being fair and equitable), and fidelity (honoring promises and commitments, being honest). In evaluation, the do-no-harm principle has traditionally focused attention on the welfare of program participants and control groups with respect to such possibilities as negative program side effects experienced by participants or lack of control-group access to viable alternative services. In a particular evaluation, a practitioner might, or might not, choose to assign great weight to this value when making ethical decisions. To the extent that evaluators are clear in their personal beliefs concerning the relative importance of these and other principles, their decisions concerning the actions to be taken in ethically problematic situations will be developed with greater confidence.

—*Michael Morris*

Further Reading

Morris, M., & Cohn, R. (1993). Program evaluators and ethical challenges: A national survey. *Evaluation Review, 17,* 621-642.

Newman, D. L., & Brown, R. D. (1996). *Applied ethics for program evaluation.* Thousand Oaks, CA: Sage.

■■ ETHNOGRAPHY

Ethnography is the art and science of describing a group or culture from the emic or insider's perspective. The ethnographer writes about the routine, daily lives of people. The patterns are a form of reliability. The ethnographer enters the field with an open mind, not an empty head. Before asking the first question in the field, the ethnographer begins with a problem, a theory or model, a research design, specific data collection techniques (such as fieldwork, participant observation, informal interviewing, and surveying), tools for analysis (including computer programs), and a specific writing style. The final product is an ethnography or an ethnographically informed report or video.

—*David M. Fetterman*

Evaluation Practice Around the World

Ethiopia

The Evaluator as Ethnographer

Within an ethnographic study, the ethnographer is not just evaluating the "field" of "other" but also her or his role in what is going on. In so doing, the ethnographer becomes what Ruth Behar refers to as the "vulnerable observer." For me, the experience of being the vulnerable observer meant challenging all my taken-for-granted assumptions about being white, Irish, middle class, and a nurse, in a situation of oppression in a Third World country where a breakdown in caring had occurred. My experience is contextualized within a culture of Western aid to the Third World and as such problematizes the notion of a neat understanding of specifics when debating national or cultural context in relation to evaluation. I was engaged in a project in Ethiopia from March 1996 to March 1997 that was working to improve nursing and patient care in a hospital there.

I provide three vignettes to illustrate the complexity of evaluation practice when judging both self and "other." The first relates to an early occasion on a ward when, due to the absence of both human and material resources, it was not possible to provide minimum, adequate care for patients.

I am desperate and I feel very angry. I ask the health assistant: "What can I do?" He suggests that I "go home." I then say to the intern and later to the surgeon (who came to visit a woman returned from the operating room) that "the situation is inhuman and desperate and people should not be at risk because they come into hospital." I suggest to them: "It is your responsibility to speak out." The surgeon replies, "I have, but nobody listens." He also states: "We can't [speak out]." He goes on to say: "Surgery is easy; it is the pre-op preparation and the post-op nursing care that makes a difference." I agree, and I add: "You need to keep saying that the situation is unacceptable until people hear you." The surgeon talks about "people's attitudes" and I say: "You must first start with your own attitude." He speaks of the energy he had when he came one year ago and of how he has lost some of it. I say: "Please don't lose your energy, you need to use it."

The second vignette was recorded 6 months later:

When leaving the School of Nursing I see two men carry a boy of about 10 years on a plastic bag. There are flies on the boy's face. I wonder if he is dead or very sick. If the latter, why is he on his way out of the hospital? They

stop to get a better grasp of the "stretcher." People look, I do too. Desperately I want to do something, [but] I have no language and they are on their way from the hospital. I walk on and once again I feel the ache of it all, the inhumanity, poverty, struggle of so many here.

Later I learn that the boy was taken from an outlying area and died when he got here. As I record this I feel the pain. Tears come to my eyes; I am aware that such responses drain me. If I lived here permanently would I survive this level of emotional pain? Perhaps I too would learn to ignore it; that is to appear to be indifferent to it, to act inhumanly. We in the West live very privileged lives and all by accident of birth.

The third vignette situates the historical context with which those wishing to engage in patient or nursing care, and the evaluation practices that are inherent within such activities, had to contend. It contains the words of an Ethiopian man working for the donor aid agency.

There is no history of speaking out; we accept what is said from the top. The security [under the previous regime] was very tight; one could be put to jail for openly speaking out. Say something, go to prison, be punished. We still do not speak about the government; there is still a fear. They won't complain about things.... It is a kind of culture; we have to accept what is given by others. If you do something [negative or wrong] people will tell you in an indirect way...people have no confidence. From their family, you have to accept what the family is telling you, it is the way we were brought up, no freedom. If you decide [what to do] for yourself, the family will want to keep you [to control you].

In seeking to recall telling moments within my ethnographic experience, what is noteworthy is the implied difference between my earlier attempts at appraising or judging the situation and my growing awareness of the struggle of "other" to be involved in such endeavors. The struggle locally was to deliver care in an environment of fear, poverty, and oppression, whereas my framework for caring was born of the luxury of a Western structural, cultural style of nursing care. In seeking to explicate this reality, I am reminded of the term *outsider within*, used by Patricia Hill Collins to describe the experience of involvement with marginality by Black women working for White families. Within my White privilege, I was marginal to the lived experiences of the patients and of the people with whom I worked. My involvement was transient; my experience did not include all of the interlocking systems of their reality.

— Jean Clarke

Further Reading

Behar, R. (1996). *The vulnerable observe: Anthropology that breaks your heart.* Boston: Beacon.

Clarke, J. (2001). *Oppression and caring: A feminist ethnography of working to improve patient care in Ethiopia.* Unpublished Ph.D. thesis, Trinity College, University of Dublin.

Collins, P. H. (1999). Learning from the outsider within: The sociological significance of Black feminist thought. In S. Hesse-Biber, C. Gilmartin, & R. Lydenberg (Eds), *Feminist approaches to theory and methodology: An interdisciplinary reader* (pp. 155–178). Oxford, England: Oxford University Press.

ETIC PERSPECTIVE

An *etic perspective* is the external, social scientific perspective on reality. Most ethnographers start collecting data from the emic or insider's perspective and then try to make sense of what they have collected in terms of both the native's view and their own scientific analysis. An external view without an emic or external foundation is unusual and uncharacteristic of ethnographic work. The etic perspective is typically adopted after multiple, and often conflicting, emic or insider views are collected. The etic view involves stepping back from the insider's views in an attempt to explain how groups are communicating or miscommunicating.

—David M. Fetterman

EVALTALK

EvalTalk provides a vehicle for open discussions concerning evaluation issues. Sponsored by the AEA, the list is open for use by anyone. The archives can be accessed at http://bama.ua.edu/archives/evaltalk.html.

EVALUABILITY ASSESSMENT

Evaluability assessment was thrust on the evaluation scene in the 1970s and was initially thought to show great promise for improving programs and saving valuable evaluation resources that might have been wasted by evaluating programs that were not ready to be evaluated. After a short burst of interest and activity, the process appears to have lost much of its appeal among evaluators. This entry provides a definition of evaluability assessment and offers some conjectures as to why a tool with such demonstrated promise seems to have all but disappeared from the practice of evaluation—at least as the practice is described in published literature.

EVALUABILITY ASSESSMENT: A DEFINITION

Evaluability assessment (EA) is a systematic process for describing the structure of a program and for analyzing the plausibility and feasibility of achieving objectives; their suitability for in-depth evaluation; and their acceptability to program managers, policy makers, and program operators. This is accomplished by the following process:

1. Program intent is clarified from the points of view of key actors in and around the program.

2. Program reality is explored to clarify the plausibility of program objectives and the feasibility of program performance.

3. Opportunities to improve program performance are identified.

Two primary outcomes are expected from an EA:

1. *Definition of a program's theory.* This includes the underlying logic (cause and effect relationships) and functional aspects (activities and resources), with indications of types of evidence (performance indicators) for determining when planned activities are implemented and when intended and unintended outcomes are achieved.

2. *Identification of stakeholder awareness of and interest in a program.* This means stakeholders' perceptions of what a program is meant to accomplish, their concerns or worries about a program's progress toward goal attainment, their perceptions of adequacy of program resources, and their interests in or needs for evaluative information on a program.

When an impact evaluation is anticipated, both of these outcomes should be attained before the evaluation is designed. When a program is being planned, or when improvement is the intent, only Outcome 1 may be pursued: Having a defined program framework increases the likelihood that program staff will manage their programs to achieve intended impacts, whether or not the impacts are to be measured. When the purpose is a preparatory step to further evaluation, these outcomes permit a clear indication of whether an intensive evaluation is warranted and, if so, what components or activities in the program can provide the most desirable data. In essence, they prevent evaluators from committing two types of error: Type III, measuring something that does not exist, and Type IV, measuring something that is of no interest to management or policy makers (Scanlon, Horst, Nay, Schmidt, & Waller, 1979).

Type III error exists when the program has not been implemented, when the program is not implemented as intended, or when there is no testable relationship between the program activity carried out and the program objectives being measured. Type IV occurs when the evaluator brings back information that policy makers and management have no need for or cannot act on. Both types of error are avoidable if an evaluability assessment is conducted. Type III errors may be avoided by defining the program and describing the extent of implementation; Type IV, by determining from the stakeholders what they consider important about the program and the evaluation.

ORIGIN AND DECLINE IN USE

Evaluability assessment originated in the early 1970s for the purpose of improving summative program evaluations. Such evaluations, then and now, were often perceived by policy makers as expensive wastes of time that produced little in the way of timely, useful information. Evaluators, on the other hand, often found that programs had grandiose goals and few concrete objectives. This led them to produce evaluations that angered policy makers by highlighting program deficiencies or else the evaluations were as muddled and vague as the programs. Joseph Wholey and his associates at the Urban Institute in Washington, DC, decided that an impasse had developed between stakeholders of programs and evaluators of those programs because of differences between rhetoric (i.e., claims about a program) and reality. They explored ways of aligning rhetoric with reality, and evaluability assessment was born.

For a few years the process flourished, but use dropped off dramatically after Joe Wholey left the U.S. Department of Health and Human Services. (He was the Deputy Assistant Secretary for Planning and Evaluation at the Department of Health, Education, and Welfare, the forerunner of the Department of Health and Human Services.) Debra Rog (1985) attributed this pattern of diffusion and decline in use to Wholey's advocacy: While he and the other associates who conceived the process were active in its implementation, its use increased; when they became less active, its use declined. However, it is more likely that the scarcity of concretely defined methodology had as much or more to do with the minimal adoption of EA as the advocacy of its creators. In other words, an evaluation process needs to meet the same implementation requirements as a program if it is to be successful. In this case, that would mean clearly defined outcomes for an EA and clearly defined and plausible activities (methods, steps, tasks) for reaching those outcomes— and neither of these (outcomes or methods) were products of the early work done by Wholey and his associates. They did discuss tasks that needed to be accomplished, such as document analysis, meetings of work groups, and site visits, but they did not identify specific guidelines on how to accomplish these tasks.

In 1984, Smith and her colleagues in the U.S. Department of Agriculture (USDA) initiated a project to define the evaluability assessment process in a methodological sense and to encourage adoption in the USDA's Cooperative Extension Services throughout the United States. Implementation proceeded iteratively, in a different major programming area, in five different states. After each iteration, procedures were analyzed and revised to clarify and, where possible, to simplify to make the process more usable and more "operator robust." The outcome from the project was a set of guidelines for implementing evaluability assessments. Ten tasks were described for the production of a successful EA, and methods were defined for the accomplishment of those tasks.

Wholey and his associates had developed EA as a method for analyzing a program's structure to determine the extent to which it was suitable for effectiveness evaluation, and they later recognized it as a way for determining the extent to which a program was capable of being managed to obtain successful results. Smith (1989) demonstrated EA's contribution to program planning for developing programs capable of providing evidence of that achievement.

It is not known why the decline in published literature on the use of evaluability assessment occurred, but a number of factors may have contributed to the phenomenon:

1. *EA Unreported.* Evaluability assessments often go unreported. Most EAs lead to the conclusion that the program under review is not ready for an impact study, if the intent is to show that the program is making intended impacts (e.g., those mandated by Congress). Reports of such studies usually fail to meet the criteria for publication or are written by persons who are not interested in publishing them. Also, when the purpose is to improve a program, these types of studies are often done in house and are not reported or shared with those outside the program or organization.

2. *Methodology Unavailable.* Methodology for conducting evaluability assessments was not available early in EA's history and was not easily accessible later. As already discussed, the early promoters of EA provided scant methodology for the actual conduct of such a study, and what they did publish was not readily available (e.g., Schmidt, Scanlon, & Bell, 1979) or was hard to interpret into action steps (e.g., Nay & Kay, 1982). In addition to this early void of methodology, the first set of specific guidelines for how to conduct EA (Smith, 1989) received scant attention in the United States, partly because the publisher did not promote the text among evaluators in the United States and partly because the price of the book made it mostly unattainable ($80+ was a lot for an evaluation book in 1989). Also, the book may not have been held in high esteem because agriculture, the subject of the programs used for the methodological research, was not recognized as a leader in evaluation theory and methodology.

3. *Implementation Difficult.* Good evaluability assessments are difficult to implement effectively; the process requires much skill and experience. Nay and Kay discussed the fragility of negotiating relationships with and among policy makers, program implementers, and other stakeholders to achieve the understandings necessary to determine what was expected and being implemented as a program, and they suggested that senior evaluators be the ones to carry out these tasks. To develop a plausible theory of program implementation, persons representing all levels and aspects of a program must be involved in describing program actions and resources, and their input must be in depth and thoughtful, revealing what is being done and why. Such descriptions are not easy to elicit because (a) they begin to reveal a person's beliefs and values (e.g., about the people they are trying to serve with the program), (b) they can reveal inadequacies of skills and work habits of staff (e.g., that something less than or different from expected is being done), and (c) many staff will think the exercise is not wise use of their time (i.e., it takes them away from their programming duties). Many hours, much savvy (program, political, and policy), and a wide repertoire of skills are needed by the evaluator to negotiate all the tasks necessary to navigate a successful EA, and not all evaluators possess the essential skills or have the interest in spending evaluation resources in this way.

4. *Name and Promotional Confusion.* The name given to the approach and its promotion during the height of interest in it suggested that EA was not an evaluation approach in its own right. The original developers of the evaluability approach promoted the process as a preliminary step to an impact evaluation, as something to do before conducting an evaluation. They described evaluability assessment as the beginning of a four-step evaluation process, to be followed by rapid feedback evaluation; performance monitoring; and, where there was sufficient program implementation, intensive study of program results. The usual pressure evaluators face for results pushes many to proceed directly to the intensive evaluation instead of doing the preliminary work.

5. *Objectivity Loss.* Evaluability assessment evaluators may lose program objectivity, in appearance or in reality. In each of the three purposes for implementing an evaluability assessment, the conductor becomes very involved in the program. In each case, involvement with the staff is intense and personal, especially as assumptions and values surface, as they

must in theory definition. In later steps, conclusions of evaluability (when the purpose is summative) or recommendations for improvement (when the purpose is formative or summative) or conclusions of plausibility (when the purpose is program planning) all represent assessments of program value—all indicate that the program is worthy of investment of additional resources. Although these are appropriate positions for evaluators to take, problems can occur when the same person who conducted the EA conducts a subsequent evaluation of program performance or impact. The problem can be a loss of credibility of evaluation results with those who are in positions to make decisions about the program.

6. *Assumption of Rationality.* Evaluability assessment is based on an underlying assumption of rationality; that is, that organizations and their programming efforts are tightly coupled and highly structured or will be at the conclusion of the assessment. It is based on a rational model of organizational decision making, with corresponding assumptions of evaluability very close to that of the problem-solving model. Further assumptions of rationality are that *the* decision makers can be identified and that programs will remain static long enough for some model of program behavior to be appropriate or measurable. In other words, programming is depicted as a deliberate process: First we think, then we act; first we formulate, then we implement. As much as some (evaluators and others) would like to see this orderly process in programs, in many practical situations the assumptions underlying the rational model do not hold; also, many evaluators refuse to accept rationality as an assumption of real-world program development or implementation.

7. The primary outputs for evaluability assessment are now being sought under separate evaluation rubrics, which are readily found in published literature. Using the metaphor of a corporate takeover, the two primary outputs of EA have been sold as program theory evaluations and stakeholder evaluations and, in so doing, have created a situation in which the whole is greater than the sum of its separate parts. The two processes practiced separately produce far less than when combined as a comprehensive evaluability assessment, in terms of (a) producing real knowledge about program intents and implementation, (b) building ownership and commitment among all levels of decision makers for creating a climate in

which changes essential for program success can and will be made, (c) facilitating the ability to manage a program for success, and (d) clarifying and improving the criteria for exercising program accountability.

—*M. F. Smith*

Further Reading

Nay, J. N., & Kay, P. (1982). *Government oversight and evaluability assessment.* Lexington, MA: Lexington Books.

Rog, D. (1985). *A methodological analysis of evaluability assessment.* Unpublished doctoral dissertation, Vanderbilt University, Nashville, TN.

Scanlon, J. W., Horst, P., Nay, J. N., Schmidt, R. E., & Waller, J. D. (1979). Evaluability assessment: Avoiding Types III and IV errors. In G. R. Gilbert & P. J. Conklin (Eds.), *Evaluation management: A selection of readings.* Washington, DC: Office of Personnel Management, Federal Executive Institute.

Schmidt, R. E., Scanlon, J. W., & Bell, J. B. (1979). *Evaluability assessment: Making public programs work better* (Human Services Monograph Series, No. 14). Washington, DC: Urban Institute.

Smith, M. F. (1989). *Evaluability assessment: A practical approach.* Boston: Kluwer.

Wholey, J. S. (1979). *Evaluation: Promise and performance.* Washington, DC: Urban Institute.

Wholey, J. S. (1987). Evaluability assessment: Developing agreement on goals, objectives and strategies for improving performance. In J. Wholey (Ed.), *Organizational excellence: Stimulating quality and communicating value.* Washington, DC: Heath.

▋▋ EVALUAND

Evaluand, a generic term coined by Michael Scriven, may apply to any object of an evaluation. It may be a person, program, idea, policy, product, object, performance, or any other entity being evaluated.

▋▋ EVALUATION

Evaluation is an applied inquiry process for collecting and synthesizing evidence that culminates in conclusions about the state of affairs, value, merit, worth, significance, or quality of a program, product, person, policy, proposal, or plan. Conclusions made in evaluations encompass both an empirical aspect (that something is the case) and a normative aspect (judgment about the value of something). It is the value feature that distinguishes evaluation from other types of inquiry, such as basic science research, clinical epidemiology, investigative journalism, or public polling.

—*Deborah M. Fournier*

EVALUATION AGREEMENTS. *See* ETHICAL AGREEMENTS, EVALUATION PLANS

▪ *EVALUATION AND PROGRAM PLANNING (EPP)*

EPP, a journal published by Elsevier Sciences Ltd., was founded in 1974 by Jonathan A. Morell and Eugenie Walsh Flaherty. It is based on the principle that the techniques and methods of evaluation and planning transcend disciplinary boundaries. *EPP* publishes articles from the private and public sectors in a wide range of areas: organizational development and behavior, training, planning, human resource development, health and mental, social services, mental retardation, corrections, substance abuse, and education. The primary goals of the journal are to assist evaluators and planners to improve the practice of their professions, to develop their skills, and to improve their knowledge base.

—*Jonathan A. Morrell*

▪ *EVALUATION & THE HEALTH PROFESSIONS*

Evaluation & the Health Professions has, for 25 years, provided a forum in which health-care practitioners, researchers, planners, policy makers, and students could examine the development, implementation, and evaluation of health-care programs and interventions. It offers a broad, multidisciplinary perspective on complex health-care issues through original research that focuses on the results of evaluation studies, instructional innovations, progress reports, and updates. Articles often influence the design of health-care programs and shape clinical practice and policy.

EVALUATION CAPACITY BUILDING. *See* CAPACITY BUILDING

▪ EVALUATION CENTER, THE

The Evaluation Center was established in 1965 at The Ohio State University and has been housed since 1973 at Western Michigan University (WMU). From 1965 to 2002, Daniel L. Stufflebeam was Director. It conducts research, development, dissemination, service, instruction, and leadership to advance theory and practice for evaluating programs, personnel, and students or beneficiaries. Center staff have created the CIPP Evaluation Model; led development of standards for evaluations; evaluated programs in various U.S. states and in other countries; evaluated evaluations and testing systems; devised procedures for evaluating teachers, administrators, and U.S. Marines; issued numerous publications; trained many evaluators; developed and staffed evaluation offices; helped establish AEA; and designed WMU's Interdisciplinary Evaluation Ph.D. Program, the first of its kind in the world.

—*Daniel L. Stufflebeam*

Further Reading

The Evaluation Center. (2004). Retrieved May 15, 2004, from http://www.wmich.edu/evalctr

EVALUATION NETWORK (ENET). *See* AMERICAN EVALUATION ASSOCIATION

▪ EVALUATION PLANS

An *evaluation plan* can serve as a contract or a memorandum of agreement between the evaluator and the client. As with a contract, it defines the roles and responsibilities of the evaluator and the client. The basic components of an evaluation include (a) a statement about the background of and rationale for the program, (b) a list of the stakeholders in the evaluation, (c) the purpose of the evaluation, and (d) the key questions to be answered by the evaluation. Each of these components will be briefly discussed.

The evaluator can obtain some initial information on the background and rationale for the program, process, or product by reviewing available documents and records. This information should be supplemented through meetings held with various stakeholders.

Each evaluation has several levels of stakeholders. In the evaluation plan, it is important to distinguish these different levels. The primary stakeholder is typically the person, group, or organization responsible for the evaluation development and funding; thus, in many cases, the primary stakeholder can be viewed as the client. Secondary stakeholders may not have financial control over the evaluation, but they may be affected by the evaluation and its results. Meetings with these various stakeholders can help the evaluator gather needed information on the background of the program, process, or product; the specific purpose(s) of the evaluation; and the key questions for the evaluation. Questions that can be asked of these stakeholders to elicit this information include (a) What is your role in the program? (b) What are your observations about the program? (c) What are the goals of the program? (d) What concerns do you have about the program? (e) What do you hope to learn from the evaluation? (f) What roles and responsibilities do you want to assume in the conduct of the evaluation? (g) What decisions do you want to make that will be based on the evaluation? and (h) When do you have to have the information from the evaluation? A dialogue among the stakeholders can help to identify areas in which views of the program, process, or product are similar or different. Such dialogue can also point out unstated goals. Indeed, the evaluator may use these meetings with stakeholders to develop a "logic model," or the expected links from the funding or initiation of the program, process, or product to the expected outcomes.

The evaluation plan should also contain a brief statement as to the purpose of the evaluation. This will help to clarify to the client, the stakeholders, and the evaluation whether the evaluation is a needs assessment, a developmental evaluation, a formative evaluation, or a summative evaluation (focused on monitoring and auditing, on outcomes, on impacts, or on performance measurement, respectively). It is also useful to include a statement about how the evaluation findings will be used.

The final element of the evaluation consists of the key evaluation questions. These are the small set of questions guiding the evaluation.

—*Darlene F. Russ-Eft*

See also ETHICAL AGREEMENTS

Further Reading

Russ-Eft, D., & Preskill, H. (2001). *Evaluation in organizations: A systematic approach to enhancing learning, performance, and change.* Cambridge, MA: Perseus Press.

■■ EVALUATION RESEARCH

Evaluation is the systematic assessment of the worth or merit of some object. *Research* is the process of studying something in a detailed, accurate manner. *Evaluation research* is a systematic process for (a) assessing the strengths and weaknesses of programs, policies, organizations, technologies, persons, needs, or activities; (b) identifying ways to improve them; and (c) determining whether desired outcomes are achieved. Evaluation research can be descriptive, formative, process, impact, summative, or outcomes oriented. It differs from the more typical *program evaluation* in that it is more likely to be investigator initiated, theory based, and focused on evaluation as the object of study.

—*Leonard Bickman*

EVALUATION RESEARCH SOCIETY (ERS). *See* AMERICAN EVALUATION ASSOCIATION

■■ *EVALUATION REVIEW: A JOURNAL OF APPLIED SOCIAL RESEARCH*

Published for 26 years, *Evaluation Review* has served as an interdisciplinary forum for researchers, planners, and policy makers who develop, implement, and use studies designed to improve the human condition. As the journal subtitle implies, the focus of this journal has been on evaluation as research. The long-time editor is Richard Berk.

■■ *EVALUATION: THE INTERNATIONAL JOURNAL OF THEORY, RESEARCH AND PRACTICE*

Evaluation was launched in July 1995 to promote international dialogue and to build bridges within the field. Edited from a European base, it is an international journal that promotes exchange among European, North American, Asian, and Australasian voices within the evaluation community. The journal is interdisciplinary, bringing together contributions from across the social sciences and related fields. Currently, the editor is Elliot Stern, of the Tavistock Institute in London.

▦ EVALUATION THEORY

Evaluation theory has been evolving and growing, although there is no single theory of evaluation, nor will there likely ever be one. Evaluation theory follows evaluation practice. Social and political demands for valuing forced the traditional social sciences into service, but over the years, evaluation has come into its own. Although the methods of evaluation are still borrowed from the social sciences (including an ever-broadening repertoire of evidence seeking and of creating methods), there is a growing awareness, beginning in the 1960s, that evaluation is more than the application of methods. It is also more than the simple discovery of what is good and right.

An evaluation theory serves to provide a plausible body of principles that explain and provide direction to the practice of evaluation. Shadish, Cook, and Leviton (1991) define the ideal theory of evaluation:

> The ideal (never achievable) evaluation theory would describe and justify why certain evaluation practices lead to particular kinds of results across situations that evaluators confront. It would (a) clarify the activities, processes, and goals of evaluation; (b) explicate relationships among evaluative activities and processes and goals they facilitate; and (c) empirically test propositions to identify and address those that conflict with research or other critically appraised knowledge about evaluation.

There are many theories of evaluation or formulations that more or less meet the specifications of this description, and they are known more widely as models of evaluation. These are theoretical formulations that attempt to provide a coherent set of principles to explain the whys and hows of evaluation. They are, at the same time, subsets of a broader notion of evaluation theory, one that *ideally* encompasses all those theories (or models) of evaluation. There has been a tendency in evaluation to see the development of evaluation theory as evolutionary—moving through time with each generation of models and ideas developing in response to earlier generations. There is, no doubt, interplay among these perspectives, but the relationship is probably not an evolutionary one. The first, second, and third generations that Lincoln and Guba discuss in fourth-generation evaluation live on; Stage 1, 2, and 3 theories, as conceptualized by Shadish, Cook, and Leviton, live on. Recent work has begun to look closely at the interplay between presumably different theories of evaluation exemplified in Deborah Fournier's work on evaluation warrants and Christina Christie's work on conceptions of stakeholders and use.

A theory of evaluation is, indeed, not a simple theory and no doubt must comprise many theories that make the practice, and the profession, of evaluation possible. Much incredibly good thought has gone into various components of evaluation theory, and this entry does not attempt to reconcile or make sense of these various formulations. Sketched here is one way of delineating these many theories that are necessary for a theory of evaluation.

The *theory of valuing* specifies

- The nature of value, especially in relation to facts
- How value is assigned to evaluands
- The nature and source of criteria and standards
- The nature of metaevaluation, including justification, validation, and verification

At the heart of evaluation, and what distinguishes it from the social sciences more generally, is that it is about value. What is value? What does it mean to assign value? How do we know if we have assigned value properly? These are questions that a theory of value would address.

The *theory of practice* characterizes

- Evaluator roles, including professional ethics
- The nature of evaluands, especially the nature of programs
- The nature of evidence
- The identification of stakeholders and how they participate in evaluation, including a conceptualization of power
- The nature of normative discourse
- Ways of synthesizing

There are ways of doing things that are a part of evaluation, and although methods for evaluation are drawn from the social sciences, there are questions that must be addressed in relation to the use of those methods by evaluators for the purpose of assigning value. What is evidence, and how do we make sense of it? What is the relationship between generalization and evaluation? How do we conceive of evaluands? What are the interpersonal, political, and social components of evaluation? What is the language of evaluation?

The *theory of prescription* delineates

- The meaning of amelioration
- The logic of prescription and its particular relationship to evaluation
- The nature of recommendations

Evaluation qua evaluation is separate from prescription, but fundamentally, as a practice and a profession, we understand that we are attempting to make things better, by (for example) identifying what is right and good and remedying what is wrong and bad. What does it mean to make things better? What counts as a social problem? What counts as a prescription? How do prescriptions relate to evaluations? These are issues that a theory of prescription would address so that the essentially social ameliorative role of evaluation as a profession and practice may be understood.

The *theory of use* specifies

- How evaluation modifies evaluands
- What makes evaluation relevant, comprehensible, credible, and just
- The authority of the evaluation

Related to a theory of prescription is the need for a theory of use. How is it that ascribing value and making prescriptions actually affects evaluands? What does it mean for evaluation to be useful? Where must evaluation draw its authority from to be useful?

Many of these questions and components of evaluation theory are covered throughout this encyclopedia, not coherently, but in small parts with cogent arguments that provide some answers to many of these questions. Definitive work that attempts to build an evaluation theory has not yet been done.

See also MODELS OF EVALUATION

Further Reading

House, E. R. (1980). *Evaluating with validity.* Beverly Hills, CA: Sage.

Schwandt, T. A. (2002). *Evaluation practice reconsidered.* New York: Peter Lang.

Scriven, M. (Ed.). (1993). Hard-won lessons in program evaluation. *New Directions for Program Evaluation, 58.*

Shadish, W. R., Cook, T. D., & Leviton, L. C. (1991). *Foundations of program evaluation: Theories of practice.* Newbury Park, CA: Sage.

Taylor, P. (1961). *Normative discourse.* Englewood Cliffs, NJ: Prentice Hall.

■■ EVALUATION USE

Evaluation use, or evaluation utilization, occurs when evaluation information in the form of findings, or evaluation practice, has influence on the actions or thoughts of stakeholders. Typically, evaluation use is differentiated from evaluation influence more generally. The former refers to situations within the direct domain of the evaluator (e.g., the program being evaluated). The two main types of evaluation use discussed in the literature are instrumental use (direct actions) and conceptual use (changes in thinking). In addition to use of findings, the evaluation process itself may have impact, instrumental or conceptual.

—Marvin C. Alkin

See also UTILIZATION OF EVALUATION

EVALUATION UTILIZATION.
See EVALUATION USE, UTILIZATION OF EVALUATION

■■ EVALUATIVE INQUIRY

Evaluative inquiry for learning in organizations is an approach to evaluation that underscores the importance of individual, team, and organizational learning as a result of engaging in evaluation processes. As such, it strives to integrate evaluation into normal organizational operations, supports organization members' interest and ability to explore critical issues using evaluation logic, relies heavily on stakeholder involvement throughout the evaluation, and values the diversity of the perspectives, values, and knowledge of those involved in the evaluation process. Evaluative inquiry for learning in organizations is based on the following assumptions:

- Stakeholders' learning occurs through social interactions during the evaluation (e.g., process use). This learning may be transformative in that stakeholders develop new perceptions and understandings of the evaluand, the organization, organization members, evaluation practice, and, ultimately, themselves.

- Stakeholders' learning occurs within an organizational context and is likely to be mediated by the organization's internal systems and structures.
- Evaluation must be responsive to the evolving information and decision-making needs of organizations.
- Evaluative inquiry should be ongoing and integrated into all work practices.
- The use of evaluation findings is of critical importance.

Although evaluative inquiry is similar in some aspects to other evaluation approaches, it is most highly reflective of an organizational learning perspective. Even before management experts started talking about intellectual capital and the coming knowledge era, Argyris and Schön were exploring the concept of organizational learning and its role in facilitating organizational change. Since then, many other researchers have identified organizational learning principles and characteristics of learning organizations. For example, Watkins and Marsick found that most organizational learning theories and models share the following attributes:

- Learning organizations focus on organizational learning and transformation. It is not enough for individuals to learn.
- Structures and systems are created to ensure that knowledge is captured and shared for use in the organization's memory.
- Leaders and employees at all levels think systematically about the impact of their decisions and work within the total system.
- Learning is built into work structures, politics, and practices.
- Learning is transformative in some ways, although it is likely that some new learning will also be adaptive.
- Learning has a greater impact when it involves a greater percentage of the employee population.
- Organizational systems and politics are structured to support, facilitate, and reward learning for individuals, teams, and the organization.
- Measurement systems benchmark current knowledge and culture and monitor progress toward becoming a learning organization.

In essence, organizational learning represents the organization's commitment to using all of its members' capabilities. It is different from individual and team learning in that organizational learning is dependent on individuals and teams sharing their learning in an ongoing, systemic way. Ultimately, organizational learning is about creating continuous processes and mechanisms for learning how to do things better.

From a learning standpoint, the evaluative inquiry approach draws heavily on constructivist and transformational adult learning theories. Constructivist learning theory proposes that learning is primarily about meaning making and suggests that individuals and groups learn by interpreting, understanding, and making sense of their experiences, often within a social context. Learners are not passive (as implied in behaviorism models of learning) but are active participants in the construction of their own knowledge. Constructivist learning theory claims that learners can determine what they need to know within the particular work context and seek out knowledge using both internal and external resources.

Taking constructivist learning theory a step farther is transformative learning theory, which "seeks to explain the way adult learning is structured and to determine by what processes the frames of reference through which we view and interpret our experience (meaning perspectives) are changed or transformed" (Mezirow, 1991, p. xiii). Therefore, transformative learning "is a process of examining, questioning, validating, and revising [these] perceptions" (Cranton, 1994, p. 26). Within the work context, transformational learning theory asks us to focus on the relationships between our work and ourselves.

Viewed through the lens of evaluation, evaluation becomes transformative when employees learn, improve their practice, and address critical organizational issues through a collaborative, dialogic, reflective, and inquiry-oriented approach. Therefore, an evaluative inquiry approach to evaluation focuses on what and how people learn from evaluation thought and practice in addition to the usual focus on evaluation findings. By acknowledging and encouraging the learning dimension of evaluation, organizations build members' capacity for engaging in thoughtful and productive evaluation work.

PHASES OF EVALUATIVE INQUIRY FOR LEARNING IN ORGANIZATIONS

Evaluative inquiry consists of three specific phases. In the *Focusing the Inquiry* phase, an evaluation team or work group is established. The role of this team is to provide input and feedback on the evaluation's design and implementation, as well as on the findings. In addition, the team might be responsible for various data collection and analysis activities. The composition of the team is likely to include a variety of stakeholders (e.g., program designers, clients, management, funders, and others who have a stake in the evaluand). Although the evaluator (internal or external) might lead or facilitate this team, it is essential that members participate fully throughout the inquiry process. During the *Focusing* phase, the evaluation team determines (a) the issues and concerns the evaluative inquiry will address, (b) who the evaluation's stakeholders are, and (c) the questions that will guide the evaluative inquiry. The team might also develop a logic model of the evaluand.

In the next phase, *Carrying Out the Inquiry,* the evaluation team determines the most appropriate inquiry design, methods of data collection, methods of analysis and interpretation, and communicating and reporting strategies. If possible, team members might also assist in the data collection and analysis activities.

The third phase, *Applying Learning,* constitutes one of the more unique features of the evaluative inquiry for learning in organizations approach. Whereas most evaluations end with the delivery of a final report, those using the evaluative inquiry approach continue working with the evaluation team, or with others as needed, to help (a) develop strategies that address the evaluative inquiry's outcomes, (b) design and implement action plans based on these strategies, and (c) monitor the progress of actions taken. The evaluator might also act as a resource for assisting organization members in locating individuals or groups that might fill any gaps in knowledge and skills necessary to implement the resulting action plans. This third phase of evaluative inquiry contributes significantly to increasing the use of evaluation findings.

EVALUATIVE INQUIRY LEARNING PROCESSES

As each of the inquiry phases (*Focusing the Inquiry, Carrying Out the Inquiry,* and *Applying Learning*) are implemented, organization members come together to engage in the learning processes of Dialogue; Reflection; Asking Questions; and Identifying and Clarifying Values, Beliefs, Assumptions, and Knowledge. As team members participate in each of the evaluation phases, they strive to create an environment in which they can trust one another, feel safe speaking their thoughts and opinions, and be able to question past

and future practices. They are particularly mindful of ensuring that real dialogue occurs, that there is time for reflection, and that assumptions are tested and validated. By participating in these learning processes throughout the evaluative inquiry, team members develop greater insights and understandings about the evaluand and the organization's context. Ultimately, these insights and understandings lead to more informed decisions regarding the evaluation's findings. It should be noted that these four learning processes occur through a dynamic, fluid, social interaction among organizational members.

ELEMENTS OF ORGANIZATIONAL INFRASTRUCTURE

In large part, the success of evaluative inquiry is based on an organization's infrastructure; that is, the strength of the underlying foundation or framework for supporting learning within the organization. An organization's infrastructure can strongly influence the extent to which organization members learn from evaluative inquiry and use their learning to support personal and organizational goals. The elements of the organization's infrastructure include Leadership, Culture, Communication, and Systems and Structures. The nature of these components provides the footing on which evaluative inquiry efforts can be undertaken and sustained: They will facilitate or inhibit organizational learning from evaluative inquiry to varying degrees, depending on how they operate within the organization.

The *Leadership* element suggests that the more that leaders (and managers) support a learning environment, the more likely organization members are to support systematic and ongoing evaluation. If organizational leaders suggest that they know it all, or that learning from experience is unnecessary, then evaluative inquiry will be more difficult to implement. On the other hand, if leaders model learning, create a spirit of inquiry, and use data to act, then evaluation practice may be more successful.

The second element, the organization's *Culture,* is fundamental to creating learning from evaluation practice. If the culture is one that supports asking questions, open and honest communication, teamwork, risk taking, valuing mistakes, and trust in one another, evaluative inquiry may be welcomed and successful. However, if organization members are afraid to offer their opinions, do not believe managers will act on evaluation results, or believe that the results will be used to punish individuals or groups, then the evaluative inquiry's findings will be less useful in helping the organization make effective decisions.

The third element, *Communications,* is closely related to the intended use of evaluation findings. The more systems and channels an organization has to communicate and report the progress and findings of an evaluation, the more likely it is that the evaluation will have an impact on individuals, teams, and the organization overall. However, if there are few means to share what is learned from the evaluation, or organization members are restricted from sharing their learning from the evaluation process, then evaluation will lose an important opportunity to enhance the organization's performance.

The fourth element, the organization's *Systems and Structures,* concerns how employees' jobs are designed, how they are rewarded and recognized for their work, how learning is expected to occur, and how the physical environment contributes to working together. The more cross-trained organization members are, the more they are encouraged to learn from each other, the more their jobs allow for teamwork, and the more employees understand the interrelatedness of their jobs, the more likely it is that evaluative inquiry will serve its learning function.

Before implementing an evaluative inquiry effort, it is often useful to understand the strengths and weaknesses of an organization's infrastructure in relation to evaluation and organizational learning. One might use, for example, the Preskill and Torres diagnostic instrument called Readiness for Organizational Learning and Evaluation. The instrument's results can be used to

- Identify the existence of learning organization characteristics
- Diagnose interest in conducting evaluation that facilitates organizational learning
- Identify areas of strength to leverage evaluative inquiry processes
- Identify areas in need of organizational change and development

When organization members come together to reflect on the results of this assessment, they may discuss not only how ready the organization is to engage in evaluative inquiry but also how the organization functions in relation to other organizational initiatives.

Evaluative inquiry for learning in organizations offers organizations a highly participative, focused, utilization-oriented approach to evaluation. Using evaluation logic, this approach becomes a catalyst for learning and change by focusing on

- Program and organizational processes as well as outcomes
- Shared individual, team, and organizational learning
- Education and training of organizational practitioners in inquiry skills
- Collaboration, cooperation, and participation
- Establishing linkages between learning and performance
- Searching for ways to create greater understanding of the variables that affect organizational success and failure
- Using a diversity of perspectives to develop understanding about organizational issues

—*Hallie Preskill*

Further Reading

Argyris, C., & Schön, D. A. (1978). *Organizational learning: A theory of action perspective.* Reading, MA: Addison-Wesley.

Argyris, C., & Schön, D. A. (1996). *Organizational learning II.* Reading, MA: Addison-Wesley.

Cranton, P. (1994). *Understanding and promoting transformative learning.* San Francisco: Jossey-Bass.

Mezirow, J. (1991). *Transformative dimensions of adult learning.* San Francisco: Jossey-Bass.

Preskill, H., & Torres, R. T. (1999). *Evaluative inquiry for learning in organizations.* Thousand Oaks, CA: Sage.

Preskill, H., & Torres, R. T. (2000). *The Readiness for Organizational Learning and Evaluation (ROLE) instrument.* Available from Hallie Preskill at www.hpreskil@unm.edu.

Watkins, K. E., & Marsick, V. J. (Eds.). (1996). *Creating the learning organization* (Vol. 1). Alexandria, VA: American Society for Training and Development.

■■ EVALUATOR

An *evaluator* is a person or group that uses credible and verifiable evidence to form conclusions about performance (e.g., program effectiveness, impact, or implementation fidelity) assessed against criteria.

—*M. F. Smith*

■■ EVALUATOR ROLES

Many textbooks on evaluation have no subject index entry for evaluator or evaluator role, suggesting that, at least for many evaluation theorists, the definition is taken for granted. In general, evaluators have been assumed to be specialists who exercise their special knowledge and skills in independent, detached ways to avoid bias in their evaluative work.

Sprinkled throughout the evaluation literature is a wide array of terms used to describe the roles of evaluators in their work. The following is a list of many of those terms.

Auditor	Judge
Change agent	Learner
Coach	Manager
Collaborator	Mediator
Consultant	Methodologist
Critical friend	Partner
Decision maker	Poet
Describer	Researcher
Educator	Social critic
Expert	Social scientist
Facilitator	Scribe
Historian	Steward
Illuminator	Storyteller
Inspector	Technician
Investigator	Therapist

The most clearly developed aspect of evaluator roles is the distinction between internal and external evaluators. External evaluators are outside of the programs, organizations, or whatever types of evaluands they are evaluating, and their virtue is in their objectivity, distance, freshness of perspective, and independence. They may, however, lack an understanding of the history and culture of the evaluand. Internal evaluators, on the other hand, operate from within programs, organizations, or other types of evaluands, and their virtue is in their familiarity with the program or organizational context and their ability to observe whether evaluation recommendations are implemented. Internal evaluators, however, are perceived as less objective and compromised by their position within their organization. There is, in addition, a hybrid external-internal role exemplified by evaluators contracted to do evaluation with a particular agency, organization, or program over an extended period of time, thus combining elements of both types of evaluator.

Evaluators' roles are defined by the knowledge and skills they need; the functions they perform; and how they interact with stakeholders, the organization or program, and the profession. The first is the aspect most fully explored, especially in discussions of the basic knowledge and skills required of evaluators. However, there remains a lack of any clear delineation of that body of knowledge and skills, which speaks to the diverse perspectives on evaluation's purpose and methodology.

Evaluators' professional obligations are, at least in the United States, codified in *The Program Evaluation Standards* and the *Guiding Principles for Evaluators*. These publications give direction for practice, provide a means for solving problems, and form a framework for judging the quality of the work evaluators do.

The development of the notion of a learning organization provides some articulation of evaluator roles vis-à-vis organizations. Seeking to transform programs and organizations, either through capacity building or targeted evaluation activities, evaluators often assume blended hybrid internal-external roles—for example, evaluator and human resource consultant or evaluator and strategic planner.

Less frequently discussed is the interpersonal and relational aspect of evaluator roles. Jennifer Greene's work has focused most specifically on this aspect in her discussions of "evaluator as engaged person," which is reflected in the way evaluators present their work and in the locations in which evaluators are engaged. Not only do evaluators have knowledge and skill, they employ these in particular contexts, and the characteristics of the contexts, in turn, define evaluators' roles. Evaluation adopts a political stance, as observed by Carol Weiss, often by disproportionately casting its gaze on the poor, the disadvantaged, the powerless, and those in need. Evaluators who agree to conduct evaluations of programs both accept and promote the notion that the program is problematic or at least that the evaluation is worthwhile. Thus evaluators play a role of legitimating some and delegitimating other programs, putting some at risk but not others.

Evaluator roles have proliferated as the profession and practice have embraced different perspectives, and this will be an area of investigation within the practice for some time to come.

See also CERTIFICATION, PROFESSION OF EVALUATION

Further Reading

King, J. A., & Stevahn, L. (2002). Three frameworks for considering evaluator role. In K. Ryan & T. A. Schwandt (Eds.), *Exploring evaluator role and identity.* Greenwich, CT: Information Age.

Evaluation Practice Around the World

Scotland

The Ancient Struggle of Evaluators: A Scottish Legend

University-based evaluators working within the Scottish National Health Services may not so far have compared themselves to Nessie, the beast said to be roaming the waters of Loch Ness. However, such a comparison produces striking similarities in the roles both species play and the dilemma they face in fulfilling these roles. Nessie is thought to be an eel-like creature that inhabits the depths of Loch Ness in the north of Scotland. She is an important role model for researchers when it comes to the "canny" way she combines two apparently contradicting activities. Being Nessie sometimes involves diving deep into murky waters, but it also involves giving memorable presentations at the right time, the right place, and to the right people.

This accords with our experience as university-based evaluators because as such we have a dual role to fulfill. In our case, we are working within an organization called the Scottish School of Primary Care on projects that are funded by Scottish Primary Care Trusts. These trusts provide and coordinate primary care services all over Scotland. They are accountable to the government and they aim to provide the most appropriate and efficient services for their patients. Part of their strategy is to fund researchers like us to evaluate the performance of various services or programs.

The evaluation of the rising number of emergency hospital admissions among the elderly provides a typical example of the dilemma we researchers face in this situation. This evaluation focuses on the development of services that prevent unnecessary hospital admissions of elderly patients. It is necessary to gather a broad range of data about the performance of existing services from a broad range of stakeholders, and this is a tricky endeavor due to a plethora of restraining factors, such as short-term funding, complex ownership of services, and complicated resourcing arrangements. The services are run by different health-care organizations, with different agendas, who compete for funding.

In the course of these evaluations, evaluators have to demonstrate diverse talents. Sometimes it is necessary to be an evaluation expert, other times an information broker, a learning facilitator, a mediator, or some other role. Living up to these challenges involves diving deep into the murky waters of politics and social dynamics, which obscures the assessment of these services. Months of negotiations are usually required to forge links between the various key stakeholders, such as general practitioners, nurses, hospital consultants, social workers, and occupational therapists, as well as the primary intended users of this evaluation, people

80 years old and older. Although potentially a full-time undertaking in itself, service development alone is not valued within academia.

University-based evaluators have to combine their developmental role with a research agenda. Evidence gained while evaluating services needs to be written up and published in peer-reviewed papers. Ideas developed in the course of the evaluation have to be transformed into successful grant proposals. The researcher's dilemma behind this dual role is that there are never enough time and personnel resources to cover the developmental and the research aspect. Therefore, like Nessie, who busies herself with her own interests in the depths of Loch Ness but manages to rekindle excitement with a few well-timed sightings, researchers must give memorable presentations of themselves and their work at the right time, at the right place, and to the right people. The longer a project has been running, the stronger the pressure from the department to publish in peer-reviewed journals, and the developmental aspect continues to be as time intensive as it has been throughout the entire project.

We are not the first researchers to have experienced the tension between research and development. In Scottish universities and among clinicians and researchers working for the National Health Services, there is a growing awareness of this dilemma. In a joint effort to tackle this challenge, Scottish Higher Education Institutions, National Health Service Trusts, the Scottish Executive Health Department, and various funding agencies have invested in establishing the Scottish School of Primary Care (SSPC). The SSPC is a virtual school aimed at bringing research, evaluation, and service development together in projects such as the evaluation of hospital admissions of older people. Health professionals and managers in the Primary Care Trusts recognized the need for this evaluation. By using the resources of the SSPC, the Trusts gain access to a broad range of university experts they can tap to run these projects. The Trusts then have access to research evidence from numerous university departments and are able to learn from one another by sharing experiences and discussing common issues. Consequently, the Trusts and the universities benefit from this situation. The Trusts pay the researchers' salaries and receive professional evaluations of their services. The universities benefit through acquiring external funding and more research staff, who go on to publish work and raise the profiles of their departments.

However, researchers working for the SSPC are still in the middle of the dilemma of how much time to invest in research and how much in service development. In struggling with this dual role, we can learn another lesson from the legendary beast of Loch Ness. Over the years, only a small number of people claimed to have caught sight of her, and fewer still have provided evidence of her existence. Her modesty and diffidence nourish the legend. Similarly, stakeholders value evaluators for their expertise in conducting evaluations and practically implementing findings and not for openly struggling with their dual roles as

researchers and developers. Evaluators' advantage, however, is that they are aware of the conflicting demands they face and, more important, their academic departments, as well as their clinical partners, are also aware of this challenge. This has proven to be a constructive step toward amalgamating academic research and the logic of evaluation. We feel that Nessie would agree.

—Markus Themessl-Huber,
Alison Harrow, and
Stephan Laske

■■ EVALUATORS' INSTITUTE™, THE

The Evaluators' Institute™ was formed in 1995 to provide short professional development courses on evaluation topics and, more recently, to offer certificates in evaluation practice. The Institute's goals are to (a) enhance the capabilities of practicing evaluators and others responsible for and using evaluation results; (b) increase the implementation and use of methodologically defensible evaluations; (c) advance the evaluation profession; and (d) implement events that are seen as relevant, of high quality, and of great utility to participants. Nationally and internationally recognized scholars in evaluation helped conceive the Institute and, each year, assist with course planning and implementation. Institute courses are endorsed by the American Evaluation Association.

—M. F. Smith

EVIDENCE-BASED PRACTICES. *See* BEST PRACTICES

■■ EXECUTIVE SUMMARY

An *executive summary* is an abstract of the evaluation, typically in ordinary, nontechnical language, and is usually no more than 10% of the original document. Executive summaries literally are written for an executive who has neither the time nor the technical expertise to read the original. Executive summaries may include recommendations.

See also RECOMMENDATIONS, REPORTING

■■ EXPERIMENTAL DESIGN

An experiment is a randomized comparison used to assess the effects of a treatment or intervention. In the simplest experiment, participants are assigned at random to one of two groups: One receives the treatment or intervention of interest and the other receives either an alternative treatment or no intervention at all. Both groups of participants are subsequently assessed on an outcome measure, and differences between the groups on the outcome measure are used to estimate the size of the treatment effects.

The alternative to a randomized experiment is a quasiexperiment. A comparison is quasiexperimental if participants are not assigned to treatment conditions at random. For example, a quasiexperiment results when the participants choose for themselves which treatment to receive or when treatments are assigned by others based on criteria such as need, merit, or convenience.

Without random assignment, the participants in the treatment groups can differ in ways that bias estimates of the treatment effect. For example, a medical intervention will look more effective than it is if the intervention is given to those who are the healthiest and the alternative treatment is given to those who are the sickest. In this case, subsequent differences in health would result simply because of the initial differences in health. Random assignment to treatment conditions equates the treatment groups on initial characteristics and thereby avoids bias due to differences in the composition of the groups. As a result, randomized experiments typically produce more valid and precise estimates of treatment effects than do quasiexperiments.

Although random assignment removes bias due to initial group differences, that advantage can be vitiated by differential attrition. Attrition results when not all the participants remain in the study until completion. Differential attrition arises when the participants in the treatment group who leave early differ in important ways from the participants in the comparison group who leave early. Incentives to entice participants to complete the study are often used to reduce biases due to differential attrition.

Randomized experiments are also susceptible to biases from differences in local history. Differences in local history arise when the interventions under study are not the only ways in which the groups of participants are treated differently. For example, if the different interventions are administered at different facilities, those facilities might interact differently with the participants in other ways as well. The best way to avoid local history effects is to control external influences so they are either avoided or distributed equally across the groups.

Randomized experiments are renowned for being difficult to implement. Participants are likely to resist being randomly assigned to treatments they perceive as differing in desirability. Administrators and service providers often prefer to distribute valuable resources based on need, merit, or individual preference rather than by lottery. Also, substantial resources, commitment, and ingenuity are often required to devise mechanisms that can deliver treatments at random.

In spite of their frailties, randomized experiments often remain the preferred method for assessing the effects of treatments when they can be implemented. Quasiexperiments can be far easier to conduct, but biases in quasiexperiments due to initial group differences can be so severe and so difficult to remove through statistical adjustments that well-executed randomized experiments are often the only way to obtain credible assessments of treatment effects.

—*Charles S. Reichardt*

See also QUASIEXPERIMENTAL DESIGN

▦ EXPERIMENTING SOCIETY

Experimenting society is a phrase associated most often with Donald Campbell. It reflects a vision of

a society that would use social science methods and evaluation techniques to vigorously try out possible solutions to recurrent problems and would make hard-headed, multidimensional evaluations of outcomes, and when the evaluation of one reform showed it to have been ineffective or harmful, would move on and try other alternatives.

An experimenting society is a liberal state committed to science as well as reform and to seeing these two as intertwined. Several volumes commemorating Campbell's contributions to evaluation include this phrase in their titles.

Further Reading
Campbell, D. T. (1991). Methods for the experimenting society. *Evaluation Practice, 12*(3), 223-260.

EXPERT JUDGMENT. *See* ACCREDITATION, CONNOISSEURSHIP

▦ EXTERNAL EVALUATION

An *external evaluation* is conducted by an evaluator who is not an employee of the organization that houses the object of the evaluation (e.g., the program). An external evaluator brings objectivity, accountability, and perspective to the problem at hand.

A key characteristic that distinguishes an external evaluation from an internal one is the objectivity of the evaluator. An external evaluation is governed by the terms of a contract between the organization and the evaluation consultant that are specific to the tasks of the evaluation project and are limited in duration to the life of the project. Contractual obligations tend to hold the evaluator's focus on the parameters of the evaluation itself and seldom allow the consultant to get involved in broader organizational issues. The bonds are easy to sever by either party, and thus the relationship tends to be both temporary and rather watchful. External evaluators are not constrained in their relations with staff and can communicate with all levels without fear of reprisal. They are at ease dealing directly with their client, who has limited influence over their careers outside of the terms of their contract.

On the other hand, internal evaluators are likely to be part of a larger group or department; they may even be part of a bargaining unit; they have a clearly defined location on the organization chart, as well as within the internal culture; and they have a personal stake in the success of the organization. Their relations with other staff members may be hampered by the implications of their judgmental role; their employer may find it difficult to sanction them due to the organization's complex contractual environment. Because of the reporting structure, they may never have access to the head of their program or organization to present their study findings.

Compensation arrangements associated with an external evaluation tend to heighten accountability. The internal evaluator receives a salary regardless of the degree of completion of the evaluation project, but timelines and penalties for noncompletion are much more stringent for the external evaluator. Clearly, the consultant will not be paid if the work is not done. The disadvantage of a focus on contractual obligations is that discussions between consultant and client can deteriorate to legalistic interpretations about milestones and deliverables. The advantages of these cut-and-dried arrangements are several: The drive to completion is likely to be stronger; the evaluation process is likely to be more transparent, or at least better documented; and the evaluator's accountability will be more pronounced.

Another key characteristic of an external evaluation is perspective. Although an internal evaluator may have a deep understanding of the context and politics within which the program is embedded, an external evaluator has a broader perspective that results from having evaluated other programs in other contexts. External evaluators often belong to a wide array of communities and bring broader influences from such areas as academia, business, and other work communities, as well as from the evaluation field itself, to the evaluation problem. Because they lack the support of the internal culture provided by membership in the organization under review, they may rely more heavily on membership in professional groups to cultivate informal support networks, again broadening the perspectives brought to an evaluation project. This cross-fertilization of ideas can result in fresher, more innovative ways of looking at organizational issues that may not be apparent from the inside. Further, through a series of engagements in different settings, external evaluators have honed their craft by developing a whole host of ways to interact with stakeholders, collect data, and present findings. Thus they are better able to respond to the unexpected as the evaluation is implemented.

The advantages and disadvantages of external as opposed to internal evaluation have been debated in the evaluation literature since the mid-1980s, but now the shifting borders between employees and consultants resulting from massive government layoffs, the changing nature of the workplace, and the growing professionalization of evaluators may be blurring the distinctions between the two types of evaluation.

In the end, it may be that the selection of either an internal or external evaluator will be situational and very likely budget driven. Internal evaluators may be available to the organization at no additional cost, although adding another task to their workload may slow down the delivery of a product, and they may not have the credibility or caché that an external evaluator may bring to the project. In some cases, a joint internal-external team of evaluators may be the best approach, particularly in very complex organizations such as the federal government, where an external view may be more credible but an internal shepherd may also be required to move study results through the bureaucracy.

—*Gail V. Barrington*

■■ EXTERNAL VALIDITY

External validity refers to the *generalizability* or *representativeness* of experimental effects or program treatments. There are several questions of representativeness that could be posed concerning the results of experimental or evaluation studies: (a) To what other groups do the study results apply, or to what population can they be generalized? These are questions of *sample generalizabilty.* (b) To what other experimental or social settings and programs do the results apply? Such questions are addressing issues of ecological *representativeness.* (c) Do the treatment or independent variables used in the study represent factors that are unique to the study (or program) or represent a stable class of variables that are universal? For example, if the construct of "respect for authority" was assessed with an attitudinal scale, would the construct remain the same in meaning across different cultural, linguistic, and class distinctions? Here, the concern is *variable representativeness.*

Campbell and Stanley remind us that issues of external validity are seldom resolved. Efforts to generalize incur the same problems encountered in inductive inference: Neither can be fully justified logically. Both involve extrapolating beyond the realm of the sample or local study and making assumptions about the regularity of occurrence of certain phenomena or relationships. For example, one might feel more comfortable making generalizations if it were discovered that the results from the local study confirmed findings from similar studies that had been conducted. Another issue that must be recognized is the role external validity plays in evaluation studies versus the role it plays in research studies. Evaluation studies can be distinguished from research by their limited generalizability; the object of evaluation may be unique, of limited duration, or developed to serve the unique needs of a given population. Program conditions are dynamic, making controlled replication nearly impossible. Because evaluation studies provide empirical justifications for making decisions related to the merit or worth of something under specific conditions, the demand for generalizing is not as great as it is in research studies. A more realistic question for evaluation studies is: Given what we now know about the program or product, what *aspects* can be useful or have merit if transported to other programs or integrated into new products? This question of *transportability* removes many of the constraints imposed by issues of external validity on evaluation studies.

—*Charles L. Thomas*

Further Reading

Campbell, D. T., & Stanley, J. C. (1963). *Experimental and quasi-experimental designs for research.* Chicago: Rand-McNally.

Worthen, B. R., & Sanders, J. R. (1987). *Educational evaluation: Alternative approaches and practical guidelines.* White Plains, NY: Longman.

FAIRNESS. *See* SOCIAL JUSTICE

■■ FALSIFIABILITY

Falsifiability is a criterion for scientific theories, hypotheses, or propositions proffered by Karl Popper in the 1930s. This criterion implies that for any of these to be scientific, they must be refutable or falsifiable, and if they are not, they are merely dogmatic stances. In other words, a scientific theory or idea that cannot be refuted provides nothing of value because any claim or event could or would be consistent with the theory or idea. For an assertion to be falsifiable, there must be empirical evidence that would show the assertion to be false. For example, the assertion "Phonics instruction is the most effective way to teach reading" could be falsified by observing one instance in which phonics instruction did not lead to the ability to read. This criterion has several limitations. There are any number of scientific theories that are true by definition (for example, Newton's laws of motion) or are approximations rather than literally true. Popper's concern was specifically with what he considered scientific rather than whether a theory, idea, or proposition was right or wrong. Indeed, throughout history, science has been wrong, and ideas that may not be scientifically sound may be right but simply beyond the ability of current science to test. The criterion of falsifiability is most often associated with the uses of experimental and quasiexperimental designs in evaluation, and although it has limitations, it can be a useful heuristic to challenge taken-for-granted ideas and the meaning and value of a theory.

Further Reading

Popper, K. R. (1992). *Logic of scientific discovery.* London: Routledge.

■■ FARRINGTON, DAVID

(b. 1944, Ormskirk, Lancashire, England). Ph.D., M.A., and B.A. Psychology, Cambridge University, England.

Farrington is Professor of Psychological Criminology at Cambridge University, President of the Academy of Experimental Criminology, and Chair of the Campbell Collaboration Crime and Justice Group, which aims to produce systematic reviews of evaluations of criminological interventions.

Farrington completed one of the first detailed reviews of randomized experiments in criminology in 1983. His work in developmental criminology and criminal career research has been influenced by Donald West, Alfred Blumstein, Rolf Loeber, Lee Robins, and Joan McCord. His work in evaluation has been influenced by Tom Cook, Robert Boruch, and Lawrence Sherman.

With Brandon Welsh, he edited a special issue of *Annals of the American Academy of Political and Social Science* in 2001 titled "What Works in Reducing Crime." In 2003, he also published papers in *Annals:* "Methodological Quality Standards for Evaluation Research" and "British Randomized Experiments on Crime and Justice." Along with Lawrence Sherman and Brandon Welsh, Farrington edited one of the first books on cost-benefit analysis in criminology, and he has written various papers on this topic. He has also edited books, including *Evidence-Based*

Crime Prevention (2002) and *Offender Rehabilitation in Practice* (2001). With colleagues Brandon Welsh and Kate Painter, he has examined the impact of street lighting and closed-circuit television in reducing crime.

Farrington has received the Sellin-Glueck Award of the American Society of Criminology in 1984 for his international contributions to criminology and the Sutherland Award of the American Society of Criminology in 2002 for his outstanding contributions to criminology. His 1986 book *Understanding and Controlling Crime* (written with Lloyd Ohlin and James Q. Wilson), which advocated longitudinal-experimental research in criminology, won the 1988 prize for distinguished scholarship of the American Sociological Association Criminology Section.

He has been President of the British Society of Criminology, the American Society of Criminology, and the European Association of Psychology and Law, as well as Chair of the British Psychological Society Division of Forensic Psychology. He is a Fellow of the British Academy and of the Academy of Medical Sciences.

FAULT TREE ANALYSIS

Fault tree analysis identifies causes of a major undesirable event (fault) in a system. Adapted from engineering, it is a technique frequently used in needs assessment. Not passing a certification examination is an example of an undesirable event that would be placed at the top of a tree. Key factors possibly causing that event would be situated under the top, followed by subfactors causing the key factors, and so forth, thus forming a tree-like figure. Key factors could be grouped into those under the control of the system and those not. Failure pathways can be ascertained through quantitative and qualitative procedures.

—*James W. Altschuld*

Further Reading

Witkin, B. R., & Stephens, K. G. (1973). *Fault tree analysis: A management science technique for educational planning and evaluation.* Hayward, CA: Office of the Alameda County Superintendent of Schools.

FEASIBILITY

Feasibility refers to the degree to which an evaluation is realistic on a number of levels: for example, design and procedures, knowledge and ability of the evaluator,

political viability, cost effectiveness, time frame for completion, and protection of human subjects.

—*Jeffrey G. Tucker*

See also Evaluability Assessment

FEMINISM

Feminism is a school of thought that has its origins in the 1800s with the suffragists who fought for women's right to vote. Currently, feminism includes many diverse perspectives, in a range that includes Marxist, race-based, cultural, and poststructural feminism. Despite these variations, the central focus of feminism is the study of women's experiences and the elimination of bias and discrimination against women. A common belief that guides feminism is that gender bias exists systemically and is manifest in the major institutions in society, such as schools, the media, business, and government. Feminism examines the intersection of gender, race, class, and sexuality in the context of power.

—*Donna M. Mertens*

FEMINIST EVALUATION

Feminist evaluation, like other evaluation approaches, is concerned with measuring the effectiveness of programs, judging merit or worth, and examining both formative and summative data to promote change. The difference between feminist approaches and other evaluation models lies in the attention paid to gender issues, the needs of women, and the promotion of change. Feminist evaluation approaches are specifically interested in promoting social justice, particularly for women, but not only for women. Attention is also paid to race, class, and sexual orientation. As a result of this concern for women and other oppressed groups, the methods used in a feminist approach are usually collaborative and inclusive and have an action orientation.

Feminist evaluation is a natural outgrowth of the influence of the feminist movement, feminist theory, and feminist research on the evaluation field. As feminists and feminist researchers have questioned and expanded the boundaries of what it means to do research, these ideas have influenced the way women and men with feminist attitudes approach evaluation. Feminist researchers such as Reinharz, Stanley, and

Wise; Fonow and Cook; Harding; hooks; and Collins have contributed to expanded and entirely different views of what it means to do research, to question authority, to examine gender issues, to examine the lives of women, and to promote social change. Feminist research has evolved over the years from feminist empiricism (using traditional research methods to examine women's issues) to feminist standpoint theory (which argues that women approach research with different perspectives and therefore different abilities to see problems than men) and finally to postmodern feminism. Postmodern feminist thought argues against the creation of new versions of an approach that is implicitly sexist, racist, and classist, that is, another grand theory of absolute truth. Feminist postmodernism advocates attending to multiple perspectives and multiple realities in the process of research and avoids the creation of grand narratives or theories.

In the evaluation field, collaborative and emancipatory evaluators and theorists have addressed some of the issues of concern to feminists and have also contributed to the development of alternative approaches to evaluation. Evaluators such as Egon Guba, Yvonna Lincoln, Jennifer Greene, David Fetterman, and Michael Patton have contributed much to the debate surrounding what is acceptable evaluation practice, what questions should or can be asked, how they should be asked, who should be included, and what methods can be used to answer questions. In spite of the inclusiveness of collaborative or empowerment-oriented evaluations, however, these can still fall short of the requirements of a feminist evaluation. Research studies have shown that even collaborative approaches can be co-opted by powerful or cultural interests and thus will not adequately represent the voices of those with less power (which often means women).

CHARACTERISTICS OF FEMINIST EVALUATION

Labeling evaluation models or approaches specifically as *feminist* is a fairly recent phenomenon. Within the evaluation field, there remains much resistance to alternative paradigms or approaches to evaluation, and in the not-so-distant past, even alternative methods were contested as being inappropriate, biased, and unreliable (e.g., the quantitative-qualitative methods debate). Backlash against feminism and feminist

work, as well as other alternative evaluation approaches, often creates a hostile environment for feminists. For this reason and others, feminist evaluators, like many women worldwide, may be reluctant to label themselves as feminist, or their work as feminist, although their approach and methods may be very feminist indeed.

Some would regard feminist evaluations as those evaluations that specifically examine women's programs, but these individuals lack understanding of a feminist approach. Feminist evaluation is not just evaluation of women's programs. It is a particular stance, a worldview, a critical eye, that promotes the asking of different questions, the use of different methods, and the sharing of knowledge in different ways in the evaluation of any program. Feminist approaches to evaluation have several commonalties, including the following:

- A central concern is that gender inequities lead to social injustice.
- Discrimination or inequality based on gender is structural and systemic.
- Evaluation is political; the contexts in which evaluation operates are politicized; and the personal experiences, attitudes, and characteristics that evaluators bring to evaluations (and with which we interact) lead to a particular political stance.
- Knowledge is a powerful resource that serves an explicit or implicit purpose. Knowledge should be a resource of and for the people who create, own, and share it. Consequently, the evaluation process can lead to powerful negative or positive effects on the people involved in the evaluation.
- Knowledge and values are culturally, socially, and temporally contingent. Knowledge is also filtered through the knower.
- There are many ways of knowing; some ways are privileged over others.

EXAMPLES OF FEMINIST EVALUATION

Recent examples of feminist evaluations are fairly limited, due to the newness of the approach and the reluctance of evaluators to call their work feminist. One example includes an evaluation of an adolescent abuse prevention program that paid special attention to the needs of young women, the psychological impacts of violence on women, and educational differences between men and women with regard to prevention education. This evaluation placed women and their material realities at the center of the evaluation and attempted to understand the problem context from a feminist perspective. Multiple perspectives were solicited during the evaluation, and in particular, the viewpoints of the evaluator (a feminist) and other feminist activists were sought out to provide alternative questions and interpretations of the resulting data. The use of mixed methods and an action orientation also characterized the study.

Another example is an evaluation of an alcohol treatment program that paid specific attention to how the program might or might not address the needs of women, structural inequities in the treatment of substance abuse in women, structural inequities in the community supports available, and physiological and psychological differences between the way men and women respond to alcohol and treatment. A collaborative evaluation approach was used; program participant input was solicited, particularly of women; and evaluation team members included feminists with an action orientation. This feminist evaluation team was consistently reflective during the evaluation process on the question of whether the evaluation promoted ongoing sociopolitical and gender analysis.

In spite of its late arrival and continued lack of acceptance in some quarters, feminist evaluation approaches are beginning to change the way evaluation work is done. Contributors to the development of feminist evaluation approaches include Donna Mertens, Jo Anne Farley, Elizabeth Whitmore, Egon Guba and Yvonna Lincoln, Denise Seigart and Sharon Brisolara, Patricia Lather, and other respected researchers and evaluators.

MAJOR ARGUMENTS

The most common arguments within the evaluation field surrounding feminist evaluation include the following:

- Feminist evaluation is not evaluation.
- Feminist evaluation is biased (it "looks under only certain rocks").
- Feminist evaluation approaches can be used in some situations, but not all evaluations.
- Only feminists can do feminist evaluation.

Some evaluators dismiss feminist evaluation approaches as being too oriented toward social action and therefore unworthy of the label *evaluation*. This argument has been made against empowerment-oriented and collaborative approaches as well, yet debate continues as to how an evaluation should be judged, what exemplifies a "quality" evaluation, and what criteria ought to be used. By the traditional standards for an evaluation with a postpositivist orientation (e.g., objectivity, neutrality), feminist evaluation does not qualify as evaluation. However, many within evaluation circles argue that these criteria are and have always been unachievable. Defining the concept of objectivity (or lack thereof) alone has contributed to the demise of many trees. The idea that an evaluator can distance him- or herself from a study and remain neutral, bringing no personal attitudes to the process, today seems quite absurd. The idea of the nonpolitical evaluation, an evaluation that can remain unaffected by the political and cultural contexts within which the evaluation takes place, is dying a slow death.

Other evaluators argue that feminist evaluators are biased and focus only on certain very specific aspects of a situation in their quest for the promotion of feminist ideals. These critics misunderstand the point of feminist approaches. Feminist evaluation and feminist evaluators do not desire a different kind of "bias" in their work. What they seek is to expand the horizon of evaluators, to eliminate a patriarchal bias, and to include perspectives that have been ignored in the past. In this sense, feminist evaluators "look under more rocks" than the typical evaluator because they add the concerns of feminists and a social justice perspective to their agenda.

Still more evaluators argue that it may be appropriate to use feminist ideas and methods in some evaluations but not all because in some situations, it may not be appropriate. These arguments also lack understanding of feminist approaches. A feminist paradigm uses a feminist eye, an eye that looks always for gender discrimination and social injustice, in every evaluation opportunity. A feminist evaluator will always use methods that work toward empowerment and the promotion of social justice, particularly with attention to gender issues. Typically, this includes the use of inclusive and collaborative methods, but feminist evaluation is not limited to these. What is of primary importance is that the views of feminists are represented in some way in the evaluation, either by including feminist evaluators on the team or by soliciting the input of feminist participants regarding the questions asked and the interpretations made.

Last but not least, some evaluators will argue (or be concerned) that feminist evaluation can be done only by feminist evaluators. It is true that nonfeminists may be able to increase attention to women's issues through the use of collaborative methods or by involving women in the evaluation process. However, it is also easy to argue that the evaluation process can be co-opted by stronger, political influences and cultural traditions. Feminist evaluation must be done by feminist evaluators or evaluators must be careful to include or seek out the input of knowledgeable feminists so that feminist perspectives can be clearly represented. The inclusion of women will not necessarily address this problem, for not all women are feminists. Some women believe, for example, that it is proper for their husbands to make all decisions for them. Cultural traditions, lack of education, and threats of violence affect the way women think and act, thus sometimes limiting their ability to see outside their own "box." The inclusion of multiple perspectives and multiple realities in evaluations can help widen the horizons of women and other oppressed groups, raise their consciousness, and permit them the space to question their current situations.

CONCLUSION

Feminist evaluation is a new model within the evaluation field. To promote social justice and a better world, for women as well as for other oppressed groups, feminist approaches to evaluation can make major contributions to program improvement, policy development, and evaluation theory. In a world where women continue to suffer from violence, poverty, and discrimination, feminist evaluations can contribute to transformations in power, increasing education, and the righting of long historical wrongs. Regardless of the methods used—quantitative, qualitative, collaborative, mixed—it is the questions asked and who holds power that determines the importance of an evaluation and how the results will be used. Feminist evaluation is a way of seeing; a critical eye that asks questions nonfeminists will not or do not ask, in every evaluation. To address issues that will foster stronger democracies and a more just world, feminist ideals and feminist evaluation approaches make an important contribution.

—*Denise Seigart*

Further Reading

Seigart, D., & Brisolara, S. (Eds.). (2002, Winter). Feminist evaluation: Explorations and experiences. *New Directions for Evaluation, 96.*

Truman, C., Mertens, D., & Humphries, B. (2000). *Research and inequality.* London: UCL Press.

▟ FETTERMAN, DAVID M.

(b. 1954, Danielson, Connecticut). Ph.D. Educational and Medical Anthropology, M.A. Education, M.A. Anthropology, Stanford University; B.A. Anthropology, B.S. History of Science, University of Connecticut.

Fetterman is a member of the faculty and Director of the MA (master's program) Policy Analysis and Evaluation Program in the School of Education at Stanford University. He was formerly Professor and Research Director at the California Institute of Integral Studies, Principal Research Scientist at the American Institutes for Research, and Senior Associate and Project Director at RMC Research Corporation. He has conducted fieldwork in both Israel (including living on a kibbutz) and the United States (primarily in inner cities across the country).

Fetterman has contributed to the theory and practice of evaluation through the use of cultural or anthropological theories and field research methods. He has developed the empowerment evaluation approach, for which he is known around the globe. His primary contributions to evaluation theory, preceding his work on empowerment, have been in ethnographic evaluation and cultural approaches to auditing and Internet and computer applications in evaluation. He has advanced theories of the insider's perspective of reality in all of his work, including ethnographic, traditional, and empowerment evaluation.

Fetterman is Past President of the American Evaluation Association, as well as of the American Anthropological Association's Council on Anthropology and Education. He received the American Evaluation Association's Paul Lazarsfeld Award for Evaluation Theory in 2000, the Perloff President Award in 1984, and the Myrdal Award for Evaluation Practice in 1995, as well as the George and Louise Spindler Award for Excellence in Educational Anthropology from the Council on Education and Anthropology. He was also awarded the Washington Association of Practicing Anthropologists' Praxis Publication Award for translating knowledge into action.

He is General Editor for Garland Publications' Studies in Education and Culture series and author of *Foundations of Empowerment Evaluation; Empowerment Evaluation: Knowledge and Tools for Self-Assessment and Accountability; Speaking the Language of Power: Communication, Collaboration, and Advocacy; Ethnography: Step by Step; Qualitative Approaches to Evaluation in Education: The Silent Scientific Revolution; Excellence and Equality: A Qualitatively Different Perspective on Gifted and Talented Education; Educational Evaluation: Ethnography in Theory, Practice, and Politics;* and *Ethnography in Educational Evaluation.*

FIELD EXPERIMENT

A *field experiment* is a randomized, controlled outcome study conducted to identify effects caused by or attributable to an intervention. It is an experiment conducted under realistic operating conditions; that is, with consumers characteristic of those targeted and within the situation in which the evaluand is expected to function. The goal is to produce conclusions that are scientifically valid and relevant to the concerns of decision makers. The challenge is to find the appropriate balance between scientific rigor and decision utility, given the circumstances in which the trial is to take place. A field experiment may be contrasted with a quasiexperiment that has similar intent and application but is not randomized.

—*M. F. Smith*

See also QUASIEXPERIMENTAL DESIGN

FIELDWORK

Fieldwork is the hallmark of research for ethnographers. The method essentially involves working with people for long periods of time in their natural setting to see people and their behavior with all the real-world incentives and constraints. This naturalistic approach avoids the artificial response typical of controlled or laboratory conditions. Immersion in the natural setting enables the ethnographer to identify patterns of behavior over time that are typical of the group. The fieldworker uses a variety of methods and techniques to ensure the integrity of the data. These methods objectify and standardize the researcher's perceptions.

Of course, the ethnographer must adapt each method to the local environment.

—*David M. Fetterman*

FITZPATRICK, JODY L.

(b. 1948, Waco, Texas). Ph.D. Educational Psychology, M.A. Government, B.A. Government, University of Texas–Austin.

Fitzpatrick is Professor in the Graduate School of Public Affairs at the University of Colorado. Before coming to academia, she conducted numerous evaluations for organizations at state and local levels. Her areas of interests are program theory, ethics, and evaluation use. She has conducted evaluations in a variety of settings with a focus on programs concerning children, women, and families. Her most recent evaluations concern programs to encourage girls' achievement in math and science and factors that influence women to choose careers in technology. Primary influences on her evaluation work include Thomas Kuhn, Carol Weiss, Joseph Wholey, and Eleanor Chelimsky.

Her contributions to the practice of evaluation include her column "Exemplary Evaluations" in the *American Journal of Evaluation,* in which she interviews well-known evaluators about the choices they made in a specific evaluation and the factors that influenced those choices. The intent of the column is to illustrate the array of choices and the difficult decisions that evaluators face, not only in methodology, but in determining the focus of their questions, who the stakeholders are that they serve, and the judgments they make.

She is a coauthor of the textbook *Program Evaluation: Alternative Approaches and Practical Guidelines* (with Blaine Worthen and Jim Sanders) and has authored numerous articles on evaluation and ethics in evaluation.

She has served on the board of the American Evaluation Association and as Associate Editor of the *American Journal of Evaluation.* She has also won the Outstanding Teaching Award from the University of Colorado, Colorado Springs.

FOCUS GROUP

A *focus group* is a small group of people involved in a research interviewing process specifically designed to uncover insights regarding the research focus. The group interview is distinctive in that it uses a set of questions deliberately sequenced or focused to move the discussion toward concepts of interest to the researcher. The focus group consists of a limited number of homogeneous participants discussing a predetermined topic within a permissive and non-threatening environment. A skilled moderator or interviewer guides the discussion, exercising limited control over the discussion and moving the conversation from one question to another.

Although this process is called a focus group interview, it is really more like a focused discussion. The moderator engages the participants in a conversation and participants are encouraged to direct their comments to others in the group. The primary responsibilities of the moderator are to keep the discussion on topic and on time and to engage the participants in the conversation.

DEVELOPMENT OF FOCUS GROUP INTERVIEWING

The term *focus group interview* is derived from Robert Merton's research just before World War II. Focus groups gained popularity during the late 1950s as market researchers sought to understand consumer purchasing behavior. At this time, focus groups were composed of 10 to 12 participants, often consisting of strangers and conducted in front of one-way mirrors that allowed the sponsor to observe. The focus groups of this period were often used to determine whether a product would be successful: Group discussion revealed the factors that influenced consumer decisions or uncovered barriers to use or adoption.

As the discipline of evaluation evolved in the 1960s, 1970s, and 1980s, there was increased attention on alternative means of gathering information. Some evaluation methods (e.g., quantitative, positivistic) were not always applicable to the changing needs of the period. For example, issues relating to motivations, needs, individual perceptions, opinions, and attitudes were increasingly important in the evaluation community. Evaluation researchers began to see the benefits of using a variety of qualitative methods, including focus group interviews. During this period, evaluators discovered that several changes resulted in better focus groups. Instead of special rooms with one-way mirrors, evaluators sought out natural environments

such as homes, restaurants, or public meeting spaces and also reduced the group size to six to eight participants to allow for discussions of greater depth. In addition, they incorporated the more rigorous analytic methods that were typical of academic research.

QUALITY OF FOCUS GROUP STUDIES

To a casual observer, focus groups can look deceptively easy, but in fact they are complicated to plan, conduct, and analyze. When focus groups are conducted without adequate preparation, planning, or skills the results are less dependable. The quality of the focus group study depends on a number of factors: careful planning, good questions, skilled moderation of the discussion, and systematic and verifiable data analysis.

Planning a focus group study consists of determining the number of groups, developing a strategy for recruitment, creating incentives, and anticipating other logistic concerns. The basic design strategy is to conduct three or four focus groups for each audience category that is of interest to the researcher. Recruiting begins by identifying as precisely as possible the characteristics of the target audiences. Participants are selected and invited because they have certain experiences or qualities in common. People who meet the qualifications of the study are invited to participate.

Questions must be developed for the focus group. These questions are designed to be conversational and easy for the participants to understand. In a 2-hour focus group, there would be approximately a dozen questions. Care is needed in the phrasing and sequencing of the questions. Focus group questions are distinctive by their focus, by their emphasis on concrete experiences, and by their tendency to elicit conversation.

Moderating is the process of guiding the discussion. It begins with helping people feel comfortable and establishing a trusting, permissive, and comfortable environment that removes barriers to communication. At the beginning of the focus group, the moderator describes the protocol of the discussion. There are several concerns that the moderator faces as the conversation continues. The moderator must know when to wait for more information and when to move on to the next question. The moderator must be able to control dominant speakers and encourage hesitant participants. The moderator guides the participants through the questions, carefully monitoring the time and moving from question to question when sufficient responses have been provided.

Analysis is the process of making sense out of the series of conversations. Not all studies require the same level of analysis. Occasionally, analysis can be done quickly because the data are clear and patterns are evident. At other times, the analytic process can be extremely time consuming. The analysis process consists of reviewing the data as captured by multiple means (memory, field notes, tape recording, video recording) and looking for the major themes that cut across groups. Often the focus group conversation is transcribed and the transcript is used in later analysis. Focus group analysis should be systematic and verifiable. Being systematic means that the analyst has a protocol that follows a predetermined sequence for capturing and handling the data. The process is verifiable in that there is a trail of evidence that could be replicated.

THE USE OF FOCUS GROUPS IN EVALUATION

Focus groups for evaluation have typically been used in the following ways:

- Trying to understand a problem, situation, or program from the perspective of a certain group. This understanding could result in the development of a program logic model, or it might be part of a needs assessment study, or it might be to gain insight into the variation of perceptions on a particular topic.
- Pilot testing of program ideas, materials, policies, services, or products.
- As a preliminary step in a series of research methods. Focus groups used in the development of a survey help ensure that the concepts are clear and the language is appropriate.
- Traditional evaluation uses, including formative evaluation, process evaluation, and impact or outcome evaluation. In these cases, the focus groups are not used for actual measurement or statistical purposes but rather as a way of gaining insight about a concept, a program, or a product.

—*Richard A. Krueger*

Further Reading

Krueger, R. A., & Casey, M. A. (2000). *Focus groups: A practical guide for applied research* (3rd ed.). Thousand Oaks, CA: Sage.

■■ FORMATIVE EVALUATION

Evaluation is considered *formative* when it is conducted during the development or delivery of a program or product with the intention of providing feedback to improve the evaluand. Formative evaluation may also focus on program plans or designs.

Formative evaluation typically focuses on determining whether a program is unfolding as planned, identifying obstacles or unexpected opportunities, and identifying midcourse corrections that will increase the likelihood of the program's success. It is a structured way to provide program staff with feedback designed to fine-tune the implementation of the program, and most often it is for internal use. Because many programs are never really complete, formative evaluation may be the primary mode of evaluation and can be critical to the development of information systems that provide continual feedback over time.

Robert E. Stake is known to illustrate the distinction between formative and summative evaluation with the following analogy: "When the cook tastes the soup, that's formative; when the guests taste the soup, that's summative."

■■ FORSS, KIM

(b. 1952, Malmo, Sweden). Ph.D., M.B.A. Stockholm School of Economics.

Forss is an economist and management specialist and one of the founders of the Andante group, a constellation of independent organizations involved in research, training, and consultant work in the field of international development cooperation. He has had assignments with the Departments of Foreign Affairs in Sweden, Norway, Denmark, and Ireland; with United Nations agencies; and with domestic public administration and private companies.

His contributions to the field of evaluation are in the design of evaluation systems, methods for quality control, participatory evaluation, and evaluation and organizational learning.

FOUNDATIONS AND EVALUATION. *See* PHILANTHROPIC EVALUATION

■■ FOURNIER, DEBORAH M.

(b. 1956, Manchester, New Hampshire). Ph.D., M.S. Instructional Design, Development and Evaluation, Syracuse University; B.S. University of Maryland.

Fournier is Assistant Professor and Director of Educational Research and Evaluation, School of Dental Medicine, Boston University. As Director, her role is to advance the School of Dental Medicine's vision of pursuing excellence in teaching and learning through the support of faculty in the (a) design, development, and delivery of instruction that is grounded in learning theory and cognitive science research; (b) evaluation of programs, policies, faculty, and students that enables continuous improvement; (c) analysis, interpretation, and use of data to sustain evidence-based decision making; and (d) study of teaching and learning to measure impact and institutional effectiveness.

Since 1996, she has served on an annual site visit team as Curriculum Consultant to the National Council on Dental Accreditation, which reviews schools of dental medicine. She is Cochair of the Curriculum Committee and Chair of the Evaluation and Dissemination Committee, School of Dental Medicine, and also a member of the Advisory Board for the Center for Excellence in Teaching at Boston University.

Her primary contributions to the field of evaluation center on exploring evaluative reasoning and the warrantability of approaches and applied inquiry methods. Primary influences on her evaluation work include the kinds of warrants used to support evidence collected by evaluators to build defensible evaluations. She is a member of the Editorial Advisory Board of the *American Journal of Evaluation* and a past Editorial Assistant of *New Directions for Program Evaluation.* She is an active member of the American Evaluation Association, where she is Past Chair of the Topical Interest Group on Theories of Evaluation.

■■ FOURTH-GENERATION EVALUATION

Fourth-generation evaluation, as its name implies, is the successor model incorporating three earlier generations of evaluation models (objectives, description, judgment) and moving beyond them to include intensive stakeholder participation in determining both the course of the evaluation and, as well, what actions should be taken on the evaluation results. In fourth-generation evaluation, the definition of stakeholder is considerably expanded to include not only program funders and managers but also targets of the program (those who, but for the program, might have had a program of their own) and other members of the community who have an interest or stake in the outcomes of the program being evaluated.

Fourth-generation evaluation begins with sharply different assumptions, which lead, in turn, to different modes of operating in the context. First, such evaluation efforts begin with the premise that it is not merely a physical, tangible reality to which stakeholders respond, but to their social-psychological *constructions*—that is, the mental meanings, values, beliefs, and sense-making structures in which humans engage to make meaning from events, contexts, activities, and situations in their lives. Thus, the collection of data on constructions assumes equal importance with collection of data on tangible realities (e.g., test scores, number of program participants, and the like). The collection, analysis, and evaluation of those constructions are central activities of the evaluation effort.

Second, it is assumed that the interaction between evaluators and stakeholders is an interactive epistemological exercise in which both sides arrive at a position that is more informed, more factual, more sophisticated, more data-rich, and more subtle. This is in sharp contrast to older models, in which stakeholders were assumed to be sources of data but not contributors to the nomination of critical issues or shaping of the evaluation effort. In fourth-generation evaluation, original program objectives are not the sole focus of evaluation data collection. Instead, objectives are joined with critical claims, concerns, and issues nominated by stake-holding audiences to enlarge the range of data gathering, discussion, and negotiation points between and among stakeholders. Furthermore, an epistemological commitment is made to expand the range of audiences that have access to data, information, and interpretations. Information is no longer concentrated in the hands of a small number of individuals but rather is shared widely in an effort to provide maximum evaluative responsiveness and the increased participation of stakeholders who have sophisticated information with which they might negotiate a program's future.

Third, fourth-generation evaluation enjoys an expanded methodological repertoire. Some evaluation efforts confine themselves to experimental and randomized-trial models, which rely heavily on mathematical and statistical models to generate data, but fourth-generation evaluation uses a data collection and analytic design that also incorporates, in additional to statistical approaches, a qualitative repertoire of methods. Although statistical and mathematical models do handle some forms of data well, it is only qualitative methods that are capable of collecting and analyzing the social constructions of stakeholders. Thus the methodological strategies of fourth-generation evaluators are often mixed in design, with *fit of method to question* rather than evaluator persuasion or training being the central methodological issue.

Fourth, this model of evaluation conceives of values in a vastly different way from many other more conventional forms of evaluation. Rather than assuming that values and valuing—an inherent part of human activity—should be marginalized in the interests of some putative scientific objectivity or disinterest, fourth-generation evaluation assumes that values are an inescapable part of human cognitive and sense-making activity. Because they are inescapable, and because evaluation itself is about the assignment of merit and worth to some evaluand, values are assigned a central role in evaluation activities. Values that inhere in the context or program site, values that are held by stakeholders, and values uncovered as conflicting between and among stakeholders are believed to be critical data sets in formulating judgments and conclusions about program usefulness. Values also feed into such evaluation arenas as competition between programs, decisions about expansion or reduction of the target base, administrative and delivery personnel requirements, and cost-benefit analyses. The recognition of and explicit dialogue on values, particularly where there is conflict that needs to be mediated between stakeholding groups, is an especially important role for fourth-generation evaluators. In recognition of this role, evaluators should have

training in mediation, small- and large-group facilitation, leadership, and other skills normally not considered as a part of those advanced theoretical and experiential degrees usually seen in evaluation programs.

Fourth-generation evaluation begins with philosophical assumptions (axioms) deriving not from logical positivism but rather from phenomenology and critical theory. The phenomenological statement of ontology (the study of the nature of reality) asserts that reality is not necessarily tangible or physical but rather consists of the mental and social *constructions* of individuals and groups. Because constructions emanate from the sense-making, meaning-imputing cognitive activities of humans, there is no single, necessarily tangible reality that can be referenced or subdivided atomistically for study. Rather, constructions are multiple (dependent only on the number of constructors) and they exist holistically, "fitted" with other constructions that tend to reinforce or buttress them. Treating individual and group constructions in ways that preserves their holism also permits evaluators to uncover and examine the values, beliefs, and attitudes that form the foundations for those constructions. Uncovering these values helps to ensure that when values are in conflict, stakeholders have an opportunity to optimize along more treasured values in open, negotiative ways.

The derivation of fourth-generation evaluation from critical theorist perspectives means that the various realities are also amenable to being treated as historical reifications—that is, as historical artifacts that can be altered or redirected toward increased democratic participation, increased civic involvement, or increased social justice.

The *epistemology* undergirding fourth-generation evaluation is likewise radically different from that which is basic to logical positivism. The first way in which it is different is that it is likely to be multiple and highly influenced, if not completely shaped, by race, ethnicity, gender, able bodiedness, sexual orientation, linguistic status, and other characteristics of constructors that are reasonably stable. Thus we can speak of multiple epistemologies, not a single epistemology: a critical theorist perspective on ways of knowing that influence how truth is constructed, delivered, and acted on. The phenomenological philosophy directs attention to the relationship between inquirer and respondent and proposes that that relationship is interactive, interdependent, and intersubjective. Maximum opportunities exist for evaluators to "trade roles," becoming at times the teacher, teaching stakeholders what needs to be known about the program (and therefore what information needs are critical from the perspective of funders, sponsors, and managers), and at times the learner, learning from stakeholders what is critical to them for decision making and for understanding program success.

While the axiological position of logical positivism is that of value freedom, objectivity, and scientific disinterest, the *axiology* of phenomenology understands that no human activity is value free. Consequently, values are most appropriately held to be central to fourth-generation evaluation. Because values are central, strenuous efforts are made both to take account of the various value positions brought to bear and to uncover assumed values of which individuals and groups may themselves be unaware.

Methodology (the overall design strategy for an evaluation) is also construed very differently under the umbrella of phenomenology than it is under that of logical positivism. Randomized, controlled experimentation is not likely to uncover the social constructions of stakeholders (although it can do some other things), and as a result, chosen methods may be (and often should be) mixed between quantitative and qualitative. Qualitative methods will, however, always be a foundational part of any phenomenological inquiry or evaluation because they are the only methods appropriate for and able to garner the mental sense-making, meaning-making activities of human beings. Other kinds of data may also be needed, and thus many fourth-generation evaluations are themselves mixed designs. Mixed-methods designs are always appropriate when data are needed that respond to different definitions of reality and different perspectives on what constitutes critical data (e.g., cost-benefit analyses).

Fourth-generation evaluation also differs significantly from other types of evaluation in the criteria posed to judge its worthwhileness, its rigor, and its validity and value. Originally, four criteria were proposed for trustworthiness judgments of constructivist evaluations (as well as inquiries more broadly, including research, evaluation, and policy analyses). These were credibility, roughly analogous to internal validity; transferability, analogous to the requirement for generalizability, or the ability to be useful beyond the generating context; dependability, a form of reliability estimate that enables the conclusion that sound methodological decisions were made in the field and that appropriate processes were employed; and confirmability,

or the ability to trace data back to their sources and verify information that was collected in the evaluation effort. These criteria represent a major shift in the constitution of rigor for evaluation studies, principally for two reasons. First, they assume that the ability to use the study's findings beyond its own local contexts is a matter for consumers of evaluation reports (e.g., those who might wish to transfer one evaluation's findings to their own contexts) rather than a matter of statements by evaluators, as in the case of generalizability. Second, trustworthiness judgments reside not in methods (as they do, for example, in classical experimentation) but in the data themselves: Can data be traced back to a primary source? Are they verifiable? Are the conclusions reached logical, sensible, plausible? This represents a major shift in standards of rigor and validity, as experimental models typically assert generalizability via strict adherence to appropriate statistical methods and techniques, but constructivist models rely rather more on judgments of transferability from those seeking to transfer and use the findings in their own, local contexts.

Fourth-generation evaluation, however, also has its own, intrinsic, nonexperimental criteria for determining how authentic the evaluation's efforts might be. Called *authenticity criteria*, these criteria include judgments regarding the fairness, or balance, in the evaluation report; ontological authenticity; educative authenticity; catalytic authenticity; and tactical authenticity. Fairness refers to the evaluation's efforts to make certain that all stakeholder views are represented in a balanced way in the final report. Ontological authenticity references the extent to which the evaluation effort helps individual and stakeholder groups to understand more clearly their own, perhaps previously unarticulated beliefs and values. Educative authenticity refers to the characteristic of the inquiry that permits stakeholders to understand and appreciate the standpoints and value positions of other stakeholders and groups affected by the evaluation. Catalytic authenticity arises from the efforts of the evaluation to prompt action on the part of stakeholders. Fourth-generation evaluation was in fact developed, in part, as a response to the nonuse of evaluation findings; catalytic evaluation—or the ability of any evaluation efforts to be so framed as to move decision makers and stakeholders to action—is therefore intrinsic as one of the validity judgments that might be rendered about an evaluation's effectiveness.

Tactical authenticity, the final of the five intrinsic criteria of authentic fourth-generation evaluation, speaks to an issue that many detractors simply find impossible to accept. Tactical authenticity recognizes that not all stakeholders enter evaluation efforts with the same skills or ability to take action, or even with the request that action be taken on evaluation findings. The corridors of power frequently seem forbidding to stakeholders who feel themselves marginalized. Thus one final task for the evaluator is one that is frequently perceived as an advocacy role. It is, however, not an advocacy role as much as it is an effort to level the playing field in the interests of having all stakeholders' voices heard and ensuring that input into claims, concerns, and issues comes from all interest sectors.

A clear distinction can be made here between criteria for validity and rigor. The trustworthiness criteria are foundational; that is, they are responsive to the concerns of the more classical paradigm, which we call the scientific method. Those criteria are primarily directed at ensuring that methodological decisions (decisions about design strategy and method) are logical, sound, and feasible and may be inspected by the public. The authenticity criteria are aimed at larger paradigmatic issues. Because of their inherent relationship to the evaluation model's central premises or axioms, they are less about method and rather more about the intrinsic relationships between evaluators and stakeholders. Thus the authenticity criteria are grounded in professional ethical standards and in reasonable and just ways of making certain that all voices have an equal say in the valuing of the merit or worth of some program (curriculum, policy, and the like).

Fourth-generation evaluation was designed to counteract several problems with classical experimental or quasiexperimental designs in evaluation. The first problem was the rampant nonutilization of evaluation findings, despite the expenditure of millions of dollars on national, statewide, and local evaluative efforts. The second problem, long identified by feminists and other theoreticians, was the objectification of human beings in classical scientific models of research. The third problem this model hoped to address concerned the relationships between evaluators and program stakeholders, as well as between stakeholders and policy formulation personnel. The deep and authentic involvement of program "targets" in evaluating programs designed for them was meant to provide grassroots input to policy processes as a way of democratizing and extending citizen involvement (i.e., parent involvement, teacher involvement,

and the like). Finally, the paradigm was designed to take account of critical social data that had been largely ignored in the social sciences since the turn of the 20th century: the social meaning-making and sense-making processes by which thinking humans make sense of their own worlds and those of others.

—*Yvonna S. Lincoln*

Further Reading

Guba, E. G., & Lincoln, Y. S. (1981). *Effective evaluation: Improving the usefulness of evaluation results through responsive and naturalistic approaches.* San Francisco: Jossey-Bass.

Guba, E. G., & Lincoln, Y. S. (1982). Epistemological and methodological bases of naturalistic inquiry. *Educational Communication and Technology Journal, 30,* 233-252.

Guba, E. G., & Lincoln, Y. S. (1989). *Fourth generation evaluation.* Newbury Park, CA: Sage.

Lincoln, Y. S., & Guba, E. G. (1985). *Naturalistic inquiry.* Beverly Hills, CA: Sage.

Lincoln, Y. S., & Guba, E. G. (1986). Research, evaluation and policy analysis: Heuristics for disciplined inquiry. *Policy Studies Review, 5*(3), 546-565.

Lincoln, Y. S., & Guba, E. G. (2000). Paradigmatic controversies, contradictions and emerging confluences. In N. K. Denzin & Y. S. Lincoln (Eds.), *Handbook of qualitative research* (2nd ed., pp. 163-188). Thousand Oaks, CA: Sage.

■■ FREEMAN, HOWARD E.

(b. 1929, New York City; d. 1992, in flight between Washington, DC, and Los Angeles). Ph.D., M.A. Graduate School of Arts and Sciences, New York University; B.A. New York University.

Freeman began his career as Assistant Social Scientist at the RAND Corporation, followed by a position at the Harvard School of Public Health (1956-1962). He became the Morse Professor of Urban Studies at Brandeis University, where he served for 12 years. Freeman was Social Science Advisor for Mexico, Central America, and the Caribbean for the Ford Foundation in Mexico City from 1972 to 1974.

Later, during his tenure at UCLA, he was Professor and Chair of Sociology, Director of the Institute for Social Science Research, and a contributing faculty member in several UCLA departments. Freeman was also Senior Research Advisor to the Robert Wood Johnson Foundation, a consultant to the RAND Corporation, and a member of the Institute of

Medicine and the National Academy of Sciences. He was a consultant on evaluation and research to many foundations and organizations, including the National Science Foundation, Russell Sage Foundation, American Academy of Sciences, MacArthur Foundation, the National Institutes of Mental Health, the National Center for Health Services Research, and the Japan Academy for Health Behavioral Science.

Freeman was one of the first to delineate medical sociology as a field in sociology. He and Ozzie Simmons received the Hofheimer Prize from the American Psychiatric Association for the best book on behavior from 1960 to 1963 for *The Mental Patient Comes Home*. In 1991, Freeman received the Myrdal Award for Evaluation Practice from the American Evaluation Association. Freeman wrote and edited many books on evaluation research. He also was the coeditor of several evaluation research journals.

His interest in the social sciences allowed him to elevate evaluation research to a more rigorous and scientific endeavor. His textbook, well known in the field of evaluation, *Evaluation: A Systematic Approach*, coauthored with Peter Rossi and others, is widely used today. In fact, Freeman passed away on the airplane after finishing one of the editions of the book. He had authored more than 100 books and articles.

▪▪ FRIERSON, HENRY T.

(b. 1944, Weir, Kansas). Ph.D. Educational Psychology, Michigan State University; M.Ed. Educational Psychology, B.S. Psychology, Wayne State University.

Frierson is Director of the Research Education Support Program and Professor of Educational Psychology, Measurement and Evaluation, University of North Carolina at Chapel Hill. He has been at the University of North Carolina since 1974 and has served as the Associate Dean of the Graduate School and a Professor in the School of Medicine, where he founded and directed the Learning and Assessment Laboratory. Since 1996, he has directed the Research Education Support Program, which is largely supported by funding from the National Institutes of Health and the National Science Foundation.

His recognition of the mentoring needs of minority graduate students has focused his attention on increasing the number of individuals of color in doctoral

programs and research and evaluation careers. His work has supported the development of culturally responsive approaches in evaluation. David Fetterman and Ernest House, writers he admires for their deep understanding of the value of evaluation for program improvement, especially when participants are involved, have influenced Frierson.

Frierson has been a member of the American Evaluation Association's Task Force on Diversity in Evaluation and American Educational Research Association's Commission on Research in Black Education. He has been recognized for his contributions to higher education and received the 1993 Award for Excellence in Research and Education from the Research Focus on Black Education Special Interest Group of the American Education Research Association and the Fifteenth Anniversary National Association for Minority Educators Tribute Award in 1990.

▪▪ FUNNELL, SUE

(b. 1951, Sydney, Australia). M.A. Education, B.A. Psychology, University of Sydney

Funnell's work in evaluation stems from a mixed group of intellectual influences, including realist philosophy; evaluation approaches that focus on "the why of the outcomes"; stakeholder values; social justice and distributive considerations; and taxonomies of objectives, including those of Bennett, Bloom, Hastings, and Madaus.

Funnell's primary contribution to evaluation has been the development of a particular approach to program theory (program logic), beginning in the mid-1980s in Australia, that overcomes some of the shortcomings of mechanistic input-process-output-outcome models, gives explicit recognition to the complexities of causality, and incorporates evaluation criteria, including those that represent different stakeholder perspectives. The methodology helps to avoid simplistic and goal-displacing approaches to performance monitoring and is an antidote to black-box approaches to evaluation. The methodology, including the development of a taxonomy of program logics, was informed by evaluation theory but developed from the ground up as Funnell was working with hundreds of program managers and evaluators across many different areas of the public sector. The methodology has been influential throughout Australia and internationally with respect to program planning and design, performance monitoring, and program evaluation at both policy and practitioner levels.

Highlights of Funnell's career include a 6-month research scholarship to study at the Center for Instructional Research and Curriculum Evaluation at the University of Illinois, two terms as President of the Australasian Evaluation Society, and receiving the Australasian Evaluation Society Evaluation Training and Services Award (its highest award) for Outstanding Contributions to Evaluation in Australia.

FUZZY METHODS. *See* COMPLEX ADAPTIVE SYSTEMS, SYSTEMS AND SYSTEMS THINKING

GAY, LESBIAN, AND BISEXUAL ISSUES IN EVALUATION. *See* LESBIAN, GAY, BISEXUAL, AND TRANSGENDER ISSUES IN EVALUATION

■■ GENDERED EVALUATION

Gendered evaluation is contingent on the meanings given to the terms *sex* and *gender:* whether sex and gender are understood to be a fact of nature or socially constructed; whether to view the experiences of a particular gender as homogeneous or see that gender can be constructed and experienced differently based on the intersections of race, ethnicity, class, and sexual identity; and whether to accept the bifurcation of sex (female and male) and gender (masculine and feminine) or to explore the inclusion of more than two sexes (i.e., intersexed individuals) and two genders (i.e., transgendered individuals).

—*Denice A. Cassaro*

Further Reading

Seigart, D., & Brisolara, S. (Eds.). (2002). Feminist evaluation: Explorations and experiences. *New Directions for Evaluation, 96.*

■■ GENERAL ACCOUNTING OFFICE (GAO)

The General Accounting Office is the audit, evaluation, and investigative arm of the U.S. government.

The GAO was created in 1921 as a result of the Budget and Accounting Act, and its "watchdog" role has evolved over the decades. The Budget and Accounting Act transferred auditing responsibilities, accounting, and claims functions from the Treasury Department to the new agency. The GAO was created because federal financial management was in disarray after World War I. Wartime spending had driven up the national debt, and Congress saw that it needed more information and better control over expenditures. The act made the GAO independent of the executive branch and gave it a broad mandate to investigate how federal dollars are spent. The act also required the president to prepare an annual budget for the federal government. Later legislation clarified or expanded the GAO's role, but the Budget and Accounting Act continues to serve as the basis for its operations.

The GAO exists to support Congress in meeting its Constitutional responsibilities and to help improve the performance and ensure the accountability of the federal government to the public. The GAO examines the use of public funds; evaluates federal programs and activities; and provides analyses, options, and recommendations to help Congress make policy and funding decisions. The GAO performs a range of oversight-, insight-, and foresight-related engagements, the vast majority of which are conducted in response to congressional mandates or requests. The GAO's engagements include evaluations of federal programs and performance, financial and management audits, policy analyses, legal opinions, bid protest adjudications, and investigations.

The GAO employs professionals who hold degrees in many academic disciplines, including accounting, law, engineering, public and business administration, economics, computer science, and the social and physical sciences. These professionals are arrayed in 13 research, audit, and evaluation teams. The teams are backed by staff offices and mission support units. About three quarters of the more than 3250 employees are based in Washington, DC; the rest are deployed in 11 field offices.

The GAO conducts its work within a particular sociopolitical climate and thus its focus changes from time to time. For example, in 2003, the focus was on the challenges that most urgently engaged the attention of Congress. Issues such as terrorism, Social Security and Medicare reform, the implementation of education legislation, human capital transformations at selected federal agencies, and the security of key government information systems were investigated to support congressional members and their staffs in developing new federal policies and programs and oversee ongoing ones.

The GAO has contributed substantially to the theory and practice of evaluation in the United States. Because it is the largest internal, independent evaluation unit in existence, its operations have contributed to an understanding of internal evaluation. The work of the GAO has also been instrumental in understanding evaluation utilization, as it must be defined to be accountable. In the past year, the GAO made 1950 recommendations to improve government operations, and four out of five recommendations made during the past 4 years have been implemented. A number of prominent evaluation theorists (for example, Nancy Kingsbury, Eleanor Chelimsky, Lois-Ellin Datta) have been employed by the GAO.

Further Reading

U.S. General Accounting Office. (n.d.). *GAO: Accountability, reliability, integrity.* Retrieved May 20, 2004, from http://www.gao.gov/

▉ GENERALIZATION

Generalization refers, broadly, both to the process of drawing a general conclusion from specific observations (e.g., generalizing about a large population from a much smaller sample) and to the conclusion that results (e.g., a generalization drawn about whether males or females more strongly prefer a specific political candidate). In the context of evaluation, the relevant question typically is: How well, based on a specific set of observations made in a particular evaluation conducted in a given setting at a particular time, can one draw more general conclusions about the policy, program, or practice in question?

Researchers often think about generalization in terms of generalizing from a sample, preferably a random sample, to a population. However, in evaluation (and elsewhere), the generalizations in which we are interested are typically more complex. Evaluators (and evaluation audiences) may be interested in whether we can generalize from a sample of one population to another population (e.g., can we generalize from a school evaluation in Georgia to the school system in California? Can we generalize to rural poor from a welfare reform evaluation that included only urban poor?). We may also be interested in generalizing across time and historical context (e.g., can we generalize findings about a job-training program in 1998, when the economy was strong, to 2003, when the economy was weak?). As Lee Cronbach reminded us, we may sometimes actually be interested in generalizing from a sample that participated in an evaluation to an individual case (e.g., can a school principal generalize to *her particular school* based on findings reported for the many schools that took part in an evaluation?). In the influential validity framework of Donald T. Campbell and his associates, the preceding forms of generalization all fall under the rubric of external validity, which refers to the extent to which one can generalize the findings of a study to other persons, settings, and times.

Evaluators (and consumers of evaluation) are also interested in how well we can generalize from research on concrete operations to more abstract constructs. This generalization issue is exemplified in debates about how well a specific achievement test supports conclusions about the more abstract construct of student learning. In Cook and Campbell's validity framework, this generalization issue falls under construct validity.

Ernie House suggests that three methodological traditions have taken hold in evaluation in an attempt to deal with the challenges of generalization (and other challenges that beset early large-scale, quantitative evaluations). First is the qualitative tradition in evaluation, which, as advocated by some prominent evaluation figures such as Bob Stake, eschews attempts to generalize beyond the local context. Stake argues that the focus of evaluation should be on particularization rather than generalization. A second, very different tradition House cites is meta-analysis. As illustrated in the work of Mark Lipsey, meta-analysis attempts to facilitate generalization by combining studies from different contexts and times. A third recent tradition is the set of approaches that rely on program theory, including the theory-driven approach of Huey Chen. These theory-based approaches attempt to support generalization by identifying underlying processes and by specifying the conditions under which a given program will have the desired effects.

More generally, Lipsey suggested that the common methodological recommendations about how to support generalization relied on three underlying principles or assumptions. First is a "similarity principle," which assumes that one can predict from like instances. For example, both Cronbach and Cook and Campbell suggested studying cases similar to those to which you wish to generalize. The second, the "robustness principle," assumes that generalization is more warranted if a given finding has been observed over diverse circumstances. Again, both Cook and Campbell and Cronbach discussed the value of studying diverse cases for generalization. Third, an "explanation principle" presumes that knowledge about why an effect does (or does not) occur helps in attempts to extrapolate to other persons, settings, or times. Cronbach especially emphasizes the importance of explanation. (More recently, Shadish, Cook, and Campbell have provided a somewhat similar set of five principles to support generalization).

Interestingly, Melvin A. Mark's three principles are linked to the three evaluation approaches identified by Ernie House. Qualitative methods, with limited attempts to generalize beyond the current setting, rely on the similarity principle (assuming the ability to generalize, e.g., from a school in 2003 to the same school in 2004). Meta-analysis, in combining studies from different contexts, relies largely on the robustness principle. The program theory approach to evaluation, clearly, relies on the explanation principle.

Although the term *generalization* is widely used, and evaluators rarely discuss its meaning, some nontrivial ambiguity exists about what, precisely, it means to say that a finding is generalizable. Does it mean, for example, that the size of the treatment effect in a new setting will be precisely what it was in an evaluation? Probably not, for we would rarely expect *exactly* the same treatment effect in different settings (or even in an exact replication, in the same setting). Alternatively, does generalization simply mean that the treatment effect in a new setting will be of the *same sign* as it was in the evaluation? In other words, would a treatment that had a positive effect in an evaluation also have a positive effect in the new setting? Some authors explicitly adopt this meaning of generalization. However, it may be unsatisfying simply to conclude, when an evaluation finds a large positive treatment effect, that the program's effect is likely to be positive, but perhaps far smaller, in a new setting of interest. Rather than talking about generalization in general terms, evaluators might be better off talking about an expected range of treatment effects for the persons, settings, or times to which we wish to generalize. Alternatively, we could talk about the expected "robustness" of findings.

The pathways of an evaluation's influence typically involve generalization. Evaluation findings in one state may influence policy deliberations in another state or at the federal level. Evaluation findings at a limited number of sites may influence program offerings at many other sites. Even if we think of evaluation findings as particularized and try to restrict use to the specific setting in which the evaluation was conducted, generalization is involved. Even in this limited case, generalizations must be made from one time and one set of participants to later times and to other sets of participants. Generalization is a central part of the work of evaluation.

—*Melvin M. Mark*

Further Reading

Cook, T. D., & Campbell, D. T. (1979). *Quasi-experimentation: Design and analysis issues for field settings.* Skokie, IL: Rand McNally.

Cronbach, L. J. (1982). *Designing evaluations of educational and social programs.* San Francisco: Jossey-Bass.

House, E. R. (2001). Unfinished business: Causes and values. *American Journal of Evaluation, 22*(3), 309-315.

Mark, M. M. (1986). Validity typologies and the logic and practice of quasi-experimentation. In W.M.K. Trochim (Ed.), *Advances in quasi-experimental design and analysis* (pp. 47-66). San Francisco: Jossey-Bass.

Shadish, W. R., Cook, T. D., & Campbell, D. T. (2002). *Experimental and quasi-experimental designs for generalized causal inference.* Boston: Houghton-Mifflin.

GEORGHIOU, LUKE

(b. 1955, Beirut). Ph.D., B.Sc. (Hons) Liberal Studies in Science (Physics), University of Manchester.

Georghiou is Professor of Science and Technology Policy and Management and Executive Director of Policy Research in Engineering, Science and Technology, University of Manchester, an institute focusing on evaluation of research and innovation policy and programs. He is a consultant to several ministries in the United Kingdom, the Organisation for Economic Co-operation and Development (OECD), the European Commission, several major companies, and several foreign governments. Georghiou co-led the United Kingdom's largest research evaluation exercise, the evaluation of the Alvey Program for Advanced Information Technology, from 1983 to 1990.

His research includes evaluation of R&D and innovation policy, foresight, national and international science policy, and management of science and technology. He developed the concept of "behavioral additionality," now widely used in European policy development rationales. Georghiou's work has been influenced by the work of Richard Nelson and Stan Metcalfe in evolutionary economics. The Manchester tradition of evaluation science policy, begun by Bruce Williams and further impressed on Georghiou by his doctoral supervisor and first employer Michael Gibbons, has shaped his theory and practice of evaluation.

Georghiou has chaired several international evaluation panels, such as the European Union Biotechnology program, the EUREKA Initiative, and the German Futur Initiative and has been a member of many others. He currently chairs committees on the effectiveness of direct measures for R&D support for the European Commission. He is also on numerous committees, including the Finnish Public Research Funding Evaluation Committee, the Medical Research Council Steering Group for the Monitoring and Evaluation of Research Funding Schemes, the Swedish KK-stiftelsen (Knowledge Foundation) International Advisory Committee on Evaluation of Research Doctorates, the Executive Board of the Save British Science Society, and the Steering Committee of the Technology Strategy Forum.

Georghiou has authored or coauthored several works, including *Evaluation of Research: A Selection of Current Practices, Post-Innovation Performance—Technological Development and Competition,* and *Evaluation of the Alvey Program.*

GLASS, GENE V

(b. 1940, Lincoln, Nebraska). Ph.D. Educational Psychology, M.S. Educational Psychology, University of Wisconsin; B.S. Mathematics and German, University of Nebraska.

Glass is Professor of Education Policy Studies and Professor of Psychology in Education at Arizona State University at Tempe, where he has held appointments in three departments, headed the Ph.D. program in Education, and served as Associate Dean of Policy for Research in the College of Education. Before moving to Arizona State University in 1986, he held faculty positions at the University of Illinois, Urbana-Champaign, and the University of Colorado at Boulder. In 1975, he was elected President of the American Educational Research Association; he was the youngest president the association had had in its 80-year history. Glass has been Visiting Scholar at the Max-Planck-Institute for Psychiatry in Munich and the Center for the Study of Evaluation at UCLA.

His primary contribution to the field of evaluation was his invention in 1976 of the statistical technique for the synthesis of empirical research studies currently known as meta-analysis. Trained originally in statistics, his interests include psychotherapy research, evaluation methodology, and policy analysis. Primary influences on his work include Robert E. Stake, Michael Scriven, and Paul E. Meehl. He served as Review Editor of *Educational Research* (1968-1970), Methodology Editor for *Psychological Bulletin* (1978-1980), and Coeditor of *American Educational Research Journal* (1983-1986) and, in 1993, he created and still edits the first all-electronic scholarly journal in education on the Internet, *Education Policy Analysis Archives.* He is also Editor of *Education Review* and Executive Editor of *International Journal of Education & the Arts.*

He has published more than a dozen books, including *Design and Analysis of Time-Series Experiments* (with V. L. Willson and J. M. Gottman), *Benefits of Psychotherapy* (with M. L. Smith and T. Miller), *Meta-Analysis in Social Research* (with B. McGaw and M. L. Smith), and *School Class Size: Research and Policy* (with L. S. Cahen, M. L. Smith, and

N. N. Filby), as well as nearly 200 articles in scholarly and professional journals. His work on meta-analysis of psychotherapy outcomes (with M. L. Smith) was named as one of the "Forty Studies That Changed Psychology" in the book of the same name by Roger R. Hock (1999).

Besides winning the Creative Talent Award in Psychometrics from the American Institutes for Research for his dissertation, recognition for his work includes the American Educational Research Association's Palmer O. Johnson Award (received twice, in 1968 and 1970), the American Evaluation Association's Paul Lazarsfeld Award (1984), the Cattell Award of the Society of Multivariate Experimental Psychology, and the Lifetime Achievement Award of the Arizona Educational Research Organization (1998). He is also a member of the National Academy of Education (2000).

■ GOAL

A *goal* is a general statement of an intended outcome of a particular program; it is usually operationalized into a measurable objective.

—Jeffrey G. Tucker

See also OBJECTIVES-BASED EVALUATION

■ GOAL-FREE EVALUATION

This approach, developed by Michael Scriven, rests on the premise that an evaluation should examine the value of a program by investigating what it is doing rather than what it is trying to do. It is, in large part, an approach designed to reduce a particular kind of bias in evaluation. In other words, the organization of the evaluation is not based on what the program's goals are but rather on what the program is actually doing. If the program is meeting its goals and objectives, this should become apparent through an investigation of the program's activities and outcomes. The orientation in goal-free evaluation is more toward the ways in which a program meets the needs of its target clients or population and less on what managers and developers assert to be their intentions. Therefore, goal-free evaluation relies heavily on needs assessment to judge the quality and fit of the program to client needs.

In many ways, the idea of goal-free evaluation has been a powerful rhetorical device within evaluation practice, cautioning evaluators to examine more than what program managers and developers say they intend to do. Such goal statements often serve many purposes, both pragmatic and political, but provide a poor grounding for conducting an evaluation. Examining only stated goals diminishes the likelihood of uncovering unintended and unanticipated outcomes, either positive or negative.

Goal-free evaluation is unlikely to be a popular approach with managers and program administrators, in large part because it decreases their control over the focus of the evaluation and, therefore, the evaluation's conclusions. The notion of goal-free evaluation very explicitly takes the perspective of the consumer, the client, the recipient of services. Scriven uses consumer examples to illustrate this difference. For example, when one evaluates a product to purchase, such as a car, one is uninterested in the goals and intentions of the car manufacturer and instead makes a judgment about which is the best car based on an assessment of one's own needs.

Further Reading

Scriven, M. (1976). Prose and cons about goal-free evaluation. In G. V Glass (Ed.), *Evaluation studies review annual* (Vol. 1). Beverly Hills, CA: Sage.

■ GOALS 2000

Goals 2000: Educate America Act, a bipartisan bill, was signed into law on March 31, 1994. The U.S. federal government pledged to form a new and supportive partnership with states and communities in an effort to improve student academic achievement across the nation. Goals 2000 was a direct outgrowth of the state-led education reform movement of the 1980s. The 1989 Charlottesville Education Summit, convened by then President George H. W. Bush and the nation's governors and led by then-Governor Bill Clinton, further underscored the need for a national response to address educational needs by establishing the following national education goals to be achieved by the year 2000:

- All children in America will start school ready to learn.
- The high school graduation rate will increase to at least 90%.

- All students will leave grades 4, 8, and 12 having demonstrated competency over challenging subject matter in the core academic subjects.
- U.S. students will be first in the world in mathematics and science achievement.
- Every adult American will be literate and will possess the knowledge and skills necessary to compete in a global economy and exercise the rights and responsibilities of citizenship.
- Every school in the United States will be free of drugs, violence, and the unauthorized presence of firearms and alcohol and will offer a disciplined environment conducive to learning.
- The nation's teaching force will have access to programs for the continued improvement of their professional skills and the opportunity to acquire the knowledge and skills needed to instruct and prepare all U.S. students for the next century.
- Every school will promote partnerships that will increase parental involvement and participation in promoting the social, emotional, and academic growth of children.

Goals 2000 is widely recognized as the initial impetus for standards-based reform in U.S. education and schools.

—*Jeffrey G. Tucker*

GOALS-BASED EVALUATION. *See* OBJECTIVES-BASED EVALUATION

▪▪ GOVERNMENT AND EVALUATION

The degree of interest in evaluation shown by governments, where evaluation is seen as a systematic assessment of government interventions, can be explained by a number of factors. One of the overall preconditions for the occurrence of evaluation is a democratic system. Even though democracy is neither a sufficient nor necessary factor for conducting evaluations, it is still a very important one, at least for some comprehensive types of evaluation. It is, for example, difficult to imagine evaluations that question government programs on the basis of their aim and relevance or an independent (free from government oversight)

evaluation of programs in monolithic societies such as some communist countries.

Another general overall observation is that, with one or two exceptions (for example, the United States), governments and not parliaments are the main players in either conducting evaluations themselves or having them done externally. The reason is quite simple. The implementation of different programs is usually a task for governments, and the evaluation of these programs is usually requested or demanded by parliaments.

GOVERNMENT AND EVALUATION: ORIGINS

The fact that evaluation activities are normally carried out by governments and not parliaments does not explain why some countries have more evaluation activities or started earlier than others. This is not an easy question to answer. A comparison of evaluation activities in eight countries reveals a first and second wave of countries according to degree of maturity in evaluation. The first wave countries, for example, the United States, Canada, and Sweden, were characterized by an interest in evaluation as such. One of the common features of these early pioneers was that they shared stable institutions with access to basic information about the state of things; for example, institutions that registered the development of important welfare indicators. This coincided with an interest in empirical evidence for the decision-making process. Evaluation was supposed to serve as an *information* source within a rationalistic planning procedure. The name of one of the leading concepts of the 1960s, Planning, Programming and Budget Systems, gives an indication of this view. Another feature uniting these first wave countries was a large public sector and, as a consequence of this, lots of programs to evaluate. A further explanation is the entry of academics with a social science background and with more training in evaluation, in contrast to evaluators who mainly had a legal background.

If the need for information affected evaluation activities in the 1960s, the perspective was different in the 1970s and the 1980s. Evaluation was seen as a means to help governments cut expenditure in the public sector. Still, evaluation was regarded as a rationalistic tool. Governments believed empirical evidence could provide them with answers to the decisions they should make. In the wake of financial crisis, ministries of finance emerged as leading players in the field of evaluation. Concepts or expressions such as management by results, value for money, and "new public management" became commonplace. In this development, a mishmash of terms, such as *monitoring, follow-up, quality assurance, audits, performance indicators, service standards,* and other jargon emerged, all under the umbrella of evaluation. The term *evaluation* became a semantic magnet. This is also the time when the second wave countries, for example, Australia, The Netherlands, and Norway, appeared on the evaluation map.

The interest in evaluation as an information source and the financial crisis were the prime movers for the first and second wave countries where evaluation was concerned. For others, this was not enough. The international or intranational community has different rules for the members of its own organizations, and it may force countries receiving loans or subsidies to fulfill different demands made on them. External pressures have been the point of departure or the prime mover for evaluation activities in these countries. Membership in the European Union has, for example, forced countries such as Spain, Ireland, and Italy to conduct evaluations that would not have been necessary without the European Union. Sponsors, such as the World Bank, require or help recipient countries with capacity building in the area of evaluation. All these efforts directly encourage governments to be active in evaluation.

THE INSTITUTIONALIZATION OF GOVERNMENT AND EVALUATION

The institutionalization of evaluation activities in governments differs. This can be explained to some extent by the organization of different governments, as well as by the intensity with which countries have chosen to implement evaluation activities. The idea that an evaluation function should be embedded in all departments or that all programs should be evaluated according to evaluation plans is something that has been approved by parliaments in, for example, Australia and The Netherlands, but to a lesser degree in most other countries. Other countries have created separate evaluation authorities, committees or, in for example Sweden and Norway, agencies that are

required to show the results they have achieved in their annual reports. Another way for governments to obtain evaluation information is via special research institutes established in certain areas, for example in the regional area, labor market area, crime prevention, and so forth.

GOVERNMENT AND EVALUATION: NATURAL PARTNERS?

The relation between governments and evaluation is not without complications. In a democratic society, evaluation results are open to the public, the political party in office, and politicians in opposition. This means that if programs are not doing well, a chance arises for criticizing the government. Politicians who stipulate both the scope and the types of information they need are probably the most decisive parties for evaluation success. Different political parties have varying degrees of interest in evaluation. Although evaluation activities in many countries have increased, evaluation activities in, for example, the United States and Canada have decreased, at least at the federal or central level. Making thorough evaluations takes time, and politicians in general are impatient. Evaluation information is, to a great extent, history, and it has to compete with a political perspective, which usually looks ahead.

It is therefore not surprising that one of the more powerful words today is *control*. If we look in retrospect at the types of evaluation that are normally conducted in different countries, only a few countries, mainly the early pioneers in evaluation, have a balance between different kinds of evaluations (i.e., output, process, and outcome evaluations). The newcomers mostly conduct output and process evaluations. Evaluation is dependent on the concept that knowledge-based information is important, but perhaps the modern world moves too fast for the reflective knowledge-based information that evaluations are supposed to generate.

—*Rolf Sandahl*

Further Reading

Furubo, J.-E., Rist, R., & Sandahl, R. (Eds.). (2002). *International atlas of evaluation.* New Brunswick, NJ: Transaction.

Rist, R. (Ed.). (1990). *Program evaluation and the management of government: Patterns and prospects across eight nations.* New Brunswick, NJ: Transaction.

Evaluation Practice Around the World

Belgium

Policy Evaluation in Belgium: Toward Institutionalization?

A number of European countries (France, Switzerland, The Netherlands, Sweden, and others) in which evaluation is developed have taken measures toward institutionalizing it (e.g., by creating parliamentary or executive bodies, evaluation clauses, national societies of evaluators). It is generally accepted that Belgium is lagging behind in this area, even though the Belgian National Audit Office is the headquarters of the European Evaluation Society. What is the real situation regarding evaluative practice in Belgium? To answer that question, a distinction must be drawn between the various levels of power extant in the country.

At the federal level, a representative survey carried out among secretaries and directors-general in ministries and public undertakings and chairmen of standing parliamentary committees, parties, and trade unions reveals that most public bodies claim that they use one or another form of evaluation as a tool in managing and piloting policies. The evaluations carried out generally relate to an action program. They are conducted ex post facto by an internal evaluator who employs qualitative and quantitative methods and involves the administration and officials concerned in the process. According to those who replied to the survey, evaluation results are released to a large public and are very often taken into account. Furthermore, they give rise to modifications of margins in regard to both the policy under evaluation and the organization in charge of implementation.

Finally, 88% of the public bodies questioned, irrespective of whether they carry out evaluations already, are in favor of enhanced policy evaluation at the federal level.

However, a metaevaluation indicated the limits of the survey in terms of scientific quality and political reappropriation of the findings contained in the reports. Evaluation specifications are often incomplete or even nonexistent. The number of partners involved in evaluative processes is quite small: The administration generally takes pride of place, whereas the political arm (executive and legislative) and the beneficiaries of public action are underrepresented. Moreover, political exploitation of evaluators' conclusions and findings is on the low side, given a perceived lack of interest on the part of political decision makers. That holds true both in cases where the evaluation is decided on and carried out at the administration's own behest and in cases where the evaluation is the result of an evaluation clause or political request.

With regard to quality standards determined by professional evaluation organizations and already applied in many countries, we would emphasize that, in general, Belgian evaluations do not give rise to any deontological problems. They would appear to be satisfactory but capable of considerable further improvements in terms of their practical feasibility (e.g., the cost-benefit ratio of the evaluation) and scientific accuracy (e.g., presentation of the context of the policy evaluated, verification and validity of data, explicit grounds for conclusions). On the other hand, the standard of political usefulness of evaluations is clearly not so well met. The following points in particular are worthy of discussion: failure to identify all the parties involved in the policy under evaluation, excessively restricted choice of information gathered, difficulty in distinguishing conclusions from value judgments, poor readability of certain reports, and inappropriate timing in publication of evaluation results.

In conclusion, evaluative practice is (perceived by public bodies as) developed within the administration despite a low degree of formal institutionalization. Mention must be made here of the recent development of the tasks of the National Audit Office, which in 1998 was allocated new powers regarding the proper use of public funds, enabling it to carry out a check as to effectiveness, efficiency, and economy alongside the traditional review of legality and regularity.

The situation we have just described is similar to that obtaining in the northern regions of the country. Both in (Flemish-speaking) Flanders and in the region of Brussels, evaluations are ordered unsystematically and outside any institutional framework regulating the practice.

The situation is different in (French-speaking) Wallonia, where evaluative practice has developed as a result of the conditions attaching to grants from the European structural funds. The obligation to carry out an evaluation of programs (Feder, Leader, Urban, etc.) financed by the European Union gives rise to twin consequences.

First, it has made possible the recent development of encouraging initiatives such as the creation of the Walloon Society for Evaluation and Foresight and of a Walloon Institute for Evaluation, Foresight, and Statistics. It is interesting to note that in the Walloon region, the concept of evaluation is closely bound up with the concept of foresight. Second, it promotes use of evaluation by extending the scope of policies evaluated to a variety of fields (energy, waste, etc.) and even to the contract for the future of Wallonia (a 10-year regional development program launched by the current government). However, as do other levels of power, the Walloon regional authorities pay little heed to the quality of evaluations carried out (using meta-evaluation, for instance). In addition, the executive is also the dominant player in this process, even if, as in this case, it is the government bureaucrats who are more active and more encouraging than the executives of the administration.

The three major challenges that must be overcome to enhance evaluative capacities in Belgium are as follows:

1. The development of an epistemic community. Scientific investigations have recently been carried out at widely attended symposia and study work-shops and have shown the practices being devel-oped in Belgium. To that we must certainly add the need to engage in the training of officials in evalua-tion methods and the framing of quality standards for evaluators.

2. Some strengthening of the role played hitherto by parliamentary and supervisory bodies to overcome the problem of evaluation being made the preserve of the executive (both administrative and governmen-tal). So far, the federal, regional, and community parliaments have been singularly missing from evaluative practice.

3. The introduction of multilevel cooperation. Because of Belgium's federalist structure, many policies are administered by several levels of power (examples being security contracts and employment policy), and that situation is not effectively taken into account by evaluation. Good governance and evidence-based policy making imply the need for multilevel evaluation in Belgium.

—*Steve Jacob and Frédéric Varone*

Further Reading

Jacob, S., & Varone, F. (2001). L'évaluation des politiques publiques en Belgique: État des lieux au niveau fédéral, dans administration publique [The evaluation of public politics in Belgium: The state of venues at the federal level in public administration]. *Revue du Droit Public et des Sciences Administratives, 2,* 119-129.

Jacob, S., & Varone, F. (2002). L'évaluation des politiques publiques en Belgique: Six études de cas au niveau fédéral [The evaluation of public politics in Belgium: Six case studies at the federal level]. *Courrier Hebdomadaire, 1764-1765,* 44-49.

De Visscher, C., & Varone, F. (Eds.). (2001). *Evaluer les politiques publiques: Regards croisés sur la Belgique* [Evaluating public politics: Crossed perspectives on Belgium]. Louvain-la-Neuve, Belgium: Académia-Bruylant.

GOVERNMENT PERFORMANCE AND RESULTS ACT (GPRA)

Part of the Clinton administration's effort to "rein-vent government," the Government Performance and Results Act of 1993 was designed to shift the focus of government decision making and accountability away from the activities that are undertaken to the results of those activities, such as real gains in employability, safety, responsiveness, or program quality. Under GPRA, federal departments and agencies are required to develop multiyear strategic plans, annual perfor-mance standards, and performance reports.

—*Jeffrey G. Tucker*

GRADING

The determination of the merit or worth of some-thing in an absolute (rather than relative or comparative)

sense (see Ranking). Evaluation questions that call for grading include, "Is this intervention (or product or individual) good enough to implement (or buy or hire)?" and, "How should we characterize this level of performance (on a particular dimension or overall)? Is it excellent? Good? Satisfactory? Poor? Completely unacceptable?" Grading does not necessarily involve the use of letter grades, but it does always involve gen-erating an evaluative claim about the absolute quality or value of an evaluand, using explicitly evaluative terms such as "excellent," "adequate," "worth imple-menting statewide," and so on.

—*Jane Davidson*

GRASSO, PATRICK G.

(b. 1945, Newark, New Jersey). Ph.D. Political Science, M.A. Political Science, University of Wisconsin–Madison; B.A. Political Science, University of Illinois.

Grasso is with the Operations Evaluation Department of the World Bank, Washington, DC. Throughout his career, Grasso has been concerned with how government affects economic development and human betterment. Over the past 3 years, he has led a team testing various modalities of knowledge management as mechanisms to both strengthen the quality of evaluation work and increase its dissemination and use by practitioners within the international economic development system.

He has focused on the use of public policy as a lever for improving economic performance at the local, state, and national levels. Grasso's work in this area has addressed a number of substantive issues, particularly in the tax policy area, that are not the traditional domain of program evaluation but rather of macroeconomics. His work on employee stock ownership plans as mechanisms to improve economic productivity and provide financial benefits to workers, for example, was groundbreaking in its application of a quasiexperimental design to tax expenditure analysis. A culmination of this body of work came with the publication of a *New Directions in Evaluation* issue titled "Evaluating Tax Expenditures."

Grasso credits David Easton's work applying systems theory to politics and public policy analysis for providing a solid framework for his understanding of the forces at work in the policy arena. Ira Sharkansky, Grasso's graduate mentor, has been a continuing influence, helping him to see the importance of thinking outside the conventional terms of analysis; in particular, his work as a graduate assistant on Sharansky's book *The United States: A Study of a Developing Country* deeply influenced his subsequent thinking on the importance of understanding the hidden continua in apparently discontinuous processes. His work at the U.S. General Accounting Office with Eleanor Chelimsky and Lois-ellin G. Datta were critical in helping him to master the practice of evaluation. Chelimsky's insistence on rigor in design and analysis and clarity in reporting moved his thinking beyond the mechanics of evaluation research to a deeper understanding of the social and political functions of evaluation, especially to the distinction between evaluation and advocacy. Datta's support for thinking unconventionally and applying old methods in new ways opened up many opportunities for Grasso's intellectual exploration and growth, leading to important studies with real impacts on public policy. Finally, working

with Robert Picciotto at the World Bank showed Grasso how to put together these many influences—systemic thinking, unconventional analysis, rigorous application of methods and clear communication of results, adaptation and intellectual exploration—behind a vision worthy of a committed professional life, such as the alleviation of poverty around the world.

■ GREAT SOCIETY PROGRAMS

Lyndon B. Johnson called on the federal government to create a "great society" in America. That phrase has since become synonymous with the domestic record of the two Democratic administrations of the 1960s, and the programs of the Great Society constituted the most important expansion of the American state since the New Deal. New legislation addressed civil rights, voting rights, and discrimination in housing and established the Medicare and Medicaid programs. For the first time, federal aid was provided for elementary, secondary, and higher education. The Department of Housing and Urban Development and the Department of Transportation were created, and the National Endowments for the Humanities and the Arts and the Corporation for Public Broadcasting were established. Federal housing subsidies were dramatically expanded, and environmental legislation to protect air and water was passed into law. Finally, a "War on Poverty" was designed to eliminate hunger and deprivation from American life.

The centerpiece of the War on Poverty was the Economic Opportunity Act of 1964, which created an Office of Economic Opportunity to oversee a variety of community-based antipoverty programs, among them the Job Corps, whose purpose was to help disadvantaged youths develop marketable skills; Volunteers in Service to America, a domestic version of the Peace Corps, which sent middle-class young people on "missions" into poor neighborhoods; the Model Cities program for urban redevelopment; Upward Bound, which assisted poor high school students entering college; legal services for the poor; the Food Stamps program; and Project Head Start, which offered preschool education for poor children.

These combined efforts had a huge impact on the mostly unknown field of evaluation: Politicians and citizens alike wanted to know if these new social programs were working, who was being affected, and how. A presidential executive order gave employment and financial support to those who wished to apply their analytical skills to examine questions relating to efficiency and effectiveness and gave birth to large social policy organizations such as Abt Associates and the Urban Institute, for example.

—*Jeffrey G. Tucker*

■■ GREENE, JENNIFER C.

(b. 1949, Palo Alto, California). Ph.D. Educational Psychology, M.A. Education, Stanford University; B.A. Psychology, Wellesley College.

Greene is Professor of Educational Psychology at the University of Illinois, Urbana-Champaign. Previously, she held faculty positions in the Department of Policy Analysis and Management at Cornell University and in the Department of Education at the University of Rhode Island.

Her contributions to evaluation have been substantial and center on work that has done much to legitimize participatory, value-engaged, democratizing approaches to evaluation. Greene's work on stakeholder-based evaluation and stakeholder involvement in evaluation is foundational work that has provided the basis for understanding how and why stakeholder involvement is important. More recently, she has extended this work through her analysis of the democratizing potential of dialogue and discussion in evaluation. Greene can also be credited with some of the most comprehensive work on mixed-method approaches to evaluation. This work provides both a conceptual framework and pragmatic guidance for mixed methods.

Greene's work in evaluation has been strongly influenced by Lee Cronbach's mentorship, especially his ideas on the importance of understanding the full contextual complexities of programs being evaluated and the use of evaluation to educate the "Policy-Shaping Community." She also was encouraged by Egon Guba, especially his quiet insistence that Greene learn something about qualitative methods, and by the political ideas of Ernie House, in particular the very notion of doing evaluation for expressly political purposes, specifically social justice. More general intellectual influences, such as progressive politics, antiwar protests, and the feminist movement of the 1960s and 1970s, and "liberation" theories, such as

those of Paulo Friere, are also evident in Greene's work. Being a true evaluation practitioner, Greene's contributions to the field are also born of her early evaluation work, which involved extensive fieldwork. Learning on the job and stretching her methodological repertoire at that early stage in her career were key experiences in shaping her intellectual interests and contributions to the theory and practice of evaluation.

As Coeditor of *New Directions for Evaluation* (with Gary Henry) from 1997 to 2004, Greene brought her appreciation of multiple approaches in evaluation to her work, in the selection of both topics and authors. She is on the Advisory Boards of the *American Journal of Evaluation, Evaluation,* and *International Journal of Educational Technology.*

■■ GROUNDED THEORY

This is a form of comparative analysis developed by some Chicago sociologists from the 1920s onward. Categorization of incidents and events begins tentatively, as if to test the robustness of the first level of understanding. Some incidents and events do not meet the criteria for placement in first-sweep categories. These items are retained and the categories reconsidered to see if all the items are justified in their inclusion. This process of iteration continues intermittently as new data are collected, and some of these new data are sought on the basis of absence and presence of items in the developing structure of categories. The aspiration is to devise, by analytic induction, a grounded theory of the action yet to be employed as a main methodology in evaluation. Nias' work with elementary teachers is one example.

—*Clem Adelman*

See also Constant Comparative Method, Inference

Further Reading

Glaser, B., & Strauss, A. (1967). *The discovery of grounded theory: Strategies for qualitative research.* Chicago: Aldine.

Nias, J. (1989). *Primary teachers talking: A study of teaching as work.* London: Routledge.

■■ GROUP INTERVIEW

A *group interview* involves an interviewer discussing a topic with between 4 and 12 people simultaneously, thereby enabling a different perspective on an evaluation problem not possible through individual interviews. The interaction can be directed in a structured or unstructured way, depending on the purpose of the interview. This can be to explore a phenomenon, pretest facets of survey design, triangulate with other methods used in an evaluation, or determine attitudes and behaviors.

The skills needed by a group interviewer are similar to those required for a one-on-one interview, but in addition, the person requires group process skills such as not allowing one person to dominate and bringing in shyer participants. The advantages of the technique are that it is cost effective, creates rich data, allows flexibility, and is generally enjoyable for participants.

—*Rosalind Hurworth*

▐▌ GUBA, EGON G.

(b. 1924, Chicago, Illinois). Ph.D. Educational Inquiry, University of Chicago; M.A. University of Kansas; A.B. Valparaiso University.

Guba is Professor Emeritus, School of Education at Indiana University–Bloomington. He has also been Associate Dean for Academic Affairs of the School of Education. Previous faculty positions have included teaching statistics and measurement at the University of Chicago and the University of Kansas, and Community Studies, Inc., at The Ohio State University, where he served first as Head of the Division of Educational Research and then Director of the Bureau of Educational Research and Service.

His primary contribution to the field of evaluation was in raising serious questions about conventional approaches to evaluation and inquiry more generally. These doubts evolved toward the formulation of a monograph, *Naturalistic Inquiry,* which was a precursor to a lifelong collaboration with Yvonna Lincoln, resulting in many contributions to evaluation theory and methodology. His work has been influenced by Ralph W. Tyler, J. W. Getzels, and Edgar Dale.

He is the author of numerous journal articles and chapters, and the coauthor, with Yvonna Lincoln, of *Effective Evaluation, Fourth Generation Evaluation,* and *Naturalistic Inquiry.* He is Editor of *The Paradigm Dialog.* Along with Yvonna Lincoln, he is the 1987 recipient of the Paul F. Lazarsfeld Award from the American Evaluation Association.

▐▌ GUIDING PRINCIPLES FOR EVALUATORS

A mark of the maturity of a profession is the development of professional codes of conduct. Such codes describe the ethics and standards that the professionals should abide by in their work. The codes are usually developed by relevant professional associations.

The American Evaluation Association (AEA) is a professional association devoted to the study and practice of evaluation. AEA began in 1986 with the merger of two predecessor organizations, the Evaluation Network and the Evaluation Research Society. Over the ensuing years, the AEA board of directors and membership expressed increased interest in drafting a code of professional conduct. In 1992, the AEA board of directors formed a task force with the goal of drafting a code of conduct for the evaluation profession. The resulting document was the AEA Guiding Principles for Evaluators, adopted in 1994 and published in 1995.

Evaluators had considered matters related to professional conduct prior to the formation of the AEA task force in 1992. For example, the Joint Committee on Standards for Educational Evaluation published the *Standards for Evaluations of Educational Programs, Projects, and Materials* in 1981, and the Evaluation Research Society had its own ethical code, as well. However, AEA never formally adopted any of these codes of conduct, largely because the AEA board believed that AEA needed to develop its own code rather than adopt one from another group.

The AEA board specifically charged the task force with developing general guiding principles rather than standards. Principles are general and abstract guides to professional conduct, whereas standards are specific and detailed recommendations for how the principles should be operationalized in practice. Development of such standards specifically for AEA is a task that remains for the future. The hope was that, by virtue of their generality, the principles would apply to evaluators of all kinds in all the diverse settings in which they work.

The task force comprised volunteers from members of the board in 1992. The four task force members worked in a variety of evaluation job settings, including academics, private practice evaluation, and government administration. The task force reviewed pertinent literature and relevant codes from other professional organizations and developed an initial draft.

The task force then obtained feedback on the content of the draft from the AEA board of directors and membership through meetings, written correspondence, and several symposia at the 1993 AEA annual conference. The AEA board of directors accepted the final draft of the Guiding Principles in January 1994. A membership vote led to the adoption of the Guiding Principles later that year.

The Guiding Principles are intended to guide the behavior of evaluators proactively and to inform clients, stakeholders, and the public about what to expect from professional evaluation. The five AEA guiding principles for evaluators are as follows:

1. *Systematic inquiry.* Evaluators conduct systematic, data-based inquiries about whatever is being evaluated.

2. *Competence.* Evaluators provide competent performance to stakeholders.

3. *Integrity and honesty.* Evaluators ensure the honesty and integrity of the entire evaluation process.

4. *Respect for people.* Evaluators respect the security, dignity, and self-worth of the respondents, program participants, clients, and other stakeholders with whom they interact.

5. *Responsibilities for general and public welfare.* Evaluators articulate and take into account the diversity of interests and values that may be related to the general and public welfare.

The principle of *systematic inquiry* includes adherence to the highest appropriate technical standards and effective communication with clients about the strengths and shortcomings of the evaluation questions and of the methods used for answering those questions. *Competence* refers to evaluators' responsibilities to possess the appropriate skills to undertake the tasks required to do the evaluation and to continue their professional development. The principle of *integrity and honesty* involves evaluators' responsibilities to be forthcoming with regard to costs, limitations of the methodology or results obtained, changes to project plans, conflicts of interest, and sources of financial support. In addition, this principle includes evaluators' responsibility to try to prevent the misuse of their work by others. *Respect for people* encompasses evaluators' responsibilities to abide by other relevant professional ethics and standards, to maximize benefits and minimize risks to participants and clients, and to respect individual, group, and cultural differences among participants. The section on *responsibilities for general and public welfare* stresses that evaluators take into account the implications of their work with regard to clients, stakeholders, and the public good, that evaluators foster free exchange of information with stakeholders, and that evaluators maintain balance between client needs and other needs regarding the general and public welfare.

The order of the principles is arbitrary. They are not independent of one another, and depending on the situation may sometimes even conflict with each other. At such times, evaluators must use their best judgment in resolving the conflict or seek the guidance of colleagues. Compliance with the principles is voluntary and is not monitored by AEA, and the principles are not used to sanction the behavior of individual evaluators.

Many authors have commented on the Guiding Principles since their publication. Early commentaries were published in the same volume in which the Guiding Principles first appeared. Some comments pertained to the generality of the principles, essentially calling for more specific standards. Other comments questioned whether the principles gave adequate guidance to evaluators in some specific evaluation settings, such as internal evaluators or evaluators who work in international or culturally diverse settings. Such comments reflect one intention of the Guiding Principles, to stimulate continued debate about the professional conduct of evaluation. Consequently, the Guiding Principles call for their own periodic review and amendment as the profession further matures. Such matters are the purview of the AEA board of directors in general and of the AEA ethics committee, which assumed responsibility for the periodic review of the principles after the task force disbanded in 1994.

—*William R. Shadish and Jason K. Luellen*

Further Reading

Shadish, W. R., Newman, D. L., Scheirer, M. A., & Wye, C. (Eds.). (1995). Guiding principles for evaluators. *New Directions for Program Evaluation, 66.*

Joint Committee on Standards for Educational Evaluation. (1981). *Standards for evaluations of educational programs, projects, and materials.* New York: McGraw-Hill.

HALL, BUDD L.

(b. 1943, Long Beach, California). Ph.D. Comparative and International Education, UCLA; M.A. Education, B.A. Political Science, Michigan State University.

Hall is Dean of the Faculty of Education at the University of Victoria, Canada, and was previously Chair of the Adult Education Department and taught participatory research and evaluation at the Ontario Institute for Studies in Education, University of Toronto. He served as Secretary-General of the International Council for Adult Education from 1979 to 1991 and worked as the head of evaluation and research in the Institute of Adult Education, University of Dar es Salaam, Tanzania, from 1970 to 1974.

Hall's primary contributions have been to the theory and practice of participatory research and evaluation. His first publication, in 1975, was a special issue of the journal *Convergence* that included a number of international articles on the then new field of participatory research. Hall has applied participatory evaluation in many contexts, such as a large-scale project on community learning that explored renewal options for coastal communities in British Columbia facing economic collapse in the wake of contraction of resource-based economies.

His work has been influenced by the ideas of the late Julius Nyerere, former present of Tanzania, and Paulo Freire. Julius Nyerere had a profound belief in the capacity of ordinary women and men to know their own environment and to learn how to change the conditions that affect their lives. Hall met Paulo Freire in 1971 when he visited Tanzania. Freire's exploration

of the thematic ideas of rural peoples was an early elaboration of an approach to research, and ultimately to evaluation, in which identification of ideas came directly from the women or men most closely involved with the issues at hand. Hall and his colleagues at the Institute of Adult Education began to experiment with participatory approaches to evaluation.

Hall is a lifetime member of the National Institute for Adult and Continuing Education of England and Wales and has delivered more than 40 keynote addresses in 27 countries.

HASTINGS, J. THOMAS

(b. 1911, Louisville, Kentucky; d. 1992, Urbana, Illinois). Ph.D., University of Chicago; B.A., Ball State University.

Hastings was instrumental in developing the connection between the school curriculum and educational testing, program evaluation, and higher education. He studied at the University of Chicago with Ralph Tyler and was a contemporary of Benjamin Bloom and Lee J. Cronbach, and with some of his contemporaries (Bloom, Hastings, and Madaus) he published the seminal works *Handbook on Formative and Summative Evaluation of Student Learning* and *Evaluation to Improve Learning*.

His only campus was the University of Illinois, where he had a profound impact, as well as being a colleague to measurement people around the world, including Ralph Tyler, William F. Connell, Robert Stake, Christine McGuire, Ben Bloom, Jack Easley, George Madaus, Jack Merwin, and Barry MacDonald.

He started work in 1942 as the University of Illinois' University Examiner (a position similar to that held by Ralph Tyler at The Ohio State University), assisting faculty in improving evaluation of their courses.

With Lee Cronbach, he cofounded the Center for Instructional Research and Curriculum Evaluation (CIRCE). He was the first Director of the Illinois Statewide Testing Program, the main focus for CIRCE at the time, and one of the organizers of the group called the Directors of Statewide Testing Programs.

He was among the first faculty in the Bureau of Research and Service in the College of Education and was instrumental in recruiting additional faculty. He was sought over and over again for committees and assignments involving contentious issues because everyone knew that he would give them a fair and honest hearing. The scope of Hastings' work was far reaching, as is well demonstrated by his key role in the reorganization of Japan's national education system after World War II.

According to Mary Anne Bunda, one of Hastings' many students, he once hooked up a washing machine motor to run a desk calculator to do a factor analysis for his dissertation. He was Cronbach's Boswell.

■■ HAUG, PEDER

(b. 1947, Ørsta, Norway). Cand. Paed. Educational Research, Oslo University; Ph.D. Education, Stockholm Institute of Education.

Haug is Professor of Education and Vice Dean of the Faculty of Education at Volda University College of Norway. Prior to taking his Ph.D., he was a school-teacher, and his work in evaluation has been focused on evaluating educational reforms and educational policy, both in public schools and in teacher education programs. As a member of the Research Council of Norway, he has been the research director of two multiyear, comprehensive evaluation projects of national educational reforms in special education and in elementary and secondary education. He has held a variety of research positions in institutes throughout Norway and lectured extensively on issues in educational reform throughout Norway.

His primary contribution to the field of evaluation is twofold. On the one hand, he has contributed to the development of the Swedish model of theory-oriented evaluation, and here, his major intellectual influence has been Ulf Lundgren. On the other hand, influenced early by his work with educational sociologist Anton Hoëm, Haug has contributed to sociological studies of developing, implementing, and evaluating educational policy.

He is the author or coauthor of more than 40 research and evaluation reports, as well as numerous articles in publications directed at teachers; his scholarly journal articles and book chapters have appeared in both Norwegian and English-language publications. His books include *Seksåringer—Barnehage Eller Skole?* (The 6-year-olds—kindergarten or school?); *Pedagogisk Dilemma: Specialundervisning* (Educational dilemma: Special education); *Skolebasert Vurdering—Erfaringer og Utfordringer* (School-based evaluation: Experiences and challenges; with L. Monsen). He also coedited *Den Mangfaldige Spesialundervisninga* (Diverse special education), *Theoretical Perspectives on Special Education,* and *Evaluating Educational Reform: Scandinavian Perspectives.*

■■ HENRY, GARY T.

(b. 1953, Clark County, Kentucky). Ph.D. Urban Social Institutions, University of Wisconsin, Knapp Dissertation Fellow; M.A. Political Science, B.A. Political Science and Latin American Studies, University of Kentucky.

Henry is Professor in the Departments of Public Administration and Urban Studies, Political Science, and Educational Policy Studies at Georgia State University. During his time at Georgia State, he has also been Director of the Applied Research Center. Previously he held faculty positions at Virginia Commonwealth University, and he was also a visiting faculty member at the University of Liege, Belgium, and Huang He University, People's Republic of China. Henry was Deputy Superintendent of Public Instruction for Policy, Assessment, Evaluation, Research, and Information Systems, Department of Education, Commonwealth of Virginia, and Deputy Secretary of Education, Commonwealth of Virginia.

His primary contributions to the field of evaluation have been generated by his interest in evaluation methods, evaluating state and federal programs, and understanding evaluation's influence in democratic societies. Often the evaluations he conducted have attempted to inform and influence policy as well as improve programs. Henry has evaluated preschool programs, public information campaigns, and merit-based financial aid programs and has developed performance indicators for schools. His evaluation practice has allowed him to stay involved in the day-to-day details of collecting and analyzing evaluation data, working with stakeholders and the policy community, and disseminating findings about policies and programs to parents, program staff, policy makers, and the public.

Three people he reported to in the formative stages of his career have been the primary influences on his work: Gordon Garner, Ray Pethtel, and Don Finley, who emphasized the social mission of public service and evaluation, the need to be accurate and concise in providing information, and the importance of looking at alternative interpretations of the data and who might push them in the policy process.

Henry is the author of numerous book chapters, journal articles, and evaluation reports, as well as the author or coauthor of several books: *Evaluation: An Integrated Framework for Understanding, Guiding, and Improving Policies and Programs* (with Melvin Mark and George Julnes); *Graphing Data: Techniques for Display and Analysis;* and *Practical Sampling.* He was also a coeditor (with George Julnes and Melvin Mark) of *Realist Evaluation: An Emerging Theory in Support of Practice* and the editor of *Creating Effective Graphs: Solutions for a Variety of Evaluation Data.* He was Coeditor with Jennifer C. Greene of *New Directions for Evaluation* (1996-2003) and is on the Editorial Board of the *American Journal of Evaluation.*

Henry is the recipient of the 1998 Outstanding Evaluation of the Year Award from the American Evaluation Association and the 2000 Joseph Wholey Award for Outstanding Scholarship on Accountability from the American Society for Public Administration and the Center for Accountability and Performance.

HERMENEUTICS

Hermeneutics broadly refers to the theory of interpretation. The object of interpretation is the meaning of some human action, artifact (e.g., a work of art), or text. The principal schools of hermeneutic thought and their leading theorists include philosophical hermeneutics (Hans-Georg Gadamer, Charles Taylor), critical theory (Jürgen Habermas), and deconstructionism (Jacques Derrida), and there is a lively debate among their respective positions. The term is also used as a synonym for *interpretive,* such as in interpretive social science. Whether directly acknowledged or not, ideas central to the hermeneutics schools of thought are influential in some forms of interpretive, qualitative, and transformative (e.g., critical, feminist) approaches to evaluation.

—*Thomas A. Schwandt*

Further Reading

Bernstein, R. J. (2002). The constellation of hermeneutics, critical theory, and deconstruction. In R. J. Dostal (Ed.), *The Cambridge companion to Gadamer.* Cambridge, England: Cambridge University Press.

Rabinow, P., & Sullivan, W. M. (Eds.). (1987). *Interpretive social science: A second look.* Berkeley: University of California Press.

HISTORY OF EVALUATION

Evaluation is probably as old as the human race, dating from the time humans first made a judgment about whether building campfires and using weapons helped them to survive. Indeed, evaluation is an essential human activity that is intrinsic to problem solving, as humans (a) identify a problem, (b) generate and implement alternatives to reduce its symptoms, (c) evaluate these alternatives, and then (d) adopt those that results suggest will reduce the problem satisfactorily. As humans, we will always be faced with problems whose solutions require evaluation so that effective action can be taken.

Evidence of more formally organized evaluation goes back thousands of years. Chapter 1 of the Book of Daniel in the Old Testament describes a quasiexperiment evaluating the effects of a Hebrew versus a Babylonian diet on health. Evidence suggests that personnel evaluation dates back more than 4000 years in China, to about 2200 B.C. Philosophers have written about the nature of valuing for millenia. Most evaluation textbooks have many other examples of formal evaluations over the last several centuries.

Today, there are many different fields of evaluation, including but not limited to program evaluation, policy evaluation, personnel evaluation, product evaluation, and student evaluation. Each of these specialties has its own history, and it is not possible to cover all of them here. Instead, this entry focuses mostly on the history of program evaluation, the field that was primarily responsible for the explosive growth of evaluation theory and practice over the past 40 years. The emphasis is mostly on U.S. history, given the centrality of the United States to how program evaluation developed, although this entry will comment briefly on international efforts.

Many developments in the first half of the 20th century contributed to the modern era of program evaluation. Primary among them was growth and refinement in the theories and methods of the social sciences, with examples of their application to practical problems in education, political science, and psychology. For instance, educational researchers developed methods to improve the evaluation of student achievement, and in psychology, Kurt Lewin's action research movement led to applications of social psychology to social problem solving, with the concurrent need to evaluate those efforts in field settings. The apparent successes of such efforts led to growing optimism that social science could contribute to social problem solving, following the successful model of the physical sciences in technological problem solving in the first half of the 20th century.

The largest single influence on modern program evaluation was the expansion of government social programs throughout the 20th century. The first stage of this expansion occurred as a result of the Great Depression in the 1930s. The crash of the stock market and the subsequent run on the banks crippled the nation's economy. Many Americans were left unemployed and living below the poverty level. A multitude of relief agencies was legislated under the rubric of President Franklin D. Roosevelt's New Deal. Such agencies provided aid in the form of employment relief and opportunity, housing assistance, and health provisions. None of these programs put an end to the Great Depression, but federal support for social programs was growing.

Government support expanded further after World War II, a time when the United States experienced rapid economic growth. People held science in high esteem, given the contributions made by scientists in areas such as physics and chemistry to winning the war (e.g., the atomic bomb) and to improving quality of life in the decades immediately after the war (e.g., television, jet travel). During the first few decades after World War II, social scientists were highly optimistic about being able to do the same thing that physical scientists had done by transferring social science methods and theories to solving practical social problems. A plethora of such problems needed to be addressed,

including poverty, access to medical care, civil rights, and coping with educational needs in the wake of the launching of Sputnik by the Soviet Union. Numerous social programs were initiated under the leadership of President John F. Kennedy, with the goal of protecting national prosperity and providing for the well-being of American citizens. Following Kennedy's assassination in 1963, Lyndon B. Johnson was sworn in as president. He followed through on Kennedy's initiatives and expanded social programs to conduct a "War on Poverty" in his quest for a "Great Society." During these years, government began to take on more responsibility for the general welfare of its citizens, a role that previously had been the nearly exclusive province of individuals, families, and private charities. Social programs in health, education, and housing, among others, grew to account for billions of dollars in government spending. For example, funding for social programs increased from about $23 billion in 1950 to about $428 billion by 1979 (without accounting for inflation).

These were massive expenditures. Concurrent competition for these federal dollars was intensified by growing defense budgets, due to the Vietnam War and the Cold War; increasing inflation rates that were exacerbated by oil embargoes; and mounting federal budget deficits. Many members of pertinent branches of the government were growing concerned about how social programs disbursed their funds and whether those programs actually achieved expected outcomes. Program managers wanted information about how they could better manage their programs. Social scientists viewed these programs as fertile ground for developing both social science theory and methods. All these factors contributed to the demand for more formal social program evaluation.

Thus, beginning in the 1960s, evaluation grew and flourished as a profession. Vital to its establishment as a profession was legislation mandating and funding it. This development can be traced only inexactly. Early federal programs to require evaluation included the juvenile delinquency program and the Manpower Development and Training Act, both in 1962; the Economic Opportunity Act of 1964; and the Title I (compensatory education) section of the Elementary and Secondary Education Act. These acts, and others, provided major funding for evaluation. Between 1968 and 1978, more than 100 federal statutes called for evaluation in the area of education alone. Many of these mandates were accompanied by funds specifically appropriated for evaluation. In addition, state and local governments also funded program evaluations, never to the degree of the federal government but still stimulating substantial additional activity, the value of which is difficult to estimate, given the dispersal and independence of state and local governments. Hence, although the exact number of dollars allocated and spent at the federal, state, and local levels on evaluation is unclear, it was surely in the hundreds of millions of dollars by 1980 and is no doubt above $1 billion dollars today. This large amount of funding created the incentive for people to do evaluations.

Given the demand for evaluation services, who would be the supply? The public sector was not well equipped to meet the burgeoning demand for evaluation services. Those persons who managed or staffed social programs typically lacked the personnel or the skills to perform evaluations. Public sector specialists, such as auditors, economists, budget directors, and planning and systems analysts, were called on to provide feedback about social programming, but too few existed or were available to meet the demand. For example, planning and systems analysts were mostly in the Department of Defense. To borrow them meant to weaken the Department of Defense workforce at a time when that department's demands were increasing as well. Furthermore, the skills of these public specialists, which were grounded in the theories and methodologies of accounting, auditing, surveying, and forecasting, were only partly relevant to drawing conclusions about the role that social programs played in addressing social problems. Consequently, the government also looked to those in the private sector and in academia to fill the demand.

Evaluation-related activities were common in the private sector, usually with the aim of improving company profitability. Toward that end, companies had accountants to monitor their financial activity, management consultants to improve their operations, and research and development teams to design and provide feedback regarding products. Some of these personnel could play a role in social program evaluation, as well, although that role was inherently limited, given that social programs are not judged by whether they make a profit.

Universities were a more fertile source of evaluators and, eventually, of the training programs to produce evaluators with the skills that were relevant to social program evaluation. Academicians clearly had

pertinent expertise in social science methods, so many graduates of professional schools and social science departments were drawn to work in the field of evaluation. With the increase in employment opportunity provided by federal, state, and local evaluation funds, graduate schools experienced an influx of students seeking professional training in social science disciplines, including economics, education, political science, psychology, and sociology. U.S. Census data indicated an 895% increase in doctoral production, from 1469 in 1950 to 13,153 in 1986. Many of these social scientists went into evaluation work either part- or full-time.

All these public sector, private sector, and university-based scientists responded to government requests for evaluation in three settings. First, some formed contract research firms with as many as 800 doctoral specialists. Good examples are Abt Associates in Boston and Manpower Development Research Corporation in New York. Second, academicians obtained contracts and, to conduct evaluations, served as consultants, acted as consultants, and advanced knowledge regarding theory and methods. Academicians also started many evaluation training programs to produce more and better qualified evaluators. Third, federal, state, and local agencies established public-sector offices dedicated to evaluation. All three of these settings continue to produce evaluations in large numbers today.

The field of program evaluation prospered during the 1960s and 1970s. Numerous evaluations were conducted in response to federal mandates, state mandates, and local program managers. They were conducted for many different reasons, including providing insight into which of several alternative actions tended to produce desirable results, improving operations, identifying needs to which programs could respond, justifying a program's budget, and creating support for a proposal or for continued funding of the program. The evaluations were diverse in the substantive areas studied. Education, health, and mental health probably saw the largest number of evaluations. As a result of the diversity of questions asked and of sectors in which evaluation was needed, evaluators were necessarily diverse in fulfilling their roles, both substantively and methodologically. All of this funding and activity gave credibility to evaluation and helped establish it as a profession.

Signs of the transition of evaluation to professional status during these years included the creation of professional publications, professional societies, and professional codes of conduct. Perhaps the earliest of the journals was *Evaluation Review,* established in 1976; other important evaluation journals include the *American Journal of Evaluation, New Directions for Evaluation,* and *Evaluation and Program Planning.* In addition, two professional evaluation societies, the Evaluation Research Society (ERS) and the Evaluation Network (ENet), were founded in the 1970s to foster evaluation as both a profession and a science. ERS and ENet merged in 1986 to form the American Evaluation Association, which currently has approximately 3000 members representing all 50 states in the United States, as well as more than 50 foreign countries. Evaluators also developed professional codes of conduct. Early codes included the ERS ethical code and the Joint Committee educational evaluation standards. AEA oversaw the development of guiding principles of good professional evaluation conduct that were adopted by its members in 1994, and the Joint Committee has since published an updating of its program evaluation standards.

Another indicator of professionalization is the accumulation and transmission of a unique transmittable knowledge base. The early knowledge base of evaluation reflected the existing methods and theories of the diverse backgrounds from which early evaluators were drawn—for example, many psychologists and educators did experimental evaluations, many educators focused on testing during evaluation, many anthropologists used qualitative methods, and many of those from management used management information systems. From this early collection of methods, a specialized body of evaluation knowledge evolved, as well as training programs to transmit knowledge to new evaluators.

Theories changed as the years went by, or more accurately, they expanded and diversified. Early theories dealt primarily with methods for doing evaluation in field settings, but as practical experience with evaluation accumulated, subsequent theories began to address the politics of applying methods in field settings and how research fits into social policy. Those theories provided perspective on five fundamental issues of program evaluation: (a) how social programs and policies develop, improve, and change, especially in regard to social problems; (b) debates about the best ways for constructing knowledge about social programs; (c) the ways that value can be attached to program descriptions in a highly charged political process; (d) how social science information is used to modify programs and policies; and (e) the tactics and strategies evaluators follow in their professional work, especially given the constraints of time and money that they usually face.

As a result of all these influences and developments, by the 1990s, evaluation had matured considerably as a profession. However, at the same time that these developments were occurring during the 1970s and 1980s, fiscal and social conservatism was on the rise, leading to a backlash against the expansion of government programs. Some commentators argued that social programs seemed to show small gains, gains not worth the funding, given inflation, the federal deficit, and the discontent of many Americans with the tax burden. The backlash came to a head in the 1980s, when the Republican administrations of Ronald W. Reagan and George H. W. Bush responded with cuts in federal domestic spending, many of which were directed at social programs. In turn, funding for evaluation declined in many sectors, although the absolute number of evaluation dollars was still large.

The politics of the 1990s were dominated by the Democratic presidency of William J. Clinton and a Republican majority in Congress. The country experienced unprecedented growth in the economy, but funding for social programs remained restricted because of an emphasis on a balanced budget and deficit reduction. A trend of diverting the administration of many social programs to the state level continued. Consequently, some of the responsibility for conducting evaluations was diverted to the state level.

As all these developments show, evaluation has clearly been influenced over the years by the social and political climates of the day. Its funding and the sets of questions it studies often change with political tides. However, the need for evaluation seems to be here to stay, as citizens and their representatives prioritize programs and the social problems addressed, as existing programs continue to be scrutinized, and as new and modified programs are proposed.

—*William R. Shadish and Jason K. Luellen*

Further Reading

Shadish, W. R., Cook, T. D., & Leviton, L. C. (1991). *Foundations of program evaluation.* Newbury Park, CA: Sage.

Rossi, P. H., Freeman, H. E., & Lipsey, M. W. (1999). *Evaluation: A systematic approach* (6th ed.). Thousand Oaks, CA: Sage.

HONESTY

Eleanor Chelimsky writes, "Telling the truth to people who may not want to hear it is, after all, the chief purpose of evaluation." Honesty is critical to the practice of evaluation. Audiences look to evaluators to provide honest assessments of the quality of products, programs, or policies. Honesty plays a prominent role in evaluators' ethical codes. But what do we mean by honesty? Dictionaries define *honesty* as being truthful, adhering to the facts. Evaluators recognize that there are many versions of truth, but through the use of systematic inquiry; thorough exploration of program context and stakeholders' views; and accurate, comprehensive, and balanced reporting, evaluations can produce more honest appraisals of programs than can other means. Honesty includes practicing within one's limits of competence, identifying potential conflicts of interest that can influence the evaluation, thoroughly describing procedures and results, justifying conclusions, and managing the evaluation in a fiscally responsible manner.

—*Jody L. Fitzpatrick*

Further Reading

Chelimsky, E. (1995). Comments on the guiding principles. In W. R. Shadish, D. L. Newman, M. A. Scheirer, & C. Wye (Eds.), Guiding principles for evaluators. *New Directions for Program Evaluation, 66,* 53-54.

HOOD, STAFFORD L.

(b. 1952, Chicago, Illinois). Ph.D. Education, University of Illinois, Urbana-Champaign; M.S. Guidance and Counseling, B.A. Political Science, University of Wisconsin, Whitewater.

Hood is Professor of Education at Arizona State University. His contributions to understanding and promoting an African American perspective in evaluation have been widespread and influential. Hood published the initial inquiry into the untold legacy of African American scholars and practitioners in educational evaluation during the 1930s, 1940s, and 1950s. He is the founding Codirector of the Relevance of Assessment and Culture in Evaluation annual national conference, established in 2000 at Arizona State University. Hood also established the Relevance of Culture in Evaluation workshop for women and minority teachers in predominantly minority school settings (funded by the National Science Foundation). Hood works diligently as a member of the American Evaluation Association and the Research Focus on Black Education Special Interest Group of the American Educational Research Association to influence evaluation and research.

Hood was inspired by W.E.B. Dubois and Fredrick Douglass (especially his famous quote: "Power concedes nothing without a demand. It never did, and it never will.") His career was influenced by evaluators Leander Boykin, Ernest House, Reid E. Jackson, and Robert Stake. He acknowledges James D. Anderson, Terry Denny, Henry Frierson, Gordon Hoke, and Frederick Rodgers as personal intellectual influences.

Hood was selected as a Fellow of the American Council on Education (2001-2002), is in the Leo High School Hall of Fame (Chicago), and is a member of Omega Psi Phi fraternity.

HOPSON, RODNEY

(b. 1965, Huntington Station, New York). Ph.D. Educational Evaluation, M.Ed. Educational Evaluation, M.A. Linguistics, B.A. English Literature, University of Virginia.

Hopson is Associate Professor of Foundations and Leadership and a member of the Center for Interpretive and Qualitative Research at Duquesne University.

His *New Directions in Evaluation* issue "How and Why Language Matters in Evaluation" has provided evaluators across disciplines with a comprehensive analysis of the relationship of language policies and politics to evaluation theory and practice. He has contributed to the practice of evaluation through his focus on developing appropriate evaluation strategies for oppressed and marginalized others, and he is committed to mentoring and encouraging evaluators of color. Hopson's work has been influenced by Dell Hymes and Carol Camp Leakey and, more specifically in evaluation, by Michael Q. Patton, Jennifer Greene, Robert Covert, and Stafford Hood.

He received a National Institute of Drug Abuse postdoctoral fellowship, which he spent at the Johns Hopkins School of Hygiene and Public Health in 1997 and 1998; the American Evaluation Association Marcia Guttentag Award for promising young evaluator in 2001; and a Fulbright scholarship to the Republic of Namibia in 2001. Hopson's research in Namibia followed an early period spent there as a missionary in

South Africa through the Harvard Institute for International Development's WorldTeach program. He currently serves on the American Evaluation Association board of directors (2004-2006) and is Project Director for the AEA/Duquesne University Internship Program.

■: HOUSE, ERNEST R.

(b. 1937, Alton, Illinois). Ed.D. Education, University of Illinois, Urbana-Champaign; M.S. Education, Southern Illinois University; A.B. English, Washington University.

House is Professor Emeritus in the School of Education at the University of Colorado at Boulder. Previously, he was at CIRCE at the University of Illinois, Urbana-Champaign. He has been a visiting scholar at UCLA, Harvard University, and the University of New Mexico, as well as at universities in England, Australia, Spain, Sweden, Austria, and Chile.

His influence on the field of educational evaluation and policy analysis is felt both nationally and internationally. He has contributed substantially to a growing discussion on the role of values, ethics, and social justice in evaluation, as well as to metaevaluation, evaluative reasoning, and the philosophical basis of evaluation. His work has helped alter the discourse in evaluation from one of technique to one that regards evaluation as a powerful social practice that should embody the values of democratic society. His work has been influenced by John Rawls' *Theory of Justice,* Perelman and Olbrechts-Tyteca's *The New Rhetoric,* Roy Bhaskar's *Realist Theory of Science,* and the work of Michael Scriven, Robert Stake, and Barry MacDonald. He has conducted numerous evaluations, critiques, and studies, including an assessment of environmental education policies in Europe for the OECD; a 5-year study of the evaluation office in the National Science Foundation; an assessment of the Michigan Accountability Program for the National Education Association; a critique of the National Follow Through Evaluation for the Ford Foundation; and a critique of the evaluation of Jesse Jackson's Push/Excel program for the U.S. Department of Education.

He is the author of many journal articles, chapters, and books, including *Values in Evaluation and Social Research* (with K. Howe), *Where the Truth Lies, Schools for Sale, Professional Evaluation: Social Impact and Political Consequences, Jesse Jackson and the Politics of Charisma, Evaluating With Validity, Survival in the Classroom* (with S. Lapan), and *The Politics of Educational Innovation.* House was Coeditor of *New Directions in Program Evaluation* and a featured columnist for *Evaluation Practice.* In 1999 and 2000, he was a Fellow at the Center for Advanced Study in the Behavioral Sciences at Stanford University. He is also the 1989 recipient of the Harold E. Lasswell Prize in Policy Sciences and the 1990 recipient of the Paul F. Lazarsfeld Award for Evaluation Theory from the American Evaluation Association.

■: HUGHES, GERUNDA B.

(b. 1951, Miami, Florida). Ph.D. Educational Psychology, Howard University; M.A. Mathematics, University of Maryland, College Park; B.S. Mathematics, University of Rhode Island.

Hughes is a faculty member and coordinator of the secondary education program in the School of Education, Howard University. She is a co-principal investigator of the Center for Research on the Education of Students Placed at Risk classroom assessment project, an interdisciplinary research project examining the problems of effective classroom assessment in mathematics and reading. This project, and other work, reflects her contributions to understanding the best ways to judge the educational achievement of minority children. Hughes' work has been primarily in educational measurement, including serving on the National Assessment of Educational Progress (NAEP) validation studies panel as a mathematics and test- and item-bias consultant. She has a strong commitment to mentoring and affirmative action and is a member of the American Educational Research Association's Division D Affirmative Action Committee.

Her work in evaluation has been influenced by Floraline Stevens and Stafford Hood, as well as Edmund Gordon and, especially, Sylvia T. Johnson, who was known as a crusader for quality and fair testing for minorities.

■: HUMAN SUBJECTS PROTECTION

Every evaluation, in one way or another, involves collecting information from people—by observation, interviews, surveys, tests, existing documents, and records. Ethical evaluators need to take precautions to ensure that the rights of the people from whom they collect data are protected. These rights include, but are not limited to, the right to privacy, the right to confidentiality, and the right to choose whether to participate in a study without penalty and with an understanding of the benefits and risks.

Concern for the protection of human subjects first received prominent attention in the 1970s. The National Commission for the Protection of Human Subjects of Biomedical and Behavioral Research held hearings and published *The Belmont Report,* which brought attention to some of the abuses of human subjects in social science research. In 1974, the Department of Health and Human Services established procedures for the review of research involving human subjects. The National Research Act (Public Law 93-348) established Institutional Review Boards (IRBs) within universities and other organizations conducting research to review procedures used in research involving human subjects. Today, 17 federal agencies make use of these federal regulations, and undergoing an IRB review is common practice in university settings. Other laws, such as the Buckley Amendment, have also established guidelines to regulate the use of data.

Although these federal regulations provide some protection for human subjects, their focus is primarily on research. Many evaluations may not make use of an IRB process for a variety of reasons—it may not be required by the funder, the agency may not have established an IRB, or the nature of the data collection may exempt the evaluation from formal IRB review. Further, although review by an IRB can be helpful in protecting the rights of human subjects, federal regulations do not cover all areas pertinent to evaluation, and members of IRBs may not be sufficiently sensitive to the nature of evaluation methods and the environment in which it is practiced to recognize all threats. Thus the ultimate responsibility for the protection of the rights of human subjects lies with the evaluator.

Protecting the rights of human subjects plays a prominent role in the two major ethical documents guiding evaluators, the Guiding Principles for Evaluators and the Program Evaluation Standards. *Respect for people* is one of the five guiding principles of the American Evaluation Association. This principle notes evaluators' obligation to "respect the security, dignity and self-worth of the respondents, program

participants, clients, and other stakeholders with whom they interact." Respect for people includes concerns regarding informed consent and confidentiality, as well as maximizing benefits, minimizing harm, and being sensitive to subjects' cultural differences. *Rights of human subjects* is one of the Proprietary Standards defined by the Joint Committee: "Evaluations should be designed and conducted to respect and protect the rights and welfare of human subjects."

Human subjects protection in evaluation studies entails different complexities and concerns than that facing the typical social science researcher. *The Belmont Report* identifies three principles evaluators can use in considering these protections: beneficence, respect, and justice. *Beneficence* prompts the evaluator to avoid unnecessary harm and to strive to obtain good outcomes for participants and society as a whole. *Respect* reminds the evaluator to protect the autonomy of individuals taking part in the evaluation so that they may choose to participate in an informed and free manner. The principle of *justice* encourages the evaluator to protect and defend the equitable treatment and representation of different groups in both the evaluation and the program. These principles influenced the development of evaluation codes of conduct and are useful in considering ways to protect human subjects in the context of evaluation work.

Consider beneficence. In an evaluation study, human subjects can include program clients and people who work in the program. Clients may suffer harm from results of an evaluation that contribute to the demise of certain program services that clients may view as effective. Data from an evaluation may point to the ineptitude of staff in delivering program services. The Guiding Principles note that such harm can occur from "justified negative or critical conclusions" and that the evaluator is bound to "maximize the benefits and reduce any unnecessary harms that might occur, *provided this will not compromise the integrity of the evaluation findings*" (italics added). Unlike research, evaluation takes place in a public setting and has implications for program and policy decisions. The evaluator has an obligation to serve societal or public interests, as well as those of program stakeholders. Thus protecting human subjects must be balanced by the obligation to serve the public good.

The principle of respect is generally addressed through informed consent procedures. However, ensuring that respect is maintained can become more difficult and complex in an ongoing evaluation study, where the evaluator often acts as a participant observer, talking with staff and clients and observing program activities. As the participant observer develops rapport and even friendly, collegial relationships with staff and clients, the nature of the evaluator's role and the consent that client and staff may have provided can begin to fade from the consciousness of these human "subjects." Evaluators need to get to know the program and its stakeholders to effectively portray the nature of the program and its effects, but to what extent can evaluators use comments or observations obtained in these more relaxed settings as data and, ultimately, evidence for program success or failure without violating the principle of respect for human subjects? The answers to these questions depend on the context of the program, the nature of the evidence, and the manner in which the evaluation has been presented and will be used.

Protecting the rights of human subjects extends to other complex areas in evaluation: determining appropriate uses of control groups that can result in the denial of potentially beneficial services, ensuring sensitivity to cultural differences regarding privacy and confidentiality, maintaining confidentiality of data in times of increasing technological sophistication, and balancing the rights of different stakeholder groups.

—*Jody L. Fitzpatrick*

See also INFORMED CONSENT

Further Reading

Sieber, J. E. (1992). *Planning ethically responsible research.* Newbury Park, CA: Sage.

Newman, D. L., & Brown, R. D. (1996). *Applied ethics for program evaluation.* Thousand Oaks, CA: Sage.

■■ HYPOTHESIS

A *hypothesis* is a tentative statement about the world involving conjecture about relationships that are not yet verified: It is a prediction. Hypothesis testing is done to determine what is true—what would explain certain observations or phenomena. A hypothesis is an a priori statement of expectation that includes who is involved, what treatment or intervention they will be exposed to, the outcome measures to be used, and the comparison group. A good hypothesis is clear and concrete. Although the hypothesis (often denoted as H_1), the prediction, is a statement of anticipated outcomes, it is actually the null hypothesis, or the negation of the hypothesis (often denoted as H_0), that is tested, not the hypothesis.

IDEAL TYPE

Max Weber argued that no scientific method could reveal all of reality or do justice to the diversity of particular phenomena. He developed the construct of the *ideal type* to deal with the dilemma created by using constructs that are too general and thus devoid of specifics or using constructs that are so particularized as to defy general application. The ideal type is not ideal in a normative sense, nor is it an average of all instances of a phenomenon; rather, it is a constructed ideal that approximates reality by selecting elements and characteristics of the phenomena. In evaluation, examples of ideal types are program, treatment, intervention, and stakeholder.

Further Reading

Weber, M. (1949). *The methodology of the social sciences* (E. Shils & H. Finch, Eds.). New York: Free Press.

ILLUMINATIVE EVALUATION

To an English teacher, *illuminative* may simply be an adjective. To a historian of ideas, this adjective carries connotations of enlightenment. To evaluators, however, it has a more specific denotation: "Evaluation as Illumination: A New Approach to the Study of Educational Innovations," a paper written at the University of Edinburgh, Scotland, by a lecturer (Malcolm Parlett) and one of his doctoral students (David Hamilton). The article took 18 months to prepare. Drafts were sent out for comment and (such was the power of the emergent democracy of the photocopier)

bootleg copies circulated widely. For this reason, scientific journals eventually declined to publish it.

"Evaluation as Illumination" originally appeared in mimeo form, in 1972, as an occasional paper of the Department of Educational Sciences, University of Edinburgh. Thereafter, it was reprinted, to the authors' knowledge, 11 times between 1976 and 1988. By the latter date, the novelty of the term had dissipated or merged with cognate ideas. Nevertheless, the label survived. In early 2003, an Internet inquiry using "illuminative evaluation" as a search term generated 84 pages of references (almost 500 entries).

It would be easy, therefore, to write this entry as a fireside memoir, a victory narrative, or, what amounts to the same thing, a paean of self-justification. This encyclopedia entry, however, has a different aspiration. It puts illuminative evaluation into its historical context, as an example of a professional field in the making. It addresses four questions: Why was "Evaluation as Illumination" written? What did it say? Why is it still cited? How should it be regarded, in hindsight?

In its simplest form, "Evaluation as Illumination" was the outcome of joint collaboration. It was composed—a more accurate characterization than "written"—by two people who came together with different backgrounds. They found a point of contact; they negotiated a view of writing as composing, and, word by word, they struggled with each other to find a common language to harmonize and express their shared interests. Thereafter, they continued their intellectual journeys in different directions. Within a decade, Malcolm Parlett had left the university world and became a Gestalt therapist; David Hamilton followed a conventional academic career—a path that, in his case, would have been unlikely without the cultural capital he accumulated through coauthoring "Evaluation as Illumination."

At the outset of their collaboration, Malcolm Parlett had acquired a doctorate in experimental psychology and David Hamilton had been a science teacher. Their point of contact was that they shared a disillusionment with inherited models of educational research. Parlett had suffered a profound reaction against the "methodolatry" of experimental psychology that, in the event, was alleviated by the clinically or person-oriented social scientists he met while working at Massachusetts Institute of Technology as a postdoctoral fellow. David Hamilton's intellectual angst stemmed from the gulf that existed between the universalist assumptions of educational research and the situated assumptions of practitioners, with rescue coming in the form of writings about classroom research by Louis M. Smith and Philip Jackson. Both of us felt, in effect, that there was merit in moving toward practice and practitioners.

The immediate catalyst for writing "Evaluation as Illumination" was a commission, given to Malcolm Parlett by the Nuffield Foundation (London), to explore evaluation alternatives with respect to a nonprogrammatic English curriculum innovation, Resources for Learning. "Evaluation as Illumination" became the foremost outcome of that commission. It may have had highly local origins, but it also had wider ramifications. It can still be read as an expression of the wider reaction against logical positivism that built up in the 1960s. More important, it retains a strong sense that critique should always be concrete and transcendental rather than oppositional or, worse still, ad hominem. Critique, that is, should reach beyond the status quo and offer fresh horizons. In combination, these ideas mean that "Evaluation as Illumination" was a text of salvation and delivery.

The article began life as an analysis of the shortcomings of existing research. However, as drafts took shape, we gave more and more attention to the *new approach* prefigured in its subtitle. We realized that although it is easy to criticize through hindsight, it is more difficult to offer alternative practices. It was paramount, we felt, to communicate both with and through something that practitioners could understand even if, at the time, we assumed that all practitioners were male.

From the outset, "Evaluation as Illumination" was envisaged more as a communication than as a statement. We were well aware that the impact of texts is related

to their readability. We took great pains to search out (borrow, poach) images, analogies, and metaphors. We eschewed jargon as a barrier to communication, and we tried to think, instead, in terms of what we termed "quotable quotes." These, perhaps, are the phrases—such as "illuminative evaluation"—that have remained in the collective conscience of the evaluation community and that, somehow, have fostered its survival.

Here is an abridged version of the original.

Innovation is now a major activity. Curricula are restructured, new devices introduced, forms of teaching permutated. More recently—to aid decision-making—innovation has been joined by evaluation. The "evaluator" has emerged as a new and influential figure. As a new field, program evaluation has encountered a wide range of problems. It proceeds in the absence of coherent or agreed frames of reference. Generally, however, two paradigms can be discerned in educational research. Dominant is the agricultural-botany paradigm. Almost all evaluation studies have resided within this tradition. More recently, a few empirical studies have been conceived outside the agricultural-botany paradigm. They relate instead to social anthropology, psychiatry, and participant observation. We outline here an approach that belongs to this alternative or "social anthropology" paradigm.

Recently, there has been an increasing resistance to agricultural-botany evaluations. For instance, strict control is rarely followed; researchers are constrained from adapting to the changed circumstances that arise; artificial and arbitrary restrictions are placed on the scope of the study; it is insensitive to local perturbations and unusual effects; and it rarely acknowledges the diversity of questions posed by different interest groups. The traditional evaluator is restrained, therefore, by the dictates of the agricultural-botany paradigm.

The primary concern of illuminative evaluation is with description and interpretation rather than with measurement and prediction. Its aim is to study the innovatory program, its significant features, recurring concomitants, and critical processes. Central to an understanding of illuminative evaluation are two concepts: "instructional system" and the "learning milieu." Educational catalogues, prospectuses and reports characteristically contain formalized plans and statements that relate to particular teaching arrangements. These summaries define an instructional system, including its pedagogic assumptions, syllabus, techniques and equipment.

An instructional system, when adopted, undergoes modifications that are rarely trivial. To switch from discussing the instructional system to describing its implementation requires another concept. The learning milieu is the social-psychological and material environment in which students and teachers work together. It represents a nexus of cultural, social, institutional, and psychological variables. Acknowledging the complexity of the learning milieu is a prerequisite for the serious study of educational programs. They cannot be separated from the learning milieu of which they become a part. If an evaluation hinges on the supposed perpetuation of the instructional system, it makes an arbitrary and artificial distinction.

Illuminative evaluation comes in diverse forms. It is not a standard methodological package, but a general research strategy. It aims to be both adaptable and eclectic. The problem defines the methods used and not vice versa. No method (with its built-in limitations) is used exclusively or in isolation.

Illuminative evaluation has three overlapping stages: investigators observe; inquire further; and then seek to explain. The transition from stage to stage occurs as problem areas become progressively clarified and redefined. This "progressive focusing" permits unique and unpredicted phenomena to be given due weight. Within this three-stage framework, an information profile is assembled using data collected from observation, interviews, questionnaires and tests, documentary and background sources. With respect to observation, the illuminative evaluator builds up a continuous record but, in the process, is cautious about using observation schedules because they do not uncover more meaningful features. Interviews vary as to the type of information or comment that is sought. Questionnaire and test data can sustain or qualify earlier tentative findings. Documentary evidence is relevant because innovations do not arise unheralded. It provides historical perspective, indicates areas for inquiry, points to topics for intensive discussion, and exposes aspects of the innovation that would otherwise be missed.

First encounters with illuminative evaluation prompt a number of important questions. First, can "personal interpretation" be scientific? The "subjective" nature of the approach is inevitable; and the use of interpretative human insights and skills is, indeed, encouraged. Second, does the presence of the evaluator have a distorting effect on the conduct of the scheme under review? Illuminative evaluators recognize this hazard and attempt to be unobtrusive without being secretive, supportive without being collusive, and non-doctrinaire without appearing unsympathetic. Third, is illuminative evaluation restricted to

small-scale innovations? There can be a full progression from small studies to larger scale inquiries. Illuminative evaluation can yield more generally usable insights and abstracted summaries that can be extended to the overlapping phenomena that accompany teaching, learning and innovation.

Overall, illuminative evaluation concentrates on the information gathering rather than the decision-making component of evaluation. The task is to provide a comprehensive understanding of the complex reality (or realities) surrounding a program: in short, to "illuminate." In his report, therefore, the evaluator aims to sharpen discussion, disentangle complexities, isolate the significant from the trivial, and to raise the level of sophistication of debate.

In summary, the theatre provides an analogy. An agricultural-botany evaluator is rather like a critic who reviews a production on the basis of the script and applause-meter readings, having missed the performance. There is no play that is director-proof, any more than an educational innovation is teacher-proof or student-proof. If this is acknowledged, it becomes imperative to study an innovation through the medium of its performance and to adopt a research style and methodology that is appropriate. By discarding a spurious "technological" simplification of reality and by acknowledging the complexity of the educational process, the illuminative evaluator is likely to increase rather than lessen the sense of uncertainty in education. On the other hand, unless studies such as these are vigorously pursued there is little hope of ever moving beyond helpless indecision or doctrinaire assertion in the conduct of instructional affairs.

With hindsight, "Evaluation as Illumination" can be read in various ways. First and foremost, it was a comment on Anglo-American educational research in the 1960s, a time when attention turned to program evaluation. Reaction against Descartes' dream of a idealized and calculable universe fostered a diaspora of postpositive responses, both inside and outside evaluation. "Evaluation as Illumination" was but one example. Nevertheless, its message of salvation and deliverance had an appeal that, seemingly, lingers on.

Second, "Evaluation as Illumination" was an argument against "methodolatry," against closed systems of analysis. At that time, we did not fully appreciated how Donald Campbell and Julian Stanley's "Experimental and Quasi-experimental Designs for Research on Teaching" (1963) could be seen both as the high point and the downturn of logical positivism in social and evaluation research. Its pivotal postpositivist idea is that all research is open to external threats to its validity, and this sense of uncertainty is symbolized in Campbell and Stanley's use of *quasi* (near or almost). Insofar as all research is logically open, "Evaluation as Illumination" was offered as a resource, not as a template. We accepted that it could be interpreted in diverse ways. We never tried, therefore, to police its ideas and their interpretation. To write a text is to release its meanings.

Third, "Evaluation as Illumination" was self-consciously crafted as a "good read." We tried, that is, to practice what we preached. We paid much attention to the rhetorical dimension of our argument, following the classical definition of rhetoric as an art of persuasion rather than of decoration. In one sense, this feature could be seen as our Achilles heel. Our attention to narrative clarity may have brought illumination to some, but the glister associated with our use of English (or, more accurately, hybrid Anglo-American English) brought others to a different view; namely, that "Evaluation as Illumination" is a crisp example of the representation problem in modern science. Postmodernists, for instance, highlight the representation problem in the claim that it is impossible to establish a secure link between language and its referents. To this extent, "Evaluation as Illumination" became a more open text than originally intended.

My own view is, ironically, that the representation problem brings evaluation back to where Malcolm Parlett and I began our collaboration at the end of the 1960s—with the problem, not of language, but of practice. Evaluation, like education, is a practical science. It is about creating knowledge about practice, a language of "what to do Monday." Illumination assumes such insightful knowledge. It creates power—the power to act and rearrange the world according to particular values. A key problem within evaluation, then and now, is the relationship between knowledge and values and the practice of democratic power in civil society. Insofar as "Evaluation as Illumination" foreshadowed such questions, it may still be as relevant to the beginning of the third millennium as it was to the democratic debates of the 1960s and 1970s.

—*David Hamilton*

Further Reading

Parlett, M., & Hamilton, D. (1972). Evaluation as illumination: A new approach to the study of innovatory programs. In D. Hamilton, B. MacDonald, C. King, D. Jenkins, & M. Parlett (Eds.), *Beyond the numbers game* (pp. 6-22). Berkeley, CA: McCutcheon.

■■ IMPACT ASSESSMENT

Impact assessment is an evaluation focused on the outcomes or impact of a program, policy, organization, or technology. Impact assessments typically try to make a casual inference that connects the evaluand with an outcome. Empowerment evaluation regards impact assessments as a process for describing performance in a way that will influence change and improvement. Impact assessment is also referred to as *outcome, impact,* or *summative evaluation.* The latter focuses on the judgment of worth or merit of the evaluand. This form of evaluation contrasts with process or formative evaluation, in which the purpose is to describe how a program operates (process) or to provide feedback on program improvement.

—*Leonard Bickman*

■■ IMPARTIALITY

Impartiality is an evaluation stance implying the lack of preference in the evaluator for the values or aims of any constituency or interest group in a program and expressing a formal disinterest in respect to outcomes. A position of impartiality involves the evaluator setting aside personal judgment to concentrate on feeding the judgments of participants. As Stenhouse put it, "instead of discriminating between alternative courses of action, [such an approach] seeks to make actors more discriminating." This is a methodological principle, not an ontological claim. We may consider a difference between evaluators being impartial and being value free. Acknowledging the inevitability of evaluators' holding values in relation to program goals or activities, we may, nonetheless, conceive of an act of cognitive editing in which evaluators set aside their preferences to become procedurally disinterested in program decisions and directions. Impartiality also need not imply lack of engagement or personal commitment to evaluation participants. The refusal of evaluators to express a preference (i.e., expose their values) may inspire confidence in participants, promoting the expectation of equal treatment with others, unmitigated by evaluators' own beliefs. Nonetheless, some see this as optimistic, given the impossibility of suppressing evaluator subjectivity, and tantamount to seeking (an equally implausible) objectivity.

—Saville Kushner

Further Reading

Stenhouse, L. (1980). *Curriculum research and development in action.* London: Heinemann.

■ IMPLEMENTATION

Implementation describes (a) the act of putting into practice the plans to complete an evaluation and (b) a type of evaluation. To implement plans is to use resources in intended ways to accomplish evaluation goals. An implementation evaluation assesses the extent to which planned activities and operations are in place. It is common in evaluation literature to see *process* and *implementation* used interchangeably to describe the same type of study; for example, of a program that is in place and using resources earmarked for specified goals. The conclusions from an implementation evaluation are more likely to be estimates of the extent of compliance with a plan rather than a yes or no determination. Such studies are essential because implementation problems are a common cause of program failure.

—M. F. Smith

■ IMPROVEMENT

Improvement refers to the act of making something better in some way—more efficient, productive, cost effective, and so on. In evaluation, formative evaluation is evaluation done for improvement because it provides information to enable program staff to make appropriate improvements (additions or changes) before a summative evaluation measures outcomes for an external audience of funders or other decision makers. Data for improvement come in a variety of forms, both quantitative and qualitative, including the following: interviews, surveys, observations, and document analyses. Due to the interactive nature of evaluation, improvement may also come from participants' involvement in the evaluation process.

—Jean A. King

See also Formative Evaluation

■ INCLUSION

Inclusion refers to meaningful involvement of all stakeholders in the evaluation process. It is meant to include the stakeholders who have traditionally been recognized, such as funders, administrators, staff, and participants, as well as seeking out accurate and credible representation for members of groups who have been traditionally excluded from or misrepresented in the evaluation process. Inclusion carries with it an implicit directive to be consciously aware of the bases for exclusion or misrepresentation, such as gender, race or ethnicity, disability, sexual orientation, religious preference, economic status, language, or other characteristics commonly associated with discrimination or oppression.

—Donna M. Mertens

■ INCLUSIVE EVALUATION

Inclusive evaluation emerged in response to increasing pressures to be responsive to cultural pluralism, as well as a redefinition of the role of the evaluator in relation to social change. The transformative paradigm provides the underlying philosophical assumptions that guide the work of the inclusive evaluator. Methodologically similar to democratic deliberative evaluation in its use of collective deliberation, stakeholder inclusiveness, and dialogical data collection methods, inclusive evaluation derives its difference from its deliberate emphasis on including groups that have historically experienced oppression and discrimination on the basis of gender, culture, economic level, ethnicity or race, disability, sexual orientation, language, or religious preference.

The role of the evaluator in an inclusive context is to function as a member of a team whose function is to bring about social change. This work is conducted with a conscious awareness of the social injustices that are part of the everyday living experience of many groups of people. The recognition of social injustice is accompanied by a willingness to challenge the status quo. For example, schools are failing the poorest children of color, prisons are inordinately full of men of color, programs for youth are not universally successful in preventing drug use or teenage pregnancy, and the burden falls more on the poor, minorities, and other known segments of the population. Thus the evaluator's job is to seek to uncover the weaknesses in the present system that contribute to a continuation of poor education, poverty, and other social ills. The evaluator can encourage those in power to go beyond a "blame the victim" stance to a position in which the failures within the system can be revealed. The challenge lies in finding ways to bring the thinking of critical theorists, feminists, and others who write from the antidiscriminatory paradigm to the evaluation community and the stakeholders. Society expects evaluators to be objective, and thus it is incumbent upon the inclusive evaluator working within the transformative paradigm to explain the meaning of objectivity thusly: *Objectivity,* within this framework, means a lack of bias that is achieved by inclusion of all relevant stakeholders in such a way that authentic and accurate representations of their viewpoints are considered.

In terms of actual practice of evaluation, the application of an inclusive approach to evaluation has implications for every step in the process: design of the study, definition of the problem, selection of indicators of success, sampling and data collection decisions, development of intervention strategies, addressing power differentials in the study, and setting standards for a good evaluation.

THE DESIGN OF THE STUDY

An inclusive approach to evaluation is amenable to quantitative, qualitative, or mixed methods designs. One underlying principle that guides the choice of design is that members of the community affected by the evaluation would be involved to some degree in the methodological and programmatic decisions. Several issues arise related to design choice, including being responsive to the community's perceptions and involvement, ethical issues concerning denial of treatment, and sharing of perks with those involved in the study.

Ethical concerns arise in design choice when the design involves denial of treatment, lack of community involvement in the decision to participate, or lack of fully informed consent as to the consequences of participating, especially as these relate to the use of a control group or a placebo. Denial of treatment is one strategy used in experimental designs to establish a control group. However, this is viewed as especially problematic in terms of the ethics associated with the transformative-emancipatory paradigm. Assignment to treatments or denial of treatment on a random basis

is also considered to be unethical and illegal in many schools and social service agencies. In those settings, reliance on a true experimental design with random selection and random assignment to conditions is not possible. Evaluators can recommend designs that avoid such ethical dilemmas, such as use of the next best current treatment, mixed methods, qualitative approaches, time series designs, use of known alternative treatments, comparison with an extant group, or comparison with a larger statistical base in terms of known levels of incidence.

THEORETICAL FRAMEWORK FOR DEFINING THE PROBLEM

Theoretical frameworks that place the blame for failure inside individuals or their culture are dysfunctional, deficit models. For example, the deficit model leads to framing the problem of poverty and underachievement of children in poor urban or rural schools in terms of social deficiency or cultural deficits rather than in terms of the marginal resources of their schools and the racialized politics of local, state, and federal governments. The inclusive framework views gender, race or ethnicity, disability, sexual orientation, and other bases of diversity from the perspective of a social, cultural, or minority group such that the defining characteristic is perceived as a dimension of human difference (not a defect). Within this paradigm, the category of diversity is recognized as being socially constructed such that its meaning is derived from society's response to individuals who deviate from cultural standards.

Evaluation Questions and Indicators of Success. The evaluator needs to work critically to develop appropriate questions and performance indicators that reflect those factors that are related to transformation. For example, evaluators can raise questions to ensure that the products of a program are appropriately inclusive of the pluralism in the community. They can also ask about the cultural appropriateness of data collection methods and the indicators that are established for success.

Sample Definitions and Inclusiveness. A prerequisite to being more inclusive is the development of an appropriate sensitivity to the diversity within the populations that are served by a program and an understanding of the complexity of the characteristics and the cultural implications. Not all deaf people are the same. Not all Latino people are the same. Not all African Americans are the same. What are the differences within the population that are important within this context? How are the services distributed within different subgroups? What are the values that underlie the distribution of services?

For example, a study of deaf and hard of hearing people can include the following dimensions: those who are highly educated and proficient users of American Sign Language; deaf adults with limited education and reading skills, some of whom communicate with sign language and gestures and pantomime; deaf and blind individuals who use an interpreter at close range; highly educated hard of hearing adults who use personal assistive listening devices; deaf adults from other countries who use their indigenous sign language; and deaf adults who rely on oral communication (reading lips and printed English). In addition, diversity in the sample was sought on the basis of gender, race or ethnicity, and any other important characteristics germane to the study.

Evaluators can use such question as these to help assess the inclusiveness of their samples:

- Are we including people from both genders and of diverse abilities, ages, classes, cultures, ethnicities, families, incomes, languages, races, disabilities, and sexualities?
- What barriers are we erecting to exclude a diversity of people?
- Have we chosen the appropriate data collection strategies for diverse groups, including providing for preferred modes of communication?

Data Collection Strategies. Probing to discover the complexities of the populations is a first step. The evaluator must figure out the best way to obtain authentic data from the various subgroups. This might involve using different languages or dialects, which has implications for the evaluator's own expertise linguistically or the acceptability of using an interpreter. This will definitely involve determining the appropriate method of data collection. For some populations, a survey sent home from school or through the mail may be incomprehensible, possibly a threat, or just one more thing a person who is struggling to survive cannot deal with. Is a focus group a

better way to collect data? Is a meeting in the school, church, or community center a better approach? Are meetings better scheduled during the day or at night? Is it necessary to provide food, transportation, or child care? Sensitive, careful probing can help identify appropriate data collection methods and instruments that can lead to the attainment of authentic and accurate data.

Addressing Power Differentials. Intertwined with such methodological decisions are issues related to differential power for the various stakeholder groups. The evaluator's job is to make sure that strong power imbalances do not distort the study's findings. Power differences can be addressed by the evaluator adopting a role that facilitates the involvement of those who have had a traditionally less powerful role in discussions of social and educational programs and their impacts. For example, in an evaluation of the accessibility of court systems for deaf and hard of hearing persons, an advisory council represented the diversity of the deaf and hard of hearing community in terms of preferred communication modes. However, input was also sought from that community that was inclusive of other types of diversity, such as gender, ethnicity or race, language, and experience with the court system.

Power differences can be addressed by using focus groups or other data collection methods to obtain information prior to the design of an intervention from the perspective of members of marginalized groups. In addition, opportunities can be provided during the project for the involvement of members of underrepresented groups in decisions about possible data collection methods, interpretation of findings, or implementation of results. These are some examples of ways to recognize and accommodate differences in traditional positions of power among various stakeholders. Evaluators who seek to be inclusive must also seek ways to redress power imbalances by issuing invitations throughout the process to those with the least power to be part of the conversation.

STANDARDS FOR EVALUATION

The evaluator's role is to ensure that a quality evaluation is planned, conducted, and used. To this end, the evaluation community has engaged in the development of various sets of standards for good evaluations. The Program Evaluation Standards were developed in

1994 by the Joint Committee on Standards for Educational Evaluation. This document provides one guide for evaluators to use in explaining to their clients the characteristics of a good evaluation. An addition of standards for a good evaluation based on the transformative function of evaluation would lead to a greater degree of inclusivity of previously marginalized groups. Additional standards could be incorporated to increase the appropriateness of an evaluation in terms of multicultural and power issues, using such categories as methodological validity, interpersonal validity, consequential validity, and multicultural validity.

Using this expanded set of standards, evaluators could ask such questions as follow:

- What are the influences of personal characteristics or circumstances, such as social class, gender, race and ethnicity, language, disability, or sexual orientation in shaping interpersonal interactions, including interactions among evaluators, clients, program providers, consumers, and other stakeholders?
- What evidence is there that the evaluation was conceptualized as a catalyst for change (e.g., a shift in the power relationships among cultural groups or subgroups)?
- Were the time and budget allocated to the evaluation sufficient to allow a culturally sensitive perspective to emerge?
- Did the evaluator demonstrate cultural sophistication regarding the cognitive, affective, and skill dimensions? Was the evaluator able to have positive interpersonal connections, conceptualize and facilitate culturally congruent change, and make appropriate cultural assumptions in the design and implementation of the evaluation?

Adoption of the inclusive evaluator's role does not mean that the evaluator's traditional tools should be discarded. The Program Evaluation Standards have value, as do the other tools that evaluators learn to use in evaluation and research methods, statistics, and policy analysis classes. The role of the inclusive evaluator is enriched by the addition of units in methods-oriented classes on the understanding of groups that have been traditionally underrepresented, through the examination of scholarly literature that has emerged from feminists, people of color, people with disabilities, and their advocates, and by interacting with members of those communities in a sustained and meaningful way.

—*Donna M. Mertens*

Further Reading

Hopson, R. K. (Ed.). (2000). How and why language matters. *New Directions for Evaluation, 86.*

Mertens, D. M. (2003). The inclusive view of evaluation: Visions for the new millennium. In S. I. Donaldson & M. Scriven (Eds.), *Evaluating social programs and problems: Visions for the new millennium* (pp. 91-107). Mahwah, NJ: Lawrence Erlbaum.

■■ INCREMENTAL CHANGE

Incremental change is the concept that programs and organizations develop over time by making small alterations; that is, by changing components or activities in increments, thereby building on the status quo. This type of change is evolutionary and gradual, creating minor improvements without addressing basic assumptions about organizational goals or operations. It contrasts with *radical* or *revolutionary change,* in which people are encouraged to question basic assumptions about the program and its structure, activities, and outcomes, leading potentially to dramatic actions that can transform an organization. Given its adaptability, program evaluation can support both types of change.

—*Jean A. King*

■■ INDEPENDENCE

Taken to signify a political stance for an evaluation that is not subject to the control of or that does not provide privileged access to any particular stakeholder group or constituency. Independence has been implied and advocated in a number of ways. For example, Scriven's goal-free evaluation seeks to uncouple evaluation from program prescriptions; Weiss' stakeholder evaluation seeks to honor the significance of all stakeholder agendas, not just those of the powerful; Stake's responsive evaluation was designed to broaden the data reach of evaluation beyond the limited concerns of the administrative system.

It is in MacDonald's democratic evaluation, however, that independence is explicitly discussed—in fact, well expressed in the maxim attributed to MacDonald: "An evaluation can be sponsored but not bought." Independence is designed to strengthen the public credibility and undeniability of the evaluation by demonstrating that the evaluation has no preference for or obligation to any partial view and to ensure that it is a general resource for the citizenry. Independence does not imply freedom from contractual obligations or from the obligation to provide a service to the sponsor. It does, however, imply the need to negotiate an appropriate political role for the evaluation in which the power of the sponsor does not overwhelm the obligations of the evaluation to report to multiple audiences. A component of independence, and closely related to it, is impartiality: the formal disinterest of the evaluation in respect to program value positions and its outcomes.

—*Saville Kushner*

See also DEMOCRATIC EVALUATION, GOAL-FREE EVALUATION

■ INDEPENDENT EVALUATION

For an evaluation to be considered independent, the evaluator must be impartial, objective, unencumbered, and balanced. Further, because perceived independence is as important as independence itself, the evaluator must be accountable for every step in the research process and able to document all key decisions and actions for the client organization, other evaluators, and the community at large. Overall, external evaluations tend to hold more credibility than internal ones because the external evaluator appears to have less to gain or lose from the evaluation findings and is less likely to experience a conflict of interest.

—*Gail V. Barrington*

■ INDICATORS

An *indicator* is the operationalization of a variable used in an evaluation. It is what is measured to signify performance. For example, if an intelligence quotient is a variable, its indicator might be the score on a Stanford-Binet test. Indicators are descriptions of what can be empirically observed that will signal the occurrence of the aspect or facet of the evaluand under study.

—*M. F. Smith*

INDUCTION. *See* INFERENCE

■ INFERENCE

Inference is a conclusion drawn from premises or observations: if drawn from premises, a deductive inference; if from observations, an inductive inference. The common form of a deductive inference is *if p, then q. Not q, therefore not p.* In other words, the conclusion (not q) must follow from the premise (if p, then q). Inductive inferences are passed when sufficient observation of events have been made so that it is possible to conclude with confidence that something is the case. For example, an evaluator observes instances of client satisfaction with services in adequate numbers and under appropriate varying conditions and can then conclude that clients are satisfied with the services. Statistical conclusions are inductive inferences expressed in probabilistic terms. Inductive inferences carry a certain degree of risk in determining how many instances of observation, and of what kind, are adequate. Statistical conclusions include safeguards, such as confidence intervals and significance tests.

■ INFORMED CONSENT

Informed consent is a central ethical principle in collecting data from people. Awareness of the need for informed consent arose from the Nuremburg trials of Nazi scientists, who had used concentration camp prisoners for horrifying medical experiments. The Nuremburg Code, developed after the trials, established subjects' right to give voluntary informed consent prior to participation in research. The Program Evaluation Standards and the Guiding Principles for Evaluators both reinforce evaluators' obligation to obtain informed consent for data collection.

Informed consent is based on the principles of respect and autonomy. Individuals have the right to choose whether to participate in a study and may discontinue their participation at any time. *Informed consent* means that the person being asked to participate knows what a reasonable person in the same situation would want to know before giving consent. Consent forms typically describe the purposes of the study, what participants will be asked to do, potential risks and benefits to participants and others, and the confidentiality of the information collected; they also inform people of the voluntary nature of their participation and their right to withdraw.

A good informed consent form is clear and understandable, free of jargon, and provides an appropriate level of detail for the respondent. The nature of the interaction between the respondent and the person obtaining consent is important. The form should be provided in a friendly and open, but respectful, manner that encourages the recipient to ask questions or express concerns. Precautions should be taken so that the respondent does not feel intimidated by any perceived higher status of the person giving the form. When data are collected from individuals whose culture or norms differ from those of the evaluator, representatives of that group should be recruited to ensure that the form addresses concerns that those respondents might have regarding privacy, confidentiality, or other issues and uses language and terms that are familiar to the respondents.

Particular care should be taken to help individuals who may feel pressured to participate recognize that their choice is voluntary. In evaluation, these groups are common sources of data and include prisoners, employees, and recipients of services who may feel that their eligibility for services could be threatened by failure to participate. Other groups, such as children, developmentally delayed adults, and persons with mental illness or senility, may be unable to give full informed consent. They may assent to participate, but parents or other guardians must also give full consent.

When data are collected through surveys or telephone interviews, voluntary consent is obtained when the respondent chooses to complete the survey or phone interview. However, evaluators should ensure that the cover letter or instructions contain sufficient information for respondents to be informed and recognize their right of refusal.

Informed consent is often neglected in evaluation. Evaluations take place in public programs where data are often collected routinely, and clients may unknowingly be assigned to different services, later used for evaluation, by service providers. Nevertheless, evaluators should remain sensitive to the principles of informed consent and actively balance its requirements with other ethical obligations.

—*Jody L. Fitzpatrick*

Further Reading

Sieber, J. E. (1992). *Planning ethically responsible research.* Newbury Park, CA: Sage.

Newman, D. L., & Brown, R. D. (1996). *Applied ethics for program evaluation.* Thousand Oaks, CA: Sage.

▦ INGLE, ROBERT

(b. 1926, Detroit, Michigan; d. 1998, Milwaukee, Wisconsin). Ph.D., Wayne State University; M.A., B.A., University of Michigan.

Ingle was the cofounder, with William Gephart, of the Evaluation Network (ENet) and a significant force behind the merger of ENet and the Evaluation Research Society into the American Evaluation Association. He was Professor in the Department of Educational Psychology at the University of Wisconsin from 1962 through 1992. During his tenure, he served on the university governance committee twice, developing policy for faculty governance.

He is remembered as a "friendly curmudgeon who was dedicated to developing the evaluation profession" and was supported in these endeavors by his lifelong wife, Maria. He served as conference chair for the annual evaluation conference from the inaugural conference in 1981 (then the ENet and ERS joint meeting) in Austin, Texas, through the 1991 American Evaluation Association conference in Chicago, Illinois. The Robert B. Ingle Award was created by the American Evaluation Association Board of Directors to honor all the service contributions Ingle made to the association. This award continues to be presented at the annual meeting to a member who has been particularly instrumental in promoting the interests and operations of the American Evaluation Association.

▦ INPUTS

Inputs are one aspect of an evaluand that may be a partial or entire focus of an evaluation. Inputs are those elements dedicated to the evaluand, as well as the context of the evaluand, such as money, staff, time, facilities, equipment, and supplies, as well as laws, regulations, and funders' requirements. A number of evaluation approaches pay special attention to inputs, including logic models, CIPP, the countenance model, and discrepancy approaches.

▦ INSPECTION

In evaluation, the term *inspection* is associated with the evaluation conducted by an office of inspectors general, a particular governmental agency, or international agencies such as the United Nations. Offices of inspectors general are common throughout the world and serve both internal and external evaluation purposes, including reporting to an agency manager as well as to a government officer or body outside the agency being inspected. In some cases, the public may also be a primary audience for inspections. Inspections are often conducted within a short time frame and focus on policy issues, fiscal management, and compliance with sanctions, abuse, and fraud.

See also AUDITING

Further Reading

Hendricks, M., Mangano, M., & Moran, W. C. (Eds.). (1990). Inspectors general: A new force in evaluation. *New Directions of Program Evaluation, 48.*

▟ INSTITUTIONAL SELF-EVALUATION

Institutions whose members are willing to describe their activities and actions to each other and to organizations that provide accreditation may be said to be engaged in *institutional self-study.* Such accounts may incidentally influence practices.

Institutional self-evaluation is more intrusive in that it entails explanation of activities and actions, thus making the members of the institution and the institution more vulnerable to those making decisions about the distribution of scarce resources. The politics of the institution are embodied in the preconditions for the evaluator and should, as far as possible, be taken into account when writing and negotiating the self-evaluation contract or agreement. Reputation, tenure, promotion, and the accountability relationships within an institution may become challenged, yet vulnerability is a condition in the quest to find more profound approaches to innovation and possible change for the better. The institution's members constantly test the sensitivity of the evaluator to these uncertainties. The evaluator is often based in the institution and has to be accessible to all members equitably. Institutional self-evaluation tests any claims of democratic procedures, trust, confidentiality, and authenticity.

Beginning in 1974, protocols for such institutional self-evaluation were devised during the process. In 1982, Adelman and Alexander independently tried out ideas from evaluation, action research, and organizational behavior in the two separate university colleges in which they were based. Before the endeavor could commence, an agreement on procedures, confidentiality, pseudonymity, and purposes was negotiated with

members of both colleges, leading to an institutional agreement.

Adelman and Alexander experienced similar problems as their work proceeded, problems that related to those in the qualitative evaluation literature; for instance, those arising from attempts to voluntarily change curricula in schools. These problems included devising procedures for identifying issues without blame or praise; further exploration on disputed issues arising from discussion; extent of feedback of information; commenting on self-evaluation reports and refraining from comment on substantial points, persons, or other appraisals; and making any judgments, positive or negative.

Inevitably, institutional evaluators seek information and members' judgments about the worth of their activities and actions. In most evaluations, interim or terminal reports are required, even in the most politically fraught cases. During institutional self-evaluation, members' reports may be issued at any point. Their significance pertains to the impact on the work of the institution. Reports by the institutional evaluator may comment on the worth of particular activities and actions in the context of structural developments of the institution. Both sources of report usually have some impacts on internal politics, some anticipated but often unanticipated.

Internal resident evaluators may legitimately be requested by the institution's members to investigate particularities. On their own initiative, internal evaluators may seek potential sites for critical incidents, sites where converging streams of activity would reveal the gap between aspiration and practice. In this regard, the internal evaluator theorizes about the institution from the privileged position of being able to visit all its sites, at least by request. Members of the institutions may ask for evaluators' judgments. Although evaluators cannot answer one on one, the answers to these requests often becomes incorporated into subsequent reports. For example, I had been moved by a conversation with a faculty member to collect information from the student enrollments on courses that were taken to reach published standards and grades to teach initial literacy. A large group of staff was teaching these courses, and no one person was formally responsible for literacy. The report described the lack of guidance in combining courses leading to the standard in literacy. The problem was structural. The report was placed on the agenda of the representative committee for teacher preparation.

There was little discussion, and some denied the validity of the data on the grounds that students learned more than was stated in the prospectus of courses. The problem was referred upward for the most senior managers to consider, one of whom was chairing the meeting. After several invited reports were met with similar responses, I decided to work with specialist groups of faculty on ways to identify and self-evaluate course content and structure. As for the wider institutional issues, these were monitored by attendance at specific meetings, even of the most senior managers. For the evaluator, the realization of the gaps and sometimes chasms between some of the senior managers' knowledge and understanding of the institution's activities and the actual activities was truly alarming. This was made more poignant because the college was under threat of closure by the government on the grounds that it was too small to be economical. The college did have options for survival, one of which was to combine with the large local university, one of whose most senior administrators was part of the steering group for the wider study, which involved two more colleges. The internal resident evaluator only discovered this political situation about 6 months after the commencement of the contract.

PROCEDURES DEVISED AND THEIR WEAKNESSES

Initially, the internal evaluator wrote reports and requested comments from faculty. Comments were to be in type and without attribution. The evaluator would collate and summarize the comments and then convene or attend a meeting of the faculty involved. The evaluator found that a minority of the faculty sent in comments, making the feedback inadmissible. The evaluator ceased this approach. Instead, the evaluator attended the regular meetings of a subject group of faculty and, after several meetings and with knowledge of previous minutes of meetings, suggested some additional issues that seemed worthy of discussion by the faculty. The faculty were willing to talk about these and be tape-recorded on condition of confidentiality.

The evaluator was allowed to comment on the procedures for the discussions and was able to gain acceptance for the discussion to move toward explanation and so to self-evaluation. However, not all subject groups and few program groups were willing to engage in such explicit discussions. Trust and security were lacking, faculty felt vulnerable, and a small minority were willing to accuse individuals without a sufficient understanding of the context. The ordinary situation was silence or platitude or asking for further time before making a reply. Occasionally, the questions would be turned back to the evaluator for a response, to which I would reiterate my nonreactive, nonintervention position.

As an internal and resident evaluator, I had to be on guard from the outset to display an equitable relationship with all members. I resisted any attempts by the senior management or anyone else to co-opt me into their judgment processes. I declined offices in the senior executive suite, for some were in a most isolated place on the campus.

The discussion, issues, discussion, and evaluation method did work well and demonstrated that professors could not only make self-critical and well-evidenced judgments of their own and colleagues' work and its contribution to the whole but also plan adjustments and even changes to all aspects of courses.

Self-evaluation has been shown to be feasible and useful where protocols are established and followed by more than a minority in the institution. In the college, the program committees, which oversaw all or most of a complete degree, were not amenable, and yet it was at this level that the major structural decisions were made. The college was divided by its programs and by the quite different ways of dealing with problems and persons among the directors, from power-coercive to technical-rational to normative-reeducative.

The aspiration to promote self-evaluation in institutions is in contradistinction to power-coercive means of promoting adjustment and change; possible, but with many safeguards, in technical-rational; and probable when the administration takes a normative-reeducative approach.

Self-evaluation can enhance understanding and help to formulate more effective decisions if the evaluation flows into a plan of institutional development, given the constraints mentioned here. Self-evaluation may become part of cycles of action or participatory research in situations where time and resources for employee and employer development are allowed.

—*Clem Adelman*

Further Reading

Adelman, C. (1984). *The politics and ethics of evaluation.* Houndsmills, UK: Palgrave Macmillan.

Adelman, C., & Alexander, R. (1982). *The self-evaluating institution: Practices and principles in the management of educational change.* London: Methuen.

Dressel, P. (1976). *Handbook of academic evaluation.* San Francisco: Jossey-Bass.

Simons, H. (1987). *Getting to know schools in a democracy: The politics and process of evaluation.* London: Taylor & Francis.

▪▪ INSTRUCTIONAL DESIGN AND EVALUATION

Like program evaluation, instructional design emerged as a distinct field of study in the mid-20th century. However, although large government programs drove the application of evaluation, it was the very modest accomplishments of behaviorism's teaching machines and programmed instruction that suggested there is much to be learned about instructional design.

Although piecemeal at first, a knowledge base examining varying methods of instruction and their effects on goals, content, and learners has produced a thriving and stable field of study whose reach extends into K-12 education, community education, higher education, and training in business and industry. Like evaluation, instructional design considers itself a transdiscipline, blending the processes of curriculum development, instructional materials development, and instructional management and delivery. The general aim of instructional design is to construct optimal "blueprints," or knowledge about what methods of instruction will produce desired learning outcomes under the variety of conditions that may exist.

Literally hundreds of instructional design models bear similar characteristics by being reciprocal in nature and generally bearing comparable components. Every model also identifies evaluation as one of its key steps, as the seminal Dick and Carey model (Figure 1) illustrates. Instructional design also employs and makes very clear distinctions between formative and summative evaluation.

The role of formative evaluation in instructional design is for course or curricular improvement. Frequently, formative evaluation is internal, but it may involve subject matter experts or others external to the design process. Various evaluation models are also applied at this stage of design and include but are not limited to connoisseur, decision-oriented, and objectives-driven approaches. Field or pilot testing is also considered a strategy of formative evaluation. After formative evaluation, instructional designers hope to have as close as is possible to an error-free version of their instructional designs and materials for delivery to their target audience.

Summative evaluation in instructional design matches learning outcomes to learning goals. Not all summative evaluation is goal based, but instructional

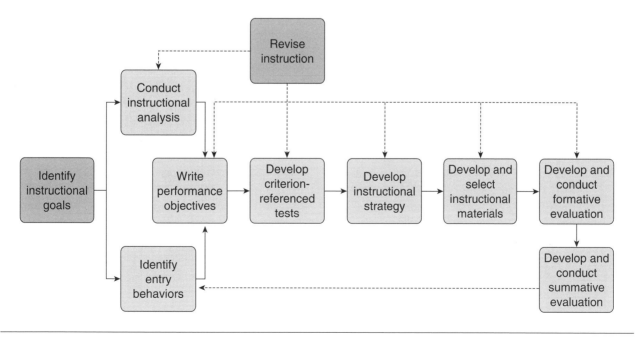

Figure 1   *Dick and Carey Design Model*

objectives are the basis for key evaluation questions. Related elements of the summative evaluation are institutional impacts, learner and content congruence, and programmatic costs. Summative evaluation is generally reserved for the external evaluator, who applies both qualitative and quantitative data collection and analysis methods. Although learner assessment data is used in both forms of instructional design evaluation, summative evaluation makes more frequent use of standardized assessments in education.

Recently, instructional designers have adopted "confirmative evaluation" as an evaluative stage aimed at the terminal objectives for a stated program or curriculum. Although timing plays the key role from an instructional design perspective, confirmative evaluation takes up where summative evaluation leaves off. Smaller samples of target learners and more indirect measures may be used at this point, but the emphasis is still on performance in a realistic context. For example, confirmative evaluation of a substance abuser prevention program will focus on participant quality of life and citizenship indicators. Confirmative evaluation of a primary grade literacy program will focus on middle school competencies in reading, creative writing, and verbal expression.

—*Mark Hawkes*

Further Reading

Dick, W., & Carey, L. (1978). *The systematic design of instruction.* New York: HarperCollins.

■■ INSTRUCTIONAL TECHNOLOGY, EVALUATION OF

Instructional technology (IT) is a broad term that covers traditional media, computer-based training, games and simulations, multimedia, distance education, electronic performance support systems, and virtual reality. IT can be found as both hardware and software in schools, businesses, corporate training departments, and even on the Web. However, the majority of the evaluation work focused on IT over the last decade takes place in educational settings. Why? A $7 billion annual investment in educational technology has left policy makers and administrators fielding questions from the public about the value, return on investment, and conditions of optimal use of school-based instructional technology.

THE EVOLUTION OF SCHOOL-BASED IT EVALUATION

When desktop technology became affordable enough for K-12 schools to buy in bulk, the emphasis was on building school, district, and statewide technology infrastructures. As these networks emerged, implementation was the initial interest for evaluators and their stakeholders. Evaluations focused on technology implementation applied a variety of strategies (e.g., the Computer Aided Education and Training Initiative). These studies attempted to determine the tractability of technology implementation and document how challenges were addressed. "Adoption of Innovation" studies applied the instrumentation of proven models (e.g., Apple Computers of Tomorrow) to compare IT project development to the blueprint of efficient and comprehensive technology adoption in schools.

Eventually, evaluations focused more intensively on such IT components as professional development, equity of access, integrative capacity, learner control, and technical support. These evaluations provided important project-level information on the formative development of school-based IT systems. As useful as these evaluation data were to stakeholders at the time, however, little information was directly linked to student achievement. Because of the enormous capital invested in IT, demonstrating technology's vital effectiveness has become a political, economic, and public policy necessity.

In focusing on learning impact, evaluators are cautious about treating technology as a discrete and isolated entity. Because technological applications evolve so quickly and because these evolutions limit the utility of past evaluations, careful IT evaluation embeds technology use in the larger process of school change. Still, pinpointing IT-induced learning outcomes is problematic. Evaluators often find the effectiveness of IT fixed in the effectiveness of other school improvement efforts. Disentangling technology-induced learning outcomes from learning resulting from other school programs is difficult and requires evaluation methodologies and data sources unique from oft-used survey and observation. When standardized test scores are used as a measure of learning impact, evaluators find they provide limited formative information with which to drive the development of a school's technology program. Consequently, alternative forms of documenting learning impact are needed.

A hybrid form of school-based IT evaluation suggests that evaluation apply three levels of indicators.

Leading indicators emerge from the first stages of an evaluation and address implementation and curriculum development concerns. A next level of indicators shows impact at an intermediate point in the form of behavioral indicators and performance on curriculum-embedded measures. A trailing set of indicators speaks to policy makers and the public about standardized tests and graduation rates. This *distributed* evaluation approach places the responsibility for evaluation at multiple levels and uses local capacity (teachers, schools) to identify and collect data. It is an approach with the potential to get formative evaluation data quickly into client hands, be flexible to types of indicators and measures, and be more resistant to criticisms than were previous evaluations.

DISTANCE AND ONLINE LEARNING

Ever-increasing access to the Internet and World Wide Web has made the online environment a fertile field for IT products and practices. Add to this the growing use of room-based interactive video systems, and almost every sector of education, business, and industry is affected.

When distance and online learning programs are evaluated, a familiar pattern emerges. Evaluations are generally drawing from criteria involving a combination of the following elements: interface design, instructional design, student satisfaction, technology access, faculty satisfaction, economic viability, departmental capacity, interdepartmental collaboration, and the educational-level infrastructure. Methodologically, multiple approaches are applied, and this usually involves a statistical analysis of the overall quality of the online program and a descriptive-interpretive analysis of the program through the eyes of participants.

Although curriculum, policy, and organization questions are important in the evaluation of online learning systems, there is a lack of questions related to the technology itself. Questions in two technological domains appear necessary to address information needs appropriately in online learning evaluation. The *delivery domain* is characterized by the equipment, computers, machines, and media that provide access to the instruction. Modern adaptations of delivery include room-based and desktop interactive video and text- and audio-based synchronous and asynchronous communication. The *instructional domain* seeks to harness the technology for motivation, engagement, and communication to enhance student learning.

As a medium, or vehicle for transporting information between learners and instructor, the delivery technology influences student access to the information and the cost and timeliness of delivery. The instructional technology, however, is more directly related to the impact of the instruction on the consumer. Evaluators working in the online environment have been careful to apply approaches that separate the influences of delivery and instructional technologies so that attributions about impact can be more accurately made.

IT EVALUATION IN BUSINESS AND INDUSTRY

In market demand, the private sector has perhaps the most efficient approach to the evaluation of instructional technology products. Whether the product is hardware or software related, industry-developed IT products are heavily influenced by consumer needs and market analyses. Initial stages of product or process evaluation are driven by internal beta testing. Subsequent evaluation involves several iterations of field testing.

When hardware is the target of evaluation, several key evaluation criteria apply: platform interoperability, system compatibility, ease of use, functionality, and application. For software products' interaction, the ease of use, surface features, and motivation are applied as key evaluation criteria. Even for Web products, developers are interested in content credibility, customer navigability, and critical information accessibility.

—Mark Hawkes

Further Reading

Baker, E., & Herman, J. L. (2000). *Technology and evaluation.* Los Angeles: National Center for Research on Evaluation, Standards, and Student Testing. Retrieved May 22, 2004, from http://www.sri.com/policy/designkt/baker2.doc

▨ INTENDED USERS

Evaluations have many potential stakeholders and audiences. The concept of *intended users* moves from the general, passive concepts of stakeholders and audiences to specific and active focus on actual primary intended users and their commitments to concrete uses. Intended users are those who have the responsibility to apply findings and implement recommendations. In working with intended users, the evaluator facilitates judgment and decision making by specific people. The values and questions of intended users inform and guide the evaluation. In this way, evaluation use can be planned for and facilitated with those who have real interest in and responsibility for evaluation use.

—Michael Quinn Patton

Further Reading

Patton, M. Q. (1997). *Utilization-focused evaluation.* Thousand Oaks, CA: Sage.

⠿ INTENDED USES

Evaluations have many potential uses, such as improving programs, rendering judgments of merit and worth, generating lessons about effectiveness, assuring accountability, testing program theory, calculating costs and benefits, and building organizational capacity. No single evaluation will serve all these potential uses well. Establishing utilization priorities focuses an evaluation. The concept of *intended uses* moves from the general idea of doing a useful evaluation to a specific and concrete focus on the priorities of intended uses for a particular evaluation's primary intended users. The goal of the evaluation then becomes intended uses by intended users.

—Michael Quinn Patton

Further Reading

Patton, M. Q. (1997). *Utilization-focused evaluation.* Thousand Oaks, CA: Sage.

⠿ INTERNAL EVALUATION

Internal evaluation is the use by an organization of evaluators who are employees of that organization to evaluate the organization's own programs. During the last decade, internal evaluation has grown rapidly worldwide. In North America, internal evaluation is estimated to account for between half and three quarters of all evaluations.

There are three characteristics that distinguish internal evaluations from external evaluations:

1. The primary responsibility for internal evaluation lies with the organization itself. Internal evaluation is viewed as an essential tool for managers and an integral part of the management process.

2. The issues addressed by internal evaluation are the concerns of the managers, staff, and clients of the organization. In contrast, the focus of external evaluations typically are the concerns of persons outside of the organization; for example, policy makers or funding bodies.

3. Internal evaluators are directly accountable to the organization they are evaluating, whereas external evaluators are independent of the organization they are evaluating.

STRENGTHS AND WEAKNESSES OF INTERNAL EVALUATION

Within the organizational context, internal evaluation has many strengths. The relationships that internal evaluators build over time enable them to reduce the anxiety and fear often associated with external evaluations. As staff members of an organization, internal evaluators tend to know more about the organization's programs, organizational context, and political processes. This knowledge allows them to select evaluation strategies that fit the unique characteristics of their situation and to have their findings accepted more readily. Internal evaluators can become a valued corporate resource by communicating relevant evaluation findings in a timely fashion, supplying crucial evaluation information for strategy planning and policy decisions, creating a "corporate memory," and building an evaluation culture.

The major weakness of internal evaluation is that it is perceived as being less objective. This perception may be crucial when there are financial or legal concerns and when accountability is a major focus. The pitfalls of internal evaluation, however, can be largely overcome by careful attention to evaluation methodology and by strategies such as having an external evaluator validate the internal evaluation process.

ROLES OF INTERNAL EVALUATORS

Internal evaluation is an applied research activity that supports organizational development and learning. To accomplish this mission, internal evaluators need to assume proactive and challenging roles that include identifying best practices, identifying organizational factors that influence performance, and monitoring the implementation of solutions based on evaluation findings. They need to avoid negative roles such as those of number cruncher, whistleblower, or spy for senior management.

MODELS OF INTERNAL EVALUATION

There are several popular internal evaluation models. The "internal departmental" is a common model in larger organizations that have a separate internal evaluation unit. The head of this unit usually reports directly to the chief executive or senior vice-president of the organization, thereby giving the unit significant independence and influence. A second model is the "embedded" internal evaluation function. In this model, managers or project team leaders carry part-time evaluation responsibility. They are part of the team and use evaluation to strengthen programs by identifying potential problems and monitoring implementation. A third model is the "hybrid" that couples the skills and objectivity of an external evaluator with the organizational savvy of internal evaluators.

THE PROCESS OF INTERNAL EVALUATION

The internal evaluation process differs considerably from the process used in external evaluations. In the usual external evaluation, although program managers and staff may have the responsibility to provide data to an external evaluator, they may benefit little from the evaluation study because the focus of the evaluation and evaluation reports address the information needs of the sponsor.

In contrast, internal evaluation places considerable emphasis on front-end analysis of the information needs of various stakeholders, especially those within the organization. This front-end process ensures that the right questions are being addressed, and it disciplines the selection of evaluation methods by carefully assessing the "return on investment" for the fiscal and staff resources that the program expends on the evaluation. This process results in highly focused evaluations that make good use of limited time and money. The internal evaluation process also promotes utilization and reflective practice. Because it is highly participatory and interactive, internal evaluation empowers program managers and staff to understand their program theory and practice better. The internal evaluation process requires program managers and staff to generate fact-based recommendations and

action plans, and then through monitoring, it ensures that the changes are implemented. In short, the findings of internal evaluations are transformed into action by a highly effective process that emphasizes organizational development and learning.

KEY FACTORS IN BUILDING INTERNAL EVALUATION CAPABILITY

There are several important factors that contribute to developing effective internal evaluation capability. High-impact internal evaluation units demonstrate top management support for evaluation, positive leadership by the head of the internal evaluation unit, an organizational culture that supports continual learning and critical program review for decision making, adaptation by the internal evaluation units to the culture and decision-making style of the organization, and a highly visible public image of an evaluation that is achieved by soliciting topics for evaluation, publicizing the results of evaluations, and using evaluations for program improvement.

RECENT TRENDS IN THE PRACTICE OF INTERNAL EVALUATION

There are several recent trends in the practice of internal evaluation that have important implications for the field of evaluation as a whole. These include the following:

- Replacing "wall to wall" evaluations that review all programs with monitoring systems to identify "hot spots" that require in-depth evaluations
- Shifting from large databases to smaller program-level "data marts" and distributed networks with rapid access to information, which encourages the strategic use of information and a quick response to changing conditions
- Replacing written evaluation reports with new reporting formats designed to provide information when it is really needed, such as writing letters to flag a concern, having evaluators sit on program committees, and holding a wrap-up session rather than writing a final report
- Working with managers, staff, and clients to articulate clear outcomes and developing tools for measuring the outcomes and best practices that contribute value for money

—Arnold Love

Further Reading

Love, A. J. (1991). *Internal evaluation: Building organizations from within.* Newbury Park, CA: Sage.

Mathison, S. (Ed.). (1991). Authority in internal evaluation. *Evaluation and Program Planning, 14*(2, special section), 157-198.

■■ INTERNAL VALIDITY

Internal validity refers to the evidence that the interpretations and conclusions reached in the evaluation can be attributed to program functions rather than to other factors. Poorly designed outcome evaluations, by definition, have questionable integrity because of insufficient safeguards against alternative explanations for program effects; program outcome effects are intractably enmeshed with extraneous factors. The design challenges for evaluation studies are similar to those in traditional research in that a system of logic must be applied that enables the designer to construct procedures that will reduce the irrelevant sources of program outcome variability before the evaluation is conducted.

For example, gathering evidence of *program fidelity,* that is, evidence that the program features that are the object of the evaluation were actually implemented, should be part of the evaluation plan. If such evidence is collected early or periodically, the evaluator may even be instrumental in prompting program staff to activate the identified program features, hence removing this threat to internal validity. Some sources of program outcome variability, however, may be beyond the control of the evaluator. For example, if any events occurred between the pretest and posttest for all or some of the program participants that affect their responses to the posttest, there may be little the evaluator can do about it. This threat to the subsequent explanation of program effect is commonly called *history.* When discovered, at minimum, the evaluator should adequately describe the situation. Some threats to internal validity can be statistically controlled.

Several threats to internal validity of both research and evaluations have been identified and discussed in the literature:

1. *Unreliability of measures.* Use of unreliable data collection procedures makes it nearly impossible to disentangle actual program outcome variance from variance reflecting measurement error.

2. *Attrition.* Differences in groups' standing on measured program outcomes may be due to differential changes in their composition over time rather than to program interventions. For example, if loss of program participants is disproportionately occurring among those with low standing on the measured outcomes, scores will rise due to the survivors' initial higher standing.

3. *Statistical regression.* Groups that are selected based on their initially very low (or high) standing on some measure are likely to show changes in their standing in the opposite direction on subsequent testing due to the measurement errors in the assessment procedures used in initially classifying them. Statistical procedures are available to control for this phenomenon.

4. *Selection.* Participation in such programs as community-based health centers or social service agencies is generally voluntary. This self-selection process may be associated with other personal characteristics, such as motivation, interest, and education, that may influence the participants' responses to program interventions, making them respond differently than would individuals in the general population or nonparticipant comparison groups and thus leading to differences due to factors other than program effects.

—*Charles L. Thomas*

Further Reading

Posavac, E. J., & Carey, R. C. (2003). *Program evaluation methods and case studies* (6th ed.). Upper Saddle River, NJ: Prentice Hall.

Campbell, D. T., & Stanley, J. C. (1963). *Experimental and quasi-experimental designs for research.* Chicago: Rand-McNally.

■■ INTERNATIONAL DEVELOPMENT EVALUATION ASSOCIATION (IDEAS)

Until the creation of IDEAS in 2002 at a Constituent Assembly in Beijing, China, there was no professional organization for those evaluators whose main focus and concern was with development. IDEAS fills a gap in the international evaluation architecture. It is focused on the evaluation needs of developing countries and transition economies through capacity building, providing global knowledge, and supporting the networking of development evaluation professionals. IDEAS is a voluntary professional association guided by a 10-member board; each member is from a different country. Membership is open to all those interested in development evaluation.

—Ray C. Rist

INTERNATIONAL DEVELOPMENT RESEARCH CENTRE (IDRC)

The International Development Research Centre (IDRC) is a public corporation created by the Canadian government to help communities in the developing world find solutions to social, economic, and environmental problems through research. Its in-house evaluation unit focuses on promoting evaluation as a planning and management tool, building capacity for evaluation, and assessing the use and impact of research for development. The IDRC is particularly sensitive to the need to redress the pervasive control of evaluation agendas by donor agencies. The IDRC's evaluation unit emphasizes working with the emerging evaluation associations in developing nations.

INTERNATIONAL ORGANIZATION FOR COOPERATION IN EVALUATION (IOCE)

The International Organization for Cooperation in Evaluation (IOCE) is a loose coalition of regional and national evaluation organizations from around the world. The IOCE seeks to legitimate and strengthen evaluation societies and associations by promoting the systematic use of evaluation in civil society. It builds evaluation capacity, develops principles and procedures in evaluation, encourages the development of new societies and associations, procures resources for cooperative activity, and is a forum for the exchange of good practice and theory in evaluation. The IOCE inaugural assembly was held in Lima, Peru, in March 2003.

—Craig Russon

Further Reading

International Organization for Cooperation in Evaluation. (2002). *IOCE mission.* Retrieved May 22, 2004, from http://home.wmis.net/~russon/ioce/

INTERNATIONAL PROGRAM IN DEVELOPMENT EVALUATION TRAINING (IPDET)

Founded in 2001, IPDET is a month-long summer program for executive training in development evaluation. It is cosponsored by Carleton University in Ottawa, Ontario, and the World Bank. The impetus for the program originates in a growing global demand for professional evaluation of developmental policies, strategies, programs, and projects, especially those related to poverty reduction, social development, and governance. The first 2 weeks of the program offer an 80-hour core course on development evaluation. The second 2 weeks offer a set of technical workshops on a broad array of development evaluation topics. Combining the totals from the two programs in 2001 and 2002, more than 275 persons from 52 countries attended.

—Ray C. Rist

Further Reading

International Program for Development in Evaluation Training. (2001). Retrieved May 22, 2004, from http://www.carleton.ca/ipdet

INTERPRETATION

Interpretation involves explaining findings, attaching significance to particular results, making inferences, drawing conclusions, and presenting patterns within a clear and orderly framework. It occurs after description has taken place and begins after the evaluator has extracted meaning from, and has tried to make sense of, data from transcripts, photographs, and statistics. Interpretation can also arise from a need to make comparisons across cases, examine causes and consequences, and answer particular evaluation questions. For interpretations to be considered trustworthy and viable, the evaluator will need to use techniques such as seeking alternative explanations, carrying out negative case analysis, and peer debriefing.

—Rosalind Hurworth

INTERPRETIVISM

Interpretivism is based on a philosophical framework that promotes plural perspectives in evaluations relying on qualitative approaches and natural settings. It arose as an alternative to positivist methods, and many associated ideas can be traced back to the work of Guba and Lincoln in the 1980s. Basically, interpretivism is about contextualized meaning involving a belief that reality is socially constructed, filled with multiple meanings and interpretations, and that emotions are involved. As a result, interpretivists see the goal of theorizing as providing an understanding of direct lived experience instead of abstract generalizations.

In addition, there is no separation between the evaluator and those evaluated, and the underlying principles are based on openness and dialogue. Interpretivist inquiry is, therefore, subjective, dialectic, and value laden, and consequently, this has led to diverse and debatable findings within evaluations.

—*Rosalind Hurworth*

Further Reading

Lincoln, Y. S., & Guba, E. G. (1985). *Naturalistic inquiry.* Beverley Hills, CA: Sage.

Smith, J. K. (1989). *The nature of social and educational inquiry: Empiricism versus interpretation.* Norwood, NJ: Ablex.

▚ INTERVENTION

Any planned effort that is designed to produce specific changes in peoples' thoughts, feelings, or behaviors may be classed as an *intervention*. An intervention may be simple (e.g., the use of dental floss) or a complex array of program activities and elements (e.g., a transition-to-work program).

—*Jeffrey G. Tucker*

See also CIPP MODEL, PROCESS EVALUATION

▚ INTERVIEWING

Interviewing has played a significant role in evaluation methodologies. From the question a doctor might pose a patient to the widespread use of opinion polling in social research, people have relied on question and answer exchanges to gather and share information, opinions, feelings, ideas, and experiences. Interviewing in the context of evaluation is a form of instrumentation used in both quantitative and qualitative study designs to collect data. Interviewing can occur through the mail, over the telephone, in person, or in groups. Most evaluation designs employ several types of interviews.

Interviews are often defined as being either structured or unstructured. However, all interviews have structure in that they involve purposeful thinking on the part of the interviewer and a desired outcome from the exchange. Whether to understand the lived experiences of a subject, as in phenomenological interviewing; contrast perceptions on a common topic, as in focus group interviewing; or construct joint understandings of a social practice, as in ethnographic interviewing, all interviewing is based on some assumption about human interaction.

In structured interviews, the interviewer generates a series of questions that she or he will ask all the respondents the same way and in the same order, with little follow-up probing. The interviewer is expected to remain detached and "neutral" so that the responses provided by the interviewee can be objectively compared and contrasted with other interviewees' responses.

In unstructured interviewing, the interviewer does not believe the interview can or should be neutral, and she or he constructs the interview around the personal and unique perspective of each respondent. The outcome of the interview is understood to be a jointly constructed and contextually imbued response.

A shared feature, however, in all forms of interviewing is that they are social relationships and therefore filled with the power dynamics, inequalities, social norms, and expectations inherent in such relationships. In fact, it is the social nature of these interactions that provides the opportunity for meaningful exchanges between individuals as well as creating a variety of methodological, ethical, and epistemological issues for evaluators.

Current dilemmas in the field of evaluation include how to reach hard-to-reach stakeholders; what to do with contextual factors, such as gender, social class, educational level, personal experience, and ethnicity, within both the interview contexts and the program being evaluated; and the basic question: For what purpose, ultimately, do we interview?

Evaluation is meant to serve the interests of the public, and in this task, it is still evolving. The social practice of interviewing has provided evaluators with the means to shift the process of evaluating programs from a detached and technical approach that often relies on externally developed tests and measures to an approach that builds an understanding of the program values, beliefs, assumptions, and processes of the participants within the program context itself. Interviewing, especially in groups, opens up opportunities for questioning and engagement, understanding and empathy, critique and consensus, action and praxis. It is because evaluators understand the power and potential of human conversation that stakeholder-based, responsive, collaborative, participatory, and deliberative democratic approaches to evaluation have emerged.

—Melissa Freeman

See also DELIBERATIVE FORUMS, FOCUS GROUP

IUCN. *See* WORLD CONSERVATION UNION

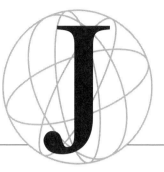

JACKSON, EDWARD T.

(b. 1951, Ottawa, Ontario). Ed.D., M.Ed. Adult Education, University of Toronto; B.A. Psychology, University of Western Ontario.

Jackson is Chair of the Centre for the Study of Training, Investment and Economic Restructuring and Associate Professor of Public Administration and International Affairs, Carleton University, Ottawa. He is also President of E. T. Jackson and Associates Ltd., an international management consulting firm that provides services to the Canadian International Development Agency, other development agencies, government agencies, and nongovernmental organizations.

Since 1982, Jackson has been a leader in evaluations of rural development, water management, education, and public sector reform projects in 30 developing countries for the Canadian International Development Agency. His work has promoted participatory evaluation throughout the world, and he has published two coedited volumes (with Yusuf Kassam), *Knowledge Shared: Participatory Evaluation in Development Cooperation* and *Voices of Change: Participatory Research in the United States and Canada,* related to this work. He cofounded the World Bank and Carleton University International Program on Development Evaluation training in 2001, a professional development program. He is also a member of the advisory board of the international journal *Action Research.*

Jackson, like many participatory evaluators, has been influenced by Paulo Freire's *Pedagogy of the Oppressed,* as well as the participatory research movement of the 1970s and 1980s, project management by activity in the 1980s, and results-based management in the 1990s.

JOINT COMMITTEE ON STANDARDS FOR EDUCATIONAL EVALUATION

The Joint Committee was created in 1975 and is a coalition of major professional associations concerned with the quality of evaluation. Sponsoring organizations have included the American Association of School Administrators, American Counseling Association, American Educational Research Association, American Evaluation Association, American Psychological Association, Association for Supervision and Curriculum Development, Canadian Evaluation Society, Canadian Society for the Study of Education, Consortium for Research on Educational Accountability and Teacher Evaluation, Council of Chief State School Officers, Council of the Great City Schools, National Association of Elementary School Principals, National Association of Secondary School Principals, National Council on Measurement in Education, National Education Association, National Legislative Program Evaluation Society, and the National School Boards Association. The sponsoring organizations appoint equal numbers of committee members to represent perspectives of evaluation specialists and users. The Joint Committee is housed at the Evaluation Center, Western Michigan University. The Joint Committee is accredited by the American National Standards Institute.

The Joint Committee has issued three sets of standards for evaluations that are now widely recognized: *The Personnel Evaluation Standards* (1988), *The Program Evaluation Standards* (2nd ed., 1994), and *The Student Evaluation Standards* (2003). Each set of between 21 and 30 detailed standards requires evaluations to meet requirements for utility, feasibility, propriety, and accuracy. The joint committee reviews and updates each set of standards approximately every 5 years.

—*Daniel L. Stufflebeam*

Further Reading

The Joint Committee on Standards for Educational Evaluation. (n.d.). Retrieved May 23, 2004, from http://www.wmich.edu/evalctr/jc/

⊞ JUDGMENT

Judgment is an essential element of evaluation that involves comparison and discrimination to arrive at knowledge of value and the relationship of things to each other, such as moral qualities, intellectual concepts, logical propositions, and material facts. Judgments occupy a space between what are ordinarily considered facts and opinions. A critical element of judgment is that it is not mere personal preference or arbitrary but rather is considered and thoughtful.

As such, judgments may be good or bad, and evaluation as a practice and profession promotes and incorporates skilled and justifiable judgment. Skilled judgment is something on which one relies; for example, when undergoing surgery, sending one's child to school, or driving a car in traffic.

⊞ JUDICIAL MODEL OF EVALUATION

The early 1970s saw a proliferation of new models for evaluation, including some extrapolated from fields such as art, literature, and justice. Though still discussed as part of evaluation theory, only a few of these extrapolated approaches have thrived. Most seem to have gone extinct. The models based on jurisprudential procedures may be among the latter.

More specifically, in the Western approach to jurisprudence, hearings are among the chief methods of

sorting out the most convincing conclusion from often incomplete or biased evidence. There are several variations. Hearings can be used for clarification or illumination purposes without a decision being reached, such as hearings before Congressional committees. Hearings can be used for review purposes, such as hearings on the fitness of candidates for key appointments. Hearings can also be used for reaching a legal decision, such as hearings before a judge and jury on specific charges. Usually, the judge or hearing officer ensures that the rules of fair argument are observed and a jury reaches conclusions based on evidence presented by the defense and prosecution attorneys.

Among the defining elements of a hearing is the assumption that there are two (or more) sides to almost every question, sides that are adversaries to each other. The hearing process recognizes this through providing a forum for presenting the best case for or against a position, with cross-examination to identify weaknesses in arguments by the defense or advocate and the prosecution or adversary. In this sense, the judicial process is similar to the formal debate process.

The intriguing parallels between judicial processes and evaluation, particularly with regard to possible biases in favor of or against a program, seem to have been discussed first by T. R. Owens in 1971. In the next few years, some evaluators tried out what was then called the adversarial or judicial evaluation model. Since the early 1980s, however, there seem to be no instances of a real-world application of the approach. The last full-on sighting may have been around 1980 and 1981 in the National Institute of Education's national hearing on minimum competency testing. Nonetheless, in texts on evaluation, the judicial, adversarial, or clarification approach often is included as if it were no more or less flourishing than, say, case study approaches, experiments, and mixed methods. Although judicial, adversarial, and clarification concepts are not quite entirely interchangeable, for purposes of this entry, the term "clarification hearing" will refer to all three variants because it seems best to reflect the underlying purposes.

CHARACTERISTICS OF THE CLARIFICATION HEARING APPROACH

The underlying purpose in this approach is to provide a balanced picture of strengths and weaknesses, illuminate the complexities of the issues, and reveal where evidence is more or less strong. The program is put on trial, with a judge hearing arguments from the defense that evidence shows the program has succeeded and receiving from the prosecution evidence, including witnesses, showing that the program has failed. The process requires the following:

- Selection of a "judge" to organize and be arbitrator of the proceedings
- Selection of a "jury" of stakeholders who give the "verdict," or plans for videotaping and distributing the proceedings to a larger audience
- Criteria of effectiveness with which both prosecution and defense evaluators agree
- Generation of possible issues
- Selection of issues to be argued
- Preparation of the case, including locating evidence and witnesses
- Rehearsal of the arguments
- Statement of appropriate "charges" or assertions
- Opposing presentation, including cross-examinations

THE CONTEXT OF THE 1970s

The experimental or quasiexperimental approach characterized many of the early evaluations of Great Society demonstrations and programs. These included randomized experimental evaluations of income maintenance programs (the Seattle and Denver Income Maintenance Experiment demonstrations) and quasiexperimental studies such as those of Head Start. The methodological limitations of these experimental studies were of concern to many evaluators, who searched for improvements and alternatives, both in quantitative and more qualitative modes. The alternative approaches developed at this time include—but are by no means limited to—Eisner's examination of methods from art, such as connoisseurship; Stake's countenance model, combining description and judgment, and his 1971 responsive evaluation approach; Scriven's goal-free evaluation; Parlett's illuminative model; adversarial evaluation; and Guba and Lincoln's 1981 discussions of constructivist knowing and naturalistic and participatory evaluation, ideas developed more fully in their fourth-generation evaluation. The context for the clarification hearing approach thus is somewhat analogous to an explosion of new life forms, each searching for its own niche and struggling to predominate, to survive, and to avoid extinction.

APPLICATIONS IN PRACTICE

The clarification hearing approach seems to have been more talked about than applied, at least in applications that can be reasonably located at present. Most of the applications took place in the 1970s or early 1980s. These included a 1976 evaluation of a team teaching program in Hawaii for grades K-3 (conducted in 1977 by the Northwest Regional Educational Laboratory), a 1981 application to an employment and training program, an experimental comparison of the outcomes of an interaction advocacy, and an adversarial evaluation and discussion of the minimum competency testing (MCT) process.

Perhaps the largest scale application was the National Institute of Education National Hearings on MCT, presided over by Representative Barbara Jordan. The purpose of these hearings was primarily methodological: to test out, systematically, the potential of the approach itself for program evaluation using the hot topic of minimum competency testing in the schools. Funded by the institute's Division of Teaching, Learning and Assessment, the hearings brought together distinguished experts in measurement and evaluation under the leadership of James Popham and George Madaus in the roles, respectively, of representatives of the for (pro) and against (con) positions. Representative Barbara Jordan was the judge or presiding officer. Many months went into organizing the rules for the hearing, developing the issues, collecting evidence, identifying witnesses, rehearsing the arguments, and organizing the videotaping and subsequent national PBS presentation of the tapes. The hearings themselves were held in Washington, DC.

More recently, third party reviewers assessed the quality of an evaluation of the Summerhill School in Great Britain by presenting the evaluation report in formal legal proceedings. At issue was whether or not the evaluation was sufficiently unbiased for the government to use as a basis for decisions on whether funding should be continued. This was not conceived, however, as a clarification hearing, and the parties involved were not comfortable with the procedure as an appropriate way of presenting the evaluation's strengths and limitations.

RETROSPECTIVE ASSESSMENTS OF THE APPROACH IN PRACTICE

By and large, those writing about the applications such as the Hawaii team-teaching evaluation and the

MCT clarification hearings concluded that as a way of helping ensure full, fair exposition of evidence, the approach was at best a limited success, and, more bluntly, it was a failure as a workable evaluation model. Concerns include the time required (which was prolonged, although a second trial might have gone more quickly, building on lessons learned); the cost, which was well over $100,000 in 1970s money; and a sense that preconceptions, personalities, debating skills, and other factors not directly associated with quality of evidence played too great a role (Popham & Carlson, 1983). The approach seemed too vulnerable to influences of the better lawyer over the better case, and too "yes or no" for complex, nuanced issues. Scriven suggested, "it is best thought of as a possible method rather than an analytic insight into evaluation in general. For example, there are many cases in which there are no funds or time for setting up the apparatus required and many others in which the format of a debate is more useful." The most thorough analysis, comparing the clarification hearing model to 21 other approaches on checklists of characteristics, strengths, and limitations, is Stufflebeam's 2001 review. It is decidedly not among the nine approaches he recommends.

A DEAD END? ANY DESCENDANTS IN CONTEMPORARY EVALUATION PRACTICE?

Because it appears to be no longer practiced—if indeed it ever really was—the clarification hearing model seems to be a dead end among the approaches developed in the 1970s. Even though, as noted, some reviews and texts describe it as if it were, it may be time to write off the approach as being primarily of historical interest. Postings in Evaltalk, the Assessment Reform Network, and elsewhere indicate an incompatibility with contemporary approaches emphasizing stakeholder participation, collaboration, "appreciative inquiry," and consultancy and a certain discomfort with approaches likely to emphasize differences, confrontations, and adversarial stances. In an asymmetrical contrast, advocacy-based evaluation approaches can be found easily in the theoretical and practice literature.

Nonetheless, there seem to be some descendants of clarification hearings. For example, the consensus panel is a flourishing approach in active contemporary practice, and it contains many elements of the clarification hearing. Perhaps the most notable, long-running, best-defined operational instance is the National Institutes of Health Consensus Panel hearings. On the recommendation of a director of one of the National Institutes of Health, a medical practice, procedure, or approach currently regarded as experimental may be reviewed to see if it is of such proven effectiveness that federal health-care funds may be spent on it. If the director's arguments are persuasive, the procedure can be scheduled for formal review by a consensus panel. Experts take much time to bring together evidence presented to a panel of experts in a hearing. Among the procedural elements are identification of issues, development of clear ground rules for discussion, a "judge" or hearing examiner keeping the proceedings on an even keel, extensive reviews of the literature and advance organization of the arguments for and against, in-depth consideration of the quality of the evidence, and a voted-on decision by the "jury" of experts. Variants of this approach have been applied to decision making by the Environmental Protection Agency and, in review of evidence of program effectiveness, by the U. S. Department of Education.

Another descendant, also in widespread and active use, may be metaevaluation procedures, meaning here a thorough review of an evaluation, not an evaluation synthesis. Stufflebeam and Scriven, among others, have been productive in developing criteria, checklists, and guidelines for conducting these assessments of evaluation quality. Metaevaluation has been used by organizations such as the U.S. General Accounting Office to reach conclusions about the value and worth of a program. It is a well-established procedure whose results are accepted by refereed journals and is recommended at both the beginning and conclusion of an evaluation to cumulate knowledge.

A third descendant is the forum or debate on substantive or methodological issues about which opinion may be sharply divided, and experts take the roles of advocate or adversary. The topic of the 1980 National Institute of Education National Hearing, for example, continues to be a lightning rod today in debates on high stakes testing, although with possibly less openness to the rules of evidence developed in the clarification hearing model.

Arguably, where the stakes are high, it might be well to revisit the full clarification hearing model, finding the resources to do it well, applying lessons learned about its shortfalls, and helping ensure a full, fair, in-depth review of the evidence.

—Lois-ellin Datta

Further Reading

Braithwaite, R. L., & Thompson, R. L. (1981). Application of the judicial evaluation model within an employment and training program. *Center on Evaluation, Development and Research Quarterly, 14,* 13-16.

Clyne, S. F. (1982). *The judicial evaluation model: A case study.* Unpublished doctoral dissertation, Boston College.

Estes, G. D., & Demaline, R. E. (1982). Outcomes of the MCT clarification process. In E. R. House, S. Mathison, J. A. Pearsol, & H. Preskill (Eds.), *Evaluation studies review annual* (Vol. 7, pp. 227-258). Beverly Hills, CA: Sage.

Kourilsky, M. (1973). An adversary model for educational evaluation. *Evaluation Comment, 4,* 3-6.

Kourilsky, M., & Baker, E. (1976). An experimental comparison of interaction advocacy and adversary evaluation. *Center on Evaluation, Development and Research Quarterly, 9,* 4-8.

Levine, M. (1974). Scientific method and the adversary model: Some preliminary thoughts. *American Psychologist, 29,* 661-677.

Levine, M. (1982). Adversary hearing. In N. L. Smith (Ed.), *Communication strategies in evaluation* (pp. 240-258). Beverly Hills, CA: Sage.

Northwest Regional Educational Laboratory. (1977, January). *3-on-2 evaluation report, 1976-1977* (Vols. 1-3). Portland, OR: Author.

Owens, T. R. (1971, April). *Application of adversary proceedings for educational evaluation and decision making.* Paper presented at the Annual Meeting of the American Educational Research Association, New York.

Owens, T. R. (1973). Educational evaluation by adversary proceedings. In E. R. House (Ed.). *School evaluation: The politics and process* (pp. 295-305). Berkeley, CA: McCutchan.

Popham, W. J., & Carlson, D. (1983). Deep dark deficits of the adversary evaluation model. In G. F. Madaus, M. Scriven, & D. L. Stufflebeam (Eds.), *Evaluation models* (pp. 205-214). Boston: Kluwer-Nijhoff.

Smith, N. L. (1985). *Adversary and community hearings as evaluation methods* (Paper and Report Series No. 92). Portland, OR: Northwest Regional Educational Laboratory, Research on Evaluation Program.

Stenzel, N. (1976). *Adversary processes and their potential use in evaluation for the Illinois Office of Education.* Springfield: Illinois Department of Education.

St. John, M. (n.d.). *Committee hearings: Their use in evaluation* (Evaluation Guides, No. 8). Portland, OR: Northwest Regional Educational Laboratory.

Wolf, R. L., & Arnstein, G. (1975). Trial by jury: A new evaluation method. *Phi Delta Kappan, 57*(3), 185-187.

Wolf, R. L. (1979). The use of judicial evaluation methods in the formulation of educational policy. *Educational Evaluation and Policy Analysis, 1,* 19-28.

Worthen, B. R., & Rogers, W. T. (1980). Pitfalls and potential of adversary evaluation. *Educational Leadership, 37,* 536-543.

■■ JULNES, GEORGE

(b. 1954, Cincinnati, Ohio). Ph.D. Psychology-Clinical/Community, University of Hawaii—Manoa; M.B.A., M.P.P. Public Policy, University of Michigan; B.S. Psychology and Philosophy, University of Wisconsin–Madison.

Julnes is Associate Professor in the Research and Evaluation Methodology Program in the Department of Psychology at Utah State University. Previously he was on the faculty at Fairleigh Dickinson and Old Dominion Universities.

Julnes has contributed to the field of evaluation primarily through his development of a pragmatic approach to evaluation, created by combining the neo-Vygotskian notion of "assisted performance"; Weick's ideas on sense making; the realist foundations of many evaluation theorists; and the value theory of the pragmatists, wherein we arrive at judgments of value first and only afterwards divine the balance of the abstract principles responsible for those judgments. This unique approach reconciles many of the previously accepted qualitative versus quantitative debates. Incorporating insights from his collaborations with Melvin M. Mark and Gary Henry, Julnes' work emphasizes the role of social programs in supporting available individual and social capacities and the role of evaluation in supporting the natural decision-making capacities of stakeholders.

Julnes was taught and influenced by Larry Mohr, particularly in regard to his outcome line approach to program theory and his multiple regression framework for evaluation analysis; by Roland Tharp, in regard to his vision of community psychology and the neo-Vygotskian developmental concepts, such as "assisted performance"; and by Karl Weick, in regard to his constructivist "sense-making" view of what people do naturally in organizations and other social settings. Julnes' intellectual influences are the early pragmatists, such as John Dewey and Oliver Wendell Holmes; the neorealist philosophers Hilary Putnam, Richard Boyd, Roy Bhaskar, and Rom Harré, who have articulated alternatives to the traditional empiricist-constructivist debates; and the work of Don Campbell and Lee Cronbach.

JUSTICE. *See* SOCIAL JUSTICE

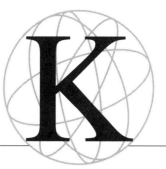

KASA. *See* KNOWLEDGE, ATTITUDES, SKILLS, ASPIRATIONS

■ KELLY CONFERENCE, THE

The Edward F. Kelly Evaluation Conference was established in 1987. It is dedicated to the memory of Dr. Kelly, who was a professor at the University at Albany and at Syracuse University. The conference provides budding evaluation scholars with an opportunity to share ideas and to network with colleagues. Students from Queens University, the University at Ottawa, Cornell University, Syracuse University, and the University at Albany rotate the responsibilities of hosting the conference on an annual basis. The gathering is an icon for Dr. Kelly's devotion to the field of evaluation.

—*Cheryl MacNeil*

■ KEY INFORMANTS

Key informants, or key actors, are typically articulate and culturally sensitive. Key actors play a pivotal role in the theater of ethnographic research, linking the fieldworker and the community. They provide detailed historical data, knowledge about interpersonal relationships, and a wealth of information about the nuances of everyday life. They generally answer questions about the group in a comprehensive, albeit meandering fashion. Key informants are typically cultural brokers straddling two cultures. This position gives them a special vantage point in describing their culture. Ethnographers try to speak to as many people as possible, but they traditionally rely most heavily on key informants.

—*David M. Fetterman*

■ KING, JEAN A.

(b. 1949, Glens Falls, New York). Ph.D., M.S. Curriculum and Instruction, A.B. English, Cornell University.

King is Associate Professor of Education, University of Minnesota. She has served as Co-coordinator of the University of Minnesota's Patrick Henry High School, has been a member of the faculty at Tulane University, and has taught secondary school English in New York State.

Her primary contributions to the field of evaluation include the development of participatory evaluation practice, evaluation capacity building, free-range evaluation, and interactive evaluation practice. King works primarily in K-12 education and underfunded social service agencies, providing assistance conducting high-quality, useful evaluations with limited resources. She is known for her commitment to pragmatic solutions in evaluation and her valuing of reflection on practice. King's position as Coordinator of Research and Evaluation at Anoka-Hennepin ISD #11, Coon Rapids, Minnesota, from 1999 to 2002 demonstrates these attributes. Her main intellectual influences are the late measurement expert Jason Millman,

Marv Alkin and his studies of evaluation utilization, and Michael Quinn Patton's utilization-focused evaluation.

King's involvement in the American Evaluation Association as Associate Conference Chair and Conference Chair from 1992 to 1999 and as the founder of the topical interest groups on collaborative, participatory, and empowerment evaluation and evaluation in precollegiate education demonstrate her commitment to the profession of evaluation. She is also committed to the improvement of quality education for evaluators. She is Founding Director of the Center for Applied Research and Educational Improvement at the University of Minnesota. She has been Coordinator of Evaluation Studies, helped to establish a program evaluation minor and a post–master's certification program, and founded the Minnesota Evaluation Studies Institute. She is Editor of *New Directions for Evaluation.*

King is a Phi Beta Kappa member and has received the American Evaluation Association's Myrdal Award for Evaluation Practice and the Ingle Award for Service to AEA. She received the University of Minnesota Robert Beck Award for Faculty Excellence in 1999 and the Distinguished Teaching Award in 2002.

⊞ KIRKHART, KAREN

(b. 1948, Pomona, California). Ph.D., M.S.W. Social Work, University of Michigan; B.A. Psychology, Pomona College.

Kirkhart's earliest mentor in evaluation was Marcia Guttentag, to whom she dedicated her dissertation in posthumous tribute. However, it is unquestionably Michael Scriven who has had the greatest influence on her work, through his focus on values, the power of unintended outcomes, metaevaluation, and the Key Evaluation Checklist. Kirkhart's commitment to evaluation centers on the potential for social change, and this drew her to theorists and practitioners who focused on roles and contexts of evaluation: Ernest House (justice and fairness), Lee J. Cronbach (the policy-shaping context of evaluation influence), Samuel Messick (social consequences of our understandings and actions), Michael Q. Patton (the personal factor in evaluation), Anna-Marie Madison and Stafford Hood (inclusion of racial and ethnic diversity), and Jennifer Greene (power, privilege, and the participatory process). Kirkhart also credits her conversations and debates with Will Shadish for pushing her work toward greater precision and clarity. Like Donald Schön, Kirkhart views evaluation as a combination of technical rationality and professional artistry, and from the artistic perspective she cites as influences John Baldessari, for never taking one's expertise too seriously, and Ed Ruscha, for humor and an unyielding California sensibility.

Kirkhart has taught, practiced, and written about evaluation for more than two decades, with an emphasis on local-level evaluation of educational and human service programs. Her publications have made significant original contributions to evaluation theory in two areas: multicultural validity and evaluation influence. In the first area, she examines the relationship between evaluation and social justice, framed within the broader context of validity. Her writings on the topic of multicultural validity draw on classic validity theory, postmodern perspectives, and standpoint epistemologies to examine the many ways in which culture bounds understanding in general and judgments of program merit and worth in particular. In the second area, her theoretical work places evaluation use in the broader context of power, influence, and consequences, interweaving ethics and validity. Her Integrated Theory of Influence advances the study of evaluation by providing a unifying framework for examining evaluation impact and clarifying conversations on use.

She has served on the governing boards of ENet (1977-1978, 1980-1982; President, 1981), the Evaluation Research Society (1983-1985), and the American Evaluation Association (1986, 1993-1995; President, 1994). Within the American Evaluation Association, she has served on the Diversity Committee (1998-2003), Nominations and Elections Committee (1988-1990; Chair, 1988-1989), Advisory Committee, the Initiative for Building Diversity Among the Evaluation Community (2000-2003), Task Force on Guiding Principles for Evaluators Working Across Cultures (2001-2003), and multiple TIGs (Chair, TIG on Evaluation Use, 2003-2005). Within the American Psychological Association, Kirkhart served as President of Division 18 (1990-1991) and chaired its Section on Evaluation (1986-1988). She has served on numerous editorial advisory boards and received award recognition for both teaching and service.

She married fellow evaluator Nick L. Smith in 1984. Their son, Dylan, grew up attending annual AEA meetings, leading him to a career interest in building hotels.

■ KIRKPATRICK FOUR-LEVEL EVALUATION MODEL

By far the most popular approach to the evaluation of training in organizations today is Kirkpatrick's "four levels" framework. This evaluation model delineates four levels of training outcomes: reaction, learning, behavior, and results. Level 1 includes assessment of training participants' reaction to the training program. Kirkpatrick originally discussed reactions in terms of how well participants liked a particular program. In practice, measures at this level have evolved and are most commonly assessments of trainees' affective responses to the quality (e.g., satisfaction with the instructor) or the relevance (e.g., work-related utility) of training. Learning measures, level 2, are quantifiable indicators of the learning that has taken place during the course of the training. Level 3 behavior outcomes address either the extent to which knowledge and skills gained in training are applied on the job or result in exceptional job-related performance. Finally, level 4 outcomes are intended to provide some measure of the impact that training has had on broader organizational goals and objectives. In recent practice, the typical focus of these measures has been on organizational-level financial measures.

THE POPULARITY OF THE FOUR-LEVEL MODEL

The Kirkpatrick model has served as the primary organizing design for training evaluations in for-profit organizations for more than 30 years, and its popularity can be traced to several factors. First, the model addresses the need for training professionals to understand training evaluation in a systematic way. It provides a straightforward system or language for talking about training outcomes and the kinds of information that can be provided to assess the extent to which training programs have achieved certain objectives.

Second, Kirkpatrick insisted that information about level 4 outcomes is perhaps the most valuable or descriptive information about training that can be obtained. For training professionals in organizations, this bottom-line focus is seen as a good fit with the competitive profit orientation of their sponsors. The four-level model has therefore provided a means for trainers in organizations to couch the results of what they do in business terms. Many see this as critical if the training function is to be seen as contributing to organizational success.

Finally, the popularity of the four-level model is also a function of its potential for simplifying the complex process of training evaluation. The model does this in several ways. First, the model represents a straightforward guide to the kinds of questions that should be asked and the criteria that may be appropriate. Second, the model reduces the measurement demands for training evaluation. Because the model focuses the evaluation process on four classes of outcome data that are generally collected after the training has been completed, it eliminates the need for pre-course measures of learning or job performance measures. In addition, because conclusions about training effectiveness are based solely on outcome measures, the model greatly reduces the number of variables with which training evaluators need to be concerned. In effect, the model eliminates the need to measure or account for the complex network of factors that surround and interact with the training process.

There is no doubt that Kirkpatrick's model has made valuable contributions to training evaluation thinking and practice. It has helped focus training evaluation practice on outcomes, fostered the recognition that single-outcome measures cannot adequately reflect the complexity of organizational training programs, and underscored the importance of examining multiple measures of training effectiveness. The model promoted awareness of the importance of thinking about and assessing training in business terms. The distinction between learning (level 2) and behavior (level 3) has drawn increased attention to the importance of the learning transfer process in making training truly effective. The model has also served as a useful heuristic for training evaluators and has been the seed from which a number of other evaluation models have germinated.

LIMITATIONS OF THE FOUR-LEVEL MODEL

There are at least three limitations of Kirkpatrick's model that have implications for the ability of evaluators trained in this model to deliver benefits and further the interests of organizational clients. These include the incompleteness of the model, the assumption of causality, and the assumption of the increasing importance of information as the levels of outcomes are ascended.

The Model Is Incomplete

The four-level model presents an oversimplified view of training effectiveness that does not consider individual or contextual influences in the evaluation of training. A broad stream of research over the past two decades has documented the presence of a wide range of organizational, individual, and training design and delivery factors that can influence training effectiveness before, during, or after training. This research has led to a new understanding of training effectiveness that considers what Cannon-Bowers and others refer to as the "characteristics of the organization and work environment and characteristics of the individual trainee as crucial input factors." For example, contextual factors, such as the learning culture of the organization; organizational or work unit goals and values; the nature of interpersonal support in the workplace for skill acquisition and behavior change; the climate for learning transfer; and the adequacy of material resources such as tools, equipment, and supplies, have been shown to influence the effectiveness of both the process and outcomes of training. Kirkpatrick's model implicitly assumes that examination of these factors is not essential for effective evaluation.

The Assumption of Causal Linkages

Kirkpatrick's model assumes that the levels represent a causal chain such that positive reactions lead to greater learning, which produces greater transfer and, subsequently, more positive organizational results. In one of Kirkpatrick's more recent publications, he states that "if training is going to be effective, it is important that trainees react favorably" and that "without learning, no change in behavior will occur." Research, however, has largely failed to confirm such causal linkages. Meta-analyses of training evaluation studies using Kirkpatrick's framework by Alliger and Janak and, more recently, by Alliger, Tannenbaum, Benett, Traver, and Shotland have found little evidence either of substantial correlations between measures at different outcome levels or evidence of the linear causality suggested by Kirkpatrick.

Incremental Importance of Information

Kirkpatrick's model assumes that each level of evaluation provides data more informative than at the previous level. This assumption has generated the perception among training evaluators that establishing level-4 results will provide the most useful information about training program effectiveness. In practice, however, the weak conceptual linkages inherent in the model and the data it generates do not provide an adequate basis for this assumption.

—*Reid Bates*

Further Reading

Alliger, G. M., & Janak, E. A. (1989). Kirkpatrick's levels of training criteria: Thirty years later. *Personnel Psychology, 42,* 331-342.

Holton, E. F., III. (1996). The flawed four level evaluation model. *Human Resource Development Quarterly, 7*(1), 5-21.

Kirkpatrick, D. L. (1994). *Evaluating training programs: The four levels.* San Francisco: Berrett-Koehler.

Newstrom, J. W. (1995). Review of "Evaluating training programs: The four levels by D. L. Kirkpatrick." *Human Resource Development Quarterly, 6,* 317-319.

■■ KNOWLEDGE, ATTITUDES, SKILLS, ASPIRATIONS (KASA)

KASA refers to knowledge, attitudes, skills, and aspirations that influence the adoption of selected practices and technologies to help achieve targeted social, economic, and environmental outcomes. Changes in KASA may occur when people react positively to their involvement in program activities. This is one element in a hierarchical model of program development and evaluation based on the work of Claude Bennett, which is similar to other hierarchical stage approaches to evaluation, such as Kirkpatrick's Four-Level Model of Evaluation, commonly used in human resource development. An evaluation of a program may therefore focus on the degree of change in KASA.

■■ KONRAD, ELLEN L.

(b. 1953, Los Angeles). M.S. Public Affairs, University of Oregon, Eugene; B.A. Psychology, Lewis and Clark College, Portland, Oregon.

Konrad started her professional and evaluation career as a federal presidential management intern at the U.S. Department of Health, Education and Welfare. Over the course of her career, she has conducted evaluations in the public sector at the county, state, and federal government levels. Her main intellectual influences were Donald Campbell, Thomas Cook, Robert Boruch, Carol Weiss, Eleanor Chelimsky, Judith Gueron, and Joseph Wholey.

Along with Jules M. Marquart, Konrad was Coeditor of the Spring 1996 issue of *New Directions for Evaluation* (Vol. 69), "Evaluating Initiatives to Integrate Human Services." A major focus of her work has been conceptualizing, characterizing, and evaluating human services integration initiatives. She is Cofounder of the American Evaluation Association Topical Interest Group on Social Services Evaluation and served as its Chair between 1986 and 1993.

Konrad cofounded and served as Vice President (1996-1997) of the Arizona Evaluation Network, a local affiliate of the American Evaluation Association. She cofounded the Oregon Program Evaluators Network (another AEA local affiliate) and served as its President (1999). Konrad was an ex officio member of the Board of Directors for the American Evaluation Association, serving as the Topical Interest Group and Local Affiliate Coordinator from 1997 to 1998.

■ KUSHNER, SAVILLE

(b. 1947, Leeds, U.K.). Ph.D., University of East Anglia; Dip. Ed., Bristol University; B.Sc. Economics, London University.

Kushner is a program and policy evaluator by professional practice, as well as Professor of Applied Research in Education and Director of the Center for Research in Education and Democracy at the University of the West of England.

He has, for many years, been a member of a transatlantic group of evaluation practitioners and theorists developing democratic and case study methodologies for program evaluation. He has conducted evaluations in fields as diverse as schooling, the performing arts, research funding, police training, computer technology, and health services. His primary contribution to evaluation theory and practice has been an elaboration of democracy and case study through the concept of "personalizing evaluation."

Kushner was Lawrence Stenhouse's research student at the University of East Anglia and learned educational values and philosophy from him, developing his educational ethics and concept of curriculum from Stenhouse. Kushner worked with Stenhouse's close friend and colleague Barry MacDonald for 20 years and learned, through him, a commitment to evaluation as democratic action and to case study for portraying the drama of institutional struggle. Evaluation experiences at Summerhill School had a significant influence on Kushner's educational ethic, and A. S. Neill now assumes equal position with Stenhouse as an influence. Intellectually, Kushner has been most influenced by the work of Bob Stake in the United States and MacDonald in Europe, but he also acknowledges the impact on him of inspirational writers on existentialism, including Peter Berger and Donald Schon; an aspiration to write narrative portrayals with the economy and drama of Dashiel Hammett; and a desire to emancipate youth by challenging the icons of older generations from the work of surrealist Andre Breton.

Kushner's recent book *Personalizing Evaluation* (which was also translated into Spanish) provides a fresh, new perspective on evaluation, one that begins with the experiences and narratives of participants from various programs.

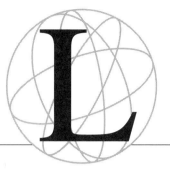

LEARNING ORGANIZATION

The concept of the *learning organization,* promoted by scholars such as Garvin and Senge, has been enthusiastically embraced by many organizations as a means of enhancing their capacity for change and renewal. To transform themselves, organizations must first be able to create, acquire, and transfer knowledge. Only then do they form a basis on which to modify practice to reflect the new learning.

Success in becoming a learning organization relies not only on a commitment to learning on the part of the organization itself but on a realization of the centrality of individuals to the change process. Organizations need to engage with individual perspectives as a basis for initiating change. These may involve a notion of the disciplines of a learning organization, which involve ideas such as *personal mastery* (individual commitment to lifelong learning), *mental models* (the capacity of individuals to scrutinize and share their own thinking and assumptions), and *shared vision* (the fusion of individual and organizational vision), or Garvin's approach, which promotes the building blocks of a learning organization such as systematic problem solving, learning from past experience, and the transfer of knowledge through a variety of mechanisms. All these approaches imply that change is a continuous process and involves an element of reflection and analysis.

The strong emphasis on organizational problem solving in the use and dissemination of new knowledge is encapsulated in the problem-solver perspective of change described by Havelock. This model of change implies that organizations have the ability to identify and solve their own problems and that this ability is practiced at all levels in the organization. All areas must therefore be involved in the creation and dissemination of new knowledge, which forms the basis of the change process. This process should be dynamic: Responsibility should not lie with the individual alone or be confined to a particular department or section of the organization. However, individuals at each level of the organization take different responsibilities for the creation and transfer of learning. These individuals and the roles that they play can be summarized in the following way.

Managers play a key role in providing the broad conceptual framework for a learning organization and in supporting individual efforts to adopt its principles and practices. They are the principal and most visible advocates of the learning organization. Senge describes the manager in the learning organization as a "researcher" and "designer" who researches the organization or unit as a system, uncovers the internal and external forces that drive it, and designs the learning processes that drive change.

Trainers and human resource (HR) personnel are in a position to provide a direct link between individual and organizational learning. Rather than acting as the passive conduit for management-initiated HR policies, the HR professional in a learning organization is directly involved with the alignment of organizational and individual learning objectives and is able to act, in Havelock's description, as the outsider who is the "Catalyst Consultant" or "Collaborator for Change." The HR staff member also has direct involvement with participants in their learning and so is in an excellent position to be able to identify barriers to learning transfer.

A number of researchers have written about an extended role for the evaluator as an agent of change and the implications this has for the skills that evaluators must employ in working with individuals and groups during the change process. In many ways, this role is similar to that of the HR consultant. The evaluator also has a key role in disseminating the results of learning and so must employ strategies that are aimed at maximizing organizational communication about the aims and benefits of individual learning. The evaluator must be able to integrate the three components that promote the transfer of learning: reflection, dialogue, and action planning.

Individual employees as the "experts" in their roles are encouraged to take responsibility for identifying their own learning needs and any barriers, including external elements, that may affect the potential for change to occur. With the assistance and support of HR personnel or experienced evaluators, they are encouraged to research their own jobs and seek feedback regarding their performance.

—*John M. Owen*

Further Reading

Havelock, R. G. (1971). *Planning for innovation through dissemination and utilization of knowledge.* Ann Arbor, MI: Center for Research on Utilization of Scientific Knowledge.

Senge, P. M. (1990). *The fifth discipline: The art and practice of the learning organization.* Garden City, NY: Doubleday.

■■ LEEUW, FRANS L.

(b. 1953, Maastricht, The Netherlands).

Leeuw is Chief Review Officer with The Netherlands' Inspectorate for Education, Utrecht, and is responsible for higher education, knowledge management, and evaluation studies and international affairs. Also, he is Professor of Evaluation Studies on the faculty of Social Sciences at Utrecht University. Previously he was Dean of The Netherlands Open University, director of performance auditing and evaluation of The Netherlands National Audit Office, and a faculty member at Leyden University. Leeuw is an advisor for the Operations Evaluation Department of the World Bank.

Leeuw's work in evaluation focuses on theory-based evaluations and program theories, education,

development, and managing evaluations. He has written numerous publications in these areas, including *Collaboration in Public Services: The Challenge for Evaluation* (with Andrew Gray, Bill Jenkins, and John Mayne.) Leeuw was President of the European Evaluation Society from 1999 to 2002.

■■ LEGISLATIVE MONITORING

Legislative monitoring is the process of reviewing and reporting on pending legislation, including committee discussions, drafts, lobbying, and other activities that have an impact on the legislation. This monitoring is done by a host of groups, including government watch groups; professional associations; unions; and local, state, and federal government agencies. Monitoring focuses typically on a particular issue, such as health care, environmental pollution, educational reform, or workplace safety, that is relevant to a profession, industry sector, or geographic region. As such, legislative monitoring is often done to inform lobbying and to create strategies to influence legislation.

■■ LESBIAN, GAY, BISEXUAL, AND TRANSGENDER ISSUES IN EVALUATION

One of the many challenges an evaluator faces is designing and implementing an evaluation process that is inclusive and safe for individuals who choose to be open about their sexual identity. An effective evaluator must grapple with the complexity of what it means to identify as lesbian, gay, bisexual, or transgendered (LGBT) if she or he hopes to be inclusive.

People who identify as LGBT are diverse in terms of their socioeconomic class, race, ethnicity, religion, and sex, and they are hidden because their sexual identity is not known with certainty unless they self-identify. Assumptions are often made about one's sexual identity if one's gender identity or gender presentation is deemed incongruent with one's sex. For example, if a male's gender presentation is considered overly feminine through behavior or appearance, he may be considered gay. If a female's gender presentation is considered overly masculine, she may be considered a lesbian. These types of assumptions are based on the meanings Western culture gives to the conjoining of sex and gender. A binary system of two sexes (female and male) and two genders (feminine and masculine) exists with a perceived inherent relationship between sex and gender (male = masculine, female = feminine). (In this entry, the use of the term *opposite sex* has been deliberately avoided and *other sex* used in its place to stay away from oppositional binary thinking about sexes.)

Embedded in this understanding is the belief that male or masculine is superior to female or feminine, thus laying the foundation for sexism or male supremacy in our culture, and the belief that the "natural" sexual relationship between males and females is heterosexual, thus providing the groundwork for heterosexism or heterosexual supremacy. LGBT people and heterosexuals who do not identify as transgendered yet deviate from the sex and gender norm are exposed to discrimination, threats of violence, and even death due to the practice of sexism and heterosexism in our culture. Coupled with the political nature of evaluation, the effects of sexism and heterosexism have serious implications for evaluators and the evaluation process.

Although lesbian, gay, bisexual, and transgendered identities are categorized together, there are distinct and important differences between each identity and within each identity. The differences between and within each identity are especially significant when considered with the intersections of other identities, such as race, class, ethnicity, and religion. The intersections of these identities affect how gender is defined within the framework of those identities. The meanings given to the concepts of man and woman can vary by culture, class, and religion. Within that context, what it means to be LGBT and the consequences for being identified or self-identifying as LGBT can vary greatly.

Some similarities and differences between the sexual identities include the following:

- Lesbians experience sexism as women and as lesbians, with sexism getting increasingly virulent as a woman's gender presentation gets more masculine; lesbians experience heterosexism.
- Gays experience privileges as men but face increasing hostility as the man's gender presentation gets more feminine; gays experience heterosexism.
- Bisexuals experience sexism and heterosexism similarly to lesbians or gays if they are involved in a same-sex partnership. If in a heterosexual partnership, they would experience privileges as heterosexuals,

and they would be given more latitude with their gender presentation.

There exists a multiplicity of meanings within each LGBT identity, with an overlap of sexual identities depending on the definitions used (whether the definition is in terms of one's behavior or one's proclaimed identity). An example of the complexity can be seen within the possible variations existing under the term *lesbian*. These include

- Lesbian identity with lesbian activity
- Lesbian identity with bisexual, heterosexual, or celibate activity
- Bisexual identity with lesbian activity
- Heterosexual identity with lesbian activity
- Transsexual male-to-female with lesbian activity

Transgender is an overarching term encompassing anyone whose gender identity is not completely congruent with her or his sex. Included are people who identify as intersexed (those born with physical characteristics associated with both males and females), transsexual (those who desire to live permanently as a member of the sex other than their birth sex and may choose to have sex reassignment surgery), transgenderist (those who live almost full-time to full-time in the gender societally incongruent from their birth sex but do not desire sex reassignment surgery), bigendered (those who live a dual life, with one role as a man and another as a woman), cross-dresser (those who dress in clothing associated with the sex other than their own physical sex), and gender queer (individuals who identify as neither "man" or "woman" but instead refer to their gender as "queer"). The gender movement is constantly evolving, so terms and meanings will change over time. Within the transgendered population are bisexuals, gays, heterosexuals, and lesbians.

Taking into account the complexity of LGBT issues due to the multiplicity of meanings of identities and the consequences of heterosexism and sexism, the following three considerations are important for an evaluator when designing and implementing an inclusive evaluation process.

1. Genuineness of the evaluator in her or his acceptance of LGBT individuals and efforts in providing a safe and inclusive environment for LGBT participants. In some contexts, an evaluator's support and desire for inclusivity could go against the beliefs of

some constituencies in an evaluation process, and the evaluator will be seen as unfavorably biased.

2. Awareness that as a hidden population, LBGT individuals may be present even if no one openly identifies as LGBT. A way to communicate openness to diversity is through the use of language (whether in a quantitative or qualitative format) that avoids promoting heterosexual dominance and a binary perspective of gender and sex. Terms such as *married* or *divorced* refer most often to heterosexual relationships, but either including or substituting the terms *partnered* or *committed relationship* would invite not only LGBT individuals but also heterosexuals in relationships other than a marriage. When collecting demographic information, inquiring about both sex and gender and providing evaluation participants with more than the usual binary options will make space for complexity of identities. For example, when asking a person to identify sex, offer female, male, intersexed, transsexual, and other (or "what best describes your sex, if the preferred option is not offered"); when asking about gender, offer masculine, feminine, androgynous, transgendered, and other (or "what best describes your gender, if the preferred option is not offered"). Providing an explanation for the distinction between sex and gender and for the terms people may find unfamiliar will help raise awareness of the existence of LGBT individuals. When asking about sexual identity, offering the identity options in alphabetical order does not privilege heterosexuality and would signal inclusivity. For example, the options could be listed as bisexual, gay, heterosexual, lesbian, questioning, and other (allowing for comment to self-identify). For clarity of identity, explicit and detailed questions need to be asked, as appropriate, in a given context. Qualitative approaches tend to yield a better understanding of identity and experiences. The evaluator will need to be prepared to handle some of the confusion and even hostility people may express when exposed to the choices or concepts.

3. Attention is warranted in examining who is able to "come out" (identify as LGBT) and why. For some, the privileges of their class, race, ethnicity, and religion may make it easier to be open about sexual identity. For example, the most visible and powerful members of the LGBT population advocating for equal rights are primarily white, middle to upper class gays and lesbians whose gender presentations do not deviate greatly from society's gender expectations

based on their sex. They mirror the dominant group in our society (predominantly white, middle to upper class, heterosexual). For others, to be who they are requires them to be more public about their identity. For example, a person who is transsexual will have to engage with the legal and medical institutions to be able to transition from one sex to another and successfully function in our society. Each of the identities within the LGBT population brings different issues to the forefront.

—*Denice A. Cassaro*

LESSONS LEARNED. *See*
Best Practices

⊞ LEVIN, HENRY M.

(b. 1938, New York City). Ph.D., M.A. Economics, Rutgers University; B.S. Economics and Marketing, New York University.

Levin is William Heard Kilpatrick Professor of Economics and Education at Teachers College, Columbia University, and Director of the National Center for the Study of Privatization in Education. He is the David Jacks Professor Emeritus of Higher Education and Economics and former Director of the Center for Educational Research at Stanford University, whose faculty he joined in 1968. Previously, he was Research Associate at the Economics Studies Division of the Brookings Institution in Washington, DC; Founder of the Accelerated Schools Project; Founding Director of the Institute for Research on Educational Finance and Governance; and a visiting scholar at the Russell Sage Foundation. He has also been Visiting Professor at Peking University, a consultant to the World Bank, and Fulbright Professor in Spain and Mexico.

He is a specialist in the economics of education and has focused extensively on the cost effectiveness of educational approaches, the educational outcomes related to a variety of finance options and sources (e.g., vouchers, private versus public), the educational implications of technologies, and strategies such as accelerated schools, a program he conceived and developed for high-risk students designed to accelerate the learning of disadvantaged students to successfully integrate them into the mainstream. His work has been influenced by Thomas D. Cook, as well as many economists.

He is the author, editor, coauthor, or coeditor of numerous articles and 13 books, including *Resource Guide for Accelerated Schools, Effective Schools in Developing Societies, Comparing Public and Private Schools, Schooling and Work in the Democratic State,* and *Public Dollars for Private Schools.* His best selling book, *Cost-Effectiveness Analysis: Methods and Applications,* is now in its second edition. He is Editor of *Review of Educational Research* and is on the Editorial Board of *Urban Review, Evaluation and Program Planning, Public Finance Review,* and *Economics of Education Review.* He is a member of the International Academy of Education and served as President of the Evaluation Research Society. He is the winner of the 1992 Dana Award for Pioneering Achievement and the 1985 Alva and Gunnar Myrdal Evaluation Practice Award of the American Evaluation Association.

■■ LEVITON, LAURA

(b. 1951, Chicago, Illinois). Ph.D. Psychology, University of Kansas; Postdoctoral Fellow, Northwestern University; M.A. Psychology, University of Kansas; B.A. Psychology, Reed College.

Leviton is a Senior Program Officer for Research and Evaluation at the Robert Wood Johnson Foundation. Previously, she was on the faculty of the University of Pittsburgh and University of Alabama, Birmingham.

Leviton has contributed to evaluation theory, practice, and the profession in four different areas: (a) her evaluations of community-based health and social service programs; (b) coauthoring the widely used text *Foundations of Program Evaluation,* with William R. Shadish and Thomas D. Cook; (c) conducting one of the earliest HIV prevention evaluations and, to date, still the largest randomized experiment evaluating methods to encourage safer sexual practices in gay and bisexual men; and (d) her published works on evaluation utilization in education.

Among the many people who have influenced her work in evaluation are Gloria Ladieu Leviton, Charles A. Kiesler, Donald Campbell, Jack W. Brehm, Thomas D. Cook, Robert F. Boruch, Beaufort Longest, Jr., Russell G. Schuh, Thomas Allen Bruce, and Mary Guinan.

She was President of the American Evaluation Association in 2000 and AEA Board Member from 1999 to 2001, coeditor of a special issue of Public Health Reports concerning the CDC's HIV community-based prevention activities, and a contributing author to a wide range of evaluation journals and books. She has served on the National Institutes of Mental Health's Mental Health, AIDS and Immunology Review Committee and the NIH Study Section for Review of HIV/AIDS Prevention Research, the CDC National Advisory Committee on HIV and STD Prevention, and was a member of the Institute of Medicine Committee to Evaluate the Metropolitan Medical Response Systems Program of the Department of Health and Human Services (preparedness for biological, chemical, or radiological terrorist attack).

Leviton received the Award for Distinguished Contributions to Psychology in the Public Interest from the American Psychological Association in 1993 and the Edgar Hayhow Award of the American College of Healthcare Executives for article of the year in Hospital and Health Services Administration in 1987. She was a W. K. Kellogg National Fellow from 1981 to 1984.

■■ LICENSURE

Licensure refers to permission (usually granted by the state) to conduct evaluations. The law usually specifies the qualifications of the evaluators. This typically entails the assessment of an applicant's competence in a core set of standards accepted within the profession or the applicant's experience. Licensure ensures a foundational level of knowledge of evaluation and potentially protects society from incompetent evaluators by delimiting the scope of practice of practitioners. Licensure can also protect a profession from competition. Currently there is no licensing process for evaluators in the United States; however, some evaluation organizations worldwide are exploring the possibility of certification.

—Leonard Bickman

■■ LIGHT, RICHARD J.

Ph.D. Statistics, Harvard University.

Light is Walter H. Gale Professor of Education in the Graduate School of Education and Kennedy School of Government at Harvard University.

Light's work emphasizes applications of statistics and research design to challenging problems in American education. He has contributed to understandings of how to collect and analyze information to improve program management, including analyzing how evaluators can play a vital role in shaping public policy. Light coauthored *Summing Up* (with Judith Singer and John Willett) and *By Design* (with David Pillemer), and he is the author of *Making the Most of College,* which won the Stone Award for the best book on education and society.

He is Board Member of the American Association of Higher Education, Board Member of the Fund for the Improvement of Postsecondary Education (FIPSE), member of the U.S. General Accounting Office National Advisory Board, and Chair of the Changing Demographics in Colleges Project at the American Academy of Arts and Sciences. Light is Past President of the American Evaluation Association and recipient of AEA's Paul Lazarsfeld Award for Distinguished Contributions to Scientific Practice in 1991. He was named one of America's great teachers by Vanderbilt University's Chancellor's Lecture Series. In 1998, Light was elected a trustee of Wellesley College and a Fellow of the American Academy of Arts and Sciences.

■■ LINCOLN, YVONNA S.

(b. 1944, Tampa, Florida). Ed.D. Higher Education, Indiana University–Bloomington; M.A. Medieval History, University of Illinois–Urbana; B.A. History, Michigan State University.

Lincoln is Ruth Harrington Chair of Educational Leadership and Distinguished University Professor of Higher Education in the Department of Educational Administration and Human Resource Development at Texas A&M University. She has held faculty positions at Vanderbilt University, the University of Kansas, Indiana University, and Stephens College.

She is most widely known for the creation of a new paradigm in evaluation theory, with Egon Guba, based on her understanding of the inability of the "scientific method" to answer evaluation questions satisfactorily or with appropriate responsiveness to those most affected by evaluation's findings. She has published numerous journal articles. Her special interests are program review processes in higher education, organizational analysis, and alternative paradigm research. She is the coauthor, with Egon Guba, of *Effective*

Evaluation, Naturalistic Inquiry, and *Fourth Generation Evaluation,* and she is Editor of *Organizational Theory and Inquiry: The Paradigm Revolution.* She is also Coeditor (with Norman Denzin) of two editions of the *Handbook of Qualitative Research.*

Her work has been strongly influenced by her education in history, which has given her an awareness of how constructed history is, how incomplete the resources are on which we lean to create history for ourselves, and on how much interpretation of evidence—in the absence of complete context—takes place, even when our sources appear thorough and rich. In evaluation, she has been much influenced by Robert Stake and his work on responsive evaluation, especially his focus on the democratic and social justice aspects of stakeholder responsiveness. She was also greatly influenced by Parlett and Hamilton, Lawrence Stenhouse, and others working to create widespread involvement in evaluation decision making.

With Egon Guba, she is the recipient of the American Evaluation Association 1987 Paul F. Lazarsfeld Award for Outstanding Contributions to Research and Scholarship in Evaluation Theory. She is also the recipient of the 1990 Distinguished Researcher Award, Division J, American Educational Research Association; the 1991 Sidney Suslow Distinguished Research Award, Association for Institutional Research; the 1993 Research Achievement Award, Association for the Study of Higher Education; and the 2002 Indiana University College of Education Distinguished Alumna Award. She has served as President of the American Evaluation Association and on the executive boards of the Association for the Study of Higher Education and of Division J (Postsecondary Education) of the American Educational Research Association.

■■ LIPSEY, MARK W.

(b. 1946, Iowa City, Iowa). Ph.D. Psychology, Johns Hopkins University; B.S. Applied Psychology, Georgia Institute of Technology.

The main focus of Lipsey's work has related to the synthesis of evaluation research findings to describe the cumulative evidence about the effects of social programs. This has involved application of meta-analysis techniques, with which he focused mainly on the area of antisocial behavior. He has also contributed to the methodological discussion in evaluation, especially with regard to the statistical power and "design sensitivity" of experimental and quasiexperimental designs for field research.

His interest and orientation to evaluation were strongly influenced by Don Campbell, especially his works on quasiexperimentation and evolutionary epistemology that appeared during the years when Lipsey was in graduate school. Initially Lipsey was a physics major at Georgia Tech, but he was lured into psychology by some interesting elective classes in social psychology that hooked him on the idea that one could use scientific methods to understand and, perhaps, alleviate social problems. This path was further consolidated in graduate school, where his cohort came through during the days when "social relevance" was the hot issue for psychology.

Lipsey had the good fortune to be recruited to a faculty position in a new program in public affairs psychology that Arthur Brayfield was launching at Claremont Graduate School to develop the contribution of psychology to social issues. Expansion of his interest in Campbell's methods for field experimentation and quasiexperimentation followed naturally, and he joined the movement at the time (the early 1970s) that launched program evaluation as a research specialty area. Over the 20 years he was at Claremont Graduate School, and continuing to this day, an extraordinary number of doctoral students have been trained in evaluation and gone on to make careers in that or related areas.

Lipsey has authored or coauthored several books aimed at graduate students and new evaluators on meta-analysis, design sensitivity, and general evaluation methods, including the most recent edition of the widely used text *Evaluation: A Systematic Approach* (with Rossi and Freeman).

■■ LITERATURE REVIEW

A *literature review* is both process and product. The literature review process entails a systematic examination of prior research, evaluation studies, and scholarship to answer questions of theory, policy, and practice. Literature review as a product persuasively presents new knowledge synthesized from prior inquiries. Its value lies in the opportunities it affords for articulating continuities and contradictions across diverse groups of studies, for reflecting on the quality of normative understandings and methods, and for facilitating discourse among research and evaluation communities that might not communicate directly.

In its most familiar role, literature review prefaces proposals for and reports of new empirical investigations. As a preface, a literature review articulates a context of antecedent investigations for the new inquiry, demonstrating how the new work can make important contributions to current understanding of a problem. The preface identifies communities of inquiry and stakeholders to which the new research seeks to speak.

A literature review can also constitute an independent evaluative and scholarly achievement. In one form, often called *integrative review,* a reviewer looks for consistent findings across approximate methodological replications addressing a common question. When statistical or mathematical tools are used to evaluate these consistencies, the integrative review is called a *meta-analysis.* A literature review also can be used to build or evaluate theory. Conclusions drawn across many individual studies can be used to create more encompassing constructs or to determine the strengths and weaknesses of a conventional theory to describe real events adequately. A literature review also can articulate and reflect on the ways in which practical interventions—and research or evaluation methods—are implemented and how innovation might be introduced to practice conventions. Finally, a literature review can elucidate historical trends, chronicling social factors that led to current norms of understanding, policy, and practice. Needless to say, these roles intertwine, and a given literature review might serve several purposes simultaneously.

The literature review process entails a number of methodological paradoxes. Selection and analysis of prior studies serve predetermined questions, but these predetermined questions often change as the reviewer interacts with the available studies. Second, although more comprehensive reviews might be more convincing, larger collections of studies are more difficult to interpret and may be unnecessary if limited or tentative proposals are the persuasive intent of the review. Third, a reviewer's biases are more likely to operate in study selection that is more exclusive, but including all research regardless of quality of method or relevance risks the persuasiveness of the reviewer's arguments. Finally, the best reviews will capitalize on the diversity of the studies they collect, synthesizing new knowledge from an apparently inchoate mass, but the greater the diversity of the studies, the more difficult it is to identify convincingly common themes and patterns.

Literature review demands a disciplined balance, acknowledging both consensus and contradiction, creating knowledge in the process of criticizing current understanding and practice, requiring commitment to significant questions with flexibility to allow those questions to change, refining the quality of evidence but continuing to invite ideas and contrary indications even from remote and unlikely sources. Literature review requires rigor, integrity, and transparency to draw new illumination from old coals.

—*Robert L. Bangert-Drowns*

Further Reading

Fink, A. (1998). *Conducting research literature reviews.* Thousand Oaks, CA: Sage.

Hart, C. (1998). *Doing a literature review.* Thousand Oaks, CA: Sage.

■■ LOGICAL POSITIVISM

In the literature on evaluation, *logical positivism* usually refers to some version of a scientific philosophy developed by members of the Vienna Circle in the 1920s and 1930s (largely as a reaction to then-dominant Continental philosophies of phenomenology and idealism). The philosophy rests on three key ideas: (a) the verifiability principle, or criterion of meaning: To be considered genuine, legitimate, and meaningful, a knowledge claim about the world must be capable of verification; (b) the doctrine of meaningful statements: The only statements capable of verification, and hence of meaning, are those that can be verified through observation or those that are demonstrable logically; (c) all justified knowledge ultimately rests on noninferential self-evident observations (i.e., foundationalism).

—*Thomas A. Schwandt*

Further Reading

Friedman, M. (1999). *Reconsidering logical positivism.* Cambridge, England: Cambridge University Press.

■■ LOGIC MODEL

An articulated model of how a program or project is understood or intended to contribute to its specified outcomes and that focuses on intermediate outcomes rather than tightly specified processes is a *logic model.* Such models are usually shown diagrammatically but can be reported in narrative form. Although logic models have become increasingly popular in recent years, their use can be traced back at least to the 1960s, when Suchman suggested that evaluation might address the achievement of a "chain of objectives."

Logic models can be developed prospectively for planned new programs or retrospectively for existing programs. Logic models can be used in various ways: (a) to guide an evaluation; (b) to provide staff and other stakeholders with a common, motivating vision; and (c) to report a performance story to funders and senior decision makers. Ideally, a performance story based on a logic model does not simply report evidence to support the causal chain but addresses the extent to which the outcomes can reasonably be attributed to the program and the influence of external factors.

Logic models can be drawn with the causal sequence going from left to right, from top to bottom, from bottom to top, or even from the outside into the center of a circle.

Where there are multiple strands of a program logic, it can be important to make it clear whether these are *alternative* causal paths or *complementary* paths. For example, in Figure 1, the program logic diagram for a home visiting service for parents of young children, the two strands are complementary—it is understood that both are needed for the program to succeed—which has implications for both practice and evaluation.

Nurses need to balance their advice on infant nutrition with a concern not to undermine parental confidence. Evaluation of such programs needs to focus on both these intermediate outcomes. Logic models that show such complementary strands can identify points at which programs need to achieve a reasonable balance between competing imperatives rather than optimizing one of them at the cost of the other.

It can also be important for practice and for evaluation to identify *alternative* causal paths—different ways in which participants might achieve the intended outcomes. These can be particularly important in making valid comparisons between the outcomes of participants in the program and of nonparticipants. It cannot be assumed that the program is the only way in which the intended outcomes can be achieved or that the program works in the same way for all participants. In some cases, it is possible to show the particular contexts in which particular causal paths will operate, taking a realist approach to thinking about programs and evaluations.

There is some debate as to whether a diagram of boxes labeled Inputs, Processes and activities, Outputs and short-term outcomes, and Outcomes and long-term outcomes (sometimes preceded by a fifth box, labeled Context) is sufficient to constitute a logic model (see Figure 2 for an example used by the United Way).

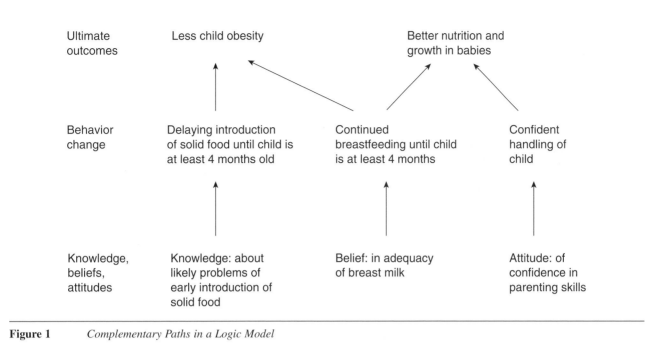

Figure 1 *Complementary Paths in a Logic Model*

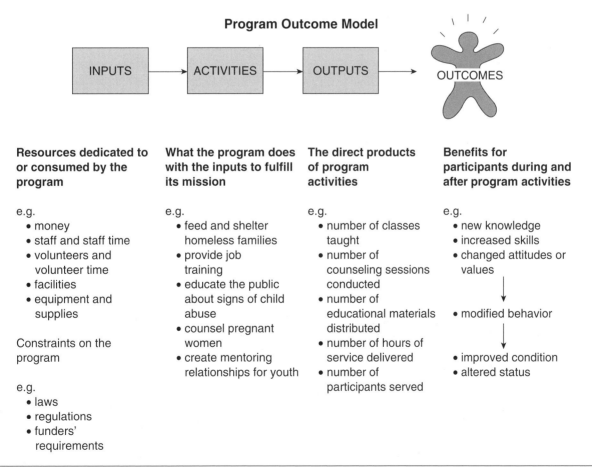

Figure 2 *Illustration of a Simple Logic Model*

SOURCE: Reprinted from *Measuring program outcomes: A practical approach* (1996). Used by permission, United Way of America.

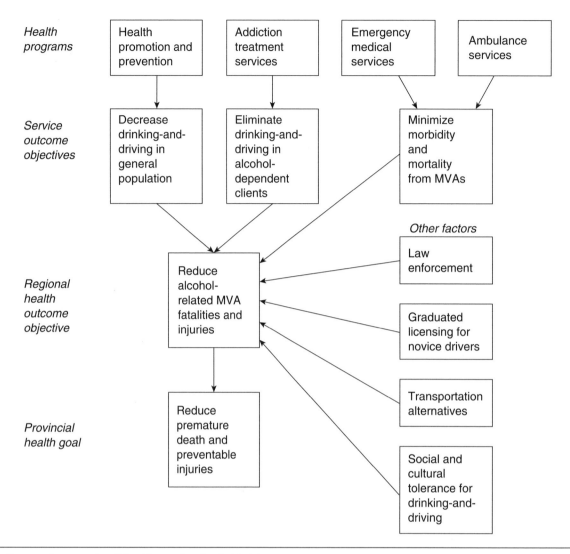

Figure 3   *Representing Other Factors in a Logic Model*

SOURCE: From Halpern, G., "From hubris to reality: Evaluating innovative programs in public institutions," in *The Innovation Journal,* 3(3), copyright © 1998. Reprinted with permission.

Some would argue that it is the simplest version of a logic model and a useful starting point for organizations that have not previously articulated the intended outcomes from their various activities. Others have argued that the model needs to articulate the actual causal mechanisms that are thought to be involved and the specific connections between various inputs, processes and outputs or outcomes.

There is a risk in using logic models that are excessively focused on intended processes and outcomes, as they can lead to evaluations that search only for confirming evidence and not for evidence of unintended outcomes and the influence of other factors. It can be useful for logic models to explicitly show the factors that are likely to influence outcomes (see Figure 3).

Two other types of logic models can be useful in evaluation. Negative program theory explores how the program, even if competently implemented, might result in negative outcomes—either the reverse of the intended outcomes, or some other outcomes that would be seen as problematic. For example, negative program theory of a policy of increasing teacher pay to improve student performance might explore how such a policy might instead contribute to worse student performance or to other negative outcomes, such as increased financial pressure on parents.

The second type of logic model is a diagram showing the causal processes of a problem that the program is intended to change; for example, car theft or school failure.

Because developing a logic model can take significant time and skills, it is often useful for an organization to use or develop a generic logic model for all projects as a common framework or starting point. Some generic logic models require the specification of the intended participants (or *reach*) to communicate what will be done with whom and why. Some versions require specification of external factors. *Logframes,* or the logical framework approach, are a particular form of generic program logic commonly used in international development, having been originally developed in the 1960s. The logframe matrix consists of a narrative summary, analogous to a program logic, divided into four levels of objectives linked in a cause and effect sequence: goal, purpose, outputs, and activities. For each level, the matrix records verifiable indicators, means of verification, and important assumptions.

The advantages of using a generic logic model can include increased ability to communicate about different projects across an organization and a quicker process for developing the logic model, which leaves more time for actually using it. Disadvantages can include failure to encapsulate the specific features of the project adequately, as the project is framed in ways to suit the generic model, and program stakeholders may not identify with the logic model. It may be that a sensitive combination of idiosyncratic and generic program logic is the best approach, where stakeholders' emerging articulations of how the program works are progressively revised into simpler and more general diagrams.

—*Patricia J. Rogers*

Further Reading

Roger, P. J. (2000). Causal models in program theory evaluation. In P. J. Rogers, T. A. Hacsi, P. Petrosino, & T. A. Huebner (Eds.), Program theory in evaluation. *New Directions for Program Evaluation, 87.*

Suchman, E. R. (1967) *Evaluative research: Principles and practice in public service and social action programs.* New York: Russell Sage Foundation.

■ LOGIC OF EVALUATION

The *logic* of a subject concerns such matters as its definition and the definitions of its major concepts, the nature of its relations with other subjects, the rules of inference that operate within it and in applying it, and logical disputes about these matters. What follows is a rather condensed treatment of some of these matters. It should be noted that these issues are not of merely academic interest because from them there follow many practical conclusions—for example, about what training is appropriate for evaluators, what kind of insurance coverage they need, how other disciplines can contribute to and can learn from them, and so on.

THE DEFINITION OF EVALUATION

Synthesizing the dictionary definitions of *evaluation* and *an evaluation* yields this: "determining the merit, worth, or significance of things; a report of such a determination." There is no need to deviate from the common meaning, and it avoids confusion in other people's minds to stay with it. Objections are often raised that such a definition excludes certain approaches to evaluation, such as utilization-focused evaluation, but of course it does not: They are simply approaches to this task, and the definition is strictly neutral about what approaches are best. Evaluators often feel that it would be more appropriate to define evaluation as what evaluators do, but that is a mistake. Evaluators do many things, such as conduct surveys and interviews and statistical analyses and, no doubt, going to church and watching television. The issue of definition requires us to focus on what they do that distinguishes them as evaluators, and the answer is just exactly their concern with determining value (i.e., merit, worth, or significance, depending on the context). Of course, evaluators do many other things that are not intrinsically evaluative, both on the way to an evaluative conclusion and in the course of business dealings that request these other services, for which many evaluators are extremely well qualified. If these other things were all that they did, an evaluator would be only a social scientist—a perfectly respectable, but somewhat limited profession. It is taking the extra step, from empirical or merely factual research to an evaluative conclusion that marks the evaluator as a practitioner working, at least partly, in a different discipline. That is the answer to the important question about the difference between evaluation and the usual kind of research in the social sciences. Someone once said that the usual kind of empirical research is an attempt to answer the question, "What's so?" whereas the evaluator tries to answer the question, "So what?" One might add that the social scientist is often also concerned to find out "Why so?" and the policy analyst is often concerned with the question, "Now what?" Of course, for almost all of the history of the social sciences, social scientists' answer to the question "So what?" was simply that there could not be any scientific answer to it or, indeed, any rational answer. Evaluative questions were beyond the domain of science and reason, a mere matter of preference or taste. If that were true, there could be no legitimate field of evaluation.

THE VALIDATION OF EVALUATIONS

Which brings us face to face with the most central question in the logic of evaluation: How is it possible to justify answers to questions about value in a scientific or other disciplinary way? The skeptical answer to this question given by the social scientists—the doctrine of value-free science—did not come out of the blue. It was preceded by more than a century, beginning with Hume, in which the answer to this question was that it is logically impossible to do this; attempts to do it were said to have "jumped the is-ought gap" or, using Moore's later term, to have "committed the naturalistic fallacy." However, it has become clear that, like Hume's skepticism about the legitimacy of *causation,* his view, and Moore's, on this point, and hence that of the doctrine of value-free social science, was based on an oversimplified analysis of the logic of language. We can in fact infer validly from factual premises to evaluative conclusions by using definitions that bridge the gap: Because they are definitions, they do not count as value premises; that is, imported assumptions about values. The simplest cases are those in which propositions unpacking the meaning of "a good (or bad) X"—for example, "a good watch," combined with a number of facts about the performance of a particular watch—fully justify the conclusion that this is a good or bad watch (or X). This is what product evaluations do routinely, and it is logically impeccable. We commonly use exactly this kind of template in program evaluation and personnel evaluation, as well as in product evaluation.

There is a second way to justify evaluative conclusions, however—the barefaced way. Here we do use premises that express values and that are not definitionally true. They are value premises, which can be directly validated in commonsense ways. There is no shortage of these: For example, premises expressing legal requirements or severe needs are often validated by legal research or systematic needs assessment and combine with facts about a program's performance to imply the merit (or lack of merit) of the program. Of course, they will be accepted only by those who regard adherence to the law or attention to needs as obligatory, but that includes the context of most program evaluations because they are done in a value-imbued context. Does this show that we have validated the evaluative conclusions? It does if we consider the assumptions of practical life to be sensible ones, and it does not involve making highly contested assumptions of an ethical or political kind. Of course, these assumptions lie outside the domain of the axioms of conventional social science, so accepting them marks another significant difference between evaluation and social science. It does not rule out the possibility that we might think it more sensible to expand conventional social science so that it takes on the support or refutation of such assumptions and could then claim that evaluation was part of social science. Many evaluators would favor that alternative, but until it is generally accepted, we must concede that this second method of validating evaluative conclusions marks a difference between the two disciplines.

However, the first approach to jumping the is-ought or facts-values gap (they are not quite the same, but both illustrate the same logical point) shows that we can bypass the great logical obstacle that was held to render our field inaccessible to scientific validation. How did this obstacle impede progress for so long?

TYPES OF VALUE CLAIM

One of the sources of the fallacious belief that science was (or should be) value free was an oversimplified paradigm of value claim. It was generally taken that the prototypical example was exemplified in a claim like, "I value loyalty over industriousness in my employees" or, more simply, "I like white wines in general much more than red ones." This is, of course, a mere statement of personal preference and as such cannot be validated as having any wider applicability. Even if it asserts that "Italians value red wines well above white ones," it will still be merely a local truth, and a truth about a matter that is in one sense subjective. Still, one needs to be clear that such claims are perfectly verifiable by observation and evidence of other kinds, such as buying habits, conversation, and so on, and hence are not subjective in the pejorative sense that puts them outside the domain of scientific testability. For many of the enemies of evaluation as a discipline—Ayer, Stevenson, and others—that was too much of a concession, and they argued that one should not treat these claims as proper claims at all; that is, as propositions or statements of a factual kind. They tried to subsume them under mere noises, but the effort to do so was implausible then and absurd now that we are less obsessed by the threat of legitimating evaluative statements.

In any case, there are other types of value claim that need to be distinguished from this one. For example, there are market value claims, such as a claim about the value of a house for sale in a particular location, and these have a standard method of verification recognized by the law and common sense; so these, again, are entirely testable and much less "subjective" because they do not have any particular connection to private states of the mind.

Then there are what might be called contextual value claims—claims that are prima facie factual but in a certain context refer to properties that are highly valued in that context and hence carry the import of an assertion of value. In the context of recruiting basketball players, for example, statements about an athlete's height are value imbued.

Finally, there are what we might call essentially evaluative claims, claims about the brilliance of Einstein or Chopin or Leonardo or about the excellence of the workmanship in a piece of Faberge jewelry or a great cathedral or the superiority of highly interactive modes of instruction over the lecture format or the disappointing results from the most heavily supported and widely implemented models of school reform or addiction reduction of recent years. These are what the fight is all about, and they are very unlike assertions of personal preference. Although in some cases they lack the support that entitles them to be called provable, in many other cases (e.g., in the claim about Einstein), they have more than enough support to justify the view that they are as well supported as the usual kind of particular or general scientific claim.

These are the kinds of claim that evaluators aim to support by their work, and the suggestion that they are any less objective than claims about the advantages of one engineering design over another for certain purposes is no longer plausible—especially as that claim from engineers is simply one example of an evaluative claim, a type that is found throughout every scientific or other discipline and is known as an intradisciplinary evaluation. Throughout the long fight over the legitimacy of evaluation as a discipline, it was conveniently ignored that no discipline exists without standards of merit for the methodological entities with which it deals—the data, experiments, hypotheses, and work of its professionals—the application of which, of course, is simply one branch of the supposedly "forbidden" subject.

BRANCHES OF EVALUATION

There are a dozen named branches of evaluation, of which the Big Seven are sometimes said to be the evaluation of products, performances, personnel, programs, policies, proposals, and portfolios. Some of these were practices half a million years ago and became skilled practices with specialist practitioners thousands of years ago, guilds after that, and then professions that blithely ignored the alleged impossibility of their subject across a century or more. Two fields of special importance and late emergence into recognition, although long practiced, are intradisciplinary evaluation and *metaevaluation* (the evaluation of evaluations). There are also many pseudoevaluative activities, thought by their practitioners to be branches of a legitimate discipline and often of considerable history, in which all the language and attitudes of evaluation are present but the basic requirements of testability and validated standards do not exist. Most (but not all) of literary criticism, art criticism, and wine connoisseurship clearly exemplify this syndrome. There are also subareas with great achievements that are still making many mistakes because they have not awakened to the fact that evaluation has evolved independently of their subarea, and they have lessons to learn from it. Consumer product evaluation is an example: The Consumers Union in the United States does great things but makes many mistakes because it thinks statistics and engineering alone are all it needs to design and do its work. The road-testing magazines are in the same category.

APPLIED FIELDS OR AREAS OF EVALUATION

Most of the branches of evaluation can be applied to areas within each of the traditional subject matter areas. For example, within the fields of public health or social work or physics, there is plenty of program, performance, and personnel evaluation; some product evaluation and policy evaluation; and, of course, intradisciplinary and metaevaluation. Although there is not the slightest advantage to doing more evaluation if it is not good evaluation, in most areas, the commitment to evaluation is too small, both in resources and attitude, to achieve the maximum benefits. This is largely because of deficiencies in the training of professionals about evaluation; they all too often pick up a sense of defensiveness about it or a sense that it is something one has to do to get funded. The correct attitude is simpler: It is a minimum requirement of professionalism to ensure regular skilled external evaluation of one's work. Evaluation is a *professional imperative,* an obligation that is not only part of valuing good work in itself but a part of discharging one's obligation to society to do good work. Now that evaluation as a discipline has developed considerably, this obligation entails at least some effort to keep up with what is going on in the field itself, not just in already-implemented applications to one's own area. What has emerged in evaluation that might be useful to busy practitioners in applied areas?

THE FUNDAMENTAL OPERATIONS IN EVALUATION

In many applied areas, there is continuing carelessness and consequent errors in distinguishing among the core evaluation operations. Even in areas that pride themselves on precision and scientific method, such as measurement and testing, these errors are quite common. There are essentially five fundamental operations, with a couple of minor variations. The basic operations are grading, ranking, scoring, apportioning, and synthesis: All of these are familiar terms and practices, but it is extremely rare to find a practitioner or text that can define them correctly or distinguish them precisely. Quite different designs are required for each of these, and major failures to provide the help that is needed result from failing to distinguish them correctly. A horse race is a great approach to

ranking, but not to grading, which will also require scoring—and, in fact, measuring (a particular approach to scoring)—in this case, by using a stopwatch. If you have ever seen a scale in a survey in which the anchors are something like excellent, very good, average, below average, poor, or unacceptable, you have seen a design that confuses grading with ranking, which will produce uninterpretable results.

Two additions to the basic list are of great practical value: Profiling is the exhibition of grades (not scores) in several dimensions in bar-graph format: It is extremely useful in that it avoids the difficult and disputable task of synthesis in many cases where it makes it possible to do ranking without synthesis. Gap ranking is a refinement of ranking in which qualitative estimates of the intervals are added. It is standard practice in horse racing: "The winner is X by a head in front of Y; a length back is Z by a nose over W." It is extremely useful in a common context where ranking is required; for example, in the award of funds or prizes, where splitting the pot is possible.

Other topics in the logic of evaluation that may help indicate its utility today include the distinction between roles and goal of evaluation, where the *formative-summative* classification comes in: the function of program goals in program evaluation; the relation of explanations and recommendations to evaluations, which brings up the legitimacy and necessity of *theory-based evaluations* and evaluation-based recommendations; the distinction between criteria and indicators and how this shows that personnel evaluation cannot use style variables; and ethics as a branch of evaluation.

—*Michael Scriven*

Further Reading

Scriven, M. (1991). *Evaluation thesaurus* (4th ed.). Newbury Park, CA: Sage.

Scriven, M. (1994). Product evaluation—The state of the art. *Evaluation Practice, 15*(1), 45-62.

■■ LOGIC OF EVALUATION— WORKING LOGIC

General logic can be found across various fields and settings in evaluation practice. What does vary across practice in these fields and settings is how the general logic is followed; that is, the type of questions posed, what or how criteria are selected, what or how standards are constructed, how performance is measured, and how data are synthesized.

For example, in a consumer approach to product evaluation, a source of criteria is the properties inherent in the product being evaluated. Tools of the trade include needs assessment, using idealized and contextual functional analyses to identify what the product is suppose to do, and how consumers actually use the product. Absolute standards are generated from minimal acceptable performance, set by the industry, and relative standards are constructed by comparison to critical competitors. Performance trials are used that include in-house staff and experts in alpha trials and consumers in beta trials.

In contrast, a source of criteria and standards in a stakeholder approach to program evaluation is what stakeholders value in a particular program. Audience participation techniques and iterative group processes are typically used. In a program theory approach, criteria and standards are established from the underlying social theory that exists in the research literature. Experimental and quasiexperimental research methods are used to measure performance. With a connoisseurial approach, criteria and standards come from values personally held by an expert. Measurement of performance relies significantly on firsthand observation, interviewing, and document review.

This variation in the detail of the general logic is called *working logic*. Working logic guides evaluators in how to build a logical chain of reasoning using a specific model or approach or when designing an evaluation. To justify conclusions made in evaluation, evaluators follow the same general logic and employ a particular instance of it—working logic. Subsumed under general logic are many individual types of working logic.

PARAMETERS OF WORKING LOGIC

The reason there is variation in the details of the four steps of general logic is that evaluation models and approaches vary along four key parameters: problem, phenomenon, questions, and claims. The particular kind of problem addressed in an evaluation influences how the object of evaluation under study is (or can be) defined or operationalized, the kinds of questions that can be raised about the object, and the kinds of claims that can be made. These differences across key parameters in each of the models are important because

they orient the logical foundation for building an argument structure that works to establish and justify conclusions. The reasoning used by evaluators is directed toward a particular set of parameters. The model or approach selected and used by an evaluator advances not only a particular point of view but a particular set of parameters, a specific working logic. When evaluators use a particular model or approach, they are committing themselves to using a specific working logic.

For example, in a consumer approach to product evaluation, the focus is on determining the extent of performance (type of problem to solve) of functional products, such as computers or cars (type of phenomenon), by asking questions such as, "Is X good? Is X better than Y and Z?" (type of questions) to establish performance and comparative value conclusions (type of claims).

In contrast, in a connoisseurial approach to program evaluation, the focus is on describing the unique qualities of a program (type of problem to solve), defined as a *collection* of qualities (type of phenomenon), by asking questions such as, "What does it feel like to be in this program?" (type of questions) to establish descriptive and value conclusions (type of claims).

In a causal approach to program evaluation, the focus is on determining the intervention effectiveness of a program (type of problem to solve), which is defined as a set of treatment-outcome relationships that have been structured in such a way as to ameliorate a particular educational or social problem (type of phenomenon) by asking questions such as, "Is A better than B because A is more effective than B at producing C?" (type of questions) to establish causal and value conclusions (type of claims).

In these three examples, the kinds of problems, phenomena, questions, and claims are different. The connoisseurial and causal examples both deal with the programs but differ in the way they each define or conceptualize a program (the phenomenon). The connoisseurial model defines a program as a set of unique qualities; the causal model defines a program as a set of treatment-outcome relationships.

REASONING PATTERN OF WORKING LOGIC

The parameters of working logic orient the logical foundation for building an argument structure or reasoning pattern that works to establish and justify conclusions. Toulmin examined different types of inquiry and identified six logical features that are common to all kinds of inquiry (see Figure 1). All six features work together to form a reasoning pattern resulting from a process of inquiry:

- *Claims* conclude what is to be taken as legitimate and most likely the case.
- *Evidence* is the facts that form the basis or foundation for the claim.
- *Warrants* legitimate the inferences drawn from evidence to the claim by appeal to some authority. They confer varying degrees of strength or forcefulness on the claim they justify.
- *Backings* are added authority that support the warrant by appeal to some more general authority, especially when others are skeptical or not willing to accept the warrant at its face value.
- *Conditions of exception* point out circumstances in which the warrant may not hold or will hold in only a limited way. They anticipate certain objections that could be advanced against the claim.
- *Qualifiers* identify the strength or forcefulness of the claim. They may be expressed in such terms as *probably, possibly, conclusively,* or *most likely the case.*

This reasoning pattern can be useful in mapping out the overall reasoning process in any evaluation design plan, model, or approach. The structure can also be used to identify multiple chains of reasoning that are linked together in an evaluation, as an evaluation contains a complex collection of subarguments. The evidence-warrant-backing relationship can be a means for examining how a particular evaluation allows support for conclusions, and the conditions of exception can be viewed as means for examining how the evaluation rules out alternate explanations that can potentially weaken conclusions. The reasoning pattern illuminates the ways in which building a credible evaluation is influenced and makes clear the features that need to be considered when drawing conclusions in evaluation and where conclusions can be open to challenge and criticism.

WARRANTABILITY OF EVALUATIVE CONCLUSIONS

In drawing inferences from evidence to make claims, evaluators design evaluations that use different kinds of warrants. The warrant functions to legitimate the inferences drawn from evidence by appeal to some sort of authority—because it is the rule, because I personally observed it myself, because it is the law, because a reputable expert said so, because the test is proven reliable, because the phenomenon possesses the same major attributes as previously accepted instances, because the situation bears similarity to previous cases, because it reflects the needs and values that are held by stakeholders, because the study was randomized. As distinguished from evidence that answers the question, "What do you have to go on to support your claims?" the warrant answers the question, "How can you say that?"

For example, in a connoisseurial approach to evaluation, to assert that a program is good based on expert opinion means that the warrant appeals to the personally held values of an expert and functions to affirm the credibility and reliability of the expert. One way to challenge the warrant is to show that the expert is not an authority at all or that there is a conflict of interest: The expert states that Program A is a good art program based on his or her direct observations of the program (evidence), thus this is most likely the case (claim) because the judgment of the expert is reliable in the area of art education (warrant), and the expert is highly experienced and respected by colleagues and has a long history of credibility (backing of the warrant) and can be shown to have nothing to gain or lose that might reduce reliability in judgment (conditions of exception).

Warrants in evaluation can be categorized into two types: warrant using and warrant establishing. Warrant-using types of warrants are well established, uncontested, and generally accepted as given. The warrants used to support causal claims in experimental and quasiexperimental studies are warrant using. In a causal approach, where randomization is possible, warrantability of causal claims is grounded in sampling theory. It is broadly accepted that sampling theory ensures that randomization achieves comparative equivalence by dispersing influences on the dependent variable equally over treatment groups, resulting in a no-difference pretest comparison. Randomization, comparison groups, and pre-post measures serve as warrants to establish and legitimate the making of causal inferences—relationships were identified under reliable methods. In instances in which randomization is not possible, the warrantability of claims changes. The key to strong defensible claims

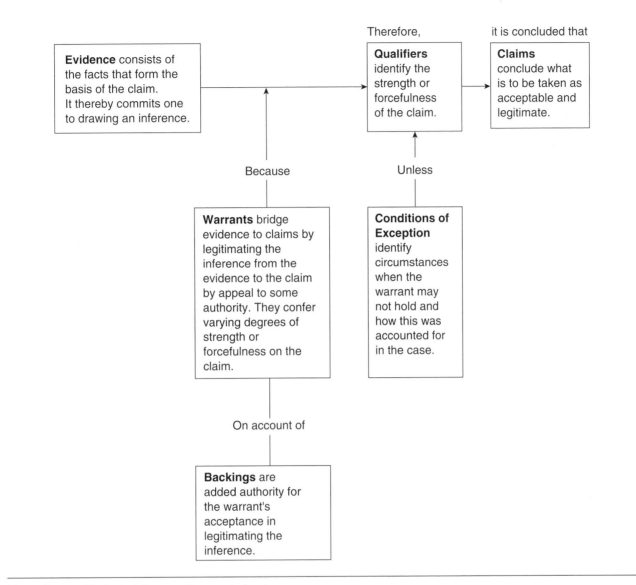

Therefore,

it is concluded that

Evidence consists of the facts that form the basis of the claim. It thereby commits one to drawing an inference.

Qualifiers identify the strength or forcefulness of the claim.

Claims conclude what is to be taken as acceptable and legitimate.

Because

Unless

Warrants bridge evidence to claims by legitimating the inference from the evidence to the claim by appeal to some authority. They confer varying degrees of strength or forcefulness on the claim.

Conditions of Exception identify circumstances when the warrant may not hold and how this was accounted for in the case.

On account of

Backings are added authority for the warrant's acceptance in legitimating the inference.

Figure 1   *Six Logical Features Common to Inquiry*

with quasiexperimentation is the use of pattern matching of causal predictions to the obtained data (verification) and the ruling out of alternative explanations (falsification). Point specificity and complex causal predictions of anticipated effects are matched to obtained data to support inferences about treatment impact.

Many warrants used in evaluations are not of this type. They are often warrant establishing. This refers to warrants that are not uncontested and must be constructed and tried out by application in a number of cases over time. They are unfamiliar, controversial, or newly introduced from another discipline, and thus the validity of the assumptions underlying the inferences must be established through justification of the

warrant and additional backing. This is evident, for example, in evaluation approaches that use warrants that are grounded in the needs, interests, or values of stakeholders or in participative, empowerment, or community capacity-building approaches that warrant claims through audience participation and collaboration. In such instances, evaluators often seek to use and defend the legitimacy of the warrant, as well as the claims. What is interesting to note is that what is deemed as warrant establishing in evaluation may be warrant using in another area of inquiry. For example, a connoisseurial approach in program evaluation has been warrant establishing, but such an approach is warrant using in art and literary fields, where it is widely accepted and uncontested.

In addition to these types of warrants, evaluators use a variety of other warrants in designing and implementing evaluations, such as parallel case–type warrants that affirm that the evidence bears an essential similarity to other instances of this type that have been already been accepted and documented: When X is like Y in terms of qualities A, B, and C, then X will be like Y in similar respects. Analogy-type warrants affirm that the evidence shows that a certain kind of relationship exists between two instances, based on a similar relationship that has been already been accepted and documented: When X is like Y in terms of A, B, and C, then X will be like Y in other respects. Generalization-type warrants affirm that the evidence is a case or instance of something already known that is based on many previous instances: When many instances of X have the qualities A, B, and C, then other Xs can be characterized by A, B, and C. Sign-type warrants affirm that the evidence possesses the attributes that are symptoms of behaviors or conditions: When X symptomatically occurs before, after, or with Y, then X is a sign of Y.

The warrant-establishing nature of evaluation is expected, given its markedly diverse practices and its history of annexing methods and perspectives from other disciplines. Professional inquiry activities, both intellectual and practical, are guided by the goals of the inquiry and its logic. Discrepancies between what the inquiry aims to achieve and what it can actually achieve through its existing methods and tools influences the theoretical and methodological developments that take place.

—*Deborah M. Fournier*

Further Reading

Fournier, D. M. (Ed.). (1995). Reasoning in evaluation: Inferential links and leaps. *New Directions for Program Evaluation, 68.*

Scriven, M. (1980). *The logic of evaluation.* Inverness, CA: Edgepress.

Scriven, M. (1993). *The evaluation thesaurus.* Newbury Park, CA: Sage.

██ LONGITUDINAL STUDIES

A study that follows an individual or group over a substantial and extended period of time is considered *longitudinal.* Longitudinal evaluations may examine the influence of an intervention over time, as well as the interaction between maturation, context, and the intervention. Such studies often entail the creation of large data sets collected from a large sample of individuals over time. Examples of longitudinal studies are the U.S. Early Childhood Longitudinal Study, the U.S. National Longitudinal Study of Adolescent Health, the Australian Longitudinal Study on Women's Health, and the Finnish Jyväskylä Longitudinal Study of Personality and Social Development.

██ LUNDGREN, ULF P.

(b. 1942, Värmland, Sweden). Ph.D., Licentiate, M.A. Social Sciences, University of Göteborg, Sweden.

Lundgren is Professor and Head of the Research Unit for Studies in Educational Policy and Educational Philosophy, Uppsala University, and Director of the Education Policy Institute, which focuses on the politics of education, educational policy making, and the governing of educational systems. He also held faculty appointments at the University Centre of Aalborg, Denmark, and Stockholm Institute of Education (where he was also the Vice Chancellor), and he was Director General of the National Agency for Education in Sweden.

Lundgren has contributed to the practice of educational evaluation in many countries, notably Sweden, Norway, Portugal, and Swaziland. He has written extensively on evaluation as an instrument for policy and governance and on evaluation as politics. Much of his earlier work is published in an edited collection, *Ulf P. Lundgren's Skrifter 1966-1991.* His work has been influenced by the linguistic traditions of Bellack, Halliday, and Bernstein; by the philosophies of Durkheim and Dewey; by Urban Dahllöf's frame-factor theory; and by Robert Stake's and Ernest House's work on the politics of evaluation.

Lundgren's work has been recognized by many professional associations. He has received the Australian-European Award in Social Sciences, the Bicentennial Award from the American Education Research Association, University of Saskatoon Award, and the Order for Honourable Service (Sweden). Lundgren is a permanent member of the Royal Academy for Art and Science in Uppsala; an honorary member of the Nation of Värmland, Uppsala; Board Member and Chair (1990-2000) of the OECD Center for Educational Research and Innovation, and a member of France's Haut Conseil de l'évaluation de l'école.

⊞ MABRY, LINDA

(b. 1948, Austin, Texas). Ph.D. Educational Psychology, University of Illinois, Urbana-Champaign; B.Ed., University of Houston.

Mabry is the great-granddaughter of the proprietor of one of Austin's first five businesses, Weed's Livery and Undertaking. Her own undertaking was education, beginning when she was 10 years old and teaching younger siblings and neighbors in her backyard "Sunshine Club." A decade later, she was teaching third grade full-time as an intern in a racially transitional, impoverished north Houston school, for which she was named the Outstanding Graduating Senior in the College of Education at the University of Houston. She stayed home with her three children until they had all entered school and, after a 7-year hiatus, returned to teaching in Illinois.

With an interest in how computers might enhance individualized learning, she left the classroom 6 years later to complete a master's degree in computer-assisted instruction. Discouraged by the state of educational technology in the mid-1980s but stimulated by academic thinking and research, she began doctoral studies in aesthetic foundations, then switched to program evaluation, beginning with the evaluation of arts education programs as a teaching and research assistant in the Center for Instructional Research and Curriculum Evaluation. When her evaluations of educational programs revealed the destructive power of high-stakes standardized testing, she moved into the field of K-12 student assessment. In that field, Phi Delta Kappa recognized with an Outstanding Dissertation designation her first research, an examination of a teacher-developed performance assessment system at Walden III High School in Racine, Wisconsin.

In the areas of research and evaluation, she found stimulating the debates regarding ethics and professional responsibility (particularly regarding advocacy) in an era that recognizes the mutability of truth and questions authority. Her thinking and contributions have especially focused on ethics, postmodernism, and their intersection with methodology, validity, advocacy, and responsibility. In the area of assessment of student achievement, admiring especially Sam Messick's work regarding consequential validity, she has concentrated on performance assessment, validity, and high-stakes testing for educational accountability.

Her research and evaluation has resulted in a book on each topic and has been conducted with research grants or fellowships from the Spencer Foundation–National Academy of Education, National Endowment for the Arts, Proffitt Endowment, Bagley Endowment, Washington Educational Research Association, State of Washington Office of the Superintendent of Public Instruction, Ameritech Corporation, Hewlett-Packard Corporation, and others. She has served on the Board of Directors of the American Evaluation Association, the Board of Directors of the National Center for the Improvement of Educational Assessment, and the Performance Assessment Review Board of New York City. She was part of the team that authored AEA's first public statement on high-stakes testing, an effort funded by the National Science Foundation.

▊ MACDONALD, BARRY

(b. 1932, Aberdeen, Scotland). Ph.D. (Honoris Causa), University of Valladolid, Spain; M.A., Dip.Ed., M.Ed., University of Aberdeen, Scotland.

MacDonald was Director of CARE (the Centre for Applied Research in Education) at the University of East Anglia. Following studies in modern languages, education, and educational psychology at the University of Aberdeen, he spent some time as a teacher and teacher educator in Scotland, where he experimented with case study approaches to the building of teacher confidence in the classroom. In 1968, he moved to London to undertake the role of evaluator of Lawrence Stenhouse's controversial Humanities Curriculum Project.

MacDonald was the first to articulate a political typology of evaluation, and he contributed substantially to the development of a case study approach to evaluation. Stenhouse and MacDonald eventually used the Humanities Curriculum Project as an intellectual base to found CARE. The necessity to observe and understand this complex project across 36 school sites led MacDonald to experiment with the intensive study and dissemination of individual cases. In this, he was working in parallel with Robert Stake, Louis Smith, and others in the United States. This shared perspective resulted in the formation of an enduring transatlantic group through the Cambridge Conferences, which codified and articulated democratic and case study principles for evaluation. MacDonald went on to direct the Ford Success and Failure and Recent Innovation (SAFARI) project (1973-1975), in which case study and democratic evaluation methodologies were further elaborated and published. A central feature of the SAFARI project was the generation of teacher biographies as a basis for theorizing about innovation. Other large-scale evaluation projects (e.g., the Understanding Computer-Assisted Learning Evaluation) followed and became further demonstrations for democratic, case-based approaches. In 1978, MacDonald was invited by the Ford Foundation to conduct a policy evaluation of bilingual schooling in the United States. The study was founded mainly on a single school case study (its historical and contemporary contexts) in Boston. In 1999, MacDonald received an honorary doctorate from the University of Valladolid, Spain, in recognition of his contributions to educational evaluation, in particular, and to the post-Franco democratization of Spanish education in general.

▊ MADISON, ANNA MARIE

(b. 1947, Palestine, Texas). Ph.D., University of Southern California.

Madison is Professor in the College of Public and Community Service at the University of Massachusetts at Boston. She teaches in the Master of Science in Human Services Program, specializing in public and nonprofit sector management, public policy, performance monitoring, and evaluation. Her evaluation career represents multiple roles as educator, practitioner-consultant, and applied researcher and has been influenced by public policy and urban studies. She has conducted evaluations of human services, management capacity building, youth programming, disease prevention, and education.

Her primary contributions to the field of evaluation center on policies and practices affecting minorities, management, and evaluation; mission-based evaluation; participatory evaluation; and evaluation capacity building. Her recent evaluation work focuses on evaluation capacity building in community-based progressive organizations that promote the principles of active democracy by involving constituents directly in governance and in shaping their communities.

She has published in the areas of evaluation education in management, language in evaluation, new paradigms in evaluation practice, and performance and accountability in human services. She has made domestic and international presentations on evaluation practice and theory. She provides evaluation training and continuing education to practicing professionals in New England and has served as a trainer to develop evaluation capacity in Africa. She is Editor of *Minority Issues in Program Evaluation* and *New Directions for Program Evaluation,* has served on the editorial boards of the *American Journal of Evaluation* and *New Directions for Program Evaluation,* and is the cofounder of the Minority Issues TIG of the American Evaluation Association. Madison is a former board member of the American Evaluation Association and has served on the Ethics, Nominations, Awards, and Annual Program Committees.

▊ MARK, MELVIN M.

(b. 1953, Grand Island, Nebraska). Ph.D., M. A. Social Psychology, Northwestern University; B.A. Psychology, University of Nebraska–Lincoln.

Mark is Professor of Psychology and Senior Scientist at the Institute for Policy Research and Evaluation, Pennsylvania State University.

Mark's current work focuses on the theory, methods, and practice of evaluation and the appropriate use of social science research in social policy, particularly in the context of program evaluation, and includes several areas of the intersection and interaction between affect, cognition, and motivation in psychological processes. He has conducted federally funded evaluations in the areas of prevention programs for at-risk youth, federal personnel policies, and industrial modernization and has also been involved in evaluations of state and local programs. Mark is a coauthor (with Gary Henry and George Julnes) of *Evaluation: An Integrated Framework for Understanding, Guiding, and Improving Policies and Programs* and *Realist Evaluation*. In these works, Mark and his collaborators provide an evaluation theory that captures the sense-making contributions from postpositivism and the sensitivity to values from constructivist traditions.

As an undergraduate, Mark was inspired to study social psychology by Muzafer and Carolyn Sherif's Robbers Cave Experiment, a classic experiment conducted in the 1950s on building positive intergroup relations. Mark currently lives in the house formerly occupied by the Sherifs. His graduate studies at Northwestern University were motivated by an interest in doing social psychology in real-world settings. It was at Northwestern that he was drawn to evaluation and especially methodological issues by the work and intellectual charisma of Tom Cook and Don Campbell.

Mark, in his role as Editor of the *American Journal of Evaluation,* has contributed to promoting quality dialogue in and about evaluation. Mark was the 2000 recipient of Pennsylvania State University's College of Liberal Arts Outstanding Teacher Award.

▚ MATHEMATICA POLICY RESEARCH

Mathematica is known for its high-quality, objective research on a wide variety of social problems and policy formation. The firm has conducted comprehensive studies of health care, welfare, education, employment, nutrition, and early childhood policies and programs in the United States. For more than three decades, Mathematica has offered policy makers a combination of evaluation expertise, direct data collection services, and insight into the socioeconomic issues that drive public policy. Clients include federal agencies, state and local governments, foundations, universities, professional associations, and businesses.

—*Jeffrey G. Tucker*

▚ MATHISON, SANDRA

(b. 1954, Calgary, Alberta, Canada). Ph.D., M.A. Educational Psychology, University of Illinois, Urbana-Champaign; A.B. (with distinction) Sociology, University of Alberta.

Mathison is Head of the Department of Educational and Counseling Psychology and Special Education at the University of British Columbia and has been a faculty member at the University at Albany, State University of New York, and the University of Louisville. She was Director of Evaluation for the University of Chicago School Mathematics Project, where she conducted local and national evaluations of math curriculum and teacher professional development projects.

Her contributions to evaluation theory and practice include qualitative methods in evaluation, internal evaluation, and the role of standardized testing as a form of evaluation in K-12 schools. Her article "Why Triangulate?" is widely recognized as a seminal work for qualitative researchers and evaluators alike. Mathison's contributions include work that has promoted a greater understanding of the democratic potential of evaluation; for example, through her explication of deliberation in evaluation. As an evaluation theorist and practitioner, she has contributed significantly to research on the use of standardized testing in K-12 schools, including analyses of its social, political, and ethical dimensions.

Mathison's main intellectual influences include social theorists Karl Marx, Jürgen Habermas, Paul Feyerabend, Brian Fay, and cultural anthropologist Clifford Geertz. She was introduced to these authors as an undergraduate and continues to read and reread their works. In evaluation, Mathison was influenced by Robert Stake's work on naturalistic, responsive, and case study evaluation; Ernest House's work on justice and fairness; Michael Scriven's philosophical analysis of evaluation and development of evaluation as a discipline; Carol Weiss' seminal work on the political nature of evaluation; and Terry Denny for introducing her to Paul Taylor's *Normative Discourse.*

Mathison has been a member of the American Evaluation Association Board of Directors and Chair of the first ever AEA public affairs task force, which developed a widely cited position statement on high-stakes testing in K-12 education.

■■ MATRIX SAMPLING

Matrix sampling is a methodology to enhance the efficiency of measurement. In conventional measurement, every person in a group (e.g., every evaluation participant) completes every item on an instrument. In matrix sampling, each person completes only a sample of items, thereby reducing testing time for individuals. By averaging over persons who are measured, the performance of a group (e.g., evaluation participants) on a variable of interest can be estimated. Matrix sampling is used in situations where efficiency and economy are concerns, including large-scale summative evaluations and student assessment systems for nations, provinces, or states.

—*Joseph M. Petrosko*

■■ MDRC

MDRC was established in 1974 by the Ford Foundation and six agencies of the federal government. The "Great Society" programs of the 1960s had been launched with great fanfare and hope that they would end poverty in America, but because clear measures of their effectiveness were lacking, these programs were the subjects of unsubstantiated claims of both success and criticism. MDRC's founders sought to establish a new kind of organization that would build a compelling body of evidence on whether social programs improve the lives of low-income individuals and families and are a cost-effective use of taxpayer dollars. MDRC has broadened its original focus on programs targeted to low-income youth and adults to include evaluations of a wide variety of programs' effects on children, families, inner city neighborhoods, education, childcare, housing, and health.

—*Jeffrey G. Tucker*

■■ MEANING

Meaning and action frame the interpretive approach to educational and social research and evaluation, within which *meaning* is understood to be constructed during the telling of narratives. Some basic elements of an interpretive framework for meaning in evaluation include the understanding that (a) the meaning of an action or event can be separated from that action or event itself; (b) the contextual elements of the field of meaning are crucial to understanding the meaning expressed by stakeholders; and (c) although meaning is an individual creation, it can be shared by a group or community. Therefore, an evaluator's approach to data gathering helps to frame the meaning stakeholders are able to articulate.

—*Leslie K. Goodyear*

Further Reading

Atkinson, R. (2002). The life story interview. In J. F. Gubrium & J. A. Holstein (Eds.), *The handbook of interview research* (pp. 121-140). Thousand Oaks, CA: Sage.

Smith, J. K. (1989). *The nature of social and educational inquiry: Empiricism versus interpretation.* Norwood, NJ: Ablex.

■■ MEANS-ENDS RELATIONS

Simplistically, *means* are processes, activities, ways of doing or being, and *ends* are the achievements, outcomes, states of being that result from means. Means and ends are sometimes also thought of as process and outcome, the more common manifestation in evaluation. In this context, there is a focus on the instrumental understanding of means-end relations. Particularly in realist approaches to evaluation, means-ends relations are key to determining when a program or process has an intended effect. In evaluation, there is concern over what takes precedence—the means or the ends or how to balance the two. Some evaluation approaches more naturally focus on means (for example, participatory, responsive, appreciative inquiry) and others focus on ends (for example, realist and experimental approaches), although both are relevant to all evaluation approaches. In the former case, the means can become the ends, but in the latter, the means cannot be ends in and of themselves.

Understanding means-end relations is necessary not only in the empirical scientific disciplines but is also a consideration in moral philosophy. Questions about the universality of means and ends has vexed moral philosophers for centuries and is an abiding topic in religious studies. The ubiquity of means-end relations is communicated through common discourse, such as "the means justify the ends," "the ends do not justify the means," and "a means to an end."

■■ MEASUREMENT

Measurement may be defined as the set of rules for transforming behaviors into categories or numbers. Constructing an instrument to measure a social science variable involves several steps, including conceptualizing the behaviors that operationally define the variable, drafting items that indicate the behaviors, administering draft items to try out samples, refining the instrument based on item analysis, and performing reliability and validity studies. These studies are necessary to ensure that scores on the instrument are consistent and have evidence of adequately representing a construct. Two theoretical approaches dominate the field of measurement: classical test theory and item response theory.

—*Joseph M. Petrosko*

Further Reading

Nunnally, J. C., & Bernstein, I. H. (1994). *Psychometric theory* (3rd ed.). New York: McGraw-Hill.

■■ MERIT

Merit is the absolute or relative quality of something, either overall or in regard to a particular criterion (see *Criteria*). To determine the merit of an evaluand in regard to a particular criterion, it is necessary to collect relevant performance data and to *explicitly ascribe value* to it; that is, to say how meritorious the evaluand is in that particular dimension. To determine the overall merit of the evaluand, a further step is required: synthesis of performances with multiple criteria (see *Synthesis*). Merit determination and synthesis are two of the core methodological tasks that distinguish evaluation from the collection and reporting of descriptive data for interpretation by others.

—*Jane Davidson*

■■ MERTENS, DONNA M.

(b. 1951, Spokane, Washington). Ph.D., M.S. Educational Psychology, University of Kentucky; B.A. Psychology, Thomas More College.

Mertens is Professor in the Department of Educational Foundations and Research at Gallaudet University. Her theoretical contribution to evaluation has centered on bringing the implications of the transformative paradigm to the evaluation community. The transformative paradigm places central importance on the lives and experiences of those who suffer oppression and discrimination, whatever the basis of that may be—sex, race or ethnicity, disability, sexual orientation, or socioeconomic status. Evaluators working within this paradigm are consciously aware of power differentials in the evaluation context, and they search for ways to ameliorate the effects of oppression and discrimination by linking their research activities to social action and wider questions of social inequity and social justice.

Many people contributed to broadening Merten's understanding of effective evaluation. Yvonna Lincoln and Egon Guba influenced her thinking about the importance of philosophical assumptions and paradigms in guiding evaluation practice. Patti Lather shaped the directions of her theorizing about the emancipatory paradigm and the potential contribution of feminist thinking in evaluation. Carole Truman, John Stanfield, Ricardo Millett, Rodney Hopson, and Carol Gill illuminated the intersections of race and ethnicity, gender, disability, and sexual orientation. Elizabeth Whitmore and Amy Wilson stretched her understandings of the transformative paradigm in international development work. Amy Szarkowski and Carolyn Williamson, two of Merten's Ph.D. students at Gallaudet University, brought the optimistic perspective to her theory of a transformative paradigm in the form of positive psychology and resilience theory, which they used as the theoretical bases for their dissertations. Michael Patton's emphasis on utilization of evaluation and the personal factor has influenced her thinking as well.

Mertens has served as a member of the American Evaluation Association's Board of Directors, as President in 1998 and as a board member. During that time, she addressed two major initiatives, one of which was the Building Diversity Initiative, a project funded by the W. K. Kellogg Foundation to increase the number of evaluators of color, as well as to improve the evaluation skills of all evaluators working in culturally diverse communities. She also served as the board liaison to the planning group that resulted in the founding of the International Organization for Cooperation in Evaluation. She has conducted many different evaluations, ranging from a national evaluation of court accessibility for deaf and hard of hearing people to the transformation of the nation's teacher preparation programs for teachers of the deaf to the effects of international development efforts for people who are deaf, blind, and mentally retarded in Egypt, Costa Rica, and Mexico.

She has authored, coauthored, edited, and coedited several books, including *Parents and Their Deaf Children: The Early Years* (with Kay Meadow Orlans and Marilyn Sass Lehrer), *Research and Inequality* (with Carole Truman and Beth Humphries as coeditors), *Research Methods in Education and Psychology: Integrating Diversity;* and *Research Methods in Special Education* (with John McLaughlin), as well as journal articles published in the *American Journal of Evaluation, American Annals of the Deaf,* and *Educational Evaluation and Policy Analysis.*

■ META-ANALYSIS

Gene V Glass coined the term *meta-analysis* in his 1976 presidential address to the American Educational Research Association. Glass bemoaned the state of educational research, and scientific and evaluative enterprises more generally, left fragmentary and incoherent through failure to integrate conclusions across the burgeoning number of studies and disciplinary specialties. What if, he asked, we applied statistical analysis to groups of studies just as researchers and evaluators statistically analyze groups of humans? What if we could compare study conclusions on a common metric, determine not only the likelihood but also the strength of an intervention's effects, and test whether different intervention conditions influence effectiveness? Glass argued that conventional statistical techniques could be used to create a higher order analysis *beyond* ("meta") the analysis presented by primary researchers and evaluators.

By his own admission, Glass was not the first to think of statistically integrating findings from independent studies. Examples of systematic reviews in medicine, agriculture, and the physical sciences can be drawn from the early 20th century. Statistical research integration did not receive systematic or widespread attention, however, until Glass's articulation. Meta-analysis is now a commonplace in many disciplines and continues to grow in the scope and frequency of its application.

In practice, meta-analysis has significant limitations. Meta-analysis integrates findings only from studies that yield quantitative results. Research and evaluation relying on narrative, interpreted observation, and explorations of personal meaning making and felt experience do not easily yield to statistical integration and are often excluded. Meta-analyses require collections of rough replications, investigations of the same question using approximately the same "quantitative" research method. When a researcher uses an especially sophisticated investigatory strategy or looks at a phenomenon from an unconventional angle, that study may be excluded from meta-analysis even if it yields important insight. Meta-analysis depends on the quality of the research as reported in available documentation. If a field is plagued with poor research designs or fails to report information relevant to an important issue, meta-analysis often cannot repair these deficiencies. Also, the kinds of insights that meta-analysis yields are predominantly correlational; meta-analysis can detect relations between study conditions and study outcomes, but the analyst can only speculate about the causes of these relations.

However, society could derive enormous benefits from meta-analysis. Meta-analysis can estimate the central tendency of study outcomes and test whether outcome variations fit a pattern, no mean feat in the face of prodigious research productivity. Detection of patterns among study outcomes should, on the one hand, save funding agencies and researchers from investing in yet more replications in the same area and, on the other hand, identify issues deserving further investigation. Also, meta-analysis can estimate the expected strength of variables' effects or relationships under specifiable conditions. In matters of policy and evaluation, estimating the relative efficacy of different interventions can provide important data in decision making. In short, meta-analysis could make the research enterprise more efficient and intervention and evaluation more effective.

Meta-analysis typically proceeds through four stages: searching for and selecting relevant studies, coding study features, translating study outcomes to a common metric, and analyzing and interpreting relations between study features and outcomes. Each stage entails significant decisions by the meta-analyst that make it unlikely that any two meta-analyses on the same issue will exactly correspond in their conclusions.

The question or problem the meta-analyst seeks to address frames search and selection strategies applied to primary studies. How the initiating question is framed, and which constructs and operationalizations are presumed relevant to the question, make an enormous impact on which studies will be investigated. Further, meta-analysts may differ about criteria for study conclusion. Some may apply stringent standards on research quality, some may include only studies with a particular research design or investigate subjects with particular characteristics, others may be comprehensive and inclusive.

Similarly, the central focus of the meta-analysis greatly influences which study features will be coded. Each coded study feature represents a hypothesis to be tested: Does feature X explain variance in the findings among these studies? The initiating questions of the review filter ideas for these hypotheses, drawn from prior reviews and meta-analyses, theoretical frameworks, public or academic debates, issues of practice, and concerns for research quality. The meta-analyst determines how each factor is to be coded (e.g., categories of a variable, scales of measure), taking into account the kinds of information made available in the study reports themselves. Outcomes are translated into some measure of effect size, usually the standardized difference between comparative means or the correlation coefficient. These translations are not always straightforward; complex designs or problematic reports can complicate effect size calculation and cause disagreement about how to best represent a study's findings.

Currently, most meta-analysts assess effect sizes for homogeneity, comparing the variance among effect sizes to the expected variation estimated from sampling error within the studies. Essentially, effect sizes are subjected to analyses of variance that are weighted by sampling error; studies with larger samples are given greater weight because their findings are presumed to be more reliable. However, such weighted analyses are not always superior to alternatives. A few large-sample studies could overwhelm findings from a larger number of small studies, even though the larger studies are not necessarily superior to smaller studies in quality. When sample sizes vary widely among studies or when an analyst determines that larger and smaller studies should have equally important contributions to an overall conclusion, weighted analyses would not be recommended. Unweighted statistics, nonparametric tests, and visualization strategies are viable alternatives to analyses weighted by sampling error.

The burgeoning research literature has made systematic research integration an imperative, but the future of meta-analysis is difficult to predict. Some suggest that meta-analysis would no longer be needed if there were better mechanisms with which researchers could directly share and coordinate their original data. Others imagine a two-tier research society, differentiating the data collectors from the research synthesizers. Some insist on the universal applicability of weighted tests of homogeneity; others press for more precision from meta-analytic estimates. Still others argue for a mixed review process that combines statistical with narrative analysis, differential weighting of "best" evidence, and inclusion of interpretive research forms. Given the many ways in which human judgment and the qualities of research literature operate against consistency and precision, it is probably best to think of meta-analysis as an enormously useful exploratory tool for detecting patterns in research findings and suggesting new directions for evaluation, research, theory, and policy.

—*Robert L. Bangert-Drowns*

Further Reading

Bangert-Drowns, R. L. (1986). A review of developments in meta-analytic method. *Psychological Bulletin, 99,* 388-399.

Bangert-Drowns, R. L., & Wells-Parker, B. (2001). Meta-analysis without the mantra: A reply to Wilson and weighted analysis. *Addiction, 96,* 981-985.

Glass, G. V, McGaw, B., & Smith, M. L. (1981). *Meta-analysis in social research.* Beverly Hills, CA: Sage.

Hedges, L. V., & Olkin, I. (1985). *Statistical methods for meta-analysis.* San Diego, CA: Academic Press.

▊ METAEVALUATION

Metaevaluation is the evaluation of evaluations (and of evaluators). It must not be confused with meta-analysis, which is a particular and relatively recent development in research integration; namely, the synthesis of multiple research studies of the same phenomenon, studies that may or may not be evaluative, into an overall conclusion. Meta-analyses in the social sciences are typically syntheses of merely empirical studies, not evaluative studies. The literature review that is often part of an evaluation project will often conclude with a meta-analysis that has an evaluative conclusion because it is integrating a number of evaluative studies; however, that is not, as such, a metaevaluation but merely a synthesis of evaluations. The key element in metaevaluation (here, MEV) is that it *evaluates* the evaluations to which it refers; it does not merely summarize them. Of course, a review of prior evaluations might also be evaluative about them as well as about the evaluands to which they refer, in which case it would be both a meta-analysis and a MEV.

The importance of MEV arises particularly from two implications of its present incarnation. On the one hand, it is ethically and symbolically crucial because it shows that evaluation is a reflexive (self-referent) subject and hence that the evaluator is not above being evaluated—what's sauce for the goose is sauce for the gander. This is often reassuring to those being evaluated, but it is not a mere therapeutic gesture: The metaevaluation should be incorporated into serious evaluations because it shows a commitment to self-improvement, perhaps even a touch of humility, nearly always well-justified in a youthful discipline such as evaluation. This feature is reminiscent of the requirement in psychoanalytic certification that analysts themselves be psychoanalyzed, a requirement that shows that psychoanalysis is also a self-referent discipline. Although one might argue that the general professional imperative is to ensure that one is regularly evaluated by someone else with the required skills, for evaluators this means there is an obligation to ensure that one's work is, at least from time to time, subject to MEV.

The second key point about MEV stems from the fact that, loosely speaking, MEV is a reflection of the general scientific commitment to independent confirmation of one's conclusions. It has by now been developed to a level where it can provide a very sophisticated check on the validity of the evaluation under examination. There are a number of significantly different ways to do MEV, and doing more than one is rarely redundant. The simplest consists of replication of the original study and its methodology followed by critical comparison of the results from the two efforts. This is the straight confirmation approach to MEV. An approach that is somewhat more powerful involves using a different methodology to evaluate the same evaluand; this reflects part of what is meant by triangulation in the usual discussions of scientific methodology. Both those approaches involve a cost that is likely to be comparable to the cost of the original study. There are other approaches that, although much less expensive, are still powerful and often fruitful: They focus on design critique. The usual genesis of these is from some standard set of requirements that have been proposed as necessary elements in a good evaluation design. One then reviews an evaluation by comparing it to this list. The most common of these approaches to MEV involves applying the Program Evaluation Standards to the evaluation. A detailed guide to using this approach for MEV has been developed by Dan Stufflebeam and is available on the checklist Web site (http://www.wmich.edu/evalctr/checklists/checklistmenu.htm). Another approach uses Scriven's Key Evaluation Checklist as the template for judging an evaluation: This checklist can be found at the same site. A special use of this kind of MEV is its use by the original evaluator as a way to review his or her own work in the draft stage. Obviously, evaluators cannot do a full-scale confirmation or triangulation study in the available time or resource framework, but they can run it through a comparison with one of these general-purpose checklists. If the one used in the MEV is not the one used in the original design, the evaluator gains a degree of triangulation from this procedure. The General Accounting Office has also developed its own checklist for doing MEVs.

Taking the design critique approach a step toward further specificity—that is, toward checking content or component coverage—one can often use subject-specific checklists as templates for MEV. Again, this will introduce an element of triangulation if the checklists were not the ones on which the original design was based. This is easiest to do in an area such as product evaluation, where, for example, a number of well-researched but different checklists for evaluating common items such as computers, cars, or houses are available, but it can also be applied in personnel and performance (testing) evaluation. In program evaluation, where one might hope to apply it to programs such as addiction-termination programs, the differences in the underlying theories may make the resulting checklists too different to work well together. That problem also shows up in program evaluation, even at the more general design critique level, when deep theoretical splits emerge, as has, for example, occurred recently over what is to count as a satisfactory proof of causation.

The simplest of all approaches to MEV involves a commitment to error identification and correction that shows up in the practice of showing final drafts of evaluation reports to those evaluated or directly implicated in the evaluation. To make this a serious commitment, one needs to guarantee that either what are perceived as errors will be corrected to the satisfaction of the evaluee or the complaint will be appended to the final report. However, there has to be some quid pro quo about this: To have this opportunity, the evaluee must agree not to appeal against the report in other ways until it has been submitted under the conditions just described. Otherwise, boards of trustees find themselves swamped by complaints from fundees about reports they have not yet seen, which is likely to make them very unhappy.

—*Michael Scriven*

Further Reading

House, E. R., Glass, G. V, McLean, L. D., & Walker, D. F. (1978). No simple answer: Critique of the follow-through evaluation. *Harvard Education Review, 48,* 128-160.

Scriven, M. (1969). An introduction to meta-evaluation. *Educational Product Report, 2,* 36-38.

▦ METAPHOR

Evaluators acknowledge the importance of the language embedded in evaluation practice and the power of language in conveying meaning about the social complexities found in evaluations. By examining the implicit language in evaluation practices, *metaphors* can reveal the power of language in shaping the realities communicated through evaluation reporting. Illuminating the metaphoric language in evaluations can serve an educative function.

"Metaphor is, at its simplest, a way of proceeding from the known to the unknown. It is a way of cognition in which the identifying qualities of one thing are transferred in an instantaneous, almost unconscious, flash of insight to some other thing that is, by remoteness or complexity, unknown to us" (Nisbet, 1969, p. 4). Metaphors are pervasive in our communication. They are a fundamental structure in our everyday thoughts and actions. "Metaphors draw attention to the mental tools we use in representation" (Radnofsky, 1996, p.387). We represent our world symbolically

through the selection of these word images. Often unconscious, metaphors can be considered linguistic tricksters. If we systematically link our metaphorical expressions to metaphorical constructs, we can understand the unconscious nature of activities.

Bringing to the surface the terminology embedded in the evaluations of programs helps us to think about the programs and the evaluations independently of what they are supposed to be. Ernest House has written about how evaluations can metaphorically represent social service delivery as industrial production. "Program elements are defined as *time, costs, procedures,* or *product. A monitoring evaluation* is an assessment of whether the program conforms to the design and reaches the target" (House, 1986, p. 34).

The language, symbols, metaphors, and images projected in evaluative representations are shaped by and will shape thinking about evaluands. If evaluators seek to become better in practice and to make better the world in which they live, then it is useful to look with a critical lens at the levels of meaning projected in evaluative representations. For example, if evaluators talk about inputs and outcomes and units and measurements and then juxtapose that with language found in programs (e.g., recipients, contracts, specialists, treatments), a picture devoid of personable images can be created. What that means to the people represented in evaluation reports is that they can become unconsciously objectified in ways that may serve to create or maintain a devalued social status, such as a commodity, to the program and evaluation industries.

Metaphors shape language and language shapes discourse. Looking at the metaphors embedded in evaluative representations can assist evaluators in thinking and communicating differently about evaluation practice. Critical reflection about the metaphoric language in evaluation practice creates the potential to think more broadly about the function of evaluation in our society. Making conscious the meanings of metaphors in evaluation practice can help to promote a larger agenda for the greater social good.

—*Cheryl MacNeil*

Further Reading

House, E. R. (1986). How we think about evaluation. In E. R. House (Ed.), *New directions in educational evaluation.* Philadelphia, PA: Falmer.

Kaminsky, A. (2000). Beyond the literal: Metaphors and why they matter. In R. K. Hopson (Ed.), How and why language matters in evaluation. *New Directions for Evaluation, 86,* 69-80.

Lakoff, G., & Johnson, M. (1980). *Metaphors we live by.* Chicago: University of Chicago Press.

Nisbet, R. A. (1969). *Social change and history: Aspects of the Western theory of development.* London: Oxford University Press.

Radnofsky, M. L. (1996). Qualitative models: Visually representing complex data in an image/text balance. *Qualitative Inquiry, 2,* 385-408.

▪▪ MILLETT, RICARDO A.

(b. 1945, Panama City, Florida). Ph.D., M.S.W. Social Planning and Research, B.A. Economics, Brandeis University.

Millett is President of the Woods Fund of Chicago, a grant-making foundation whose goal is to increase opportunities for less advantaged people and communities in the metropolitan area, including the opportunity to contribute to decisions affecting them. He is a veteran foundation professional with deep experience and expertise in the areas of foundation performance evaluation and strategic planning. Previously, he was Director of Evaluation at the W. K. Kellogg Foundation, Senior Vice President of Planning and Resource management for the United Way of Massachusetts Bay, Deputy Associate Commissioner of the Department of Social Services for Massachusetts, and Senior Analyst at Abt Associates. He has served as Director for Neighborhood Housing and Development for the Boston Redevelopment Authority, Executive Director of Roxbury Multi-service Center, Associate Professor of Research and Evaluation at Atlanta University, and Director of the Martin Luther King Center at Boston University.

Throughout his career, Millett has worked to achieve social and economic justice for all people. He has focused on making the tools of evaluation more relevant, useful, and user-friendly to nonprofits and foundations. His efforts are apparent in a number of manuals he authored while at the Kellogg Foundation, perhaps most especially his work on cluster evaluation. He has actively supported initiatives to build pipelines for evaluators of color as well as providing support for the development of international evaluation associations.

His work has been influenced by Michael Q. Patton, Ernest R. House, Paulo Freire, and Berger and Luckman's seminal text *The Social Construction of Reality.*

Millett is on the Board of Directors of the Center for Effective Philanthropy. For his contributions to evaluation, he was awarded the American Evaluation Association's Myrdal Award in 2001 and the Michigan Evaluation Association Award in 2002.

▪▪ MINORITY ISSUES IN EVALUATION

Evaluative judgments are, by their nature, inextricably bound up with culture and context. Thus, where there is sociocultural diversity, there very likely is some diversity in the expected and preferred evaluative processes and practices that undergird judgments of merit, worth, value, quality, significance, and congruence. Maximizing accuracy, appropriateness, respect, and excellence calls for openness to the decentering realities and complexities of difference and diversity. The presumption of similarity and single reality theories often leads evaluators—as well as other practitioners—to overlook, if not explicitly dismiss, such diversity as extraneous nuisance variation and noise.

When not dismissible in such oversimplifying ways, socioculturally grounded differences are often defined as problematic targets for amelioration and correction. Difference tends to be almost automatically interpreted as deficient and deviant. It is not surprising, then, that patterns of sociocultural diversity have become intimately intertwined with systemic processes of asymmetric power relations and privilege. This has resulted in systematic patterns of difference in access, resource opportunities, and life chances associated with major diversity markers such as race and ethnicity.

Such patterns are often related to and exacerbated by minority status. Minority—versus majority—status, and related issues, may revolve around several dimensions:

- *Sociodemographic representation.* Who is physically present (structural diversity)?
- *Sociopolitical voice and power.* Who defines, who determines, who decides?
- *Socioeconomic access and opportunity.* Who has control over and benefits from valued material resources and assets?
- *Sociocultural presence.* Whose ways of being, doing, thinking, knowing, and engaging define the "mainstream" rules, roles, and normative expectations (the disposition of social mirrors and windows)?

In general, minority issues in the evaluation spotlight involve considerations related to underrepresented or unrepresented persons, perspectives, concerns, and so on that have an impact on accuracy, value, validity, or utility. Not attending to these issues often results in myopic inaccuracies, truncated understandings, and twisted representations, especially when such differences are associated with minority status that is treated as a deviant or extraneous variation.

The AEA Guiding Principles spotlight the need to attend mindfully and proactively to the full spectrum of diversity issues as a necessary prerequisite for ethical practice. This is particularly critical when diversity is associated with underrepresented "minority" persons, positions, and views. Guiding Principles D and E are especially relevant. Guiding Principle D, respect for people—with its focus on respecting "security, dignity and self-worth"—requires empathic competencies if respect is to be offered in ways that are perceived and received as respectful. To discern and make that judgment accurately, one needs to be able to engage in cognitive and affective frame shifting and probably also behavioral code switching—notably, standing and sitting in another's perspective. Such skills constitute the core infrastructure for intercultural and multicultural competencies. Guiding Principle E, responsibilities for general and public welfare, is a logical follow-up to Principle D: "Evaluators articulate and take into account the diversity of interests and values that may be related to the general and public welfare." This ethical principle challenges evaluators to know the spectrum of interests and perspectives as they attend to the "full range of stakeholders."

To embrace these principles effectively, evaluators need refined awareness of and openness to diversity as well as an understanding of how to engage such diversity authentically. Presumed similarity through sociocultural invisibility—regardless of intent—is problematic. As the default condition for many, that ethnocentric presumption poorly prepares evaluators to honor these guiding principles in actual practice. What ultimately matters is not personal intent but rather interpersonal impact. To what extent do the persons whom evaluators engage discern and feel that the evaluative processes, protocols, practices, and products used are congruent with, are responsive to, and accurately reflect their internal sociocultural structures and rhythms (experiential validity)? This is a critical question that deserves to be asked and substantively answered.

Within the American Evaluation Association, the first organized champion for these issues was the Minority Issues in Evaluation Topical Interest Group (MIE-TIG), which has since been joined by several other TIGs that spotlight evaluation issues related to sexual orientation, disability, special needs populations, and so on. The MIE-TIG was founded in 1987 by Anna Madison and then–AEA President Bob Covert, and it continues to advance a two-pronged agenda:

1. *Expanding the pipeline and access agenda.* Increase the racial and ethnic diversity among evaluation professionals.

2. *Capacity-building agenda.* Increase and deepen intercultural and multicultural competencies within the evaluation profession: notably, enhanced knowledge and skills for more effective work within diverse communities.

The second agenda item has relevance for all evaluators who work with diverse stakeholders and within diverse communities. This capacity-building agenda does not presuppose or privilege any one or only one particular evaluative approach. Instead, it spotlights the beginning-to-end importance of substantively incorporating and engaging diversity concerns and issues—from conceptualization and design through implementation, meaning-making interpretation, and meaning-sharing dissemination.

In 2000, the MIE-TIG's long-standing dual agenda was expanded to a broad AEA organizational development agenda. This expansion was prompted by outreach from the Kellogg Foundation via Evaluation Director Ricardo Millett. The invited proposal development process was initially spearheaded by three AEA board members: Charles Thomas, Donna Mertens, and David Chavis. In 2000, the AEA Board of Directors received the Building Diversity Initiative grant for a comprehensive planning and infrastructure-development process that was subcontracted to the Association for the Study and Development of Community (see the MIE-TIG's Web site for more information and downloadable copies of products: http://www.obsidcomm.com/aea/). AEA continues its efforts to breathe life into this comprehensive diversity plan.

Minority issues in evaluation invites and challenges the evaluation profession to expand its line of sight and the capacities of its practitioners to more authentically perceive and receive the voices, vantage points, and experiences of the full spectrum of stakeholders. Embarking on this learning and reflective-practice journey requires mindful, "light-on-one's-feet" responsiveness to stand inside the internal contours and rhythms of that which one seeks to evaluate. More specifically, it demands proactively discerning and tapping into diverse socially patterned ways of thinking, knowing, being, doing, engaging, and so on to maximize what Karen Kirkhart calls "multicultural validity."

Walking pathways toward culturally competent evaluation demands a decentering capacity to stand beside respectfully—if not inside—given one's recognition of the gifts, as well as the limits, of one's own repertoire. More specifically, it calls on evaluators to engage the self as a pivotal instrument through regularly refining awareness of one's blank spots (know that you do not know) and blindspots (not knowing that you do not know), as well as one's conscious competencies and unconscious competencies ("autopilot"). Blindspots often are a source of major sociocultural blunders that undermine responsiveness, congruence, relevance, and thus excellence in evaluation design, development, and delivery. Moving from periphery to center, minority issues in evaluation are not simply optional or minor opinions and views but rather fundamental ethical prerequisites for excellence in evaluation processes, protocols, practices, and products.

—*Hazel Symonette*

▉ MISUSE OF EVALUATIONS

Evaluation processes and findings can be misrepresented and misused. The profession recognizes a critical distinction between *misevaluation,* in which an evaluator performs poorly or fails to adhere to standards and principles, and *misuse,* in which users manipulate the evaluation in ways that distort the findings or corrupt the inquiry.

The profession has become increasingly concerned about problems of misuse, whether the source be politics, asking the wrong questions, pressures on internal evaluators to present only positive findings, petty self-interest, or ideology. Misuse, like use, is ultimately situational. Consider, for example, an illustrative case. An administrator blatantly quashes several negative evaluation reports to prevent the results from reaching the general public. On the surface, such an action appears to be a prime case of misutilization. Now consider the same action (i.e., suppressing negative findings) in a situation in which the reports were invalid due to poor data collection. Thus misutilization in one situation may be conceived of as appropriate nonuse in another. Intentional nonuse of poorly conducted studies can be viewed as appropriate and responsible. Here are some premises with regard to misuse:

1. Misuse is not at the opposite end of a continuum from use. Two dimensions are needed to capture the complexities of real-world practice. One dimension is a continuum from nonuse to use. A second is a continuum from nonuse to misuse. Studying or avoiding misuse is quite different from studying or facilitating use.

2. Having conceptualized two separate dimensions, it is possible to explore the relationship between them. Consider the following proposition: As use increases, misuse will also increase. When people ignore evaluations, they ignore their potential uses as well as abuses. As evaluators successfully focus greater attention on evaluation data and increase actual use, there may be a corresponding increase in abuse, often within the same evaluation experience. Donald T. Campbell formulated a discouraging law that the more any social indicator is used for social decision making, the greater the corruption pressures on it will be.

3. Misuse can be either intentional or unintentional. Unintentional misuse can be corrected through the processes aimed at increasing appropriate and proper use. Intentional misuse is an entirely different matter that invites active intervention to correct whatever has been abused, whether the evaluation process or findings. As with most problems, correcting misuse is more expensive than preventing it in the first place.

4. Working with multiple users who understand and value an evaluation is one of the best preventives against misuse. Allies in use are allies against misuse. Indeed, misuse can be mitigated by working to have intended users take so much ownership of the evaluation that they become the champions of appropriate use, the guardians against misuse, and the defenders of the evaluation's credibility when misuse occurs.

5. Policing misuse is sometimes beyond the evaluator's control, but to the extent possible and realistic, professional evaluators have a responsibility to monitor, expose, and prevent misuse.

—Michael Quinn Patton

Further Reading

Alkin, M., & Coyle, K. (1988). Thoughts on evaluation misutilization. *Studies in Educational Evaluation, 14,* 331-340.

Patton, M. Q. (1997). *Utilization-focused evaluation.* Thousand Oaks, CA: Sage.

■■ MIXED METHODS

Mixed-method evaluation involves the planned use of two or more different kinds of empirical designs or data gathering and analysis tools in the same study or project. A substantial amount of contemporary evaluation practice routinely involves a variety of different kinds of methods—structured and unstructured, quantitative and qualitative, standardized and contextually responsive. Evaluators routinely use a variety of methods because the field now accepts the legitimacy of various methodological traditions and because diverse methods enable better understanding of the complex, multifaceted, real-world social phenomena evaluators aim to understand. What distinguishes mixed-method evaluation is thus the *intentional* or *planned* use of diverse methods for particular mixed-method purposes using particular mixed-method designs.

Methods are intentionally mixed in evaluation for purposes of (a) triangulation, or enhancing the validity or credibility of evaluation findings through results from the different methods that converge and agree, one with the other; (b) development, or using the results of one method to help develop the sample or instrumentation for another method; (c) complementarity, or extending the comprehensiveness of evaluation findings through results from different methods that broaden and deepen the understandings reached; (d) initiation, or generating new insights in evaluation findings through results from the different methods that diverge and thus call for reconciliation via further analysis, reframing, or some other shift in perspective; and (e) value diversity, or incorporating a wider diversity of values and thus greater consciousness about the value dimensions of evaluation through the use of different methods that themselves advance different values. Because practice is characteristically more complex than theory, many mixed-method evaluation studies incorporate two or more of these mixed-method purposes.

Beyond the intentional identification of purpose, mixed-method evaluation involves considered attention to the philosophical assumptions that underlie or accompany the use of social scientific methods. These assumptions—as captured in philosophical paradigms, frameworks, or mental models—pertain most importantly to views of the social world (for example, realism or constructionism), perspectives regarding the nature of social knowledge (for example, objective or value laden), and positions regarding what is most important to know (for example, generalizable causal relationships or contextual meaningfulness). The controversial issues here are, (a) When evaluators mix methods, are they also mixing philosophical assumptions? and (b) Should they? There are currently three primary stances on this issue. First, proponents of aparadigmatic stances argue that philosophical assumptions are useful conceptual tools, but they should not drive practice decisions. Rather, practical decisions about evaluation design and method should be steered by the demands of the context or by the constructs and parameters of the relevant substantive or program theory. So, within this stance, paradigms are not really relevant to mixed-method (or any other kind of evaluation) practice. Second, proponents of a dialectical stance argue in favor of intentionally mixing philosophical assumptions when mixing methods. From this perspective, philosophical assumptions do and should meaningfully influence practice decisions. Because all sets of philosophical assumptions (all paradigms or mental models) are partial and limited, more comprehensive and insightful mixes are attained via the intentional inclusion of more than one methodological tradition or framework. In this dialectical perspective, possible tensions and dissonance from different paradigmatic assumptions are welcomed as generative. Third, proponents of pragmatic stances advance an alternative, inclusive paradigm or philosophical framework within which multiple assumptions and diverse methods can comfortably reside. In this third stance, as in the first, differences in paradigmatic traditions are de-emphasized and thereby not considered either particularly beneficial or problematic in mixed-method work. Various forms of contemporary realism and pragmatism are the most popular alternative frameworks advanced within this pragmatic perspective.

Mixed-method designs differ along several key dimensions. One is whether the methods are integrated throughout the study or rather kept separate until the end, at which point conclusions and inferences are compared or connected. A second is whether the different methods involved are considered of relatively equal importance and weight or whether one methodology is dominant and the other less dominant. Third, different methods can be implemented concurrently or sequentially. Additional design dimensions involve the mixing of methods within a single study or across studies, mixing within an evaluation team or a single evaluator, and the nature and degree of the differences in the methods used (for example, in known biases).

Some decisions about mixed-method designs are inherent in prior decisions about purpose and paradigmatic stance. For example, a triangulation purpose requires concurrent implementation of different methods to assess a given phenomenon, and a development purpose involves, by definition, sequenced methods. Both purposes and designs are best conducted within an aparadigmatic or pragmatic philosophical stance because these enable consistent conceptualization of the phenomena being studied, and such consistency is required for convergence.

Planning a mixed-method evaluation involves an iterative negotiation of macro- and microdesign lenses, best accomplished by starting with the various constructs or variables to be assessed in an evaluation. For example, an evaluation of a substance abuse prevention program for youth includes both process and outcome questions. One key outcome to be assessed is substance abuse behavior, both in the present and the future. The evaluator envisions using both a standardized questionnaire and an innovative role-play method to assess this outcome, with the methods equally weighted and implemented concurrently and their analysis highly integrated, under a mixed-method purpose of initiation and a dialectical stance on paradigms. The evaluator then repeats this design process for the next construct to be assessed, making adjustments in the mixed-method plans for the first construct as necessary. Thus it proceeds, balancing microplans for each construct with a coherent and sensible overall plan.

More than any other applied social scientists, evaluators *are* mixed methodologists. Now that the field of mixed methodology includes some robust and useful ideas about purpose, paradigms, and design, evaluators can be more thoughtful mixed methodologists and thereby enhance the quality and potential impact of their work.

—*Jennifer C. Greene*

Further Reading

Greene, J. C., & Caracelli, V. J. (Eds.). (1997). Advances in mixed-method evaluation: The challenges and benefits of integrating diverse paradigms. *New Directions for Evaluation, 74.*

Tashakkori, A., & Teddlie, C. (Eds.). (2003). *Handbook of mixed methods in social and behavioral research.* Thousand Oaks, CA: Sage.

◼◼ MODELS OF EVALUATION

Different approaches to evaluation, whether the differences are based on methodology, epistemology, or ontology, are typically subsumed under the phrase *models of evaluation.* It is the way in which differences in evaluation theory and practice can be acknowledged and commonalities and differences in approaches are marked.

CHARTING EVALUATION MODELS

There has been a proliferation of attempts to categorize models of evaluation, usually in charts that provide a comparison on a common set of characteristics. These charts name models and provide detail on some or all of the following:

- Purpose
- Assumptions
- How the evaluation is organized
- Questions asked
- Strengths and weaknesses
- Intended users
- Primary methodology
- Proponents of the model
- Epistemology
- Ethics

In 1974, Robert Stake prepared a chart with nine approaches to educational evaluation, a fugitive document that nonetheless provided the basis for many categorization schemes to follow. Ernie House analyzed many of these evaluation models, based on their epistemological and ethical premises, in an article that appeared first in 1978 in the *Educational Researcher,* again in his book *Evaluating With Validity* in 1980, and later in the first edition of *Evaluation Models* in 1983. Indeed, most evaluation textbook authors feel compelled to include some version of an evaluation models chart. A recent overview of models in this vein is Dan Stufflebeam's *New Directions for Evaluation* issue "Evaluation Models," published in 2001. In this monograph, he identifies 22 evaluation models categorized into four groups, as follows:

I. Pseudoevaluation
   A. Public relations–inspired studies
   B. Politically controlled studies

II. Quasievaluation studies
   A. Objectives-based studies
   B. Accountability
   C. Objective-testing programs
   D. Outcome evaluation (value-added assessment)
   E. Performance testing
   F. Experimental studies
   G. Management information systems
   H. Benefit-cost analysis
   I. Clarification hearing
   J. Case study
   K. Criticism and connoisseurship
   L. Program-theory based
   M. Mixed-methods studies

III. Improvement or accountability oriented
   A. Decision oriented
   B. Consumer oriented
   C. Accreditation or certification

IV. Social agenda or advocacy
   A. Client centered or responsive
   B. Constructivist
   C. Deliberative democratic
   D. Utilization focused

Even a comprehensive analysis of the variation in how we think about and do evaluation, such as Stufflebeam provides, immediately falls short because using this strategy is necessarily incomplete. The most obvious way in which any chart is incomplete is in what it includes and excludes. Why, for example, would one include pseudoevaluation in an analysis of models of evaluation? Why exclude participatory approaches or realist evaluation? The point here is not to critique Stufflebeam's work but to illustrate that enumerating and categorizing evaluation models is itself a theoretical task based on a priori assumptions about the nature of models and their definitions.

This charting of evaluation models has a pragmatic purpose as well. Delineating the attributes of different approaches to evaluation provides evaluation practitioners with the detail to make choices. Models as described in these charts, even though there will be inevitable disagreement about some elements of the charting, provide the practitioner with direction regarding the parameters, purpose, and processes within any evaluation approach. Presumably one can then make informed choices about how to do evaluation within a particular local context.

MINING EVALUATION MODELS

Perhaps the best extant work that digs beneath the surface characterization of differences and similarities in evaluation theory and practice is the work of Shadish, Cook, and Leviton in *Foundations of Program Evaluation*. In this work, the authors develop a stage theory of evaluation theory. To do this, they focus on what they perceive to be key and foundational shifts in the conceptualization of evaluation by "sampling from theoretical writings in the field," rather than using the more encyclopedic charting approach. This analysis samples the works of Michael Scriven, Donald Campbell, Carol Weiss, Joseph Wholey, Robert Stake, Lee Cronbach, and Peter Rossi. The focus is the theory of evaluation, and characterizations of evaluation approaches are thus organized around assumptions about (a) social programming, (b) knowledge construction, (c) valuing, (d) knowledge use, and (e) evaluation practice or methods. This work provides one of the first steps toward the development of a coherent theory of evaluation, which concludes the book.

Although they provide a less fully developed scheme, Guba and Lincoln use a similar strategy in *Fourth Generation Evaluation* by characterizing the evaluation models as generational (measurement, description, judgment), leading up to a fourth generation of evaluation (responsive constructivist).

Christina Christie's work on the practice-theory relationship in evaluation also mines the models of evaluation more deeply than the charting strategies of categorization. In the *New Directions for Evaluation* issue "The Practice-Theory Relationship in Evaluation," she surveys eight evaluation theorists (Boruch, Eisner, House, Fetterman, Chen, Patton, Cousins, and Stufflebeam) who vary in perspective on methods, values, and use. The comparison among them then focuses on a number of dimensions, seeking the areas in which these approaches are similar and different. This analysis suggests that the categorizations of the charting strategy are not always confirmed (for example, there are important nuanced differences between Fetterman's empowerment evaluation and House's deliberative democratic evaluation).

BUILDING A THEORY OF EVALUATION FROM MODELS OF EVALUATION

These approaches to analyzing evaluation models that mine the models to build a general theory of evaluation demonstrate a natural growth in the discipline. On the one hand, this approach encourages dialogue about what constitutes good evaluation. For example, Stufflebeam concludes his *New Directions for Evaluation* monograph by examining his 22 models' compliance with the Program Evaluation Standards; he identifies 9 that make the grade, so to speak. Guba and Lincoln's work has always been motivated by understanding what it means to formulate better evaluation theory and practice. This focus on models of evaluations has also contributed to improved practice in more pragmatic ways. In some senses, the practice of evaluation, albeit with implicit theoretical notions, preceded without the development of a theory of evaluation. Also, much of the charting of models early in the formalization of evaluation as a discipline (or "transdiscipline," as Scriven refers to it) was groundwork for the current theory-building focus. Of course, this is not the only path to the development of a theory of evaluation.

Further Reading

Christie, C. C. (Ed.). (2003). The practice-theory relationship in evaluation. *New Directions for Evaluation, 97.*

House, E. R. (1980). *Evaluating with validity.* Beverly Hills, CA: Sage.

Stufflebeam, D. L. (2001). Evaluation models. *New Directions for Evaluation, 89.*

Stufflebeam, D. L., Madaus, G. F., & Kellaghan, T. (2000). *Evaluation models* (Rev. ed.). Boston: Kluwer.

■■ MODUS OPERANDI

Michael Scriven introduced this term to evaluation. *Modus operandi* refers to the identification of the cause of a certain effect by means of a detailed analysis of the preceding chain of events and the ambient conditions of those events. The term is often used in police work, abbreviated "MO," referring to the particular way in which a certain criminal performs criminal acts.

MONITORING. *See* INSPECTION, PARTICIPATORY MONITORING AND EVALUATION, PERFORMANCE-BASED MONITORING

■■ MOOS, RUDOLF H.

(b. 1934, Berlin, Germany). Ph.D. Psychology, B.A. (Honors) Psychology, University of California, Berkeley; Postdoctoral Fellowship, Biobehavioral Sciences Training Program, University of California School of Medicine, San Francisco.

Moos is Professor in the Department of Psychiatry and Behavioral Sciences at Stanford University and Senior Research Career Scientist at the Palo Alto Veterans Affairs (VA) Hospital. He is Emeritus Director of the Center for Health Care Evaluation at the Palo Alto VA and Stanford University Medical Centers. Previously at the Palo Alto VA, he was Director of the Program Evaluation and Resource Center and Codirector for Health Services Research of the Cooperative Studies Program Coordinating Center.

Moos has made numerous contributions to the theory and methods of the field of community psychology. He has identified and conceptualized key factors in diverse social environments and contributed to the development of theory and methods in research on stress and coping. Specifically, he developed methods to identify psychosocial risk factors associated with psychiatric and substance abuse disorders. He developed a set of 10 Social Climate Scales to operationalize and measure underlying risk factors in diverse social environments. These scales have been translated into more than 25 languages and are widely used in many hospital and community-based treatment programs. His interest in the relationship between social resources and stressors led him to develop the Life Stressors and Social Resources Inventory and the Coping Responses Inventory. These inventories are widely used to assess the coping strategies individuals use to manage personal crises.

Moos serves on many editorial boards, including those of the *Journal of Studies on Alcohol* and the *American Journal of Community Psychology*. He has published hundreds of articles, reports, and books on the utilization, costs, evaluation, and outcome of mental health services, community settings, and substance abuse treatments. Books he has written pertaining to evaluation include *Evaluating Treatment Environments: The Quality of Psychiatric and Substance Abuse Programs; Evaluating Residential Facilities* (with S. Lemke); *Evaluating Educational Environments: Procedures, Methods, Findings and Policy Implications;* and *Evaluating Correctional and Community Settings.*

He is the recipient of many awards and honors, notably the Hofheimer Award for Research, American Psychiatric Association; Distinguished Contribution Award, Division of Community Psychology, American Psychological Association; MERIT Award, National Institute on Alcohol Abuse and Alcoholism; the 1992 Paul Lazarsfeld Award for Evaluation Theory, American Evaluation Association; Distinguished Research Award, Association of Medical School Psychologists; Outstanding Achievement in Health Services, Department of Veteran Affairs; and the 2002 Seymour B. Sarason Award, Division of Community Psychology, American Psychological Association.

■■ MORAL DISCOURSE

Following a usage described by Foucault, a *discourse* is more than just language-in-use; it refers to a system of thought that simultaneously takes up ideas, ideologies, attitudes, actions, and concepts informing our understandings of self, world, and others. The notion of a *moral* discourse specifically directs attention to ways of thinking and acting about morality. Morality, broadly speaking, is concerned with systems of public thought (about moral rules, ideals, virtues, etc.) that informally govern our behavior as it affects others. Defining morality as an informal system contrasts it with systems of law and religion. In the former, unlike the latter, there is neither a decision procedure nor a source of authority that can, once and for all, settle contested questions. Morality is thus, in a fundamental sense, always an open question.

Moral discourse takes up questions of ethics and value. The study of ethics may be taken as synonymous with the study of morality, or it can more narrowly refer to the study of the moral principles of a particular

group, as, for example, the professional ethics of evaluators. Questions of value have to do with the worth of something (or someone or some action)—including just what "having value" means in terms of a property or characteristic of something, and whether value is an objective or subjective matter. Moral discourse also encompasses discussion of political morality: that is, why people should accept and obey the decisions of a political system (especially in cases where some people disagree with those decisions). Depending on what value is placed at the center of social and political decision making (for example, personal liberty, democratic participation, community), approaches to answering this question differ—thus the debates between theories of classic liberalism, deliberative democracy, and communitarianism.

The subject matter of moral discourse is different in important ways from the subject matters of scientific and technical discourse. The former, generally, is concerned with matters of what it is right to do and good to be in our interactions with each other and is governed by questions of value or substantive rationality: Where am I (are we) going? What should I (we) be? Is this desirable? What should be done? The latter is concerned with the production of knowledge and with the design and testing of means to achieve agreed-on ends. It is governed by questions of analytic or instrumental rationality—What is knowledge? How do you know? What is effective for in reaching this goal?

Evaluation theory and practice participate in and contribute to both kinds of discourse, although it may be the case that more time in the education and training of evaluators is formally devoted to the study of the subject matters of scientific and technical discourse than to moral discourse. Nonetheless, here are a few examples of how evaluation is involved in moral discourse: When evaluators contend that the purpose of evaluation is the judgment of value; when evaluators debate the primary orientation or aim of evaluation (e.g., as objectivist, empowerment, transformative); when evaluators argue that a particular program or project (or person) that has been the object of the evaluation has (or does not have) value; when evaluators consider what professional values (honesty, integrity, credibility, competence, serving the public good, etc.) are and ought to be promoted in evaluation; when evaluators argue the merits of advocacy and debate their obligations to clients, to the public good, and to promoting social justice in evaluation practice; when evaluators consider what *fairness* and *balance* in evaluation reporting mean; when evaluators assess their actions as evaluators—for example, whether actions are to be judged in terms of their consequences or in terms of a set of virtues of what makes a "good" evaluator.

—*Thomas A. Schwandt*

Further Reading

House, E. R. (1980). *Evaluating with validity.* Beverly Hills, CA: Sage.

Schwandt, T. A. (2002). *Evaluation practice reconsidered.* New York: Peter Lang.

■ MORELL, JONATHAN A.

(b. 1946, Brooklyn, New York). Ph.D. Psychology, Northwestern University; B.A., McGill University, Montréal, Québec.

Morell's primary contributions to the evaluation profession have been in the evaluation of information technology's impact on organizations and the application of complex adaptive systems perspectives to evaluation theory. He was influenced by his studies with Donald Campbell; his analysis of the comparative epistemology of science and engineering; and his interdisciplinary work with automotive industry experts, computer scientists, and product engineers. Three broad principles guide his work in designing and implementing evaluation and his strategies for data analysis: an eclectic acceptance of multiple methodologies, the principle of sociotechnical systems, and the dynamics of complex adaptive behavior.

He is Founding Editor (with Eugene Walsh Flaherty) of *Evaluation and Program Planning.* Morell was instrumental in initiating the presession tradition at the annual meetings of the American Evaluation Association. He is a recipient of the American Evaluation Association's Distinguished Service Award, a Fellow of the Society for Community Research and Action, and an avid bicycle rider.

■ MORRIS, MICHAEL

(b. 1949, Washington, DC). Ph.D., M.A. Community-Social Psychology, B.A. Psychology, Boston College.

Morris is Professor of Psychology at the University of New Haven and serves as Evaluator for the Commission on Institutions of Higher Education, New England Association of Schools and Colleges. He has worked as an organizational consultant in the human services, nonprofit, and public sector for many years.

Morris has contributed substantially to research on the ethics of evaluation. He conducted the first U.S. national survey of evaluators' encounters with ethical conflicts in their professional work. Morris built on this seminal investigation and follow-up study of the reasoning underlying evaluators' perceptions of behavior in evaluations as being either ethical or unethical. His interest and scholarship in ethics is manifest in the variety of his contributions to the profession. He is Former Chair of the Ethics Committee of the American Evaluation Association; Coeditor (with Jody Fitzpatrick) of a volume of *New Directions for Evaluation,* "Current and Emerging Ethical Challenges in Evaluation"; and Inaugural Editor of the Ethical Challenges section of the *American Journal of Evaluation.*

Morris' work has been influenced by William Ryan's book *Blaming the Victim.* While in college, Morris took the class in which Ryan first used this text, and the experience impressed on him the crucial roles social science—scientists—play in defining, perpetuating, and ameliorating social problems. Morris also gained an appreciation for the importance of "use" from Michael Q. Patton's *Utilization-Focused Evaluation,* and he learned much about organizational dynamics from Daniel Katz and Robert Kahn's *The Social Psychology of Organizations.* He credits the Katz and Kahn book with providing him with the "conceptual anchor" for his evaluation practice.

Morris is the recipient of the University Award for Distinguished Teaching from the University of New Haven and has authored numerous publications in evaluation.

■ MOSTELLER, FREDERICK

(b. 1916). Ph.D., M.A., Princeton University; M.S., B.S., Carnegie Institute of Technology.

Mosteller is Roger I. Lee Professor of Mathematical Statistics and Professor Emeritus of Statistics at Harvard University. He has chaired the Departments of Statistics, Biostatistics, Social Relations, and Health Policy and Management at Harvard University, making him the only person in Harvard's history to serve as chair of four different departments. He directs the Center for Evaluation of the Initiatives for Children Project at the American Academy of Arts and Sciences, where he was named a Fellow in 1954. He is also a Fellow of the American Philosophical Society, Institute of Mathematical Statistics, American Statistical Association, American Association for the Advancement of Science, American Society for Quality Control, American Sociological Association, and an Honorary Fellow of the Royal Statistical Society.

He is the author of more than 340 journal articles concerning mathematics, statistics, psychology, sociology, epidemiology, and education, and he has written, edited, or contributed to more than 60 books, the most recent of which is titled *Evidence Matters: Randomized Trials in Education Research* (edited with Robert Boruch). Mosteller has served on the editorial boards of a dozen journals, including *Journal of the American Statistical Association, Psychological Review,* and *Science.* He has also held the office of President at the American Association for the Advancement of Science, the American Statistical Association, the Institute of Mathematical Statistics, the Psychometric Society, and the International Statistical Institute. He has been a member of the Board of Directors of the Russell Sage Foundation, Social Science Research Council, and American Medical Review Research Center, as well as being a member of the Board of Trustees of the National Opinion Research Center and the Center for Advanced Study in the Behavioral Sciences.

He has received numerous honors, including three honorary doctor of science degrees (Chicago, Carnegie Mellon, and Wesleyan Universities), an honorary doctor of social science (Yale), and an honorary doctor of laws (Harvard). He is the recipient of numerous prizes and awards, including the American Statistical Association's Founders Award, the Marvin Zelen Leadership Award in the Statistical Sciences, the Lifetime Membership Award from the American Psychological Association, and the 1978 Alva and Gunnar Myrdal Science Award from the American Evaluation Association.

■: MOST SIGNIFICANT CHANGE TECHNIQUE

The *most significant change (MSC) technique* is a dialogical, story-based approach designed to run throughout the life of a program. In what is basically a form of continuous *values inquiry,* examples of significant program outcomes are collected and presented to designated groups of stakeholders who deliberate on the value of these outcomes in a systematic and transparent manner. In evaluation, its primary purpose is to facilitate program improvement by focusing the direction of work toward explicitly valued directions and away from less-valued directions. Other possible roles are to provide decision makers with a vicarious experience of the project, encourage recognition of diversity in values among stakeholders, identify unintended outcomes, and provide performance information in the form of client success stories.

Initially devised for the evaluation of a social development program in Bangladesh, MSC has so far largely been used for monitoring and evaluating international development programs. As the MSC approach has developed and spread, the name has evolved too, with the technique having been referred to as the "evolutionary approach to organizational learning," the "story approach" and "monitoring without indicators."

MSC has points in common with critical incident technique and Kibel's results mapping. Critical incident technique focuses on variations from prescribed practice and generates negative information, whereas MSC searches for significant outcomes through an inductive process and tends to generate mainly positive information. Kibel's results mapping differs from MSC in that stories are coded by experts against a results ladder and a contribution analysis, whereas MSC stories are filtered up through the organization using a participatory process involving values inquiry.

OVERVIEW OF MSC METHODOLOGY

The MSC approach has three main stages:

- Establish domains of change
- Collect and review stories of change
- Monitor the process and verify the stories

Stage One: Establish Domains of Change

The first step is for the people managing the MSC process to identify the domains of change they think should be evaluated. Selected stakeholders are asked to identify loosely defined areas, such as "changes in people's lives," that can be flexibly interpreted by the people who collect the stories. This discrete activity need occur only once, although it can be worth revisiting. It helps to have one category that is broad enough to include unintended and unanticipated outcomes.

Stage Two: Collect and Review Stories of Change

Stories of significant change are collected from beneficiaries, clients, field staff, and others directly involved in the program. A simple question is used to help collect the stories: "During the past month, in your opinion, what was the most significant change that took place in the program?" Respondents are asked to allocate their stories to a domain category. They are also encouraged to report why they consider a particular change to be the most significant one.

Next the stories are analyzed and passed up through the levels of authority commonly found within an organization or program. Each level of the program hierarchy reviews the stories sent to them by the level below and identifies the single most significant account of change in each domain. The "winning" stories are then passed on to the next level, and the number of stories is gradually reduced through a systematic and transparent process. At every stage of story selection, the selection criteria are recorded and made available to all interested stakeholders. This means that subsequent stages of the collection and selection process are informed by feedback from previous rounds. In this way, the organization effectively records and adjusts the direction of its attention—and the criteria it uses to assess the events it observes there.

After a suitable time period, such as a year, all the stories selected at the highest level over that period are put into a single document, together with the reasons they were selected. The program funders are then asked to look at the full set of stories and identify those that best represent the kinds of outcomes they wish to fund. They are also asked to explain the reasons for their choices. The results of the program funders' deliberations are conveyed to program managers.

Stage Three: Monitor the Process and Verify the Stories

Program managers and stakeholders can verify the winning stories by visiting the locations of the events described in the stories. This step makes it possible to check that storytellers are reporting accurately and honestly and to gather more detailed information about particularly significant events. If a visit takes place some time after the original event, there is also an opportunity to see what has happened since the event was first recorded.

Quantification can take place at two different stages. When an account of change is first described, the person recording the story can also include quantitative information. It may also be worthwhile assessing the extent to which the most significant changes identified in one region have taken place in other locations within a specific time period. The optional step of monitoring the monitoring system might involve looking at who participated and how they affected the content of the stories, as well as how often different types of changes have been reported.

PURPOSE OF MSC IN EVALUATION

The primary purpose of MSC is program improvement. This is facilitated by focusing the direction of work toward explicitly valued directions and away from less valued directions. MSC was originally framed as a tool to enable organizational learning. When an organization's observation and judgment processes are made more visible, the organization becomes more open to change. This representation of the organizational learning process is based on evolutionary epistemology, which uses the Darwinian theory of evolution, adaptation, and natural selection to describe organizational change. As applied to MSC, the idea is that the fittest (most significant) reported changes are identified using a selection process that is part of the evaluation system. Because these are endorsed as the most desirable outcomes, the whole organization can then create more of these explicitly valued outcomes.

MSC is not intended to provide a stand-alone approach to summative evaluation, but it can offer some very useful "accessory" functions to complement core summative evaluation techniques that include examination of overall program performance. MSC can also contribute to summative evaluation through values inquiry and by providing information about unexpected outcomes and success stories.

—*Jessica Dart*

Further Reading

Dart, J. J., & Davies, R. J. (in press). A dialogical, story-based evaluation tool: The most significant change technique. *American Journal of Evaluation.*

Davies, R. J. (1996). *An evolutionary approach to facilitating organizational learning: An experiment by the Christian Commission for Development in Bangladesh.* Swansea, UK: Centre for Development Studies. Retrieved May 27, 2004, from http://www.swan.ac.uk/cds/rd/ccdb.htm

■■ MULTICULTURAL EVALUATION

Multicultural evaluation is evaluation conducted with special attention to racial-ethnic cultures. This special attention can involve one or more of a variety of different aspects surrounding evaluation; these include the context in which evaluation occurs, evaluation planning, stakeholder designation, implementation, design-method selection, measurement selection, reporting, and dissemination. This special attention to racial-ethnic cultures can also vary in degree, from being a central, dominant feature of an evaluation to being a secondary, peripheral feature. In general, evaluations that have the label of multicultural involve racial-ethnic issues in many aspects of the evaluation, and they have racial-ethnic issues as one of the central features of the evaluation.

When evaluation began to be codified as a field and discipline in the United States in the second half of the 20th century, multicultural issues were not central concerns of evaluators. At that time, evaluators generally were White, and they worked in a White culture. As evaluation progressed, ethnic-racial issues began to become more apparent. For example, the area of education was a primary setting for early evaluation work. The U.S. government launched the "Great Society" programs to address, among other issues, disparities in educational opportunities and achievement between Whites and Blacks. Evaluators working in these settings, therefore, began to confront cultural issues to which they had not had to attend before. Other factors were also operating that brought racial-ethnic issues to the forefront in evaluation. One important factor was that U.S. society was focusing more attention on racial-ethnic issues generally. U.S. society was also growing and becoming more multicultural. Evaluators found that they were working with a more diverse group of stakeholders than had been the case earlier. Another factor was the growth of evaluation beyond the U.S. borders, into other cultures where the majority culture was different from the majority culture in the U.S. or where there was a multiplicity of racial-ethnic cultures rather than one dominant culture. Evaluators working in these multiethnic cultures attended to these aspects of the evaluation context, as good evaluators would do in regard to any aspect that had a dominant role in the setting surrounding an evaluation.

In the U.S. culture, another factor was also at work to foster multicultural evaluation: the increase in trained evaluators from non-White cultures. These evaluators were very aware of racial-ethnic issues on many levels and brought this awareness to their evaluation work. These culturally aware evaluators made other evaluators aware that evaluation issues that at first seemed to have no relation to cultural issues could indeed have racial-ethnic aspects and overtones. The growing importance of these viewpoints in the U.S. was demonstrated by the formation of two topical interest groups within the American Evaluation Association: the International and Cross-Cultural TIG in 1990 and the Minority TIG shortly thereafter. These groups and others outside the United States, within both national and local evaluation associations, have continued to focus the evaluation profession on the importance and relevance of cultural issues in evaluation work.

Multicultural evaluation can be the central focus of an evaluation in different ways. One example would be an evaluation in which the project focus and related evaluation questions relate to racial-ethnic cultural differences. In the health area in the United States, for instance, there are significant disparities in health-related outcomes among different racial-ethnic groups, with racial-ethnic groups generally having worse outcomes than Whites. Some programs established to address and reduce these differences focus on interventions in different racial-ethnic cultural groups. Evaluations of these programs have multicultural questions at their core, such as, "Does the program to increase breast screening for cancer result in the same change among women who are Chinese, Korean, and Hispanic?" Multicultural issues will also infuse other aspects of the evaluation, such as the need to include women from these cultures in planning, implementing, and interpreting the results from the evaluation. The evaluation team will probably need to include Chinese-speaking, Korean-speaking, and Spanish-speaking staff members and have a high level of sensitivity to these cultures among all staff.

Multicultural issues can be involved in evaluation in less prominent ways. The program being evaluated can be one that does not have cultural issues at its core but may, for example, involve participants from several different racial-ethnic groups. Consider a reading enrichment program for an inner city school in a large metropolitan area in the United States or abroad. This school is likely to have children from several, and in some cities many, different racial-ethnic cultures. Multicultural issues enter into this evaluation in terms of the participants and considerations that the evaluation team will need to attend to (for example, involving a diverse group of advisors in planning the evaluation and creating and implementing surveys and tests in several languages). In this evaluation, multicultural issues are not core but are still key in achieving a successful evaluation.

—Ross Conner

Evaluation Practice Around the World

Israel

Learning to Understand Multiculturalism

Israel is a small, unique country composed of many diverse communities from a vast array of backgrounds. The current population of 6.2 million citizens is made up of 78% Jews (of which more than 50% are immigrants) and 21.5% non-Jews, most of whom are Arabs. More than 90% of the population lives in urban centers. The Bedouin population in the southern part of the country is undergoing dramatic changes in lifestyle, moving from a centuries-old lifestyle to a modern one in the space of a quarter of a century. Many Jewish communities have large numbers of immigrants, originating from more than 70 different countries, who have arrived in waves throughout the 53 years of Israel's existence.

I want to tell a story about a recent workshop in parenting that I evaluated for an NGO. The group included members of multiple cultural backgrounds: native Israeli–Jewish; native Israeli–Arab; and immigrants from Ethiopia, the Caucasus, and Bukhara. The group examined any issue central to the workshops (issues affecting young children and their families) on several levels. The subject of the workshop was young children growing up in multilingual settings (Hebrew and Arabic, Hebrew and Amharic, Hebrew and Russian, etc.). In the last session of the workshop, each participant was asked to share a story representing how culture had been passed on to her as a child. The group then selected one of the stories to elaborate and convert into a story for young children that would include both text and illustrations.

The participants excitedly shared their stories, both in their native tongue and in Hebrew. Each story in the "storytelling" became an opportunity to learn about and appreciate the other. The Bukharan woman told of her parents' stories, about how they struggled to find food and survive during World War II. An Ethiopian woman told a story of the day in the life of a shepherd. Another told a story of how a child assisted her mother in the day's chores. Another woman told a traditional Ethiopian tale that her father taught her that caused another participant to giggle hysterically and later cry.

It was Fauzia, one of the Arab home visitors who wears Muslim traditional dress, who gained resounding applause from the primarily Jewish group of 35. Fauzia told a simple story of a little girl named Fatmeh. Fatmeh, promised a present from Mecca, waits impatiently for a whole month for her grandparents to return from their Muslim pilgrimage to Mecca for the Haj. Fauzia brought the house down, as all of the participants learned something about Arab culture, heard a story in Arabic, and saw a drawing of typical dress from the Haj. One participant remarked that this was the first time she had been able to understand Arabic.

Each of these stories helped to elicit information from and empathetic understanding of the participants. The common grounds of motherhood, multiple generations, and parents as teachers were evident within all of the diversity.

Such a workshop is an important contribution to me as the evaluator: to my understanding of the life of the participants; of their perceptions of reality; and especially of their views of child rearing, which was the focus of the project. Without this knowledge and understanding, it would be impossible for me to evaluate a program that works in a cross-cultural setting.

Sometimes diversity has several layers; for example, in a program for the empowerment of Bedouin women. As the evaluation manager, I have to work with the foundation, which is a European foundation that knows very little about the Bedouin situation, culture, or way of life. Communication with the foundation is in English. I have to work with the Israeli project management, which is composed of Jewish and Bedouin professionals. Communication with them is in Hebrew. I have to work with the people who operate the program in the field, Bedouin professionals and paraprofessionals. The language here is mixed Hebrew and Arabic. Then I have to work with the women, the clients of the program, who are illiterate, poor, deprived, and very traditional Bedouin women. The language here is purely Arabic, with the special dialect of the southern Bedouins.

As an evaluator in a country such as Israel, you must have the ability to live with diversity in the deep sense of that meaning: to use all your senses to listen to many different voices in different languages (both verbal and nonverbal) and to live with the idea that your academic knowledge is just not good enough, and other bodies of knowledge, such as different cultures, ideas, and perceptions of reality, are always elusive and difficult to reach.

—Miri Levin-Rozalis

MULTITRAIT–MULTIMETHOD ANALYSIS

Multitrait-multimethod analysis is a methodology used to assess the construct validity of an instrument. The technique requires that subjects be measured on at least two variables with at least two methods of instrumentation; for example, reading and mathematics each measured with multiple-choice items and open-response items. A trait correlation is the correlation coefficient between the same variable, measured with two different methods (e.g., reading multiple-choice scores correlated with reading open-response scores). A method correlation is the correlation coefficient between the two different variables, measured with the same method (e.g., reading multiple-choice scores correlated with mathematics multiple-choice scores). A relatively high trait correlation, coupled with a relatively low method correlation, is evidence of the construct validity of a variable.

—Joseph M. Petrosko

Further Reading

Nunnally, J. C., & Bernstein, I. H. (1994). *Psychometric theory* (3rd ed.). New York: McGraw-Hill.

NARAYAN, DEEPA

Ph.D., Iowa State University.

Narayan is Senior Adviser in the Poverty Reduction and Economic Management Network of the World Bank and Lead Author and Team Leader for Voices of the Poor, a multicountry research initiative to understand poverty from the perspective of the poor.

She has more than 20 years of development experience in Asia and Africa and has worked for NGOs, national governments, and the United Nations system. Her work with the Voices of the Poor project has critically analyzed development assistance and its lack of success because outsiders presume to know what is best in a particular environment without building on the knowledge that already exists there. Among her most recent publications are three volumes about and for Voices of the Poor, *From Many Lands, Can Anyone Hear Us?* and *Crying Out for Change,* as well as a joint World Bank–World Health Organization publication on health issues titled *Voices of the Poor: Dying for Change.* She is also the author of *Empowerment and Poverty Reduction: A Sourcebook.* Currently, she is leading the development of an empowerment framework (that has influenced empowerment evaluation) for the World Bank.

NARRATIVE

The Latin root of *narrative, narratio,* means *telling.* It is considered a primary act of mind. Because the meaning of events is not given, we make sense of and construct *meaning* by imposing a certain *form* on experiences and events. In stories, events are connected in actual space and time. Stories can reveal the ambiguity of everyday situations and lived experiences. Stories also serve as vehicles in learning processes because they are open to social negotiation and dialogue. If evaluators listen to different stories and facilitate a dialogue about stories, a narrative approach to evaluation can enhance mutual understandings and promote democratic principles.

—Tineke A. Abma

Further Reading

Abma, T. A. (Ed.). (1999). *Telling tales: On evaluation and narrative.* Stamford, CT: JAI.

NARRATIVE ANALYSIS

Policies and programs can be understood as *practices* constituted by narratives. Narratives serve psychological, cultural, social, and political functions. People tell stories to find out what happened and what this means for their role and (group or national) identity. Stories are directed to others and told to influence actions and social practices. Program participants will, for example, try to convince others of their point of view with the use of rhetorical devices, such as metaphors. This means that a practice is shaped by the communication between storytellers and their narratives. In this process, certain stories and voices will be taken seriously and lead to changes, and others will gain no hearing. As such, narrating is a political act.

Stories told and enacted in practice can be analyzed with the help of narrative analysis. Commonly, qualitative researchers and evaluators analyze narratives using a grounded theory approach or comparable type of analysis. These types of analysis have various shortcomings.

In the search for general and abstract theoretical concepts, the uniqueness and the ambiguity of personal experiences is ignored. With the focus on the content of narratives, no attention is paid to the meanings embedded in the form (language and structure). Furthermore, this type of analysis often lacks an interest in the larger interactive and discursive context. Narrative analyses serve as an alternative. In the context of evaluation, we identify the following types of narrative analysis:

- *Life history analysis.* This is an integral analysis of a personal history, performed by identifying certain themes and connecting these with major life markers.
- *Discourse analysis.* In a discourse analysis, the focus switches to the use of a more or less coherent form of language.
- *Performative analysis.* This analysis focuses on the implicit or explicit claims that are made to motivate people to *act* in a certain way so that the program is continued or changed.
- *Rhetorical analysis.* This is an analysis of the *linguistic devices*—intensifiers, markers, qualifiers, and metaphors—that are used to get a message across.
- *Argumentative analysis.* This is a structural analysis of the arguments, pro and con, regarding a certain program or policy.
- *Storytelling workshop.* This is an organizational learning intervention in which 8 to 10 participants engage in a dialogue and relate to a set of presented stories.

An important and distinct characteristic in the emerging heuristic for narrative evaluation is communication and dialogue. Evaluators not only want to gain insight into the different stories of stakeholders (the story as a *source of information*), they also share an interest in the *social construction* of meaning through stories. They ask, "Why did this person tell that story at that particular moment, and what were the consequences?" This question will shed light on the misunderstandings, conflicts, and dynamics that flow from the differences and vertical asymmetry between personal stories and collective narratives or between personal and collective narratives. This social construction process can be analyzed from a more distanced position. Evaluators may also act as facilitators of storytelling processes and workshops to enhance mutual understandings between participants.

—*Tineke A. Abma*

Further Reading

Abma, T. A. (Ed.). (1999). *Telling tales: On evaluation and narrative.* Stamford, CT: JAI.

Abma, T. A. (2001). Reflexive dialogues: A story about the development of inquiry prevention in two performing art schools. *Evaluation, 7*(2), 238-252.

■■ NARRATIVE REPRESENTATION

As *narrators,* evaluators make some things visible and allow others to remain invisible. Although evaluation reports take many forms and functions, they commonly have the character of a scientific text and factual account. This kind of text is, however, not very appropriate for communicating and facilitating reflexive dialogues. Polyvocal texts give voice to those who feel marginalized and leave more room for interpretation to stimulate dialogues. A self-reflexive text makes readers more aware of the fact that the stories are retold and inevitably colored by the author's biography, personal projects, and persuasions.

—*Tineke A. Abma*

Further Reading

Abma, T. A. (1998). Writing for dialogue: Text in evaluative context. *Evaluation, 4*(4), 434-454.

■■

Evaluation Practice Around the World

South Africa

A Lonely Black Elderly Man Smiled

South Africa and its people are consistently being challenged to deal with changes on various levels. Since the political changes in 1994, exciting possibilities have arisen that allow for innovative training and transformational community work initiatives. Initiatives in community intervention shed light on the multicultural nature of the population, as well as its limited financial resources, and set the stage for the development of an evaluation approach that highlights the historical, sociopolitical, and collective nature of people in a particular context.

The political agendas of apartheid and integration of the South African society were and still are a challenging process for the perpetrators, as well as the victims. This may be illustrated by a community initiative in the context of an old age home, consisting of mainly White elderly people and only one Black elderly man. Volunteers from the student community were asked by the management of this retirement home to interact with the residents because many of the elderly had been abandoned by their families and would welcome contact with young people.

A final-year undergraduate student, Refilwe, who was able to communicate with the only Black resident, Mr. Buys (not his real name), in an African language, visited him once a week over a period of 10 weeks. According to the staff, Mr. Buys did not want to talk to any of them or with the other residents. He spent most of his time sitting in the sun and waiting for the days to pass. Refilwe entered into the relationship with the intention of understanding Mr. Buys' expression of integrity or despair (based on Erikson's stages of development) and to learn from the process.

The context described here illustrates the mismatch between traditional evaluation, the changed sociopolitical situation, and dynamic learning environments, and it sparked interest in developmental evaluation. Developmental evaluation has sustained interest in participatory and experiential learning processes. Experiential learning proposes a cycle of concrete experiences, reflective observation, abstract conceptualization, and active experimentation. To make sense of an experience, it is necessary to think about it and to reflect on it; to be actively involved in construing experiences; and to maintain a holistic view of the social, cultural, and emotional context in which learning occurs. Refilwe's seventh visit with Mr. Buys is an illustration of the reflective observation that is part of this process: "Today we spoke about the regrets in his life and he told me that the biggest regret in his life is not finding himself a wife. From where I was sitting I could feel a mountain of regrets overwhelming him. His life has been one big regret. It was written all over his face."

Maintaining a constant awareness of their subjective involvement in the process implies that evaluators should reflect constantly on their role and position in the process. Critical reflection requires the examination of past incidents and events, to make sense of them and to create a framework of ideas and values. Refilwe kept a diary reflecting on the visits and also discussed her observations with Mr. Buys, other students, and lecturers. She wrote: "The process was not as difficult as I thought. Mr. Buys always looked at me as a child and maybe that is why he never went too deep in the details of his life. Mr. Buys' response came as a shock—he left me thinking—I wondered why? Through my visits, Mr. Buys and I have developed from complete strangers to good friends. Even though he still cannot pronounce my name."

Developmental evaluation is also about challenging interactional patterns. Refilwe's second-to-last visit can be described as a challenge to Mr. Buys' usual way of interacting with people and the world: "He was ready to tell me all about how unfair the staff is and how they have not given him his pension yet. I stopped him and told him that I would like to hear about some good times in his past. He started talking. An experience we both enjoyed. And then I got to see his aged face smile."

Developmental evaluation should reflect sensitivity. It is not about imposing information on people but about creating conditions in which there is a deep respect for the diversity within and between people. Refilwe writes: "The major difference between Mr. Buys and me is our age. However when I gave him the respect he expected and time he needed, he started talking to me."

When using the metaphor of a story to describe developmental evaluation, researchers should not take the story away from its readers but rather add their own narrative about it to the already rich tapestry of experience. We can say that the boundaries between readers and author are differentiated by the responsibility taken by each party. In the beginning of a story, the writer assumes responsibility for providing a clear description of the context and characters involved. Refilwe describes this as follows: "When one enters into a community he or she needs to know what the needs of the community are. In this case entering into an old age home—how an old person perceives his or her life, will give an indication of what to do." The responsibility then gradually shifts to the reader, community, or person to understand these descriptions to follow the progress of the story. In Mr. Buys' and Refilwe's story, they engaged in creating a collage about his life. Mr. Buys insisted on making the final decision about the pictures to be pasted on the poster and where to hang it in his room.

We may conclude that developmental evaluation is not a linear progression of activities carried out with one intended objective. Rather, it is a multifaceted process, including continuous assessment and incorporating the participants' expectations. In this way, researchers are able to intervene holistically and ethically in communities to coconstruct rich stories of experiences that seek to transcend historical, cultural, and sociopolitical barriers.

—*Vera Roos*

◼◼ NATHAN, RICHARD

(b. 1935, Schenectady, New York). Ph.D. Political Economy and Government, M.A. Public Administration, Harvard University; B.A., Brown University.

Nathan is Distinguished Professor of Political Science and Public Policy, Rockefeller College, University at Albany, State University of New York. Previously, he was Professor of Public International Affairs and Director of Princeton Urban and Regional Research Center, Woodrow Wilson School, Princeton University. He has served as an advisor to the U.S. General Accounting Office and was Deputy Under-Secretary for Welfare Reform, U.S. Department of Health, Education and Welfare.

He has authored or coauthored numerous publications, including his most recent book, *Regionalism and Realism: A Study of Governments in the New York Metropolitan Area* (with Gerald Benjamin). He has written extensively on government policy and practices and has been called to provide testimony to the U.S. House of Representatives on matters of welfare reform and reducing extramarital births.

Nathan was the 1989 recipient of the American Evaluation Association Paul Lazarsfeld Award. He was honored as a Distinguished Scholar by the American Political Science Association Section on Federalism and Intergovernmental Relations. He received the Charles E. Merriam Award from the American Political Association and the James E. Webb Book Award from the National Academy of Public Administration.

◼◼ NATIONAL ASSESSMENT OF EDUCATIONAL PROGRESS (NAEP)

The National Assessment of Educational Progress (NAEP) is an assessment program operated by the National Center for Educational Statistics of the U.S. Department of Education. The purpose of NAEP is to act as the nation's "report card" by providing an estimate of the achievement of students at grades 4, 8, and 12. Nationally representative samples of students are tested in basic subjects, such as reading and mathematics, and in other areas, including civics, geography, and literature. NAEP also reports data on school characteristics and the results of teacher surveys. Information from NAEP can be used to address issues such as how various instructional practices relate to achievement and what policy changes are being made in U.S. schools.

—*Joseph M. Petrosko*

◼◼ NATIONAL INSTITUTES OF HEALTH (NIH)

The NIH is the steward of medical and behavioral research for the United States. It is an agency under the U.S. Department of Health and Human Services, with headquarters in Bethesda, Maryland, and the surrounding area. The NIH comprises the Office of the Director and 27 institutes and centers employing more than 18,000 people. The mission of the NIH is to uncover new knowledge that will lead to better health for all, and NIH works toward that mission by

- Conducting research in its own laboratories
- Supporting the research of nonfederal scientists in universities, medical schools, hospitals, and research institutions throughout the country and abroad
- Training research investigators
- Fostering communication of medical information

The NIH sets aside 1% of its budget to conduct evaluations of programs under its auspices, thus making a continual contribution to knowledge about public health and human service programs. NIH maintains an online database of evaluation studies in these areas.

—*Jeffrey G. Tucker*

◼◼ NATIONAL SCIENCE FOUNDATION (NSF)

The National Science Foundation (NSF) has been instrumental in supporting the development of evaluation theory and practice in the United States. NSF's Division of Research, Evaluation and Communication was formed in 1992 in response to a Congressional request for external, third-party evaluations of education programs. NSF has provided resources for evaluating science, math, and technology programs; has collaborated with universities to prepare the next generation of evaluators; has made a commitment to support the recruitment and mentoring of evaluators of color; and has supported evaluation capacity building and research on evaluation.

—*Conrad G. Katzenmeyer*

■ *A NATION AT RISK*

A Nation at Risk is a report published by the U.S. Department of Education's National Commission on Excellence in 1983. This report is the origin of many current reforms in education. Using military metaphors to illustrate the proclaimed mediocrity of American education, the commission's recommendations included more stringent high school graduation requirements, the adoption of higher and measurable standards of academic performance, increased time spent in school, and higher standards of performance for teachers. Although the means to correct the perceived problems of schooling and education have varied, this document is a critical historical event that focused federal and national attention on educational issues.

■ NATURAL EXPERIMENTS

A *natural experiment* is a naturally occurring instance of observable phenomena that approach or duplicate a scientific experiment. Notable events such as elections, disasters, and policy implementation often provide the basis for natural experiments that permit examination of alternate reactions and explanations for them. Such occurrences may lend themselves to the examination of reactions of subgroups or straightforward comparisons of data collected before and after an event. The 2000 presidential election in the United States and the events of 9/11 are events that have spawned many natural experiments. An example of a natural experiment occurred in Helena, Montana, while a public smoking ban was in effect. Helena is geographically isolated and served by only one hospital. Data collected by the hospital indicate that the rate of heart attacks dropped by 60% while the smoking ban was in effect.

■ NATURALISTIC EVALUATION

Naturalistic evaluation combines the assumptions and methods of naturalistic inquiry with various approaches that attempt to blend evaluation into the cultures and lives of the people involved. The term *naturalistic* has both paradigmatic (basic beliefs and assumptions) and methodological (procedural and practical) meanings. In recent years, other labels, such as constructivist and interpretivist, have been used to emphasize various dimensions of the naturalistic paradigm, but the methods have continued to be mostly, though not exclusively, qualitative. Schwandt, in his *Dictionary of Qualitative Inquiry,* notes that these terms also suggest the study of human life with the assumption that "meaning of human action is inherent in that action, and that the task of the inquirer is to unearth that meaning." The main objective is to use those meanings to judge the merit or worth of an evaluand in ways natural to the setting, expectations, values, assumptions, and dispositions of the participants, with minimal modification due to the inquiry processes used and assumptions held by the evaluator.

The argument for naturalistic evaluation makes the assumption that if evaluators are sensitive to the cultures, assumptions, and ways of the people, they are helping with the evaluation process, and results will emerge naturally through the human interactions evaluators have with the people they are serving. Further, naturalistic evaluators believe that the people they serve will be more forthright and able to share their values and perspectives and thus will be more likely to use the results if evaluations emerge naturally from the questions, ways of knowing, and values of those people.

Ironically, naturalistic evaluation is based philosophically on antinaturalism. Naturalism is a philosophy that equates the aims and methods of the social and human sciences with those of the natural sciences—prediction and control through the discovery of physical law explanations of matter in motion, including human behavior. Antinaturalists reject this view of science and the efforts to achieve physical law explanations of human action. They argue instead that, unlike objects in nature, human phenomena are best known through understanding of the meanings inherent in their experiences and actions. Therefore, antinaturalists seek to understand human action by exploring the meaningful ways in which people experience their world. Thus, to the philosopher, naturalistic evaluation is actually antinaturalistic in its assumptions. However, psychologists, sociologists, and others have used the terms *naturalistic, constructivist,* and *interpretivist* to represent this antinaturalist view of inquiry into human action and meaning.

The naturalistic inquiry paradigm and associated methods grew out of a long tradition in several fields of human inquiry, including anthropology, sociology, psychology, the humanities, and other disciplines.

Willems and Rausch defined naturalistic inquiry as "the investigation of phenomena within and in relation to their naturally occurring contexts." They emphasized that there are degrees of naturalness that depend on how much the investigator influences or manipulates "the antecedent conditions of the behavior studied" and "the degree to which units are imposed by the investigator upon the behavior studied." Denzin claimed that the logic of naturalistic inquiry encourages the inquirer to resist using methods that oversimplify the complexity of everyday life.

Lincoln and Guba built on these ideas to propose that naturalistic inquiry is principally a paradigm, a distillation of what we think about the world but cannot prove, or a system of our basic metaphysical beliefs or axioms together with their accompanying methods. They emphasized that naturalistic inquiry is not just a method but that many varieties of qualitative and quantitative methods may be used in conducting inquiry from this paradigm. In later years, they and others have argued that the naturalistic paradigm is essentially constructivist and interpretivist because it involves at least these assumptions or beliefs:

1. Regarding the ontological question of the nature of reality, the naturalistic paradigm assumes that "there are multiple, constructed realities that can be studied only holistically; inquiry into these multiple realities will inevitably diverge (each inquiry raises more questions than it answers) so that prediction and control are unlikely outcomes, although some level of understanding (*verstehen*) can be achieved."

2. Regarding the epistemological question of the relationship of the knower to the known, the naturalistic paradigm holds that "the inquirer and the 'object' of inquiry interact to influence one another; knower and known are inseparable."

3. Regarding the possibility of generalization and the goal of prediction and control, the naturalistic paradigm's "aim of inquiry is to develop an idiographic [focused on the particular and distinct] body of knowledge in the form of 'working hypotheses' that describe the individual case."

4. Regarding the possibility of establishing causal linkages, the naturalistic paradigm assumes that "all entities are in a state of mutual simultaneous shaping so that it is impossible to distinguish causes from effects."

5. Regarding the axiological question of the role of values in inquiry, the naturalistic paradigm holds that "inquiry is value-bound" by the inquirer's values as expressed in the choice and framing of a problem, evaluand, or policy option; the choice of the paradigm that guides the investigation; the choice of the substantive theory used to guide the collection and analysis of data in the interpretation of findings; and through the values inherent in the context.

These assumptions suggest a variety of methodological implications for doing naturalistic inquiry. Most items in the following list were suggested by Lincoln and Guba and have been expanded by others:

- Inquiry should be done in the natural setting or context of the entity being studied rather than in contrived, manipulated, or artificial laboratory settings.
- Humans are employed as the primary data-gathering instruments.
- Tacit (intuitive, felt) knowledge is as important as propositional (expressible in language) knowledge.
- Qualitative and quantitative methods are used.
- Purposive or theoretical sampling and random or representative sampling are used.
- Inductive and deductive logic guides analyses.
- Emerging theory development is emphasized over a priori theory development.
- The inquiry design emerges rather than strictly following a preordained plan.
- Meanings and interpretations associated with data are negotiated among participants to account for their different views of reality and their unique as well as common values.
- Case study reporting is preferred over scientific or technical reports.
- Data are interpreted in terms of the particular case from which they are drawn rather than in terms of law-like generalizations and are tentatively applied to other sites based on boundaries set by the emerging focus.
- Alternative criteria for judging the trustworthiness of the inquiry may be employed (credibility,

transferability, dependability, and confirmability are proposed).

Paralleling the evolution of the naturalistic inquiry paradigm and methods, the field of evaluation has expanded to include a wide variety of approaches to the judgment of merit and worth of programs, personnel, learning, policies, and other evaluands. A dominant theme in this growth pattern has been the appropriateness of the naturalistic paradigm to many different evaluation approaches.

One of the first indicators of this theme was in Robert Stake's discussion of naturalistic generalizations. He argued that evaluation audiences primarily need help deciding what they should do in their particular situations rather than general conclusions about a population of situations or grand theory. Stake expanded on this theme when he proposed an approach called "responsive evaluation," which encourages evaluators to use both qualitative and quantitative methods in response to the needs and values of stakeholders. His proposal included the following elements, which echo the themes of naturalistic inquiry cited earlier.

- Evaluators should assume value pluralism among stakeholders or constituencies interested in their evaluations and should not press for consensus on values, issues, perspectives, and so on if consensus does not already exist.
- Evaluators should know the circumstances, problems, and issues well and provide stakeholders with well-crafted stories that invoke vicarious experiences and portray complexity, holistic impressions, mood, personal knowings, and subjective understanding of those points as a basis for making judgments.
- Diversity, the particular, and the local should be emphasized more than the general in evaluation studies, as opposed to evaluation research studies.
- The evaluator should be open to what is going on and not restrict attention to initial issues or questions.
- Judgment occurs during description and observation as well as during and after analysis. Descriptions and values come out at about the same time in most people's minds.
- New interpretations are always possible by the evaluator and by anyone reading the evaluator's summaries.

- Audiences should use the evaluator's judgments in combination with many other influences as they make their decisions about the evaluands.
- Case study methods are very appropriate for evaluations because they are concrete, contextual, and open to different interpretations. Thus they fit people's natural ways of making sense of the world.
- Local knowledge, naturalistic generalizations, and transferability (application of results in making practical decisions by the reader rather than inferences from results by the evaluator) are the ideal of most evaluations, not theory building and universal generalizations.
- Evaluators should think of themselves as teachers who share what they learn with stakeholders both didactically (explicitly stating their value judgments) and through discovery learning (so that the readers of reports can make their own value judgments from rich and thick descriptions).
- Acknowledging that social inquirers either implicitly or explicitly advocate certain values throughout their work, evaluators should include multiple advocacies rather than explicitly advocate for one position or another, and should also remind the reader of their fallibility, humanity, and probable biases.
- Evaluators should provoke readers to problematize issues they have not questioned and to consider alternative interpretations and constructions of the evaluands and their values.
- Rather than seek for one universal truth, evaluators should pay attention to context; situational variations; and the multiple character of various kinds of reality across time, place, and players. Descriptions, shared meanings and the individual's responsibility to interpret and use interpretations in action are some of these multiple realities.
- Criteria for judging goodness of evaluations and of evaluands should remain open to change across time, place, and social situations. We should be humble about what we are striving for.

Many evaluation theorists have built on the foundations offered by Stake and the naturalistic inquiry literature, although they often chose to focus on the predominant use of qualitative methods. Many theorists have also identified collaborative approaches suggested by Stake's invitation to be responsive to stakeholders and have developed various participant-oriented approaches to evaluation. Guba and Lincoln built explicitly on responsive evaluation in their effective evaluation approach, then elaborated, modified, and extended those ideas in their fourth-generation evaluation approach. Lincoln continues to elaborate the approach in various articles and chapters on interpretivism. They changed their focus from the naturalistic paradigm to the constructivist (and then interpretivist) paradigm, apparently because they felt these better represent their thinking, are easier to communicate to others, and allow a broader world of philosophical ideas from which to stimulate improvements. Although the term *naturalistic* was dropped, the ideas proposed by Guba and Lincoln represent extensions of the naturalistic evaluation approach and should be considered relevant to the history and evolution of this kind of evaluation.

The shift to fourth-generation evaluation involved combining the five axioms from Guba and Lincoln's explication of the naturalistic paradigm into two constructivist beliefs they call "relativist ontology" and "monistic, subjectivist epistemology." They also added a third constructivist belief, called "hermeneutic methodology," to make methodology explicitly part of their basic beliefs. It involves a continuous dialectic of iteration, analysis, critique, reiteration, reanalysis, and so on, leading to the emergence of a joint (among all the inquirers and respondents, or among etic and emic views) construction of a case.

Guba and Lincoln presented theorems specifically associated with evaluation (in addition to 14 other theorems associated with all forms of inquiry), derived from these beliefs:

- Evaluation is a form of constructivist inquiry and hence has all the attributes of that genre.
- Evaluation produces reconstructions in which "facts" and "values" are inextricably linked.
- Accountability is a characteristic of a conglomerate of mutual and simultaneous shapers.
- Evaluators are subjective partners with stakeholders in the literal creation of evaluation data.
- Evaluators orchestrate a negotiation process that aims to culminate in consensus on better informed and more sophisticated constructions.
- Constructivist evaluation data have neither special status nor unique legitimacy; they represent simply

another construction to be taken into account in the move toward consensus.

To decide if naturalistic evaluation would be appropriate for a given setting, the following several questions are offered for consideration:

- Can most of the evaluation issues and criteria for making value judgments be clearly defined before the study is initiated, or would it be helpful to explore the context and nature of the evaluands as part of the evaluation and allow issues and criteria to emerge during the study?
- Is thick contextual description of the evaluand and its setting desired?
- Is an evaluation needed of the processes by which the evaluand is addressing its outcomes?
- Do evaluation recipients want judgments of the evaluand as it is operating in its natural state?
- Is there time to study the evaluand through its natural cycle?
- Can the evaluand be studied somewhat unobtrusively, as it operates naturally, in an ethical way?

These questions clarify that naturalistic evaluation is sometimes a very useful approach, though not always. Alignment with paradigm assumptions described herein is an essential way of ascertaining whether this approach might be appropriate for any future evaluations.

—*David D. Williams*

Further Reading

Denzin, N. K., & Lincoln, Y. S. (2000). *Handbook of qualitative research* (2nd ed.). Thousand Oaks, CA: Sage.

Greene, J. C., & Abma, T. A. (Eds.). (2001). Responsive evaluation. *New Directions for Program Evaluation, 92.*

Guba, E. G., & Lincoln, Y. S. (1981). *Effective evaluation: Improving the usefulness of evaluation results through responsive and naturalistic approaches.* San Francisco: Jossey-Bass.

Guba, E. G., & Lincoln, Y. S. (1989). *Fourth generation evaluation.* Newbury Park, CA: Sage.

Lincoln, Y. S., & Guba, E. G. (1985). *Naturalistic inquiry.* Beverly Hills, CA: Sage.

Stake, R. E. (1986). *Quieting reform: Social science and social action in an urban youth program.* Urbana: University of Illinois Press.

Williams, D. D. (Ed.). (1986). Naturalistic evaluation. *New Directions for Program Evaluation, 30*(whole number).

Evaluation Practice Around the World

Spain

The Problem With Taking Qualitative Evaluation Home

She came back after living in England and New York for 3 years—3 years of learning about evaluation. It had been a period of intense work and many opportunities, attending seminars and meetings conducted by exponents of the most innovative trends in the field, at which she was able to hear their opinions and learn their theories. However, in the last months of her study, one thing guided her work: the return to her country to work as an evaluator, to perform evaluations, to evaluate educational and perhaps social programs, implementing what she had learned. She wished to be an independent evaluator and contribute to establishing an evaluation culture in the changing setting of education in her country. She imagined the environment she would find and carefully prepared for the first challenges she would have to face. She gathered the articles, books, and magazines she thought she would need for the main debate she would face: qualitative methodology as opposed to the use of more quantitative means of research in evaluation. This discussion in the American scientific community was drawn out, and the arguments put forward were diverse and complex.

It was not easy to fit back into the academic life of the traditional university she had left, where the tradition was limited to the study of sciences, engineering, and medicine. What she had learned seemed to be of value only to her and of no use in the world of education in which she found herself. The demand for evaluations was scarce and the number of evaluations in the educational sector insignificant; indeed, their usefulness seemed unknown. Only those nearest to the concept of educational curriculum seemed interested in knowing their proposals, approaches, trends, and developments.

The first seminars, conferences, and courses she organized at a university in Madrid were attended by inspectors; by policy makers from autonomous governments mainly involved in training, educational, and social programs; and by Army specialists. The first evaluation she was asked to perform was requested by one of the course attendees who worked for the Autonomous Government of Madrid—an evaluation of a program to train teachers, to introduce a new primary curriculum in which "trainer trainers" were to be involved. These were mainly secondary school teachers who had worked for the Ministry of Education and Science in preparing the curriculum documents that was undergoing the experimental phase of the educational reform.

Writing case studies and using of qualitative methodology in the evaluation was allowed because new ways of working were considered a priority, and the policy maker understood the usefulness of the evaluation to the development and improvement of the program. A team of four (including the policy maker) was formed, with the commitment to provide practical training throughout the evaluation process.

The fieldwork was shared equally by the team members. Meetings were scheduled to plan the gathering and processing of information; to study in depth the theoretical aspects that arose; and to implement the evaluation approach, which was used for the first time in the educational context.

Data gathering began with the seminars given by the trainer trainers to primary school teachers already teaching the new curriculum. Notes were taken in the classes, and primary teachers to be trained were interviewed. Each one of the members of the evaluation team worked on a case study, concentrating on the training designed for each one of the subjects of the new curriculum. Language, mathematics, history, and natural sciences were chosen, among others. The work by the evaluation team was carried out with a high degree of agreement. The case studies were written, and each provided a detailed record of the peculiarities of the training process of each subject but also allowed the team to establish the common features of the curriculum and innovation. The program documents were studied and the trainer trainers interviewed.

The first intermediate evaluation report was prepared as a basis to gather more information on the training process and was presented to the three groups involved in the program. These groups were the trainer trainers, the program director and coordinator, and the primary school teachers. The data in the report had been negotiated so there would be no surprises.

The meeting with the trainers was stormy—the report had been provided to them in advance, and they reacted strongly. They did not recognize what the primary teachers said about their seminars and their innovation proposal, which was that the ideas were not well argued out and were only slightly innovative, especially regarding student roles in the teaching and learning. Displeased, the trainers criticized the qualitative methodology used, questioning its validity because it did not include conclusions but rather was markedly descriptive in nature. They questioned the images of the training process evaluators had built up with the remarks and points of view provided by the teachers.

The report turned out to be the element that led to discussion within the program not only in regard to the training provided but in regard to features of the curriculum that seemed to be insufficiently defined, aspects of learning proposed, and communication between pupils and teachers. The report revealed that the qualitative methodology had provided a picture of what was happening that

injured sensibilities, partially due to its precision, although it could be used as a basis for changing teaching practice. The program director and those responsible for the program appreciated hearing primary school teachers' voices directly; they also appreciated the policy-related task of the evaluator. In this evaluation, the evaluators became aware of their power and of the need to position themselves as independent professionals, without whom this evaluation could not have been concluded.

The evaluation contributed to the process of change, which is always difficult, as was the introduction of this qualitative evaluation methodology by this new, enthusiastic evaluator.

—María José Sáez Brezmes

NEEDS ASSESSMENT

Needs assessment is a process or a systematic set of procedures undertaken for the purpose of setting priorities and making decisions about program or organizational improvement or allocation of resources. The priorities come from identified needs, which are measured discrepancies (gaps) between the current (what is) state of affairs of a group or organization and the desired (what should be) state in regard to variables of interest. A prioritized need can be thought of as representing a problem or situation that should be rectified for the good of the organization and the groups it serves.

The general steps in the needs assessment process are initial focusing on an area of concern for the assessment; determining and prioritizing the "what should be"s; ascertaining the current status, or "what is"; identifying discrepancies between what is and what should be; rank-ordering discrepancies; causally analyzing the greatest discrepancies; selecting a solution strategy; and designing an action plan for implementation. The needs assessment process itself should be evaluated, although this is not often done.

The seemingly simple procedure of assessment and the idea of need quickly become complicated due to factors such as organizations' having many needs with insufficient resources to resolve all of them, multiple constituencies (with different needs) being served by one organization, stakeholder groups within and outside of organizations having varied perceptions of what needs should be accorded high priority and what

strategies should be used to resolve them, obtaining agreement on the what-should-be status, collecting sufficient and meaningful information about the what-is condition, and using multiple methods to assess the what-is condition that either might not triangulate or might even be in conflict. Let us briefly examine the subtle nature of the determination of the what-should-be and what-is states.

With regard to the what-should-be side of the equation, most needs are value driven in areas related to health, education, social welfare, and mental health. It is relatively easy to ascertain what should be for some dimensions of health. Recognized standards exist and are commonly accepted. If an individual's temperature is 105°F and a small range around 98.6 degrees is normal, that individual clearly has a health need. The same line of thinking can be applied to blood pressure and levels of low and high density lipids in cholesterol as well as overall cholesterol. Even here, however, there is a subtle yet apparent distinction between short-term needs (a fever) and long-term needs (elevated cholesterol).

Further, in what seems like a straightforward topic such as health, the what-should-be condition can be value laden and tenuous to describe. If the concern is wellness, what does that mean to the general public, to health practitioners, and so forth? Undoubtedly myriad connotations and meanings could and would be ascribed to the term, and these play a major role in any attempt to come up with a comprehensive and accepted general description of it. Moreover, what would be the specific indicators of wellness and what would be the standards that are to be expected (e.g., running a certain distance in a specified time every other day, running that distance faster, running more regularly at a slower pace, etc.)? What does it mean to be physically fit? Would the average person have a different view from an individual who routinely follows a strenuous daily workout regimen?

Shifting to schooling, what should a high school graduate know or be able to do as a result of his or her education? The perspective of the academically inclined secondary educator about that question is likely to be markedly different from that of a career and technical educator. How are such value positions adjudicated when we deal with identifying and prioritizing needs in the face of the pluralism of values and philosophies that is considered to be so important in a democratic society?

For a number of variables representing serious societal problems, the what-is state is equally difficult to assess. How are the smoking rates of the U.S. population measured, and how can reliable data be obtained for teenage rates of smoking, as well as rates for subgroups of teenagers—females, males, ethnic populations? How do we measure or assess the well-being of the American population or that of another country? How do we deal with variables that are not easily defined operationally?

Child, spousal, and sexual abuse; driving while under the influence of alcohol; and rape are not only complex to define, the prevalence of these variables is usually underestimated and, in turn, predicting incidence is compromised. In so many instances, child abuse and rape are seriously underreported due to the shame felt by the victim or the issues inherent in our legal system when a case is reported (a rape victim my feel more on trial than a perpetrator) or because of substantial variations in the way the variables are interpreted in local and regional jurisdictions.

In addition to the problems cited here, the needs assessor must always be aware of political issues in needs-related decisions. Attending to and assessing needs is inherently a political act (what might be called the needs assessment cauldron), and those working in needs assessment must recognize the political dimensions of what they are doing. Dealing with an identified and prioritized need will require the commitment of finances, time, motivation and energy, and administrative support from a finite pool of such resources, thus diminishing what can be used for other needs. Needs are in competition, and vested interests will automatically and immediately emerge to

challenge selected priorities. Examples abound across sectors in the public domain, as well as within them. To illustrate the across-sectors case, note that in times of national emergencies, military needs must take precedence over educational and social welfare concerns. Within a sector, the competition can be just as keen, as is evident in what treatments and drugs will or will not be subsidized in health-care systems.

—*James W. Altschuld and David D. Kumar*

Further Reading

Witkin, B. R., & Altschuld, J. W. (1995). *Planning and conducting needs assessments: A practical guide.* Thousand Oaks, CA: Sage.

■■ NEGATIVE CASES

A *negative case* is a strategy used especially in qualitative, naturalistic evaluation approaches to develop claims of fact or value that apply to all instances of cases. Data are analyzed iteratively with a working hypothesis or proposition in mind—cases that support the proposition strengthen the proposition; those that do not are called negative cases. The occurrence of a negative case contributes to the development of a more comprehensive proposition, such that all cases can be explained by it. A critical issue is the identification of negative cases that matter and are useful for strengthening the proposition. In evaluation, negative cases may be defined by the context of the evaluation. For example, the experience of every person receiving services matters, and so each is a case—some of which may be negative cases in a working hypothesis about the quality of the program.

See also CONSTANT COMPARATIVE METHOD, FALSIFIABILITY

NEUTRALITY. *See* BIAS, OBJECTIVITY, SUBJECTIVITY

■■ NEVO, DAVID

(b. 1939, Poland). Ph.D., The Ohio State University.

Nevo is Professor of Education at Tel Aviv University in Israel and Chief Scientist for the Ministry of Education, State of Israel.

Nevo has contributed to the field of evaluation through his work on evaluation in schools, specifically in promoting the combination of student assessment with program evaluation as a basis for the professional development of teachers and principals. Nevo has been instrumental in promoting the use of program evaluation in educational systems around the world. In this work, he is one of the pioneers of the idea of dialogic evaluation, an approach that accepts that evaluators can do many, but not all, things and that acknowledges evaluators are not the sole source of influence on changes in programs. He helped shape contemporary understandings of evaluation concepts in an analytic review of evaluation published in the *Review of Educational Research.*

As a graduate student, Nevo was involved in the Evaluation Center, which he followed when it moved to Western Michigan University (WMU). He was an active participant in the Consortium for Research on Accountability and Teacher Evaluation (CREATE) projects of the WMU Evaluation Center.

Nevo is Editor-in-Chief of *Studies in Educational Evaluation,* has conducted many large-scale evaluation studies, and has been Israel's representative at the International Association for the Evaluation of Educational Achievement since 1986. He is the coauthor (with Glasman) of *Evaluation in Decision Making: The Case of School Administration,* the author of *School-Based Evaluation: A Dialogue for School Improvement,* and the editor of *School-Based Evaluation: An International Perspective.*

■ NEWCOMER, KATHYRN

(b.1949, Omaha, Nebraska). Ph.D. Political Science, University of Iowa; M.A. Political Science, B.S. Secondary Education/Social Studies, University of Kansas.

Newcomer's main intellectual contribution to evaluation has been sorting out the relationships between performance measurement and program evaluation in public and nonprofit agencies. In practice, Newcomer has helped train hundreds of master's degree and doctoral students over two decades in evaluation skills and has overseen dozens of pro bono evaluation projects conducted by students for many nonprofit (and some public) agencies over the years.

J. Wholey and H. Hatry have served as her intellectual mentors, having collaborated on research, conferences, evaluations, and textbook design. Wholey's thinking about logic modeling and the use of evaluation work and performance measurement has been especially influential in shaping Newcomer's evaluation teaching and writing. Hatry's ideas about practical performance measurement have also greatly shaped her work.

Newcomer has served in leadership roles in several professional associations, and she was Chair of the Center for Accountability and Performance of the American Society for Public Administration. She has received teaching awards on being nominated by her students: the Peter Vaill Award (1996) and the George Washington Award (2000).

■ NEW DIRECTIONS FOR EVALUATION (NDE)

New Directions for Evaluation (NDE) and the *American Journal of Evaluation* are the two official publications of the American Evaluation Association. The editors of each are appointed by the AEA Board. The publications represent the professional excellence sought by the association and fulfill one of AEA's missions in promoting the development of evaluation as a field. The contents are consistent broadly with the policies, practices, and standards of AEA.

Conceived as a sourcebook, in which an issue or approach can be examined in more depth than it could be in a journal article, *New Directions in Evaluation* began under the editorship of Scarvia Anderson, with its roots in the national conventions of the Evaluation Research Society, which joined in 1986 with the Evaluation Network to become AEA. Many panel discussions at these meetings had outstanding presentations. At the time, there were books on evaluation but no refereed evaluation journals, and there was an expressed need for a monograph-length, relatively fast publication. The periodical was called *New Directions for Program Evaluation* at the beginning, but Michael Scriven successfully argued for a more inclusive journal title, a change that started with issue 68, "Reasoning in Evaluation," edited by Deborah Fournier.

For many years, *NDE* has been a refereed publication. A proposal for an issue, which must be on a single topic with contributions organized by the guest editor or editors, is sent to the editors-in-chief of *NDE*. The proposal is in a sense a mini-issue, presenting a comprehensive discussion of the proposed theme and its justification. Summaries of the proposed chapters by the prospective authors are extensive and complete. Proposals in turn receive thorough written reviews, according to the established protocol, by several (usually four to six) members of the Editorial Board. The proposal additionally may be reviewed by relevant substantive experts. This permits fairly detailed interaction between issue editors and the editors-in-chief, helping ensure the quality and relevance of the issue. The guest editor and the editors-in-chief also review the final manuscript before its publication and distribution by Jossey-Bass.

Over the past 15 years, more than 100 issues of *NDE* have appeared, under the guidance of editors-in-chief that have included Scarvia Anderson, Ronald Wooldridge, Ernest House, Mark Lipsey, Neil Smith, Willam Shadish, Lois-ellin Datta, Jennifer Greene, and Gary Henry. The first issue, edited by Scarvia Anderson and Claire Coles, was "Exploring Purposes and Dimensions," followed by Charlotte and Robert Rentz's "Evaluating Federal Programs." Subsequent topics have included (a) forums on methodology and theory, such as evaluation models, secondary analysis, survey research, and qualitative and quantitative methods; (b) examinations of the intersection of evaluation and broader social questions, such as multicultural evaluation, evaluation as a democratic process, and diversity in evaluation; (c) shared experiences and lessons learned—sometimes rueful, sometimes encouraging—such as experiences with control group designs in evaluation and in conducting multisite evaluations in real-world settings; and (d) presentation of newer approaches, such as the use of templates in evaluation, program theory, and appreciative inquiry.

Shorter than a book, much longer than an article, *NDE* has provided a forum for empirical, methodological, and theoretical work in evaluation. The common thread is a reflective approach, seeking balance and examination of a topic, more than advocacy for (or against) issues in these three broad areas.

—*Lois-ellin Datta*

NEWMAN, DIANNA L.

(b. 1951, Stuart, Nebraska). Ph.D. Educational Methodology and Evaluation, University of Nebraska–Lincoln; M.A., University of Nebraska; B.A. Education, Nebraska Wesleyan.

Newman is Associate Professor in the Department of Educational and Counseling Psychology and Director of the Evaluation Consortium. In addition to teaching and conducting research in higher education settings, she has served as a full-time evaluator for a K-12 school system and a public utility company.

Newman's research interests include utilization of evaluation, the ethics of practice, methods of documenting technology programs, and evidence of systemic change. She has actively practiced program evaluation in multiple settings, including K-12 education, higher education, mental health, social service, and the addictions field. As part of this practice, she has developed and validated replicable models of technology evaluation, systemic change evaluation, K-5 affective assessment, and long-term outcomes of professional development.

Newman is the author of numerous publications in leading evaluation journals and is actively involved in both the American Evaluation Association and the American Educational Research Association. She is coauthor (with Robert D. Brown) of *Applied Ethics in Program Evaluation,* served on the development committee of AEA's Guiding Principles for Evaluators, and has represented AEA on the Joint Committee on Standards for Educational Evaluation.

NO CHILD LEFT BEHIND (NCLB)

NCLB is the 2001 reauthorization of the Elementary and Secondary Education Act that funds the majority of federal K-12 education, including American Indian education, teacher training, Head Start, early literacy, school libraries, bilingual education, technology, and school safety, as well as, of course, Title I, which remains at the center of the legislation. In 2003, Title I gave $11.7 billion to schools serving low-income children, 64% of whom are students of color, in approximately 47,000 (about half of all) American public schools.

Although federal oversight of education has been in place since the Sputnik era, NCLB represents a dramatic increase in federal control over local educational decision making. While previous versions of the ESEA focused on fiscal accountability, NCLB demands accountability for outcomes, expressed as student achievement, for continued federal funding. The demands of NCLB directly affect the nature of evaluation in education by specifying how the quality of schools will be judged (for example, by specifying educational resources such as teacher qualification, parental involvement, and so on), what the indicators will be (mandatory statewide standardized student assessment and participation in NAEP), and what the standards will be (the key standard being demonstration of annual yearly progress by every subset of students).

Although NCLB had bipartisan support, it is highly controversial legislation because it amounts to an unfunded mandate for states, exercises unprecedented federal control over local educational decision making, advocates evaluation practices that are not consistent with professional standards, and contains "remedies" (such as transfers out of "failing schools") that are not workable.

See also ELEMENTARY AND SECONDARY EDUCATION ACT

■ NORM-REFERENCED TESTS

Norm-referenced tests yield scale scores that permit comparison of local test takers' performance to the test scores of specified groups (i.e., reference populations). The statistical tabulations of the reference population's test scores are considered the norms, and they serve as the basis for interpreting the local test takers' relative standing. Percentiles, percentile ranks, and normal standard scores are examples of relative scale score systems. In the context of educational evaluation, norm-referenced tests have been used when there was a justification for comparing local program outcomes to districtwide, regional, or national norms.

—Charles L. Thomas

Further Reading

American Educational Association, American Psychological Association, and National Council on Measurement in Education. (1999). *Standards for educational and psychological testing.* Washington, DC: American Educational Research Association.

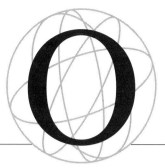

O

OBJECTIVES

Objectives state the specific outcomes an individual, program, or organization expects to accomplish within a given or stated time frame. They are detailed enough to provide an overall sense of exactly what is desired without outlining the specific steps necessary to achieve that end. Objectives link "upward" to goals (more abstract statements of intention), "downward" to strategies (specific, action-oriented plans), and directly to outcome or effectiveness measures. The acronym SMART (specific, measurable, appropriate, realistic, and time-bound) identifies the elements of objectives.

—*Jeffrey G. Tucker*

OBJECTIVES-BASED EVALUATION

Objectives-based evaluation refers to a class of evaluation approaches that centers on the specification of objectives and the measurement of outcomes. Specifically, objectives-based evaluation (sometimes referred to as objectives-oriented or objectives-referenced evaluation) focuses on generating information for accountability and decision making by developing and measuring the appropriate objectives for these purposes.

Ralph Tyler, often noted as the father of educational evaluation, has been credited with being a principal proponent of objectives-based evaluation approaches. Tyler, in his seminal 1942 manuscript *General Statement on Evaluation,* states that objectives-based evaluation entails (a) formulating a statement of educational objectives, (b) classifying these objectives into major types, (c) defining and refining each of these types of objectives in terms of behavior, (d) identifying situations in which students can be expected to display these types of behaviors, (e) selecting and trying promising methods for obtaining evidence regarding each type of objective, (f) selecting on the basis of preliminary trials the more promising appraisal methods for further development and improvement, and (g) devising means for interpreting and using the results. This approach of linking program objectives to outcome measures organized the tasks and goals of educational evaluation in a framework that was the dominant paradigm for almost half a century.

Tyler's influential work on the Eight Year Study, a longitudinal study of progressive education through the 4 years of secondary school and the 4 years of college, was the first large-scale evaluation to be designed using such an approach. This study, for a number of reasons (only one of which is the evaluation approach), has been noted as one of the most significant evaluations of the 20th century. Indeed, Madaus and Stufflebeam, in their 1989 book *Educational Evaluation: Classic Works of Ralph W. Tyler,* state, "Tyler's work on the Eight Year Study is still the best available description of how evaluators can work cooperatively with teachers to clarify instructional objectives and develop indicators of students' continuous progress toward the mastery of a whole range of learning outcomes" (p. xii).

POST-TYLER OBJECTIVES-BASED MODELS

Objectives-oriented evaluation had a strong influence on educational evaluation for many decades and, as part of that influence, several notable objectives-based theoretical models were developed, particularly during the 1960s and 1970s. These objectives-based models focus on behavioral objectives, performance objectives, and measurable objectives—which were all, more or less, synonymous terms for a specific objective that described exactly what was expected of students after instruction. These explicit objectives were distinguished from the more nebulous educational goals and objectives educators had been previously admonished for articulating. With more precise, unambiguous objectives, it was argued that one could determine with more confidence when they had been met.

In 1962, Robert Mager published a primer on how to write instructional objectives. The primer had a large impact on those interested in objectives-based evaluation models. Mager's approach to developing instructional objectives was central to many objectives-based evaluation models, and it played a particularly pivotal role in the work of W. James Popham.

Popham, following the Tyler model, developed and promoted a popular objectives-based evaluation approach that focused primarily on the championing of behavioral objective specification. Popham's evaluation model relied heavily on measuring educational outcomes, and as such, de-emphasized the focus on the instructional process. In his text *The Uses of Instructional Objectives: A Personal Perspective* (1973), Popham wrote, "The single most important deficiency in American education is its preoccupation with instructional process. This overriding concern with procedures rather than results produced by those procedures manifests itself in myriad ways. Teachers design classroom instructional sequences by asking, 'What shall I do?' rather than the appropriate question, which is 'What do I wish my learners to become?'" (p. 53).

Although he touted very focused, well-defined objectives and outcomes related to them, Popham cautioned that objectives alone were not enough. Instead, he maintained that a precise objective is most helpful when planning an instructional sequence. The evaluation of such a sequence is best when focused on the degree to which the objective has been achieved, which requires the development of measures that are based explicitly on the objectives. This meant that test items had to be developed based on instructional

objectives that specifically observed students' cognitive and noncognitive behaviors. Popham saw this as a step in the right direction because he argued that "if a school district had access to sets of objectives plus test items for each objective it could readily assess the degree to which its instructional approaches were successful," which would, in turn, encourage educators to initiate criterion-referenced instructional strategies. In support of this notion, in 1968, the UCLA Center for the Study of Evaluation (CSE) launched the Instructional Objectives Exchange (IOX).

IOX was built on the premise that instructional improvement is facilitated by clear definition of desired outcomes and the subsequent measurement of postinstructional learner attainment of those outcomes. With this as its foundation, IOX developed, collected, and maintained a vast pool of instructional objectives and related measurement tools for widespread use. Thus IOX acted as a "broker" for school districts, teachers, and groups of teachers, making it possible for objectives and related measurements for a variety of subjects, grades, and topics to be obtained. In addition, IOX served as a clearinghouse for all U.S.-based instructional objectives projects. In 1970, IOX spun off from CSE and became a nonprofit organization headed by Popham and others. IOX continues to develop state assessment systems and objectives-based assessments for other agencies.

Other notable objectives-based evaluation models were developed by Metfessel and Michael and by Hammond. Metfessel and Michael's work follows Tyler's evaluation step progression but pays greater heed to expanding the range of alternative instruments. Hammond includes Tyler's views in a behavioral objectives dimension that is part of a model that also includes a more precise definition of instruction and the institution.

In additional to the evaluation approaches that emerged, it is also important to mention Bloom, Engelhart, Furst, Hill, and Krathwohl's taxonomy of educational objectives for the cognitive domain and Krathwohl, Bloom, and Masia's taxonomy for the affective domain, both of which were derived from Tyler's objectives-based work.

Bloom et al.'s taxonomy, which originally received sporadic attention, gained the interest of educators in the 1960s when the discussion of instructional objectives became more prominent. In this taxonomy, Bloom et al. define and classify the ways in which information is used. They developed six categories of behavioral objectives—knowledge, comprehension, application, analysis, synthesis, and evaluation—which are ranked in order from the most simple to the most complex, with knowledge being the most simple objective. The affective taxonomy developed by Krathwohl et al. attracted less interest than the cognitive taxonomy but was still well known. Its focus is on students' interests, attitudes, and values. As with the cognitive taxonomy, categories range from the lowest level of awareness to the highest. The five categories are receiving, responding, valuing, organization, and characterization. Taxonomies such as these served to bring increased clarity and precision to objectives.

AN OBJECTIVES-BASED EVALUATION CLASSIFICATION SCHEME

Inspired by the increased demand for developing school accountability systems that required the specification of objectives and the need to clarify how objectives and objectives-based evaluation systems could be meaningful, in 1972, Alkin developed a classification scheme for objectives-based evaluation. This simple taxonomy classified objectives-based evaluation systems in terms of two inherent purposes: evaluation scope and program generality. With respect to evaluation scope, an objectives-based evaluation system might be used by a teacher as an instructional tool designed to help determine student achievement on incremental, or "en route," objectives, which generally represent "individual units of learning." That is, the information yielded is intended primarily for use in a single context. Alternatively, the evaluation scope may be framed by expected behavioral outcomes and would therefore be concerned mostly with measuring "terminal objectives." These objectives rely less on the manner in which a teacher might teach the objectives and more on the intended behavioral outcome.

Another dimension by which an objectives-based evaluation system could be classified is related to program generality. That is, the extent to which the evaluation is related to one particular program; for example, a textbook publisher that provides, as part of a teacher's manual, tests to be administered. This is a single-purpose objectives-based evaluation system: The related tests are "keyed to the specific objectives formulated for the program and explicit in the textbook." On the other hand, an evaluation system might also be multiprogram, meaning that it is not related to

the use of a specific instructional program or set of materials. As a result, an objectives-based evaluation system could also be classified based on program generality.

CRITERION-REFERENCED MEASUREMENT

The focal point of objectives-based evaluation shifted from the precise, unambiguous statement of objectives to how objectives are to be measured and, as a result, objectives-based evaluation became more popularly referred to as *criterion-referenced measurement*. We should note that although the terms *criterion-referenced tests* and *objectives-based tests* have been used interchangeably, *criterion referenced* is often used as a more general term and describes a test measuring instructional performance criteria; *objectives based* refers to tests measuring well-defined behavioral objectives. These measures are designed to measure performance in relationship to a behavioral domain, in contrast to *norm-referenced tests,* which measure an individual's performance in relationship to the performance of others who have also taken the exam. Criterion-referenced measures provide information about an individual's performance with respect to a defined set of behavioral criteria. As such, what is being measured is what one can do (individual performance is referenced to a defined behavioral domain) rather than how one performs in relation to others. Consequently, the criterion-referenced test is interpreted based on absolute terms (percentages) and the norm-referenced test is interpreted relative to the normed group performance (percentiles). Criterion-referenced test data, therefore, are useful in determining whether an educational program accomplished its objectives.

There are now countless examples of larger-scale, standardized, criterion-referenced measures. One of the more notable ones is the National Assessment of Educational Progress (NAEP) Exam. Although this exam was constructed later in his career, Tyler greatly influenced the development of the NAEP. First administered in 1969, NAEP is know as the nation's "report card." NAEP assesses a sample of students from across the county intermittently in reading, math, science, writing, U.S. history, civics, geography, and the arts. Results regarding subject-matter achievement are reported for particular student populations (e.g., fourth graders) and subgroups of those populations (e.g., female students, Hispanic students) rather than individual students. In 1990, NAEP began administering the exam so that states could also receive results. Following the NAEP approach, nearly all states have developed their own criterion-referenced tests to measure student performance annually.

CRITICISMS OF OBJECTIVES-BASED EVALUATION

Objectives-based evaluation gained increased consideration by professionals during the 1960s and early 1970s, but criticism of this evaluation approach soon emerged. Indeed, objectives-based evaluation came under much scrutiny and condemnation for several reasons.

First, objectives-based evaluation approaches require that program staff (and researchers) write very specific, detailed, precise objectives. This process is extremely time consuming, and teachers are often just too busy to engage in the process of developing measurable objectives for each program activity. Another related serious shortcoming of the approach is that it requires the development of valid measures for each instructional objective. Test item development, again, is time consuming and, if done correctly, can be relatively costly. Because objectives-based evaluation has been used most extensively in education, when considered within the context of a teachers' working day, these tasks seem rather awesome. In some schools, staff were spending so much time and energy stating everything they wanted to teach in terms of behavioral terms that they hardly had time to teach. In addition, the preciseness in instructional objectives advocated by many of the earlier proponents of objectives-based evaluation resulted in an excessively long list of objectives that often proved to be overwhelming and even, sometimes, meaningless. In response to such criticism, those who had once called for a narrow scope of educational objectives resulting in a massive number of objectives (see Popham, 1973) later (see Popham, 1988) recognized this problem and called for a focus on a manageable number of broad-scope objectives and the use of the taxonomies of educational objectives only as "gross heuristics."

A second set of limitations centers on the objectives-based evaluation process. Critics argue that because the emphasis is on the measure of objectives (rather than on judging the merit of a program), objectives-based evaluation does not have a true evaluation component,

capture the unintended impact of a program, describe the variation in results due to context, or assess the relationships among objectives. In addition, objectives-based evaluation findings are provided only at the end of a project. Agencies and schools needed an evaluation process that could be integrated into the development and operation of projects and that would help them improve project operations.

Criterion-referenced measures have also been scrutinized, and NAEP in particular has received criticism. As previously mentioned, NAEP results regarding subject-matter achievement are reported for populations of students rather than on an individual level. Consequently, results have been used largely for accountability and informing public policy. As such, the exam has been criticized for not having an impact on instruction at the classroom level.

Furthermore, there is the potential that the preoccupation with specified objectives that can accompany a system using criterion-referenced measures could deter teachers from teaching a wide-ranging curriculum. Thus the preestablished specificity inherent in objectives-based measures could set the stage for teachers "teaching to the test."

WHERE ARE WE NOW?

Over the past decade or so, with respect to evaluation theory development, there has been relatively little work in the area of objectives-based evaluation. Nevertheless, objectives-based evaluation approaches continue to be used to guide evaluation practice (in addition to the relatively widespread use of criterion-referenced tests used to measure student performance). For example, the World Bank's Operations Evaluation Department uses an objectives-based evaluation approach to evaluate development work. The World Bank claims that this approach to evaluating its work has three important advantages: It enhances accountability, promotes efficiency, and allows comparisons.

It is apparent that objectives-based evaluation approaches have been and remain an important option for framing evaluations. It was the exceptional work of Tyler that ushered the notions of objectives-based evaluation to the forefront of early evaluation practice—where it remained for decades. Although continued theory development in this area has seemed to taper off, theoretic notions from objectives-based evaluation continue to have influence on evaluation theory development. These models also serve as a noteworthy example of how early evaluation theoretic work could be and indeed was modified based on the field experiences of those using the approach. As a result, large-scale, significant evaluations continue to be designed using objectives-based evaluation approaches.

—*Christina A. Christie and Marvin C. Alkin*

Further Readings

Alkin. M. (1972). *A classification scheme for objectives-based evaluation systems* (CSE Report No. 79). Los Angeles: Center for the Study of Evaluation.

Bloom, B. S., Engelhart, M. D., Furst, E. J., Hill, W. H., & Krathwohl, D. R. (1956). *Taxonomy of educational objectives: Handbook I. Cognitive domain.* New York: David McKay.

Krathwohl, D. R., Bloom, B. S., & Masia, B.B. (1964). *Taxonomy of educational objectives: Handbook II. Affective domain.* New York: David McKay.

Madaus, G., & Stufflebeam, D. (Eds.). (1989). *Educational evaluation: Classic works of Ralph W. Tyler.* Dordrecht, The Netherlands: Kluwer Academic.

Mager, R. F. (1962). *Preparing instructional objectives.* Palo Alto, CA: Fearon.

Metfessel, N. S., & Michael, W. B. (1967). A paradigm involving multiple criterion measures for the evaluation of the effectiveness of school programs. *Educational and Psychological Measurement, 27,* 931-943.

Popham, W. J. (1973). *The uses of instructional objectives: A personal perspective.* Belmont, CA: Fearon.

Popham, W. J. (1988). *Educational evaluation* (2nd ed.). Englewood Cliffs, NJ: Prentice Hall.

Tyler, R. (1942). General statement on evaluation. *Journal of Educational Research, 35,* 492-501.

OBJECTIVITY

The term *objectivity* usually refers to a notion of the truth based on factual evidence obtained through scientific methods or reasoning and a belief that that truth is really the way things are. This idea is based on *objectivism,* or the assumption that there is an external world that exists in and of itself and independent of our apprehension or comprehension of it. Objectivism has both an epistemological basis (relying on the scientific method for the apprehension of truth) and a value basis. In the latter case, values are presumed to exist independently in the external world, and objects or activities are perceived or experienced as desirable when the intrinsic existing quality in them is discerned. Objectivity is typically contrasted with subjectivity.

OBSERVATION

Observation refers to a data collection strategy in evaluation that relies on first-hand and eyewitness experiences of places, activities, events, and so on. Observations can be formal (such as with the use of preordinate protocols or checklists) or informal (describing the sense of having been there), as well as participant (the observer assumes some role relevant to that social context) or nonparticipant (such as observation through a one-way mirror or noninteractively). Reports of observations are most useful when they are low inference; that is, more descriptive and less evaluative. The quality of observation is presumed to improve with prolonged periods of time.

ONTOLOGY

Ontology is a theory about the nature of being and existence. The term is used in many different senses, but basically, ontology is a branch of metaphysics that specifies fundamental properties and relations of existence, the very elementary categories of the world. Ontology is often the background (principles and causes) that informs the formulation, description, and analysis of phenomena in the world. Examples of ontological questions are, What is existence? What does it mean to say that an object exists? What are an object's properties, and how are they related to the object? When does something cease to exist? For evaluation, ontology matters when attempting to understand the variations in approaches to evaluation and the quantitative-qualitative debates, as well as in the development of a theory of evaluation.

OPPORTUNITY COSTS

Opportunity costs refer to cost in terms of forgone alternatives. These costs may be measured in many ways, including dollars, but also in time, good will, knowledge, and so on. For example, if a school district decides to purchase new textbooks, the opportunity cost is that something else might have been done with that money. In buying new textbooks, the school district has relinquished the opportunity to provide professional development of teachers, build a playground, or reduce the budget deficit. Particularly in program evaluation, the concept of opportunity cost can be useful, although, in fact, there is seldom a serious analysis of the opportunity costs of the evaluand.

This is, in part, because one must step outside the parameters of the evaluand as it is and examine it in a context of what might have been.

◼ ORGANISATION FOR ECONOMIC CO-OPERATION AND DEVELOPMENT (OECD)

The OECD is made up of 30 member countries that share a commitment to democratic government and market economy. The OECD is probably best known for its publications and its statistics, work that covers economic and social issues, including macroeconomics, trade, education, development, and science. Evaluation and decision making by the OECD take the form of "peer review and pressure":

> Peer review can be described as the systematic examination and assessment of the performance of a State by other States, with the ultimate goal of helping the reviewed State improve its policy making, adopt best practices, and comply with established standards and principles. The examination is conducted on a non-adversarial basis, and it relies heavily on mutual trust among the States involved in the review, as well as their shared confidence in the process. (Pagani, 2002, p. 4)

This peer review process is complemented by a peer-pressure effect that can take a number of forms, including "(i) a mix of formal recommendations and informal dialogue by the peer countries; (ii) public scrutiny, comparisons, and, in some cases, even ranking among countries; and (iii) the impact of all the above on domestic public opinion, national administrations and policy makers" (Pagani, 2002, p. 5).

Further Reading

Pagani, F. (2002). *Peer review: A tool for co-operation and change* (OECD No. JT00131206). Paris: OECD Publications Service. Retrieved May 28, 2004, from http://www.oecd.org/dataoecd/33/16/1955285.pdf

◼ ORGANIZATIONAL CHANGE

Organizational change is defined here as processes by which an organization alters its structures and or culture due to internal or environmental factors. A fundamental aspect of change is that it is a process, not an event. Various synonyms for *change* appear in the management literature, such as *reform, renewal,* and *improvement.* Change can be regarded as a fact, but it is not the same as improvement, which is based on judgment. A major implication for evaluation is that empirical evidence should be a major factor in decision making about change. This is usually achieved by ongoing cooperative interactions between evaluators and organizational management.

—*John M. Owen*

See also LEARNING ORGANIZATION

◼ ORGANIZATIONAL CULTURE

An organization can be categorized by two defining elements: its structure and culture. *Culture* refers to those norms and values that characterize the operations of the organization. A key aspect of organizational culture is openness to change. This involves being willing to challenge the status quo, to examine the environment for new knowledge, and to accept the need for continuous improvement. There are implications for evaluation as a means of providing evidence on which to base change and improvement. Over the past decade, a significant theoretical position has been developed that sees evaluators working cooperatively with organizational staff to instill a culture that routinely accepts evaluation as an input to learning and decision making.

—*John M. Owen*

Further Reading

Louis, K. S. (1998). Reconnecting knowledge utilization and school improvement: Two steps forward, one step back. In A. Hargreaves, A. Lieberman, M. Fullan, & D. Hopkins (Eds.), *International handbook of educational change* (Vol. 2, pp. 1074-1095). Boston: Kluwer.

ORGANIZATIONAL LEARNING. *See* LEARNING ORGANIZATION

◼ O'SULLIVAN, RITA

(b. 1948, Brooklyn, New York). Ed.D. Educational Leadership and Curriculum and Instruction, Auburn University; M.A. Educational Administration, California Polytechnic State University, San Luis

Obispo; A.B. Anthropology, University of California, Berkeley.

O'Sullivan is Associate Professor, Assessment and Evaluation, in the School of Education at the University of North Carolina at Chapel Hill.

Her primary contributions to the field of evaluation have been the development of collaborative evaluation theory and techniques that enhance evaluation capacity and utilization among educators and public service providers. She has successfully used collaborative evaluation approaches with education, health, community development, and family support programs in North Carolina; nonprofit organizations in the southeastern United States; and national program initiatives in education and community development. Recently, O'Sullivan traveled to Siberia to conduct evaluation training for 160 staff from the emerging nonprofit sector in the newly independent states of the former USSR and Durban, South Africa. While there, she co-led a workshop for 60 cooperative extension staff from six different countries. Working collaboratively with program people as they use evaluation findings to improve the quality of their services has been a sustaining influence.

In addition to her contributions to the field of evaluation via articles and presentations, O'Sullivan authored *Evaluation Practice: A Collaborative Approach* and served as Secretary-Treasurer of the American Evaluation Association from 1992 to 1997. Currently she cochairs the Collaborative, Participatory, and Empowerment Evaluation TIG. In 2001, she was presented with the first lifetime Distinguished Service Award from the North Carolina Association for Research in Education, and in 2002, she received the Outstanding Research Paper Award from the same association, as well as the Robert Ingle Service Award from the American Evaluation Association.

■■ OUTCOMES

Outcomes are changes, results, and impacts that may be short or long term; proximal or distal; primary or secondary; intended or unintended; positive or negative; and singular, multiple, or hierarchical. Outcomes are enduring changes, in contrast to *outputs,* which are more specific. Evaluations, especially summative evaluations, measure outcomes at the individual level (changes in knowledge, skills, attitudes), organizational level (changes in policies, practices, capacity), community level (changes in employment rates, school achievement, recycling), and the policy or governmental level (changes in laws, regulations, sources of funding).

See also Logic Model, Outputs

■■ OUTPUTS

Outputs are the tangible products that result from a program's activities. In an evaluation of a communications campaign, for example, outputs might be the number of public service announcements placed or the number of brochures distributed. Output measurement can also involve assessing the number and type of people who receive the program services. Outputs are a standard component of logic models, where they fall between activities and outcomes. If a program is effective, its outputs should lead to the desired outcomes. Measuring outputs is usually easier and cheaper than measuring outcomes, but this does not suffice for good summative evaluation.

—*Melvin M. Mark*

■■ OWEN, JOHN M.

(b. 1943, Bendigo, Australia). Ph.D., Monash University, Australia; M.Ed. University of Melbourne, Australia.

Owen is a Principal Fellow in the Centre for Program Evaluation, Australia. From 1992 to 2002, he was Director of a major evaluation center in Australia. During this time, he supervised the planning and development of an innovative postgraduate teaching program, which is offered online. Interests are in typologies of evaluation approaches that enable policy managers and evaluation practitioners to plan effective evaluations. He has written a major text on evaluation, *Program Evaluation: Forms and Approaches.*

He undertook a major study of education innovation diffusion for a Ph.D. at Monash University that led to an academic interest in knowledge utilization. This has underpinned his concerns for evaluation that meets the needs of stakeholders.

Owen received the Australian Evaluation Society's award for outstanding contribution to evaluation in 1994. He spent 4 months as a visiting professor at Hiroshima University in Japan in 2002.

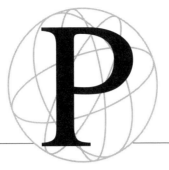

PANEL STUDIES

Panel studies involve a special type of reflexive control, which means that the target subjects who receive an intervention are compared to themselves by use of before and after measurements. Panel studies are a repeated-measures design and typically use survey methods for data collection, although interviews and other qualitative data collection methods may also be involved. Panel studies that embed qualitative samples inside a large-scale survey design can be conducted in ways that will yield valuable information to policy makers and administrators. These embedded subsamples may be representative of the whole survey universe or may be purposive and designed to understand one particular category.

—*Jeffrey G. Tucker*

PARADIGM

Paradigm is a term used to capture a worldview or perspective that, in the case of research and evaluation, includes conceptions of methodology, purposes, assumptions, and values. In evaluation, a common use of the term is in characterizing the distinction between quantitative and qualitative approaches, as well as in contrasting positivism, postpositivism, constructivism, interpretivism, feminist theory, critical theory, and so on. The term's popularity stems from Thomas Kuhn's use of it in his classic work *The Structure of Scientific Revolutions*. Although Kuhn used the term *paradigm* in various ways, in one sense he considered the standard practices of science that consist of shared ways of solving problems and definitions of classic problems to be a paradigm. He also used the term to refer to a discipline that shares assumptions, beliefs, methods, and other facets. A paradigm typically consists of an ontology (the nature of reality), an epistemology (what is knowable and who can know it), and a methodology (how one can obtain knowledge).

Further Reading

Guba, E. G. (Ed.). (1990). *The paradigm dialog.* Newbury Park, CA: Sage.

PARETO OPTIMAL

Named after Italian economist Vilfredo Pareto, *Pareto Optimal* refers to a situation in which making somebody better off does not make anyone else worse off. Pareto optimality is essentially a state of equilibrium and does not address overall fairness. This is a key concept and limitation in Rawls' theory of justice, particularly in regard to the "difference principle." Pareto Optimal is a stringent criterion in evaluation that may limit changes in programs, organizations, or policies.

See also SOCIAL JUSTICE

PARETO PRINCIPLE

The *Pareto Principle* is also known as "the 80:20 rule" and "A minority of input produces the majority of results." Italian economist Vilfredo Pareto studied the distribution of wealth in a variety of countries around 1900 and found that about 80% of the wealth in most countries was controlled by a consistent minority—about 20% of the people. The principle has been expanded beyond its economic use and reflects the notion that most of the results (of a life, of a program, of a financial campaign) come from a minority of effort (or people, or input).

PARTICIPANT. *See* STAKEHOLDERS

■ PARTICIPANT OBSERVATION

A data collection strategy inherited from cultural anthropology and, more specifically, ethnography. The strategy consists of the dual roles of participation and observation, which are best understood as a continuum from mostly observer to mostly participant, and variants between. A common caution about participant observation is the potential for "going native," in which case the evaluator completely adopts an insider's perspective and thus loses the evaluator persona. Participant observation requires that the evaluator spend time immersed in the context of the evaluand; take part in day-to-day activities; and record dialogue, interactions, and events through field notes, photography, artifacts, and interviews. An underlying assumption is that understanding the evaluand will be enhanced by an insider or empathetic view, one that requires assuming at least marginally a position of being in the context.

■ PARTICIPATORY ACTION RESEARCH (PAR)

PAR has been described as a three-pronged activity involving investigation, education, and action. Research is conceived of as a developmental process in which, through the involvement of less-powerful stakeholders in investigation, reflection, negotiation, decision making, and knowledge creation, individual participants and power dynamics in the sociocultural milieu are changed. Evaluators using PAR discover that it is more than performing particular types of activities; it becomes part of who they are, because working in this way involves a commitment to a set of values and principles beyond the simple act of collecting and understanding information. PAR is far more than a methodology; it involves a focus on process and a commitment to action. Participatory evaluation (PE) has emerged at least partly from PAR.

PAR emerged in the early 1970s, primarily, but not exclusively, in the developing world. This was, in part, a reaction to positivist models of inquiry that were seen as exploitive and detached from the urgent social and economic problems that people in much of the world were facing. Although PAR has spread to university classrooms and texts and, more recently, to major multilateral institutions, it is deeply rooted in community and international development, adult education, and, more recently, the women's movement. In North America, important work has been done at the *Highlander Center for Research and Education.*

Key concepts and principles include the following:

1. *PAR begins with an understanding of the context.* Social, political, economic, cultural, and spiritual factors are not assumed to be "given" but rather need to be understood and critically examined as part of the totality within which one is doing research.

2. *Who creates and controls the production of knowledge is essential.* One important aim of PAR is to empower people through participation in the process of constructing and respecting their own knowledge (based on Freire's notion of "conscientization") and through their understanding of the connections among knowledge, power, and control.

3. *Popular knowledge is assumed to be as valid and useful as scientific knowledge produced by "experts."* Though often dismissed as "anecdotal" and "subjective," what ordinary people know, based on life experience and often years of trial and error, needs to be respected and validated.

4. *Focus on the process—how is the research conducted?* The distance between researcher and researched is lessened; all participants are contributors working collectively. Initiating and sustaining genuine dialogue among actors leads to a deep level of understanding and respect.

5. *Critical reflection is an integral part of doing research.* This requires participants to question, to doubt, and to consider a broad range of social, political, and cultural factors, including their own biases and assumptions.

6. *Research needs to lead to action and social transformation.* Most research is about "finding truth," predicting, and verifying. PAR not only questions that, it adds an action component as an essential aspect. Praxis (action-reflection) is one of the key dynamics, a continual process of learning and doing.

—*Elizabeth Whitmore*

Further Reading

Hall, B. L. (1992). From margins to center? The development and purpose of participatory research. *American Sociologist, 24*(4), 15-28.

Maguire, P. (1987). *Doing participatory research: A feminist perspective.* Amherst, MA: University of Massachusetts, Center for International Education.

■■ PARTICIPATORY EVALUATION

Participatory evaluation is an overarching term for any evaluation approach that involves program staff or participants actively in decision making and other activities related to the planning and implementation of evaluation studies. The reasons for participant involvement, which vary among different types, include the desire to effect change in individuals, in programs or organizations, and, in some cases, in society at large, as well as building the capacity of a group or institution to conduct additional evaluations. The origins of participatory evaluation are multiple, reflecting roots in disparate traditions and disciplines literally from around the world, each pointing to the importance of participants interactively helping to study their own programs. Examples range from staff in an American social service agency working collaboratively with an evaluator to improve their program's effectiveness to clients of Australian mental health services examining their own experiences in an institution to British educators trying over time to increase their use of data collection and analysis for ongoing improvement to farmers in rural India studying ways to increase productivity.

Participatory approaches are distinguished by several characteristics. First, direct and active participant involvement over time in evaluation planning and implementation is a hallmark of participatory evaluation. It is stakeholder based, which is to say participant or consumer focused, and responsibility for the

evaluation can ultimately devolve to those who manage or participate in the program rather than to professionals with evaluation credentials. It is important to note that, in and of itself, participatory evaluation is not a social movement but rather a way to democratize the evaluation process by involving people meaningfully in studies of the programs in which they participate. Second, these approaches foster participant ownership during the evaluation process through a variety of interactive activities—question generation, periodic discussions, collaborative data analysis, reflection sessions, and so on. Evidence suggests that such interaction and ownership increases the likelihood that people will then use the studies' results. Third, the role of the professional evaluator in these approaches is that of partner, facilitator, or coach—a teacher and consultant to program participants, who is willing to share or even relinquish power for decision making in the study, but who is available for technical assistance as needed. Fourth, through the purposeful use of the evaluation process, participatory evaluation approaches may increase—intentionally or not—the evaluation capacity of individuals or of an organization over time. By taking part in studies (i.e., learning evaluation by doing it) participants may better understand the evaluation process and gain program evaluation skills. Weaver and Cousins (2001) provide five dimensions for analyzing participatory evaluation studies: the extent to which stakeholders control decisions, the diversity of individuals selected to participate, the depth of people's participation, the power relations of participants, and the study's feasibility.

The exact nature of people's involvement in participatory evaluations ranges on a continuum from shared evaluator-participant responsibility for evaluation questions and activities to participants' complete control of the evaluation process. At the shared end of the continuum, the evaluator and program staff and/or participants collaborate to identify issues, frame evaluation questions, collect and analyze data, and suggest next steps. The evaluator assumes responsibility for the quality of the process and its outcomes in conjunction with people involved in the program. Ongoing interaction throughout the study ensures its successful implementation and, it is hoped, the use of its results. Although the terms *collaborative* and *participatory* evaluation are sometimes used interchangeably, if distinguished, collaborative evaluation is a type of participatory evaluation midrange on the continuum. The notion of working together, of "colaboring," may suggest more coequal responsibility for the evaluation process, with program people concerned with issues of the evaluation's utility and feasibility and the evaluator concerned with issues of its propriety and accuracy.

At the other end of the continuum, the evaluator's role changes entirely to that of a coach or facilitator, available on call with technical skills but not charged with responsibility for the evaluation process. Studies at this end of the continuum therefore require minimal involvement from an evaluator. Program staff or people who receive services take responsibility for the study, managing and running the evaluation and using the evaluator as a resource for technical issues when needed; for example, to edit survey items, to draw a sample of respondents, or to audit a qualitative analysis. In such situations, the evaluator may serve primarily as quality control, making sure that the technical quality of the evaluation meets professional standards. This helps to ensure that the evaluation results are worth using.

Numerous terms are associated with participatory studies conducted in the absence of or with minimal involvement of an evaluator. Seven types of action research (collaborative, critical, emancipatory, participatory, practical, technical, and traditional) technically meet the criteria of participatory evaluation. All actively involve practitioners in addressing problems grounded in real-world practice; engage people consistently; create ownership through a cyclic process of planning, acting, observing, and reflecting; and may, through the process, teach evaluation skills. Two distinct forms of participatory action research, for example, that which emerged from the field of organizational learning in business, industry, and agriculture and that stemming from work with oppressed peoples in the Third World, could appropriately be labeled participatory evaluation. The literature and practice of action research, however, developed separately from that of participatory evaluation, and, like other concepts in program evaluation, *participatory evaluation* remains a broad term with multiple interpretations encompassing varied practice.

There are two common misunderstandings of the term *participatory evaluation*. First, novices may assume that an evaluation that involves program staff or participants in any way—for example, by asking people their concerns or by collecting data from them—is by definition a "participatory" evaluation.

This is incorrect—or perhaps it is more appropriate to say that, in a sense, all evaluations are participatory to a certain degree. Since the emergence of the stakeholder-based approach in the 1970s, good evaluation practice has noted the importance of interacting with stakeholders to determine their concerns and, in most cases, to frame evaluation questions. Data collection typically and unavoidably involves interaction with participants. However, mere contact between an evaluator and participants is not the defining characteristic of a participatory evaluation. What makes participatory evaluation different is the role that participants actively play throughout the evaluation process in making decisions about any number of things—what issues to study, what instruments to use, how to collect data and from whom, how to analyze the data, and so on.

A second misconception about participatory evaluation stems from the frequent but incorrect assumption that any evaluation using qualitative methods—that is, any study that necessitates an evaluator's interaction with program staff and participants for an extended period of time—is, by definition, participatory. Again, the confusion stems from a misunderstanding of the interaction between evaluator and evaluation participant. It is not this direct contact that defines a participatory evaluation; evaluators routinely interact with program staff and people who participate. Rather, it is the nature of the relationship between them that determines whether or not the study is participatory. If the evaluator retains complete control of decision making for the study, regardless of the data-collection methods used or the time spent on site, the study is not participatory.

Theorists typically categorize participatory evaluation into three distinct types, two of which build on the work of Cousins and Whitmore (1998): (a) practical participatory evaluation (P-PE), (b) transformative participatory evaluation (T-PE), and (c) participatory monitoring and evaluation (PME). Practical participatory evaluation evolved from a pragmatic desire to increase ownership of the evaluation process and the use of evaluation results by involving program staff and participants. Its concerns relate to improving evaluation practice by purposefully applying the "personal factor" of utilization-focused evaluation (see Patton, 1997). The personal factor suggests the value of connecting with primary intended users, people who are interested in the evaluation process and outcomes, and collecting information they can use in specific ways.

The evaluation setting may not allow evaluation participants to make major decisions or control resources for the organization, and participants, who are often staff members or administrators, are not necessarily from oppressed or disenfranchised groups. In P-PE, which is at the interactive end of the participatory evaluation continuum, evaluators can take a leadership role; for example, by arranging logistics, asking probing questions, and generally keeping the evaluation process moving. P-PE can provide data for accountability purposes, enabling organizations to respond to external demands for evaluation in a manner that may simultaneously help them build an infrastructure for additional evaluation activities.

By contrast, transformative participatory evaluation explicitly targets oppressed and disenfranchised groups, and program participants, in theory, become the leaders of evaluation efforts to support social change and social justice through the development of empowered citizens. The contrast is important. P-PE may help to improve the status quo, as staff members use evaluation to make programs more efficient or effective (for example, improving social service delivery to new citizens). The evaluation process may engage consumers but not necessarily with a broader social concept in mind. King proposed the term *meliorative participatory evaluation* as a category label for studies that sought both outcomes.

At its extreme, T-PE poses a more dramatic evaluation question: In what ways can this program or society more generally meet the needs of groups who have not traditionally held roles of power? "People" take leadership roles in the evaluation process and, in so doing, become empowered to effect meaningful change in their lives. The setting must include the capacity for the evaluation team to make decisions and to control resources; otherwise the empowerment process is limited in its effects. T-PE at its best provides data for program development and self-accountability, helping to shape society through a deliberative democratic evaluation process. It is a process that seeks to better the world for oppressed people; for example, by reducing poverty among rural communities in developing countries. In practice, the term encompasses a number of citizen-based evaluation approaches from the past half-century, including some forms of participatory action research and, more recently, empowerment evaluation. The implementation of empowerment evaluation has raised the question of what it means to be disenfranchised; some, for example, would question the extent to which program staff in social programs represent an "oppressed population" as they conduct an evaluation.

Both P-PE and T-PE tend to be episodic in nature; that is, they are approaches to individual evaluation studies, although typically with the commitment to increasing the organization's capacity to conduct additional studies. The third type of participatory evaluation, participatory monitoring and evaluation, attends to the continuous monitoring of program activities, as well as to periodic evaluation efforts. Arising from international development work and participatory rural appraisal (renamed participatory learning and action), PME is an ongoing, organic process that makes explicit the routine oversight of day-to-day program activities and more formal studies as needed.

Given participatory evaluation's commitment to interaction between evaluator and participants, certain contexts lend themselves more readily to participatory evaluation. A first and primary consideration is the extent to which those administering programs support the participatory process. Without autonomy, control of key resources, and the opportunity to address any issue of concern, participatory evaluation efforts face an uphill battle. Second, the organizational climate should model trust, respect, openness, and especially a willingness to acknowledge problematic areas of concern. Third, a commitment to building an evaluation infrastructure or evaluation capacity supports initial efforts as models for long-term, ongoing work. Finally, a number of resources can facilitate the participatory process: incentives for participation, sufficient funding for key activities (for example, money to copy and mail a survey), a flexible timeline that structures the evaluation process, and technical evaluation skills.

As is true of other approaches, participatory evaluation presents both advantages and challenges. Proponents identify a number of potential benefits because, in and of itself, people's involvement in evaluation studies may lead to a number of positive outcomes. These include (a) increased ownership of both the means and ends of program evaluation, and hence the more likely use of its results; (b) the ability to provide meaningful data for decision making, leading to improved practice; (c) evaluation skills training, both for individuals, who learn how to conduct an evaluation as they experience one, and for organizations, which benefit from people have increased skills and appreciation for evaluation; and (d) a cost-effective way to conduct evaluations in settings that lack resources for doing them. In addition, working together during a participatory evaluation may increase camaraderie, as people collect data and reflect on issues that are important to them. Although these claims have not been thoroughly validated, existing research does support the claim that participation helps to foster ownership and use.

By contrast, critics of participatory evaluation point to theoretical and practical concerns. Primary among these is the fear that by "giving the evaluation process away," the technical adequacy of studies will decrease, with a resultant loss of rigor, leading potentially to inaccurate or misinterpreted data, incorrect results, and flawed recommendations. Exactly how participants in a participatory evaluation will attend to the multiple and competing demands of the Joint Committee Standards raises a difficult challenge, particularly in settings unused to evaluation and in conducting a study with limited resources. The field of evaluation has, to date, built more on theorists' ideas than on systematic research evidence, and there is little formal research validation to challenge this claim. A second concern is that because evaluation involves a predictable set of skills for which people can receive formal training, on-the-job training during an evaluation may be less effective, more time consuming, and potentially frustrating for those involved. Some even question whether or not program staff and participants, who often have challenging workloads, should be encouraged or mandated to take on a technical role not rightly theirs. A third issue is the participatory potential for pseudoevaluations in which individuals push a specific agenda and,

in the absence of a trained evaluator, co-opt the study to reach predetermined conclusions. Related to this is a final concern, the dilemma of institutionalization. On the one hand, if participatory evaluation efforts are to be sustained, the active involvement of evaluators may be important to ensuring that activities take place. Absent such intervention, participatory studies often fail to continue. On the other hand, to the extent that evaluation professionals intervene in a study, participants may never take the necessary ownership to institutionalize the process, and the ideal of capacity building will go unrealized. The challenges facing participatory evaluation raise the question of viability; that is, the extent to which these efforts truly hold the capacity to build evaluation infrastructure in organizations over time.

—*Jean A. King*

Further Reading

Cousins, J. B. (2003). Utilization effects of participatory evaluation. In T. Kellaghan, D. L. Stufflebeam, & L. A. Wingate (Eds.), *International handbook of educational evaluation* (pp. 245-266). Dordrecht, The Netherlands: Kluwer Academic.

Cousins, J. B., & Whitmore, E. (1998). Framing participatory evaluation. *New Directions for Evaluation, 80,* 5-23.

King, J. A. (1998). Making sense of participatory evaluation practice. *New Directions for Evaluation, 80,* 57-67.

Patton, M. Q. (1997). *Utilization-focused evaluation* (3rd ed.). Thousand Oaks, CA: Sage.

Weaver, L., & Cousins, B. (2001, November). *Unpacking the participatory process.* Paper presented at the Annual Meeting of the American Evaluation Association, St. Louis, MO.

Evaluation Practice Around the World

Uganda

Empowering Ugandan Communities to Fight AIDS Through Participatory Evaluation

In response to an invitation to hear and comment on the evaluation results from a community-based AIDS program, more than 100 people gathered in front of a two-room mud brick house in the village of Kakoma in southwestern Uganda. The women sat on grassy mats on the ground and the men sat on portable benches, all under

makeshift bamboo scaffolding topped with banana leaves. They listened intently to Rakai AIDS Information Network (RAIN) Peer Education Trainer Eddie Mireego, who said, "Among the questions you wanted to know was about condoms....We asked about people's feelings toward condoms preventing HIV infection. People were free to say yes

AUTHOR'S NOTE: This story is dedicated to Connie Wamala, my research assistant for this evaluation, who died of AIDS in Rakai Districty in April 2003.

or no. Last year, 25 people out of 100 believed that condoms could prevent infection. We then trained [community members] and came back to evaluate. What [do you think] came out?"

Several men guessed answers ranging from 85 to 96. Eddie filled in the chart with the actual result of 86%. He then went on, "After that, we asked about really using a condom. Last year, 8 people out of 100 reported to have ever used a condom....After 1 year [of the program], what result do you expect?" After several guesses, Eddie wrote 32% in the chart and asked, "What do you get from these figures when you compare these two results?" A young man replied, "It shows that people know what to do but do not put it into action." A heated discussion then ensued in which community members argued that, for the village to survive, more villagers needed to reduce their number of sexual partners or use more condoms.

This dialogue about evaluation results occurred in 1994 during an effort to combine participatory evaluation methods with more traditional techniques to assess the progress of RAIN. Before beginning its programs in 1992, RAIN, with assistance from its donor, the U.S. Agency for Development (USAID), conducted a baseline knowledge, attitudes, practices, and behavior (known as a KAPB) survey and focus group discussions. Nearly 18 months later, RAIN conducted a follow-up survey and group and individual interviews. In addition to meeting donor requirements and learning how to improve its programs, RAIN also wanted the evaluation to further empower communities to combat AIDS. To this end, we integrated several participatory methods and events that involved community members in nearly all stages of the evaluation.

Community Involvement in Evaluation Design. To involve community members in the design of the evaluation, we conducted a community evaluation design session with about 60 village representatives. Through interactive exercises, RAIN staff demonstrated the meaning and importance of evaluation and presented the results of the baseline survey. In smaller groups, community members identified the specific questions they wanted answered in the evaluation and the ways in which they wished to benefit.

Community Involvement in Data Collection. Because of the need to maintain confidentiality and the technical skills required, community members did not conduct the survey or interviews, but they were involved in data collection in other ways. For example, to select households to be included in the survey, we numbered all the houses, wrote those numbers on slips of paper, and asked community members to pick a number of the folded-up slips from a bowl. This involvement helped people understand the concept of random selection and dispel their suspicions that RAIN visits only those who

are infected with the "slim disease." This exercise helped community members to better understand and support the evaluation, as well as, later, to accept the evaluation results as accurate. Community members also served as escorts for the RAIN interviewers, which helped the interviewers gain entrée into people's homes.

Community Involvement in Data Interpretation and Dissemination of Results. Because of resource constraints, community members did not help analyze raw data. Instead, and through evaluation presentation and feedback sessions like the one in Kakoma, we presented preliminary results to community members and facilitated a process in which they interpreted the results. We did this by presenting results community members said they wanted to know, in ways that made sense in their own lives. Presenters began by asking the audience to predict the results of a particular question, then provided the actual results. The audience was then asked to interpret what the results meant for the community and, finally, what they wanted to do with the results. As a result of these sessions, community members later reported that they had learned more about how HIV is transmitted and prevented and what fellow community members are doing to avoid infection. Others reported that the program implementers gained greater credibility and recognition and that the program received more community support.

Community Use of Results. To better use the results of the evaluation, we helped communities devise action plans in which participants identified specific issues from the evaluation; defined related objectives; and decided who would do what, where, when, and how. In addition, participants selected indicators for each objective. We later helped community members assess their progress in achieving the action plans. As a result, community members reported that they felt more responsible for the program and that there was greater unity among groups and great impetus to work together. Community members also reported that because of the plans, there were increases in people knowing how HIV is transmitted and prevented, using condoms, reducing their number of sexual partners, and being tested for HIV.

Overall, community members reported that the different participatory methods had resulted in greater program ownership and self-determination in addressing HIV/AIDS. Perhaps more revealing, particularly in a setting that had seen little change except for an increasing number of deaths, is the way the evaluation enabled participants to recognize their own efficacy in preventing HIV infection. As a Kakoma community leader explained, "We have been encouraged...and hope for better things after preventing this virus. We have been made to have hope which we did not have."

—Anne T. Coghlan

■■ PARTICIPATORY MONITORING AND EVALUATION

Participatory monitoring and evaluation (PME) is an approach to performance review in which stakeholders in an intervention (local citizens, policy makers, funding agencies, and nongovernmental organizations) work together to decide how to assess progress, conduct data collection and analysis, and take action on their findings. Participatory monitoring is mainly concerned with short-term performance assessment of outputs and outcomes; participatory evaluation is primarily focused on longer term outcomes and impacts. Both activities encourage mutual learning and knowledge production by stakeholders and adjustment of the design or operations of the intervention in light of what is learned.

The purpose of participatory monitoring and evaluation may be transformative in respect to its focus on seeking to give voice, knowledge, and justice to marginalized social groups. More often, PME has been undertaken for more instrumental reasons; that is, to render interventions more effective and sustainable. PME has been widely practiced at the project, program, institutional, and (more recently) policy levels in international development in Africa, Asia, and the Americas. This approach has also been applied to social-service programs in North America and Europe. Antecedents and derivations of PME include participatory impact assessment, participatory rapid appraisal, participatory action research, participatory learning and action, beneficiary assessment, institutional self-assessment, self-evaluation, empowerment evaluation, and fourth-generation evaluation.

There are 10 key steps in the PME cycle: deciding who participates, forming a multistakeholder vehicle to lead the process (a committee, task force, or working group), establishing goals for the PME exercise, identifying key performance issues for assessment, developing results indicators, gathering relevant data, analyzing the findings, preparing the report, sharing the findings, and taking action on the findings. A wide range of data collection techniques can be used in PME that blend qualitative and quantitative research methods. Qualitative methods may include open-ended interviews, focus groups, community meetings, and group visualization techniques (e.g., asset mapping). Quantitative methods may include large-scale, closed-ended household surveys, computerized statistical analysis, cost-benefit studies, and economic modeling. Gender-sensitive procedures can and should be used across all methods.

As with all participatory processes, the quality of stakeholder participation can range from low-level participation, in the form either of information sharing (one-way communication) or of consultation (two-way communication), to high-level participation, in the form of shared control over decisions and resources or of an outright transfer of control over decisions and resources to citizens or program participants. In the latter three forms, the role of the professional is that of a facilitator among stakeholder interests, ensuring that the weaker voices in particular are heard and exert influence in the process.

Participatory monitoring and evaluation can be time consuming and expensive at the front end of the process. Authentic stakeholder engagement takes time. Additional professional involvement adds costs to the budget, although other stakeholders—especially citizens—contribute their time and absorb opportunity costs. However, experience has shown that the downstream benefits significantly outweigh the front-end costs of PME. The insights, solutions, and new knowledge generated by the PME process yield improvements in the effectiveness of the intervention that translate into important short-term and long-term gains and savings. At the same time, managers of PME processes need senior-level champions inside the institution, as well as allies outside, to support the longer (compared to more conventional approaches) timespans of PME initiatives.

—*Edward T. Jackson*

Further Reading

Estrella, M. (Ed.). (2000). *Learning from change: Issues and experiences in participatory monitoring and evaluation.* Ottawa, ON: International Development Research Centre.

Jackson, E. T. (2000). The front-end costs and downstream benefits of participatory evaluation. In O. Feinstein & R. Picciotto (Eds.), *Evaluation and poverty reduction: Proceedings from a World Bank conference* (pp. 115-126). Washington, DC: World Bank, Operations Evaluation Department.

Jackson, E. T., & Kassam, Y. (Eds.). (1998). *Knowledge shared: Participatory evaluation in development cooperation.* West Hartford, CT: Kumarian Press.

Whitmore, E. (Ed.). (1998). Understanding and practicing participatory evaluation. *New Directions for Evaluation, 80*(whole number).

World Bank Group. (2002). *Participation and civic engagement: Participatory monitoring and evaluation.* Washington, DC: Author. Retrieved May 29, 2004, from http://www.worldbank.org/participation/pme/partme.htm

Evaluation Practice Around the World

Cambodia

Cambodia suffered terribly from the effects of the 1970s war and from genocide, particularly in regard to the lack of human resources available to manage the reconstruction process after the fighting ended. Of the Cambodian population, 63% over the age of 15 years were recently estimated to be functionally illiterate (Godfrey et al., 2001).

A study conducted from 1998 to 1999 by the Cambodia Development Resource Institute (CDRI) found that the large influx of overseas development assistance following the 1991 peace settlement had made some contribution to the development of individual human resources but little headway in developing sustainable institutions capable of facilitating national development and reducing dependence on external assistance. Reasons included the fact that donor-driven projects with little local participation in identification, design, monitoring, and evaluation resulted in no sense of local ownership (Godfrey, Chan, & Toshiyasu, 2000).

The author evaluated a 3-year youth reproductive health (YRH) project in December 2001 that suffered due to lack of local participation in planning and the fact that donor-driven monitoring and evaluation processes were inadequate for effective project management. The design showed poor understanding of the local context, with overambitious objectives in a large remote rural area where communities were uncomfortable talking about sex. Parents were initially highly suspicious of a reproductive health intervention targeted at young people. Reproductive health education content and methods were considered inappropriate for youth, especially females, who were expected to be virgins at marriage. "Inappropriate" content and methods included the use of "bad words," videos containing sexually explicit material, photos of reproductive organs, and handing around condoms. Although it seemed generally accepted that male youths were sexually active, parents were worried that increased knowledge about sex might encourage "bad behavior" and lead to promiscuity.

The assumption that it would be possible to get educated, experienced Cambodians to accept low salaries to live and work in a rural area with difficult living conditions resulted in a late start to project implementation. Insufficient time and resources to develop the staff capabilities necessary to ensure effectiveness also jeopardized the project's potential.

An external midterm assessment was late and negative, which was demoralizing for local project staff. They deserve special commendation for their positive response to assessment recommendations. This response came despite the fact that the international executing agency responsible for project design used findings as a basis for deciding to discontinue support for the local organization at the end of the project. This cannot have been easy in a culture in which such criticism usually results in loss of

face. A new expatriate program coordinator employed by the executing agency worked with the local team during the second half of the project to implement the evaluation recommendations. The active participation of parents was strongly encouraged, together with an increased use of participatory monitoring and evaluation tools, networking, and sharing of lessons and experience with similar projects in Cambodia.

The final external evaluation concluded that although the project had not achieved the original goals, it had made an important contribution to

- increased open discussion in communities about YRH. Parents gave embarrassment and ignorance as reasons for not talking to children about YRH at the beginning of the project. At the end of the project, some claimed that they had been able to learn from their children when they shared knowledge gained from education sessions. This had been complemented by information from television and radio.
- enhanced local knowledge about the importance of sexual YRH. All communities had experienced cases of HIV/AIDS, and fear of an unfamiliar, potentially fatal disease seemed to have resulted in a pragmatic and socially acceptable stance: If youths cannot be good, they should know how to be careful. Parents claimed to advise their children about reproductive health care, but the advice was superficial and of a "take care" nature. Cultural shyness and ignorance about sexuality still seemed to inhibit in-depth conversations about sex and complete understanding of YRH problems.
- increased understanding of HIV transmission mechanisms, which increased community support for HIV/AIDS victims and their families, most particularly their willingness to visit infected people and attend funerals of those suspected to have died as a result of AIDS.
- the development of local staff capabilities.

The project was considered a relative success from the perspectives of local NGO staff and the communities. Both stakeholder groups expressed disappointment about its noncontinuation during the final evaluation process. Parents and youths were anxious to have more in-depth knowledge about HIV/AIDS, as they believed the risk of disease would increase as more young people migrated to urban areas for work.

When the Cambodian project staff members were asked how the project might have been improved, they all believed that the midterm assessment should have been conducted earlier, as it marked a critical turning point in the efficiency and effectiveness of project implementation. They felt that they had gained from the increased use of participatory methodologies. Project effectiveness also seemed to have been enhanced through the application of lessons generated through regular monitoring and reflection processes during the final year.

This experience suggests that if monitoring and evaluation were introduced to local organizations as a participatory process for learning, they might contain promise for a strategic approach to increase the efficiency of overseas development assistance in Cambodia. Employers could use PME techniques to develop the critical thinking and creativity of their staff, which they expressed as a priority in a 2001 marketing survey (Mahe, 2001). The increased capabilities of local people to conduct evaluations would lessen reliance on external technical assistance, which would also further effective use of aid money.

The introduction of PME as a tool for learning would not only contribute to the development of individual human resources, it would encourage the development of institutionalized learning processes and methods for capturing and storing impact data. This would increase the ability of local organizations to market their achievements, generate resources, retain competent staff, and move toward sustainability.

Unfortunately, in a country that lacks strong accountability institutions in the public sector, where corruption is rife and culture makes it almost impossible to criticize superiors, vested interests are likely to jeopardize the objectivity of PME. For some time to come, monitoring and evaluation are likely to remain externally driven, discrete, peripheral, upward accountability mechanisms rather than an integral part of Cambodia's development process.

—Cathy Shutt

Further Reading

Godfrey, M., Chan, S., & Toshiyasu, K. (2000). *Technical assistance and capacity development in an aid-dependent economy: The experience of Cambodia* (CDRI Working Paper 15). Phnom Penh, Cambodia: CDRI.

Godfrey, M., Sovannarith, S., Saravy, T., Dorina, P., Katz, C., Acharya, S., et al. (2001). *A study of the Cambodian labour market: Reference to poverty reduction, growth and adjustment to crisis* (CDRI Working Paper 18). Phnom Penh, Cambodia: CDRI.

Mahe, J. (2001). *Marketing survey of the training needs of development organizations in Cambodia*. Private Agencies Collaborating Together.

■■ PARTICIPATORY RURAL APPRAISAL

Participatory rural appraisals were developed as an approach for international funders such as the World Bank to use in determining the viability of proposed projects in developing countries. The appraisal process typically involved a team of international experts working with local people to conduct intensive fieldwork aimed at identifying key project assumptions, establishing baseline data where possible, examining local resources, and determining commitment to and interest in the project. This process was also sometimes used for end-of-project evaluations. Farming systems initiatives emphasized interdisciplinary teams and farmer collaboration in rural appraisals. This approach eventually influenced agricultural extension practices in more developed countries.

—Michael Quinn Patton

See also Rapid Rural Appraisal

Further Reading

Shaner, W. W., Philipp, P. F., & Schmehl, W. R. (1982). *Farming systems research and development: Guidelines for developing countries*. Boulder, CO: Westview.

■■ PATEL, MAHESH

(b. 1951, New York City). Ph.D. Public Health, M.A. Economics, University of Manchester, U.K.; Postgraduate Certificate in Education, University of Leicester, U.K.; B.A. Honors Economics, University of Sussex, U.K.

Patel is Regional Monitoring and Evaluation Advisor for UNICEF.

His contributions to the field of evaluation include a framework for evaluation of the implementation of International Human Rights Conventions, such as the Convention on the Rights of the Child; adaptation of the Program Evaluation Standards to make them suitable for use in developing countries; support to the systematic usage of the Program Evaluation Standards in evaluation of joint government and international development agency programs; and the promotion of publication by evaluators from developing countries, especially in the *Journal of Evaluation and Program Planning.* He has been instrumental in the creation of national evaluation associations in Africa (16 to date); a continental African association; and organization of the first two African Evaluation Association conferences, with international agency and donor funding. He participated in the initiative to create the International Organization for Cooperation in Evaluation (IOCE). Influences to his work have been Amartya Sen in the areas of development, economics, social choice and human rights; Socrates Litsios in primary health care and planning for the "Health for All by the Year 2000" initiative; John Hey in economic and mathematical modeling, especially in the fields of prevention and microeconomics; and Urban Jonsson in human rights theory and programming and community-based development.

He is on the Editorial Advisory Board of the *Journal of Evaluation and Program Planning,* for which he has been involved in the production of two special issues, "Interesting UNICEF Program Evaluations" and "UNICEF and UNAIDS evaluations of HIV/AIDS programs in Africa." He has also published poetry and financed a large part of his academic studies by teaching Tai Chi Ch'uan.

◼◼ PATTON, MICHAEL QUINN

(b. 1945, Pewee Valley, Kentucky). Ph.D. Sociology, M.S. Rural Sociology, University of Wisconsin, Madison; B.A. Anthropology and Sociology, University of Cincinnati.

Patton is a faculty member of the Union Institute and University Graduate College and a consultant on independent organizational development and evaluation. His reach is worldwide, both through his scholarly work and as a speaker and consultant. He was the keynote presenter for the launching of the African Evaluation Society in Nairobi, Kenya, in 1999 and at the European Evaluation Society in 2000. He has twice keynoted American Evaluation Association and Canadian Evaluation Society conferences, as well as international evaluation conferences for the United Kingdom Evaluation Society, the Australasian Evaluation Society, the Japan Evaluation Society, and the World Bank's professional development seminars.

Patton is best known for his utilization-focused evaluation model, which emphasizes intended uses of evaluation by intended users. This work, as well as his work on qualitative methods for research and evaluation, makes him a seminal thinker in contemporary evaluation.

His work on the utilization-focused model was heavily influenced by his time in the Peace Corps. From 1967 to 1969, Patton worked in Burkina Faso on community and agricultural development projects. His challenge was to figure out what rural villagers there wanted and needed, an experience that contributed to the development of evaluation methods and models that focus on users' needs and interests. Patton also prizes the mentorship of Vito Perrone in the areas of pragmatism, qualitative ways of knowing, and humanism.

Patton has demonstrated his commitment to the profession of evaluation as President of the American Evaluation Association in 1988 and through his many workshops. He has conducted a workshop on utilization-focused evaluation at every American professional evaluation conference, beginning with ENet in St. Louis in 1975 and every AEA conference since AEA was founded, with the exception of the earthquake conference in San Francisco in 1989.

He is the author of five books on program evaluation, including *Utilization-Focused Evaluation: The New Century Text,* a book that has been used in more than 300 universities. His other books are *Qualitative Research and Evaluation Methods, Creative Evaluation, Practical Evaluation,* and *How to Use Qualitative Methods in Evaluation* (part of the Program Evaluation Kit). He was Editor of a *New Directions in Evaluation* issue on culture and evaluation, and his nonfiction book *Grand Canyon Celebration: A Father-Son Journey of Discovery* was a finalist for the Minnesota Book Award in 1999.

Patton has received many awards for his work in evaluation, sociology, and teaching. He is the only recipient of both the Alva and Gunnar Myrdal Award, from the Evaluation Research Society, for "outstanding contributions to evaluation use and practice" and the Paul F. Lazarsfeld Award, for lifetime contributions to evaluation theory, from the American Evaluation Association. The Society for Applied Sociology honored him with the 2001 Lester F. Ward Award for Outstanding Contributions to Applied Sociology. He received the 1979 Morse-Amoco Award from the University of Minnesota for Outstanding Teaching for his innovative course on evaluation.

⬛ PAWSON, RAY

Ph.D., University of Lancaster; B.A., University of Essex.

Pawson is a sociologist. All of his published work is narrowly methodological, although the coverage is prolix (pure and applied, practical and philosophical, quantitative and qualitative, micro and macro, contemporaneous and historical). The best-known work from his early period is *A Measure for Measures: A Manifesto for Empirical Sociology* (1989). He entered evaluation, quite by accident, when he was asked to research the effectiveness of a prisoner education program. He has been an inmate (of evaluation, not prison) ever since.

His primary contribution to evaluation is *Realistic Evaluation* (with Nick Tilley). "Realism," in the United Kingdom, at least, constitutes the prime methodological backbone of many forms of social research, and the book is an attempt to spread the word to evaluators. Mark, Henry, and Julnes are prominent members of the evaluation community caught under the same spell. Unaccountably, there are many nonbelievers. Pawson's current work on realism in evidence-based policy may be found at http://www.evidencenetwork.org.

Among his main influences are the following: the sociologist R. K. Merton—on the concept of "middle range theory," an idea whose time is still to come in evaluation; R. Bhaskar (first two books only) and Rom Harré—on the development of realist philosophy; the poet William Carlos Williams—for a salutary line for all evaluators about "the rare occurrence of the expected"; and finally, a certain prisoner—for the thought that evaluators (of prison programs) are lower even than prison guards.

Pawson has been active in the United Kingdom and European Evaluation Societies. With this in mind, he is thinking deeply about founding the English English in Evaluation Campaign (EEEC). Manifesto examples would include such items as program = program, tidbits = tidbits, gotten = no such word, and so on.

⬛ PEER REVIEW

Peer review refers generally to the evaluation of professional performance or products by other professionals and, more specifically, to a set of procedures for evaluating grant proposals and manuscripts submitted for publication. For peer-reviewed journals, content-matter specialists are asked to judge a manuscript, often using specified criteria and blinded to the author's identity. The journal editor considers reviewers' comments and decides whether the paper should be published, rejected, or revised and resubmitted. Similar procedures are used to review grant applications. Critiques of the peer review process focus on the low reliability of reviewers' recommendations, but the goal of peer review is to make good and defensible judgments rather than to have high reliability. Peer review is an example of an expertise-oriented approach to evaluation.

—Melvin M. Mark and Poh-Pheng Chua

PERFORMANCE APPRAISAL.
See PERSONNEL EVALUATION

⬛ PERFORMANCE ASSESSMENT RESOURCE CENTRE (PARC)

PARC supports international efforts to improve performance assessment in international development practice to develop quality, effectiveness, and sustainability of poverty-focused interventions. This resource center supports the evaluation work of development partners, including the governments of developing countries, agencies providing and receiving international aid, project managers, and consultants. Because the resource center seeks to link evaluators across agencies, most resources are available on the Web at http://www.parcinfo.org.

⬛ PERFORMANCE-BASED MONITORING

Over the past two decades, there has been a movement within governments across the globe to reform and reshape the ways in which they function. Demands by citizens for government accountability for results, transparency, and provision of more efficient and effective services echo now from continent to continent. The paradox of citizens asking for more services and programs despite steady-state or even

NOTE: The views expressed here are solely those of the authors and no endorsement by the World Bank Group is intended or should be inferred.

fewer government resources, for more responsiveness from fewer civil servants, and for accountability at the same time they press for decentralization has left governments experimenting with a multitude of strategies in response. These pressures are helping to drive a global public management revolution.

Although this revolution has taken hold mostly in the OECD countries, it has not stopped there. Indeed, in the developing world, a poorly functioning public sector has emerged as a key factor in the lack of progress toward sustainable economic growth (World Bank, 1997). Thus public sector reforms are now also clearly emerging in developing countries as varied as, for example, the Philippines, the Kyrgyz Republic, India, Ghana, and Malaysia, which are all facing increasing pressures from their citizens, their private and civil society sectors, and the international community to improve both the structures and processes of governance.

One important lesson learned from many OECD reform experiences is that when a government switches its focus from measuring whether a program is "on track" to whether the program is achieving its desired objectives or goals (results), the program's overall performance improves. (*Performance* means here to assume a measurable level of program and policy effectiveness and efficiency.) Improvements can come in different forms—for example, emphasizing more productivity, more public reliance on private markets, more decentralization from national to subnational units of government, clear lines of responsibility and accountability, more responsiveness to citizens as clients, and an increased capacity to monitor and evaluate the performance of the public sector.

Whatever the chosen means, these strategies emphasize that governments should achieve the results they promise to their citizens. It also then follows that if governments are to achieve these promised results, they should be able to provide to their citizens evidence of having done so. That evidence should be transparent, trustworthy, and readily available. A performance-based or results-based (we use the terms interchangeably) monitoring and evaluation (M&E) system is an important tool that allows governments to acquire this evidence.

The challenge is how governments can begin to build performance-based monitoring and evaluation systems so as to provide credible and trustworthy information for their own use and to share with their citizens. The reality is that putting in place even a rudimentary system of monitoring, evaluating, and reporting on government performance is not easy in the best of circumstances. The obstacles for developing countries are even greater and more formidable, even as they begin to construct more traditional M&E systems. These more traditional systems typically are used to assess the progress and track the implementation of government projects, programs, and policies.

It should also be acknowledged that it is not a new phenomenon that governments monitor and evaluate their own performance. For this reason, a theoretical distinction needs to be drawn between traditional M&E and performance-based M&E. Traditional M&E focuses on the monitoring and evaluation of inputs, activities, and outputs; that is, project or program implementation. Governments have over time tracked their expenditures and revenues, staffing levels and resources, program and project activities, numbers of participants, goods and services produced, and so on. Indeed, traditional efforts at M&E have been a function of many governments for several decades or longer. In fact, there is evidence that the ancient Egyptians (5000 BC) regularly tracked their government's outputs in grain and livestock production (Egyptian Museum, Cairo, Egypt).

Performance-based M&E, however, combines the traditional approach of monitoring implementation with the assessment of results (Mayne & Zapico-Goni, 1997). It is this linking of implementation progress with progress in achieving the desired objectives or goals (results) of government policies and programs that makes performance-based M&E most useful as a tool for public management. Implementing this type of M&E system allows the organization to modify and make adjustments to the implementation processes to more directly support the achievement of desired objectives and outcomes.

WHY BUILD A PERFORMANCE-BASED M&E SYSTEM ANYWAY?

A performance-based M&E system can help policy makers answer the fundamental questions of whether promises were kept and goals were achieved. If governments are promising improved performance, there should be some means of demonstrating that such improvements have or have not occurred (i.e., there is a need for measurement). The issue is not measurement per se, however. There is a general need both to document and to demonstrate government's own performance to its stakeholders as well as using the performance information to continuously improve. As Binnendijk (1999) observed:

> One key use is for transparent reporting on performance and results achieved to external stakeholder audiences. In many cases, government-wide legislation or executive orders have recently mandated such reporting. Moreover, such reporting can be useful in competition for funds by convincing a skeptical public or legislature that the agency's programs produce significant results and provide "value for money." Annual performance reports are often directed to ministers, parliament, stakeholders, customers, and the general public. (p. 3)

Performance information should also be used for internal purposes, such as for management decision making and identifying areas of improvement. This requires that performance information be integrated into key management systems and processes of the organization such as in policy formulation, in project and program planning and management, and in budget allocation processes.

Implicit in Binnendijk's analysis is that performance measurement is a management tool for both government officials and stakeholders. First, by using the performance information in policy making and program management, governments are indeed achieving higher levels of performance. Also, it is through the reporting on how well government is doing compared to real or desired criteria that numerous parties can participate in "the business of government." We have seen these phenomena in many developed countries where performance information and other official documents, such as the budget, are regularly published by the media or made otherwise available to citizens. Citizens in the United States and the United Kingdom, for example, regularly pressure their national and subnational governments to be responsive to their needs as well as being accountable for the funds put into the trust of lawmakers and officials.

IF PERFORMANCE INFORMATION IS THE KEY, THEN WHERE DOES IT COME FROM?

Performance information can come, essentially, from two sources: a monitoring system and an evaluation system. Both are needed, but they are not the same. The distinction between monitoring and evaluation is made here for conceptual and practical purposes.

Performance monitoring can be viewed as periodically measuring progress toward explicit short-, intermediate-, and long-term results. It also can provide feedback on the progress made (or not made) to decision makers, who can use the information in various ways to improve performance.

Monitoring involves measurement, and what is measured is the progress toward achieving an objective or goal (result). However, the goal cannot be measured directly. It must first be translated into a set of indicators that, when regularly measured, will provide information about whether the goal is being achieved. For example: If country X selects the goal of improving the health of children by reducing childhood morbidity by 30% over the next 5 years, it must now identify a set of indicators that translate childhood morbidity into more specific measurements. Indicators that can help assess the changes in childhood morbidity might include (a) the incidence and prevalence of infectious diseases, such as hepatitis; (b) the level of immunization converge; and (c) the degree to which children have access to sanitary water supplies. Measuring a disaggregated set of indicators provides important information as to how well government programs and policies are working to support the overall goal. If, for example, it is found that over time fewer and fewer children have clean water supplies available to them, the government can use this information to reform programs aimed at improving water supplies or to strengthen those programs that provide information to parents about the need to sanitize water before providing it to their children.

Understanding the utility of performance information for various users is a key reason for building a monitoring system in the first place. Key users in many societies who are often left out of the information flow are citizens, NGO groups, and the private sector. Monitoring data have both internal (governmental) and external uses (societal) that need to be recognized. It is important to note here that performance information obtained from a monitoring system reveals only the performance of what is being measured at that time—although it can be compared against both past performance and some planned level of present or anticipated performance. Monitoring data do not reveal why that level of performance occurred or provide the probable cause of changes in performance from one reporting period to another. This information comes from an evaluation system (see Boyle & Lemaire, 1999).

An evaluation system serves a function complementary to but distinct from that of a monitoring system within a performance management framework. Building an evaluation system allows for a more in-depth study of performance outcomes and effects; can bring in data sources other than just extant indicators; can address factors that are too difficult or expensive to monitor continuously; and, perhaps most important, can tackle the issue of why and how the trends being tracked with monitoring data are moving in the directions they are. Such data on impacts and causal attribution are not to be taken lightly and can play an important role in an organization making strategic resource allocations. As Binnendijk (1999) notes: "Because of timing as well as the need to use more rigorous methods and in-depth analysis, some performance issues, such as long-term impact, attribution, cost effectiveness, and sustainability, can probably be better addressed by evaluation than by routine performance monitoring reports" (p. 17).

An additional point to make in this regard is that an M&E system can be designed for and applicable to the project level, the program level, the sector level, and the country level. (For a global overview of the development of evaluation in this context, see Furubo, Rist, & Sandahl, 2002.) The specific indicators may necessarily be different (as the stakeholders' needs for information will also be different at each level), the complexity of collecting the data will be different, the political sensitivity on collecting the data may change, and the uses of the information may change from one level to another.

In the end, it is the creation of a system that is aligned from one level to the others (there is a "line of sight" between levels) that is most critical—in this way, information can flow up and down in a governmental system rather than being collected at only one level or another, stored and used at that level, and never being shared across levels. Blocking the information from being shared ensures that the linkages between policies, programs, and projects stay disconnected and uncoordinated. At each level, performance information is necessary, and there should be means to collect it. Although different levels will have different requirements that need to be understood and respected, the creation of an M&E system requires interdependency, alignment, and coordination across levels (see Kusek & Rist, 2001a, 2002).

PERFORMANCE-BASED MANAGEMENT AND THE INTERNATIONAL EXPERIENCE

In addition to understanding the rationale of *why* governments are moving to an increased focus on results and *what* a results-focused M&E system is, there is a need to understand *how* governments are beginning to move toward a results focus in public management. For the past two decades, governments in developed countries and, more recently, developing countries have been working to improve the quality of their public services. These governments have embarked on long-term reform agendas to change the culture from one that focuses on input management to output and outcome management, with the goal of being able to demonstrate that public expenditures are being not only efficiently spent but effectively used.

Over the last two-plus decades, we have seen many developed countries—including Australia, New Zealand, Canada, the United Kingdom, and the United States—making progress in implementing new practices to better account for the results being achieved with public expenditures. There are also several developing countries moving in this direction—the Philippines, Thailand, and Costa Rica, to name just three. The strategies used to introduce results-based management have varied across these countries; however, there appears to be a number of similar elements that contribute to a successful shift to a results-based culture.

Among these key elements are the following seven:

1. A clear mandate for making such a shift

2. The presence of strong leadership, usually through a strong champion or champions at the most senior level of government

3. The use of reliable information for policy and management decisions

4. Economic pressures and other incentives for change (often a concerned citizenry or the need to reduce the cost of burdensome civil service payrolls)

5. Clear links to budget and other resource allocation decisions

6. Involvement of civil society as an important partner with government

7. Pockets of innovation that can serve as beginning practices or pilot programs

As recently reported by OECD, reforms are maturing in many OECD countries, mainly in the English- and Scandinavian-speaking parts of the world. These countries have substantial experience with introducing a results focus and are either implementing or contemplating a new generation of results reforms. Other OECD member countries, notably those with strong legal traditions, such as France and Germany, have only recently embarked on such reforms. In France, reform efforts were boosted in 2001 with the enactment of the new results-focused budget law (OECD, 2002, p. 6). In Germany, most reforms are taking place at the local level. In Japan and Korea, reforms are centered more on ex ante and ex post policy evaluation than on results-focused management and budgeting, but reforms are aiming at increasing an outcome focus in the public sector.

In many developing countries, the desire to move toward results-based management has been linked to government efforts in long-term development and capacity building. This has been primarily driven by rising concerns over resource scarcity, increasing service demands by both clients and stakeholders, and awareness of the pressing need to cope with an increasingly competitive and global marketplace. Egypt, India, Bolivia, and Ghana are but a few of the countries that see reforms in institutional management practices as key to long-term development.

Regardless of whether the country is developed or developing, implementing a results-based management system is not an easy task. Developed countries, such as Canada, the United Kingdom, and the United States, would agree that numerous implementation problems still need to be overcome, even after years of implementation of this type of system. Examples of problems include budget structures and classification systems that are not supportive of outcome assessment and a management culture that continues to reward based on inputs.

The introduction of performance-based management strategies in developing countries is still in its infancy. As these governments move forward with their own strategies, they are trying new and innovative approaches that are enriching the pool of data and experiences. Thus far, though, one thing is clear: There is no one strategy or approach that is best for all countries. First, reform involves multiyear efforts, and strategies inevitably evolve over time. Second, each country is unique in its sociocultural and political context and its views of what is feasible in results-based

management. In practice, countries may use a combination of approaches and may adapt and test experiences from other countries to their own circumstances. As countries now move to develop their policy strategies, it is appropriate to simultaneously explore their options for how they will link their M&E systems to these policy strategies.

Designing and building a reporting system that can produce trustworthy, timely, and relevant information on the performance of government policies, programs, and projects requires experience, skill, and real institutional capacity. This capacity has to include, at a minimum, the skill and understanding to know what to do with the information once it arrives in the hands of the intended users; the ability to successfully determine objectives, logic models, and construct indicators; and the ability to collect, aggregate, analyze, and report on performance data vis-à-vis the indicators and their baselines (Kusec & Rist, 2001b).

Furthermore, there has to be capacity to move the information both vertically and horizontally within the government and to share it in a timely fashion with the parliament, civil society, and the public. Building the capacity in governments for such information systems is a long-term effort. If such requirements are difficult in developed countries (as we have learned from many OECD examples), they will be even more difficult for developing countries.

POSTSCRIPT

Building an M&E system is easier said than done. Otherwise, we would see these systems as an integral part of good public management practices in governments, and there would not be the need to consider this issue. However, the reality is otherwise. There are few such systems (in whole or in part) fully integrated into the public management strategies of developed countries and still fewer in developing countries. It is not that governments are not trying—many are. It is just that creating such a system takes time, resources, stability in the political environment, and champions who do not become faint of heart.

This takes us to the significant challenge of sustainability. Indeed, governments willing to use performance-based information to assist in the governance of the political system and frame public policies give evidence of some level of democracy and openness. Even in these countries, however, there is often a reluctance to measure and monitor for fear that the process will present bad news to the leadership and other stakeholders. Presenting one's performance shortfalls to others is not typical bureaucratic behavior. Thus the efforts to build such a system should recognize the inherent and real political limitations, start with a simple approach, work with stakeholders to help them recognize that it is their right to be regularly informed on the performance of their government, and continue to stress time and again that information can help improve policy making and public management. The possibility of achieving these modest goals should then be reason for longer term optimism.

—Jody Zall Kusek and Ray C. Rist

Further Reading

Binnendijk, A. (1999, October). *Results based management.* Paper presented at the International Conference on Evaluation Capacity Development, Beijing, China.

Boyle, R., & Lemaire, D. (Eds.). (1999). *Building effective evaluation capacity.* New Brunswick, NJ: Transaction Books.

Furubo, J., Rist, R., & Sandahl, R. (Eds.). (2002). *International atlas of evaluation.* New Brunswick, NJ: Transaction Books.

Kusek, J. Z., & Rist, R. C. (2001a). Building a performance-based monitoring and evaluation system. *Evaluation Journal of Australasia, 1*(2).

Kusek, J. Z., & Rist, R. C. (2001b). Making M&E matter—Get the foundation right. *Evaluation Insights, 2*(2).

Kusek, J. Z., & Rist, R. C. (2002). Building results-based monitoring and evaluation systems: Assessing developing countries' readiness. *Zeitschrift fuer Evaluation, 1*(1).

Mayne, J., & Zapico-Goni, E. (Eds.). (1997). *Monitoring performance in the public sector.* New Brunswick, NJ: Transaction Books.

Organization for Economic Cooperation and Development. (2002). *Glossary of key terms in evaluation and results based management.* Paris: Author.

World Bank. (1997). *World development report: The state in a changing world.* Washington, DC: Author.

Evaluation Practice Around the World

South Africa

Making Monitoring and Evaluation Work: How Resource-Poor Farmers Focus on Sustainability

The Agricultural Research Council–Institute for Soil, Climate and Water (ARC-ISCW) is currently involved in a number of projects under the National Landcare Programme (NLP) of South Africa. The vision of the NLP is to have communities and individuals adopt an ecologically sustainable approach to the management of South Africa's environment and natural resources that will also improve their livelihoods. Hence, through these NLP projects, the ARC-ISCW is aiming to develop and implement sustainable land management practices among farming communities living on the eastern seaboard of South Africa. These communities, which are populated mainly by Zulu, Xhosa, and Swazi tribes, have serious problems with soil acidity, low soil fertility, and soil erosion, resulting in low crop production and poverty.

The development approach followed by the project teams is based on a process of "true participation" that takes local farmers on a learning path toward sustainability. This participatory approach has worked because individual communities and groups have shown the benefits of working collaboratively—of developing a collective vision and learning and adapting their management practices together. The approach aims to empower people by building skills, interests, and capacities that continue even after the project ends. A prerequisite is the formation of a strong platform of human activities among the stakeholders that is based on shared learning, negotiation, and accommodation. This platform is necessary to manage the natural resources in a sustainable manner.

Monitoring and evaluation is a critical element of the development approach adopted by the ARC-ISCW. It is the "propeller" that drives the whole process; it continuously ensures integration, communication, focus, and learning, especially within the social platform. The participation of primary stakeholders in all the phases of the M&E process is seen as mandatory. Using an improvement-oriented M&E, the process helps to improve project elements such as technology, communication, training, participation, experimentation, and group work. In addition, the use of a multilevel stakeholder framework concept improves the M&E practice. It helps to identify key stakeholders and their level and degree of involvement, which, furthermore, lead to the initiation of new M&E processes. In other words, where a major new activity involving a specific stakeholder group exists, a new M&E process is initiated.

Three separate, but linked, M&E processes are usually initiated in these NLP projects. On the project (typical district, ward, or subward) level, the training of trainers, group activities, experimentation, soil health, and production are some project-level outcomes that are being evaluated in a farmer forum through a *reflective practice process*. Key stakeholders are the leader farmers and extension officers. Farmer-to-farmer training is another major activity on a lower (community or group) level, which necessitates the initiation of another M&E process among the group of leader farmers. The key stakeholders are the farming communities. A third judgment-oriented evaluation process might be necessary to demonstrate impact and accountability (e.g., with provincial and national government departments and funders) and negotiate new strategies and projects.

Different methodologies are being used within the respective M&E processes. At the project level, a logframe, or logical framework, is generally used to develop goals, objectives, outcomes, indicators, and targets. Different types of indicators are identified and monitored over space and time. The leader farmers, extension officers, and ARC-ISCW researchers participate in the M&E process, which includes data collection, reflection, and planning activities. In the lower level M&E system, a process is facilitated whereby leader farmers conceptualize their own implementation-outcomes hierarchy through a typical chain of events or theory of action. The leader farmers use this theory of action as a road map to attaining ultimate social and economic goals (i.e., increased agricultural production, increased soil health, and decreased poverty). They climb the ladder (outcomes hierarchy) together, select indicators, and monitor their progress. They reflect on indicator trends in a monthly forum and plan different strategies to improve or maintain the theory of action. They reach out to other farmers and work with individuals and groups and train them in new or improved land management practices. They monitor changes in knowledge, attitude, and skills, as well as in practice and behavior among the farming communities. They set up targets and interactively work toward them as a group of "movers and shakers" in agricultural development in their region.

By maintaining a proper evaluation processes, the NLP project stakeholders stay focused on their vision of sustainable land management. In view of sustainable rural livelihoods in Africa, the use of such approaches is essential. The platform for this approach is laid by working with local people in groups and by improving their social interaction and capacity to evaluate, plan, and act.

–Hendrik J. Smith

PERFORMANCE INDICATOR

Performance indicator is a term used to describe a range of techniques for monitoring performance by using a standardized measure. It is often expressed as a percentage, index, or rate and is monitored at regular intervals. For example, if a program or organization is attempting to improve parenting skills, a performance indicator could be the proportion of parents who feel they are coping better with parenting their children at the end of the program. There are many standard instruments available that are used as performance indicators, such as quality of life surveys, health inventories, sales records, and so on.

PERFORMANCE PROGRAM

Performance program is a term used in personnel evaluation that refers to a written statement of the scope of work and expectations of performance that constitute the basis for the personnel evaluation. A performance program is thought to encourage open, ongoing communication between the employee and supervisor about performance issues, job-related concerns, and goals. In addition, it is meant to promote effective job performance and provide feedback about past performance. In some cases, the evaluator or supervisor and employee must agree to a performance program.

See also PERSONNEL EVALUATION

PERFORMANCE STORY

A *performance story* is a succinct summary of the performance of a program. As well as explaining *what* a program has achieved, a performance story also describes the causal links that show *how* the achievements were accomplished. Performance stories are structured around some form of outcome hierarchy;

for example, results ladders, results chains, program logic, or program theory.

Performance stories are best developed along the following lines:

1. During program development, create an outcomes hierarchy that shows how program activities might plausibly lead to intermediate outcomes that will eventually contribute to the end goal.

2. Develop performance measures or key evaluation questions that can track the extent to which these intermediate outcomes are realized.

3. Collect evidence relating to these measures or questions.

4. Annotate the outcome hierarchy with the evidence collected.

Although performance stories vary in content and format, most are short, mention program context and aims, relate to a plausible results chain, and are backed by empirical evidence. The Office of the Auditor General of Canada suggests that credible performance stories should also note intended accomplishments, report achievements against expectations, discuss what was learned and what will be changed, and describe steps taken to ensure the quality of the data presented.

The following practical example of the term comes from the Department of Primary Industries in Victoria, Australia. In this department, *performance story* is defined as a plausible explanation of program results, based on a program theory that articulates the gap between inputs and outcomes. These stories (see Table 1) summarize longer evaluation reports and include additional information about unexpected outcomes and verification of data quality. The results ladder is based on Bennett's hierarchy. Ideally, program accomplishments are measured at each level to illuminate causal relationships and provide a more credible account.

Table 1 Summary Example of a Performance Story for an Agricultural Extension Program

Program Aim: To enhance the viability of the Victorian dairy industry through programs that will profitably increase the consumption of pasture per hectare by 10% on 50% of Victorian dairy farms over 5 years	
Results Ladder	*Examples of Accomplishments*
Social, economic, and environmental consequences	• Overall return to industry of $38 million • Average annual return to farmers of $15,000 • Infrastructure developed for major emerging industry issues
Behavior change	• Participants' cows are eating an extra 21% of available pasture, compared to 6% increase for nonparticipants • 63% of participants said the program encouraged them to change their practices
Knowledge, skills, attitudes, and aspirations	• 65% of participants said the program helped them develop new skills • 61% said their expectations of their farm's potential had changed
Reactions	• 92% of participants responded positively • 72% of nonparticipating dairy farmers felt program was good for the industry
People	• Participants were younger and had higher debt levels than the average dairy farmer • Enrollments represented 40% of dairy farmers
Activities	• 149 core programs (8–10 days each), 140 discussion groups
Inputs	• $5.8 million over 3 years, involving more than 300 people

The Department of Primary Industries places a high value on these performance stories because they strike a good balance between depth of information and brevity and are easy for staff and stakeholders to understand. They help build a credible case that a contribution has been made. They also provide a common language for discussing different programs and helping teams focus on results.

—*Jessica Dart and John Mayne*

See also PROGRAM LOGIC, PROGRAM THEORY

Further Reading

McLaughlin, J. A., & Jordan, G. B. (1999). Logic models: A tool for telling your program's performance story. *Evaluation and Program Planning, 22,* 65-72.

Mayne, J. (2003, April). *Reporting on outcomes: Setting performance expectations and telling performance stories* (Discussion paper, Office of the Auditor General of Canada). Retrieved June 1, 2004, from http://www.oag-bvg.gc.ca/domino/other.nsf/html/200305dp1_e.html/$file/200305dp1_e.pdf

PERSONALIZING EVALUATION

Personalizing evaluation is in the tradition of responsive and democratic evaluation. This process grew out of concerns about the distortions generated when we document a program as the principal or exclusive context within which to attribute significance to people's lives and work. It proposes, instead, the portrayal of people's lives and work as contexts within which to read the significance of a program—in pursuit of certain ameliorating effects. First, as well as holding people to account for the realization of program or policy aims, we can hold programs and policies to account for their capacity to respond to participants' aspirations and actions. Second, by contextualizing a program in a life or an event, we can better measure its significance independent of its political meaning. Personalizing evaluation also means legitimating the person of the evaluator as a bearer of values. Although stopping short of approval for advocacy, and recommending that evaluators remain impartial and disinterested in outcomes, personalized evaluation promotes the view that evaluators must be their own methodologists and seek personal voice and personal meaning in their evaluations.

—*Saville Kushner*

Further Reading

Kushner, S. (2000). *Personalising evaluation.* London: Sage.

PERSONNEL EVALUATION

Personnel evaluation refers to the systematic assessment of a person's qualifications or performance in relation to a role and larger defensible purpose. Personnel evaluation applies to a wide range of appointments, including the complex of unskilled, skilled, and professional roles in factories, stores, restaurants, airline companies, sports teams, schools, universities, hospitals, churches, government agencies, nongovernment service organizations, law firms, military services, and many others. Any enterprise's effectiveness and propriety is dependent on the intelligence, special talents, values, ethical behavior, attitudes, personal demeanor, social skills, motivation, efforts, and achievements of its personnel. Many organizations invest heavily to compensate and support their personnel during active employment and later during retirement. To make personnel costs pay off, organizations need to address a wide range of personnel matters. Among the most important are valid evaluations to guide personnel decisions and actions, ensure accountability, and foster and assess ongoing development of human resources.

Practices of personnel evaluation are discernible in virtually every sector of society—pilot selection systems, military personnel efficiency reports, and faculty evaluation systems, to name a few. However, sound personnel evaluation is not an integrated, mature professional area. The different areas of personnel evaluation tend to be idiosyncratic and not congealed by professional societies, shared literatures, or unified sets of standards. Overall, personnel evaluation is vital to the public good but is primitive, fragmented, and in need of substantial development and integration.

This entry identifies nine key attributes of sound personnel evaluation. Write-ups of the attributes are intended, in general, to characterize and comment on the landscape of personnel evaluation.

MAIN ATTRIBUTES OF SOUND PERSONNEL EVALUATION

Sound, mature enterprises of personnel evaluation require (a) clear institutional or professional missions to serve as backdrops and values bases for judging the performance of individuals, (b) one or more professional organizations for advancing and helping ensure the quality of personnel evaluations, (c) professional standards by which to plan and assess personnel evaluations, (d) ongoing research and development and a growing professional literature to help advance the theory and practice of personnel evaluation and maintain an examined record of the field's progress, (e) clear specifications of each worker's responsibilities and required competencies, (f) clear definition of roles for personnel evaluations, (g) methods and tools for validly assessing and judging worker qualifications and performance, (h) personnel who are trained and engaged in effectively practicing personnel evaluation, and (i) mechanisms for reviewing and strengthening personnel evaluation practices.

Institutional or Societal Mission. Personnel do not perform their job assignments in a vacuum but, along with other workers, help fulfill some larger mission. For example, a nation's different soldiers, whatever their ranks and particular military specialties, all should contribute to the nation's defense. A school's teachers, counselors, and administrators have varying assignments, but each must help educate the school's students. The mission of major universities is to produce outstanding research, service, and teaching, and, whatever their individual assignments, individual professors typically must contribute to all three areas to earn tenure and promotion. U.S. representatives and senators represent their constituencies' interests and collectively help preserve liberty, human rights, national defense, and the nation's welfare.

Individual professionals may work outside institutional contexts but nevertheless are expected to serve given clients and also help fulfill some broader mission. Physicians diagnose and treat the illnesses of their patients and should contribute more broadly to public health; for example, by continually upgrading their medical knowledge and skills and publishing what they learn in their practices. Farmers produce and sell crops but also contribute to a safe, nutritious food supply. Auditors assess enterprises' financial accountability, and society expects them to help ensure public confidence in a nation's economic enterprises and monetary system. Attorneys address individual disputes in the broader service of helping ensure that a nation's laws are upheld and that no one is above the law.

No person who accepts responsibility to do a job or practice a profession is an island. Personnel evaluations should assess how well workers both carry out particular responsibilities and contribute to a larger, important purpose.

Professional Societies for Personnel Evaluations. A hallmark of a profession and of many trades is that members belong to one or more professional or specialty societies dedicated to advancing and helping ensure quality in members' practices. More than 20 countries have professional evaluation societies, the largest and most mature of which is the American Evaluation Association. However, all of the national evaluation associations have concentrated on program evaluation and have done little to advance or to help ensure the quality of personnel evaluations.

One exception is the U.S.-based Consortium for Research on Educational Accountability and Teacher Evaluation (CREATE). Established in 1995, this organization is focused on advancing the theory and practice of evaluating teachers and other educators. Many of its members' writings appear in the *Journal of Personnel Evaluation in Education.* However, CREATE's membership is small, and only about 100 individuals attend the annual conferences. Other notable, focused, professional efforts in personnel evaluation are those of the American Psychological Association in its divisions of industrial psychology and personnel psychology. Members of these groups have contributed substantially to the methodologies of job analysis, exam credentialing, and supervisory evaluations. Overall, though, the widely ranging personnel evaluation enterprises are not adequately served by professional societies.

Professional Standards for Personnel Evaluations. Widespread professionalization of personnel evaluation would require personnel evaluators everywhere to adhere to some validated, consensual set of standards. Although these evaluators' different national contexts and disciplinary or service areas require different sets of such standards, few sets of standards for personnel evaluations have been developed and applied.

One positive example is the *Personnel Evaluation Standards* (Joint Committee on Standards for Educational Evaluation, 1988). Fourteen professional societies in the United States and Canada—collectively representing about 3 million professionals—appointed and sponsored the personnel evaluation standards–setting efforts of this 18-member group. Although designed for application in evaluating education personnel, the resulting standards have proven useful for personnel evaluations in other sectors. These include General Motors Corporation's evaluations of executives and the U.S. Marine Corps' evaluations of officers and enlisted personnel.

The *Personnel Evaluation Standards* provide a valuable example of principles and guidelines and standards development processes for other groups to consider, should they undertake to develop their own personnel evaluation standards. Basically, these standards require evaluations to meet four basic requirements. *Propriety standards* require evaluations to be ethical and fair to the affected parties, including beneficiaries as well as service providers. *Utility standards* require evaluators to issue results that are credible, informative, timely, and influential. The results should help individuals and groups improve their performance and help supervisors make needed personnel decisions and guide staff development and other personnel actions. *Feasibility standards* require that evaluation procedures be efficient, politically viable, relatively easy to implement, and adequately funded. *Accuracy standards* require that evaluations provide sound information about a person's qualifications and performance. The results should be grounded in an up-to-date position description, take account of the particular work environment and institutional or societal mission, be based on systematic collection and analysis of data, and be validly interpreted and reported. In explicating these requirements, the Joint Committee developed and illustrated detailed standards, with input from national and international review panels. Moreover, the Joint Committee is a standing body that periodically reviews and, as needed, updates the standards.

Research and Development on Personnel Evaluation. Sound systems of personnel evaluation should be serviced by ongoing research and development and a growing professional literature to help advance the theory and practice of personnel evaluation and record the field's progress. Pertinent research is needed because personnel evaluation is one of the most complicated, challenging, vulnerable to attack, least developed and understood, yet vital sectors of the evaluation field. Unfortunately, the research base for personnel evaluation practice is inadequate and grossly underfunded, contributing to the poor state of affairs in personnel evaluation.

Without the backing of a strong body of supportive, instructive research, it is difficult to design, conduct, and apply nontrivial personnel evaluations that will withstand rejoinder and legal challenge. Any administrator knows that consequential personnel evaluations are threatened by many legal, social, and psychological pitfalls. Employees who believe they have been evaluated unjustly often sue for corrective action and damages. Administrators and their institutions are at risk of legal judgments against them when they cannot show that their personnel evaluations were conducted in accordance with sound research and based on validated evaluation procedures and tools. To avoid challenge and retaliation, supervisors often conduct only superficial, benign, inconsequential evaluations. Such typically ritualistic evaluations ruffle no feathers, treat competence and incompetence the same, and make little difference—except for wasting time and money.

Those organizations and supervisors who employ strong evaluation measures to reward outstanding performance, weed out incompetence, or punish moral turpitude often are attacked, embroiled in endless appeal processes, or threatened with costly lawsuits. Subsequently, they often tone down and extract the teeth from their personnel evaluations.

The potential payoff of sound research on personnel evaluation is evident in three examples in education. The National Board for Professional Teaching Standards (Bond, Smith, Baker, & Hattie, 2000) has sponsored extensive, credible research and validation activities in the course of developing its procedures for credentialing highly accomplished, experienced teachers. This challenging, potentially controversial approach to identify and certify extremely competent teachers has an exemplary record of acceptance and success, precisely—I believe—because of its ongoing, well-funded (about $25 million per year) program of research and development. Similarly, the Educational Testing Service has enjoyed success in its Praxis Program (Dwyer & Villegas, 1998) for evaluating new teachers, again due largely to the underlying, ongoing systematic process of research and development. As another example, the U.S. Air Force has a long history of conducting ongoing, substantial research as a basis for selecting pilots (Hunter & Burke, 1995). The airline industry has adopted and built on this extensive program of research, which began at Wright-Patterson Air Force Base about the time of World War II. Although these and other good R&D efforts are to be acknowledged and lauded, a great deal more research and development in personnel evaluation as applied to the full range of jobs is needed. For example, the school principal has been shown to be one of the most important variables affecting the quality of any school, but principal evaluation has almost no credible base of research and development (Glasman & Heck, 2003).

Society and its institutions need effective systems of personnel evaluation to help ensure that consumers receive safe, effective, state-of-the-art services. Evaluators of personnel need to employ defensible, "bulletproof" procedures that are grounded in validated principles. This need cannot be met in the absence of ongoing, systematic research on personnel evaluation. Unfortunately, funding organizations and the evaluation establishment are investing far too few resources and effort into the vitally important area of personnel evaluation.

Defined Responsibilities and Competencies. According to the Joint Committee on Standards for Educational Evaluation (1988), "All parties to the evaluation process should have the same understanding of the position requirements. . . . Position requirements have three parts: (1) position qualifications . . . (2) position responsibilities . . . and (3) performance objectives" and, "This [defined role] standard specifies the crucial foundation step in any personnel evaluation process" (p. 85).

In evaluating a given person's competence and performance, an evaluator should obtain a valid description of the person's job, then define evaluative criteria and obtain procedures and instruments that comport with the job description. Only in this way can the ensuing personnel evaluation be fair to the evaluatee, useful for strengthening performance, legally viable, and valid. Unfortunately, many personnel evaluations fail this essential requirement.

Roles for Personnel Evaluations. Personnel evaluations have several important roles pertaining to virtually all work assignments, and it is important to clarify up front what roles a particular personnel evaluation will serve. Such roles should be considered across a range of institutions and through the various stages in a person's preparation for and engagement in a job or profession. Possible roles include providing assessments of use in preparing, credentialing, selecting, supervising, promoting, retaining, terminating, developing, and rewarding individual personnel.

Evaluations in preparation programs involve assessing applicants' interests, aptitudes, and prior achievements; documenting and confirming students' mastery of course and field experience requirements; and certifying fulfillment of graduation requirements. Such evaluations are clearly important because, if done poorly, employers may unwittingly hire persons who are credentialed but not well qualified. Preparation programs need to collaborate with licensing and certifying bodies and pertinent employers to clarify the competencies that graduates will need to succeed in the jobs for which they are being trained.

Evaluations for licensing or certification provide added checks, beyond those made by preparation programs, on the capabilities of persons intending to work in particular areas, such as plumbing, professional secretarial service, psychological counseling, teaching, medicine, and law. Such evaluations may include reviews of coursework and degrees; performance and objectives tests of skills and competencies; reviews of examinee-prepared portfolios that pertain to prior, pertinent work; assessments by prior employers; and interviews. These evaluations are usually carried out by a government agency or professional society. The licensing or certifying body's main responsibility is to ensure that the examinee meets the minimum requirements for a given area of service.

Evaluations for selection are required when organizations have to choose among position candidates. Such evaluations should be keyed to a valid job description and look at each candidate's pertinent qualifications. Assessments of applicants typically focus on records of training, experience, and social behavior; substance and persuasiveness of application materials; testimonials by credible key informants; performance in a job interview; and, sometimes, site visits to a finalist's current or previous work site. When there are many applicants, the evaluation process may include an initial screening procedure to eliminate weak and marginal candidates. Subsequently, the evaluators do an in-depth investigation of the remaining pool of most (apparently) appropriate candidates. In many cases, evaluation of a tentatively chosen applicant will proceed through an official probationary period.

Evaluation on the job is an essential requirement of supervising and making decisions about employees. These kinds of evaluations should be keyed to assigned job responsibilities and the organization's mission and priorities. Evaluation results are needed to give employees feedback on their strengths and weaknesses and point up areas requiring improvement. On-the-job evaluations are also employed to guide decisions on such matters as promotion, tenure, and continuation.

Typically, supervisors keep a file of critical incidents related to an employee's performance and may also ask employees to submit a self-report on fulfillment of job requirements. The supervisor may periodically observe and record information on the employee's performance in an appropriate work setting (e.g., a teacher's performance in a classroom). Individual peers or a personnel evaluation committee may also be asked to assess the employee's performance. Periodically, the supervisor or evaluation committee compiles, assesses, and interprets the available information, then reports it to the employee and others as appropriate. The reports may then lead to pertinent decisions and actions—including improvement plans and training—and, in positive cases, be used to reinforce the employee's good efforts and accomplishments.

Personnel Evaluation Methods and Tools. Sound personnel evaluation requires a range of potentially relevant methods and tools. Examples are interview protocols, police background checks, observation schedules, checklists, critical incident records, employee- and supervisor-prepared portfolios, document analysis, objective knowledge exams, performance tests, attitude and personality inventories, questionnaires to the employee's clients, supervisor ratings, role-play sessions, examined internships and apprenticeships, and assessment centers. These need to be carefully developed and validated in the first place. Users also should carefully select and apply only those procedures or instruments that fit the needs of particular evaluations. Subsequently, users should adapt and validate the methods and tools they chose to apply so that these are demonstrably valid for assessing the particular person's competence and performance of assigned job responsibilities.

In general, evaluators must validate the inferences they make about the qualifications, performance, and contributions of individuals. This requires access to and selective use of a wide range of potentially relevant procedures and tools that have been researched in similar situations. Ultimately, the evaluator must show that the employed procedures and tools led to defensible conclusions about the evaluatee's qualifications and performance.

Qualified Personnel Evaluators. In almost all personnel evaluations—like it or not—someone has to be "the judge." This awesome responsibility requires that supervisors and others who conduct personnel evaluations have to be credible. The Joint Committee on Standards for Educational Evaluation (1988) stipulated that personnel evaluators should "possess the necessary qualifications, skills, sensitivity, and authority, and . . . should conduct themselves professionally, so that evaluation reports are respected and used" (p. 57).

The evaluator credibility imperative brings a pervasive requirement for personnel evaluation training. Some of this should be provided in the graduate and other programs that prepare supervisors. Also, institutions need to train their supervisors to carry out effective personnel evaluations.

The needed training applies not just to evaluation specialists but to all who formally evaluate another person's work. The training should be grounded in professional standards for personnel evaluations and should draw from pertinent research and development. It should also reflect relevant institutional contexts, including missions and priorities that should be considered in the evaluations. Because institutional priorities and employee assignments change over time, supervisors and other personnel evaluators should receive training updates as appropriate. For example, the U.S. Marine Corps annually trains those who will evaluate other marines in the performance review system. Also, institutions should assess supervisors for their fulfillment of personnel evaluation responsibilities. This is a critical job responsibility that all too often is overlooked in evaluating supervisors.

Mechanisms for Reviewing and Strengthening Personnel Evaluation Practices. An imperative of all systematic evaluations is that they themselves be subject to evaluation. In personnel evaluations, this requirement is played out in two ways.

First, evaluations of individuals typically are subject to a review and appeal process. Thus, an evaluatee may request that an evaluation by her or his supervisor be reviewed by a higher level administrator or evaluation committee. Such "metaevaluations" (see Stufflebeam, 2001) should be keyed to the evaluatee's assigned responsibilities and the pertinent professional standards.

In addition, personnel evaluation systems should be evaluated and revised periodically as appropriate.

These metaevaluations should take account of problems and complaints related to past evaluations conducted under the system and should be keyed to the appropriate set of professional standards for personnel evaluations, such as those associated with propriety, utility, feasibility, and accuracy.

CONCLUSION

Personnel evaluation is critically important to the effectiveness of organizations and society. It is a vital tool for guiding personnel decisions and helping workers improve their contributions. Key dimensions of sound personnel evaluations are clear institutional and societal missions, professional evaluation societies, standards for evaluations, instructive research and development, clear job assignments, defined roles of evaluations, defensible data collection methods and tools, trained evaluators, and appeal processes plus evaluations of personnel evaluations. Some progress and exemplary work is evident in relation to each of these dimensions. In general, however, practices of personnel evaluation are often poorly grounded, superficial, and inconsequential. A clear need exists for extensive, well-funded efforts to advance the theory and practice of personnel evaluation across all enterprises that serve the public good.

—*Daniel L. Stufflebeam*

Further Reading

Bond, L., Smith, T., Baker, W. K., & Hattie, J. A. (2000, September). *The certification system of the National Board for Professional Teaching Standards: A construct and consequential validity study.* Washington, DC: National Board for Professional Teaching Standards.

Dwyer, C. A., & Villegas, A. M. (1998). *Guiding conceptions and assessment principles for "The Praxis series: Professional assessments for beginning teachers."* Princeton, NJ: Educational Testing Service.

Glasman, N. S., & Heck, R. H. (2003). Principal evaluation in the United States. In T. Kellaghan & D. L. Stufflebeam (Eds.), *International handbook of educational evaluation.* Dordrecht, The Netherlands: Kluwer.

Hunter, D. R., & Burke, E. F. (1995). *Handbook of pilot selection.* Aldershot, UK: Ashgate.

Joint Committee on Standards for Educational Evaluation. (1988). *The personnel evaluation standards.* Newbury Park, CA: Sage.

Orris, M. J. (1989). *Industrial applicability of the Joint Committee's personnel evaluation standards.* Unpublished doctoral dissertation, Western Michigan University, Kalamazoo.

Stufflebeam, D. L. (2001). The metaevaluation imperative. *American Journal of Evaluation, 22,* 183-209.

■■ THE PERSONNEL EVALUATION STANDARDS

The Personnel Evaluation Standards was published in 1988. Fourteen professional societies in the United States and Canada, collectively representing about 3 million professionals, appointed and sponsored the standard-setting efforts of this 18-member group. Although designed for application in evaluating education personnel, the resulting standards have proved useful for personnel evaluations in other sectors.

The Personnel Evaluation Standards provides a valuable example of principles and guidelines and standards development processes for other groups to consider should they undertake to develop their own personnel evaluation standards. Basically, these standards require that evaluations meet four basic requirements. *Propriety standards* require that evaluations be ethical and fair to the affected parties, including beneficiaries as well as the service provider. *Utility standards* require that evaluators issue results that are credible, informative, timely, and influential. The results should help individuals and groups improve their performance, help supervisors make needed personnel decisions, and guide staff development and other personnel actions. *Feasibility standards* require that evaluation procedures be efficient, politically viable, relatively easy to implement, and adequately funded. *Accuracy standards* require that evaluations provide sound information about a person's qualifications and performance. The results should be grounded in an up-to-date position description, take account of the particular work environment and institutional or societal mission, be based on systematic collection and analysis of data, and be validly interpreted and reported. In explicating these requirements, the Joint Committee developed and illustrated detailed standards, with input from national and international review panels.

—*Daniel L. Stufflebeam*

See also PERSONNEL EVALUATION

Further Reading

Joint Committee on Standards for Educational Evaluation. (1988). *The personnel evaluation standards.* Newbury Park, CA: Sage.

◫ PERSUASION

Persuasion is the act of encouraging people to embrace a point of view, change their minds, or do something. It can rely both on reasoning (logical argument) and on personal appeal (the characteristics of the individual). In evaluation, persuasive use is one of three traditional forms of use, occurring when decision makers take the content of an evaluation report and seek to move others to support a position. Such use contrasts with instrumental or conceptual use. Persuasion also underlies debates in the field about whether evaluators should advocate for the programs they study or for the results generated.

—Jean A. King

◫ PHENOMENOGRAPHY

Phenomenography is an approach to qualitative inquiry that focuses on human experience. It is associated most often with the work of Swedish educational psychologist Ference Marton. Although it is often considered a method, Marton focuses more on the object of inquiry. He is interested in conceptions and ways of understanding and experiencing the physical and social world. Phenomenography examines how different ways of conceptualizing or experiencing something evolve, but it also has a normative or pedagogical aspect: It examines how different ways of conceptualizing and experiencing something can be brought about.

Further Reading

Marton, F. (1981). Phenomenography: Describing conceptions of the world around us. *Instructional Science, 10,* 177-200.

◫ PHENOMENOLOGY

Human beings create their views of the world through the accumulation of sense experiences (also called data). Further, they revisit and report these experiences when completing questionnaires and interviews designed to gather attitudes, observations, and judgments. Phenomenology is relevant to evaluation because it problematizes the interpretation of reported experiences, as in, "Was that a blink or a wink?" or "I saw a blink, but you saw a wink." Phenomenology's ultimate source is the distinction pioneered by the German philosopher Immanuel Kant that sense experiences could be registered as phenomena, but "things in themselves," also known as *noumena,* are inaccessible.

—David Hamilton

◫ PHILANTHROPIC EVALUATION

Funders have long struggled with identifying and implementing measures of evaluating their performance as a way to gauge both internal performance and social impact achieved through grantmaking. Perhaps due in part to the tenuous nature of evaluation in philanthropy, a wide variety of evaluation tools and models have emerged.

PURPOSES OF EVALUATION

Philanthropic evaluation generally aims to measure two things: the effectiveness of a grant or grantee program or the social impact or effectiveness of the funder. According to a 2002 study conducted by the Center for Effective Philanthropy, evaluations are the most commonly used tool for assessing overall foundation performance. In the study *Indicators of Effectiveness,* 72% of foundation chief executives said they use grant, grantee, and program evaluations to assess the performance of their foundations in achieving social impact and operational goals.

However, attempts to assess funder effectiveness through evaluation of grants can be burdensome to grantee organizations and fail to yield the data a funder seeks. In some cases, the information that funders require to evaluate their own social impact is not the same information that would help grantees evaluate their own programs. Such evaluation requirements cost grantees time and energy in collecting and reporting information that is useless to them. In many circumstances, the data are not being used to inform the funder's strategy or practice. Funders are becoming increasingly aware of this disconnect and are working to align their information needs with that of their grantees. Some funders (for example, the Roberts Enterprise Development Fund) ask grantees what information they would find useful to track and report and use that for their own evaluations.

CHALLENGES OF EVALUATION

Funders lack accountability measures and external incentives for evaluation. Grantmakers are ambivalent and perhaps confused by the concept of accountability. In contrast to many highly regulated fields, the parameters surrounding funder accountability are limited and basic.

Performance information is limited, collected inconsistently, and not focused strategically on the outcomes of funders' work. Recently, funders have moved to assume greater responsibility for the outcomes of their work. The efforts, however, tend to be more focused on funder processes and grantee outcomes, leaving the linkages between the two undetermined.

The organizational learning agenda generated excitement but failed to link to institutional mission and the needs of fields. Over the past several years, funders have embraced ideas associated with learning organizations. Grantmakers have developed agendas focused on learning from the past, including studying "best practices" and sharing project lessons among staff. However, the relationship between learning and accountability has assumed a highly polarized tenor. In some organizations, learning and accountability are seen as competing functions. The issues are especially contentious when the same personnel, often evaluation staff, are responsible for both functions. In these situations, program staff members fear being exposed by the process of evaluation. They find it difficult to discern when an evaluator is functioning in learning mode or accountability mode, "who the evaluators work for," where their loyalties lie, and whether they can be trusted.

Evaluation is expected to fill a diversity of roles—as a learning device and as a device for judging accountability, effectiveness, management, and strategy. The ambiguity about the proper role of evaluation heightens program officers' natural fears about having their work observed and assessed. Staff members generally are unsure about the purposes of evaluation, how the process will unfold, and how the data ultimately will be used. Moreover, they tend to see that evaluation often operates in seemingly contradictory roles, and they react with understandable suspicion.

COLLABORATION TO ADVANCE THE FIELD

To overcome these challenges and to advance the field of philanthropic evaluation, grantmakers interested in and responsible for evaluation are coming together in ways both formal and informal to share experiences and expertise, with an ultimate goal of advancing evaluation practices in philanthropy. Through Grantmakers for Effective Organizations, for example, funders share evaluation experience and knowledge with colleagues by sharing documents via a Web site, contributing to an evaluation-specific e-newsletter and discussion board, and participating in case study teachings. In 2002, independent consultant Patricia Patrizi convened a gathering of nearly 50 funders with staff dedicated to evaluation to discuss common challenges faced when working to demonstrate results. The conversation was summarized in a report that describes the current state of the evaluation field. Grantmakers for Effective Organizations and Patrizi will continue the roundtable discussion annually as a way to gauge progress and set agendas for future work in the field.

WHAT WORKS

Although no definitive research has yet been conducted to identify best practices in philanthropic evaluation, what foundation evaluation staff have learned throughout their work serves as recommendations for fellow funders:

- Engage the evaluator at the beginning of the grant or program you are evaluating.
- Determine whether the utility of evaluation is sufficient to warrant its intrusiveness.
- Be able to answer the question, "This evaluation is to what end?"
- Think critically about reporting requirements—be able to determine efficiently how much and what you need to know.
- Create customized approaches for different evaluation goals and different types of programs.

—*Lori Tucker*

Further Reading

Patrizi, P. (2002). *The inside perspective.* Retrieved June 3, 2004, from http://www.geofunders.org/_uploads/documents/live/Results%20PP%20paper.doc

▉ PHOTOGRAPHY

Photography for evaluations can be considered an extension of, or variation on, participant observation or document analysis. Either existing or new photos can be used for evaluation purposes and can be analyzed either qualitatively or quantitatively.

It is interesting that photos are an underused form of data for evaluation purposes and that little has been written about them in relation to evaluation practice. Exceptions include Templin (1981) and Hurworth and Sweeney (1996).

Photography is particularly useful in evaluations in which

- there is a range of activities to be documented
- program participants are unable to undertake other forms of data collection (such as surveys or in-depth interviews). Examples include small children, non-English speakers, the physically and mentally handicapped, and the general public
- the visual image would be more "hard hitting" than prose
- programs are highly visual in themselves (e.g., programs in art, dance, drama)
- a program's effects lead to marked changes over time, such as before and after a land-care program, where an initial picture shows an eroded slope and the same slope, postintervention, is shown to have been reforested
- the physical and locational context of a program is important (e.g., for postoccupancy evaluations carried out by architects)

Photographs can add a great deal to evaluations. They provide visual communication that helps to develop insights, imagery not available by other means, the means to evoke powerful emotional responses, improved understandings about program contexts, assistance in documenting cultures, and a way of creating variety within reporting.

However, selection and analysis of photographs have to be undertaken rigorously. So, photos must not be just "happy snaps" but be sampled properly. Sampling techniques advocated by Templin include the following:

- *Fixed-time sampling.* Pictures are taken from a fixed position at regular intervals.
- *Sampling across time.* In this case, the photographer moves around, taking regular photos of a full range of activities.
- *Event-based sampling.* Only events in a certain category are photographed to address particular evaluation questions.

- *Dimensionally based sampling.* This is desirable when constraints of time make it impossible to cover all events. In this case, in conjunction with an evaluation question, a possible range is chosen.
- *Shadow sampling.* One person or group is followed throughout a certain time period or routine.
- *Snowball sampling.* A stakeholder is asked what, or who else, might be photographed.
- *Theoretically informed sampling.* Photographs are taken from different vantage points. For instance, one might take photos nearer the ground to see the world from a child's perspective or lie down on a hospital bed to see a ward from a patient's viewpoint.

Aside from rigorous sampling, there are other ways to enhance trustworthiness. These include the following:

- Ensuring there are no alterations or distortions so that photographs are evaluation evidence rather than "art"
- Ensuring that the photo is characteristic of what it purports to show
- Using photos as part of multimethod triangulation
- Explaining any selection bias caused by the client, the political situation, or social taboos
- Determining and explaining any influence the photographer might have had on the behaviors of those being photographed (prolonged engagement will help to avoid this)
- Posing a strong evaluation question so that there is a reason for the image and its content

Finally, ethical issues associated with the presentation of photographs in evaluation reports abound. If individuals and sites can be identified, informed consent will be necessary. This issue may be alleviated if photographs are taken from behind or from the side.

—*Rosalind Hurworth*

Further Reading

Hurworth, R., & Sweeney, M. (1996). The use of the visual image in a variety of Australian evaluations. *Evaluation Practice, 16*(2), 153-164.

Templin, P. A. (1981). *Handbook in evaluating with photography.* Portland, OR: Northwest Regional Educational Lab.

▪▪ PLANNING

Planning is the means by which organizations seek to achieve goals, objectives, and tasks in a stable, known, or predictable environment. To some extent, planning can be seen as the antithesis to *strategy,* which is the means by which organizations seek to achieve goals, objectives, and tasks in an *un*stable, *un*known, or *un*predictable environment. For this reason, some management commentators (e.g., Henry Mintzberg) consider planning and strategy as essentially separate endeavors and that attempts to blend them (as in strategic planning) will generally result in unstable plans and poor strategies.

—Bob Williams

■ PLANNING, EVALUATION

Planning is a process for determining what will be accomplished by an evaluation (i.e., defining the boundaries of a study) and for specifying methods and resources to achieve evaluation intents. Evaluation planning requires the definition of key evaluation questions, descriptions of information to be acquired and sources that can provide the information (including any sampling procedures), data collection and analysis techniques, reporting protocols, and required resources.

—M. F. Smith

See also EVALUATION PLANS

■ POETRY

Poetry has been used as an alternative form of representation in evaluation reporting. As an educative tool, poetry can communicate complex findings in ways that create a learning dissonance for the readers of the report. Evaluations that use poetry in this regard seek to provoke critical dialogue among evaluation stakeholders about a particular phenomenon under investigation. By constructing a poem and creatively using the language from the narrative data obtained during the inquiry, evaluators can enhance the conceptual utility of an evaluation report, advancing understandings about an experience in a program or the influence of a policy.

Poetry can move people into conversations beyond the case at hand. As the poetry in an evaluation report influences the meanings and values held by the different stakeholders regarding an evaluand, higher moral, social, and political issues for reflection can surface. In and of itself, the presence of poetry in an evaluation report can promote discussions among readers about processes and products of evaluative inquiry. Poetry as a form of evaluative representation has the potential to create dialogue about what is and what is not an evaluation and why this is perceived as so. It can serve as a useful springboard for discourse about higher ontological, epistemological, and methodological assumptions associated with evaluation.

Including poetry in an evaluation document can also be thought of as a strategy for making the evaluation report more accessible to audiences who may not be drawn to reading a technical piece of writing. For some report readers, poetry is an engaging way of thinking about evaluation findings. Poetry can be a useful medium for including diverse audiences who may not otherwise be attracted to participating in the reporting phase of an evaluation.

Poetry can be fashioned for an evaluation report in different ways. Poetic transcription is a specific form of analytic writing that combines the voices of the evaluation participants with an interpretive analysis conducted by the evaluator. The constructed evaluation findings embody a new collective third voice. Evaluation participants can also be asked to submit poetry that communicates their meaning of experience about a particular issue. Likewise, evaluators can reflect on the thoughts, feelings, or perspectives of evaluation participants and transform them into their own words.

An evaluation report is likely to be more vulnerable to questions of credibility when poetry is introduced. Whether an evaluator infuses another's poetry or adopts the role of poet in his or her own report writing, it is important that the narrative fidelity of the poem is attended to. As with any assertion that is embedded in narrative ways of knowing, an evaluator is responsible for exploring the verisimilitude of the poetry with the audience it is intended to represent and the audience of readers it has been created to influence.

—Cheryl MacNeil

Further Reading

Chin, M. (2003). *An investigation into the impact of using poetry and cartoons to communicate findings in an evaluation report.* Unpublished doctoral dissertation, Florida State University, Tallahassee.

MacNeil, C. (2000). The prose and cons of poetic representation in evaluation reporting. *American Journal of Evaluation, 21,* 359-367.

Evaluation Practice Around the World

Guyana

Personal Growth Through Self-Evaluation

Two groups of community researchers were trained in participatory learning and action techniques to give support to an education project. During the first 2 years of the project, the researchers worked alongside project staff to organize and carry out activities with groups in the community, conducting literacy training as well as small research projects.

After 1 year of involvement with the project, the researchers participated in a 4-day workshop to improve their report-writing skills and to gain an introduction to proposal writing. The workshop facilitator used self-evaluation as the means of introducing the researchers to report-writing skills.

The researchers began by identifying positive and negative perspectives of themselves, representing these in drawings. Several said at first that they could not draw, but they did, in fact, produce an image. They then discussed the significance of the images chosen, reasons for their self-perceptions, and the impact of these self-perceptions on their behavior and attitudes. This initial individual self-evaluation helped researchers learn more about themselves and appreciate themselves better. One researcher stated, "I was able to see myself for what I am. I could see the good sides of me and also the bad ones. I saw how much I know and how much I did not know about myself."

As a group, researchers examined the nature of self-evaluation and its importance to individual development, as well as to their functioning as a group. They identified the aspects of the individual, as well as the collective self-evaluation that they would undertake, and agreed to begin writing components of the individual self-evaluation at home. On the second day of the workshop, each researcher presented what he or she had prepared. Some were fearful of making their efforts public but eventually developed the confidence to share their work. With feedback from the facilitator and the other researchers, all continued refining the document until each had an individual self-evaluation of which he or she was proud. By using a uniform outline for the self-evaluation report, the facilitator was able to assess the analytical and writing capabilities of each researcher.

On the third day, researchers discussed the nature of their involvement in the project and prepared a general outline of the collective self-evaluation. This they refined as a large group; they then worked in small groups to outline each section of the report and to divide the task among themselves.

On the fourth day, the researchers compared what they had written, clarified their thoughts, and finalized their self-evaluations. They presented their collective self-evaluation to the large group with a sense of achievement. They were challenged, but they rose to that challenge. They recognized that they do have the capability to assess activities in which they are involved and were pleased to learn that the project officials welcomed and appreciated their perspectives on the development of the project in the field.

Using individual and collective self-evaluation as the medium for strengthening report-writing skills enabled the researchers to take ownership of their learning. It promoted increased self-esteem, cohesiveness, and an improved knowledge base with respect to the purpose and activities of the project itself. As the researchers noted, it drew out hidden aspects of themselves, including creative talents as exemplified by the two poems appearing here, which formed part of the evaluation of the workshop.

—Janice M. Jackson

Conclusion

Ulric Harmon

We looked at ourselves in August of last year
And within us was much fear
Our community was unclear in our many
    perceptions
Before we allowed our depression to leave an
    impression
We were recruited into a group that evolved into FREED
Though before there was a need for the alleviation
    of poverty
And a demand for education.

Which called for the project GEAP's
    implementation.
We now will introduce FREED to the nation
With qualifications to maintain the GEAP-
    generated situation.

NOTE: FREED stands for Friends Restoring Economic and Educational Development; GEAP, Guyana Education Access Project.

Progress

Smeayah
(Ernestine Logan)

All alone
In a crowd
seeking
And then light
a bright light
a hand
shone down on me
shone through me

a hand
turned me around
to look within me
to see through me
the way
outside me
opening here
opening there
opening everywhere
to others
all around me.
all around me.

POINT OF VIEW

All evaluation is conducted from a particular point of view, although this point of view is frequently implicit and often unacknowledged. Nonetheless, the particular point of view from which an evaluation is conducted suggests the forms of reasoning and criteria that will be relevant for a particular evaluation. Examples of points of view are aesthetic, economic, historical, mathematical, political, religious, and scientific. Within any point of view there are numerous value systems. Thus, for example, within a religious point of view there are value systems that might be described by major religions such as Buddhist, Christian, Moslem, and so on. These many value systems within a particular point of view are often contradictory to one another. A point of view is, therefore, cross-cultural, although value systems are culture bound.

A judgment about the value of an evaluand can and often does vary depending on the point of view taken. For example, if one evaluates a painting from an economic point of view, one might judge it to be a good painting because it has high likelihood of increasing in value. However, if this same painting is evaluated from an aesthetic point of view, the evaluative conclusion might be that it is not a good painting because it violates aesthetic standards for paintings of its type.

To take a point of view is to adopt certain canons of reasoning to use in determining the justification for assertions, including evaluative conclusions. This is important especially from a metaevaluation perspective. At one level, an evaluation of an evaluation must first examine the extent to which the evaluation being evaluated used reasoning and evidence consistent with the point of view taken and at another level must examine the extent to which the point of view was appropriate.

Further Reading

Taylor, P. (1961). *Normative discourse.* Englewood Cliffs, NJ: Prentice Hall.

POLICY STUDIES

Policy studies are closely linked with evaluation and focus particularly on policies. There is substantial overlap between the methods and strategies used in policy studies and evaluation, although policy studies are more often explicitly normative and require prescriptions or plans for future actions, often within a relatively short time frame. Policy studies may be prospective and involve a comparative analysis of future scenarios, given policy alternatives, or may be retrospective and examine the consequences of a particular policy. An example of the overlap of policy studies and evaluation is exemplified in the journal *Educational Evaluation and Policy Analysis.*

POLITICS OF EVALUATION

Like any organized social practice, evaluation is unavoidably implicated in matters of politics. The ways in which politics and evaluation are interrelated are many. Consider, for example, the following sampling of topics addressed in the literature: evaluation as a political ritual, political participation in evaluation, the politics of identifying stakeholders, evaluation as a political activity in a political context, evaluation in the service of political rationality, the political morality of evaluation practice, the politics of applying methods in evaluation, the political accountability of evaluation. A not uncommon view is that even though evaluation results are surely implicated in the arena of politics, political concerns inevitably represent an intrusion into the conduct of evaluation. The inevitability of this state of affairs is owing to the facts that (a) programs are created and maintained by political forces; (b) higher echelons of government, which make decisions about programs, are embedded in politics; (c) the very act of evaluation has political connotations. The milieu and discourse of politics—conceived in terms of norms, values, ideology, power, influence, authority, and so forth—are often contrasted with the world of science, which is conceived in terms of facts, objectivity, and empirically warranted descriptions and explanations. The world of politics and values is thought to lie outside of the scientific practice of evaluation, the so danger is that the former will impede, constrain, unduly influence, or otherwise obstruct evaluation. Taking this into consideration, evaluators ought to be aware of political rationality, recognize that the findings of their evaluations might well be used for political purposes, and take steps to minimize the contamination of scientific rationality by political influences. In a nutshell, this is the doctrine of value-free science as applied to evaluation.

A less common view is that politics is not simply bound to the *uses* of evaluation but *always* implicated in our understandings of what evaluation is as a practice and what constitutes evaluation knowledge. In other words, evaluation is as much a political as a scientific practice. In this way of thinking, the politics of knowing can be explored at both the micro and the macro levels of evaluation practice. The micro level is the level of everyday interaction involving, for example, negotiations between evaluator and sponsor, evaluator and client, and evaluator and stakeholders. The macro level refers to the behavior of evaluation as a whole—as a social practice or institution.

At the micro level, one might examine the political motivations of evaluators. For example, it is generally understood (although not necessarily widely accepted) that many evaluators prefer case study, participatory, empowerment, utilization-focused, and collaborative forms of evaluation because they want evaluation to be more directly helpful to those being studied. To promote stakeholder engagement, self-determination, and ownership of an evaluation process is to endorse a particular set of political values. Conversely, to practice evaluation in such a way that the evaluator intentionally focuses solely on producing an objective (i.e., interest neutral and value neutral) assessment of program performance and avoids any substantial involvement with participants in an evaluation (beyond using them as data sources or informants) is to promote a different political orientation to evaluation. At the micro level, the politics of negotiating evaluation contracts may also be considered, including access to and control of data, as well as the politics involved in the myriad types of interactions between evaluator, sponsor, client, and stakeholders. In a value-free ideology for evaluation, the point of such political negotiations is actually to minimize the intrusion of politics! The Joint Committee Program Evaluation Standards, for example, contend that for an evaluation to be politically viable, it must be planned and conducted in such a way that the cooperation of various interest groups is obtained and that any efforts by these groups to curtail or otherwise influence the conduct or conclusions of the evaluation are averted or counteracted. However, it may be overlooked here that a broad political orientation characterized by values of cooperation, accommodation, and "getting along" is the foreground of this way of thinking. One could equally well imagine a different political orientation of which the foreground is the political viability of evaluation in values of confrontation, ideology critique, and emancipation. An additional consideration of the micropolitics of evaluation focuses on the rhetorical construction and presentation of evaluation arguments. In Ernest House's famous argument, evaluation is fundamentally a matter of persuasion and argumentation, not demonstration or proof. The task of persuading an audience that such and such is the case inevitably takes up matters of rhetoric and the crafting of appeals to reason and evidence suited to various audiences. Thus the politics and poetics of evaluation reporting are intertwined. A final illustration of micropolitical considerations in evaluation has to do with the politics of methods choice and use. Two examples illustrate different considerations here. Consider first the politics involved in the construction of a procedure to generate data. For example, Michael Oliver, a long-time activist and scholar in disability research, argues that social researchers working for the British government promoted the view that disability is a problem "in the person" by asking survey questions such as, "Are your difficulties in understanding people mainly due to a hearing problem?" "Have you attended a special school because of a long-term health problem or disability?" Oliver maintains that if the researchers had taken the view that the problem of disability is "in society," they might have asked instead, "Are your difficulties in understanding people mainly due to their inabilities to communicate with you?" "Have you attended a special school because of your education authority's policy of sending people with your health problem or disability to such places?" Second, consider that MacDonald saw the use of case study evaluation (i.e., the idea of studying a social program as itself a case) as a means of bringing within the boundaries of a case agencies and actors at all levels of the power structure. In this way, case study methodology served the goals of democratic evaluation, for it opened programs to greater public scrutiny and accountability and served as a counterforce to bureaucratic evaluations that served to maintain and extend managerial power.

Macro-level considerations have already been touched on, demonstrating that micro- and macro-level matters are not neatly separable. Democratic evaluation or democratic evaluation theories are macro-level conceptions of the political framework for and role of evaluation in society. For example, MacDonald cast democratic evaluation largely in the context of classic liberal democratic theory, viewing evaluation as a strategy for equalizing power relationships in which centrally funded social programs are embedded. In this context, the evaluator was to serve as a broker of program knowledge serving the public's right to know. Although objecting to some aspects of MacDonald's conception, Cronbach and colleagues promoted a democratic theory of evaluation in line with a political philosophy of pluralist accommodation of multiple and competing interests. Like MacDonald, they were highly critical of conceptions of evaluation that developed almost solely around an image of the context of command in which evaluation information flows to a manager or policy official who is firmly in control of a situation and has the authority and responsibility to make the correct decision that subordinates then dutifully follow. House's version of democratic evaluation holds that evaluation is (or ought to be) an institution for democratizing public decision making. Accordingly, he situates evaluation in the political theory of deliberative democracy and argues that evaluation ought to serve the deliberative

process and its underlying values of justice, impartiality, and equality of participation. Like MacDonald, he holds that evaluators ought to be advocates for democracy and the public interest and should especially focus on the views of program beneficiaries, not simply those of program managers or sponsors. However, he views the evaluator as more than a neutral broker of information and a facilitator of understanding on the part of different stakeholders. He argues that evaluators are professionally obligated to ensure equality and inclusion as key principles of deliberative democratic participation. This obligation entails taking special care that the voices of groups historically excluded from the deliberative process are fully represented.

Given this variety of ways in which evaluation is situated within or linked to political theory, it becomes obvious that interpretations of how evaluation serves society are contested. Consider, for example, one of the American Evaluation Association's Guiding Principles for Evaluators, responsibilities for general and public welfare: "Evaluators should articulate and take into account the diversity of interests and values that may be related to the general and public welfare." Just what it means to "take into account" such interests and values will depend a great deal on the theory of political morality assumed in the practice of evaluation.

Macro-level considerations extend beyond consideration of the ways in which various evaluation theories are linked to theories of political morality. One can also examine the manner in which politics act *through* the social practice of evaluation to create its authority. In this view, evaluation (particularly given the growing influence of performance-auditing practices) is becoming one of the practices of those administrative, management, and professional authorities (and their respective intellectual and cultural discourses) that organize, regulate, lead, and direct capitalist societies. Evaluation, like other professions, exercises power to define the world by virtue of its epistemological or cognitive authority. This is a conceptual practice of power: a power to define the sociopolitical world through objectified knowledge. Defenders of this view argue that to address the nature and consequences of the politics that acts through the practice of evaluation, one must resist the tendency to depoliticize evaluation as a conceptual practice of power. To depoliticize a practice of cognitive authority is to close the question of authority in favor of the experts; to politicize the expertise of evaluation (and audit) professionals is to open the question of their cognitive authority to the critical scrutiny of society at large. A depoliticized practice "certifies as value-neutral, normal, natural, and *not political at all* the existing scientific policies and practices through which powerful groups can gain the information and explanations that they need to advance their priorities" (Harding, 1992, pp. 568-569, italics added).

—*Thomas A. Schwandt*

Further Reading

Cronbach, L. J., Ambron, S. R., Dornbush, S. M., Hornik, R. C., Phillips, D. C., Walker, D. F., et al. (1980). *Toward reform of program evaluation.* San Francisco: Jossey-Bass.

Fuller, S. (1988). *Social epistemology.* Bloomington: Indiana University Press.

Harding, S. (1992). After the neutrality ideal: Science, politics, and "strong" objectivity. *Social Research, 59*(3), 567-587.

House, E. R. (1980). *Evaluating with validity.* Beverly Hills, CA: Sage.

House, E. R. (1993). *Professional evaluation: Social impact and political consequences.* Newbury Park, CA: Sage.

House, E. R., & Howe, K. R. (1999). *Values in evaluation and social research.* Thousand Oaks, CA: Sage.

Proctor, R. N. (1991). *Value-free science? Purity and power in modern knowledge.* Cambridge, MA: Harvard University Press.

Simons, H. (1987). *Getting to know schools in a democracy: The politics and process of evaluation.* London: Falmer.

Smith, D. E. (1990a). *The conceptual practices of power.* Boston: Northeastern University Press.

Smith, D. E. (1990b). *Texts, facts, and femininity: Exploring the relations of ruling.* London: Routledge.

Weiss, C. H. (1991). Evaluation research in the political context: Sixteen years and four administrations later. In M. W. McLaughlin & D.C. Phillips (Eds.), *Evaluation and education: At quarter century* (pp. 211-231). Chicago: University of Chicago Press.

■■ POLLITT, CHRISTOPHER

(b. 1946, Stafford, England). Ph.D. Government, London School of Economics and Political Science; M.A. (Honors) Modern History, Oriel College, Oxford University.

Pollitt is Professor of Public Management at the Erasmus University of Rotterdam. Previously, he was Professor of Government as well as being Codirector of the Centre for the Evaluation of Public Policy at Brunel University. At Brunel, he served as Dean of the Faculty of Social Sciences (1994-1997). In 1994, he was the Elliot-Winant Visiting Lecturer at five U.S.

universities and has been a Visiting Professor or Visiting Research Fellow in several universities in the United States, Canada, the United Kingdom, and other European countries. He was the first elected President of the European Evaluation Society (1996-1998), contributing to its early development.

He has been a consultant to various public sector organizations, including the OECD, the European Commission, and the World Bank, as well as national public sector organizations. In the past he has undertaken consultancy for the U.K. Treasury, the Organisation for Economic Co-operation and Development, the European Commission, the Finnish Ministry of Finance, and a number of other public bodies. Currently he is working with Hilkka Summa and others on a five-country comparative study. His main focus has been on the management and organization of central government and public services. He has been continuously concerned with the problems of evaluating organizational change in central government and with the reasons that such changes, although costly in various ways, are often not evaluated at all. His current research concerns the nature of performance auditing and its relationship to "the new public management." His work has been influenced by people from a variety of disciplines, notably Lindblom, Dahl, and Brian Barry in politics; Habermas, Elster, and David Held in social theory; and Michael Q. Patton, Michael Scriven, and Carol Weiss in evaluation.

Pollitt is the author of many books and articles in the field of public management and evaluation, including *Public Management Reform: A Comparative Analysis* (with Geert Bouckaert); *Quality Improvement in European Public Services* (with Geert Bouchaert); and *Managerialism and the Public Services.* From 1980 to 1989 he was the Joint Honorary Editor of *Public Administration.*

■■ PORTEOUS, NANCY L.

(b. 1966, Winchester, Ontario, Canada). M.Sc. Social Research Methods, University of Surrey, Guildford, England [Commonwealth Scholar]; Honors B.A. Sociology, McGill University, Montreal, Quebec.

Porteous began her career with Ekos Research Associates, an Ottawa-based applied social research firm. It was at Ekos that she worked with Shelley Borys and Benoît Gauthier, two experienced evaluators whom she considers role models. After several years at Ekos,

Porteous began planning, evaluation, and performance measurement work in local government for the City of Ottawa, first with public health and then in social services, where she led the Planning and Performance Measurement Unit. Also while with the city, she worked briefly on special projects in environment and transportation. Her last post was with strategic initiatives in the City Manager's Office. For several years, Porteous was a Research Associate with the University of Ottawa's Community Health Research Unit. Recently she moved to the federal level and is now working for the Centre for Chronic Disease Prevention and Control at Health Canada. Valued colleagues such as Helen Durand Charron, Barbara Sheldrick, and Paula Stewart have greatly influenced her approach to the field of evaluation.

Porteous served as President of the Canadian Evaluation Society (CES) from 2000 to 2002. She was awarded the Contribution to Evaluation in Canada Award by the CES in 1998 for her contribution to the theory and practice of evaluation in Canada. In part, the award recognized Porteous' role in codeveloping an educational resource called the Program Evaluation Tool Kit. She has been an active member of the National Capital Chapter of the CES since 1993 and was elected Chapter President in 1998. She has also played a key role in nurturing the growth of the CES Student Evaluation Case Competition, along with the competition's founder, Michael Obrecht.

She has published manuscripts and presented papers and workshops at conferences in Canada, the United States, and Russia and has served as Guest Editor of the *Canadian Journal of Program Evaluation*. She chaired the event-planning group for the Inaugural Assembly of the International Organization for Cooperation in Evaluation in Lima, Peru, in March 2003.

Porteous is active in her community, volunteering in many different ways, such as organizing Oxfam Canada's international development education program, chairing her community association, fundraising for international women's hockey tournaments, and supporting the Women's Voices Music Festival. Always drawn to music, she toured with the international performance troupe Up With People. Her real passion is drumming. She connected with African drumming and dance while doing volunteer work in Botswana. Porteous jams with Women Off the Beat and the Boom Chicks, two local hand drum and percussion ensembles. She also delights in helping others experience the energizing effect of rhythm. She

has facilitated dozens of workshops, community drum circles, and rhythm-based events at conferences for children and youth, the gay and lesbian community, women's groups, and faith organizations.

▒ PORTFOLIO

In the field of education, a *portfolio* is a collection of a student's work that documents achievement in one or more areas. "Best works" portfolios demonstrate mastery or summary achievement. Alternatively, portfolios may serve to show progress or a range of accomplishment, including strengths and weaknesses. Portfolios and portfolio entries may be unassessed or may be assessed separately and may involve self-, peer-, and teacher evaluations and assessments by others. The criteria for evaluating student work may be explicit or intuitive, external or negotiated, preordinate or emergent. Because of the opportunity to include many examples of work over time, portfolios as an assessment technique offer an unparalleled means of enhancing the validity of inferences of student achievement and of displaying student growth.

—Linda Mabry

▒ PORTRAYAL

A central proposition in Robert Stake's "The Countenance of Educational Evaluation" was the reporting of program transactions as full descriptions. Later, he provided a different perspective on this idea in a three-page paper presented at the 1972 Annual Meeting of the American Educational Research Association, "An Approach to the Evaluation of Instructional Programs: Program Portrayal vs. Analysis." On that occasion, then, he emphasized portrayal at the expense of focus: "what the evaluator has to say cannot be both a sharp analysis of high-priority achievement *and* a broad and accurate reflection of the program's complex transactions." An abridged version appears in *Beyond the Numbers Game* (Hamilton, MacDonald, King, Jenkins, & Parlett, 1977, pp. 161-162).

—David Hamilton

Further Reading

Hamilton, D., MacDonald, B., King, C., Jenkins, D., & Parlett, M. (Eds.). (1977). *Beyond the numbers game: A reader in educational evaluation*. Berkeley, CA: McCutcheon.

■ POSAVAC, EMIL J.

(b. 1939, Pittsburgh, Pennsylvania). Ph.D., M.A. Psychology, University of Illinois, Champaign; B.D., Concordia Theological Seminary; B.S. Civil Engineering, Carnegie-Mellon University.

Posavac is Professor of Psychology at Loyola University of Chicago. He brings an eclectic background in engineering, theology, and psychology to the evaluation field. His scholarship reflects this eclectic background in his publications on statistics and research methods, evaluation, and social psychology.

Posavac's textbook (coauthored with R. G. Carey) *Program Evaluation: Methods and Case Studies* (currently in its sixth edition) is widely used in teaching evaluation and espouses a pragmatic approach to evaluation that encourages program staff and management to engage in self-evaluation. From its first edition in 1980, it has focused on the skills internal evaluators need as they work with managers and staff and endorsed the use of both quantitative and qualitative methods. With this text, Posavac's influence over a generation of evaluators is notable.

His work has been strongly influenced, as have so many others, by the work of Donald Campbell. Posavac identifies the dynamism of contemporary society and rapid technological change as creating ever more challenging demands on program evaluators. In this context, he finds inspiration in the work of Michael Scriven and Mark Lipsey. In particular, they remind evaluators that the search for the truth, elusive though it may be, about services, programs, and policies is what evaluation is about.

Posavac was awarded the American Evaluation Association's Myrdal Award for his contributions to evaluation practice in 1990.

■ POSITIVISM

Although the terms *positivism* and *logical positivism* are often used interchangeably, they are not quite the same. The French philosopher Auguste Comte (1798-1857) coined the term *positivism* to describe the philosophy presented in his six-volume opus *Cours de Philosophie Positive,* published between 1830 and 1842. Two of the many ideas argued in this work are the source of popular conceptions of positivism: first, that a "scientific" form of knowledge is the most advanced form of knowledge. Comte

argued that all branches of knowledge inevitably pass through three different "theoretical states"—"the theological or fictitious state, the metaphysical or abstract state, and the scientific or positive state." Second, Comte advocated a strict form of empiricism that was both antirealist and instrumentalist.

—Thomas A. Schwandt

Further Reading

Hollis, M. (1994). *The philosophy of social science: An introduction.* Cambridge, England: Cambridge University Press.

■ POSTMODERNISM

A movement encompassing art, philosophy, linguistics, and science, *postmodernism* is marked by fundamental skepticism about truth and distrust of the political implications of language and action. Postmodernism may be considered a philosophy or the mood or condition of an era. Alternatively, postmodernism might be seen as a logical (perhaps inevitable) development in human understanding that began with ancient Greek, Chinese, and Muslim attempts to demystify the natural world and progressed toward a reaction to 18th-century Enlightenment and modern insistence on empiricism for economic, physical, and social engineering. Postmodernists observed that in the effort to order, control, and improve human life through religion, science, and government, some people prospered and some suffered—that some always suffer, that matters cannot be arranged to ensure the good of all, and that what constitutes the "social good" is determined in large part by those empowered by society, who can manipulate "knowledge" for their own ends.

First used to describe a style of painting considered more modern than Impressionism, the term was applied in literary criticism in the 1960s to new literary styles. In the 1980s, invigorated by feminist thinking, French poststructuralists announced "a crisis of representation," signifying their doubts about language's capacity to describe reality and about received truths and "a crisis of legitimation," signifying their distrust of authority and science. As modern art had reacted against representational truth by offering instead allusions to that which cannot be directly represented, postmodern philosophers reacted to the hidden relationship between truth and power.

Among the prominent poststructuralists, Foucault objected to the presumption of authority by those (e.g., propagandists, historians, ethnographers—and, by implication, evaluators) who purport to tell the stories of others, materially diminishing others' rights. Derrida exposed the author behind the text, insisting that text—and, like Wittgenstein, Derrida said that all is text—must be deconstructed to reveal hidden and unintended agendas and to recognize how language constructs self, other, and reality. Lyotard criticized metanarratives that position real persons as nameless obscurities in such grand epics as those of Christianity and capitalism. Beaudrillard decried hyperreality, in which technology's capacity for unlimited reproduction of objects and images blurred the distinction between the real and unreal and reconstituted persons as media projections.

Postmodernist doubt aligns with poststructural recognition that language plays an important role in constructing reality and also with constructivist recognition that each person constructs an idiosyncratic understanding of the world such that objective reality, if it exists, is comparatively irrelevant. Postmodernism is a reaction against the inevitable discrepancies between tidy theory and messy reality and against science's failure to produce unequivocal truth and its record of such disasters as thalidomide deformities and the nuclear nightmare. Postmodernism opposes the use of science to legitimate privilege and power, opposes claims of proof for what is merely preference, opposes nominal or enforced consensus that marginalizes minority views and individual experience.

Extreme versions of postmodernism disavow not only the power imbalances evident today but also strategies for improvement, as even the most well-intentioned altruists have failed to create Utopia, producing instead new marginalizations and brutalizations. Extreme postmodernism spurns not only religion, history, and authorship but also rationality, criteriality, politics, and empiricism. Postmodernism's radical take on diversity denies the legitimacy of any particular ideology or strategy, leaving only one course—disengagement from the public sphere and retreat into the personal through either play or exile.

Moderate or affirmative versions of postmodernism closely resemble critical theory (in the United States) or cultural studies (in the United Kingdom) in promoting recognition of oppression so that it may be countered. Moderate postmodernists reposition rather than condemn social science, rejecting extremists' cynicism regarding inquiry and political action. This stance permits advocacy for the disenfranchised in preferring populist motifs to consolidations of power among the few but, unlike Marxism, which it otherwise resembles, recognizes that empowering the oppressed will surely turn them into oppressors. Although truth is not absolute and representations are inevitably distortions, affirmative postmodernism realizes that attempts to achieve clarity and communication may sometimes help and, despite uncertainty and the flaws of science and scientific theory, that some understanding may be possible through sensitive inquiry, that some explanations may be better warranted than others, and that some criteria may be more appropriate than others for deciding among them.

—*Linda Mabry*

Further Reading

Mabry, L. (Ed.). (1997). *Evaluation and the postmodern dilemma.* Greenwich, CT: JAI.

Mabry, L. (2002). Postmodern evaluation—or not? *American Journal of Evaluation, 23*(2), 141-157.

■■ POSTPOSITIVISM

Postpositivism is used to refer to alternatives to the philosophy of positivism. Understood very broadly, it can mean something like "nonpositivism"—that is, any philosophy other than positivism, including, for example, critical theory, feminist philosophy, philosophical hermeneutics, interpretivism, and so on. Used in a more restricted sense, it refers to a mixture of those ideas comprising the contemporary philosophy of science, including a moderate empiricism, the hypothetico-deductive method, nonfoundationalism, and acceptance of objectivity as a regulative ideal.

—*Thomas A. Schwandt*

Further Reading

Phillips, D. C., & Burbules, N. C. (2000). *Postpositivism and educational research.* Lanham, MD: Rowman & Littlefield.

■■ *PRACTICAL ASSESSMENT, RESEARCH AND EVALUATION (PARE)*

Practical Assessment, Research and Evaluation is an online journal published by the edresearch.org and the Department of Measurement, Statistics, and Evaluation at the University of Maryland, College

Park. Its purpose is to provide education professionals with access to articles that can have a positive impact on assessment, research, evaluation, and teaching practice, especially at the local education agency level. The journal is edited by Lawrence M. Rudner and William D. Schafer and is available at http://pareonline.net/.

■■ PRAXIS

Praxis is a Greek term meaning both action and conduct. It has no modern equivalent in English but denotes something quite different from the English word *practice*. Praxis refers to the kind of human action required in moral-political life, and it has its own distinct form of knowledge, called wise judgment, practical wisdom, prudence, or deliberative excellence (Greek, *phronesis*). Praxis is concerned with the competence, sensibility, and sensitivity demanded in knowing what it is right to do and good to be in a particular situation, given the situation's unique circumstances, peculiarities, contingencies, and demands. The kind of action and conduct required in praxis is distinctly different from the action and conduct associated with technical expertise and instrumental (means-end) reasoning.

—*Thomas A. Schwandt*

Further Reading

Dunne, J. (1993). *Back to the rough ground: "Phronesis" and "techne" in modern philosophy and in Aristotle.* Notre Dame, IN: University of Notre Dame Press.

Flyvbjerg, B. (2001). *Making social science matter.* Cambridge, England: Cambridge University Press.

■■ PRE-POST DESIGN

A *pre-post design* is a method for assessing the impact of an intervention by comparing scores on a variable before and after an intervention occurs. The simplest type of this design involves one group—for example, program participants in a summative evaluation. Validity of the design is enhanced by adding a control group whose members do not experience the intervention and by randomly assigning persons to treatment and control conditions. The more valid the design, the greater the confidence of the evaluator in making decisions about the efficacy of an intervention.

—*Joseph M. Petrosko*

See also EXPERIMENTAL DESIGN

Further Reading

Shadish, W. R., Cook, T. D., & Campbell, D. T. (2002). *Experimental and quasi-experimental designs for generalized causal inference.* New York: Houghton Mifflin.

PRESCRIPTION. *See* RECOMMENDATIONS

■■ PRESKILL, HALLIE

(b. 1953, New York City). Ph.D. Education, University of Illinois, Urbana-Champaign; Certificate of Advanced Study, Evaluation and Policy Research, University of Vermont; M.S. Elementary and Special Education, Long Island University; B.A. Spanish, California State University at Fullerton.

Since 1994, Preskill has been Professor in the College of Education, University of New Mexico. Previously, she was Associate Professor in the School of Education at the University of St. Thomas and worked for private industry in the areas of training and evaluation. Her primary contributions to the field of evaluation focus on linking evaluative inquiry to organizational learning. She has written extensively on how evaluation can be a catalyst for individual, team, and organizational learning. Emphasizing the importance of context, she argues that the evaluation process can help organizations grow and learn from their experiences and that evaluation should be integrated with the daily work practices of organization members. Robert Stake, Ernest House, Michael Patton, Carol Weiss, and Marvin Alkin have influenced her philosophy of evaluation. Chris Argyris, Donald Schon, Edgar Schein, Victoria Marsick, Karen Watkins, and David Cooperrider have influenced her understanding of human resource development and organizational learning.

She is the author of numerous journal articles, book chapters, and evaluation reports, as well as several books, including *Evaluation Strategies for Communicating and Reporting: Enhancing Learning in Organizations* (with R. T. Torres and M. E. Piontek, 1996), *Evaluative Inquiry for Learning in Organizations* (with R. T. Torres, 1999; winner of the 1999 Book of the Year Award, Academy of Human Resource Development), and *Evaluation in Organizations: A Systematic Approach to Enhancing Learning, Performance and Change* (with D. Russ-Eft, 2001).

She is on the editorial boards of the *American Journal of Evaluation, Human Resource Development Quarterly, Evaluation Review, Human Resource Development International,* and the book series Organizational Change, Performance, and Learning. She has served on numerous committees for the American Evaluation Association, the American Educational Research Association, the Academy of Human Resource Development, and the American Society for Training and Development. She was the recipient of the 2002 Alva and Gunnar Myrdal Award for Outstanding Professional Practice from the American Evaluation Association.

■■ PROBATIVE LOGIC

Probative inferences or probative conclusions are those that establish something as a reasonable basis for proceeding—for the time being, on the evidence available at the moment. Probative conclusions are not established beyond a reasonable doubt, but, to use an approximately equivalent phrase, are established as *prima facie* likely. Their status is less precise than statistical or numerical probability conclusions, less certain than deductive conclusions, but convey more than the mere unqualified term *probable.* It is very common in evaluation work, as in all practical endeavors, up to and including life and death decisions, to use such conclusions when nothing stronger can be established, but clients need to go forward with some reassurance. The term *probative logic* derives from a legal term, although it has been slightly modified for use in the field of evaluation.

—*Michael Scriven*

See also Logic of Evaluation

■■ PROCESS EVALUATION

Process evaluation usually refers to an evaluation that focuses on the activities and events that occur as a program is delivered; that is, things that occur between a specification of inputs and occurrence or measurement of outputs. Process evaluation focuses on how a program was implemented and operates; identifies the procedures undertaken and the decisions made in developing the program; and describes how

the program operates, the services it delivers, and the functions it carries out. By documenting the program's development and operation, process evaluation assesses reasons for successful or unsuccessful performance and provides information for potential program improvement or replication.

See also CIPP Model

■■ PROCESS USE

For many years, the evaluation field has been interested in understanding the factors that contribute to the use of evaluation findings. Although much has been learned about these factors, more recent attention has focused on what and how stakeholders learn from their involvement in the evaluation process. Although the extent to which stakeholders are involved in an evaluation varies greatly, many collaborative, participatory, and learning-oriented approaches to evaluation ask stakeholders to help determine the evaluation's purpose and key questions, to carry out various data collection and analysis activities, and to aid in the development of recommendations and action plans. As evaluators have increasingly implemented more collaborative evaluation approaches, they have come to realize that learning from the evaluation may be considered another type of *use.* Patton (1997) has called this *process use,* and defines it as follows:

> individual changes in thinking and behavior, and program or organizational changes in procedures and culture, that occur among those involved in evaluation as a result of the learning that occurs during the evaluation process. Evidence of process use is represented by the following kind of statement after an evaluation: The impact on our program came not just from the findings but also from going through the thinking process that the evaluation required (p. 90).

Process use reflects constructivist-learning theory in that it focuses on how groups of people make meaning as they conduct an evaluation. By encouraging dialogue and reflection and questioning assumptions, values, and beliefs, individuals come to more fully understand the evaluand; the organization; themselves; each other; and, ultimately, evaluation practice.

Several factors appear to influence the likelihood that those involved in evaluation processes will learn from their participation (Preskill, Zuckerman, & Matthews, 2002). These include factors related to the following:

1. *How evaluation meetings are facilitated.* This involves the intentionality of learning from the evaluation process, the amount and quality of dialogue and reflection, the meeting facilitators' group process skills, the degree of trust among participants, and how much time is given to discussing various issues.

2. *The extent to which, and the ways in which, management and leadership support participants' involvement in the evaluation process.* This involves expectations managers have for participants to share their learning with others in the organization or community, and how they are rewarded for sharing and using what they have learned.

3. *Participants' personal characteristics and experiences with evaluation and the program being evaluated.* These include participants' motivation to engage in the evaluation process, their position, their rank, their previous training in evaluation, and the belief that the evaluation findings will be used.

4. *The frequency, methods, and quality of communications between and among stakeholder participants.* These include the frequency and length of communications during the evaluation, the amount and quality of interactions once the evaluation has been completed, and the methods used to communicate and report the evaluation's progress and findings.

5. *Organizational characteristics.* These include the extant degree of organizational stability, external demands, constraints, and threats and the extent to which the organization supports evaluation work.

If process use is supported, nurtured, and studied, it may lead not only to individual learning but to team and organizational learning.

—*Hallie Preskill*

Further Reading

Patton, M. Q. (1997). *Utilization-focused evaluation: The new century text.* Thousand Oaks, CA: Sage.

Preskill, H., Zuckerman, B., & Matthews, B. (2002, November). *An exploratory study of the variables affecting process use.* Paper presented at the Annual Meeting of the American Evaluation Association, Washington, DC.

■ PRODUCT EVALUATION

This entry concerns the evaluation of physical objects produced by a manufacturing process. Because space limitations preclude an in-depth treatment, a general framework is provided that can guide more detailed evaluations. In the process, my goal is to highlight relationships between the evaluation of products and the more usual targets of evaluators (i.e., programs, regulation, and legislation). It is useful to consider product evaluation as a set of issues falling into four categories:

1. Product life cycle

2. Stakeholders and frames of reference

3. Logic models and relationships among measures

4. Sources of data

PRODUCT LIFE CYCLE

Typically, product development travels a path from initial conception or high-level design through detail design, manufacturing, marketing and sales, postsales warranty and support, to retirement. Evaluation priorities, methods, and, indeed, the meaning of the term *product evaluation* change during this life cycle.

Early in the product life cycle, evaluation is an exercise in requirements analysis. Requirements are multidimensional and typically include user need, manufacturing capacity, produceability, production cost, regulatory compliance, timing of market entry, sales volume, and the relationship of a product to an entire product line. Evaluation at this stage requires assessment of both individual requirements and the overall fit of the product within a multidimensional "requirements space." Getting it right is important because the downstream consequences of wrong decisions can be extremely damaging.

Evaluation at the detail design stage focuses on whether the product development process is meeting its targets for time, cost, and functionality. However, the essential question is not whether individual milestones for individual components are met, because design is not just a cumulative function of activities that have invariant, well-defined relationships. Rather, product development is best seen as a nonlinear open system, complete with unanticipated environmental change (e.g., business climate, user needs); sensitive, cascading consequences among large and small perturbations; unpredictable dependencies among different design activities; and emergent behavior that makes it difficult to specify "part-whole" relationships. Although monitoring individual budget and milestone activity is critical, it is also critical to address the big evaluation question; that is, in the face of inevitable change, is the design process adaptable enough to meet overall targets for cost, production schedules, and functionality?

During manufacturing, evaluation should assess both the product itself and the process by which the product is manufactured. Both are important in understanding why a product behaves as it does. Typical process measures include throughput, quality, manufacturing cost, machine behavior, and achievement of production schedules. Metrics are indicators of the fit between the finished product and its design and performance specifications. The importance of evaluating both product and process often goes beyond a simple desire to cover all relevant issues. Rather, it is often the case that a specialized manufacturing process is needed to create a particular product, and in such cases, the distinction between "product" and "process" is false because understanding one requires understanding of the other. An indicator of the link between product and process lies in the choice of methodology for product evaluation. One possibility is to measure the product after it is produced. Another is to use a well-proven manufacturing process and to make sure that the process meets its performance specifications.

Once a product is on the market and in circulation, more familiar evaluation measures come into play (e.g., sales, market share, user satisfaction, product reliability, warranty costs). These traditional metrics imply a traditional set of stakeholders (i.e., manufacturers, sellers, and consumers). However, externalities are always a function of product usage, so other stakeholder interests become relevant. For instance, vehicle purchasers may not care very much about fuel economy, but the polity might. In another example, a new product may displace older technologies and thus perturb their supporting infrastructures. Consider, for instance, the social, economic, and industrial implications of transitioning from internal combustion to fuel cell vehicle engines. The fates of people, industrial sectors, and geographical regions will depend on how this change plays out. Related to the expansion of

stakeholder groups in the postmanufacturing phase is the question of product "retirement"; that is, the costs of moving a product out of the use stream. As an example, there are regulations in Europe concerning the recyclability of automobiles.

STAKEHOLDERS

Product evaluation must consider the question, "Whose opinion matters?" Consider three products: a generator in a power plant, a commercial airplane, and an automobile. The key stakeholder in the generator example are the owners of the power plant, who will care about metrics such as purchase cost, operating cost, up time, spare parts availability, preventive maintenance schedules, and reliability. The stakeholder group expands in the case of the airplane. As with the generator, one important group consists of the owners, who care about the role of the product in a commercial process. However, other perspectives are also important. For instance, the opinion of pilots about human factors is important, as are the subjective feelings of passengers about comfort, noise, and other variables that may affect their flying experience. With the automobile, the dominant stakeholder group is the drivers. Typical facets for this group would include prepurchase consumer appeal, buying decisions, and satisfaction with the purchased product. However, dealers and manufacturers must make a profit on sales, and their needs count. Reasonable people will disagree about who the important stakeholders are and on how much effort should be put into satisfying each group. These arguments can never be resolved perfectly, but they must be resolved well enough so that it is possible to reach consensus, allocate resources, and execute an evaluation.

LOGIC MODELS

As in all evaluation, logic models are useful in product evaluation. Two examples follow that illustrate why this is so. To continue the example with the generator, there are logical relationships among the variables. There is a direct causal relationship between up time and reliability and between up time and spare parts availability. Reliability is more important than parts because parts for scheduled maintenance are likely to always be available. Thus the parts variable comes into play only on the rare occasions when the generator experiences unanticipated failure. Preventive maintenance can both increase and decrease up time. By its nature, it decreases up time, because some preventive maintenance will require taking the generator offline. But effective preventive maintenance increases reliability and thus decreases very costly unanticipated breakdowns. When the model's elements are laid out on a timeline, the model can guide the timing of evaluation activity. Imposing a timeline would show that although up time, reliability, and operating cost can begin to be assessed within the first year of operation, assessing repair under conditions of unexpected breakdown will require an extended period of observation.

Logic modeling in product evaluation is useful, but it is important to consider that relationships among important measures may be tenuous or even nonexistent. To illustrate, consider the automobile example. Two sets of variables were identified, one that measured consumers' engagement with the product and one that measured the economic viability of the product. On the surface, it seems as if these two sets of variables have a clear relationship—higher levels of consumer approval lead to greater profitability. However, this relationship may be mediated by so many other factors as to be useless for practical purposes. To name but a few of the complications: Profitability is a function of sales volume and profit per vehicle. Sales volume may depend on competition from other manufacturers and the state of the economy, and profit per vehicle may depend on the vehicle's design. (Were older components reused? Were development and tooling needed?) Any logic model attempting to show relationships here would contain so many components and multiple, overlapping causal pathways that even if the data were available, it is unlikely that decision makers would derive insight that was either actionable or generalizable. Sometimes, multiple causal models are needed.

Finally, it is important to realize that products often represent complex systems that do not conform to linear assumptions. To illustrate, consider two examples, one at the design stage and one at the marketing and sales stage. During design, one cannot assume that a product will perform as intended just because each of its components meets its own individual performance specifications. Two difficulties get in the way. First, the act of setting specifications for components entails the assumption that one knows which component

specifications are important for understanding the behavior of the product as a whole. This assumption may be false. For instance, a seemingly small change in the location of a structural support in an automobile may have major consequences for harmonic vibration that develops when the vehicle travels at a particular speed. Problems like this are difficult to detect before a prototype is tested. Second, even if a specification is known in the abstract, reliable measurement may be difficult. As an example, consider the sheet metal in the door of an automobile. That sheet-metal part must attach to various other components, and the whole assembly must fit with great precision, along with the hinges, into the automobile. As a part of that door assembly, the metal deforms and stresses. Under these circumstances, how many measurements, over how broad a surface, are needed to specify how that sheet metal part will affect the fit between the door and the frame? The answer is by no means obvious, and to complicate matters, taking those measurements will require fixing the piece in place, which distorts the measurements that are taken.

As an example of the difficulties of logic modeling at the marketing and sales stage of the product life cycle, consider how the commercial success of nearly identical products can vary dramatically. For some years in the 1980s and 1990s, the Chevrolet Prism and the Toyota Corolla were essentially the same vehicle in parts and design. Most were actually produced at the same factory. Although the Corolla was priced higher than the Prism, the Corolla sold well and the Prism did not. Cost and performance specifications certainly cannot account for the differences in market acceptance. Whatever is going on must involve market strategies and consumer belief systems that are interacting in ways that are not amenable to traditional evaluation logic modeling. Moreover, phenomena like these occur frequently.

SOURCES OF DATA

Product evaluation data can emerge from four sources, each with different utility at different stages of the product development life cycle. The basic choices are to (a) observe or measure the product, (b) embed data collection in the process of creating a product, (c) query users or other relevant stakeholders, and (d) use information external to the product or stakeholders.

Measurement of the product itself can take place across almost the entire life cycle, starting with the emergence of the product as a prototype and ending with product retirement. Measurement can be "hands on" (e.g., measurement of tolerances between parts or proxy indicators of product performance, as would be the case in tracking repair rates). Although data of this type seem hard and reliable, problems abound in the real world of data collection. For instance, products in the prototype stage of development see frequent changes in hardware and software components, as engineers swap out parts and run continual tests. Version control tracking is often not good enough that the exact content of a prototype can be known.

As another example, consider the need to monitor product reliability from the time the product is out of warranty until it is retired. Here are three of the many problems that may arise. First, with no warranty protection, owners lack incentive to return the product to dealers, but it is only the dealers, not the independent repair shops, that provide good data to manufacturers on vehicle repair history. Second, owners may live with a problem and not fix it. Third, it is not always clear that broken parts indicate the true problem. A run on hoses, for example, may mean a quality control problem in hose production or a design problem in the cooling system.

When a focus on product is chosen, another choice presents itself. One possibility is to rely on final inspection once a product is completed. A second possibility is to measure the product at intermittent steps during production. In-process inspection can avoid costly rework, but the technique is not applicable if three conditions are present: (a) a small failure in one of many components will result in overall product failure, (b) testing consumes too much time or money relative to the cost of production, (c) product functioning depends not only on individual components but on the quality of their connections and interactions. Many electronics products, for instance, meet these conditions. Another example is chemical processing, in which success requires a precise combination of ingredients combining under narrow ranges of temperature, pressure, and humidity.

A special case of product measurement arises when data acquisition is embedded in a manufacturing process. In these cases, repeated measures of the outcome of repetitious activities are monitored with respect to past behavior and trends. This is essentially a statistical process control approach and is particularly useful for that subset of manufacturing activity that produces high volumes of similar products.

Data from people are particularly important at two parts of the product life cycle. First, such data are needed during early stage design activity to set product requirements. Once a product sees the light of day, data from people are needed to assess consumer appeal, buying behavior, and customer satisfaction. A wide range of data collection techniques is used at these times, including questionnaires, focus groups, interviews, tracking of Web use patterns, and observation of people's engagement with mockups and prototypes.

Finally, data may come from external sources; that is, they may be neither measurements of the product nor information derived from people. These data are useful for two purposes. They may help define requirements for products with long development lead times, or they may be useful in logic modeling to explain a product's acceptance. As examples, consider implementation timelines for regulations (e.g., automobile safety for cars and high-definition capability for television sets), demographic changes in a customer base, energy costs, and the state of the economy. This information could be critical in the development stage of a product, to make sure of market acceptability when the product is introduced. The information also becomes useful after product introduction as a way in which to explain market acceptance.

—Jonathan A. Morell

■ PROFESSION OF EVALUATION

Whether evaluation is a profession has been debated for years. The American Evaluation Associations claims "promoting evaluation as a profession" as part of its mission. However, others argue that the field has not met the traditional criteria to qualify as a profession. This ambivalence of the status of evaluation is apparent in the Australasian Evaluation Society's homepage, which refers to evaluation as a *process* used by many other professions; at the same time, the AES claims to be the premier *professional* evaluation organization in Australia and New Zealand.

Why should there be concern about whether evaluation is profession? First, if the field is a profession, this provides potential benefits to society. A hallmark of a profession is certification or licensing of members of that profession. A major purpose of certification is to provide consumers with some assurance of the quality of the procedures and personnel used in the evaluation process. Certification can help ensure that the process and results of the evaluation are fair and accurate. Incompetent performance would reflect negatively on all evaluators, and those who lack core competencies in evaluation would not be allowed to practice.

If the field were a profession, this would also provide benefits to evaluators through legitimacy, selectivity, and the ability to influence public policy. As professional organizations, evaluation organizations would be able to set curricula, determine eligibility for licensing, and help shape policy.

How a field may be strengthened when it is viewed as a profession can be seen through the comparison of the field of accounting to that of evaluation. Accounting bears some similarity to evaluation in that they both have an auditing function. Accountants could be viewed as the evaluators of financial systems.

Accountancy is a successful profession. It wields tremendous power throughout the world, the job prospects are plentiful, and the pay is good. Accounting departments exist in virtually every university in the United States, but there is not a single department of evaluation. There are hundreds of thousands of accountants but only a few thousand evaluators. Accounting has a licensing process through the certified public accountant (CPA) exam, which is considered to be the measure of entry-level competence. The CPA exam has a major influence on the educational content of accounting programs. Evaluation has no licensing procedure. The CPA exam is developed and administered by professional associations, and it is the basis for the CPA designation in most states. Evaluation has no accreditation process for training, and its organizations are not very powerful.

The designation of profession, for better or worse, brings with it a guild or union orientation. That is, examinations are designed not only to keep the unqualified from practicing but to limit the competition. The competition in evaluation is not only from less qualified evaluators but from other professions, including accounting. Auditors now include in their practice the evaluation of nonfinancial data, such as performance indicators. Accounting is poised to assume some roles that evaluators perform in the public sector.

There are significant trends in our society that can offer challenges and opportunities for evaluation. These include the emphases on outcomes, quality, and evidence-based practices, all of which need evaluative data. In addition, the consumer movement is also hungry for evaluative data. Who is going to provide these data? It can be argued that a group recognized as a profession would be the one to gain ascendance.

Some have attempted to answer the question of whether evaluation is a profession by applying criteria that the field of sociology has articulated for what qualifies as a profession. According to many sociological theorists, a profession must have specialized knowledge and skills. Professional development must include preparation programs for teaching and testing (certifying) core knowledge and skills. There must be stable career opportunities available for those in the profession and an association devoted to furthering the professional development of practitioners.

The field of evaluation satisfies many of these criteria but not all. Although there are theories and skills practiced in evaluation, there is little agreement about which are essential or unique to evaluation. Some organizations, such as the Canadian Evaluation Society, have articulated a set of skills they view to be essential for evaluation; other specialized areas that use evaluation skills have established standards for their specific topic. For example, the Joint Committee on Standards for Educational Evaluation has issued student evaluation standards, program evaluation standards, and personal evaluation standards. Books on evaluation practices often stress different aspects of the field, with only some overlap in theory or skills. Currently there are no universal standards of knowledge and skill for evaluation.

Although training programs in evaluation exist, there have been many fluctuations in their numbers over the past 50 years. Most of these changes have occurred in the United States, where evaluation has meandered in and out of federal priorities. The largest increase in evaluation training was sparked by the U.S. Congress' 1965 decision to fund graduate training in educational research and evaluation. By 1971, there were more than 100 evaluation preparation programs nationwide. When federal support of this education waned in the 1980s, training moved to nonacademic settings, such as state agencies, schools, and private businesses. Currently there are a handful of graduate degree programs in evaluation throughout the world, several professional development centers, and many programs that offer some coursework in evaluation. The American Evaluation Association's Web site listed nine programs in the United States that offered a master's or doctoral degree in evaluation as of March 2003. These programs are located in diverse university settings that include psychology departments, policy programs, and departments of educational administration. Many evaluators report learning how to conduct evaluations through direct practice or working as an apprentice to an experienced evaluator instead of undergoing a course of formal training.

In addition to having no systematic method for educating evaluators, the field of evaluation currently has no licensure or certification requirements for practitioners. Licensing is a legal function performed by the state; certification is typically a process managed by professional associations. However, many practitioners have advocated for the establishment of certification as a method for increasing the reputation and credibility of the discipline. The Canadian Evaluation Society conducted an in-depth study of this possibility, and the AEA's president advocated the establishment of voluntary certification in 1997. A recent survey of AEA members found that most did not see a need for licensure. The debate continues, and so far, no process for certification has been initiated.

The establishment of a professional organization as a criterion for a field's being viewed as a profession has clearly been met. There are several professional associations for evaluation throughout the world. Some of the largest organizations are the African Evaluation Association, American Evaluation Association, Australasian Evaluation Society, Canadian Evaluation Association, Danish Evaluation Society, European Evaluation Society, French Evaluation Society, German Evaluation Society, Ghana Evaluators Association, Israeli Association for Program Evaluation, Italian Evaluation Society, Japan Evaluation Society, Malaysian Evaluation Society, Nigerian Network of Monitoring and Evaluation, the Program for Strengthening the Regional Capacity for Evaluation of Rural Poverty Alleviation Projects in Latin America and the Caribbean, Russian International Project Evaluation Network, Spanish Public Policy Evaluation Society, Sri Lankan Evaluation Association, Swiss Evaluation Society, United Kingdom Evaluation Society, Utvärderarna, and Walloon Evaluation Society. These organizations maintain growing membership and regular conferences in which members can meet and discuss the field of evaluation. However, there is

little or no selectivity in the membership in these organizations, which is not limited to practitioners of evaluation or those with evaluation-focused training. Because many disciplines use evaluation techniques and evaluators often come from diverse backgrounds, there are currently no criteria for inclusion in professional evaluation organizations.

Some professional evaluation organizations are influencing the content of evaluation training. For example, the U.S.-based Evaluator's Institute provides American Evaluation Association–endorsed training, and the Canadian Evaluation Society provides courses on evaluation through 31 different universities. However, no professional organization accredits evaluation education programs.

Many of these professional organizations have created standards of behavior to guide evaluators. These guidelines are often in the form of ethical guidelines. They require competence, accountability, and integrity but do not specify how to assess them. Moreover, the existence of several different paradigms of evaluation is a challenge to establishing a clear set of ethics that satisfies all these viewpoints. Without licensing requirements, there is no way to enforce these recommended ethical standards.

Job options in the field of evaluation appear plentiful. Each professional organization provides links and advertisements for job opportunities. The AEA Web site listed more than 100 employment opportunities in March 2003. In addition, many funding sources, such as federal agencies, require program evaluation plans for grant proposals. Presently there seems to be more demand for evaluation than there are evaluators.

Of the criteria for qualifying as a profession, the field of evaluation meets most, at least partially. The largest shortfalls of these criteria are the lack of evaluation education training specialization and a process for certifying professionals.

Additional criteria included by others who have questioned the designation of profession in regard to evaluation are the extent to which practitioners devote their entire working day to evaluation and how much autonomy they experience in their practice. Many evaluators are housed in academic settings, in which they are primarily professors and researchers who also happen to conduct evaluations. Evaluators may also specialize in a content area, such as education or public policy, and evaluate programs within that capacity. For these individuals, evaluation is, at best, a secondary activity. In addition, some view evaluation as a methodology rather than as a profession. However, a growing number of the members of the evaluation professional organizations identify their primary career activities as evaluation. They label themselves *evaluators* and their career *evaluation.*

If evaluation is to be considered a profession, then an articulation of the boundaries of the field has yet to be defined. We are still without a statement describing evaluation's unique contributions and limits.

The field of evaluation has grown dramatically over the past half century. Students are now able to receive graduate degrees in evaluation, professional organizations are numerous, and jobs are plentiful. However, where evaluation currently stands as a practice or a profession is still unclear. The debate does not seem to be settled yet.

—*Leonard Bickman and Stephanie Reich*

Further Reading

Altschuld, J., & Engle, M. (Eds.). (1994). The preparation of professional evaluators: Issues, perspectives, and programs. *New Directions for Program Evaluation, 62.*

Bickman, L. (1997). Evaluating evaluation: Where do we go from here? *Evaluation Practice, 18*(1), 1-16.

Long, B., & Kishchuk, N. (1997, October). *Professional certification: A report to the National Counsel of the Canadian Evaluation Society on the experience of other organizations.* Retrieved June 4, 2004, from http://www.evaluationcanada. ca/txt/longkishchukreport.pdf

PROGRAM. *See* PROGRAM EVALUATION

■ PROGRAM CULTURE

We may talk of a program as a *culture,* by which we refer to the texture of its social life. Programs exhibit all the characteristics of cultures—rules, roles, relationships, rites, and rituals—as well as the archetypal cultural condition of an essential tension between individual and collective. All cultures define conditions of collective association, but culture can be realized only through individual thought and action. It is important for evaluators, even those unconcerned with portraying experience, to be aware of how and when a program exhibits a robust culture. *Successful program culture* means social and organizational conditions

that help to create shared understanding about what words and actions mean and within which interactions can take place with the minimum of negotiation but a tolerance for argument. These are conditions that encourage people to orient their individual actions toward the goals of the program. Such conditions would be made up of a common vocabulary, sustained personal contact, and a core (not a totality) of common values and interests, together with tolerance concerning the areas in which those values and interests diverge. A program culture is an achievement rather than a design; it is recognized through a feeling of community more than through statements of allegiance to common goals; that is to say, it is experiential rather than rational. In a successful program culture, individuals can find meaning in their work from the achievements of their working colleagues.

—*Saville Kushner*

■ PROGRAM EVALUATION

If society were content with its structure and operation, it would be unlikely to mount social and educational programs. It clearly is not, and so it does. Programs are experiments with alternative futures, models for the reform of discredited presents or extensions of favored pasts. A program is generally a set of temporary arrangements for trying out new ways of providing services or conducting professional action. Having mounted a program, the organization or funding agency is compelled to measure its productivity and its impact and to understand its experience. In a context of public skepticism about a program's own claims of success, program evaluation is commissioned as a process dedicated to making, generating, or feeding judgments about the worth or significance of a program. For some, the imperative is to measure the *quality* of a program; for others, it is to portray its *qualities.*

Purposes underpinning program evaluation vary with values and interests. We may seek judgments of significance or worth to inform decision making about a program, such as whether it merits replication or termination, to hold it to account, or to scrutinize its political sources and aims. Program evaluation may be designed or used to defend or to attack a program idea or as a basis for learning and improvement or advocacy. Program evaluation is frequently seen by evaluators (perhaps less so by the political and administrative system) as social or cultural capital in itself, with a value to community independent of that of the program. The new millennium heralded an intensifying discourse around the relationship between program evaluation and democracy, and as the relationship between evaluation and "community" assumes greater significance, so program evaluation comes to be seen as cultural or social capital.

Program evaluation can be seen as a theoretical discourse, as a set of political or technical propositions, as an ethical system. Many from the university sector speak of it as a *discipline*—some claim that it is a *transdiscipline,* signifying its metamethodological role in relation to other disciplines. It may be any of these at different moments, depending on the observer's interest. Nonetheless, much of the debate and controversy concerning program evaluation involve abstractions and generalizations of evaluators' preferred practices, so each of these aspects can be combined in a view of program evaluation as a *professional practice.* As such, program evaluation integrates knowledge and action; that is, evaluation theorizing is derived from practice and is returned to it through critical reflection in and on action. It is no accident but a prerequisite that evaluation theorists are, almost invariably, evaluation practitioners. Typical of higher forms of professional practice, program evaluation cannot be entirely summed up by a set of competencies essential to effective practice. Mastery of inquiry methods and their application is rarely sufficient in itself to guarantee completion of an evaluation task. Beyond competence, program evaluation is seen to demand qualities such as refined judgment, self-knowledge, empathy, and a commitment to impartiality.

SOCIAL PROGRAMS

A program is defined by biographies, histories, intents, resources, and observable experiences, and it usually has multiple sites. The program intent is given by specified goals and other, often more concealed and contested, purposes. Program goals are not always the best guide as to a program's logic, and there is generally more than one logic at play. Programs typically have multiple constituencies of interest groups—managers, workers, clients, political sponsors, competitors. These are people who are touched or coerced by the actions of the program.

Other people have commitments to the program, such as politicians, sponsors, and program managers. The two groups together are often referred to as *stakeholders,* although that term masks important differences and privileges.

Constituents do not have to agree with a single set of aims or values, although programs generally assume that they will share their differences in a coherent way. A program may serve as a forum for the open contest of ideas and priorities, out of which evaluators may derive criteria for judgment. Such criteria generated out of internal conversations tend to give rise to multiple, plural judgments of a program's significance. However, evaluators often arrive at programs with criteria already forged elsewhere—perhaps emanating from other value systems, and sometimes at variance with the criteria against which program people would choose to be judged. The sources of and control over judgment criteria are a key dimension of program evaluation, and these variations form much of the debate over the appropriate warrant (the public role and legitimacy) of program evaluation.

Programs typically exhibit a *program culture.* This is to say that they have rules, rituals, roles, a tension between the individual and the collective, a recognizable texture to their social processes, and a broadly agreed boundary that demarcates thoughts and actions that *are* or *are not* of the program. A program culture may be manifest in the expressed reflections of its participants, in their actions and in their social relationships. The particular nature of program experience cannot change the fact that people who work in an experiment do not lead experimental lives—people have meanings and aspirations whose stability endures beyond program goals and time scales. Cultural transactions within a program will often be particular to that program, but most program participants are located within broader priorities in life. People fit into programs, but programs also fit into people's lives.

Finally, there are always two sides to the program coin that present options for evaluation. Programs have substantive activities (e.g., teaching, nursing, policing, housing development, community action), and program people will want to be judged for their quality. "Does this program produce better police officers (better classrooms, more autonomous communities)?" "What are we learning about public order (effective pedagogy, the nature of community action)?" Still, programs under evaluation scrutiny are usually innovations, and irrespective of their substantive focus, they can be understood as mechanisms of change, provoking different kinds of question and, therefore, judgment. "Is this an appropriate or effective way of changing a professional culture?" "What are we learning about institutional responses to innovation?" Programs have multiple identities that provoke questions of who evaluates and how.

There are questions, too, about where the locus of judgment lies. For some, the evaluator is the warranted judgment maker, either as "connoisseur" of substantive program activities or as expert in innovation; for others, the evaluator collects, exchanges, and "feeds" the judgments of others but remains impartial and eschews judgment, serving more as a warranted "broker." For some, the primary source of judgment lies in measures of a program's productivity; for others, it lies in measures of a program's experience. Programs are also sites for exploration and competition among purposes and judgments of merit—sites of struggle for control.

MATURATION OF THE PRACTICE

The field of program evaluation claims to have matured as a field of professional action. Part of any coming of age is self-awareness, and in establishing the claim to maturity, evaluation theorists have reflected on the nature and internal boundaries of their professional culture: in what ways their practices resemble or differ from each other. This results in a range of classification systems that seek to document and align the repertoire of methodological approaches.

Perhaps the best known of these classification systems is the familiar distinction between *formative* and *summative* evaluation. The former is designed to support decision making internal to the program, for program improvement, and the latter is designed for decision making by external audiences, for program policy development. This contrast is somewhat paralleled by another duality distinguishing *process* evaluation from *outcomes-focused* evaluation, each of which serves the interests and favors the experience of different stakeholder and interest groups. These describe variations in the social and contractual role of program evaluation. Another influential and overarching classification system has debated between *qualitative*

and *quantitative* evaluation, which stand for differences in value systems that underpin evaluation practice and the selection of method and which have been the subject of what has been claimed to be no less than a "paradigm war."

These binary distinctions have come to be seen as too coarse grained to describe differences in the professional practice of program evaluation; they are descriptive of too narrow a range of experience to qualify as a clash of paradigms. It has been said, for example, that one person's summative or outcomes evaluation is another's formative or process evaluation, and it has been noticed that a single value system or set of methodological purposes can (often, *must*) embrace both qualitative and quantitative methods. Equally, newfound concerns with democracy and with advocating evaluation as cultural and social capital prove too demanding for these lightweight binary distinctions.

Nonetheless, the collective conviction that there are paradigm differences at work in the field sustains the search for classification systems that speak to fundamental differences. Most recently, Robert Stake has sought to address complexity with a dual classification of evaluation studies—"standards-based or criterial" and "interpretive or experiential"—although he describes this classification not as binary, but as "binocular" (their combination offering "depth of field"). Standards-based, or criterial, evaluation rests on "the analysis of descriptive variables . . . [relies] mostly on numbers and criterial thinking," and interpretive, or experiential, evaluation relies on "experiential, personal knowing . . . interpretive thinking." The key characteristic of each "ocular" set is criterial thinking on the one hand, the abstraction of experience into discrete variables readied for measurement purposes, and "episodic" thinking on the other, the attempt to avoid reducing or abstracting experience instead portraying it holistically. Criterial thinking, we might say, seeks to identify, control, and eliminate variables to understand program causes and effects; episodic thinking seeks to identify, proliferate, and embrace variables to map contingencies. The differences between them are differences, Stake suggests, of mindset.

There are many more complex classification systems that can be read about throughout the program evaluation literature. These variously address the politics, philosophy, and conduct of program evaluation and typically seek to position program evaluation in

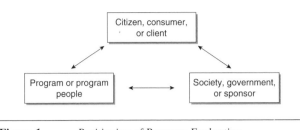

Figure 1   *Positioning of Program Evaluation Relationships*

varied ways in relation to this set of relationships, as seen in Figure 1.

Program evaluation is unusual among professional practitioner cultures in the vigor with which it has sought to structure its professional values and dispositions. This owes something to many early evaluators choosing university locations from which to conduct their work and the resulting emphasis on theory generation, but it also owes something to a collective uncertainty about the nature of the social and political warrant of evaluation. Program evaluation is a site for the resolution of ethical and democratic dilemmas—dilemmas concerning whose rights prevail over the agenda pursued by the evaluation.

METAPHORS FOR PROGRAMS

Ernest House (1972) reviewed a decade of studies of innovation and suggested that there had been a shift in the way evaluators had observed innovative programs in the post–World War II period—*"the same events will be seen differently from the three perspectives"* (p. 10): technological, political, and cultural, considered progressively. The technological view was underpinned by values of rational systems and allegiance to progress. The political perspective was brought by those who saw programs as sites for competition, conflicts, and compromises that are suppressed by assumptions of rational operations. The cultural perspective further extended the political by emphasizing pluralism in values, the diversity of experience, and the range of ways in which meaning is expressed. House's argument was that the shift in perspective and methodology was from *"the innovation, to the innovation-in-context, to the context itself."* How we see programs precedes how we construct our evaluation practice.

What follow are three alternative ways in which evaluators typically look at programs. These are metaphorical statements and are not mutually exclusive—indeed, in the context of a single evaluation, an evaluator may well shift among these models in search of different data sources and in response to different demands made on the evaluation. This is especially so in the contemporary context of advocacy for mixed-methods approaches. These metaphors echo House's analysis but are not coterminal with it.

1. Program as Production Process

The diagram shown in Figure 2 represents the broadest "church" of program evaluation. It stands for what has been labeled a "factory model," indicating its focus on performance, productivity, and outcomes, within a modernist representation of forward progress. Viewing a program in this way implies that the program is valued for those aspects that are revealed: its rational structure, its implicit access to mechanisms of causality, its yielding of comparison between intent and outcome, and the in-built assumption of moral progress. Generalizability focuses on replicability for subsequent programs and policy development. Here are located outcomes-based approaches to evaluation, including the goal-free, context-input-process-product (CIPP), utilization-focused, and realistic evaluation approaches.

Other evaluation theorists draw attention to the politics of programs; that is, programs as sites of political contest, initially arising out of multiple stakeholder interests and purposes, and the realization of early evaluation theorists that their investigative activities inevitably interacted with political process, both within and beyond the program. An alternative metaphor for program emerges as *political system,* as in Figure 3.

2. Program as Political System

Here, program is an exemplar of social and political structures, each program embedded as a case within the broad population of social and political cases. In Figure 3, for example, we see two programs portrayed–one on dental education, the other on urban housing. Each is similarly structured by levels of political action that run throughout society—politics, professional and administrative institutions, forms of organization, fields of action, and experience. Each

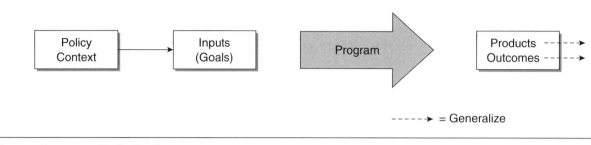

Figure 2   *Program as Production Process*

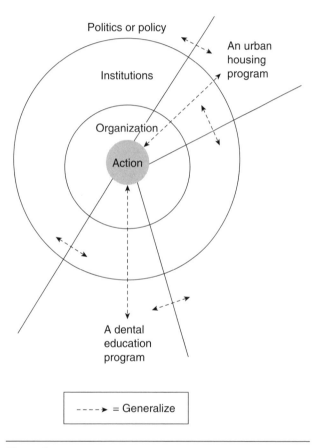

Figure 3   *Program as Political System*

program is a "slice" from the same political "cake." The emphasis in this view of program is generalization, within the case and between case and political system. Although authors and advocates of the factory model often claim a preoccupation with democracy, it is this view of program that most easily admits a direct address of issues of representation, access, rights, and participation. Here are most easily located the democratic, deliberative democratic, and multiple aims or stakeholder approaches to program evaluation.

A common theme running throughout those approaches, which provide alternatives to the production system, has been the necessity of portraying experience as a base on which to understand the change potential and the significance of a program. Counterpointing the factory metaphor has been "program as journey," but the more common usage would see program as a site of *experience*. Fueled partly by an explosion of interest in narrative, life-history methodologies, partly by an intensifying concern with the contribution of program evaluation to the improvement of welfare systems and evaluation as cultural capital, some program evaluators view programs as enveloped in participants' lives, and this builds on the view of program as a site for the struggle of agents against structures. Figure 4 represents this emphasis.

3. Program as Experience

Here, where the convention would see the circle as program, which serves as a context within which to read the significance of actions, events, and lives (x), the view of program as experience inverts that relationship such that the circle represents the life and within it is located the program. The program emerges as a generalization across individual cases and events. The principal aim here is to hold the program to account for its capacity to achieve significance in the life and work of its participants and constituents and against the range of their purposes and aims, rather than to assume that program aims and form are stable and that participants can be held accountable for sustaining them. Here are located the responsive, illuminative, dialogic or participatory, personalized, and empowerment evaluation approaches—all of them falling within the general preference for democratic evaluation.

—Saville Kushner

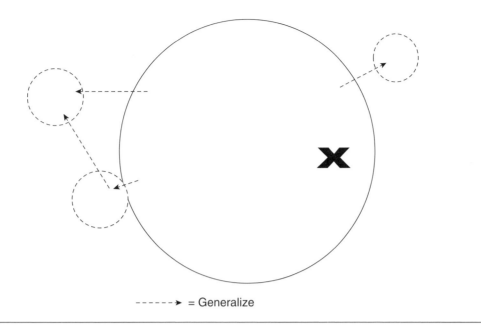

------▸ = Generalize

Figure 4   *Program as Experience*

Further Reading

House, E. R. (1979). Technology versus craft: A ten year perspective on innovation. *Journal of Curriculum Studies, 11*(1), 1-15.

Stake, R. E. (2003). *Standards-based and responsive evaluation.* London: Sage.

▪▪ THE PROGRAM EVALUATION STANDARDS

The second edition of *The Program Evaluation Standards* was published in 1994, subsequent to its initial release in 1981 as the Standards for Evaluations of Educational Programs, Projects, and Materials. These standards are the work of the Joint Committee on Standards for Educational Evaluation, housed at the Evaluation Center, Western Michigan University.

The Program Evaluation Standards provide a guide for evaluating a broad range of educational activities and were written to inform both evaluators and evaluation users. The standards are organized around four areas: utility, feasibility, propriety, and accuracy. The utility standards focus on the need for evaluation to serve the information needs of the evaluation users. The feasibility standards ensure that the evaluation is reasonable, prudent, and cost effective. The propriety standards provide direction for legal, ethical, and fiscal responsibility in evaluation. The accuracy standards focus on technical adequacy and appropriateness.

In addition to the prescriptions regarding standards for evaluation, the standards provide guidelines, note common errors made in conducting evaluation, and examine illustrative cases that provide context for understanding and interpreting each standard.

Further Reading

Joint Committee on Standards for Educational Evaluation. (1994). *The program evaluation standards* (2nd ed.). Thousand Oaks, CA: Sage.

▪▪ PROGRAM LOGIC

Program logic is sometimes used interchangeably with *program theory* to refer to an evaluation approach that begins by developing an articulated causal model of how a program is understood or intended to contribute to its specified outcomes (a logic model) and then uses this model in various ways to guide an evaluation. In many cases, the choice of term is based on local responses to the words *theory* and *logic* (each of which can be seen as unpalatable) and on the terms used in the specific texts used by the evaluators.

Like program theory, program logic can be used in two broad ways to guide an evaluation: For summative evaluations, program logic can be designed to test the articulated theory and to build evidence cumulatively to guide policy and practice; for formative evaluations, it can be designed to provide program staff and managers with timely information and helpful concepts to guide and improve their activities and decisions.

Where the terms have been used with specific meanings, there are at least four quite different ways in which they have been distinguished. First, program theory has been used to refer to causal models based on research evidence, whereas program logic is used to refer to an informal and often implicit theory of action held by program stakeholders (such as staff). Second, program theory has been used to refer to the theory of the causal mechanism, with program logic referring to the implementation theory that enacts the causal mechanism or perhaps just the processes involved in implementation. Third, program theory can be used to refer to the causal model only, with the term program logic being reserved for a detailed analysis of each intermediate outcome in the program theory in terms of the criteria and standards for success, activities that contribute to it, and other factors that influence it. Fourth, program theory can be used to refer to a range of different theories, one of which, the intervening mechanism theory, could also be labeled program logic. Given this wide variety of meanings, readers are encouraged to check just what is meant when others use these terms.

—*Patricia J. Rogers*

See also Logic Model, Program Theory

Further Reading

Rogers, P. J., Petrosino, A. J., Hacsi, T., & Huebner, T. A. (Eds). (2000). Program theory evaluation: Challenges and opportunities. *New Directions for Evaluation, 87.*

■ PROGRAM THEORY

The design and implementation of a program is usually based on a set of explicit or implicit assumptions about the actions required to solve a social problem and reasons why the problem should respond to the particular action. More specifically, there are two kinds of assumptions underlying a program: prescriptive and descriptive. The descriptive assumptions (change model) describe causal processes that lead to goal attainment. The prescriptive assumptions (action model) prescribe the program components and activities that will enable a program to function. Program theory is a systematic configuration of stakeholders' prescriptive assumptions (what actions are required to solve a social problem) and descriptive assumptions (why the problem will respond to these actions) underlying a program—whether explicit or implicit

assumptions are made by stakeholders (Chen, 1990, 2004). As the success of a program in reaching its goals depends on the validity of its program theory, an evaluation based on the conceptual framework of program theory provides information not only on whether a program is effective or ineffective but the reasons for either.

The elements of program theory and their relationships are illustrated in Figure 1.

The elements related to change model are described as follows:

Goals and Outcomes. A program needs to justify which goals it will pursue. Program goals are established in the light of certain major assumptions about them, such as their likelihood of being well understood and supported by staff and other stakeholders, their power to motivate commitment of resources and effort, and their reflection of stakeholders' aims.

Determinants. To reach goals, programs require a focus, which will clarify the lines their design should follow. More specifically, each program must identify a leverage, cause, or mechanism (called *determinant*) with which it can develop a treatment or intervention to meet a need. The assumption is that, once the program activates the identified determinants, its goals will soon be achieved. Some examples of frequently used determinants are knowledge and skills, self-efficacy, perceived vulnerability, motivation, peer pressure, and social norms.

Intervention or Treatment. Intervention or treatment comprises any activity or activities in a program that aims directly at changing a determinant. It is, in other words, the agent of change within the program. The vital assumption made in the intervention or treatment domain is that by implementing the intervention or treatment, the program changes the determinant and ultimately reaches program goals.

Elements related to the action model are discussed as follows:

Implementing Organizations: Assess, Enhance, and Ensure Its Capabilities. A program relies on an organization to allocate resources; to coordinate activities; and to recruit, train, and supervise implementers and other staff. How well a program is implemented may be related to how well this organization is structured. Initially, it is important to ensure that the implementing organization has the capacity to implement the program.

Intervention and Service Delivery Protocols. The change model for a program reflects general and

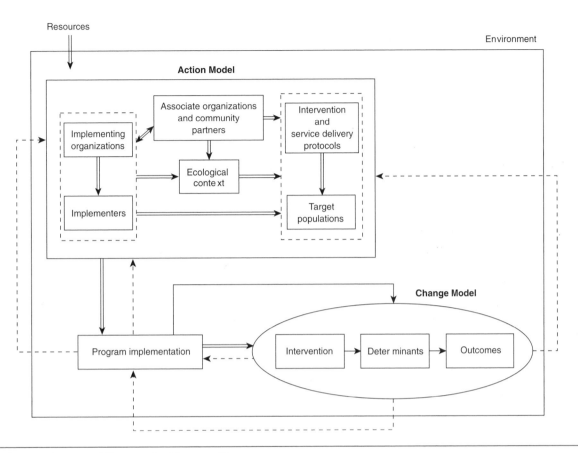

Figure 1 *Conceptual Framework of Program Theory*

abstract ideas about intervention, which must be translated into the set of concrete, organized, implementable activities constituting its programmatic model. Basically, there are two requirements for this translation: an intervention protocol and an implementation protocol. *Intervention protocol* is a curriculum or prospectus stating the exact nature, content, and activities of an intervention—in other words, the details of its orienting perspective and its operating procedures. *Service delivery protocol,* in contrast, refers to the particular steps that must be taken to deliver the intervention in the field.

Program Implementers: Recruit, Train, Maintain Both Competency and Commitment. Program implementers are the people responsible for delivering services to clients: counselors, case managers, outreach workers, schoolteachers, health experts, social workers. The implementers' competency and commitment have a direct effect, as well, on the quality of the intervention delivered to clients, and thus the effectiveness of the program in large part depends on them. It is important for a program to have a plan for ensuring competency and commitment among program implementers;

strategies such as training, communication, and performance monitoring and feedback may be used here.

Associate Organizations and Community Partners: Establish Collaborations. Programs often may benefit from, or even require, cooperation or collaboration between their implementing organizations and other organizations. If linkage or partnership with these useful organizations is not properly established, implementation of such programs may be hindered.

Ecological Context: Seek Its Support. Some programs have a special need for *contextual support,* meaning the involvement of a supportive environment in the program's work. (Indeed, most programs can be facilitated to a degree by an environment that supports the intervention processes.) For example, a program to rehabilitate at-risk juveniles is more likely to work when it obtains the support and participation of juveniles' families and friends.

Target Populations: Identify, Recruit, Screen, Serve. In the target population element, crucial assumptions at work include the presence of validly established eligibility criteria; the feasibility of reaching and effectively serving a target population; and the willingness of potential clients to become committed to, or cooperative with, or at least agreeable to joining, the program.

The relationships among components are illustrated in Figure 1 by using different types of arrows: double-bonded arrows represent a kind of "task order" relationship between components; solid arrows depict causal relationships; and evaluation feedback is represented with dotted arrows.

This is a complete list of major elements in a program theory. Some programs may have only a portion of the elements. From this list of elements, program evaluators can draw ideas about areas of potential focus within evaluations they are designing. A program theory can be based on well-defined scientific theory or, more likely, stakeholder-implicit theory. A program based on a scientific theory may increase the chance of finding that the intervention affects the outcomes. However, stakeholders may find that scientific theory is too abstract and not highly relevant to what they are practicing. The majority of programs are based on stakeholder theory. Stakeholders' perceptions and preferences may come from past experiences, from conventional wisdom, from talk with peers, from advice from experts, from acquaintance with similar programs—even from hunches. Stakeholder theory is implicit theory. It is not endowed with prestige and attention as is scientific theory; it is, however, very important from a practical standpoint, because stakeholders draw on it when contemplating their program's organization, intervention procedures, and client targeting strategies. Stakeholders' implicit theories are not (to repeat) likely to be systematically and explicitly articulated, so it is up to evaluators to facilitate or help stakeholders solidify their ideas.

The conceptual framework of program theory is useful for the following purposes:

Providing a Basis for Designing Theory-Driven Evaluations. The conceptual framework can be used as a basis for designing theory-driven evaluations for assessing implementation process or effectiveness. Following the conceptual framework, an evaluation can explain how and why a program achieves a particular result by illustrating its means of implementation as well as underlying mechanisms that influence it.

This topic is discussed in the theory-driven evaluation entry.

Facilitating Stakeholders Developing a Sound Program. The conceptual framework of program theory indicates the crucial elements that a program needs to address. In planning a new program, the framework can be used to ensure that the program addresses all the important issues; it enhances the quality of a program plan.

Contributing to the Development of a Practical Evaluation Taxonomy. The conceptual framework is useful for developing a practical program evaluation taxonomy that lays out for practitioners evaluation approaches characterizing the program planning, implementation, and outcome stages and suggests applications for these approaches.

—*Huey-Tsyh Chen*

Further Reading

Chen, H.-T. (1990). *Theory-driven evaluations.* Newbury Park, CA: Sage.

Chen, H.-T. (2004). *Practical program evaluation: Assessing and improving planning, implementation, and effectiveness.* Thousand Oaks, CA: Sage.

■ PROPRIETY

Propriety is one of the Program Evaluation Standards. It is intended to ensure that an evaluation will be conducted legally, ethically, and with due regard for the welfare of those involved in the evaluation, as well as those affected by its results.

See also ETHICS, *THE PROGRAM EVALUATION STANDARDS*

PROXIMAL OUTCOMES. *See* OUTCOMES

■ PROXY MEASURE

A measure used in the course of an evaluation in place of something that either has not been or cannot be measured directly. For example, you may not be able to measure whether a program has decreased the rate of death from motor vehicle occupant injuries among children up to 4 years old, but you can measure the use of car seats for this group. An increase in correct car seat use indicates a decrease in death and disability due to motor vehicle occupant injury, thus making this a good proxy measure.

—Jeffrey G. Tucker

PUBLIC WELFARE

Often the object of a plan or action, *public welfare* describes a state of shared prosperity, a condition of collective well-being. An extended meaning refers also to a means of mutual caring, especially economic support. Government-funded programs to assist the poor and the excluded first became known as public welfare after World War I, displacing the notion of charity, which had accrued negative connotations. Differing values fuel debate about what constitutes public welfare and what actions promote and sustain it. Such questions form the subtext, if not the explicit focus, for much evaluative inquiry. Demand for assessments of welfare expenditures was an early catalyst for formalizing and professionalizing evaluation practice.

—Bobby Milstein

PURPOSEFUL SAMPLING

Purposeful sampling involves selecting information-rich cases for study in depth, cases that offer insights into issues of central importance to the purpose of an evaluation, thus the term *purposeful sampling*. Small purposeful samples yield in-depth understanding and insights rather than empirical generalizations. For example, if a formative evaluation's purpose is to reduce the dropout rate, the evaluator could study in depth a small number of strategically selected dropouts. Several different strategies can be used to select cases, each serving a particular purpose; for example, learning from successful cases (people, programs, organizations, or communities) or documenting diversity.

—Michael Quinn Patton

Further Reading
Patton, M. Q. (2002). *Qualitative research and evaluation methods* (3rd ed.). Thousand Oaks, CA: Sage.

PURPOSES. *See* FORMATIVE EVALUATION, SUMMATIVE EVALUATION

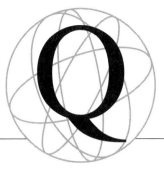

▪▪ QUALITATIVE DATA

Qualitative data is the general term given to evidence that is text based rather than numeric in representation. These kinds of data result from interviews (group, individual, focus, and so on), observations (more typically unstructured but also structured), and documents (both formal, such as mission statements, as well as informal, such as letters) that may be analyzed from a variety of perspectives. The distinction between qualitative and quantitative data is somewhat arbitrary because all evidence has dimensions of both.

See also QUANTITATIVE DATA

▪▪ QUALITATIVE-QUANTITATIVE DEBATE IN EVALUATION

Beginning in the 1970s, evaluators in the academy *and* in the field were embroiled in what has been, perhaps, the most bitter debate to date about how to do their work and why. The debate pitted quantitative methodologies against qualitative methodologies in a struggle for legitimacy and dominance in evaluation practice. The terms of the debate were primarily methodological and philosophical. The rancor ran high because the debate also involved politics and values and, thereby, fundamental definitions and understandings of evaluation as a scientific *and* a social practice. The debate was most intense in evaluation during the late 1970s and 1980s, followed by a period of rapprochement in the 1990s that signaled an acceptance of the legitimacy of multiple methodological traditions in our community, with attendant turns to the use of multiple methods and to mixed methodological thinking. Still, controversy about what constitutes legitimate and "best" practice persists in many domains of social science, including evaluation. In this entry, we briefly recount the history of the qualitative-quantitative debate, present the major points of contention, and summarize its current status.

HISTORICAL NOTES

The quantitative-qualitative debate was precipitated primarily by two simultaneous developments: a broad paradigm conflict in the larger social scientific community that occurred throughout the mid- to late 20th century but really caught fire in the 1970s and 1980s and an explosion of alternative evaluation theories in the 1970s.

The overall quantitative-qualitative debate that troubled the larger social scientific community was rooted in longstanding arguments within the philosophy of science. A quantitative paradigm, anchored in a positivist philosophy, dominated Western social science for much of the 20th century. Within this paradigm, social scientists aspired to test theories using objective methods that were valid, reliable, and replicable and experimental designs, whenever possible, that drew from successes in the physical and medical sciences. However, qualitative paradigms—rooted in interpretive, phenomenological, and constructivist philosophies and thus invested in contextual, value-laden, and contingent social knowledge—offered serious challenges to positivist dominance by the middle of the 20th century.

These challenges gradually began to make their way into the conversations of everyday researchers and evaluators. Many evaluators had to revisit the meanings of objectivity and subjectivity and learn anew about realist versus constructivist ontologies so that they could better understand where they stood on the underlying issues. As applied social scientists, evaluators were engaged in this debate, some staking out their position on the qualitative side, some on the quantitative side, and others trying to reflect on the criticisms fired from both sides and find a middle ground within which to work.

At the same time, the evaluation community itself was showing signs of frustration, primarily in response to the disappointing incidence of direct instrumental impacts of evaluations on important program and policy decisions. Evaluators who lent their expertise to the 1960s evaluations of the Great Society programs in the United States stretched to adopt the methods they had competently employed in small-scale studies, general population surveys, and controlled experiments to field settings that were frequently national in scope and targeted to special populations. These methods were not yet sufficiently refined to provide compelling evidence in the dynamic and politicized contexts of evaluation. The evaluation community responded to this failure to meet largely unrealistic expectations for immediate policy impacts by launching important research on evaluation utilization, continuing to refine and develop quantitative methods, *and* generating an explosive proliferation of alternative models for evaluation— notably, models that were responsive, decision oriented, judicial, management focused, and expert driven, as in connoisseurship, participatory evaluation, and evaluation intent on social justice. Qualitative methods and the interpretive philosophical traditions from which they drew were a good fit for many of these diverse and creative evaluation alternatives. Evaluation practice was no longer dominated by quantitative methodologies, and some of the alternative models were expressly tied to qualitative methodologies. The paradigm war was joined within the evaluation community.

WHAT THE DEBATE WAS ALL ABOUT

We have clustered the major points of contention into three key questions related to philosophy, practice,

and evaluator role. For each, we offer a modal stance of the "quants" and the "quals" as they existed when the debate was raging. The form of our presentation also intentionally captures, albeit in mild form, the often contentious tenor of this debate.

1. What Views of the Social World and Our Knowledge of It Should Frame and Guide Our Evaluation Practice?

Underlying the debates about method were different assumptions about the nature of the social world, about the nature of social knowledge, and thus about what is most important to know. Although the qualitative and quantitative traditions both have a plethora of underlying assumptions, we focus our attention on those that brought the two traditions into conflict.

Quantitative Stance. Quantitative inquiry is guided by two important tenets that offer potential conflicts with qualitative inquiry: deduction and independence. Deduction requires that expectations or hypotheses be developed from theories about how the world works. Evaluators, as well as other social scientists, test the accuracy of those expectations and, in so doing, the accuracy of the theories or explanations for how the social world actually operates. For evaluation, this implies that expectations about program effects are specified based on the theory that underlies the policy, be it a locally generated program theory or a more general theory drawn from the social sciences. These expectations are set out before an evaluation begins. The main alternative to deduction is induction, which involves creating a theory or explanation from observations. Because many theories can be devised to explain a set of observations, quantitatively oriented researchers often have an aversion to inductive explanation and are prone to be skeptical of theories developed this way until they have been directly tested and rival explanations eliminated.

The second quantitative tenet, independence, conveys a sense of distance from the program, evaluation sponsors, and program participants but not necessarily from the social goals of the program. Independence is needed to allow evaluators to make their judgments about program quality strictly on the basis of the evidence about program effects, without contamination from ideology or affiliation. Independence manifests itself in many ways, but two specific aspects have been particularly important for quantitative inquiry: the separation of fact finding from determination of value and the use of methods that allow independent judgments about accuracy of findings and replication. Quantitative researchers emphasize measuring outcomes that have been studied in prior research and evaluations or that are established outside the evaluation, usually by extrapolating them from program goals and objectives that have been consensually determined by democratic bodies. The role of a quantitative evaluator is often primarily one of getting the facts right and accurately conducting a test to see if the program influenced an important but not necessarily exhaustive set of outcomes. Independence also conveys that the systematic inquiry should be conducted in such a way that the findings are not influenced by who collects and analyzes the data. If someone else replicated the evaluation, the same results should be expected.

Invoking independence is neither a claim of objectivity nor a claim of being free from values. Independence is not an absolute but a daily struggle to maintain perspective and a commitment to learning from evidence. Because independence is measured in degrees rather than as an absolute dichotomy, it is bulwarked by transparency, which allows others to fully and completely understand the processes used to select the outcomes that were included and to make their own judgments about the adequacy of the selection and the methods used to generate the evidence.

Qualitative Stance. Qualitative inquirers reject the theory-driven, deductive, hypothesis-testing model of quantitative inquiry because they hold different assumptions about the nature of the social world, human behavior, and social knowledge. Qualitative inquirers also reject the fact-value dichotomy and maintain instead that facts and values are inescapably intertwined and therefore that inquirer independence and objectivity are neither possible nor desirable.

The theories featured in quantitative social inquiry are composed of causal propositions with intended generality, just like theories in the physical sciences. *Under conditions A and B, when Q and T occur, then Y will happen* is the kind of theoretical proposition favored in quantitative inquiry. However, argue qualitative inquirers, the social world is not the same as the physical world. Human beings, unlike molecules or sand or gravity, act with intentionality. This intentionality is rooted in the meanings that people construct of various phenomena they encounter in their daily lives as they interact with others. It is these constructed meanings that guide and shape human behavior, and

they are much more important than generalizable external forces and factors. Moreover, because different contexts present different constellations of people, interactions, and events, what is meaningful to a given individual or group is, in important measure, context specific, not universal. Such meaningfulness also cannot be derived in advance or from outside the context, say from a theory, because meanings are dynamically constructed from within a given setting. Thus understanding of human behavior is attained not by testing hypotheses derived from outside or general theories—because such theories do not well capture what matters in human behavior—but rather by discerning the diverse, contextualized meanings constructed by various participants in a given context. Social knowledge as meaningfulness is thus not really universal or propositional in form but rather multiplistic, contextual, dynamic, and contingent. Contextual understanding, not propositional theory (nor prediction and control), is the proper goal of social science.

Moreover, the knowledge that social scientists generate cannot be value free. There are no "pure facts" in social science; there are only claims to know that are generated *from within* a particular theoretical, sociocultural, and, yes, even political framework. Social scientists, that is, cannot stand outside or apart from their own histories and theoretical predispositions; they cannot gather data that are untainted or free from their own biographies and prejudices (scholarly and otherwise). Rather, the perspectives, experiences, theoretical predispositions, and values of the inquirer are inevitably present in the knowledge that is generated. No number of sophisticated methods can protect or insulate social knowledge from the biases of the knower. Thus different knowers can generate different understandings and different knowledge claims, defensibly and legitimately (a stance that is, admittedly, particularly problematic for evaluators). Warrants for social knowledge involve less an appeal to method and more a turn either to the intrinsic coherence and credibility of the knowledge claims or to their political value as social critique and catalysts for action.

2. What Kinds of Questions, Issues, and Concerns Should Our Evaluation Practice Address, and With What Kinds of Evaluation Designs and Methods?

Accompanying these different philosophical assumptions were contrasting ideas about the practical character of evaluation.

Qualitative Stance. Given the emphasis on holistic, contextualized understanding in qualitative traditions, qualitative evaluators resist the usual evaluative emphasis on outcomes and insist that understanding the character and quality of the program experience is as important as understanding what difference program participation makes in the lives of participants. In fact, these two understandings are interconnected in important ways, such that interpreting information on program outcomes requires an understanding of the character of program participation. Thus qualitative evaluators insist on pursuing evaluative questions about the quality and meaningfulness of program experiences rather than outcome questions alone.

Qualitative evaluators assume that much of what is important to know about a given evaluation context cannot be known in advance or from the outside. Rather, meanings and meaningfulness are constructed along with the program's implementation from within its places and spaces. Qualitative evaluation designs are therefore emergent and flexible in important ways, taking direction and form as evaluators develop their understanding of the inside experience of program participation. This understanding is developed primarily, although not exclusively, from intensive methods and small samples featuring on-site observation, open-ended interviewing, and review of existing documents and records. Qualitative sampling is usually purposeful, rather than random or representative, aiming for information richness within specified criteria. In qualitative evaluation, for example, purposeful sampling can emphasize diversity of program experience or perhaps focus on high-end cases or sites, aiming to learn about the program at its best. Iteration in data collection and analysis is the ideal, as emerging insights can help guide future data collection. With their characteristically small samples, qualitative evaluators are indeed challenged in evaluation to attain not only depth and contextuality of understanding but breadth and representativeness of results across multiple program participants and sites.

Finally, it is important that criteria for making judgments of program quality in qualitative evaluation are drawn both from the outside, reflecting program developers' intents or policy makers' goals, and from the inside, representing program staff's theory of action or local community aspirations. Qualitative evaluators are committed to honoring the daily lived experience of program participation and its contextual meaningfulness in all judgments about program quality.

Quantitative Stance. Without question, programs are important as the means through which democracies try to remedy social ills. Social programs reflect society's intentions to make the lives of the target population better, usually in fairly specific ways. These intentions are reflected in the outcomes that serve as indicators of improving conditions, such as having more third graders read proficiently or increasing the total earnings of former welfare recipients. Understanding programs, specifically which programs work to improve what outcomes for whom and why a program is successful, is essential for making progress, for achieving social goals. Quantitative evaluators tend to focus on selecting measures for the intended program outcomes and assessing the extent to which changes in the outcomes for the program's target population can be attributed to the program. Experience also has taught evaluators to attend to program implementation, asking and answering questions such as: Were the prescribed services actually delivered? Who received what services? What were the costs of the services? Addressing these questions allows evaluators, citizens, and policy makers to assess whether the program can and should be improved or whether another alternative has greater promise for improving the lives of the program beneficiaries.

To collect meaningful evidence for answering questions about which programs work best and whether the services actually reached the intended recipients, we need indicators of what it means to work best, and we need data that accurately represent what is happening in a specific community, across the state, or throughout the nation. Many programs are national or statewide, and the public must be given evidence to make judgments about whether the government is adequately addressing social problems. To provide this evidence, we need more than cases that showcase one local program that is successful and more than testimonies from a handpicked sample of people who benefit from the program: We need to know if the program benefits are pervasive, enduring, heading in the direction intended, and produced without triggering unanticipated negative consequences.

Beginning in the 1960s, strides were being made in the logic of research design, in sampling, in measurement, in data collection, in data analysis, and in database management and manipulation for inquiry purposes. Accuracy of the evidence about program effects, in terms of validity and reliability, was enhanced as inquiry methodology was refined and improved.

Measures have become more comprehensive, valid, and reliable indicators of program outcomes and implementation. Methods of drawing and obtaining data from probability samples that serve as accurate models of the program's intended beneficiaries have become more frequently used in evaluations. Methods for using designs that rule out other plausible explanations for program effects have been put into practice more often. The limitations that plagued our efforts to realize the promise of quantitative methods in evaluation have been diminished by continued criticism and constant innovation in the application of these methods to serious social problems.

3. What Is the Evaluator's Primary Role in Evaluation Practice? What Is Evaluation's Primary Role in Society?

Critical to this conflict were conflicting ideas about the positioning of evaluation in society.

Quantitative Stance. Evaluation in modern democracies is a means of providing evidence about policies and programs that are improving the lives of their intended beneficiaries and those that are not. The evidence can encourage adoption of effective policies and rethinking or improving ones that are less effective or ineffective. An evaluator's role is to collect, produce, and disseminate information that allows democracies to act more rationally in the pursuit of social betterment or allows organizations to act more rationally in the pursuit of their own goals. Evaluations can influence actions and attitudes but are only one of many influences. Evaluators must be credible, careful in their assertions, and independent of sponsors and other allegiances that can bias or create the impression of bias in the presentation of the findings. Evaluators can be vocal and participate directly in informing the public, stakeholders, and policy makers in making findings clear and in attempting to balance interpretations of others, including vested interest groups that seek to distort the evidence or stretch findings too far.

The role that is taken by many quantitative evaluators is one that can be characterized as a "neutral broker" of information. Some would extend this role to having the evaluator make overall judgments about a program's value to society. Others would demur and simply attempt to present evidence clearly and carefully for citizens, journalists, and policy makers to use in forming opinions and beliefs about the program or the organizations that are responsible for delivering services. Societies, in particular modern democracies, and the organizations within them need someone to provide information that is as accurate and complete as possible to inform attitudes and actions about social programs. Many evaluators have been rooted in the belief that evaluators should play this role and have lived careers fulfilling this mission as best they could.

Qualitative Stance. Yes, indeed, evaluation in modern democracies has the very important job of contributing to programs and policies that meaningfully improve quality of life for groups and individuals in need. Qualitative and quantitative evaluators agree on this point. Where they disagree is on the character of the knowledge needed to do this important job (see discussion under question #1) and on the location of evaluation within the policy arena. From a perspective rooted in meaningfulness, contextuality, and multiplicity, qualitative evaluators seek in-depth program understanding that defies simplistic decisions to support or abort a given social program and instead demands considered attention. Qualitative program understanding seeks, broadly, to inform public debate about important public issues and, specifically, to illuminate and enhance practice. Practitioners in the local context, rather than remote decision makers, are characteristically the primary intended audience for qualitative evaluation, given its respect for local context, for the insiders' lived experiences, and for the day-to-day challenges of program implementation. Qualitative evaluators also seek to educate and inform broader communities of practice and discourse. Conducting evaluation to address the interests of practitioners and to educate interested citizens, rather than to inform policy decisions more narrowly, is an important political statement about the relationship between evaluation and public policy.

In service to this vision of evaluation, the qualitative evaluator is positioned close to, even entangled with, the program being evaluated. Closeness is required for in-depth contextual understanding. Closeness is also required to ensure that the voices and perspectives of multiple program stakeholders are given space and legitimacy in the evaluation. Qualitative evaluators are sensitive to the ways in which their presence changes the program evaluated, infuses the data gathered, and colors the interpretations rendered. Some qualitative evaluators endeavor to mute this presence, although most strive to clearly track and acknowledge its effects. Some qualitative evaluators offer recommendations for program improvement and change—often developed collaboratively with program staff—and others leave such programmatic deliberation to program professionals and community activists. However, no qualitative evaluator chooses to remain at a distance, for distance cannot ensure independence and is likely only to obscure in-depth contextual understanding and voice.

THE ONCE AND FUTURE CONFLICT

The passion for direct conflict between qualitative and quantitative evaluators has faded over the past 10 years, and respectful coexistence has become the norm; still, tensions persist, and skirmishes occur from time to time. A case in point is the federal government's contemporary push for "scientifically based evidence," favoring especially experimental evidence. If the standards for what constitutes legitimate evidence relevant to policy decisions and program continuation narrow too much, excluding evidence from all but large-scale, randomized experiments, we will obtain only very limited information on very few programs. The contextual insights, program stories, and participant feedback available from case studies, in-depth interviews, surveys, and other methods will be omitted. Moreover, narrowing the types of evidence that are considered legitimate for program improvement and policy actions will silence the voices of the many program stakeholders who can and should be heard. We, quantitative and qualitative evaluators alike, should unite in worry that the absence of evidence that meets some narrowly drawn standard will become a license for actions based entirely on ideology or the force of unconstrained rhetoric. We should also unite in our commitment to enact our hard-won acceptance of multiple methods and multiple ways of knowing, to reclaim the conversation about the contributions of social science to social policies and programs and refocus it on substance and values rather than on method, and thereby to redirect our collective evaluation expertise and energy in the service of democratic social betterment and social justice.

—*Jennifer C. Greene and Gary T. Henry*

■■ QUALITY

Quality is an elusive term that gets fuzzier the closer you look at it. In organizational matters, it has two dimensions: a technical meaning that reflects the degree to which a product or service satisfies stated or implied needs and, more recently, a second "emotional" dimension that has gained prominence, as research shows that there are distinctive cultural meanings that can overwhelm technical meanings. This research shows that in general, *quality* is associated with *perfection* in Japan, *up to specifications* in Germany, *luxury* in France, *working better than last time* in the United States, and *personal identification* in Australia and New Zealand. This means that *quality* in Japan means getting it right the first time, whereas in the United States it implies continuous improvement (i.e., getting it near enough the first time) and in New Zealand, a degree of personal involvement. This has significant implications for quality control and approaches to quality management.

—*Bob Williams*

■■ QUALITY ASSURANCE

Quality assurance may be defined as a planned and systematic set of activities that provide confidence that a product or service will fulfill requirements for quality. Quality assurance is frequently confused with Total Quality Management, which is a more comprehensive organizational philosophy that engenders a commitment to, as well as the production of, quality products and services. Total Quality Management is based on the premise that quality *workplaces* produce quality products and services. Quality assurance is based on the notion that *managerial systems and standards* produce quality products and services.

—*Bob Williams*

■■ QUALITY CIRCLES

Quality circles are quality-improvement study groups composed of a small number of employees (10 or fewer) and their supervisor. Quality circles were developed in Japan during the 1960s, influenced by the work of Edward Deming (one of the originators of

Total Quality Management). They were based on the error correction principles of "plan-do-check-act" but also promoted the idea of worker involvement in decision-making processes. Widely adopted in North America and Europe, especially in the manufacturing industries, they were in some ways the forerunner of the broader concept of self-managed teams. The use of quality circles has declined in recent years, primarily because they have been replaced by broader management initiatives or more centralized quality management approaches.

—Bob Williams

■ QUALITY CONTROL

Quality control is an umbrella term for techniques and activities used to fulfill requirements for quality. Although *quality assurance* and *quality control* are often used interchangeably, quality control is the broader term. It is possible to have quality control without quality assurance, but not vice versa. The currently fashionable "Six Sigma" is a quality control method.

—Bob Williams

■ QUANTITATIVE DATA

Quantitative data generally refers to observations that are represented in numerical form. Examples include program funding level (in dollars), clients' ages, number of hours of services received, and children's standardized test scores. All of these can be expressed as numbers, as amounts, or as degrees; that is, as quantitative data. Quantitative data can be analyzed with statistics, both descriptive and inferential. Traditionally, quantitative data are distinguished from qualitative data, in which observations are represented in words (or narrative) rather than in numbers. However, the boundaries between the two are more permeable than the distinction suggests, as when qualitative data give way to frequency counts of various themes or when a statistical finding is described in everyday language.

—Poh-Pheng Chua and Melvin M. Mark

See also QUALITATIVE DATA

■ QUANTITATIVE WEIGHT AND SUM

Quantitative weight and sum (also called *numerical weight and sum,* or *NWS*) is a numerical synthesis methodology for summing evaluand performance across multiple criteria. NWS involves ascribing numerical values to criteria that represent importance, using a fixed-length numerical scale to score the evaluand on each criterion, multiplying weights by scores, and then summing these products. The resulting sum represents the overall merit of the evaluand. NWS works adequately for ranking provided that (a) there is a small number of criteria; (b) there is some other mechanism for taking into account "bars" (minimum levels of acceptable performance); and (c) there is a defensible, needs-based strategy for ascribing weights. For other ranking tasks, use qualitative weight and sum.

—Jane Davidson

■ QUASIEXPERIMENTAL DESIGN

Experiments can be partitioned into two types: randomized experiments and quasiexperiments. Both types of experiments are used to estimate the effects of treatments and interventions. Estimating a treatment effect requires comparing what happened after a treatment was implemented with what happened after no treatment (or an alternative treatment) was implemented. In randomized experiments, the different treatments are assigned to participants at random, and in quasiexperiments, the treatments are assigned nonrandomly. Four prototypic quasiexperiments are described: before-after, interrupted time-series, nonequivalent group, and regression-discontinuity designs.

BEFORE-AFTER COMPARISONS

A before-after comparison is one of the simplest and most common, but also potentially most misleading, designs for estimating a treatment effect. In a before-after comparison, measurements collected before a treatment is introduced are compared to measurements collected after the treatment is introduced. The estimate of the treatment effect is derived from the mean difference between the before and after measurements.

A before-after comparison can be misleading because a mean difference between the before and after measurements can arise from causes other than the treatment and can thereby bias the estimate of the treatment effect. The other causes that can introduce bias are called threats to validity. Seven threats to validity arise most often in before-after comparisons: history, seasonality, maturation, instrumentation, testing, attrition, and statistical regression. Each of these threats to validity is described here as it might apply to a before-after comparison used to assess the effects of a program to help parents manage problem behaviors in their children.

A threat to validity due to history arises when an event other than the treatment occurs between the times of the before and after measurements and causes all or part of the before-after difference. For example, if the program began while school was in session but ended right after spring break, changes in behavior could have resulted because the children went on vacation.

Behaviors can change because of seasonal variations, even in the absence of discrete events such as school breaks and vacations. For example, a change from winter to spring could cause differences in behavior because warmer weather leads to more time spent outdoors. Such an alternative cause is a threat to validity due to seasonality.

A threat to validity due to maturation means there is a trend in the level of the observed outcomes over time due to people getting older, or more tired, or hungrier, or similar factors. For example, some problem behaviors might lessen naturally as children mature.

If the before and after measurements were derived from the parents' self-reports of their children's troubling behaviors, a threat to validity would arise if the criteria parents used to judge troubling behaviors changed over time. For example, parents might come to realize that behaviors they perceived as troubling at the time of the before assessment were to be expected of all children; by the time of the after assessment, then, the parents would no longer view these behaviors as troubling. Such a change in criteria could make the mean of the before self-reports differ from the mean of the after self-reports even in the absence of a treatment. A change in measurement criteria is called a threat to validity due to instrumentation.

Assessing troubling behaviors on the before measure might by itself produce changes in children's behavior. For example, completing a before assessment of the degree to which their children's behaviors were troubling might cause parents to change how they interacted with their children, which correspondingly would change their children's behavior even in the absence of other treatments. The effect of such a change in before measure is a threat to validity due to testing.

Some of the parents might not have completed the after measurement, perhaps because they dropped out of the program before it was finished. If the parents who dropped out tended to be those whose children showed relatively little improvement in their behavior and if the data from those who dropped out were included in the calculation of the mean of the before measurements but excluded from the calculation of the mean of the after measurements, the before-after difference would make the program look more effective than it really was. Such a bias is due to the threat to validity of attrition.

Finally, parents are more likely to enroll in a behavior-management program at a time when their children are behaving particularly poorly than when they are behaving particularly well. Because of natural variation over time, behavior that is more extreme than usual (i.e., particularly poor) at one point in time is likely to be less extreme (i.e., more toward the usual) at a later point in time whether the program has an effect or not. A bias that arises because problems are extreme at the time of program enrollment but return to more typical levels over time is called a threat to validity due to statistical regression.

Before-after comparisons can sometimes be implemented under conditions in which all seven of the threats to validity that are described here are absent. In most cases, however, one or more of the preceding threats to validity will be present and capable of introducing substantial biases. A before-after comparison should be implemented and the results interpreted only after careful consideration of threats to validity that appear plausible in the given circumstances.

INTERRUPTED TIME-SERIES DESIGNS

An interrupted time-series (ITS) design is an extension of a before-after comparison. Instead of collecting observations once before and once after the treatment, as in a before-after comparison, observations in an ITS design are collected at multiple points in time, both before and after the intervention. The trend over time in the pretreatment observations is compared to the trend over time in the posttreatment observations, and the difference between the two trends is attributed to the effects of the treatment. For example, a treatment that produces an immediate effect on introduction would cause an abrupt break in the level of the posttreatment trend compared to the pretreatment trend (hence the name *interrupted time series*).

The analysis of data from ITS designs is complicated by the presence of autocorrelation among observations, which means that observations at adjacent times tend to be correlated. Classic statistical procedures, such as ordinary least squares regression, assume that observations are independent rather than correlated. Autocorrelation does not bias estimates of treatment effects but tends to underestimate standard errors, which makes statistical significance tests too liberal and confidence intervals too narrow. The effects of autocorrelation can be taken into account by using alternative statistical procedures, such as autocorrelated integrated moving average models.

The ITS design tends to be inferentially stronger than the before-after comparison because the ITS design rules out many threats to the validity of before-after comparisons. For example, the effects of maturation, seasonality, and statistical regression can be modeled and removed based on the trend in the pretreatment observations. In addition, the effects of testing tend to diminish across repeated pretreatment observations and so have small, if any, effects by the time the treatment is introduced.

Other threats to validity can be eliminated by adding a second (control) time series of observations in which threats to validity are present but the treatment is not. For example, the effects of history can be modeled and removed by adding a control time series of measurements of participants who are not enrolled in the treatment program but are influenced by the same historical events. If the trend in the control time series of observations does not change when the intervention is introduced, change in the experimental time series can be judged free of the effects of history.

Another advantage of the ITS design over the before-after design is that multiple posttreatment measures can reveal how the effect of a treatment varies over time. The corresponding drawback is that multiple observations over time make ITS designs more difficult to implement. ITS designs have often been implemented using archival records because such records often contain repeated measurements at regular intervals.

NONEQUIVALENT GROUP DESIGNS

In a randomized experiment, individuals (or whatever entities are the participants in the study) are assigned to treatment conditions randomly. In contrast, in a nonequivalent group design, the participants are assigned to different treatment conditions in a nonrandom fashion. Nonrandom assignment arises when, for example, participants select the treatment they are to receive based on their personal preferences. Alternatively, treatments could be assigned to preexisting groups (such as classrooms or hospital wards) to which the participants are assigned nonrandomly by administrators.

In traditional nonequivalent group designs, individuals are assessed on both a pretreatment and a posttreatment measure. Estimates of treatment effects are derived from group differences on the posttreatment measure. The pretreatment measure is used to take into account the selection differences between the groups (defined later). Usually the best pretreatment measure for taking selection differences into account is the one that is operationally identical to the posttreatment measure.

Selection differences are differences in the characteristics of the participants in the different treatment groups. Selection differences cause differences between the treatment groups on the posttreatment measure and so, to avoid bias, need to be taken into account when estimating the effect of the treatment. The primary distinction between randomized experiments and nonequivalent group designs lies in the nature of initial selection differences. In randomized experiments, initial selection differences are random. The probable size of random selection differences is easy to estimate and take into account using classic statistical procedures of confidence intervals and statistical significance tests.

In nonequivalent group designs, selection differences are nonrandom, and their probable size is seldom easy to estimate and take into account. A variety of statistical procedures is commonly used to take into account the effects that are due to nonrandom selection differences. These procedures include the analysis of covariance (with or without adjustments for measurement error in the pretreatment measures), structural equation modeling with latent variables, analysis of change scores, selection modeling, and matching based on propensity scores. Unfortunately, it is difficult to tell which, if any, of these statistical procedures will produce an unbiased estimate of the treatment effect in any given implementation of a nonequivalent group design. In most cases, the best strategy is twofold. First, implement the design using treatment groups that are as similar as possible, to minimize the size of initial selection differences. Second, use multiple statistical analyses that are based on a variety of different but reasonable assumptions about the nature of initial selection differences; this may encompass the size of the treatment effect within a plausible range of estimates.

In addition to biases due to selection differences, nonequivalent group designs are susceptible to other threats to validity, such as local history and differential attrition. A threat to validity due to local history arises when external events affect outcomes differentially across the treatment groups. Differential attrition arises when different types of individuals drop out of the different treatment conditions.

REGRESSION-DISCONTINUITY DESIGNS

In a regression-discontinuity (RD) design, participants are ordered on a quantitative assignment variable (QAV) and placed into treatment conditions based on a cutoff score on that variable. Those participants with scores above the cutoff score are assigned to one treatment condition and those with scores below the cutoff are assigned to the alternative treatment condition. Following the implementation of the different treatments, the participants in both groups are assessed on an outcome variable. The effect of the treatment is estimated by regressing the outcome scores onto the QAV. If the treatment has no effect, the regression lines will be the same in the two groups. If the treatment has a positive effect, the regression line in the treatment group will be higher than the regression line in the comparison group, with a sharp break in the lines appearing at the cutoff score on the QAV (hence the name *regression discontinuity*).

The RD design has most often been used with a QAV that is a measure of need or merit. For example, ameliorative interventions (such as food stamps or remedial educational programs) are assigned to participants in RD designs based on a QAV measure that assesses need (such as income or cognitive performance). In contrast, interventions (such as scholarships or sales awards) meant to reward outstanding performance are assigned in RD designs based on a QAV measure of merit (such as grade point average or sales volume). However, any quantitative variable could be a QAV. For example, a desirable treatment in short supply could be allocated in an RD design based on the time at which participants apply for the treatment, which would be an embodiment of the classic "first come, first served" distribution criterion.

The statistical analysis of data from the regression-discontinuity design depends on the shape of the regression surfaces between the QAV and the outcome scores in the two groups. The most common statistical analysis models the regression surface using straight lines, but if the shape of the regression surface is curvilinear, a linear fit will produce biased estimates of the treatment effect. Adding polynomial terms to the regression equation is the most frequently used method of taking curvilinearity into account.

In most instances, the regression-discontinuity design leads to more credible estimates of treatment effects than the nonequivalent group design. However, the regression-discontinuity design is relatively more difficult to implement because of the requirement that participants be assigned to treatments using a QAV. Administrators and service providers often prefer assigning participants to treatment conditions using qualitative rather than quantitative indicators.

CONCLUSION

The four designs that have been described illustrate the rudimentary types of quasiexperiments. The four basic designs can be implemented in more elaborate forms by incorporating additional design features. For example, another pretreatment observation can be added to the nonequivalent group design so that measurements are taken at two points in time before the intervention. Having two pretreatment measures collected over time can help researchers assess the patterns of change in each of the treatment groups and thereby model and take into account the effects of initial selection differences. A pretreatment measure can also be added to a before-after comparison, turning the comparison into a nonequivalent group design, which generally produces more credible inferences.

Quasiexperimental designs can also be strengthened by adding a nonequivalent dependent variable, which is an outcome measure expected to be influenced by threats to validity but not by the treatment. For example, the effect of an educational program intended to improve mathematical ability could be assessed using measures of both mathematical and verbal performance. The treatment program would be expected to affect the mathematical, but not the verbal, outcome variable, yet threats to validity such as certain types of local history would be expected to have the same effect on both variables. A biasing effect due to local history then becomes implausible to the extent that the treatment groups are similar on the measure of verbal performance.

Compared to quasiexperiments, randomized experiments tend to be inferentially stronger because they rule out more threats to validity. Randomized experiments often cannot be implemented, however, so researchers must rely on quasiexperiments. When using quasiexperiments, researchers should be particularly attentive to potential threats to validity and to ways of combining designs with design features to address the threats that are most likely to be realized.

—*Charles S. Reichardt*

Further Reading

Shadish, W. R., Cook, T. D., & Campbell, D. T. (2002). *Experimental and quasi-experimental designs for generalized causal inference.* Boston: Houghton Mifflin.

■■ QUESTIONS, EVALUATION

The key evaluation questions serve as a guide for the evaluation. As such, they indicate the scope of the evaluation and can communicate to stakeholders and other audiences the focus of the evaluation. Thus it is important that such key questions should appear as part of the contract and the evaluation plan.

One approach to developing the key evaluation questions involves holding one or more meetings with the primary stakeholder. Another approach involves meetings with all of the various levels of stakeholders.

In either case, numerous questions are likely to be generated. The evaluator must then, with the approval of the primary stakeholder or in conjunction with the primary stakeholder, identify the key questions. This can be done by (a) grouping questions by themes or categories, (b) identifying which questions within each category need an immediate answer, (c) determining which categories appear to have more questions of the "need to know now" type, (d) determining whether the categories identified in (c) are the most important, and (e) obtaining agreement from the client and primary stakeholder that this set of questions is of primary concern.

The following is an example of key evaluation questions that might be used for an evaluation of a Web-based training course:

- To what extent does the design and delivery of the Web-based training contribute to or impede trainees' learning and transfer of training to the job as compared with the design and delivery of the classroom-based training?
- To what extent are the completion rates of those experiencing the Web-based training the same or different from the completion rates of those experiencing the classroom training?
- To what extent and in what ways are those who complete the Web-based training different from those who do not complete?

Developing the key evaluation questions is not the same as creating the interview, focus group, or survey questions for the evaluation. The key evaluation questions may lead to a specific design and may help to determine the types of questions asked in the data collection effort. Nevertheless, the key evaluation questions tend to be broader and more comprehensive than specific questions used in the data collection.

—*Darlene F. Russ-Eft*

Further Reading

Russ-Eft, D., & Preskill, H. (2001). *Evaluation in organizations: A systematic approach to enhancing learning, performance, and change.* Cambridge, MA: Perseus Press.

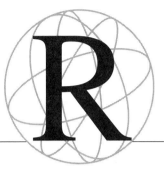

RAND CORPORATION

RAND (a contraction of "research and development") was one of the first organizations to be called a "think tank," a distinction bestowed by its original client, the U.S. Air Force (then the Army Air Force). As World War II was drawing to a close, it became apparent that complete and permanent peace might not be assured. Discussions among people in the War Department, the Office of Scientific Research and Development, and industry identified a need for a private organization that could connect military planning with research and development decisions, giving birth to the original Project RAND.

Today, RAND's work is much more diverse. Its mission is to help improve policy and decision making through research and analysis, and RAND strives to serve the public interest by widely disseminating its research findings. Current areas of research include children and adolescents, civil justice, education, energy and the environment, health and health care, international affairs, U.S. national security, population and aging, public safety, science and technology, substance abuse, terrorism and homeland defense, and transportation and infrastructure. A staff of more than 1600 is located in four principal offices, three in the United States and one in The Netherlands.

—*Jeffrey G. Tucker*

RANDOMIZED EXPERIMENT. *See* EXPERIMENTAL DESIGN, QUASIEXPERIMENTAL DESIGN

RANKING

Ranking is an evaluation process that entails placing things in an order that is based on their relative performance on a common indicator, for example a test. True ranking does not permit ties, although partial ranking does. Along with grading, ranking is a fundamental strategy for doing evaluation. This strategy is more likely to be used in evaluations where scarce resources are being apportioned, such as for the awarding of scholarships or admission to college. Unlike grades, which are criterion referenced, a rank in and of itself tells one nothing about the absolute performance of the evaluand. For example, all ranked evaluands may be bad, but still some will be ranked as first, second, and so on. The obverse is also the case. In other words, one cannot infer a grade or absolute value from a rank, although one can infer a partial ranking (with ties) from a grade.

RAPID RURAL APPRAISAL

Rapid rural appraisal (RRA) is a repertoire of informal techniques used to collect and analyze data about local situations and people. The findings are shared with the community and usually result in community actions or changes. Developed in the 1970s and 1980s to counter problems associated with outsiders conducting inquiries in developing economies, the approach draws on various inquiry methods, including some from anthropology.

To help ensure that findings are valid, RRA relies upon triangulation: cross-checking information by talking to different stakeholders, using different methods (interviews, diagrams, and observations), and having a multidisciplinary team (men and women, insiders and outsiders).

Participatory rural appraisal (PRA) evolved from RRA. PRA emphasizes local knowledge and enables local people to make their own appraisal of a situation. RRA and PRA share common methodology, but PRA researchers help local participants to conduct their own research. PRA is often used by development organizations in lower income countries to catalyze community-driven action. Originally developed for use in rural areas, modified versions of RRA and PRA have begun to be used in developed economies, with the emphasis on multidisciplinary teams and semi-structured interviews.

—*Jessica Dart*

See also PARTICIPATORY RURAL APPRAISAL

Further Reading

Chambers, R. (1994). The origins and practice of participatory rural appraisal. *World Development, 22,* 953-969.

Pretty, N. P., Guijit, I., & Scoones, I. (1995). *Participatory learning and action* (IIED Participatory Methodology Series). London: International Institute for Environment and Development.

▓ RAPPORT

Rapport is the respectful relationship that the evaluator develops with the stakeholders in the evaluation setting. Whether in negotiating the contract for services; meeting with stakeholders to frame the scope and content of the evaluation; conducting interviews, focus groups, or other data collection activities; or reporting findings and encouraging evaluation use, it is important that evaluators convey respect for stakeholders' knowledge and experiences and strive to create a positive working relationship with all those involved in the evaluation process. Rapport is particularly

important for eliciting honest, candid responses from interviewees.

—*Leslie K. Goodyear*

RATING. *See* GRADING

▓ RATIONALITY

Evaluation, in the heady days when the United States was at war with poverty, when government was thought to be capable of solving social problems, was the hope for making decisions rational. The expectation for rationality ran like this: Specify a problem that required government action, develop a list of policies that might remedy the problem, evaluate the effectiveness and cost of each of the policy alternatives, compare the results, and choose the most effective, lowest cost policy. Effective policy solutions were assumed to be abundant. Evaluations producing comparable information on the relevant policies were expected to be easy to conduct. Decisions could wait to follow the delivery of findings. Political interests would yield to the correctness of empirically determined solutions. Evaluation findings would supplant democratic debate and deliberation with instrumentally determined decisions. The petty politics of personality, vested economic interests, backroom deals, arbitrariness, and arm twisting for votes would all become things of the past. Evaluation would light the way of rationality.

Of course, few evaluators or proponents of evaluation completely bought this idealized view of the impact of evaluation, but the idea that evaluation could make decisions more rational was widely held. Passing years have circumscribed expectations for evaluation to produce greater rationality. Evaluations are much less definitive than the idealized model would require, and politics is more vital for social decision making than might have been believed. Rarely do we have evaluations that provide head-to-head comparisons of alternative policies. Many policies have been shown to produce different effects among different groups of program participants, and effects often differ in size and significance from one place to another. Experiences of everyday evaluators, as well as systematic research on evaluation use, began to show that evaluation findings were less influential in the decision-making process even when they were available and clear. Evaluation, according to the analysis of a student of politics, Majone (1989), does not so much determine the best decision as add fuel to the arguments for and against certain policies.

Not only has experience diminished the promise of evaluation leading to rational decisions, the desirability of such an outcome has been reduced, if not entirely reversed. "Epistemocracy," or the rule of knowledge that results from the model of rational decision making, has been severely challenged. Knowledge and expertise have been decried by some as simply guises for privilege. In democratic societies, issues about values and preferences must find avenues for debate and open, legitimate means for resolving differences that are too complex for technical solutions.

Melvin Mark predicts that the next great divide in the field of evaluation will separate evaluators who consider themselves neutral brokers of information from evaluators who act as advocates for a group or a set of policy preferences. Although the idealized model of rational decision making has succumbed to politics, the idea that empirical findings generated by systematic evaluations can *and* should influence public decisions made in modern democracies is being vigorously applied and vigorously contested.

—Gary T. Henry

Further Reading

Majone, G. (1989). *Evidence, arguments, and persuasion in the policy process.* New Haven, CT: Yale University Press.

Mark, M. M. (2001). Evaluation's future: Furor, futile, or fertile? *American Journal of Evaluation, 22,* 457-479.

REACTIVITY

Reactivity is an artificial effect on the research subject due to the measurement or procedures used in the study. The Hawthorne effect is an example.

—Jeffrey G. Tucker

REALIST EVALUATION

Realist evaluation, at its core, focuses on developing explanations of the consequences of social actions that contribute to a better understanding of why, where, and for whom programs work or fail to work. To this end, realist evaluators place a great deal of emphasis on (a) identifying the mechanisms that produce observable program effects and (b) testing these mechanisms and the other contextual variables or individual characteristics, often referred to as moderators, that may have impacts on the effects that are observed. Realist evaluation stands as an alternative to the two most pervasive schools of thought around which evaluation practice frequently has been organized: logical positivism and social constructivism. Rather than focusing on the contrasting philosophies, however, in this entry we will delve into the issues that everyday evaluators can use to frame their own work from a realist perspective, beginning with an example.

A number of evaluations of early education programs indicate a common pattern of results: high-quality programs accelerate increases in children's cognitive skills, but the cognitive skills of program participants and other children appear similar 3 to 5 years after the children have left the programs. However, the children who participated in these preschool programs benefit in terms of their social outcomes, such as lower incidence of retention in grade, higher high school graduation rates, and increased likelihood of employment. Patterns that repeat themselves, such as these, are the building blocks for constructing social programs that successfully improve life chances for individuals, as well as social conditions more generally. Why do these patterns occur? Many hypotheses have been offered as explanations, but one team of evaluation researchers, led by Arthur Reynolds, has shown that the cognitive advantage hypothesis is most consistent with the pattern of long-term social outcomes and that other hypotheses, such as increasing family support for the children's education or improving the children's attitudes about schooling, do not match the observed patterns of results as well. Other evaluations of the largest compensatory early childhood program in the United States, Head Start, show different patterns of long-term outcomes for European American children and African American children. Again, we have a pattern or observed regularity that begs for an explanation. Are the differences in effects attributable to differences in the quality of the Head Start centers that served European American children and those that enrolled African American children? Are the differences associated with family risk factors, such as poverty or lack of education of parents? Does the quality of later schooling explain differences? The race of the child appears to moderate the effects of Head Start, but realist evaluators would not stop with the apparent distinction. They would ask, "Does the observed difference have anything to do with the race of the child, or is race simply correlated with an underlying difference that has not been directly observed or measured?"

Beginning with the two related findings that are presented in this brief example, we can illustrate some of the more salient aspects of realist evaluation. We will present several commonly held beliefs that unify realist evaluators and some about which they differ, including the importance of ongoing social relations onto which social programs are overlaid, the investigation of patterns in the data, methods for uncovering the mechanisms that explain the observed patterns, and the importance of context.

Observable Patterns. Regular and meaningful patterns in social relations exist that can be observed and replicated to improve social conditions. The consistent finding that children who participate in high-quality preschools have more positive social outcomes is an example of a meaningful pattern that can be used to attempt to produce better social outcomes for other children. This finding has influenced states and communities to strengthen existing preschool programs and others to initiate new prekindergarten programs. To the realist evaluator, the degree of confidence about the replication does not appear as strong as a "covering law" that would govern all affected by these programs. Specifically, realist evaluators focus on contextual conditions that may limit or enhance a program's effectiveness and differences in the populations served and may moderate the effects that have been observed with other groups. *Potential* constraints on achieving similar levels of effectiveness do not undermine the findings from one setting to the extent that they should have no bearing on communities or policy makers trying to improve the life chances of children. Patterns and their replication are objects of inquiry for realist evaluators. We should learn from and take action based on regularities that have been shown to exist empirically, but we should not assume that patterns will be replicated exactly from one setting to the next.

From Explanations to Data to Explanations. The goal of evaluation or social research more generally is not to find a true theory explaining why programs succeed or fail but to move deftly from explanations to data that put the explanations to the test and then to develop more complete explanations based on empirical findings.

As the example illustrates, finding effects motivates the search for explanations that match the patterns of differences between program participants and nonparticipants. The explanation cannot be assumed to be self-evident because alternative and often contradictory explanations can fit an observed pattern. The explanations serve as working hypotheses for further analysis and future evaluations, often guiding the evaluators to important foci for the data collection. Similarly, findings that the long-terms gains from Head Start are found for some groups but not others motivate us to search for explanations. Evaluation, from a realist perspective, is an iterative process that involves developing explanations from observations, formulating working hypotheses, and testing the hypotheses on available data or collecting new data.

Programs Are Focused. Social programs are efforts that attempt to alter some ongoing social relationships while leaving others alone. The reality of social policy making and of program implementation is that social programs do not occur in a vacuum. Policies are promulgated to address a social problem or problems that have arisen as a result of existing social relationships. Early childhood education programs are means to address issues of underachievement in school and lack of social successes for children by changing a part of the child's day, replacing informal care by parents, family, and friends with more formal, developmentally oriented experiences, usually for about 9 months of the child's life. Other aspects of the children's lives are often not altered, such as the schools they will attend or their families' structure or resources. Expectations for the effectiveness of social policies should be tempered by the preexisting social circumstances.

Mechanisms May Not Be Observable. The underlying causes of the changes that are observed are known as *mechanisms* and are often not directly observed or observable. When we begin to try to explain why differences in cognitive skills diminish but differences in social outcomes persist, we need to consider the mechanisms that the program could have triggered that would be consistent with the patterns found in the data. Mechanisms are underlying causes of the changes that may not be possible to observe but that we can use as indicators in looking for patterns in the data that allow an explanation to be ruled out or supported as consistent with the data. Reynolds measured indicators of alternative mechanisms such as family support and children's social behaviors in school to test these explanations alongside the (temporary) cognitive advantage explanation and found the latter more consistent with the observed patterns of outcomes. Testing the fit of the explanation with the data is an important step for realists because the temporary cognitive advantage hypothesis is only one of the possible explanations in this case. The explanation associated with this hypothesis is actually quite elaborate and detailed. It posits that the improved cognitive skills affect the judgments of teachers and others who allow the children who received the advantage to avoid assignment to special education services, retention in kindergarten, and placement in lower level reading groups within their classrooms. Each of these variables, including teacher judgments and children's assignments, provides opportunities for recording or measuring indicators that would test the cognitive advantage mechanism.

Data May Be Quantitative or Qualitative. The data used to develop and test explanations can be either quantitative or qualitative. Realist evaluators are generally agnostic with respect to types of data, although they may be trained in a particular tradition and therefore may be more likely to use methods for which they have training. Some realist evaluators eschew experimental evaluations that used random assignment of groups to treatment and control and many types of quasiexperiments, as well. Others have noted that they are often useful and can be made more so if they provide data that can be used to sort out which mechanisms were most likely to have been responsible for the observed differences between treatment and control groups.

Data Are Used for Classification. In addition to assisting in the development of explanations, data are used to classify individuals, programs, and outcomes to make meaningful groupings. Programs often work differently for individuals who were different to begin with, as is apparently the case with Head Start in our example. Realist evaluators often speak of "natural kinds" as an attempt to understand if the groups are really inherently different or if there is an unobserved characteristic that really explains why a program works for some and not others. When programs work better for some than others, the effects are said to be

"moderated." Finding that a program is more effective for one group of individuals than another (or for one group of programs, for that matter) motivates realist evaluators to search for an underlying explanation. If an underlying explanation is found, it discounts the likelihood that the groups form natural kinds that are inherently different. Classification, whether qualitative typologies or quantitatively distinguished groupings, is an essential tool for evaluation. It enables evaluators to make better, more precise explanations, and it provides important information for people whose attitudes and actions may be influenced by an evaluation.

Context Is Important. Context is an important consideration in developing and testing explanations. Meaningful regularities do occur that transcend context, but contexts can influence whether mechanisms are triggered, and, to the extent that the program, related conditions, or the populations being served differs from one setting to the next, contexts can alter the effects. For example, if center-based early childhood programs are viewed negatively in a particular community, a high-quality preschool may not improve children's development because parents may not enroll their children. Context is sometimes used as a catch-all phrase that is meant to signify differences in the social relationships, values, and populations in different settings. Realist evaluators are prone to focus on the characteristics of setting that make a difference in terms of program outcomes and attempt to see if specific characteristics are responsible for the outcome differences. For Pawson and Tilley, context is a central concept and is used as a boundary in expectations for program effectiveness. For these realist evaluators, a task is to observe conditions before and after a program is implemented in a particular context and piece together evidence to explain why the program worked or did not work. For other realist evaluators, the comparison of treatment and control or of two or more comparison groups provides additional tests that can support or rule out plausible explanations, thereby strengthening the empirical basis for the explanation.

Societal Means for Values Judgments. Realists diverge on the explicit attention paid to values issues but find common ground in the importance of societal means for making judgments about values. Mark, Henry, and Julnes (2000) view explicit concern with values as integral to evaluation and posit that values should be a focus of inquiry in most evaluations but that they should not be the exclusive focus of any evaluation. The view of these realists about values in evaluation begins with the concept of social betterment. Social betterment is the legitimating objective of public policies and programs, and evaluators have to pay attention to societally accepted ways of measuring desired outcomes of these programs and judging social betterment, although they make the case only for societies that are democratically governed. For example, it may be self-evident to most that fewer retentions in grade and higher reading scores are outcomes that are valued in American society and that the ability of early childhood programs to improve these outcomes are important indictors of program effectiveness. These two items are thus legitimate measures of program success but are unlikely to constitute a definitive list of all the measures that an evaluation should include or that should be used to form judgments about program success.

In most cases, values inquiry, according to Mark et al. (2000), is needed to develop an accurate view of the outcomes that should be included in an evaluation. Moreover, they argue that the methods for values inquiry should strive to attain the same technical quality as the methods for explanation and classification. For example, stakeholders' attitudes about the criteria to be used to judge a program's success are very important in most evaluations, but the means used to obtain data on stakeholder attitudes should be as rigorous as the means used to measure the outcomes. However, Pawson and Tilley consider evaluation a cognitive contribution to "piecemeal social engineering" and (by and large) sidestep the issue of values and how to choose the particular outcomes for an evaluation. The examples they cite often refer to recidivism and crime rates as outcomes, which would probably receive widespread support as indicators of social problems. Clearly, realist evaluators have placed the values issue on the table and believe that it must receive explicit attention in all evaluations. However, realist evaluators have not proposed a single approach or procedure that can be used to ensure that values have been properly incorporated into an evaluation. Adequately incorporating values and value conflicts into evaluations is likely to require case studies and other evidence that exposes the current efforts to scrutiny and refinements through rounds of checking the fit between explanations and patterns of data.

CONCLUSION

Realist evaluation is a developing approach that is rooted in realist philosophy and practical experience. Its central focus is explanation, and it has a sophisticated view of how explanations about social behaviors can and should be developed. It has developed a considerable following in Europe as evaluation has risen in importance across the continent. In addition, realist evaluation has much in common with other types of evaluation, such as program theory, and may in fact be consistent with the operating principles of many evaluators who are not consciously following a particular approach to or theory of evaluation. For example, Reynolds' evaluation of the Chicago Child-Parent Centers is an exemplar of realist methods even though he did not define the approach as such. The theory and methodology of realist evaluation are works in progress. Many issues about how to conduct a realist evaluation in a particular situation have not been worked out with sufficient detail, but many of the procedures, including testing mechanisms (mediators) and examining the factors that moderate program outcomes, are being used to produce valuable information and contribute to our knowledge about public policies and social programs.

—*Gary T. Henry*

Further Reading

Henry, G. T., Julnes, G., & Mark, M. M. (Eds.). (1998). Realist evaluation: An emerging theory in support of practice. *New Directions for Evaluation, 78.*

Garces, E., Thomas, D., & Currie, J. (2002). Longer-term effects of Head Start. *American Economic Review, 92,* 1000-1012.

Mark, M. M., Henry, G. T., & Julnes, G. (2000). *Evaluation: An integrated framework for understanding, guiding, and improving policies and programs.* San Francisco: Jossey-Bass.

Pawson, R., & Tilley, N. (1997). *Realistic evaluation.* Thousand Oaks, CA: Sage.

Reynolds, A. J. (2000). *Success in early intervention: The Chicago Child-Parent Centers.* Lincoln: University of Nebraska Press.

■■ REALISTIC EVALUATION

Realist evaluation is a species of theory-driven evaluation. It has, though, a particular view about the nature of theory that is rooted in a realist philosophy of science. Realist evaluation has a distinctive account of the nature of programs and how they work, of what is involved in explaining and understanding programs, of the research methods that are needed to understand the workings of programs, and of the proper products of evaluation research. Realist evaluations ask not, "What works?" or "Does this program work?" but ask instead, "What works for whom in what circumstances and in what respects, and how?" Realist evaluation embarks on this explanatory quest on the grounds that it is panacea phobic. Programs are products of the human imagination in negotiation. They never work indefinitely, in the same way, or in all circumstances, nor do they work for all people.

THE NATURE OF PROGRAMS AND HOW THEY WORK

According to realist evaluation, programs are theories, they are embedded, they are active, and they are parts of open systems.

1. Programs Are Theories

Programs are theories incarnate. They begin in the heads of policy architects, pass into the hands of practitioners and, sometimes, into the hearts and minds of program subjects. They originate with an understanding of what gives rise to deficiencies in behavior or to discriminatory events or to inequalities of social condition and are expected to lead to changes in those patterns. They are inserted into existing social systems that are thought to underpin and account for present problems. Changes in patterns of behavior, events, or conditions are then generated through disturbances and reconstitutions of those systems. For instance, some health education theories explain the unhealthy lifestyles of adolescents by noting the undue influence of popular culture and the poor examples created by film, soap, and rock stars. This has led to the program theory of trying to insinuate equally attractive but decidedly healthy role models (e.g., sport stars) into the pages and onto the airwaves of the teen media. Programs are thus conjectures and, as in the case of this example, carry the risk of oversimplification in diagnosis and remedy.

2. Programs Are Embedded

As they are delivered, therefore, programs are embedded in social systems. It is through the workings

of entire systems of social relationships that any changes in behaviors, events, and social conditions are effected. A key requirement of realist evaluation is thus to take heed of the different layers of social reality that make up and surround programs. For instance, a program of prisoner education and training may offer inmates the immediate resources to start on the road to reform. Whether the ideas will cement depends on (a) the individual capacities of trainees and teachers, (b) the interpersonal relationships created between them, (c) the institutional balance within the prison toward rehabilitation or containment, and (d) the wider infrastructural and welfare systems that support or undermines the return to society.

3. Programs Are Active

The triggers of change in most interventions are ultimately located in the reasoning and resources of those touched by the program. Effects are thus generally produced by and require the active engagement of individuals. Take two dental health programs: the fluoridation of water and publicity on brushing twice a day. The former is a rare example of a passive program. It works whenever tapwater is swallowed and thus affects whole populations. They are not required to engage with it actively. In the health education intervention, however, the message is in the medium, and that message may be heeded and acted on, or it may be missed, ignored, forgotten, disputed, found boring, or simply overridden by the lure of sugar. So it is with the vast majority of program incentives.

4. Programs Are Open Systems

Programs cannot be fully isolated or kept constant. Unanticipated events, political change, personnel moves, physical and technological shifts, interprogram and intraprogram interactions, practitioner learning, media coverage, organizational imperatives, performance management innovations, and so on make programs permeable and plastic. Indeed, successful programs can change the conditions that made them work in the first place, the so-called arms race in crime reduction programs being a prime example. Having suffered the blows of the introduction of a new scheme, the criminal community is often able to figure out the intervention modus operandi and thus adapt its own modus operandi. A constant stream of fresh initiatives is thus required to keep pace.

Evaluations that treat programs as things or variables that directly affect passive individuals, groups, or communities misconstrue them by neglecting intentionality and interaction. Evaluations that treat programs as nothing more than participants' constructions and negotiations misconstrue them by neglecting the real systems of social relationships into which programs are inserted and the real bases for changes in reasoning and resources proffered by them.

EXPLANATION AND UNDERSTANDING OF PROGRAMS

Realist evaluation stresses four key linked concepts for explaining and understanding programs: mechanism, context, outcome pattern, and context-mechanism-outcome pattern configuration.

1. Mechanism

Mechanisms describe what it is about programs and interventions that bring about any effects. Mechanisms are often hidden, rather as the workings of a clock cannot be seen but drive the patterned movements of the hands. Many programs have multiple component interventions. The term *mechanism* is not used to distinguish these components. Interventions also often involve long sequences of steps before the outcome. Again, these are not referred to as mechanisms. Rather, *mechanism* refers to the ways in which any one of the components or any set of them, or any step or series of steps, brings about change. Mechanisms thus explicate the logic of an intervention; they trace the destiny of a program theory; they pinpoint the ways in which the resources on offer may permeate into the reasoning of the subjects. Realist evaluation begins with the researcher positing the potential processes through which a program may work as a prelude to testing them. Having established, say, that role modeling is the theory behind the emergence of the new stars of the magazines for teenage girls, the evaluator then has to ask whether the picture stories of the dreamy sporting heroes lead readers to exercise their bodies, or merely their minds.

Mechanism analysis is by no means simple. The same intervention can, of course, activate a whole series of mechanisms, each one of which is open to empirical scrutiny. The erection of closed-circuit television cameras in car parks may reduce theft by catching potential criminals unaware, through publicity that drives them elsewhere, or by attracting more customers and thus increasing natural surveillance. Moreover, even if the crucial mechanisms have been identified, it must further be assumed that they will be active only under different circumstances; that is, in different contexts.

2. Context

Context describes those features of the conditions in which programs are introduced that are relevant to the operation of the program's mechanisms. Realism uses contextual thinking to address the issues of for whom and in what circumstances a program will work. Some contexts will be supportive to the program theory and some will not. Context must not be confused with locality. Depending on the nature of the intervention, what is contextually significant may relate not only to place but to systems of interpersonal and social relationships and even to biology, technology, economic conditions, and so on. Standard measures of demographic difference in social science, in terms of sex, age, ethnicity, and class, are in themselves unlikely to capture what is contextually important but may at best be rough indicators. The salient conditions must also be identified as part of the program theory. These conditions generally suppose that certain types of subjects have a better chance and that certain institutional arrangements are better at delivering the goods. Thus, for instance, prisoner education may better aid rehabilitation in cases where there is no drug addiction, there is a family for the prisoner to return to on release, and there are employment havens that recognize qualifications gained to ease transition from prison to work.

Programs are almost always introduced into multiple contexts, in the sense that mechanisms activated by the interventions will vary and will do so according to saliently different conditions. Because of relevant variations in context and mechanisms thereby activated, any program is liable to have mixed outcome patterns.

3. Outcome Patterns

Outcome patterns comprise the intended and unintended consequences of programs, resulting from the activation of different mechanisms in saliently different contexts. Realism does not rely on a single outcome measure to deliver a pass-fail verdict on a program. Outcome patterns can take many forms, and programs should be tested against a range of output and outcome measures. For instance, it may be instructive to learn that closed-circuit television camera installation increases car park turnover as a prelude to (and potential cause of) a fall in the crime rate. Hunting down outcome patterns may also involve implementation variations, impact variations, sociodemographic subgroup variations, temporal outcome variations, personal attribute outcome variations, biological makeup outcome variations, and so on. In the case of implementation variations, it may be useful to evaluate, for example, the free distribution of smoke alarms by testing how many had been properly installed rather than relying on long-term changes in death or injury by fire.

All interventions involve multiple perturbations of preexisting regularities in behaviors, events, or social conditions, leading to the creation of many new regularities. Such outcome variations are found routinely within programs of all types. The nature and source of these internal differences is a key focus of attention in realist evaluation.

4. Context-Mechanism-Outcome Pattern Configuration

Realist evaluation is about theory testing and refinement. Context-mechanism-outcome pattern configurations (CMOCs) comprise models indicating how programs activate mechanisms, among whom, and in what conditions to bring about alterations in behavioral or event or state regularities. These propositions bring together mechanism variation and relevant context variation to predict and explain outcome pattern variation. Realist evaluation thus develops and tests CMOC conjectures empirically. The "findings" of realist evaluation are always about the configuration of features needed to sustain a program. For instance, property marking works better in reducing domestic burglary if levels of marked property are high; when crime targets are concentrated with few alternatives in small, well-defined communities providing a chance of tracing stolen property; with attendant persuasive publicity demonstrating increased risk of being caught; and thus only over a limited time period.

As well as being configurational, well-founded explanations also have scope (i.e., explain both success and failure), accuracy (i.e., explain small variations in program efficacy), and coherence (i.e., build up a useful and reuseable body of program theory).

RESEARCH METHODS

In relation to research methods, realist evaluation is critical of some methods, approaches some standard methods in unique ways, and has some distinctive methods of its own.

1. Methods Criticized

Realist evaluation is critical of the assumption that the so-called experimental methods, involving experimental and control groups, comprise a gold standard that will allow simple and conclusive findings that programs do or do not work and have a specifiable effect size. Programs as implemented are characteristically complex and variegated and applied to heterogeneous subjects and circumstances, but this fact is often ignored. Programs are not disembodied treatments. Programs are always embedded into existing flows of social conduct and produce effects because of their place in the stratified layers of social reality. Policy on–policy off comparisons are a chimera.

Realist evaluation is equally critical of the assumption that programs, their problems, processes, and products, are no more than precarious and arbitrary social constructions, (a) constituted in and through the negotiations between those involved in delivering and receiving the program and (b) of the implication that results of evaluations are and can be no more than social constructions. Programs normally involve asymmetries of power: Policy makers and practitioners rarely speak with an equal voice. Problem events, states, and behaviors addressed by programs are real: Crimes and injuries are real, poverty and sickness are real, suicide and heroin injection are real. The conditions that give rise to such problems are also real: Social divisions, physical conditions, and biological attributes are all real. The causal powers unleashed in social programs and identified in evaluation are also real.

2. Realist Use of Standard Methods

Realist evaluation is not a research technique. It is a "logic of inquiry" that generates distinctive research strategies and designs. It may be used prospectively (in formative evaluations), concurrently (in summative evaluations), or retrospectively (in research syntheses). Realist evaluation, moreover, has no particular preference for either quantitative or qualitative methods. Indeed, it sees merit in multiple methods, marrying the quantitative and qualitative. The methods used need to be selected in accordance with the realist hypothesis being tested and with the available data. Realist evaluation normally begins by eliciting and formalizing the program theories to be tested. There can be various sources of these, including documents, program architects, practitioners, previous evaluation studies, and social science literature. Hence documentary analysis, interviews, and library searches may all be involved. Interviews with program architects and documentary analysis can help articulate the formal or official program theory in CMOC terms. Interviews with practitioners are deemed especially important, as discussions of apparent program successes and failures can lead to fine-grained hypotheses about what works for whom and in what circumstances and respects.

If these hypotheses are correct, they will leave a data signature in the outputs and outcomes of the program. The next stage is to subject a whole package of CMOC hypotheses to systematic test, normally using quantitative methods with existing large data sets or with new data sets assembled to test the specific CMOC theories. The purpose of the analysis is to see if the model will explain the complex footprint of outcomes left by the program. The key to analysis is thus to devise and test multiple comparisons. Will the emerging theory explain implementation variations, impact variations, sociodemographic subgroup variations, temporal outcome variations, personal attribute outcome variations, biological makeup outcome variations, and so on?

3. Distinctive Realist Methods

Realist research is distinctive in its understanding of the research relationship between evaluators and stakeholders. The latter are regarded as key sources for eliciting program theory and providing data on how the program works. However, they are not interviewed (as in other research modes) as neutral sounding boards or for the worldviews they might impart. The realist interview recognizes the social nature of the encounter and, above all, the realist theory-testing

purpose of evaluation. Subjects are thus understood to be trying to respond to what they deem the interests of the interviewer. Interviews and questionnaires thus involve teaching (often in more or less subtle ways) the respondent, the theory at issue for the researcher so that subjects can orchestrate responses that speak in relevant ways to the realist theory being tested. The respondents, having learned the theory being tested, are able to teach the evaluator about those components of a program in a particularly informed way.

PRODUCTS OF REALIST EVALUATION RESEARCH

Realist evaluation is applicable in principle to all forms of program evaluation and to all social program areas. In every case, it produces tested theory about what works for whom in what circumstances. This end product is never a pass-fail verdict on an intervention but an understanding of how its inner workings produce diverse effects. Strong realist evaluations are thus intended to lead to better focused and more effective programs.

1. The Scope of Realist Evaluation

Realist formative evaluation is concerned with the development, implementation, and adjustment of program theory—mechanisms often need fine tuning to produce desired outcomes. Realist summative evaluations are concerned with eliciting and testing program theory in the round to give an overall indication of successes and failures and why they have come about. Realist synthesis is concerned with reading across program domains to identify the generic tools of government action and to give an indication of when favored program theories may be used and overused.

2. Middle-Range Realism

Realist evaluation steers a path between grand theorizing that aspires to universal claims about what works and a narrow focus on the descriptive particulars of specific measures in specific places relating to specific stakeholders. It aspires to develop and test theories relating to classes of condition and the types of mechanisms activated in them through forms of intervention to generate directions of change or outcome among subsets of program participants. Realist evaluation thus begins and ends with theory. It develops and tests theories about what works for whom in what context. The tests will corroborate a theory but not prove it. The realist approach is particularly keen that one evaluation should learn from another. A sequence of realist evaluations will lead to more powerful CMOCs that are increasingly refined and better tested.

3. The Payoff of Realist Evaluation

The key potential payoff of realist evaluations is programs that can be more effectively applied and targeted. Realist evaluation is skeptical about political arithmetic. It is not possible to promise net effects measurements of programs-as-a-whole that can be generalized across space and time and can thus inform exact resource allocation decisions. Variegated and changing outcome patterns are the norm in real programming. Realism thus performs an "enlightenment function" in bringing evidence into the policy fold. Understanding whole configurations of program features and contextual factors is critical to the development and implementation of improving policies and interventions. Also, although it is impossible to provide the exact recipe for success, realism can offer policy makers vital clues as to the right ingredients.

—*Ray Pawson and Nick Tilley*

Further Reading

Pawson, R., & Tilley, N. (1997). *Realistic evaluation.* Thousand Oaks, CA: Sage.

▪▪ RECIPROCITY

Reciprocity, also known as an exchange relationship, is an interchange of privileges or a give and take in the research or evaluation setting. Mutual trust, respect, and cooperation are necessary to forge a reciprocal relationship between evaluator and stakeholders in which those who are participants in the evaluation find something that they feel makes their cooperation worthwhile. An evaluator who prioritizes forging reciprocity with the evaluation stakeholders can offer useful feedback on the program's processes and products, assistance with some task, access to information, a sense of empowerment for the stakeholders, or even better relations with other stakeholders

through the use of group interviews or participatory processes.

—*Leslie K. Goodyear*

▪▪ RECOMMENDATIONS

A crucial part of an evaluation is its set of recommendations, which can provide the necessary leverage for getting concrete action for program change or improvement. Even when an evaluation contract makes no explicit mention of whether recommendations are required, evaluators often develop and include them anyway. Undoubtedly, part of this is because the evaluator's knowledge about a program at the conclusion of the evaluation is probably fuller, more insightful, and less partisan than that held by program managers or participants. The evaluator can also provide an integrated voice for a variety of stakeholders with an authority that is greater than that of any individual or group.

Readers of an evaluation report deserve to know how the recommendations were arrived at and how well grounded they are in high-quality data, logical reasoning, and sound judgment. Even some meticulously carried out evaluations include recommendations that seem to have come out of nowhere. If an evaluation shows that a program is not working at all well, it is simply not true that any change at all is better than not achieving all of the aims.

Broadly speaking, recommendations can be divided into five classes. The first three are related in that they refer to extensions or enhancements of current activity rather than to changes in strategy. The first class recommends offering basically the same program or service to a new or wider clientele; the second calls for further research, more information, increased funding, or better communication; and the third class recommends that something be done about deficiencies without being explicit about remedial courses of action.

With many of these types of recommendations, it is often difficult to decipher exactly what they entail or how much change is intended. For example, a recommendation that "consideration be given" to a particular issue or course of action is technically satisfied as soon as the program sponsor gives any attention or thought to it at all because the minimum threshold for action is so indefinite. These recommendations make it easy for decision makers to claim that they are responding to the evaluation report and yet avoid any commitment to firm action or solutions that might have negative personal or political consequences.

The fourth class consists of specific recommendations for changes in strategy or tactics. These include proposals for eliminating, strengthening, augmenting, or replacing current actions to increase the probability that the program will operate with fewer problems in the future and bring its outcomes more into line with the original intentions. These types of recommendations imply that evaluators have come to a thorough understanding of the program's internal functioning and how it operates within its context.

Tactical recommendations amount to claims that key causal links between actions and outcomes—not necessarily in one-to-one correspondence—have become known through the evaluation. If these links have been observed to apply in at least some settings, the corresponding recommendations may assume that they will hold across all settings. If the links have not actually been seen in action but rely instead on theorizing or high-level inference, the evaluator has to make more complex assumptions. In both cases, any proposals for changes are, at the time they are formulated, untried in the field and may interact with and have an impact on the context itself. Collectively, they represent a prescriptive statement about a projected reality and always, therefore, contain a conjectural element.

Making tactical recommendations amounts to engaging in program or system redesign and raises the issue of the evaluator's expertise in the design area. It also raises the matter of accountability. Once evaluators have put their recommendations together and filed their reports, they are typically out of the picture. If a particular evaluator's recommendations were all to be implemented and later turned out to be wide of the mark in achieving program goals, there are few if any penalties that can be imposed. Any intention, contractual or otherwise, to hold an evaluator accountable for the subsequent success of the program would be difficult to defend unless the evaluator also had control over how the recommendations were implemented.

Some evaluation reports specifically argue that the full set of their recommendations must be implemented as a package. Presumably, this is to forestall piecemeal implementation, which would endanger the integrity of the proposed design. Obviously, selective implementation makes it impossible to test how adequate or effective the full design might have been. When acting on a set of recommendations, therefore, it is important to focus on the intended functions of any that are either not implemented at all or are only partially implemented. It may then be possible to make adjustments elsewhere in the system to compensate.

Recommendations in the fifth class propose changes in policy or program objectives (including reordered priorities), extending, on occasion, to wholesale restructuring. However, even when an evaluation clearly demonstrates that the original conceptualization of a program was, in retrospect, inadequate or unworkable, there are risks in recommending a significant redirection because the original rationale for proposing and implementing the program would have had a strong focus on the achievement of specific goals. Consequently, the initiators of a program are likely to be more strongly attached to its goals than they are to particular strategies to achieve those goals and may therefore consider any such recommendations as lying outside the evaluator's brief. It is one thing to entertain new lines of attack to achieve fixed goals; it is quite a different matter to revisit or rework the goals themselves and possibly jeopardize future support or funding. Those situations aside, a general point is that in recommending revised goals, the evaluator is likely to have more success if an educative rather than a strictly descriptive or evaluative stance is adopted in writing the report and if the recommendations are framed with appropriate tact and diplomacy.

In summary, recommendations can provide a fitting capstone to an evaluation report. To be of greatest benefit, they must be clearly articulated, based as far as possible on detailed knowledge of why the program has been operating as it has and how it could operate better, and propose specific actions rather than vague generalities that are difficult to audit. The more radical any proposals for change, the greater the depth of explanation required. In particular, if the recommendations challenge the aims of the program, they require special care in formulation.

—D. Royce Sadler

Further Reading

Hendricks, M., & Papagiannis, M. (1990). Do's and don't's for offering effective recommendations. *Evaluation Practice, 11,* 121-125.

Posavac, E. J., & Carey, R. G. (2002). *Program evaluation: Methods and case studies* (6th ed.). Upper Saddle River, NJ: Prentice Hall.

REFLECTION

An integral part of interpretive, participatory, and collaborative approaches to evaluation, *reflection* is the basis for effective dialogue and validity testing. Within these frameworks, evaluators reflect back to stakeholders the understandings and meanings stakeholders attribute to actions and events related to the program. This back-and-forth member checking often takes place in a three-part format: descriptive reflection, evaluative reflection, and practical reflection, all part of an iterative process that involves description, analysis, critique, reiteration, and so on toward joint construction of meaning.

—*Leslie K. Goodyear*

Further Reading

Bray, J. N., Lee, J., Smith, L. L., & Yorks, L. (2000). *From collaborative inquiry in practice: Action, reflection and meaning making.* Thousand Oaks, CA: Sage.

REFLEXIVITY

Reflexivity refers to the process of acknowledging and critically examining one's own characteristics, biases, and insights, particularly as they influence participants and evaluation processes and findings. Reflexivity involves various efforts to identify the evaluators' impact and either control it or document and account for it. Ideally, evaluators keep an audit trail or fieldnotes documenting their methodological choices, their reactions to people they study, their intentions, and their interpretations. These records reflect evaluators' efforts to understand roles they play and can be helpful in interpreting the directions their studies take, how they influence the evaluand, and how they are influenced by the evaluand.

—*David D. Williams*

REGRESSION ANALYSIS

Regression is a statistical method for estimating the relationship between one or more predictor (independent) variables and a criterion (dependent) variable. Conventionally, regression studies have focused on the correlation between the predictors and the criterion variable. However, regression is a highly flexible approach to data analysis that can be used to compare differences on mean scores of the dependent variable from different categories of one or more independent variables. This application is equivalent to the statistical methods *analysis of variance* and *analysis of covariance.* An evaluator could use regression to estimate the effects of an intervention on an outcome variable, controlling for demographic variables of the program participants and control subjects.

—*Joseph M. Petrosko*

Further Reading

Cohen, J., Cohen, P., West, S. G., & Aiken, L. S. (2003). *Applied multiple regression/correlation analysis for the behavioral sciences* (3rd ed.). Mahwah, NJ: Lawrence Erlbaum.

REICHARDT, CHARLES S. (CHIP)

(b., 1951, Princeton, New Jersey). Ph.D., M.A., B.A. Psychology, Northwestern University.

Reichardt attended Northwestern during the height of its training program in methodology and evaluation research in the 1970s, when the faculty included Don Campbell, Tom Cook, Bob Boruch, and Paul Wortman. Reichardt was Don Campbell's research assistant, and the well-known volume on quasiexperimentation written by Cook and Campbell was produced during Reichardt's stay at Northwestern. Quasiexperimental design has been a central theme in his research ever since.

His interest in program evaluation was inspired by Don Campbell's "experimenting society" and a 1960s-style desire to do good. Reichardt's focus in evaluation has been on improving research methods, especially those used for assessing program effectiveness. He is Professor of Psychology at the University of Denver, where he has been since 1978.

RELATIVISM

Relativism is a view that there is no objective reality or universal truth. Sometimes equated with subjectivity and contrasted with objectivity. Richard Bernstein defines *relativism* more specifically as the belief that truth and value can be understood only in relation to some theory, conceptual framework, or cultural or social practices. There is a radical sense of relativism that is a self-refuting position (i.e., one cannot hold a relativist position relativistically) and, in any event, too skeptical as an epistemological position. However, more qualified senses of relativism, such as culture-specific knowledge and the epistemology of poststructuralism, are epistemologies that need to be considered more seriously. Indeed, these assumptions of relativism are foundational for a number of evaluation approaches, including fourth generation, participatory, responsive, and transformative.

■■ RELIABILITY

There are several definitions of *reliability* for measures of individual differences, each stressing one of its many facets. It may be defined as the *accuracy or precision* of an instrument in measuring the "true" standing of persons to whom a particular test was administered. Another definition states that reliability is an estimate of the *stability, dependability, or predictability* of a measure. This definition focuses on whether repeated measures taken on the same persons using the same or comparable instruments will produce the same or similar results. Finally, reliability is defined as the proportion of observed score variance that is attributable to true score variance.

—*Charles L. Thomas*

Further Reading

Crocker, L., & Algina, J. (1986). *Introduction to classical and modern test theory*. New York: Holt, Rinehart & Winston.

Kerlinger, F. N. (1986). *Foundations of behavioral research* (3rd ed). New York: Holt, Rinehart & Winston.

REPEATED MEASURES. *See* QUASIEXPERIMENTAL DESIGN

■■ REPORTING

Reporting has, historically, consisted primarily of comprehensive written reports prepared and delivered by the evaluator as one-way communication to evaluation audiences. This approach follows the traditions of social science research reporting, where objectivity, replicability, and comprehensiveness are standard criteria of quality. The primary burden of the evaluation's utility is placed on the content of the report and its use by evaluation clients and audiences. Indeed,

early complaints about evaluations focused on their lack of use, citing in particular that reports went unread and findings were not considered. To improve use, evaluators have more recently begun to employ varied and interactive forms of reporting—often (but not always) in addition to traditional, comprehensive written reports. The defining characteristics of evaluation reporting are its purposes, audiences, content, and format.

PURPOSES

Evaluation reporting typically serves one or both of two main purposes and generally follows the original purpose of the evaluation endeavor. First, reports can help improve a program. Formative reports are intended to inform decision making by program staff, management, and others about changes that will increase the program's effectiveness. Second, summative reports are provided to demonstrate a program's effectiveness (its merit or worth) and as a means of accountability to funders, other primary stakeholders, the public, and others interested in the type of program evaluated. The primary objective of any report is that audience members understand the information being presented. Understanding is a requisite for any type of evaluation use, whether that use is conceptual (to further understanding) or instrumental (to stimulate action).

AUDIENCES

Audiences for evaluation reports are often numerous and varied. Generally, audiences are considered to be in one of three categories. Primary audiences usually request the evaluation, are the major decision makers associated with the program being evaluated, or have funded the program. Sometimes, these groups include the program's staff, supervisors, managers, or external constituents.

Secondary audiences are involved with the program in some way. They may have little or no daily contact with the program but may have a strong interest in the results of the evaluation. Secondary audiences may use the evaluation findings in some aspects of their work and decision-making processes. These groups might include some program participants, their supervisors or managers, and individuals whose work will be affected by decisions based on the evaluation results.

Tertiary audiences are yet more distanced from the inner workings of the program but may want to stay informed about the program and would be interested in receiving the evaluation's results. These groups might include future program participants, audiences who represent the general public interest, and members of the program's profession (e.g., educators interested in professional practices related to school reform).

Identification of audiences and understanding of their characteristics are critical for ensuring that evaluation reports are used. Audiences vary across a number of characteristics that mediate the type of evaluation report that will be most meaningful for them. For this reason, evaluators have long been advised to produce as many types of reports (with varied content and using different formats) from an evaluation as may be needed to meet audience needs. These characteristics include the audience's accessibility, education level, familiarity with the program, familiarity with research and evaluation, role in decision making, and attitude toward or interest level in the program or the evaluation. Where an audience stands on any one of these dimensions plays some role in determining the evaluation report's content and/or delivery method. For example, program officers of a funding agency or other busy executives may be highly interested in an evaluation's findings but feel they do not have time to read a lengthy report or meet for a discussion about it. A single-page summary report, which they can read quickly and at the time that best suits them, is probably the best format choice. Audience access can vary in other ways too. For instance, an evaluation of a development project in a Third World country could include numerous agencies from different countries. A report formatted to be viewed from a Web site may be accessible to all parties, whereas a large document to be downloaded from the site might not.

Audiences who are very familiar with a program, such as the primary audiences for an internal evaluation, will need less background and descriptive information about the program than more distant audiences. Similarly, audience familiarity with research and evaluation, as well as the audience's education level, should affect how a report is written. The next section reviews general considerations for other aspects of report content—writing; tables and figures; graphic design; and photographs, cartoons, and poetry.

CONTENT

Almost nothing is more important to written communication than clarity and readability. In developing written reports, evaluators typically strive to reduce complexity while bearing in mind the intended audience. Complex terminology can appear in evaluation reports in two ways. Evaluators sometimes use it to describe qualitative or quantitative research methodologies, or they may use it to describe unique aspects of a particular program. Terminology specific to a program is appropriate for a detailed final report read primarily by program participants, whereas a summary of the same evaluation findings presented in a bulletin and distributed to other groups would be written in simpler terms.

More often than not, evaluation reports include tables and figures, used to present a significant amount of data with great precision in a very small amount of space. Tables present numbers or text in rows and columns to show identifiable relationships and trends. Figures include charts, graphs, or illustrations used to convey quantitative or qualitative data (or interpretations of data) in a visual form. Charts and graphs typically are used with quantitative data to show relationships, components, or trends. Illustrations include diagrams, maps, and drawings and are used to convey ideas and relationships that are difficult to express in words in a short period of time or space.

Although less frequently used, other content that can be found in evaluation reports are photographs, cartoons, and poetry. The use of photography in evaluation reports is appealing to most audiences, and photographs can more easily be included in reports now than in the past. Still, many evaluators do not use them. Photographs are particularly helpful in providing evidence in ways pure narrative cannot, allowing audiences to enter into the world of the program being evaluated and assign their own meanings and interpretations to what they see. Photographs have a tremendous capacity to provide complex information and stimulate thought and discussion. Cartoons are a combination of pictures and text that can convey the complexity of issues uncovered by an evaluation through humor and visual cues. Poetry provides a way of perceiving meaning from text about evaluation findings and can help articulate contradictions, sensitive topics, emotional reactions, and challenges in the setting. It can make findings more accessible by using participants' language and avoiding evaluation or other academic jargon.

FORMATS

Report formats can be categorized according to degree of interaction with audiences: noninteractive, written formats; potentially interactive formats; and interactive formats.

Noninteractive, Written Formats

The most common formats for reports of evaluation findings are text based and include interim or progress reports; final reports; executive summaries; newsletters, bulletins, and brochures; news media communications; and Web-site communications. Virtually all evaluations include some kind of written report, whether or not other formats are used to report findings. Written evaluation reports are most effective when they are clear, use language appropriate to the audience, and are laid out in a manner that makes their contents inviting and easy to assimilate.

Interim or Progress Reports. This type of report presents the results of partial evaluation findings. Interim reports are typically short but can be of considerable size in the case of multiyear, multisite, or very comprehensive evaluations. They are almost always produced in anticipation of a complete, final report and are typically planned for at the outset of the evaluation. The scheduling of interim reports is dictated by several factors: the life cycle of the program, when certain data collection activities can and will be completed, and specific decision-making needs of clients and stakeholders. Interim reports are important because they help keep audiences aware of evaluation activities and emerging findings, and they integrate evaluation activities and findings with key stages in the life of a program or organization.

Comprehensive Final Reports. This type of report is produced at the conclusion of data collection and analysis activities and is the most commonly used form of reporting by evaluators. The framework for these reports is found in the reporting traditions of basic social science research. This approach mandates formal, thorough treatments of a study's rationale, methodology, results, and implications. The objective is to provide sufficient documentation for readers to draw alternative conclusions and/or replicate the research.

Evaluators sometimes underestimate the time necessary to complete final reports and have faced significant criticism for delivering reports after the time at which they could have been used. Although many clients expect lengthy, comprehensive reports that are time consuming to produce, it is unclear that such reports provide the most cost-effective means for communicating evaluation findings in ways most useful to audiences. Written reports serve important archival purposes, including accountability needs, but they are not necessarily the best format for facilitating understanding or decision making for change and improvement. As will be discussed later, presentations of both interim and final evaluation findings can be delivered in a variety of formats—from highly visual, computer-generated presentations delivered via CD-ROM to interactive working sessions.

Executive Summaries or Abstracts. The executive summary is essentially a shortened version of a longer evaluation report. Very few reports are written without an executive summary, which is positioned at the front of the longer document. Its intent is to communicate the essential messages of the original document accurately and concisely. Few people may read a full evaluation report; some will skim parts of it, but most (if not all) will read the executive summary. For this reason, it is especially important that executive summaries be well written. Summaries are typically written to address the needs of busy decision makers and are especially useful for quick dissemination of findings. They can be reproduced separately and disseminated as needed, can vary in length from one paragraph to several pages, and can be tailored to address the needs of particular audiences and emphasize different program elements and findings.

Newsletters, Bulletins, and Brochures. These formats are sometimes used when evaluators want to relay evaluation findings to a broad group of individuals in a form other than that of a lengthy written report. A newsletter may be devoted solely to communicating evaluation findings from one study, or articles about the evaluation findings may be included in existing internal or external newsletters. A newsletter can be a single page containing key findings, or it can be several pages created in a newspaper format describing particular elements of the evaluation and its findings.

Bulletins look similar to newsletters but are typically characterized by their brevity, their sole dedication to reporting evaluation results, and the frequency of their publication during the evaluation. Once the study or project has been completed, bulletins are often discontinued, only to start up again when a new study begins.

Brochures are sometimes created to generate interest in evaluation findings. They can stimulate readers to find out more about a program and its evaluation results. A typical brochure is printed on standard-size paper and folded twice. It might include a description of the evaluation object, an overview of the evaluation design, and the evaluation's findings and recommendations. This form of communication can be used to invite readers to a postevaluation discussion and action planning session, or it can be used expressly to inform readers of the study's conclusions.

Mass Media. In many evaluations, findings need to be disseminated beyond the primary stakeholders. In these cases, using the news media to communicate and report evaluation findings helps reach the general public, as well as specific industry or professional groups.

The general public is reached through mass media; namely, newspapers, television, radio, and the Internet. Examples are publications such as the *New York Times, Time* magazine, and local newspapers. A newspaper's ability to reach a large audience is often the major reason for using this method. Television and radio are also well suited to reaching large segments of the public. Like videotape presentations (see below), they can transmit evaluation findings using language, sight, and sound. The Internet must now also be considered a form of mass media, and it is increasingly available to more and more segments of the general public.

Evaluation results may find their way into print media through three established routes. First, newspaper writers may obtain copies of evaluation reports from one of the stakeholder groups and write an article based on the report. A second method involves the newspaper writer interviewing the evaluator and possibly the program staff and participants. From these interviews, the reporter writes an article. The third method is the press release. An evaluator or primary stakeholders may contact a reporter by phone and provide evaluation information. On the more formal side, a written press release is produced. This is typically a one- to two-page summary of the evaluation's findings, sent to both print and electronic media. If the press release is brief and written like a news story, it may be published as is or it may be excerpted. If the

release creates enough interest in the topic, a reporter may call the evaluator for an in-depth interview. Evaluators and their clients have the least control over the content of reports conveyed via the news media. Because much of what the evaluator conveys will be abbreviated due to space and time restrictions, there are no guarantees of what will show up on the page, screen, or air.

Specialized media include newsletters, journals, and magazines published by trade and interest groups such as the American Hospital Association, American Evaluation Association, or American Association of Retired Persons. These groups report information (evaluation findings) of particular interest to their constituents.

Web Sites. Web-site communications can be used to make reports easily accessible to a very broad audience at minimal cost. Web-site postings can include summaries or feature articles and access to full reports that are available to download. Typical Web-site postings of evaluation findings provide them in a concise, scannable, written format, but they can also include photographs, sound, and animation—just as video, CD-ROM, and television presentations do. Audiences' access to and practices with respect to the Internet are important considerations prior to establishing it as a mainstay for reporting findings.

Potentially Interactive Formats

Several formats for reporting evaluation findings provide the opportunity to interact with audiences: oral presentations, videotapes, and poster sessions. These formats typically are used to increase audience access to findings (with or without interaction) and usually are developed in addition to some kind of written report.

Oral Presentations. More often than not, evaluators make oral presentations of their findings at meetings of program clients and staff. The audience of an oral presentation is able to hear findings at the same time that they can see data displayed (e.g., charts, graphs, illustrations presented on overheads or projections from a computer). Face-to-face communications are particularly useful for conveying information on complex, specialized topics. Further, the oral presentation provides an opportunity for audience members to ask questions and deepen their understanding of the findings.

Videotape or Computer-Generated Presentations. These can be an especially useful means for communicating qualitative evaluation findings because they can capture the sound, motion, subtlety, and complexity of participant experiences. Moreover, the technology to produce them is increasingly accessible and easy to master without specialized expertise. Videotape or computer-generated presentations can be used to disseminate findings to broader audiences than those directly involved with a program. They are also effective for providing evaluation findings to groups whose time is limited or who might not be accustomed to reading evaluation reports—parent and community groups, for example. Such presentations can be facilitated by the evaluator and can include the same opportunities for interaction and discussion that verbal presentations provide.

Videotape or computer-generated presentations are valuable as stand-alone presentations, too. For example, copies of videotapes might be distributed to the parent or community groups for each school within a district, allowing them to receive evaluation findings on a program with districtwide implications. If the school district is large and the evaluation staff is small—a typical scenario—this means of presentation might make evaluation findings available to groups that otherwise would not get them. Finally, videotape or computer-generated presentations can help standardize the presentation of findings across multiple evaluators and sites.

Poster Sessions. A poster session provides quick, visually oriented, easily read information to an audience who may have little or no knowledge about a program or organization. It is an informative display that can be combined with an oral presentation or discussion. Displays typically include photographs, diagrams, graphs, tables, charts, drawings, and text on poster-size boards (Velcro, magnetic, felt, etc.). The contents of the displays can be produced on 8.5" × 11" sheets and then arranged on one or more display boards.

Poster sessions are frequently used at conferences or association meetings as a way of displaying condensed evaluation information on a program or organization in an easily accessible manner. At public meetings, school or community open houses, or other situations that call for a quick transfer of information, poster sessions can create a strong impression and communicate vital information. They are useful when evaluators do not have a captive audience and must communicate main ideas and key data in a short span of time or limited space. As audience members pass by the display or stop for brief discussion, the evaluator can emphasize key ideas and issues and elicit questions. Poster sessions can also be set up to stand alone for viewing at any time by audiences who frequent their location.

Interactive Formats

Some formats are inherently interactive: working sessions, synchronous electronic communications, and personal discussions. For many evaluators, the use of interactive formats is based on the assumption that evaluations are more effective when evaluators work collaboratively with clients and stakeholders.

Working Sessions. Working sessions can be conducted at any time during an evaluation, but for reporting purposes, such sessions would typically come midway (for interim reporting) or at or near the end of an evaluation. A working session is a meeting of evaluation stakeholders that includes the presentation of findings and significant opportunities for interaction among the participants, with a specific purpose in mind—for example, to engage stakeholders in interpreting data, to solicit feedback about initial evaluation findings or interpretations developed by the evaluator, to develop recommendations based on evaluation findings, and to develop action plans based on evaluation findings or recommendations.

Teleconferences and Videoconferences. With synchronous electronic communications such as teleconferences and videoconferences, participants are available to interact in real time without being in each other's physical presence. Teleconferencing allows participants to ask questions, provide input, and openly discuss issues. Videoconferencing provides the means for face-to-face communication without the time and expense of travel. Teleconferences can be arranged through long-distance service companies and do not require specialized equipment, as do videoconferences. Both are useful when interaction is important among stakeholders and in-person meetings are difficult to arrange—for example, in the case of multisite evaluations. Either type of conferencing can be organized and carried out for the same purposes as the working sessions described previously.

Personal Discussions. Although these are not usually recognized as an explicit format for reporting evaluation findings, personal discussions do take place and serve this purpose. Personal discussions among evaluators, clients, and stakeholders are a natural part of any evaluation. They can involve the evaluators and one or more parties to the evaluation. They may be either planned or impromptu, and they may be initiated by the evaluator or by someone else. They occur face to face or over the telephone. Indeed, they constitute one of the most significant elements of an evaluation. As with other forms of interactive communication, they can occur at any time during an evaluation, but in terms of reporting, they would occur at interim or final reporting times. Sometimes personal discussions about findings occur prior to the formal presentation of findings. They have both assets and liabilities. Personal discussions can be tailored to specific individuals and can thus be highly responsive to audience needs. On the other hand, they can be impromptu and challenge the evaluator to present findings both accurately and consistently. Sometimes when noninteractive formats for presenting findings have been used, evaluators plan personal discussions (meetings) with key stakeholders to answer questions, to orient them to a formal report, or to discuss implications or plans for action.

Evaluation reporting is a complex endeavor, often no less so than the evaluation itself. Challenges for evaluators include insufficient time and political and organizational complexity. On the other hand, technological advances have increased options for formatting text; the inclusion of sight, sound, and motion; and the accessibility for audiences.

—*Rosalie T. Torres*

Further Reading

Torres, R. T., Preskill, H., & Piontek, M. E. (in press). *Evaluation strategies for communicating and reporting* (2nd ed.). Thousand Oaks, CA: Sage.

■■ REPRESENTATION

Evaluators who ground themselves in qualitative or interpretivist approaches to inquiry are confronted with the challenge of what has been labeled by postmodern scholars the "crisis of representation."

Constructivist and interpretivist approaches to evaluation and social research acknowledge the constructed nature of the social world and the multiplicity of experiential realities that might be represented through evaluation or inquiry. Evaluators who work within this frame understand that *how* they present their research or evaluation findings to audiences is at least as important as *what* they present. Presenting evaluation findings is no longer just a matter of choosing the right questions; collecting the right data; and writing a clear, succinct report. Questions of voice, style, and audience are brought to the fore for consideration in the creation of representations of evaluations. Evaluators who subscribe to a constructivist framework ask the question: Is it enough to rely on scientific writing standards for evaluation findings? Are these standards adequate for the challenges of postmodern research sensibilities, in which there is an acknowledgment of the many ways data are mediated by their social and cultural contexts? Some scholars suggest that the conventions of writing within fields such as evaluation privilege the analytic predispositions and categories of the evaluator at the expense of meanings that are closer to stakeholders' lived experience. Questions arise regarding the authenticity of evaluation reports—are they, too, just accounts of experiences, themselves grounded in particular places and perspectives? Social researchers and evaluators are testing the boundaries of representing evaluation findings and experimenting with new and different approaches to representing the evaluation process and product. These experiments include using transcripts of interviews to create poetry as a representation of a interviewee's story, creating performances that embody the experiences of stakeholders or challenge an audience to act out the part of stakeholders in the evaluation, and setting the stage for multiple readings and interpretations of the same data through interactive forums or discussions. In sum, highlighting issues of representation in evaluation challenges assumptions such as authority, the position of the evaluator, and the role of criteria in evaluation.

—*Leslie K. Goodyear*

Further Reading

Gubrium, J. F., & Holstein, J. A. (1997). *The new language of qualitative method.* New York: Oxford University Press.
Gubrium, J. F., & Holstein, J. A. (Eds.). (2002). *The handbook of interview research.* Thousand Oaks, CA: Sage.

∷ RESEARCH TRIANGLE INTERNATIONAL (RTI)

RTI is an independent, nonprofit corporation with a long history in scientific research and technology development. RTI activities both mirror and support national policies and programs, as well as diverse commercial, industrial, and academic endeavors. All activities are guided by RTI's mission: to improve the human condition through objective, innovative, multidisciplinary research, development, and technical services, setting the standard for scientific and professional excellence.

RTI headquarters are located in Research Triangle Park, North Carolina, and it also has 10 satellite offices throughout the United States and overseas. RTI scientists design, develop, and apply advanced tools and methods in five major fields of research: health, environment and natural resources, education and training, advanced technology, and economic and social development.

—*Jeffrey G. Tucker*

∷ RESPONSIVE EVALUATION

Responsive evaluation is an orientation, a predisposition, to the formal evaluation of education and social service programs. It is a disposition favoring personal experience. It draws on and disciplines the ordinary ways people perceive quality and worth. More than most other formal approaches, it draws attention to program activity, to program uniqueness, and to the cultural plurality of people. This responsive predisposition can be recognized in all evaluative research, for every composite and executive summary will include at least traces of experiences of goodness and badness.

A responsive evaluation study is a search and documentation of program quality. The essential intellectual process is a responsiveness to key issues or problems, especially those recognized by people at the sites. It is not particularly responsive to program theory or stated goals but more to stakeholder concerns. The design of the study usually develops slowly, with continuing adaptation of design and data gathering paced with the evaluators becoming well acquainted with program activity, stakeholder aspiration, and social and political contexts.

Issues of policy and practice are often taken as the "conceptual organizers" for the inquiry, more so than needs, objectives, hypotheses, group comparisons, and economic equations. Issues are organizational perplexities and social problems, drawing attention especially to unanticipated responsibilities and side effects of program efforts. The term *issue* draws thinking toward the interactivity, particularity, and subjective valuing already felt by persons associated with the program. (Examples of issue questions: Are the eligibility criteria appropriate? Do these simulation exercises confuse the students about dependable sources of information?) Stakeholders have a variety of concerns. They are proud, protective, indignant, improvement minded, troubled by costs. Responsive evaluators inquire, negotiate, and select a few concerns around which to organize the study.

These evaluators look for attainments and for troubles and coping behavior as well. To become acquainted with a program's issues, evaluators observe its activities, interview those who have some stake in the program, and examine relevant documents. These are not necessarily the data-gathering methods for informing the interpretation of program quality but are needed for the initial planning and evolving focus of the study. Management of the responsive evaluation study usually remains flexible; both quantitative and qualitative data are gathered.

OBSERVATIONS AND JUDGMENTS

Directed toward discovery of merit and shortcoming in the program, responsive evaluation recognizes multiple sources of valuing as well as multiple grounds. It is respectful of multiple, sometimes even contradictory, standards held by different individuals and groups and is reluctant to push for consensus.

Ultimately, the evaluators describe the program's activity, examine its issues, and make summary interpretations of worth, but first they observe and inquire. They exchange draft descriptions and tentative interpretations with data providers, surrogate readers, and other evaluation specialists to tease out misunderstanding and misrepresentation. In their reports, they provide ample description of activities over time and personal viewing so that, with the reservations and best judgments of the evaluators, the report readers can make up their own minds about program quality.

There is a common misunderstanding that responsive evaluation features collaborative methods. It sometimes fits well with them, but the two are not the same.

With help from program staff members, evaluation sponsors, and others, the evaluator considers alternative issues and methods. Often clients will want strong emphasis on outcomes, and often evaluators press for more attention to the processes. They negotiate. Usually the evaluation team, ultimately, directly or indirectly decides what the study will be because it is the team that knows more about what different methods can accomplish and what methods its evaluators can do well—and it is this team that will carry them out. Preliminary emphasis often, especially for external evaluators, is on becoming acquainted with the activity but also with the history and social context of the program. The program's philosophy may be phenomenological, participatory, instrumental, in pursuit of accountability, anything. Method depends partly on the situation. For it to be a good evaluation, the methods should fit the "here and now" and have potential for serving the evaluation needs of the various parties concerned.

Even so, it has been uncommon for a responsive evaluation study to be heavily dependent on instruments. Seldom does it prioritize the testing of students or other indicators of successful attainment of stated objectives. This is because such instrumentation has often been found superficial and inattentive to local circumstances. Standardized tests, for example, seldom provide comprehensive measures of the outcomes intended. For in-depth evaluation, test results have too often been disappointing—with educators, for example, probably justifiably believing that the students learned more than showed up on the tests. Even when it is possible, developing new tests and questionnaires correctly is very expensive. With a responsive orientation, data-gathering instruments are used but usually in a subordinate role.

RELIANCE ON SUBJECTIVITY AND PLURALISM

The initial proponent of responsive evaluation was Robert Stake. His 1960s thoughts about how to evaluate programs were extensions of empirical social science and psychometrics, with depersonalization and objectivity esteemed. He saw his early efforts to evaluate curriculum reform failing. Neither the designs nor the tests were getting answers to the important questions. Responsive evaluation was a response to "preordinate evaluation" and expressed opposition to immediate selection and final measurement of a few outcome criteria. Over the years, Stake and colleagues voiced the claim that disciplining impressions and personal experience led to better understanding of merit and worth.

The case study, with the evaluand as the case, became Stake's preferred way of portraying the activity, the issues, and the personal relationships that reveal program quality. Not all who have a predilection for responsive evaluation use a case study format. Many evaluators do their work responsively without calling it that, and some who call their work responsive are not responsive to Stake's issues. Different evaluators find different grounds for showing merit and worth.

Those who object to the responsive approach often do so on the ground that too much attention is given to subjective data (e.g., the testimony of the staff or the judgments of students). For description of what is happening, the evaluators try (through triangulation and review panels) to show the credibility of observations and soundness of interpretations. Part of the program's description, especially that about the worth of the program, is revealed in how people subjectively perceive what is going on. Placing value on the program is a part of experiencing it.

The evaluators' perceptions are recognized as subjective: It is the evaluator who chooses what to observe, who observes, and who reports the observations. In responsive evaluation, the evaluator tries to make those value commitments recognizable. Issues—for example, the importance of a professional development ethic—are not avoided because they are inextricably subjective. When reporting, care is taken to illuminate subjectivity in data and interpretation.

Objection to a responsive approach is partly expressed with the belief that a single authority (e.g., the program staff, the funding agency, or the research community) should specify the key questions to be evaluated. Their questions generally are worthy of study, but in program evaluation for public use, these questions are never studied exclusively. Whenever a program is informally evaluated, a wide array of concerns will be considered—and so should they be in a formal evaluation. Embezzlement, racial discrimination, inconsistency in philosophy, and thwarting of creativity may be unmentioned in the contract and not within the evaluators' expertise, but some sensitivity to all such problems belongs within the evaluation expectation, and the evaluator should try not to be blind to them.

To be sure, evaluation studies are administratively prescribed. They are created not only to gain understanding and inform decision making but to legitimatize and protect administrative decisions and program operations from criticism. Further, evaluation requirements are sometimes made more vigorously for the purpose of promulgating standards than for seeing if they are being attained. Evaluators work in political, competitive, and self-serving situations. One must hope that they portray the meanness as well as the effectiveness they find.

By seeking out stakeholder issues, evaluators try to discover how both political and corporate efforts extend control over education and social service. Few evaluators are vigorously supportive of activist reforms, but the most responsive do tend to honor the issues reformists raise. Responsive evaluation was not conceived of as an instrument of reform but as an orientation to inquiry. Some writers have found responsive evaluation democratic; others have found it conservative. It has reflected the concerns of diverse people affected personally and culturally by the program at hand—and it has regularly produced some findings each constituency does not like.

ORGANIZING AND REPORTING

The feedback from responsive evaluation studies is expected to be, in format and language, informative and comprehensible to the various audiences and responsive to their interests. Thus, even at the risk of catering to specific groups, different reports or presentations may be prepared for them. Narrative portrayals, storytelling, and verbatim testimony will be appropriate for some, databanks and regression analyses for others. Obviously, the budget will not allow everything, so these competing communications are weighed early in the work.

Responsive evaluation is an ally of participatory evaluation, organized with and around stakeholder concerns. It is not uncommon for responsive evaluation feedback to occur early and throughout the evaluation period. Representatives of the prospective audience of readers should have directly or indirectly helped shape the list of issues to be pursued. Along the way, the evaluator may ask, "Is this pertinent?" and "Is this observation evidence of success?" and might, based on the answer, change the priorities of inquiry.

Responsive evaluation has been useful during formative evaluation when the staff needs more formal ways of monitoring the program and when no one is sure what the next problems will be. It has been useful in summative evaluation when audiences want an understanding of a program's activities and scope and its strengths and shortcomings and when the evaluators feel that it is their responsibility to provide vicarious experience. Such experience is seen as important if the readers of the report are to determine the relevance of evaluator findings to their own sense of program worth.

As analyzed by Ernest House, responsive evaluation will sometimes be found to be "intuitive" or, indeed, subjective, closer sometimes to literary criticism, to Elliot Eisner's *connoisseurship,* or to Michael Scriven's *modus operandi* evaluation than to the more traditional social science designs. When the public is seen as the client, responsive evaluation may be seen as "client centered." Usually, however, it differs from those approaches in an essential feature, that of responding to the experience, issues, language, contexts, and values of an array of stakeholder groups.

When Stake proposed this "responsive evaluation" orientation at an evaluation conference at the Pedagogical Institute in Göteborg, Sweden, in 1974, he was partly reflecting the ideas of Tom Hastings, Lee Cronbach, Mike Atkin, Jack Easley, Barry MacDonald, and David Hamilton. Especially in *Beyond the Numbers Game,* they spoke of the necessity of organizing the evaluation of educational programs around what was happening in classrooms, drawing more attention to what educators were doing and less attention to what students were doing. Later refinements of responsiveness were spurred by Ernest House, Stephen Kemmis, Egon Guba, and Yvonna Lincoln and restated by Linda Mabry, Thomas Schwandt, Yoland Wadsworth, Ian Stronach, Stafford Hood, and updated in an issue of *New Directions for Evaluation* edited by Jennifer Greene and Tineke Abma.

It is difficult to tell from an evaluation report whether the investigation was responsive. A final report seldom reveals how issues were negotiated or how audiences were served. Examples of studies that were intentionally responsive can be found in the field of education (MacDonald & Kushner, 1982) as well as in health care (Abma, 2000). Stake's *Quieting Reform* (1986), a metaevaluation of Cities-in-Schools, also took a responsive approach.

—*Robert E. Stake and Tineke A. Abma*

Further Reading

Abma, T. A. (2000). Responding to ambiguity, responding to change: The value of a responsive approach to evaluation. *Evaluation and Program Planning, 23*(2), 461-470.

Greene, J. C., & Abma, T. A. (Eds.). (2001, Winter). Responsive evaluation. *New Directions for Program Evaluation, 92.*

Hamilton, D., Jenkins, D., King, C., MacDonald, B., & Parlett, M. (Eds.). (1977). *Beyond the numbers game.* London: Macmillan.

House, E. R. (1980). *Evaluating with validity.* Beverly Hills, CA: Sage.

MacDonald, B., & Kushner, S. (Eds.). (1982). *Bread and dreams.* Norwich, England: CARE, University of East Anglia.

Stake, R. E. (1974). *Program evaluation, particularly responsive evaluation* (Occasional Paper Series No. 5). Kalamazoo: Western Michigan University Evaluation Center.

Stake, R.E. (1986). *Quieting reform: Social science and social action in an urban youth program.* Champaign: University of Illinois Press.

Evaluation Practice Around the World

The Netherlands

Responsive Evaluation in a Postmodern Society Avant la Lettre

Professional evaluation is gradually gaining more popularity in The Netherlands. In the slipstream of the "new public management" trend, auditing and performance measurement were introduced in the context of public administration. At this moment, this trend seems to be on its return. Even proponents of performance measurement acknowledge negative side effects, such as "McDonaldization," proceduralism, and fear of innovation. Performance indicators may be appropriate in the context of industrial processes, such as telephone and bus services, but are less suitable within the context of professional and strategic processes in which the degree of ambiguity is high.

Recently there has been a growing interest among policy makers and researchers in evaluation approaches that acknowledge plurality, dialogue, and deliberation and participation. In 2001, for example, the Dutch Society for Public Administration nominated Egon Guba and Yvonna Lincoln's *Fourth Generation Evaluation* as a classical work. A few years earlier, several participants in an expert seminar on the future of evaluation referred to fourth-generation evaluation (FGE) as a promising perspective.

In Guba and Lincoln's "responsive-constructivist" approach to evaluation, the evaluator becomes a facilitator of a dialogical process among different stakeholders to gain an enhanced insight into their own points of view and the perspectives of others on the value of the evaluated practice or program. FGE stems from a critique on the policy-centered view of dominant approaches and clearly has an emancipatory ideal; namely, to include the voices of the silenced minorities in the process. The methodology is based on the notion that different realities exist side by side. Reality is not a given, but is constructed in social interactions and relations. Evaluation criteria are therefore based on the values, interests, and perspectives of different stakeholders, including agents, beneficiaries, and victims. They become active participants (versus information givers) in the collaborative process, negotiating the evaluation questions, methods, and interpretations of the findings. Methodologically, this means that the design gradually emerges in response to the issues raised in the process.

In The Netherlands, FGE has been implemented within various policy fields, among them social revitalization, vocational rehabilitation, supported employment, palliative care, and arts education. FGE has also been used in the evaluation of strategic processes and in the context of (medical) technology assessment. The methodology of selecting a variety of stakeholders; the generation of issues within homogeneous stakeholders groups; the formulation of an "agenda for negotiation" to be discussed within heterogeneous stakeholder groups; and the credibility criteria appear to be helpful in situations where dominant approaches fall short. The main reason to use FGE is, however, often value driven. FGE is seen as a more democratic approach that acknowledges plurality and empowers citizens, the mentally handicapped, (psychiatric) patients, and students.

The fact that FGE speaks to the imagination of Dutch policy makers and researchers is remarkable, especially when we compare it to the reception of Guba and Lincoln's work in the United States. Although their work met open hostility overseas, here it is seen as a promising perspective for the future of evaluation. There is, of course, skepticism and critique, and practitioners who have actually implemented the approach have identified cautions such as the lack of willingness among participants to be involved and problems related to asymmetrical relationships. Other authors also have suggested modifications of the FGE methodology, such as the creation of different speech contexts to prevent subtle forms of exclusion and the use of stories and narrative analysis to deepen evaluators' understanding of lived experiences. Some have used the (hermeneutic) notion of dialogue to refine the process of understanding among stakeholders. In general, however, there is an interest among policy makers and evaluators in working along the lines of Guba and Lincoln's paradigm. I believe the generous reception of FGE in The Netherlands relates to the Dutch society and culture.

All Western societies are undergoing radical changes in the direction of network societies. Globalization and computer technology play an important role in this transition. More horizontal relations replace hierarchical relationships. Power is no longer centralized but is highly distributed among different actors. This is happening on a micro level in the relationships between individuals but is also true for relationships between various organizations and nation-states. There is a growing awareness of mutual interdependencies and the importance of temporary working relationships and political coalitions on certain issues. Governments no longer claim to be central actors in the policy process but consider themselves as actors among others. The public domain is no longer the exclusive territory of public managers and policy makers.

Although this process is happening now all over the world, The Netherlands has always been characterized by mixed arrangements in the public domain. Market, government, and civil society have always shared their responsibility and worked together in the domains of health care, education, and housing. As a small country, The Netherlands has never been able to isolate itself from the rest of the world. Historically it is a merchant nation, and the Dutch have always invested in building and maintaining enduring relationships and in learning other languages. As such, The Netherlands is a postmodern society avant la lettre. Within this particular context and culture, a responsive evaluation approach finds good soil in which to flourish.

—*Tineke A. Abma*

Further Reading

Guba, E. G., & Lincoln, Y. S. (1989). *Fourth generation evaluation.* Newbury Park, CA: Sage.

RIST, RAY C.

(b. 1944, Carbondale, Illinois). Ph.D., M.A., Washington University, St. Louis; B.A. Psychology and Sociology, Valparaiso University.

Rist is Senior Evaluation Officer in the World Bank's Operations Evaluation Department. Previously he held positions at the U.S. General Accounting Office and the U.S. Department of Health, Education and Welfare. He was Director of the Center for Policy Studies at George Washington University's Graduate School of Education and Human Development, and he has taught at George Washington University, Johns Hopkins University, Cornell University, and Portland State University.

Rist's influence in evaluation is wide and deep. His work has been influential in the development of evaluation within the public sector. His work has focused on issues of governance, policy implementation, policy tools, and public sector management strategies. He has also made substantial contributions as an education policy expert. His contributions in evaluation and the public sector are reflected in the many publications he has authored and coauthored (25 books and more than 125 articles), such as the *International Atlas of Evaluation; Carrots, Sticks and Sermons: Policy Instruments and Their Evaluation;* and *Program Evaluation and the Management of Government.* His long-standing work on educational policy is marked by a number of works, including *Restructuring American Education; Desegregating Schools: Appraisals of an American Experiment; Invisible Children;* and the recently reissued *The Urban School: A Factory for Failure.*

In his evaluation work, Rist has contributed to the legitimacy and expansion of qualitative methods in evaluation. He has also had a substantial impact around the world as a consequence of his work designing and building results-based monitoring and evaluation systems in many developing countries. He has contributed to the development of better governmental evaluation in the United States by twice being a member of teams that have built federal evaluation centers, once for the General Accounting Office and earlier for the Department of Health, Education and Welfare.

Rist was a senior Fulbright Fellow at the Max Planck Institute in Berlin (1976-1977). He received the GAO Comptroller General's Special Award, and he has received the Medal of Merit from the French parliament. He demonstrates his enthusiasm for baseball as a member of the Stan Musial Society.

▟▜ RIVAL INTERPRETATIONS

Rival interpretations, a term often used in qualitative inquiry, include disconfirming cases, "exceptions that prove the rule," and competing explanations. These are interpretations or explanations of a case that challenge the findings of its analysis. Once an evaluator has described a case and its patterns, themes, and plausible explanations, it is important to look for other possible ways to explain the findings and the meaning of those findings. This means looking for other ways of organizing the case and the data toward new interpretations or digging for plausible counterinterpretations and the data to support them.

—*Leslie K. Goodyear*

▟▜ ROG, DEBRA J.

(b. 1956, New Bedford, Massachusetts). Ph.D. Social Psychology, Vanderbilt University; M.A. Social Psychology, Kent State University; B.S. American International College.

Rog is Senior Research Associate in Vanderbilt University's Institute for Public Policy Studies and Director of the Center for Mental Health Policy in Washington, DC. She has more than 20 years of experience in program evaluation and applied research and has directed numerous multisite evaluations and research projects.

Her primary contribution to the theory of evaluation is to the study of evaluation itself, beginning with her dissertation, a study of evaluability assessment, for which she received the Robert Perloff President's Prize for Promising Evaluator from the Evaluation Research Society in 1985. She has continued to reflect on the practice of evaluation, especially with respect to conducting multisite evaluations and conducting research with hard-to-reach, vulnerable populations. Putting these ideas into practice, she has conducted private foundation and federally funded, large-scale, national, cross-site studies on program and system initiatives for homeless families and for homeless and domiciled individuals with serious

mental illness and on collaborations for violence prevention. Primary influences on her evaluation work include Donald Campbell and Carol Weiss, as well as Len Bickman and Terry Hedrick, with whom she was fortunate to have worked closely.

She has been actively involved in the American Evaluation Association, having served twice on its board; worked as Local Arrangements Chair for the 1990 meeting and Program Cochair for the 1996 meeting; and served on numerous committees, including chairing the awards committee for 3 years. She has also been involved in training practitioners, especially in developing and using logic models, performing case studies, and conducting research with hard-to-reach, vulnerable populations. She is a member of the American Psychological Association, the American Psychological Society, and the American Public Health Association.

She has written a number of articles on evaluation methods, edited several volumes of *New Directions for Evaluation,* and coedited the *Handbook of Applied Social Research Methods.* Since 1980, she has coedited the Applied Social Research Methods series of textbooks. She has been recognized by the Eastern Evaluation Research Society, the National Institute of Mental Health, the American Evaluation Association, and the Knowledge Utilization Society for her contributions to evaluation and applied research and by the *American Journal of Evaluation* for the evaluation of the Robert Wood Johnson Foundation/U.S. Department of Housing and Urban Development Homeless Families Program.

▟▜ ROGERS, PATRICIA J.

(b. 1961, Melbourne, Australia). Ph.D. Education Policy and Management, Graduate Diploma in Education, B.A. Political Science, University of Melbourne.

Rogers has been driven by both the promise of good evaluation and the threat of bad evaluation. She has been influenced by evaluation pioneers Carol Weiss, Michael Scriven, and Michael Patton, whose different approaches to evaluation form a useful counterbalance, and by Jerome Winston, an Australian evaluation pioneer in systems theory and organizational learning and in asking not, "Did it work?" but, "For whom, in what ways, and how did it work?" She was subsequently influenced by the work of realists, such as Tilley and Pawson (United Kingdom) and Henry, Mark, and Julnes (United States).

Rogers' contributions to evaluation theory and practice include the following:

1. Impact evaluation, especially using nonexperimental designs and program theory. She has used program theory since 1986 to guide the monitoring and evaluation of public sector programs, including maternal and child health projects, agricultural research and extension projects, and prisoner diversion programs, and she has written extensively on this, including the program theory chapter in *Evaluation Models: Viewpoints on Educational and Human Service Evaluation* (Madaus, Scriven, & Stufflebeam, Eds.) and a *New Directions in Evaluation* issue on program theory. Rogers is currently using program theory as a unifying conceptual framework for the national evaluation of approximately 800 projects funded through the Australian Federal Government's $225 million Stronger Families and Communities Strategy.

2. Performance monitoring and performance indicators, particularly learning from others' past experiences of difficulties in developing and using them

3. The impact of evaluation, including formal utilization of results and formal and informal impacts of the process

4. Evaluating approaches to program evaluation by articulating and empirically investigating the program theory of the approach, particularly how it is understood to contribute to better programs

5. Building the evaluation capability of public sector organizations through strategies such as thinking big and starting small and paying attention to both supply and demand issues in evaluation

6. Encouraging interdisciplinary and international contributions to evaluation theory and practice

Rogers has taught graduate courses in evaluation at Melbourne since 1989 and led workshops in evaluation in Australia, New Zealand, South Africa, Malaysia, and the United States. She is a foundation member of the Australasian Evaluation Society and a former member of its board. A former Editor of the AES magazine *Evaluation News and Comment,* she is also a former Chair of the American Evaluation Association Awards committee.

Rogers received the AES 2002 Evaluation Training and Services Award (its highest award) for outstanding contributions to the profession of evaluation and the AES Caulley-Tulloch Prize for Pioneering Evaluation Literature (with Gary Hough) for a paper linking organizational theory and program evaluation.

Married, with two handsome, blue-eyed, blond sons, Rogers lives in the beautiful Australian bush just outside Melbourne.

■■ ROSSI, PETER H.

(b. 1921, New York City). Ph.D. Sociology, Columbia University; B.S. Sociology, City College.

Rossi is Professor Emeritus of Sociology at the University of Massachusetts and has held appointments at Harvard; at the University of Chicago, where he was Director of the National Opinion Research Center; and at Johns Hopkins University.

Rossi is probably best known for his text *Evaluation: A Systematic Approach,* coauthored originally with Howard Freeman and, after Freeman's death in 1993, with Mark Lipsey. The first edition was published in 1979, and the seventh in 2003. Rossi's contributions to evaluation are much broader and are reflected in a score of published research monographs. Some examples are *Families Move* (1956), a panel study of the moving decisions of a sample of households; *The Education of Catholic Americans* (1962, with Andrew M. Greeley), which estimated the effects of attending Catholic schools on the adult occupational attainment of American Catholics; *The Roots of Urban Discontent* (1974, with Richard Berk and Bettye Eidson), an analysis of how the responses of elites in 15 major cities to the needs and discontents of African Americans affect race relations in those cities; *Money, Work and Crime* (1980, with Richard Berk and Kenneth Lenihan), a report on a large-scale, randomized experiment estimating the effects of short-term income support given to released felons on postrelease recidivism; *Down and Out in America* (1989), the social epidemiology of homelessness in Chicago; *Just Punishments* (1997, with Richard Berk), a comparison of the Federal Sentencing Guidelines to sentences desired by a national sample of Americans; and *Feeding the Poor* (1999), a synthesis of research on federal food programs for poor Americans.

Rossi participated in several evaluations of major social programs, including those reported in *Reforming*

Public Welfare (1976, with Katherine Lyall), which assessed the New Jersey-Pennsylvania Income Maintenance Experiment; *Evaluating Family Preservation* (1991), which assessed evaluations of family preservation programs; and *Four Evaluations of Welfare Reform: What Will Be Learned?* (2001), which assessed major evaluations of the current welfare program, Temporary Assistance to Needy Families.

Growing up in a bilingual working class family in the Great Depression was a powerful influence on Rossi's work as a social scientist and led to a strong concern for issues involving social justice and distributive equity. In his undergraduate years he was a Marxist, but he became a social democrat, a political belief system that melds democratic government, free enterprise, and social welfare public programs. His strong interest in applied social research led quite easily to his concentration on evaluation research.

In graduate school, Rossi was profoundly influenced by the teaching and role modeling of Robert K. Merton, who introduced him to advanced social theory and the importance of empirical evidence in the testing of social theory, and Paul F. Lazarsfeld and his view that the major function of social research in public policy formation and change was to evaluate the effectiveness of public programs. Lazarsfeld became Rossi's graduate school mentor and appointed him to the research staff of Columbia's Bureau of Applied Social Research. Rossi's view of evaluation as the assessment of the effectiveness of social programs has been strongly influenced by the works of Donald T. Campbell, Lee Cronbach, and Michael Scriven.

While in graduate school at Columbia University, Rossi met and married Alice S. Kitt, a fellow graduate student. Although their scholarly interests were different, they were complementary, and Rossi considers Alice to be in many ways the better social scientist.

Rossi has won numerous awards, including the American Evaluation Association's Myrdal Award in 1981.

▞ RUGH, JIM

(b. 1941, Ithaca, New York). M.S., B.S. Agricultural Engineering, University of Tennessee; M.P.S. International Agricultural and Rural Development (participatory evaluation emphasis), Cornell University.

Rugh is Coordinator of Program Design, Monitoring and Evaluation for CARE International. His work at CARE International includes providing guidance and support to CARE and partner staff in 80 countries to strengthen their capacity for improved project design, more systematic monitoring systems, and better quality and more useful evaluations. Prior to joining CARE in 1995, he had his own consultancy service for 11 years, during which time he evaluated the international development programs of many NGOs.

He has more than 39 years of involvement in development work in Africa, Asia, and Appalachia, 23 of those years as a specialist in evaluation. This has included long-term residence in India, Senegal, Togo, and the United States, as well as frequent travel to many other countries.

He has been an especially active member of the American Evaluation Association's International and Cross-Cultural TIG. He received a Certificate of Appreciation "in recognition of many years of generous service to the International and Cross-Cultural Evaluation Topical Interest Group, American Evaluation Association" in 2002. Rugh was Chair of AEA's Nominations and Elections Committee in 2004. He is the leader of InterAction's Monitoring and Evaluation Interest Group, including the annual PVO Evaluators' Roundtable, and a founding member of the Atlanta-Area Evaluation Association.

▞ RUSSON, CRAIG W.

(b.1958, Moab, Utah). Ph.D. Vocational and Technical Education, M.A. Educational Psychology, University of Illinois, Urbana-Champaign; M.B.A., St. Ambrose University; B.A. Psychology, Utah State University.

Russon is Evaluation Manager with the W. K. Kellogg Foundation. He was a Peace Corps volunteer in Chile and Honduras between 1981 and 1983.

He has worked with many others, both within and outside the American Evaluation Association, to establish the International Organization for Cooperation in Evaluation (IOCE), a loose coalition of 45 regional and national evaluation organizations around the world. He is known within the American Evaluation Association for his establishing the Silent Auction, AEA Travel Grants, and the Book Exchange. He created and comanages XCeval (a listserv for persons interested in international and cross-cultural evaluation issues) and the International and Cross-Cultural Evaluation TIG Web site (http://home.wmis.net/~russon/icce/). Russon is Coeditor (along with Karen Russon) of *The Annotated Bibliography of International Program Evaluation.*

Russon is on the Board of Directors of the American Evaluation Association and the Michigan Association for Evaluation, one of AEA's 13 state and regional affiliates. He has worked to decentralize AEA's governance structure by transferring some of its decision-making power to the affiliates, which makes it possible to expand the market for evaluation products and services at the grassroots level.

⊞ RYAN, KATHERINE E.

(b. 1950, Dixon, Illinois). Ph.D. Educational Psychology, M.Ed. Special Education, B.S. Psychology, University of Illinois, Urbana-Champaign.

Ryan is Associate Professor of Educational Psychology at the University of Illinois, Urbana-Champaign. Before joining the Educational Psychology Department, she was Head of the University of Illinois Internal Evaluation Unit at Urbana-Champaign for 10 years.

Situated at the intersection between theory and practice, the majority of her research on evaluation is devoted to democratizing evaluation practice. In addition to framing conceptual issues, she has used work from two substantive areas in evaluation (family literacy evaluation and the evaluation of teaching) to illustrate how inclusive evaluation approaches, including democratically oriented evaluation, could be used for democratizing evaluation. Her empirical studies have elaborated existing theory in democratically oriented evaluation. Her current work looks at how description and practice may be used to inform evaluation theory.

She has authored or coauthored articles, chapters, and volumes on evaluation, including an issue on democratically oriented evaluation approaches in *New Directions in Evaluation* (with Lizanne DeStefano). She coedits a book series, Evaluation and Society, with Thomas A. Schwandt. The inaugural volume in the series, *Exploring Evaluator Role and Identity,* was published in 2003. Ryan serves on the editorial boards of *New Directions in Evaluation* and the *American Journal of Evaluation* and has served on the American Evaluation Association Board of Directors.

SAMPLING

Sampling is the process of selecting units for study that will be representative of a population so that one can make generalizations about that population. A key distinction in sampling is between the theoretical population and the accessible population. Often the theoretical population is not known or could be known only with great cost and difficulty, but the accessible population is one that is more delimited and that the evaluator can with confidence identify and thus select from. Samples can be selected randomly, purposively, or accidentally. Random, or probability, sampling involves a prespecified set of procedures for selection and may be simple, stratified, clustered, or combined into a multistage sampling plan. Purposive sampling begins with an interest in a particular group—the evaluator chooses units based on the purpose of the evaluation, although precautions to verify the extent to which the sample actually reflects the population characteristics of interest are necessary. Some types of purposive sampling are the *expert* and *snowball* techniques. Sampling may also be done based on convenience, and therefore the inclusion of certain units is, in a sense, accidental. How sampling is done depends on the purpose of the evaluation.

—*Jeffrey G. Tucker*

Further Reading

Trochim, W. (2000). *The research methods knowledge base* (2nd ed.). Cincinnati, OH: Atomic Dog.

SANDERS, JAMES R.

(b. 1944, Williamsport, Pennsylvania). Ph.D. Research and Evaluation Methodology, University of Colorado; M.S.Ed. Educational Research, B.A. Chemistry, Bucknell University.

Sanders is Professor Emeritus at Western Michigan University and was on the faculty at Indiana University where he helped to create their first evaluation program. Before he came to the Evaluation Center at WMU to assist Dan Stufflebeam with its development, serving also as the center's Associate Director, Sanders was an evaluator for the Northwest Regional Educational Laboratory. He worked extensively with foundations and community-based organizations, including the W. K. Kellogg Foundation and the United Way of America.

Sanders is a coauthor (along with Blaine Worthen and Jody Fitzpatrick) of one of the most popular evaluation textbooks, *Program Evaluation: Alternative Approaches and Practical Guidelines,* now in its third edition. Sanders also chaired the Joint Committee on Standards for Educational Evaluation from 1988 to 1998. The committee has written program evaluation standards (*The Program Evaluation Standards: How to Assess Evaluations of Educational Programs*), including a revision in 1994, which have become a common means for judging the quality of evaluation itself. *The Program Evaluation Standards* presents, explains, and illustrates 30 standards to provide a guide for evaluating educational and training programs, projects, and materials in a variety of settings. Sanders' work has been directed at practitioners and aimed at improving evaluation practice. His book *Evaluating School Programs: An Educator's Guide* (now in its second edition) is an example of this focus.

His muses and intellectual influences are Campbell and Stanley, Egon Guba, Ayn Rand, Michael Scriven, Robert Stake, and Dan Stufflebeam.

Sanders has also dedicated his time to the profession of evaluation. He was a founding member of the Evaluation Network, one of the organizations that merged to form the American Evaluation Association. He has been a board member and President of AEA and received the Friend of Evaluation Award from the Michigan Association for evaluation. As President of AEA, Sanders created the Public Affairs Program and promoted evaluators' participation in public policy debates. He supported the first AEA Public Affairs Task Force on High Stakes Testing, and was a member of the task force. He has been recognized with the Distinguished Service Award from Western Michigan University.

■ SCHEIRER, MARY ANN

(b. 1941, Akron, Ohio). Ph.D. Sociology, Cornell University; M.A. Sociology, State University of New York at Binghamton; M.A. Public and International Affairs, University of Pittsburgh; B.A. Sociology and History, College of Wooster.

Scheirer is Senior Program Officer for Evaluation, Robert Wood Johnson Foundation. Her previous positions have included Independent Consultant; Adjunct Faculty Member, Department of Public Administration, George Washington University; Social Science Analyst, U.S. General Accounting Office; and Senior Study Director, Westat, Inc. Before entering the evaluation field, she was a Peace Corps volunteer in the Philippines. Scheirer is a sociologist and health services researcher with more than 20 years experience in applied social research, with an emphasis on evaluating health and human services intervention programs.

Her primary contributions to the field of evaluation have been to open the "black box" of programs being evaluated by developing tools to describe program components and to measure the extent and types of program implementation, particularly focusing on process assessment of community health programs. Her work has been influenced by Donald Campbell, especially his application of evolutionary theory from biology to evaluation: Generate program variations, try them out to see which ones work to fill a needed niche, multiply and disseminate successful adaptations.

Scheirer is the author of *Program Implementation: The Organizational Context* and Editor of two issues of *New Directions for Evaluation,* "A User's Guide to Program Templates" and "Guiding Principles for Evaluators" (coedited with William R. Shadish, Dianna Newman, and Chris Wye).

She is active in the American Evaluation Association, American Public Health Association, Washington Evaluators, and American Sociological Association, with numerous presentations at professional conferences. She has served on the Board of Directors of the American Evaluation Association and was a member of the Task Force on Developing Ethical Principles for Evaluators. She has also served as President and currently serves as Treasurer of Washington Evaluators. She is the winner of the 1999 American Evaluation Association's President's Prize for best paper.

■ SCHWANDT, THOMAS A.

(b. 1948, Chicago, Illinois). Ph.D. Inquiry Methodology, Indiana University, Bloomington; B.A. English Literature, Valparaiso University.

Schwandt is Professor of Education in the Division of Quantitative and Evaluative Research Methodologies of the Department of Educational Psychology and affiliated faculty in the Unit for Criticism and Interpretive Theory at the University of Illinois, Urbana-Champaign. Previously he held faculty positions in the Department of Medical Education, College of Medicine, University of Illinois, Chicago, and the School of Education, Indiana University, Bloomington; served as part-time Research Professor at the National Center for Comprehensive Rehabilitation Research and Development, Bodø, Norway, and visiting faculty at Roskilde University, Denmark. He has lectured and taught extensively throughout Norway, Sweden, and Denmark.

His primary contributions to the field of evaluation center on exploring the relevance of practical hermeneutics for the theory and practice of evaluation and for reuniting moral, political, and technical evaluation discourses. His work has also contributed considerably to the clarification of philosophical assumptions underlying various forms of qualitative or interpretive methodologies used in evaluation. Primary influences on his evaluation work include Egon Guba, Robert Stake, and Ernest House, and the work of Lee Cronbach, Carol Weiss, and Donald Campbell has been influential as well. More broadly, the primary intellectual influences for his scholarship are Hans-Georg Gadamer, Charles Taylor, and Richard J. Bernstein.

He is the author of the *Dictionary of Qualitative Inquiry, Evaluation Practice Reconsidered, Evaluating Holistic Rehabilitation Praxis,* and *Linking Auditing and Metaevaluation* (with Edward Halpern). With K. E. Ryan, he has edited *Exploring Evaluator Role and Identity* and with P. Haug, *Evaluating Educational Reform: Scandinavian Perspectives.* The recipient of several teaching awards and a member of the editorial boards of *New Directions for Evaluation,* the *American Journal of Evaluation,* and *Qualitative Inquiry,* he received the American Evaluation Association Paul F. Lazarsfeld Award in 2002 for his contributions to evaluation theory.

■■ SCORE CARD

A *score card* is a system of recording performance, usually statistics. The score card is primarily meant to provide descriptive information, although it may also be an impetus for improvement. A baseball score card, for example, builds a system of descriptive information about the performance of individual players, the team, select positions, and so on that can be used to describe the game but may also suggest comparative performance. For example, recording pitches and then comparing that across the game with how deep in the pitch count hits occur provides an indicator of the pitchers' performance. Score cards are used often in business and industry for strategic management and improvement and are sometimes referred to as the balanced score card.

■■ SCRIVEN, MICHAEL

(b. 1928, in Beaulieu, Hampshire, England). Ph.D. Philosophy, Oxford University; M.A. combined honors Mathematics and Philosophy, Melbourne University, Australia; B.A. honors Mathematics, Melbourne University.

Scriven is Professor of Philosophy at Western Michigan University and was recently Chair in Evaluation at Auckland University, New Zealand. Previously he held faculty positions at the University of Minnesota; Swarthmore University; Indiana University; the University of California, Berkeley; the University of San Francisco; the University of Western Australia; Pacific Graduate School of Psychology; and Claremont Graduate University. He has taught in departments of philosophy, psychology, mathematics, the history and philosophy of science, and education. He is a former President of AERA and was the first president of one of the two organizations that merged to become the American Evaluation Association. He was also the 1999 President of AEA, as well as Founding Editor of its journal *Evaluation Practice* (now the *American Journal of Evaluation*). He has been a Fellow of the Center for Advanced Study in the Behavioral Sciences of Palo Alto, a Whitehead Fellow at Harvard, and a Senior AERA Fellow in Evaluation at the National Science Foundation.

His contributions to the field of evaluation are many. He has influenced the field through (a) the creation of discipline-specific terminology, including the terms *formative* and *summative evaluation, holistic* (versus analytic) evaluation, and *component* (versus dimensional) evaluation, as well as such terms as *metaevaluation, goal-free* (and *goal-based*) evaluation, *the synthesis step,* and *the evaluative imperative;* (b) the creation of new ways of thinking about evaluation models, such as the idea that goal-based evaluation represents a management approach and bias quite different from needs-based evaluation, which is consumer oriented, and that evaluation is an autonomous discipline, as well as a vital component of all other disciplines; and (c) the idea that evaluation in all domains is an application of the same basic logic, which has contributed to the beginnings of a logic of evaluation.

He has written extensively on the philosophy of science, particularly about the logic of science, causal inference and explanation, and values in science. He is the author of more than 300 publications, including such books as *The Logic of Evaluation* and *Evaluation Thesaurus* (now in its fourth edition). He has served on the editorial boards of 36 journals in 10 fields, as well as being Editor of six, including two on microcomputers.

He is the recipient of many awards and prizes, including the 1986 American Evaluation Association

Paul F. Lazarsfeld Award for contributions to evaluation theory, the 2001 American Evaluation Association Robert Ingle Award, the Policy Studies Association Donald Campbell Award as an "outstanding methodological innovator in public policy studies," the Jason Millman Award for lifetime contribution to evaluation awarded by CREATE, and the McKeachie Award for lifetime contribution to faculty evaluation.

■■ SECONDARY ANALYSIS

Secondary analysis involves the use of existing data, collected for the purposes of a prior study, to pursue a research or evaluation interest distinct from the original study. Although secondary analysis is most commonly used when quantitative data have been collected, qualitative data can also serve for secondary analysis. This strategy is frequently used when large data sets are available, sometimes in the public domain, such as (for example) the Trends in International Mathematics and Science Study data set of student achievement in mathematics in many countries around the world. Other examples are the National Assessment of Educational Progress and the Youth Tobacco Survey. Secondary analysis differs from research syntheses and meta-analyses, which compile and assess the evidence relating to a common construct, topic, or area of practice. Although not a common strategy in evaluation, secondary analysis of existing data can provide answers to some evaluative questions, and occasionally secondary analyses of data collected for a program evaluation may be done. The latter may be in the context of a metaevaluation or simply to corroborate evaluative conclusions or ask new evaluative questions. Secondary analysis is, of course, dependent on the availability of data sets.

SELECTION BIAS. *See* SAMPLING

■■ SERVICES

Services are the group of specific activities and resources provided to a target population, the quality of which is often the focus of an evaluation.

—*Jeffrey G. Tucker*

■■ SETTING

Setting is the specific context in which an evaluation is conducted, including both the physical location (the country and region, the city and neighborhood, the building, and the rooms where activities occur) and the institutional or organizational context (the type of organization, the relationships between and among participants, people's previous evaluation experiences, etc.). Setting can also involve physical, social, political, and psychological factors that might influence the program, as well as conducive and distracting influences present in the environment.

—*Jean A. King*

See also SOCIAL CONTEXT

■■ SHADISH, WILLIAM R.

(b. 1949, Brooklyn, New York). Ph.D., M.S. Clinical Psychology, Purdue University; B.A. Sociology, Santa Clara University.

Shadish is Professor and a Founding Faculty Member at the University of California, Merced. He was Dunavant University Professor of Psychology at the University of Memphis, where he became part of the faculty in 1981. He was also Director of the Research Design and Statistics Program in the Department of Psychology and Director, Center for Applied Psychological Research, from 1990 to 1997.

He is known for his work on program evaluation theory, especially in *Foundations of Program Evaluation* (coauthored with Tom Cook and Laura Leviton), as well as other works. *Foundations* was the first comprehensive effort at articulating a theory of program evaluation theory. In it, the authors suggest that evaluation practice is driven by four key theoretical issues: how knowledge is constructed, the role that values play in evaluation, how evaluation knowledge is used, and how social programs function and change. Shadish's contributions to methodology and design in evaluation are demonstrated in the updated *Experimental and Quasi-Experimental Designs for Generalized Causal Inference* (with Tom Cook and the late Donald Campbell). This volume might be considered the third in a generation of some of the most influential texts in social science research and evaluation, each updating and expanding on its predecessors.

This latest volume introduces a theory of causal generalizations that responds to criticisms of the Campbell tradition's failure to deal adequately with external validity.

Shadish was a postdoctoral Fellow in Methodology and Evaluation Research in Northwestern University's Department of Psychology from 1978 to 1981. His connection with Northwestern and Tom Cook, as well as with the work of Don Campbell, are strong influences on his work in methodology and program evaluation. Larry Hedges' meta-analysis work has also been influential for him.

Shadish has made substantial contributions to the professions of evaluation and psychology. He has been President of the American Evaluation Association (1997), Editor of *New Directions for Program Evaluation* (1992-1995), and Chair of the American Evaluation Association Task Force on the Development of Guiding Principles for Evaluators (1992-1994). In this position, he helped to develop AEA's ethical code for evaluators.

His scholarship and service to the profession and community have been repeatedly recognized. He has received the Outstanding Research Publication Award, American Association for Marriage and Family Therapy (1994); Paul F. Lazarsfeld Award for Evaluation Theory, American Evaluation Association (1994); Outstanding Research Publication Award, American Association for Marriage and Family Therapy (1996); James McKeen Cattell Fund Sabbatical Award (1996-1997); Robert Ingle Service Award, American Evaluation Association (2000); Catherine Rivers Johnson Award (in recognition of service helping children), Memphis Beat the Odds Foundation (2000); and the Donald T. Campbell Award for Innovations in Methodology, Policy Studies Organization (2002). Shadish is a Fellow of the American Psychological Association and the American Psychological Society.

▪▪ SHULHA, LYN M.

Ph.D. Educational Evaluation, University of Virginia; M.Ed. Curriculum and Instruction, Queen's University, Canada; Ed.Dip. Physical Education and Guidance, University of Western Ontario; B.P.E. Physical Education, B.A. Sociology, McMaster University.

Shulha is Associate Professor of Evaluation, Planning and Assessment in the Faculty of Education at Queen's University, Canada. Previous positions include Program Evaluator for the University of Virginia's Evaluation Research Center and Teacher and Department Head with Ontario's Superior-Greenstone District School Board. Shulha's work in evaluation research and practice continues to be fueled by the pragmatic concerns of program personnel, school organizations, and classroom teachers. She finds herself aligned with a number of evaluators whose primary interest is evaluation use. Her fidelity to principles of evaluation use has led her to be a strong advocate of mixed-methods inquiry, including evaluative inquiry. She has contributed to the collective knowledge about the nature of collaboration in mixed-methods research and, in particular, collaboration as mixed-methods research. This orientation informs her continuing research around critical elements and the power of university and school professional learning partnerships. It is through such partnerships that Shulha is able to pursue a parallel research agenda that focuses on the complexity of classroom and large-scale assessment practices. Influences on her evaluation work include Michael Patton, Marvin Alkin, Bradley Cousins, Hallie Preskill, and Robert Wilson.

She is the author of several articles, reports, and book chapters, including "Collaborative Mixed-Method Research" (with R. J. Wilson) in *Handbook of Mixed Methodology* (Tashakkori & Teddlie, Eds.). She is also Section Coeditor for *Who Will Teach?* (Upitis, Sr. Ed.) and a major contributor to a special section on classroom assessment investigations that was published in the *Alberta Journal of Educational Research*. Shulha serves on the editorial boards of the *American Journal of Evaluation* and the *Canadian Journal of Program Evaluation*. She was recently appointed to the Joint Committee on Standards for Evaluation as a representative of the Canadian Society for the Study of Education, and she is Director of the Assessment and Evaluation Group, Faculty of Education, Queen's University. She received a Recognition Award in 2001 from the American Evaluation Association for her work as Associate Editor of the *American Journal of Evaluation*. In 1996, the Concurrent Education Student Association, Faculty of Education, Queens University, presented her with an Award of Appreciation for her teaching and commitment to the Concurrent Program.

SIDE EFFECTS. *See* Outcomes

∷ SIGNIFICANCE

Statistical significance is a mathematical procedure for determining whether a null hypothesis can be rejected at a given alpha level. Tests of statistical significance play a large role in quantitative research designs but are frequently misinterpreted. The most common misinterpretation of the test of significance is to confuse statistical significance with the practical significance of the research results. Other indexes need to be calculated in each study to set statistical significance in proper perspective. Effect size measures, for example, is a valuable tool that estimates the magnitude of the difference, relationship, or effect in the population being studied.

—*Marco A. Muñoz*

Further Reading

Cohen, J. (1988). *Statistical power analysis for the behavioral sciences* (2nd ed.). Hillsdale, NJ: Lawrence Erlbaum.

Gall, M. D., Gall, J. P., & Borg, W. R. (2003). *Educational research: An introduction* (7th ed.). Boston: Allyn & Bacon.

∷ SIMONS, HELEN

(b. South Island, New Zealand). Ph.D., University of East Anglia, Norwich, England; B.A., University of Melbourne, Australia; Diploma of Education, Victoria University, Australia.

Trained as an educational psychologist in Melbourne, Victoria, Simons emigrated to England in 1970, where she has resided ever since. Since 1992, she has been Professor of Education and Evaluation at the University of Southampton, United Kingdom. Her contributions to evaluation theory, practice, and the profession have addressed case study evaluation; program, policy and institutional self-evaluation in education and the health professions; and ethics and politics of evaluation.

Simons' inspirations stem from a commitment to democratic processes, creative arts in evaluation, justice and fairness, qualitative inquiry, ethical practice, and representing the complexity of human experience in evaluation. Her influences include all who have aspired to generate and sustain a culture of qualitative evaluation that makes a difference to professional practice and policy development.

She is an Academician of the Academy of the Learned Societies in the Social Sciences and has been Vice-President of the United Kingdom Evaluation Society (2003-2004); currently she serves as its President (2005-2006). She holds a Trained Teachers Certificate (Dist) from Dunedin Teachers College, New Zealand, and a London Certificate in the Arts and Therapy in Education.

∷ SITUATIONAL RESPONSIVENESS

Situational factors that affect evaluation design and use include program variables (e.g., size, complexity, history), evaluation purposes (formative, summative), evaluator experience and credibility, intended users, politics, and resource constraints. An evaluator demonstrates *situational responsiveness* when strategizing how various factors affect evaluation design and use. The implication is that no one best evaluation design exists; that is, no standardized cookie-cutter approach can be applied regardless of circumstances and context. The standards and principles of evaluation provide direction, but every evaluation is unique. Situational responsiveness involves negotiating and designing the evaluation to fit the specific, intended uses of the evaluation by particular intended users.

—*Michael Quinn Patton*

Further Reading

Patton, M. Q. (1997). *Utilization-focused evaluation.* Thousand Oaks, CA: Sage.

∷ SMITH, M. F.

(b. 1942, Altha, Florida). Ph.D. University of Maryland, College Park; M.Ed. University of Florida, Gainesville; B.S. Mississippi State University.

Smith is Professor Emerita, University of Maryland, and Director of the Evaluators' Institute (based in Delaware). She previously held faculty positions in the Colleges of Education, and Agriculture, University of Florida. She has directed evaluations in a variety of fields; for example, medicine and health, parks and recreation, agriculture, nutrition, family finance, youth development, public K-12 education, and university academic instruction.

Her interest in evaluation began in 1970, when she directed a project for the University of Florida Laboratory School to develop and test curricula for kindergarten through eighth grade. This project involved an evaluative component to determine whether the programs worked. However, at that time, evaluators were not available, only statisticians. As a result, Smith returned to school, studied research and evaluation, and began her career as an evaluator. Primary influences on her early evaluation work include Michael Scriven, Dan Stufflebeam, Michael Patton, Don Campbell, James Sanders, Robert Boruch, Lee Sechrest, and others.

Smith has contributed in many ways to the field of evaluation. Her work on evaluability assessment translated the concept to a set of practical methodological steps that built on the work of Wholey, Kay and Nay, Schmidt, and others. In 1984, Smith initiated a project to define the practical and methodological aspects of the EA process and to encourage its adoption in the U.S. Department of Agriculture's State Cooperative Extension Services. Through her work with five different state extension services, the methodology was refined and resulted in the publication of *Evaluability Assessment: A Practical Approach* (Kluwer, 1989).

She served on the Board of Directors of the American Evaluation Association for 10 years and is past Editor of *Evaluation Practice* (now the *American Journal of Evaluation*). It was under her leadership that this publication moved from a focus on "news" to become a peer-reviewed journal abstracted and indexed in a number of professional sources. She co-edited the *American Journal of Evaluation*'s special issue on the future of the evaluation profession and is also Editor of the Profession of Evaluation section of *The International Handbook on Educational Evaluation*. She organized a national symposium on evaluation in state Cooperative Extension Services, whose attendees formed the first AEA TIG, Extension Education Evaluation. She is the recipient of the 1994 Robert Ingle Award for Service from the American Evaluation Association. Smith has served on a number of national committees, notably the Government Auditing Standards Advisory Council, which was responsible for revising the U.S. General Accounting Office Government Auditing Standards.

In 1996, with the help of 20 national leaders in evaluation, she began The Evaluators' Institute™, an AEA-endorsed training institute that enables practicing evaluators to acquire evaluation knowledge and skills. More than 2100 different individuals from 49 U.S. states, the District of Columbia, and 65 countries and U.S. territories have studied evaluation topics over the course of the Institute's programs.

▉ SMITH, NICK L.

(b. 1946, Kirksville, Missouri). Ph.D. Educational Psychology, B.S., University of Illinois, Urbana; M.S., Illinois State University.

Smith was given a head start in the field of evaluation by his influential advisors at the University of Illinois, especially Tom Hastings, Ernie House, and Bob Stake. His thinking has also been heavily influenced by the writings of Michael Scriven and Donald Campbell, as well as a list of colleagues too long to include.

His early evaluation work included conducting large-scale evaluation studies at the Northwest Regional Educational Laboratory in Portland, Oregon (1973-1975), and evaluations of medical education at the University of Nebraska Medical Center (1975-1976). Returning to the Northwest Regional Educational Laboratory in 1976, Smith directed a multiyear, federally funded, research and development project to produce alternative evaluation methods for use by local school districts and state departments of education (1978-1985). Since 1985, he has been on the faculty of the Instructional Design, Development, and Evaluation Program in the School of Education at Syracuse University, where he continues his study and writing on evaluation theory, methods, and practice.

Evaluation theory and the methodology of applied social science and evaluation, especially investigative approaches, are the primary areas of Smith's research interest. He is especially interested in descriptive theories of evaluation and in advocating and conducting studies of actual evaluation practice to provide an empirical basis for the improvement of subsequent evaluation theory and practice. His approach to the study of investigative methods emphasizes their reliance on the fundamental aspects of all inquiry: the development of skills and procedures of knowledge, observation, reasoning, and intuition.

Smith has held numerous leadership positions in evaluation, including President of the Evaluation Network (1980), Chairperson of the Evaluation

Section of Division 18 of the American Psychological Association (1985-1986), and President of the Research on Evaluation Special Interest Group of the American Educational Research Association (1987-1988). In the American Evaluation Association, he served as President of the Theories of Evaluation Topical Interest Group, two terms on the Board of Directors (1988-1991 and 1999-2001), and as President of AEA (2004). During this time, he also served on the editorial boards of a half dozen evaluation journals, including serving as Editor-in-Chief of *New Directions for Program Evaluation* (1988-1992).

His research and service have been recognized through such awards as the Distinguished Research Award from the Association of Teacher Educators (1984), the Distinguished Service Award (1987) and Special Achievement Award (1993) from Division 18 of the American Psychological Association, and the Robert B. Ingle Service Award (1991) from the American Evaluation Association.

■■ SOCIAL CLASS

A *class* identifies people as being members of a group based on some common attribute or circumstance. Although social scientists disagree upon a definition of *social class,* they agree that classes are not perceived to be equal in rank or social status. Hierarchy is evident in the terms most often used to identify class groups: *upper, middle, working,* and *lower.* Social class as defined by economic factors, such as wealth and occupation, appeared during the Industrial Revolution, when a new consciousness of the socially constructed nature of class emerged. The concept of class mobility was at the core of the 18th-century Enlightenment and shaped the role of research and evaluation in society. It was hoped that research and evaluation studies would point to the causes of social inequalities and identify interventions that would best redress them.

Class issues that are essentially issues of inequality in society affect the decisions made by evaluators. How class and class-related issues should be incorporated in evaluations has been widely contested. The two most influential theories of class are those of the political philosopher Karl Marx (1818-1883) and sociologist Max Weber (1864-1920). Their work has shaped the landscape of how class has been defined and analyzed in the social sciences. For Neo-Marxists,

class is an objective measure of one's relation to the means of production and a direct result of the structures of capitalism. Furthermore, a class is defined relationally: The behaviors and values of the lower classes are determined because of the practices and beliefs of the upper classes, and vice versa. Members of different classes not only have different interests; these are in conflict with each other. For these theorists, the presence of class is evidence of a deeply unjust and polarized social structure. Theorists influenced by Weber, on the other hand, view social class as a more subjective measure of a person's access to multiple economic processes, which include, among others, income and educational level, social status, and power. The interplay of these resources contributes to a person's "life chances" but does not determine his or her fate.

Class differences are created and maintained in our daily social practices, and these practices in turn are shaped by our perceptions of class. Evaluation can play an active role in understanding the formation of class values and beliefs and the relationship that the members of one class have to the others. Evaluators can take a "neutral" stance on class, treating class as one (albeit important) variable in determining the effectiveness of programs and policies (a choice that some say only serves the interests of the powerful), or they can place class relations and the social structures that shape them at the forefront in an attempt to bring to the surface those contradictions between the rhetoric of social practices and their actual effect on people. The decision to approach evaluation from one or the other position has clear political implications.

—*Melissa Freeman*

Further Reading

Burke, M. J. (1995). *The conundrum of class: Public discourse on the social order in America.* Chicago: University of Chicago Press.

House, E. R. (1993). *Professional evaluation: Social impact and political consequences.* Newbury Park, CA: Sage.

Milner, A. (1999). *Class.* Thousand Oaks, CA: Sage.

■■ SOCIAL CONTEXT

The concept of *social context* focuses on the broader social and political environment surrounding an evaluation, emphasizing the circumstances surrounding programs and grounding them in a general way within the society in which their activities take place. Social context may locate programs historically, philosophically, geographically, or culturally. It contrasts with a program's institutional or organizational context, which focuses on the organization in which the evaluation takes place.

—*Jean A. King*

See also SETTING

SOCIAL INDICATORS

Social indicators are measurements taken over time to track the course of a social problem; for example, school dropout rates or teen pregnancy rates. Social indicators are usually statistics, often longitudinal, that provide a picture of where a society or collective stands with respect to social values and goals. They can be social facts, such as unemployment rate or perinatal mortality rate, or more subjective, such as job satisfaction or happiness. Two common purposes for developing social indicators are to monitor social change and to measure the public welfare. Social indicator research is relatively recent, having become most formalized only in the mid-1960s. In the United States, the development of social indicators was born of concerns about the impact of the American space program on American society. The NASA project concluded that there was an almost complete lack of adequate data and methodology for determining the impact. Many organizations (for example, the Centers for Disease Control, OECD, United Nations) generate social indicator data (typically through surveys) that can be used in evaluation.

—*Jeffrey G. Tucker*

SOCIAL JUSTICE

The principles of social justice are used to assess whether the distribution of benefits and burdens among members (or groups) of a society are appropriate, fair, and moral. The substance of such assessments usually consists of arguments about the concepts of rights, deserts, or needs. When applied to society as a whole, the term *social justice* pertains to whether the institutions of a society are arranged to produce appropriate, fair, and moral distributions of benefits and burdens among societal members and groups. As such, social justice is linked directly to the evaluation of social and educational programs, policies, and personnel because these entities, and their evaluations, directly affect the distribution of benefits and burdens. Of course, there are competing conceptions of social justice within liberal democratic societies, and social justice remains a controversial topic in evaluation.

In spite of the conceptual link between social justice and evaluation, social justice concerns are often omitted from evaluation discussions. There are at least two reasons for this. First, evaluators are not well versed in philosophy or political science and often feel unprepared to discuss such concepts. Many evaluators have had methodological training that does not deal with social justice issues. Second, and more important, social justice concerns have long been excluded from social science research for political reasons. In her history of the origins of American social science, Dorothy Ross documented how social justice concerns were indeed topics of discussion in the social sciences during the early 20th century. However, several "Red scare" episodes stemming from fears of Marxism swept the United States and intimidated many social researchers. Some prominent economists and sociologists were dismissed from their university positions for supporting labor unions, child labor laws, and other social policies opposed by university boards of trustees, who came mostly from business backgrounds.

The result was that mainstream social scientists retreated from issues that might be seen as politically risky into concerns about research methodology. If social researchers could be persecuted for taking stands on political and "values" issues, they would be safe if they focused on which tests of statistical significance to employ or what sampling procedures to use, issues of no interest to politicians or boards of trustees. Those social researchers who remained concerned about social justice issues were relegated to the fringes of their disciplines for being too political. Social science in other countries had different origins, differences reflected in different discourses today.

This shift into safer political waters was bolstered intellectually by the ascendant philosophy of science called logical positivism, which endorsed "values-free" research. Values-free social science became the accepted research dogma. In the view of the logical positivists and those influenced by them (knowingly or unknowingly), values were not researchable. Only entities that could be confirmed by direct reference to "facts" were appropriate for scientific research. Facts were one domain and values quite another. In this view, values were emotions or political stances or projections of feelings. Because they were nonrational, value positions simply had to be accepted or rejected.

Later historic, philosophical, and sociological investigations into the nature of scientific inquiry proved that this positivist view of facts was incorrect. It was not possible to compare concepts and theories directly with the facts because one's view of the facts was determined by one's concepts and theories to begin with, even in science. The primacy of facts doctrine was revised to one that compared propositions (beliefs) to the existing corpus of beliefs. Sometimes the new scientific claim had to be changed, and sometimes the corpus of beliefs had to be changed, but theory confirmation consisted of comparing the belief in question to other beliefs, not to pristine facts (called nonfoundationalism).

Nonetheless, the positivist interpretation of values continued unchanged among social scientists, even among those who had grasped the nature of the new nonfoundationalism. Perhaps this attitude toward values reflected the political climate of the Cold War, the time period during which these changes occurred. Research methodology remained the focus of social scientists in the United States. The origins of American social science were forgotten, and young social researchers inherited concepts of values-free science. For many evaluators, social justice issues still retain nuances of illegitimacy.

The dominance of values-free social research meant that the conceptions of social justice embraced by politicians would be accepted without challenge in the evaluation of social programs and policies (except for those researchers at the fringes). For much of the 20th century, the utilitarian conception of justice prevailed, identified with one of its main formulators, John Stuart Mill. Utilitarianism is captured in the phrase "the greatest good for the greatest number," although it is a more sophisticated philosophy than such a slogan implies. The way this theory played out in social policy and programs was that the overall benefits should be increased to the maximum. Society should be organized to maximize overall benefits. Hence, everyone could have more. How those benefits were distributed was not a major issue. When applied to social policies and programs, the nuances of utilitarian theory disappeared. The politics of "more for everyone" was more appealing than the politics of distribution. As implemented in social research practices, utilitarianism focused attention on outcomes. If the gross domestic product increases, that is good, regardless of how it is distributed. The presumption is that there is more to distribute, even if not everyone actually gets more. If an educational program increases overall test scores, the amount of the increase is the focus, regardless of the distribution of scores among individuals and groups, and sometimes regardless of how the gains are obtained. Quantitative outcome measures fit well into such a framework. Furthermore, the goals of social programs and policies, being value-laden, were not subject to rational or empirical analysis by evaluators. The goals had to be accepted. In a major reformulation of moral thinking in the 20th century, John Rawls challenged utilitarian theory with his "theory of justice," which was somewhat more egalitarian than utilitarianism. With sophisticated philosophical arguments (employing concepts such as "the veil of ignorance," "the minimax principle," and "reflective equilibrium"), Rawls proposed two major principles of justice by which to assess social arrangements. The first principle was that every citizen should have basic civil liberties and rights and that these rights were inviolate, regardless of circumstances. These individual rights and liberties closely resembled the U.S. Bill of Rights, as it turns out. There was little controversial about this first principle of justice.

The second principle of justice, sometimes called the "difference" principle, was controversial. Rawls argued for the distribution of benefits to count as significant, not only the overall level of benefits. Inequalities of economic fortune were permitted in the Rawlsian framework only if these inequalities helped the "least advantaged" people in society, defined as those with the fewest resources. For example, within the framework it was permissible to have medical doctors earn high fees if such financial inducements helped poor people, who would be the recipients of these medical services. Or, the least advantaged might be given preferred access to universities. Inequalities were permitted for the benefit of the least advantaged. When the two principles of justice conflicted, the first principle of individual liberties took precedence over the second principle of distribution. Hence, Rawls' theory was not strictly egalitarian, as some critics believe, because it did allow for significant inequalities in society. The Rawlsian theory shifted the focus to how the disadvantaged were treated, and in that sense it was more egalitarian than utilitarianism, which allowed trading off the benefits of the least advantaged (e.g., the unemployed) if such a move increased the overall level of benefits for society as a whole.

Utilitarianism required actively manipulating social arrangements to maximize benefits, and Rawlsian justice also required manipulating social arrangements but, unlike utilitarianism, placed constraints on the shape that the distribution of benefits could take. In particular, social arrangements should be designed to tend toward equality in the distribution of benefits. The effects of circumstances that are arbitrary from a moral point of view (for example, who one's parents happen to be) should be mitigated to this end, and at the expense of maximizing benefits, if necessary. Distributions resulting from the operation of markets must be held in check if those distributions are unjust according to the second principle. (A third theory of justice regards any distribution that results from free markets as socially just, no matter what that distribution looks like or what effect it has. The interplay of free markets determines social outcomes. This is called libertarianism.)

Following Rawls, some evaluators applied his theory to evaluation, arguing that evaluators should be concerned not only with overall test score gains but how test score gains were distributed among groups, for example. How social benefits were distributed was important for evaluation. In addition, evaluators might have to solicit the views of stakeholders, those involved in the programs and policies, to determine what social benefits were at issue. Qualitative studies soliciting stakeholder views were called for. Of course, concerns about the distribution of benefits and calls for qualitative studies moved evaluators away from the values-free, quantitative methodology approaches that the social sciences had been nurturing for decades and that most evaluators accepted. Intense debates ensued within the evaluation community, debates usually phrased as disputes over qualitative and quantitative methods but actually encompassing broader issues. Eventually, concern about stakeholders permeated the evaluation literature, even seeping into quantitative studies, and an acceptance of multiple methods, multiple stakeholders, and multiple outcomes in evaluation studies prevailed, even among those who did not accept the Rawlsian concept of social justice.

Meanwhile, during the 1980s and 1990s, Rawls' theory of justice came under strong criticism from several perspectives. One criticism advanced by postmodernists was that this Rawlsian theory of liberal egalitarianism was insensitive to diverse group identities. In that sense, it could be oppressive and undemocratic. Rawlsian theory focused on economic inequalities with little regard for other benefits that people might deem valuable. The criticism was that liberal egalitarianism identifies the disadvantaged in terms of the relatively low economic benefits they possess and proposes eliminating these disadvantages by implementing compensatory social programs.

Typically, this planning and evaluation process is conceived as requiring little or no input from those most affected by these programs and policies. Liberal egalitarianism assumed that both the benefits to be distributed and the procedures by which the distribution would occur were uncontroversial. In fact, the defined benefits might reflect only the interests of those in dominant positions already. For example, consider a highly sexist curriculum with which girls, but not boys, have great difficulty. It is not a solution to provide only girls with help in mastering this curriculum so as to remove their disadvantage. The problem lies also with the sexist curriculum. The distributivist paradigm implied a top-down, expert-driven view. Investigators looked for maldistributions of social benefits, defined group needs, and formulated policies and practices, all in the name of equality. The views of the beneficiaries could be ignored. Many critics saw such an approach as too paternalistic.

In response to these criticisms, especially from feminists and ethnic minorities, philosophers revised the Rawlsian egalitarian theory of justice to take diverse identities into account and change the theory, moving the focus away from equality as a principle of distribution and more toward equality as a principle of democratic participation. In what might be called the "participatory paradigm," the requirements of distributive justice and those of democracy were intertwined. Justice required giving all stakeholders an effective voice in defining their own needs and negotiating their benefits, particularly members of groups that had been excluded historically. Participatory democracy is a popular topic in the current philosophical and political science literature. This shifting conception of social justice had implications for evaluation. The participatory paradigm fit views of evaluation in which equality was sought not solely in the distribution of predetermined benefits but in the status and voice of the participants themselves. Benefits, along with needs, policies, and practices, were to be examined and negotiated. Democratic functioning became an overarching ideal. Several evaluation approaches now advocate giving stakeholders roles to play in the evaluation itself, although evaluators differ on what roles participants should play. (It should be noted that many evaluators who endorse participatory approaches in evaluation do so for reasons other than social justice. They may do so for the purposes of utilization, believing that engaging participants in the evaluation will lead to better implementation of evaluation findings. They do not necessarily endorse a participatory theory of justice or an egalitarian theory of democracy.) In general, social justice continues to be a controversial topic in evaluation for historical and political reasons.

—*Ernest R. House*

See also Democratic Evaluation, Deliberative Democratic Evaluation, Participatory Evaluation

Further Reading

House, E. R. (1980). *Evaluating with validity.* Beverly Hills, CA: Sage.

Greene, J., Lincoln, Y. S., Mathison, S., Mertens, D. M., & Ryan, K. (1998). Advantages and challenges of using inclusive evaluation approaches in evaluation practice. *American Journal of Evaluation, 19*(1), 101-122.

▟ SPONSOR

The *sponsor* is the person, agency, or organization responsible for initiating an evaluation; often the primary funder of evaluation activities.

—*Jeffrey G. Tucker*

▟ STAKE, ROBERT E.

(b. 1927, Adams, Nebraska). Ph.D. Psychometrics, Princeton University; M.A., B.A., University of Nebraska.

Stake is Emeritus Professor of Education and Director of the Center for Instructional Research and Curriculum Evaluation (CIRCE) at the University of Illinois. Previously, he held faculty positions at

Teachers College University of Nebraska, where he did research on testing, instruction, television teaching, and teaching machines, becoming Faculty Research Coordinator in 1962; the University of Connecticut; Central State College of Washington; Harvard University; the University of British Columbia; Universidad do Espirito Santo; the University of East Anglia; and Simon Fraser University. He has presented workshops and seminars at numerous other universities. He was a Fulbright Fellow in Sweden in 1973 and in Brazil in 1984. He has been active in the American Educational Research Association, holding the highest office of two divisions there: Division B, Curriculum and Objectives, and Division D, Testing and Research Design. He helped start the meetings of the May 12 Group and was Associate Director of the Illinois Statewide Testing Program under J. Thomas Hastings.

Stake's contributions to the field of evaluation are many. He participated in the organization of the Evaluation Research Society and the Evaluation Network, which later merged to become the American Evaluation Association. He has been a leader in the development of what has been called "responsive evaluation," in which inquiry is focused on issues experienced by educators, sponsors, and students in a particular program context. The techniques of ethnography, case study, and investigative reporting have been prominent in his work, in addition to the traditional psychometric data gathering of testing, surveying, and attitude scaling. He describes his field study as predominantly interpretive, naturalistic, particularistic, and qualitative. CIRCE is widely recognized in educational research circles as a site for innovative designs of program evaluation and is visited by leading practitioners from around the world. Among the topics of the evaluative studies directed by Stake have been science and mathematics in U.S. elementary and secondary schools, education of the gifted and model art teaching, development of teaching with sensitivity to sex equity, education of teachers for the deaf, alternative teacher education, environmental education, the training of Veterans Affairs personnel, urban social services, and youth sports.

His doctoral dissertation, *Learning Curve Parameters, Aptitudes and Achievements,* was published as P*sychometric Monograph No. 9.* He is the author of books, articles, and reports, including *Quieting Reform,* a metaevaluation study of an urban youth program called Cities-in-Schools; *Custom and*

Cherishing: The Arts in American Elementary Schools (with Liora Bresler and Linda Mabry); *Case Studies in Science Education* (with Jack Easley); and two research methods books: *Evaluating the Arts in Education* and *The Art of Case Study Research*. In 1988, he received the Paul Lazarsfeld Award of the American Evaluation Association and, in 1994, an honorary doctorate from the University of Uppsala.

■ STAKEHOLDER INVOLVEMENT

Stakeholder involvement refers to the participation of stakeholders in one or more components of the evaluation process. *Involvement* implies a role beyond providing information or responding to data-gathering instruments. Stakeholders who are involved in an evaluation process contribute to important decisions regarding evaluation planning, implementation, and use.

There are two primary rationales for stakeholder involvement in evaluation: (a) to enhance the usefulness of the evaluation results, process, or both and (b) to advance values related to equity, empowerment, and social change within the evaluation context. The utilization rationale arose during the 1970s in the United States from within the field of evaluation itself, largely in response to the disappointing lack of influence observed for the previous 1960s evaluations of the ambitious innovations of the Great Society era. These early evaluations were conducted by applied social scientists who relied on the experimentation methods they knew at the time. However, as is well recounted in the annals of evaluation history, the logic and precision of experimentation in social science was a poor fit to the disordered and dynamic character of public policies and programs. The results of these early evaluations were neither methodologically defensible nor very useful to decision makers or any other stakeholders. Empirical studies and conceptual theorizing about how to make evaluation more useful led to the core idea of stakeholder involvement, among several other utilization-oriented practices. If key stakeholders are involved in determining the course of an evaluation, goes the reasoning, they are more likely to feel a sense of ownership in the process and thereby more likely to find the evaluation useful and to actually use the results and recommendations.

A values-driven rationale for stakeholder involvement was brought into the U.S. evaluation community from external traditions of participatory and participatory action research, particularly as practiced in less-developed countries around the world. This rationale was consonant with the growing recognition, again during the 1970s in the United States, that evaluation is an inherently politicized and value-laden enterprise. Given the value inherency of evaluation, goes this reasoning, the kinds of values that can be most defensibly promoted in evaluation are those related to equity, justice, and empowerment. A critical vehicle for advancing such values in evaluation is active stakeholder participation.

The nature and form of stakeholder involvement in evaluation varies with its rationale. Use-oriented genres focus on securing the participation of a few key stakeholders with a stated interest in the evaluation. These stakeholders, characteristically on-site program administrators and staff, are likely to contribute to initial decisions about evaluation purposes and priority questions and to later decisions about action implications of the evaluation findings. In values-based genres, the emphasis is on securing the participation of a diverse range of stakeholders, including especially those with least power in the context; notably, intended program beneficiaries. This diverse "team" is likely to have decision authority in the evaluation process from start to finish, and there will be roles as data gatherers and analysts for its members. In values-based genres, the emphasis is often as much on the empowerment benefits of participation itself as on the value dimensions of the results.

—*Jennifer C. Greene*

Further Reading

Whitmore, E. (Ed.). (1998). Understanding and practicing participatory evaluation. *New Directions for Evaluation, 80.*

■ STAKEHOLDERS

Stakeholders are people who have a stake or a vested interest in the program, policy, or product being evaluated (hereafter referred to as "the program") and therefore also have a stake in the evaluation. Stakeholders are usefully clustered into four groups: (a) people who have decision authority over the program, including other policy makers, funders, and advisory boards; (b) people who have direct responsibility for the program, including program developers, administrators in the organization implementing the program, program managers, and direct service staff; (c) people who are the intended beneficiaries of the program, their families, and their communities; and (d) people disadvantaged by the program, as in lost funding opportunities.

—*Jennifer C. Greene*

■■ STANDARDIZED TEST

The most distinguishing characteristic of the standardized test is the requirement that the instrument be administered to all test takers under the same conditions. These conditions include the directions for administration, which sometimes imposes scripts that must be followed. Other administration conditions include time of year (in the case of achievement tests), time limits, and methods of recording responses. Other features are shared to a greater or lesser degree, such as procedures for developing test specifications, item writing, pretesting items and computing item statistics, and compiling preliminary forms of the tests for field trials.

—*Charles L. Thomas*

Further Reading

Thorndike, R. L. (Ed.). (1971). *Educational measurement* (2nd ed.). Washington, DC: American Council on Education.

■■ STANDARD SETTING

Although the specification of criteria in evaluation is well developed, there is much mystery associated with standard setting. The key question for standard setting is how to distinguish defensibly between evaluands that share a particular attribute or characteristic to varying degrees. Standard setting is socially desirable and is a necessity in credentialing professionals, certifying services, labeling safe products, and equitably distributing resources. Even in cases where a clear and exact standard is set, such as in setting cut scores on tests, the process is inexact, and even when sophisticated empirical strategies are used, standard setting is, at its root, a value judgment based on sociopolitical concerns. The quality of the judgment about what constitutes an appropriate standard or level of performance is determined as much by who is making the determination as by any particular method used.

Standard setting is the process used for delineating the differences among performance levels or standards. The most well-formulated methods for standard setting are in the domain of achievement testing and are a crucial part of evaluation in high-stakes situations, such as when the test score will be the determining factor regarding some reward or punishment. Examples are graduation from high school, admission to college, eligibility for scholarships, employment, and budgeting. There are a number of strategies used for standard setting in these cases. The most common are the modified Angoff, contrasting groups, and bookmark procedures.

The *Angoff procedure* is based on expert judgment about the probability of a minimally competent person answering a particular test question correctly. Judges are selected who are presumed to have appropriate expertise in the domain being tested to make a well-educated guess about these probabilities. The probabilities for all items on a test are summed to give a cut score (actually the average of a number of expert judges), which divides the group into those minimally competent and those not.

The *contrasting groups procedure* is based on a comparison of expected and actual performance among different ability groups. One begins with a group of individuals divided into ability groups based on some other factor (such as course grades, courses taken, teacher nomination, other test scores), and the relevant test is administered to these groups. Based on the differences in performance of the different ability groups (usually plotted on a graph), the score (number of correct items) that most clearly distinguishes the group becomes the cut score.

The *bookmark procedure* uses item-response theory and was developed by CTB/McGraw-Hill in 1996. This method orders test questions on a scale of difficulty, from easy to hard. Expert judges then determine where cut scores should be set along that scale. The judges, first individually and then in consultation with one another, bookmark the scores they believe separate levels (for example, advanced, proficient, and unsatisfactory) of performance.

The standard-setting process has come under close scrutiny in situations where distinguishing different levels of performance accurately or inaccurately makes a serious difference to individuals or groups of individuals. For example, many professions and occupations (teachers, lawyers, doctors, police officers) use examination scores to determine who will be licensed or certified to practice. Product safety is another area where standard setting is contested, for example when the level of polychlorinated biphenyls in farmed salmon is considered too high. The trustworthiness of the standard-setting procedure to clearly establish an appropriate cut score for the purpose at hand is critical. There have indeed been many legal challenges to the validity of cut scores.

Further Reading

Cizek, G. (Ed.). (2001). *Setting performance standards: Concepts, methods and perspectives.* Mahwah, NJ: Lawrence Erlbaum.

Horn, C., Ramos, M., Blumer, I., & Madaus, G. (2000). *Cut scores: Results vary* (Monograph Series, Vol. 1, No. 1). Boston: Boston College, National Board on Educational Testing and Public Policy.

▪▪ STANDARDS

Standards are the levels of performance, typically expressed as a rating or grade, on a given criterion. For example, an overall "B" grade may be the standard for admission to a graduate degree program, or accuracy 99% of the time may be the standard for a die-casting machine. Standards are often expressed in a score, often referred to as a cut score, but they may also be nonquantitative, such as, for example, providing an exemplar of acceptable performance. Standards may be absolute or relative and can be used in either a criterion-referenced or norm-referenced context. A standard need not be a single level of performance but may involve multiple levels of performance, such as excellent, acceptable, unacceptable. The term *standard* is often used incorrectly when what is meant is *criterion*, which is the more general description of desirable attributes or characteristics of the evaluand.

▪▪ STANFIELD, JOHN II

(b. 1951, Rome, New York). Ph.D., M.A. Sociology, Northwestern University; B.A. Sociology, California State University, Fresno.

Stanfield is Chair of the Department of African-American and African Diaspora Studies at Indiana University. He has held faculty positions at a number of universities, including an appointment as Director of the University of California, Davis, Center for Urban Research and Policy Studies. While at Morehouse College, Stanfield was Avalon Professor, Chair of the Sociology Department, and Director of the Morehouse Research Institute.

Stanfield has influenced evaluation through his work on the epistemology and politics of cultural pluralistic evaluation. His edited books *Race and Ethnicity in Research Methods* (with R. M. Dennis) and *A History of Race Relations Research: First Generation Reflections* draw together perspectives that have contributed to the understanding of issues related to culture and evaluation.

▪▪ STANLEY, JULIAN C.

(b. 1918, Macon, Georgia). Ed.D., Ed.M., Graduate School of Education, Harvard University; B.S. Education, Georgia Southern University.

Stanley, Professor of Psychology Emeritus and Director of the Study of Mathematically Precocious Youth at the Johns Hopkins University, is one of the most influential educational and behavioral statisticians of the past half century.

The epic collaboration of Stanley's research career was in 1960 with Donald Campbell while he was at Northwestern University and Stanley was at the University of Wisconsin in Madison. They coauthored a chapter for a handbook that resulted in a separate short-book publication titled *Experimental and Quasi-Experimental Designs for Research.* Thanks to Campbell's grasp of the theory of research and Stanley's statistical contributions, this little book has been widely used (at least a quarter of a million copies have been sold) in a variety of courses in education, psychology, sociology, and even history.

Stanley credits Campbell as being "one of the most illustrious psychologists of his day." Stanley was also influenced by Frederick Mosteller, O. Hobart Mowrer, Robert R. Sears, Walter Dearborn, William O. Jenkins, Nicholas Hobbs, Lee J. Cronbach, William Kruskal, Gordon Allport, Clyde Kluckhohn, Arthur Jensen, Camilla Benbow, David Lubinski, Linda E. Brody, T. L. Kelley, P. J. Rulon, F. B. Davis, E. F. Lindquist, R. Ebel, and P. O. Johnson.

He is the author of *Educational and Psychological Measurement and Evaluation* (currently in its seventh edition) and Former President of the American Educational Research Association; the National Council on Measurement in Education; and the Divisions of Measurement, Evaluation, and Statistics and Educational Psychology of the American Psychological Association. He holds honorary doctorates from the University of North Texas and the University of West Georgia. Stanley received the Cattell Award of APA Division 1 and the Lifetime Achievement Award of APA Division 5, the AERA Research Award, the MENSA Award for Lifetime Achievement, and the Thorndike Award of APA Division 15. He was a Fulbright Research Scholar in Belgium (1958-1959) and New Zealand (1974).

STATISTICS

Statistics are mathematical techniques used to describe and draw inferences from quantitative data. Statistics are commonly divided into two branches: descriptive and inferential. Descriptive statistics are used to describe, summarize, and represent more concisely a set of data. Common descriptive statistics include frequency distributions, percentiles, the mean, and the range. Inferential statistics involve procedures for drawing inferences that go beyond the data set: conventionally, inferences about a large group (i.e., a population) based on observations of a smaller sample. Statistical inference could be used, for example, to estimate the relationship between variables (e.g., the correlation between income and amount of services received), to assess whether two groups differ (e.g., does the treatment group have better outcomes than the control group?), or to judge the fit of a complex model (e.g., how well does the program theory fit the obtained data?).

—*Poh-Pheng Chua and Melvin M. Mark*

STORYTELLING

Storytelling involves collective sharing of *stories.* A simple story might describe a particular change through depiction of the situation before and after that change. Stories differ from other forms of interview response in that they still make sense when detached from surrounding discourse. In evaluation, they tend to emerge when the teller is left to complete his or her narrative without interruption.

Evaluation stories include stakeholder stories, program performance stories, and evaluator stories. Stakeholder stories emerge from interview transcripts, diaries, or open-ended responses to questions. Evaluation techniques such as the most significant change technique (MSC) and Kibel's results mapping look for stakeholder stories. Program performance

stories are succinct, evidence-based accounts of overall program performance. Evaluator stories are shared among evaluators to help make sense of evaluation practice.

—*Jessica Dart*

See also PERFORMANCE STORY

Further Reading

Prince, G. (1973). *A grammar of stories.* The Hague, The Netherlands: Mouton.

STRATEGIC PLANNING

Strategic planning is a management tool used primarily by an organization to focus its energy, to ensure that its members are working toward common goals, and to assess and adjust its direction in response to a changing environment. Strategic planning is a disciplined effort to produce fundamental decisions and actions that shape and guide what an organization is, what it does, and why it does it, with a focus on the future. Traditionally, strategic planning has been a top-down strategy controlled by managers, although more contemporary approaches emphasize democratic and participatory approaches.

See also APPRECIATIVE INQUIRY, COMPLEX ADAPTIVE SYSTEMS, SYSTEMS AND SYSTEMS THINKING

STUFFLEBEAM, DANIEL L.

(b. 1936, Waverly, Iowa). Ph.D., Purdue University; B.A., University of Iowa.

Stufflebeam is Distinguished University Professor and Harold and Beulah McKee Professor of Education at Western Michigan University (WMU). From 1973 to 2002, he directed the Evaluation Center at WMU, which he had originally founded in 1965 at The Ohio State University, directed there until 1973, and then moved to WMU. Stufflebeam chaired the national Joint Committee on Standards for Educational Evaluation for its first 13 years and was also Founding Director of the Center for Research on Educational Accountability and Teacher Education (CREATE). His more than $20 million in grants and contracts has supported evaluation and research projects in such areas as national and state achievement testing; school improvement; distance education; science and mathematics education; historically African American colleges; housing, community, and economic development; productivity of private colleges; teacher and administrator evaluation; Marine Corps personnel evaluation; metaevaluation; and the functioning of a Catholic diocese. He directed the development of more than 100 standardized achievement tests, including eight forms of the General Educational Development tests. He has also served as advisor to many federal and state government departments, the United Nations, the World Bank, Open Learning Australia, various charitable foundations, many school districts, and several universities. He has lectured and provided technical assistance in more than 20 countries. Currently he is serving on the Government Auditing Standards Advisory Council of the U.S. General Accounting Office.

Besides his many contributions to the development and advocacy of the profession, Stufflebeam is known for having developed one of the first models of program evaluation, the CIPP Model of Evaluation. His publications (15 books and about 100 journal articles and book chapters) have appeared in eight languages. Since 1983, he has been Coeditor of the Kluwer Academic Press book series Evaluation in Education and Human Services, and he is Coeditor of the 2003 *International Handbook on Educational Evaluation.* His recognitions include Western Michigan University's Distinguished Faculty Scholar Award (1984), the American Evaluation Association's Paul F. Lazarsfeld Award (1985), the Consortium for Research on Educational Accountability and Teacher Evaluation inaugural Jason Millman Memorial Award (1997), the WMU Harold and Beulah McKee Professorship of Education (1997), and a Distinguished University Professorship (2002).

SUBJECTIVITY

Subjectivity, a term often used pejoratively, refers to individual meaning, perception, and feeling. The concept is based on the epistemological position of subjectivism, which is the theory that perception creates reality and that there is no underlying true reality that exists independent of perception.

See also OBJECTIVITY

SUCCESS CASE METHOD

The Success Case Method, developed by Robert O. Brinkerhoff, is a quick and simple process that combines analysis of extreme groups with case study and storytelling. The essential purpose of a Success Case study is to find out how well some organizational initiative (e.g., a training program, a new work method) is working. A Success Case study also identifies and explains the contextual factors that differentiate successful from unsuccessful adopters of new initiatives. A recent study, for example, discovered that the factors that explained why some trainees were and others were not able to use their new training to accomplish worthwhile results involved support from their supervisors, access to certain databases, and access to training soon after being assigned new business accounts.

The Success Case study process has two fundamental parts. First, the evaluator identifies the few program participants who were the most (and least) successful. This is usually accomplished with a brief 3- to 5-item survey. That is, all participants are surveyed through self-report to determine to what extent they are using the new methods and tools a new initiative intended them to use and what, if anything, they are accomplishing.

Survey respondents are sorted into those few that are most and least successful. The evaluator then selects a random sample from among the most and least successful and, interviewing these people (usually by telephone), "digs deep" into their experience to determine the exact nature and extent of their success. More specifically, the evaluator seeks to discover the following:

- Exactly what they used, when they used it, how, when, and so on
- What results they accomplished
- How valuable the results are (e.g., in dollars)
- What environmental factors enabled their application and results

Unsuccessful persons are interviewed to determine why they were unable to use or benefit from the program. Specifically, they are asked what got in the way, what factors kept them from being successful, and so forth.

The results of a Success Case study are communicated in "story" form. That is, the evaluator finds the most compelling and descriptive examples of success the program has achieved, then documents these examples in a few brief but richly detailed stories. In an evaluation of the business value of emotional intelligence training at American Express, for example, we told the story of how six different financial advisors, each in a different situation, had used their training to increase sales, increase customer revenues, and so forth. Comparing these stories with the stories of unsuccessful participants allowed us to pinpoint the several key performance system factors that enabled some to make very successful use of the program and others to have nowhere near that success. As a result, American Express was able to formulate new guidelines for program participation and support that were aimed at increasing the numbers of advisors who could successfully leverage the training into financial results.

The Success Case Method differs from typical, more quantitative methods in that it does not seek to learn about the "average" or modal participant in an initiative. It intentionally seeks the very best that a program is producing, to help determine whether the value a program is capable of producing is worthwhile and whether it may be possible to leverage this to a greater number of participants. A "success story" is not a testimonial or a critical review. It is a factual and verifiable account—citing evidence that would "stand up in court"—that demonstrates how and how valuably a person used some new method or tool or capability. In the American Express study, for example, the stories of successful advisors cited actual data about their financial results that was verifiable and documented in office records and reports. When necessary, the evaluator seeks corroborating information from third parties, such as peers, customers, or supervisors.

—*Robert O. Brinkerhoff*

Further Reading

Brinkerhoff, R. O. (2003). *The success case method.* San Francisco: Berrett Koehler.

Brinkerhoff, R. O., & Dressler, D. E. (2002, July). Using evaluation to build organizational performance and learning capability: A strategy and a method. *Performance Improvement, 41*(6).

◼◼ SUMMATIVE EVALUATION

A *summative evaluation* is one that is done at the end of or on completion of a program. Summative evaluations may be done internally or externally and are typically for the purpose of decision making. Michael Scriven, the originator of the terms *formative* and *summative* evaluation, distinguishes summative evaluation's aim as reporting "on" the program rather than "to" the program.

See also FORMATIVE EVALUATION

◼◼ SURVEYS

Surveys are, arguably, the most popular method for collecting data for evaluations. *Surveys* involve asking questions of specific individuals and obtaining their responses. The responses are usually tabulated or analyzed and presented as evaluation findings. Conducting a survey is a low-cost and relatively straightforward way to obtain data from many people in a short period of time. However, obtaining answers that accurately reflect the attitudes or behaviors of a study population is more difficult than it may seem on the surface. Fortunately, there has been a great deal of research on survey research methods in the past 20 years that can guide the collection of accurate data.

To develop a survey that will yield an accurate depiction of a study population for an evaluation, evaluators must consider seven important elements of survey design and administration: (a) selecting the individuals to be surveyed, (b) developing the questions for the survey, (c) determining the mode of survey administration, (d) organizing the questions into an instrument, (e) administering the survey, (f) preparing the responses for analysis, and (g) analyzing the data. Each of these elements is briefly discussed in this entry, with attention to some important sources of error and examples from evaluations presented.

The first step in identifying the individuals to be surveyed in an evaluation is to clearly define the target population for the survey; after this, ways to access the study population should be listed and the best way determined. Often evaluators will choose between surveying program participants only and surveying the larger number of individuals who were eligible to participate in the program being evaluated, of whom some participated and some did not. On the one hand, participants can respond to questions about their experiences with the program, such as amount and duration of services received and satisfaction with services. On the other hand, nonparticipants can provide information on coverage rates, services received from other sources, and outcomes in the absence of participating in the program (counterfactuals).

A second consideration in choosing respondents is whether the entire study population will be surveyed or a subset will be selected. Many evaluations, such as evaluations of training workshops, attempt to survey all participants. However, trying to survey all participants is often too costly and actually results in less accuracy than surveying a carefully selected subset of the study population. The source of the inaccuracy is nonresponse, which can bias survey results, because those who choose to respond often have different responses from those who do not.

Selecting a subset of the study population is done through probability sampling methods or nonprobability methods (Henry, 1990). Nonprobability sampling methods, such as purposive sampling or convenience sampling, are often used in evaluations, but the results that are obtained are less likely to reflect the study population accurately. Inaccuracies arise because human judgments are involved in the selection process, such as in the quota sampling methods that led to several newspapers declaring Thomas Dewey as the next president the day after the 1948 election.

Probability samples, which are sometimes called *random samples* or *scientific samples,* are defined by methods of selection that result in all members of the study population having a known, nonzero chance of being selected for the sample. Human judgment is removed from the selection process and therefore eliminated as a source of bias or error. Of course, probability samples are subject to nonresponse biases. Careful evaluators allocate resources to reduce nonresponse by following up, often several times, with sampled individuals and persuading them to respond and analyzing to the extent possible between respondents and nonrespondents (Henry, 1990).

Generally speaking, there are two kinds of survey questions, often referred to by the more general term *items:* factual or behavioral items and attitudinal or opinion items. Factual or behavioral items ask questions that can be externally verified; attitudinal items tap subjective states and can only be examined for consistency of the responses. Each type of item has its own complex way of obtaining accurate responses (Fowler, 2002). For example, in talking about past behaviors, people often bring actions from the distant past into a more recent time frame, a phenomenon

known as telescoping. Therefore, survey experts encourage questions about the most recent period possible; for example, asking respondents to begin with a salient starting point and work their way forward in the process of recollecting their behaviors. It is important to begin the process of developing survey items by searching the literature for measures successfully used in previous surveys.

Surveys can be administered by mail, over the phone, in personal interviews, in group settings, and, increasingly, directly on personal computers and through the Internet. The choice of a mode of administration will determine the type of instrument that is needed (mailed questionnaire versus phone interview), the amount of time it will take to collect the responses, and the cost of the survey. Usually, these decisions are made by weighing respondent capacities, cost, and data quality. Many evaluations employ more than one method of administration, and in many cases, alternative methods will be necessary for populations with disabilities and for those who speak other languages. Methods of accommodation can include providing large-print questionnaires for visually impaired respondents or obtaining responses from surrogates, such as caregivers for medically frail individuals.

After the mode of administration is decided, items can be organized into an instrument. In general, the instrument should be organized to begin with questions that establish rapport and capture the interest of respondents and end with demographic items that some respondents may be reluctant to provide in the beginning. Questions should be ordered to minimize the cognitive effort of the respondents: Questions referring to similar things should be placed close together. Survey length is always an issue when organizing an instrument and often requires setting tough priorities so that the most important evaluation questions are adequately addressed.

Survey administration requires careful planning and painstaking follow-through if the survey is to yield accurate data. From monitoring and coaching interviewers to making sure that surveys are properly logged in and identification numbers checked off, survey administration requires adherence to the detailed procedures no matter which mode of administration is being used.

Preparation of data for analysis and the analysis itself are intimately tied together. In surveys that rely on computer-assisted telephone interviews, the data are entered directly by the interviewers, allowing evaluators to avoid potential errors from hand entry. Scanning machines and software also eliminate having people enter data by hand but require an investment of capital.

Collecting survey data that meet current standards for accuracy requires a great deal of expertise. Numerous organizations have arisen that specialize in survey research, many of which are members of the American Association of Public Opinion Researchers. Many evaluators subcontract with these organizations for collecting survey data, depending on the scope and complexity of the survey. Whether working alone or collaborating with others, evaluators who choose to conduct surveys have a wealth of research and resources that can make their survey findings more accurate.

—*Gary T. Henry*

Further Reading

Fowler, F. J. (2002). *Survey research methods* (3rd ed.). Thousand Oaks, CA: Sage.

Henry, G. T. (1990). *Practical sampling.* Thousand Oaks, CA: Sage.

⊞ SYNDEMIC

Anthropologist Merrill Singer coined the term *syndemic* in the early 1990s to describe the mutually reinforcing nature of health crises, such as substance abuse, violence, and AIDS, that take hold in communities with harsh and inequitable living conditions. Observers throughout history have recognized that different disease processes interact, but Singer's innovation was to interpret those connections as evidence of a higher order phenomenon, which he named a "syndemic." A generic definition "is two or more afflictions, interacting synergistically, contributing to excess burden of disease in a population."

Since the 1970s, health planners have understood that effective responses to the intertwined afflictions within communities require systemwide interventions. However, the desire to achieve systemic change stands in opposition to what most public health agencies are prepared to do. Ingrained in financial structures, problem-solving frameworks, statistical models, and the criteria for professional prestige is the idea, inherited from medical science, that each affliction can be prevented individually by understanding its unique causes and developing targeted interventions. Consequently, most practitioners operate with resources

focused on one disease or risk factor, leaving other problems to be addressed by parallel enterprises.

Evaluations confirm that this single-issue approach can be effective in temporarily reducing the rate of a given disorder, but it cannot serve as a means for fulfilling society's ongoing interest in ensuring the *conditions* under which people can be healthy. The main difficulty is that an exclusively disease-focused orientation prohibits a full view of the ways in which different afflictions interact. Conceptual and analytic boundaries drawn around disease categories invite simplifying assumptions such as independence and one-way causality, as well as instantaneous and linear effects. Such assumptions make the modeling task more tractable and can produce valid insights over the short term but are eventually misleading because they fail to account for the effects of causal feedback coming from outside the chosen boundary.

Proponents of a syndemic orientation do not dispute the benefits of addressing unique problems uniquely. Rather, they acknowledge the limitations of doing so and offer a complementary approach that places multiple afflictions in context. Even as colleagues continue to address specific health problems, others operating from a syndemic orientation may devise long-range policies that engage a different set of causal processes: those that configure patterns of affliction in society. By situating unique afflictions within the dynamic systems of which they are a part, a syndemic orientation concentrates on the conditions under which people can be healthy. It questions how and why those conditions differ among groups and goes even farther to engage the struggle for directed social change.

For evaluators of health programs and policies, a syndemic orientation involves not just one but a sequence of shifts in perspective. Each view offers a conceptual and mathematical formalism that is both comprehensive and context sensitive, a combination that is notoriously difficult to achieve using conventional evaluation schemes.

The first shift in perspective involves seeing more than one problem at a time; this is the crux of the syndemic idea. Mapping connections among afflictions provides a more complete picture of the health challenge in a community. It also lays the foundation for using formal network analyses to measure the strength and structural properties of linked afflictions.

Next comes the shift from recognizing linked afflictions to understanding causality within dynamic feedback systems. To comprehend why syndemics develop and how they can be controlled, evaluators must widen their analytic boundary beyond the attributable causes of the afflictions themselves, including, at a minimum, interactions among afflictions, living conditions, and the community's strength to address them both. For problems with long delays (e.g., chronic disease), this modeling approach yields more precise information about the causal influence of forces that are neither close in time nor near in space to the health events of interest. Dynamic modeling also allows evaluators to simulate policy scenarios under given community conditions. Controlled experiments using simulation improve the search for interventions that can be effective without incurring the expense, risk, delay, and other barriers to learning that are inherent in real-world experimentation.

A final shift embraces the world of political action, where policy becomes reality. Insights from systems modeling often reveal a number of possible futures and raise questions about strategic direction and agency, questions about the ends and means of social navigation. The navigational view frames changing conditions as the result of contested choices among an infinite number of possible directions. Those directions may be represented formally with circular statistics, as they are in physical navigation; however, their meaning in a social context pertains to the contours of human values. This portrayal highlights tensions between advocates of change in one direction and advocates of another, thereby allowing an assessment of power alliances and the health implications of different policy positions. Guided by an explicit moral compass, public health leaders may use a navigational approach to transcend ad hoc problem solving and exert greater control in keeping society on course toward a safer, healthier future. The navigational view also corrects a false presumption, deeply seated in popular consciousness, that only health professionals are capable of solving health problems. In fact, genuine movement toward healthier conditions is not possible unless ordinary citizens, working individually and collectively, make healthier choices in their public and private lives.

Aspects of a syndemic orientation incorporate 21st-century systems science, but the underlying concepts are not new. Still, the implications of adhering to this orientation remain largely unexplored. Recognition of the term is growing, and a widening conversation is under way, but it will probably take decades for such transformations in thinking and practice to occur. At this early stage, it is apparent that the orientation holds promise for confronting modern public health challenges. It does not impose a single, rigid model but instead offers a systems-oriented, politically engaged, and philosophically conscious frame of reference that health professionals and other citizens can use for working effectively together. The Centers for Disease Control and Prevention coordinates a Syndemics Prevention Network dedicated to exploring what this orientation entails.

—Bobby Milstein

See also Systems and Systems Thinking

Further Reading

Centers for Disease Control and Prevention. (2002). *Spotlight on syndemics.* Retrieved June 15, 2004, from http://www.cdc.gov/syndemics

Singer, M. (1996). A dose of drugs, a touch of violence, a case of AIDS: Conceptualizing the SAVA syndemic. *Free Inquiry in Creative Sociology, 24*(2), 99-110.

⊞ SYNTHESIS

Evaluation involves the collection of data from many sources and often through many means, as well as the use of multiple criteria. This corpus of information must be rendered sensible through the process of synthesis; that is, the combining of evidence on several dimensions. Synthesis is similar to putting a puzzle together—piecing together information to create a whole. The outcome of this synthesis might be numeric, such as in an overall rating perhaps best typified in a quantitative weight and sum strategy, or through the use of meta-analysis, or the synthesis might be textual, such as in an analytic conclusion.

See also Literature Review, Logic of Evaluation, Meta-analysis, Quantitative Weight and Sum, Triangulation

⊞ SYSTEMS AND SYSTEMS THINKING

The formal origins of systems theory date back to the middle 20th century and draw from two interconnected threads. There were the physicists and biologists, such as David Bohm and Ludvig von Bertallanfy, and there were the group dynamacists and organizational developers, such as Stafford Beer, Russel Ackoff, Fred Emery, Eric Trist, Reg Revans, and, to some extent, Kurt Lewin.

The basic issue all sought to understand was the relationship between an event and its context: past, present, and future. Although they each took a different route, they built on each other's concepts and established the basis of the rich range of systems approaches that are available today.

From the range of approaches, is it possible to develop some general statements about systems and the properties of systems?

Ackoff's classic definition lists 31 properties of a system. A rather simpler list was developed in the early 1970s by John Beishon and Geoff Peters at the Open University in the United Kingdom: A system is an assembly of parts wherein

- The parts or components are connected together in an organized way
- The parts or components are affected by being in the system and are changed by leaving it
- The assembly does something
- The assembly has been identified by someone as being of special interest

Around that time, Peter Checkland at the University of Lancaster, United Kingdom, developed the following list of essential properties of a system:

- An ongoing purpose (which may be determined in advance—*purposeful*—or assigned through observation—*purposive*)
- A means of assessing performance
- A decision-taking process
- Components that are also systems (i.e., the notion of subsystems)
- Components that interact
- An environment (with which the system may or may not interact)
- A boundary between the system and the environment (that may be *closed* or *open*)
- Resources
- Continuity

These definitions are relatively old, and the systems field has broadened considerably since they were formulated. Nevertheless, they still provide a good base from which to understand the fundamental nature of systems and systems-based inquiry. Thirty years on, their main disadvantage is that they promote the idea that a system is always an observable concrete "thing" (e.g., a manufacturing supply chain) rather than the possibility that a system may be an assembly of concepts, ideas, and beliefs.

SYSTEMS THINKING: USING SYSTEMS CONCEPTS

In using systems concepts, there are several traps for the unwary. A common notion of systems-based inquiry is that it must include everything. In fact it is quite the opposite—the power of systems inquiry is that it seeks to simplify, not make more complicated. Its job is to get to the essence of what is going on, not end up with some behemoth. Producing a movie is an enormously complicated undertaking, but Charlie Chaplain once said that all he needed to make a comedy was "a park, a policeman and a pretty girl." Essence—drawing simplicity from the complicated and choosing what can be usefully and feasibly left out—is the major feature of systems-based inquiry.

Like the concept of *evaluation,* the concept of *system* has both a popular and a technical meaning. The popular meaning, as in "the health system" or "recruitment system," conjures up images of interconnected management processes. This tends to encourage the conception of systems as a series of boxes with arrows or lines between them. In evaluation language, systems are fancy program logics. Not so—or not only so. Unfortunately, when we assess these popular notions of system using the technical systems tools described later, we often find that the popular concept of system gets very fuzzy. For instance, a single recruitment system can have many environments, many purposes, many boundaries. In short, the so-called recruitment system is not a system at all but (to use some technical systems terms) a "rich picture," a "problematique" or a "mess."

Perhaps one of the largest traps is to assume that systems are concrete; that they are out there somewhere and we can fall over them—in which case, the purpose of a systems-based inquiry is to identify these objects and fiddle with them in some way. In fact, systems are purely conceptual: They are not the world, *they are a way of looking at the world.* A systems-based

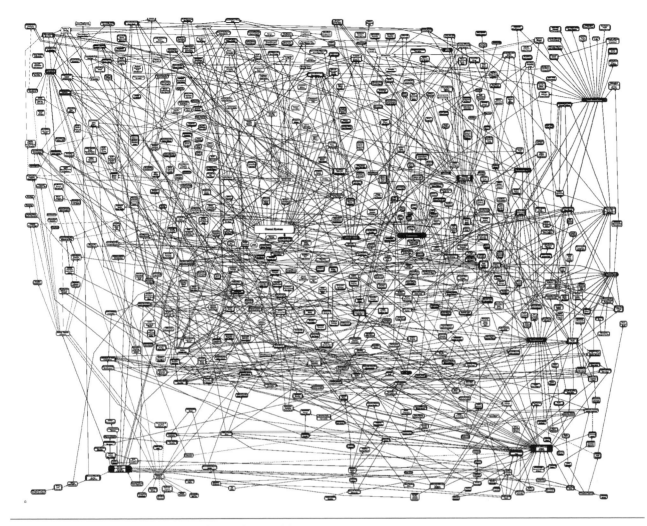

Figure 1   *Approaches to Systems Theory: Concept Map*

SOURCE: International Institute for General Systems Studies

inquiry investigates the real world *as if it were a system*. From this conceptual perspective, we gain insights about what might be going on in the real world and are thus able to form conclusions about what could be done to make real improvements.

Systems-Based Inquires

An earlier paragraph mentioned the rich range of systems-based inquires available today. How rich? Figure 1 is a concept map of several hundred approaches to systems inquiry, prepared by the International Institute for General Systems Studies.

So there is no such thing as *a* system-based inquiry. There are hundreds of techniques, methods, and methodologies to choose from, each of which might

assist a systems-based inquiry. They range from the somewhat mechanistic (e.g., system dynamics) to the essentially moral (e.g., critical systemic thinking), from "simple systems" approaches to "complex systems" approaches (e.g., complex adaptive systems), from the anthropomorphic (e.g., new science) to dialectics and learning (cultural-historical activity theory) and plain eclectic (e.g., Senge's fifth discipline). No one size fits all—the skill is to identify (a) the appropriate methodologies and methods for the job in hand and (b) the resources available.

What follows is a brief description of four different approaches, along with an assessment of their potential in evaluation. A fifth approach, complex adaptive systems, is covered elsewhere in this encyclopedia. There is nothing particularly distinctive about each

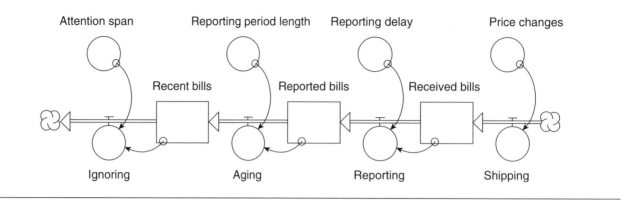

Figure 2   *A Typical System Dynamics Model*

approach—they have been chosen to provide an idea of the range of what is available. Within the systems universe, these are all very mainstream approaches. None is less than 15 years old, and all are used extensively throughout the world.

SYSTEM DYNAMICS

What Is System Dynamics?

System dynamics is essentially about exploring "feedback" and "delay." It was developed by Jay Forrester at Massachusetts Institute of Technology back in the 1960s from Stafford Beer's concepts of cybernetics. Its popularity has waxed and waned ever since. It received a boost in the 1990s when Peter Senge took system dynamics, placed it alongside organizational and personal development concepts, and called the result "Systems Thinking."

Essentially, system dynamics does three things:

- Helps us explore rigorously the implications of feedback and delay
- Maps the possible relationships among parts of the problem
- Allows us to play "what if" games with the way in which these relationships interact

System dynamics focuses primarily on identifying the main variables of a system (i.e., the parts that are able to change) and exploring rigorously the effect they have on one another *over time*. It therefore emphasizes the emergent "dynamics" of a system rather than seeking a snapshot of it.

There are many approaches to developing system dynamics models, but they invariably all end up with the kind of diagram shown in Figure 2.

This diagram is, clearly, an extremely simplified representation of the way in which a firm managed its expenses, yet the insights this system dynamics model generated reduced expense variations by 95%! One way to understand this is that we are not modeling the whole firm or even its expense processing, we are modeling the problem.

At this point in a system dynamics inquiry, we can do two things: (a) We can take all the variables and their interrelationships, plug them into a computer simulation program, and play lots of "what ifs." We achieve simplicity by seeking to identify the key variables that most affect the problem being modeled. (b) We can seek simplicity by standing back and trying to understand the essence of what is going on. Over the years, some generic simplifications have been developed with catchy names such as "fixes that fail," "success to the successful," "the tragedy of the commons," "shifting the burden," and "eroding goals." Skilled system dynamics people can spot these patterns in quite complex systems.

SOFT SYSTEMS METHODOLOGY (SSM)

What is SSM?

Soft systems methodology (SSM) is essentially about creating multiple systemic perspectives of a particular situation. Consider a basketball game. We will gain different insights if we view the game as a means of providing advertising opportunities for products, or as a means of seeing which team is better than the other, or as a means of securing highly paid employment for tall people, or as a means of allowing security companies to train staff in the control of large crowds.

SSM was developed by Peter Checkland in the late 1960s at the University of Lancaster in the United Kingdom. Originally it was seen as a modeling tool, but in later years it has been used increasingly as method of facilitating learning and identifying meaning.

At the heart of SSM is a comparison between a problem situation as it is and some simple models of the ways in which it might be perceived. Out of this comparison arise a better understanding of the situation (research) and some ideas for improvement (action).

The classic SSM method has seven stages.

1. The Problem Situation Unstructured

The problem situation is first experienced, as it is, by the researcher. That is, the researcher makes as few presumptions about the nature of the situation as possible.

2. The Problem Situation Expressed

In this step, the researcher develops a detailed description, a "rich picture," of the situation within which the problem occurs. In addition to the logic of the situation, the rich picture also tries to capture the relationships, the value judgments people make, and the "feel" of the situation.

3. Root Definition of Relevant System

Next the "root definition," the essence, of a relevant system, is defined.

Checkland provides the mnemonic CATWOE as a checklist for ensuring that the important features of a system are included: customers (the system's beneficiaries), actors (who transform inputs to outputs), transformation (from inputs to outputs), weltanschauung (relevant worldviews), owners (who have veto power over the system), and environmental constraints that need to be considered.

We then use these elements to construct a root definition. This is often in the form of "a system that does P (what) by Q (how) to contribute to achieving R (why)." Once this root definition has been developed, we then take a "cultural analysis": We explore the roles, norms, values, and politics relevant to the root definition.

4. Making and Testing Conceptual Models

This is a critical, challenging, and rigorous step. The task now is to develop systems models using *only* the elements of the root definition and cultural analysis, in a way that *flows logically from* that root definition and cultural analysis. The focus is on simplicity—the possible models should have as few components as possible (Checkland recommends no more than seven) yet demonstrate all the properties that define a system.

5, 6, and 7. From Conceptual Models to Improvements

Checkland recommends constructing several relevant models using different root definitions by choosing different CATWOE, thus creating the multiple perspectives and multiple models. The final stages of the methodology discuss, compare, and contrast these models with the problem situation. The insights these discussions bring are used to identify ways of improving the problem situation.

CULTURAL-HISTORICAL ACTIVITY THEORY (CHAT)

What is CHAT?

Cultural-historical activity theory's (CHAT) unique contribution is introducing the way in which people think and learn into systems-based inquiry. It draws from several traditions, including Vygotskyian learning theories, Marx's ideas of historical dialectics, and action research.

CHAT has five key features:

1. The starting point of a CHAT approach is a social system with a defined purpose. This purpose is affected by a range of elements, in particular mediating artifacts (e.g., tools) used in the system—including language, plus the rules by which the system operates and the roles people have in the system, especially the division of labor (see Figure 3).

2. Activity systems are multivoiced. There are always multiple points of view (such as SSM), traditions, and interests. Division of labor creates different positions for people in the system. Multivoicedness is a potential source of trouble, but it also provides sites for innovation.

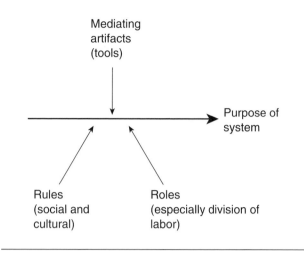

Figure 3   *The CHAT Approach*

3. Activity systems are historical. They draw strongly from the past. A system's current features and dynamics can be understood only by exploring the impact of past features and dynamics. These can be generated within the system or from its environment.

4. Changes in a system are driven primarily by contradictions. Contradictions generate tensions within the system and can result in conflicts, problems, disturbances, or innovations. These contradictions can be historically driven (e.g., an introduction of a new rule in a system of old roles or tools), can occur within elements (e.g., rules) and between elements (e.g., old rule, new tool), and can also occur between neighboring activity systems (e.g., Purpose A: Maximize organizational output; Purpose B: Provide safe work place for staff).

5. Contradictions provide primary sites for learning and development. Consequently, there is the ever-present possibility that the contradictions will transform the system. These transformations create further historical contradictions that provide further learning opportunities. And so on. In fact, the process is cyclical (see Figure 4).

CRITICAL SYSTEMIC THINKING (CST)

Churchman's critical systemic thinking (CST) approach brings ethical and moral alertness into the inquiry, which dramatically alters the possibilities of systems thinking. CST is captured in four principles and seven central concepts. The principles are as follows:

1. The systems approach begins when first we see the world through the eyes of another.

2 The systems approach goes on to discover that every worldview is terribly restricted.

3. There are no experts in the systems approach.

4. The systems approach is not a bad idea.

The four principles are embodied in the following seven central concepts of CST.

1. Purpose

CST sets out nine conditions that must be fulfilled for a system to demonstrate purposefulness. These conditions are as follows:

1. A system has a defined purpose.

2. A system has a means of assessing performance in relation to that purpose.

3. There is a defined client whose interests are served by the system.

4. Parts of the system have defined purposes.

5. A system has an environment.

6. There is a decision maker who can produce changes in the assessment of the system's performance.

7. There is a designer whose design of the system influences the decision maker, leading to changes in the assessment of the system's performance.

8. The designer aims to maximize the system's value to the client.

9. There is a built-in guarantee that the purpose of the system, defined by the assessment of the system's performance, can be achieved and secured.

2. Sweep-In

CST "sweeps in" ever more features of the problem context. This helps participants to become more aware and increasingly able to appreciate contrasting systems of meaning. Sweeping in is an attempt to raise understanding, rather than to realize absolute knowledge. Sweep-in is a process of critical reflection that helps people think or debate.

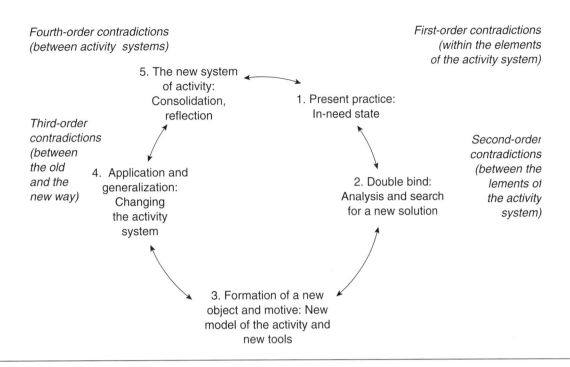

Fourth-order contradictions (between activity systems)

First-order contradictions (within the elements of the activity system)

Third-order contradictions (between the old and the new way)

Second-order contradictions (between the elements of the activity system)

5. The new system of activity: Consolidation, reflection

1. Present practice: In-need state

4. Application and generalization: Changing the activity system

2. Double bind: Analysis and search for a new solution

3. Formation of a new object and motive: New model of the activity and new tools

Figure 4   *The Contradiction-Transformation-Contradiction Cycle*

3. Unfolding

Unfolding draws upon the nine conditions of system purposefulness. This helps people to add structure and meaning to their experiences. People may use these nine conditions to bring plausible interpretations of events to the surface.

4. Boundary Setting

Boundary setting is an issue of great importance to critical systemic thinking. Put succinctly, the questions are, "Who is embraced by the action area and thus benefits?" "Who is out and does not benefit?" "What are the possible consequences of this?" "How might we feel about those consequences?" Boundary setting thus raises questions of ethics, efficiency, and effectiveness and the way in which these are inextricably linked. Boundaries are always open to further debate.

5. Securing

In today's language, *securing* is better understood as *sustainability.* Churchman argued that there was an ethical and moral obligation to explore systems and possible "solutions" with sustainability in mind.

6. Wisdom

Wisdom is thought combined with a concern for ethics.

7. Hope

Hope is the spiritual belief in an ethical future.

IMPLICATIONS FOR EVALUATION OF USING SYSTEMS-BASED APPROACHES

Systems-based approaches to inquiry provide radical and new avenues for evaluation. First, systems-based inquiry provides a very different (compared with many evaluation approaches) way of engaging with an issue. Partly this stems from systems approaches having different origins from most evaluation approaches. The roots of systems-based approaches are in the sciences of biology, engineering, organizational development, action research, psychology, and cognition, rather than in applied social science and anthropology, as are most evaluation approaches.

Second, systems-based approaches provide an opportunity for evaluation to explore areas where it is historically weak. For instance, consider the four approaches described here:

- *Systems dynamics* explores the consequences of feedback and delay and thus provides insights into the behavior of a situation from the perspective of its dynamics. These insights are frequently the opposite of those drawn from the more static investigations that characterize many evaluations.

- *Soft systems methodology* provides a means of drawing deep insights by looking rigorously at an issue from different perspectives. It has considerable potential in stakeholder-based evaluations because it provides a means by which these multiple viewpoints can be unpicked, reassembled, and assessed in a rigorous fashion.

- *Cultural-historical activity theory* provides a framework with which to identify the critical points at which a program is likely to change, innovate, succeed, or fail. It puts a substantially new spin on the utilization-focused and deliberative democratic evaluation debates. It suggests that the key issue is less about the involvement and alignment of key participants than it is about how those participants acknowledge and resolve the historical and current contradictions in the activity system of which they are a part.

- *Critical systemic thinking* draws attention to ethics and sustainability, as well as to the profound importance and political nature of identifying and setting boundaries.

Finally, systems-based approaches can provide alternative ways of understanding how to increase evaluation utilization and build capacity for program improvements.

—*Bob Williams*

See also COMPLEX ADAPTIVE SYSTEMS

Further Reading

Checkland, P. (1999). *Systems thinking, systems practice.* Chichester, U.K.: Wiley.

Churchman, C. W. (1971). *The design of inquiring systems: Basic concepts of systems and organization.* New York: Basic Books.

TACIT KNOWLEDGE

Tacit knowledge is a philosophical concept first articulated by Michael Polanyi, who wrote, "We can know more than we can tell." It is defined as the underlying or unspoken knowledge that guides people's actions and thoughts but that they may not be able to access consciously. It differs from explicit or focal knowledge. Different types exist, including expert knowledge, language competence, and basic ideas we use for everyday tasks. In organization development, tacit knowledge is a metaphor for the undocumented expertise that may be essential to guiding activities but is not written down and perhaps not even expressed.

—Jean A. King

TEACHING EVALUATION

Although evaluations are conducted in a wide variety of organizational and community contexts, most formal training in the field occurs in institutions of higher education, where classroom-based courses remain the traditional vehicle for instruction. Thus, a major challenge in teaching evaluation is to develop strategies that can facilitate—more effectively than conventional lecture methods—acquisition of the applied skills in evaluation that are needed if evaluators are to function effectively in environments that can be complex and intimidating. At the micro level, instructors have generated a rich array of in-class experiential activities (e.g., role-plays, small-group exercises) to explore specific tasks and issues that practitioners can face at each stage of the evaluation process. At the macro level, several approaches exist for giving learners the opportunity to experience firsthand the overall process of conceptualizing, designing, implementing, analyzing, and reporting an evaluation.

A major goal of most macro approaches is to have learners interact with key stakeholders (e.g., the evaluation client, agency staff, program participants, community groups) who see themselves as having a vested interest in the evaluation. Through these interactions, learners increase their ability to cope with the myriad influences that can shape the nature and quality of an evaluation. The most frequently employed macro strategies include simulations, evaluation projects, and extracurricular activities (e.g., research assistantships).

SIMULATIONS

In a simulation, the learner is presented with a detailed description of a hypothetical program that is to be evaluated, as well as the organizational or community context of the program. The learner's task is to prepare a comprehensive evaluation proposal for the program and, in some cases, to use fictitious data (provided by the instructor or the learner) as the basis for writing a subsequent evaluation report. The instructor can enrich the simulation by taking on the roles of key stakeholders in the evaluation when interacting with learners during the course. Simulations are often used in short-term evaluation courses

413

(i.e., those lasting 5 days or less) offered by training institutes.

A variation on the simulation theme is to have learners prepare an evaluation proposal for a *real* organization. The instructor usually recruits the organization in question, and agency representatives meet with the learners one or more times during the term. At the end of the course, an evaluation proposal is submitted to both the instructor and the organization. The value of this approach is enhanced when a follow-up meeting between the learners and the agency contact persons can be arranged that allows the latter to give feedback to the former regarding the proposal.

EVALUATION PROJECTS

A more ambitious strategy is to have learners, usually in teams, conduct an *actual* evaluation from start to finish, from the initial proposal to the final report. Although this goal is easier to accomplish in courses that run for two academic terms rather than one, instructors have reported success with this approach in courses that are as short as 13 weeks. Evaluation clients or projects are typically recruited and screened by the instructor prior to the start date of the course to ensure that only projects with an excellent chance of being completed by the end of the term are accepted. Screening also allows the instructor to gauge the level of evaluation skill required by proposed projects and how it matches both the level of the course and the learners' degree of expertise.

An attractive feature of this approach is that the perceived stakes are higher for learners and clients than in simulations, precisely because the evaluation is a real one. As a result, the challenges of managing both the technical (methodological) and nontechnical (political, interpersonal, cultural, etc.) dimensions of evaluation are likely to be experienced more fully by learners, reinforcing the importance of skill development in these areas.

BEYOND THE COURSE

As valuable as course-based projects are, they have significant limitations. Evaluations that would take longer than the duration of the course are usually not feasible, nor are evaluations that would require a significantly greater time commitment from learners *during the course* than is normative for the other courses in the learners' educational program. The course-based format is also not conducive to having learners participate in highly complex, large-scale evaluations.

Several strategies can be used to deal with these limitations; none of them need to be tied to a specific academic course. The simplest is the research assistant or apprentice model, in which an individual evaluator (who may or may not be a faculty member) supervises one or more learners in an evaluation he or she is conducting. The skill-development impact of this approach, as well as the ones that follow, is largely determined by how much substantive responsibility for the evaluation is actually assigned to the learner and the amount of mentoring offered by the evaluator. With respect to the latter, experienced evaluators can play an invaluable role in helping novices reflect on the lessons to be learned from tasks undertaken and stakeholders encountered.

Internships and field placements (on campus or off campus) in service-oriented settings represent a second beyond-the-course strategy. These host settings typically evaluate their program activities, and learners may become involved in multiple evaluation projects in various capacities. A third approach places learners in settings that are explicitly dedicated to research and evaluation, such as university-based evaluation centers. In theory, these learners have the opportunity to receive very intensive and sustained training in applied skills relevant to evaluation. Projects can last for several years and often include national multisite evaluations. Even in these settings, however, achieving both breadth and depth in evaluation training remains an ongoing issue.

As participatory and empowerment approaches to evaluation continue to grow in popularity, beyond-the-course strategies for educating *nonstudent* constituencies (e.g., steering committees, advisory groups) during an evaluation are likely to receive increased attention in the field. These strategies, if successful, are likely to influence the teaching of evaluation in more traditional academic settings.

—Michael Morris

Further Reading

Mertens, D. M. (Ed.). (1989). *Creative ideas for teaching evaluation: Activities, assignments, and resources.* Boston: Kluwer Academic.

Trevisan, M. S. (2002). Enhancing practical evaluation training through long-term evaluation projects. *American Journal of Evaluation, 23,* 81-92.

TEXT ANALYSIS. *See* CONTENT
ANALYSIS, GROUNDED THEORY

THEORY. *See* EVALUATION THEORY,
PROGRAM LOGIC, PROGRAM THEORY,
THEORY–DRIVEN EVALUATION

■■ THEORY–DRIVEN
EVALUATION

Theory-driven evaluation (or program theory–
driven evaluation) is a contextual or holistic assessment
of a program based on the conceptual framework of
program theory. The purpose of theory-driven evaluation
is to provide information on not only the performance
or merit of a program but on how and why
the program achieves such a result. Program theory
is a set of implicit or explicit assumptions of how
the program should be organized and why the program
is expected to work. The nature of program theory
and its conceptual framework are discussed on
pages 340 to 342 in the encyclopedia. When looking
into the crucial assumptions underlying a program,
evaluators should consider that theory-driven evaluation
provides insightful information that assists
stakeholders in understanding those components of
their program that work well and those that do not.
Theory-driven evaluation is particularly useful when
stakeholders want an evaluation to serve both accountability
and program improvement needs.

GENERAL TYPES OF
THEORY-DRIVEN EVALUATIONS

The conceptual framework of program theory is
presented elsewhere (see the Program Theory entry).
Different models of theory-driven evaluations
can be constructed depending on which part of the
conceptual framework of program theory the
evaluation is focused (Chen, 2004). The types of
theory-driven evaluations that have been commonly
applied are theory-driven process evaluation, intervening
mechanism evaluation, moderating mechanism
evaluation, and integrative process/outcome
evaluation.

Theory-Driven Process Evaluation

Theory-driven process evaluation focuses on assessing
the portion of action model implementation in the
conceptual framework (see the Program Theory entry).
More specifically, theory-driven process evaluation is a
holistic assessment of the congruency between the major
components of program theory, especially the portion of
the action model, and their actual implementation.

An example illustrating theory-driven process evaluation
is an evaluation of a large anti-drug abuse program
for middle school students in Taiwan (Chen, 1997). The
program asked school teachers to identify drug-abusing
students and provide them with counseling services.
The congruency between the action model of the program
and actual implementation is illustrated in Table 1.

Intervening Mechanism Evaluation

The model of intervening mechanism evaluation
focuses on the change model of the conceptual framework
of program theory. The change model consists
of three components: intervention, determinants, and
outcomes. The model of intervening mechanism
evaluation is illustrated in Figure 1.

Using the evaluation of a school-based anti-smoking
program (Chen, Quane, Garland, & Marcin, 1988) as an
example, program designers devised a comic book with
an anti-smoking story as an intervention for changing
students' attitudes and behaviors regarding smoking.
The *determinants* were the students' interest in reading
and keeping the comic book. The evaluation assessed
not only whether keeping the comic book affected the
number of times the comic book was read but also
whether the number of times the book was read affected
students' smoking related attitudes and behavior.

Figure 1 is a basic model of intervening mechanism
evaluation. The model can be expanded to include multiple
determinants in sequential order. To date, the intervening
mechanism evaluation is the most popular type
of theory-driven evaluation in terms of application.

Moderating Mechanism Evaluation

The moderating mechanism evaluation involves
assessing one or more factors in program implementation
that conditions, or moderates, the intervention's
effect on outcome. The factors assessed are called
moderators. The basic model for the moderating
mechanism evaluation is illustrated in Figure 2.

Table 1   Evaluating an Anti-Drug Abuse Program

Program Components	Program Plan	Actual Implementation
Target population	All drug-abusing student Drug use to be verified through urinalysis	Only those drug-abusing students who were easy to reach Urinalysis collection environment was not controlled
Implementers	Teachers provided with adequate drug abuse treatment training and information	Teachers lacked adequate drug abuse treatment training
Intervention protocol	Primary: High-quality counseling	Counseling mainly involved use of admonishment, threats, and encouragement
	Secondary: Drug education classes	Drug education classes were offered
Service delivery protocol	Compulsory individual counseling	Compulsory individual counseling, but with problems such as lack of plan and objective
Implementing organizations	Every school	Smaller schools had difficulty implementing the program
Linking with associate organizations	Effective centralized school system	Communication gap, mistrust between Ministry of Education and the schools
Ecological context Micro	Eliminating video game arcades	Video game arcades still exist
Macro	Strong public support	Strong public support, but problematic education system (elitism)

SOURCE: Adapted from *Evaluation and Program Planning, 20*(2), Chen, Huey-Tsyh, "Normative evaluation of an anti-drug abuse program," 195-204, Copyright 1997, with permission from Elsevier.

In Figure 2, the *moderating mechanism* is represented by the arrow drawn from the moderator to the midpoint of another arrow that is located between intervention and outcome, delineating the way in which the moderator conditions the intervention-outcome relationship. For example, the effectiveness of the family counseling may depend on the trust maintained between counselor and clients. Generally speaking, moderators can be clients' sociodemographic characteristics (e.g., race, gender, education, age), implementers' characteristics and styles (e.g., enthusiasm, commitment, skills, race, gender), features of client-implementer relationships (e.g., trust, compatibility of client and implementer gender and race or ethnicity), and mode and setting of service delivery (e.g., formal versus informal, rural versus urban, the intervention's integrity, and the organizational climate, whether centralized or decentralized).

Figure 2 is the basic model of the moderating mechanism. The model can be expanded by incorporating intervening mechanisms into it.

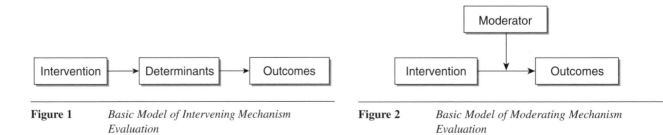

Figure 1   *Basic Model of Intervening Mechanism Evaluation*

Figure 2   *Basic Model of Moderating Mechanism Evaluation*

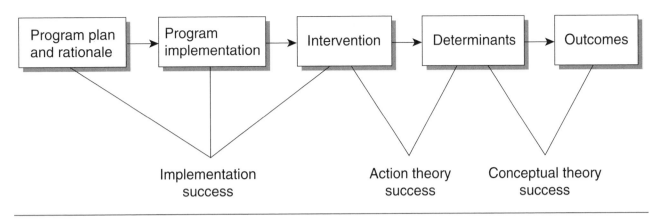

Figure 3   *Model of Integrative Process/Outcome Evaluation*

Integrative Process/Outcome Evaluation

Integrative process/outcome evaluation pertains to the systematic assessment of the crucial assumptions underlying implementation and of the causal processes of a program. This consummately comprehensive assessment provides a network of information about what works and what does not work in a program, from implementation processes to causal processes to effects on outcomes. Such a thorough analysis of potential pathways enlightens stakeholders as to how their program truly operates, providing the knowledge they will need to meet the accountability *and* program-improvement requirements they face.

For example, the application of the integrative process/outcome evaluation to the garbage reduction program (Chen, Wang, & Lin, 1997) requires a systematic evaluation of the change model and action model. The evaluation of the change model required assessment of whether the casual process underlying the program was operated as it was supposed to be. The program assumed that the new garbage collection policy would increase residents' experience of the inconvenience of storing garbage and its unpleasant smell, which in turn would lead to a drop in the amount of garbage produced by the residents. The evaluation of the action model required assessment of the following components:

- *The target population.* Were the residents well informed of the program prior to implementation?
- *Protocols of intervention and service delivery.* Had they developed? If so, they would ensure that garbage was not brought to collection points on Tuesdays.
- *Implementing organization and implementers.* Did the sanitation department have enough personnel and budget for the program? Had it provided workers with training and rehearsed them for implementation of the policy?

- *Public support and linkage with associate organizations.* Did public support for the program and links with peer organizations exist? If not, were these being created?

Integrative process/outcome evaluation, as illustrated in Figure 3, provides information on the important ingredients necessary for a program to be successful. Implementation success refers to the successful implementation of a program plan in the field so that the intervention is appropriately implemented in the field. Action theory success refers to the intervention successfully activating the desired change in the determinants. Conceptual theory success refers to the program's having successfully focused determinants so that the outcomes have been changed. Figure 3 illustrates how challenging it is to design and implement a successful intervention program. For a program to be effective, the implementation, action theory, and conceptual theory must succeed. Implementation success is vitally important to the entire change process. If implementation fails, everything fails. Even when implementation succeeds, however, the success of a program is not guaranteed. Invalidity of either the action theory or conceptual program theory could spell its doom. Comprehensive, systematic integrative process/outcome evaluation abundantly fleshes out assumed underlying mechanisms. It thus provides to stakeholders insightful information they need to have to improve their programs.

ISSUES IN AND STRATEGIES FOR DESIGNING THEORY-DRIVEN EVALUATIONS

Scope of Program Theory in a Theory-Driven Evaluation

Program theory belongs to stakeholders. However, the assumptions underlying their program theory often are not explicitly and systematically stated. One of the essential requirements in theory-driven evaluation is to clarify stakeholders' program theory or facilitate their development of one. The scope of program theory to be clarified or developed depends on which type of theory-driven evaluation stakeholders are interested in. For example, the intervening mechanism or moderating mechanism evaluation is mainly concerned with the portion of the change model in program theory. In this kind of evaluation, evaluators need to focus only on clarifying stakeholders' theory in this portion, the change model. However, if stakeholders and evaluators want to conduct the integrative process/outcome evaluation, the evaluators need to clarify the stakeholders' entire program theory.

Role of Evaluators in Clarifying Stakeholders' Theory

In clarifying stakeholders' program theory, the evaluator's role is that of facilitator. Evaluation skills and knowledge should be brought to bear to increase the productivity of the meetings at which various stakeholders attempt to articulate and refine their ideas about program theory. Stakeholders are sure to have divergent backgrounds, concerns, and interests. It is easy for them to spend much time with freeform discussions that never even approach agreement. The evaluator's job as *facilitator* is to outline for the group the salient issues to discuss, showing stakeholders where to fill in with their own experiences, thoughts, and expertise. The evaluator can synthesize the discussions and build consensus. The evaluator could fill in with his or her own evaluation expertise when stakeholders ask for advice. The evaluator is present to lay out options for stakeholders to consider. However, imposition of the evaluator's own values on stakeholders should studiously be avoided. Evaluators should make clear that stakeholders' program theory will be used as a basis for designing and conducting a theory-drive evaluation.

Participatory Modes

Evaluators can clarify an existing program theory or assist stakeholders whose program theory is under development by adopting either of two general participatory modes: the *intensive interview* and the *working group.* Choosing a mode is a prerequisite for stakeholders and evaluators preparing to work together.

The *intensive interview mode* centers on individual, intensive interviews the evaluator holds with representatives from each key stakeholder group. The aim is to record systematically the individuals' perceptions about issues within the incipient program theory. Based on these interviews, the evaluator formulates a first draft of the program theory, to be read by the representatives and other stakeholders. Their comments are considered as the final draft is prepared. Evaluators can, in addition, conduct a meeting of these individuals for the purpose of fine-tuning and finalizing the program theory. The *working group mode* similarly involves representatives from key stakeholder groups. However, in this mode the representatives are not interviewed individually but instead meet together with the evaluator to develop the program theory. Group members need to include representatives (a) of those who will be most deeply involved in formulating and designing the program, (b) of those who will be most deeply involved in implementing the program, and (c) of other key constituencies whose input will be influential in determining the direction the program will take. The facilitator, of course, (d) is an additional member. This list actually results in relatively few participating persons when the program is a small one. For a large program, however, there is a temptation to include many persons in the working group. A group that is too large can discourage members' full participation, at the same time necessitating many more sessions to finish the work.

Theorizing Procedures

As with the participatory mode, a *theorizing procedure* must be selected to help stakeholders develop their program theory. So-called *forward reasoning, backward reasoning,* and *backward/forward reasoning* are the two general options for evaluators working within the development strategies. Backward reasoning is an approach that begins with the change model, then moves backward step by step to the action model to obtain the program theory. It is "backward" reasoning in that the process moves in the reverse direction of sequences shown in the conceptual framework of program theory (as indicated in the program theory entry). More specifically, backward reasoning starts with the question, What goals will the program want to achieve? What determinants, related to goals, will be focused on by the program? What intervention will be used to affect the determinants? After the change model is completed, evaluators can facilitate stakeholders to develop an action model by asking the following questions: Which target populations need to be reached and served? What kinds of program implementers and implementing organizations are needed? What kinds of intervention and implementation protocols are required? Does the program need to collaborate with other organizations? Does the program need to seek ecological support?

Forward reasoning is the formulation of a program theory that accords with the logic flow specified in the conceptual framework of program theory—action model first, then change model. More specifically, forward reasoning concerns general program goals and grows out of the initial question about the kind of action model needed. These questions follow: What kinds of intervention and service delivery protocols are the implementing organizations good at that can solve a particular problem or assist in attaining certain goals? What target population needs reaching, how can it be reached for services, in what setting, and using what delivery mode? Are there barriers facing clients that the program could help them surmount? Should program designers seek contextual support of the intervention? How? Once the action model is complete, evaluators and stakeholders can develop a change model by asking two questions in sequence: What determinants will be affected by the intervention? What outcomes will be achieved by changing these determinants?

It is important to note that forward and backward reasoning are not mutually exclusive. The forward/backward reasoning is a use of both approaches, back and forth, to facilitate stakeholders making explicit their program theory. Evaluators and stakeholders who want the best of both worlds can apply backward reasoning first and then use forward reasoning to compensate for weaknesses attending the former procedure. For example, an evaluation focused on *both* action and change models might begin with the forward reasoning procedure to construct an action model; take up backward reasoning to establish a change model; and, finally, integrate the two to arrive at an overall program theory. This dual procedure is the better choice when program stakeholders and evaluators believe that unintended outcomes will be an important issue. Going through the theorizing procedures from different directions will alert members of a working group to the possibility of potential unintended effects. The evaluator can facilitate discussion of such unintended effects and ways to prevent them, if they are undesirable.

Consensus Among Stakeholders on Their Program Theory

Agreement among stakeholders about what the program theory should look like often is not difficult to reach. However, even if some components of the program plan do spark disagreement between key stakeholders, this is not an obstacle to evaluation. Rather, disagreement means that evaluators should test various hypotheses during the investigation of the implementation. Suppose key stakeholders in a program argue about who should be charged with implementing the program—professionals or trained peer volunteers? If implementers currently delivering services come from *both* these groups, the evaluation can ask about the relative quality of service delivery by each. Resulting data would be useful for settling differences among stakeholders as they continue planning future programs.

Research Methods

Theory-driven evaluations need to use mixed (qualitative and quantitative) methods in clarifying stakeholders' program theory. However, in terms of research design, data collection, and data analysis, some patterns are emerging from past applications of theory-driven evaluations. Quantitative methods have been heavily used in intervening mechanism evaluation and moderating mechanism evaluation. Theory-driven process evaluation and integrative process/outcome evaluation have required the collection and analysis of both qualitative and quantitative data.

—*Huey-Tsyh Chen*

Further Reading

Chen, H.-T. (1990). *Theory-driven evaluations.* Newbury Park, CA: Sage.

Chen, H.-T. (1997). Normative evaluation of an anti–drug abuse program. *Evaluation and Program Planning, 20*(2), 195-204.

Chen, H.-T. (2004). *Practical program evaluation: Assessing and improving program planning, implementation, and effectiveness.* Thousand Oaks, CA: Sage.

Chen, H-T., Quane, J., Garland, N., & Marcin, P. (1988). Evaluating an anti-smoking program: Diagnostics of underlying casual mechanisms. *Evaluation and Health Professions, 11*(4), 441-464.

Chen, H.-T., Wang, J.C.S., & Lin, L. H. (1997). Evaluating the process and outcomes of a garbage reduction program. *Evaluation Review 21*(1), 27-42.

■ THEORY IN ACTION

Theory in action refers to the mechanisms through which a program is hypothesized to work to achieve its intended outcomes—children's social and ethical development, for example. A program's theory in action is often depicted as a logic model that delineates the relationships between and among program activities, intermediate states or outcomes, and the ultimate intended outcomes of the program. A program activity and intermediate outcome for children's social and ethical development might be class meetings and children's experience of a sense of community in the classroom. Evaluations with a theory-based approach can be used to test a program's theory in action or to help define it.

—*Rosalie T. Torres*

■ THICK DESCRIPTION

A description of human action and the meanings people associate with their experiences is considered to be *thick* if it is written in concrete detail so readers may vicariously experience something similar to what the people being described are experiencing. The purpose is to help readers have a sense of being involved in the situation themselves, with a window into the meanings of the experience from the perspective of one or more of the participants. In evaluation, thick description provides the basis for interpretation of participants' involvement with an evaluand, what that involvement means to them, and why particular value judgments are justified.

—*David D. Williams*

Further Reading

Geertz, C. (1973). Thick description: Toward an interpretive theory of culture. In C. Geertz (Ed.), *The interpretation of cultures.* New York: Basic Books.

■ THINK-ALOUD PROTOCOL

Think-aloud protocol is a research strategy whereby participants speak whatever words come to mind as they complete a task, such as solving a problem or using a computer program. The task may be open ended, and it may be either of the participant's choosing or selected by the evaluator. Participants are expected to put a minimal effort into responding through the use of general prompts such as, "What are you thinking now?" or "Why did you do that?" This technique is used to identify participants' locus of attention, identify frustrations, understand language learning, and understand metacognition. The technique provides rich, direct data but is labor intensive and sometimes distracting for participants, and it may illustrate verbosity as much as it reveals thought processes.

■ 360-DEGREE EVALUATION

A *360-degree evaluation* is a type of personnel evaluation strategy in which an individual evaluates him- or herself based on a set of criteria (knowledge, skills, attitudes), as do the individual's supervisor and peers. The strategy may also be applied to evaluands other than individuals, such as programs or organizations. A gap analysis illustrates the difference between how the individual perceives him- or herself and how others perceive the individual. Feedback that is "360 degrees" may be used for coaching, formative evaluation, and organizational development.

See also PERSONNEL EVALUATION

■ TILLEY, NICK

(b. 1947, Essex, England). M.Sc., London School of Economics; B.Sc. Sociology, London University.

Tilley is Professor of Sociology at Nottingham Trent University, England, and Visiting Professor at University College London in the Jill Dando Institute of Crime Science. Since 1992, he has also worked with the Home Office Research Development and Statistics Directorate as Research Consultant. As a result of this work, an annual prize for problem-oriented policing, the Tilley Award, has been named after him and funded by the Home Office since 1998.

His primary contributions to the field of evaluation have been the conceptualization and explication of realist evaluation and the use of evaluation in the field of criminology. Primary influences for his work are Karl Popper and his writings on the open society, piecemeal social engineering, situational logic, and falsification; realist philosophy of science in the work of Roy Bhaskar and Rom Harré; rational choice theory and the significance of mechanisms in social explanation, especially in the work of Jon Elster and Raymond Boudon; middle-range theorizing as discussed by Robert Merton; and problem solving and situational crime prevention, notably as described by Herman Goldstein and Ron Clarke.

He has published widely in criminology and on realist methodology in evaluation, both for practitioners and for academics. He is the coauthor of *Realistic Evaluation* (with Ray Pawson) and Editor of *Evaluation for Crime Prevention.* He has contributed to, among other periodicals, the *British Journal of Criminology; Knowledge and Policy; Crime and Justice: A Review of Research; Evaluation;* and the *European Journal on Criminal Policy and Research.* Recent research projects have included an examination of police uses of forensic science, an evaluation of a program aiming to reduce crime against small businesses, and participation in action projects aiming to implement problem-oriented policing in Leicestershire and to reduce shootings in Manchester. He is active in many organizations and has served as President of the U.K. Evaluation Society.

TIME SERIES ANALYSIS. *See* QUASIEXPERIMENTAL DESIGN

▣ TORRES, ROSALIE T.

(b. 1955, New Orleans, Louisiana). Ph.D. Educational Psychology, University of Illinois, Urbana-Champaign; M.S. Experimental Psychology, Southern Methodist University; B.A. cum laude Psychology, Vanderbilt University.

Torres has been influenced by the works of Robert Stake, Alan (Buddy) Peshkin, Michael Patton, Clifford Geertz, Mihaly Csikszentmihalyi, and Charles Fillmore. She has been instrumental in contributing to the articulation of practice-based theories of evaluation use and thought on the relationship between evaluation and learning at individual, team, and organizational levels. She has enhanced the profession through her consideration of strategies and practices that could increase the effectiveness of communicating and reporting in evaluation. Over the past 25 years, serving in both internal and external evaluator roles, she has conducted more than 50 evaluations

in education, business, health-care, and nonprofit organizations.

She has served as an AEA Board Member, Cochair of the Evaluation Use TIG, Editorial Advisory Board Member of the *American Journal of Evaluation,* Editorial Board Member of the *Canadian Journal of Program Evaluation,* and Staff Director for the 1994 revision (second edition) of *The Program Evaluation Standards.* Torres has participated in numerous conference presentations and events with the American Evaluation Association from 1981 to the present and has coauthored *Evaluative Inquiry for Learning in Organizations* (with H. S. Preskill). She is the winner of the 1999 Book of the Year Award from the Academy of Human Resource Development.

Torres currently works, plays, and grows sweet peas in the San Francisco Bay Area.

▣ TOULEMONDE, JACQUES

(b. 1947, Roubaix, France). M.A. Economics, Paris-Sorbonne University, France; M.A. Management, Institut d'Economie Scientifique et de Gestion (IESEG), Lille, France.

Toulemonde is Scientific Director and cofounder of the Centre for European Evaluation Expertise (Eureval-C3E). He provides expertise and advice on evaluation to public organizations at the international, national, and regional levels in many countries. Besides being actively involved in building evaluation capacity in the European Union, he teaches evaluation in several French universities and is an invited speaker at international conferences. He is also a member of the International Evaluation Research Group. Previous professional experience includes being Senior Researcher in Policy and Program Evaluation and Professor of Public Economics at the National School of Public Engineering in Lyon, Officer-in-Charge of Urban Planning and Development for the French Ministry of Housing and Public Works, and Economist for the Algerian Ministry of Planning.

His primary contributions to the field of evaluation center around causality analysis, evaluation in partnership across levels of government, evaluation capacity building, and the quality and professionalism of evaluation. Besides setting up and developing the European Evaluation Society and the French Evaluation Society, he has trained hundreds of evaluation managers in the European institutions and in all European countries. He is Coeditor of *Politics and Practices of Intergovernmental Evaluation* (with O. Rieper) and author, editor, or coauthor of many journal articles, reports, and training seminars. He has contributed to several evaluation guidelines that have been widely disseminated in Europe, such as the MEANS Collection, a set of six handbooks issued in 1999 by the European Commission. He has also contributed to four books: *Intergovernmental Evaluation, Building Effective Evaluation Capacity,* the *International Evaluation Atlas,* and *Assessing Evaluative Information.*

TRANSACTION MODELS. *See* DEMOCRATIC EVALUATION, ILLUMINATIVE EVALUATION, RESPONSIVE EVALUATION

▪▪ TRANSDISCIPLINE

Michael Scriven has characterized evaluation as a *transdicipline,* a discipline that focuses on issues essential to other disciplines but has itself the attributes of a discipline. Statistics, logic, psychometrics, and evaluation are all examples of transdisciplines. Transdisciplines lead to applications of knowledge across a broad range of other disciplines. Evaluation, for example, is used in education, health, human services, engineering, environmental studies, and so on. Because evaluation is a transdiscipline, there is an ongoing debate within the profession and practice about the relative importance of knowledge about evaluation *qua* evaluation and knowledge about the discipline most closely associated with the evaluand.

Further Reading

Scriven, M. (1991). *Evaluation thesaurus.* Newbury Park, CA: Sage.

▪▪ TRANSFORMATIVE PARADIGM

The *transformative paradigm* represents a worldview, and its accompanying philosophical assumptions, that emerged from the writings of scholars from diverse ethnic and racial groups, people with disabilities, and feminists. Evaluators work in contested territory that is laden with pluralistic values and associated with real-life implications for resource allocation. These characteristics of the evaluation landscape not only differentiate it from traditional social science research but also logically connect it with the work of transformative scholars. The transformative paradigm's basic beliefs are that knowledge is not neutral: It is influenced by human interests, and all knowledge reflects power and social relationships within society. The transformative paradigm is characterized as placing central importance on the lives and experiences of marginalized groups such as women, ethnic and racial minorities, members of the gay and lesbian communities, people with disabilities, and those who are poor. Transformative scholars have as their central mission the accurate and credible representation of marginalized groups in and through the process of systematic inquiry toward the goal of bringing society to a point of greater equity and justice.

The transformative paradigm's underlying assumptions are illuminated by answering ontological, epistemological, and methodological questions. The ontological question is, "What is the nature of reality?" The transformative ontological assumption holds that there are diversities of viewpoints with regard to many social realities but that those viewpoints need to be placed within political, cultural, historical, and economic value systems to understand the basis for the differences. Evaluators need to struggle with revealing those multiple constructions, as well as with making decisions about privileging one perspective over another.

The epistemological question is, "What is the nature of knowledge and the relationship between the knower and the would-be known?" Epistemologically, the transformative assumption is that knowledge is created by a depth of understanding that can be achieved only through sustained and meaningful involvement with the community affected by the service, program, or policy. This level of involvement reflects the valuing of objectivity as much as a balanced and complete view of the program processes and effects is possible, such that bias is not interjected because of a lack of understanding of key viewpoints. This epistemological assumption underscores the importance of an interactive link between the researcher and the participants, with sensitivity given to the impact of social and historical factors in the relationship between the researcher and the participants, as well as the impact of those variables on the construction of knowledge.

The methodological question asks, "How can the knower go about obtaining the desired knowledge and understanding?" The transformative paradigm might involve quantitative, qualitative, or mixed methods, but the community affected by the research would be involved to some degree in the methodological and programmatic decisions. The research is conducted with the involvement of all relevant communities, especially the least advantaged. The research conclusions are based in data, but these data are generated from an inclusive list of persons affected by the research, with special efforts to include those who have been traditionally underrepresented.

—*Donna M. Mertens*

Further Reading

Mertens, D. M. (1998). *Research methods in education and psychology: Integrating diversity.* Thousand Oaks: CA: Sage.

Mertens, D. M. (2003). Mixed methods and the politics of human research: The transformative-emancipatory perspective. In A. Tashakkori & C. Teddlie (Eds.), *Handbook of mixed methods in social and behavioral research.* Thousand Oaks, CA: Sage.

TREATMENTS

In the context of evaluation, *treatments* refers to programs or other interventions intended to remedy or improve existing conditions. A change in policies or practices can also be called a treatment. Recent examples of treatments that have been evaluated include Early Head Start, welfare reform, and changes in Medicare capitation rates (i.e., pay schedules for various medical procedures). Quantitatively oriented evaluators often refer to estimating treatment effects; that is, to assessing how much of a difference a given treatment makes on selected outcomes. More generally, evaluation often involves assessing the implementation, effectiveness, efficiency, reach, fairness, and acceptability of a new treatment relative to current conditions or of alternative treatments.

—*Melvin M. Mark and Poh-Pheng Chua*

See also INTERVENTION

TRIANGULATION

Triangulation is typically perceived to be a strategy for improving the validity of evaluation findings; a strategy that will aid in the elimination of bias and allow the dismissal of rival alternative explanations of conclusions and propositions. Triangulation as a strategy in the social sciences dates to a 1959 paper by Campbell and Fiske in which they lay out the foundation for establishing the validity of measures through the application of a multitrait-multimethod matrix, a procedure involving both convergent and discriminant measures of traits. Eugene Webb coined the term, however, in 1966 in his now famous work, *Unobtrusive Measures.*

There are generally understood to be four types of triangulation:

1. Data triangulation, including across time, space, and person, or using several data sources

2. Investigator triangulation, or using more than one investigator

3. Theory triangulation, or using more than one theoretical perspective

4. Methodological triangulation, or using multiple methods

The basic underlying assumption in triangulation is that its use will lead to the elimination of error and bias, leaving nothing but the truth. This assumption is embedded within particular ontological and epistemological frameworks. Other conceptions of triangulation focus on an underlying assumption of clarification and elucidation as a result of triangulation. Thus, for example, different data sources or methods may lead to inconsistency and contradiction, but these are equally valuable understandings in rendering sensible accounts of what something means. Indeed, most evaluators understand that it is atypical for a single conclusion to emerge and that this does not preclude the making of evaluative claims or the drawing of evaluative conclusions.

Triangulation is often thought of as a technological solution for ensuring the validity of claims and conclusions, but it should be thought of more as a step in the process of embedding complex empirical data in a more holistic understanding of that specific situation.

In the end, the evaluator still has responsibility for the construction of plausible and justifiable claims.

Further Reading

Mathison, S. (1988). Why triangulate? *Educational Researcher,* *17*(2), 13-18.

▋▋ TROCHIM, WILLIAM

(b. 1952, Chicago, Illinois). Ph.D. Methodology and Evaluation Research, Northwestern; M.A. Experimental Psychology, Southern Connecticut University; B.A. Psychology, Loyola University (Mundelein College).

Trochim is Professor, Department of Policy Analysis and Management, and Director of the Office for the Management of Not-for-profit Institutions at Cornell University. He also holds an appointment as Visiting Scientist with the Division of Cancer Control and Population Sciences of the National Cancer Institute, the largest of the National Institutes of Health.

His contributions to evaluation are, broadly, in the area of applied social research methodology, with an emphasis on program planning and evaluation methods. Among experimentalists, he is well known for his work in quasiexperimental alternatives to randomized experimental designs, especially the regression discontinuity and regression-point displacement designs. In terms of research theory, he has extended the theory of validity through his articulation and investigation of the idea of pattern matching. In multivariate and applied contexts, he is recognized for the development of a multivariate form of concept mapping, a general method for mapping the ideas of a group of people on any topic of interest that integrates traditional group processes (e.g., brainstorming, Delphi, focus groups, nominal group technique) with state-of-the-art statistical methods (e.g., multidimensional scaling, hierarchical cluster analysis).

He has written several books, including a widely used introductory research methods text, *The Research Methods Knowledge Base,* and its online companion, *Bill Trochim's Center for Social Research Methods.* This text and its Web-based version are clear, appropriately nuanced, and transdisciplinary. They provide guidance to novice and experienced evaluators in many fields. He is also the developer of the Concept System® software and methodology and co-owner of a company, Concept Systems Incorporated, that licenses the software and provides training and consulting services to support the method.

Trochim has been an active member of the American Evaluation Association, serving multiple terms on its board.

▋▋ TRUSTWORTHINESS

Trustworthiness is a term used within interpretivist and constructivist paradigms that is the approximate equivalent of *validity.* The trustworthiness of evaluation resides primarily within the data and is addressed by questions such as, "Are data able to be traced back to a primary source?" "Are they verifiable?" "Are the conclusions reached logical, sensible, plausible?" The criteria for trustworthiness are credibility, transferability, dependability, and confirmability.

See also FOURTH-GENERATION EVALUATION

▋▋ TYLER, RALPH W.

(b. 1902, Chicago, Illinois; d. 1994, San Diego, California). Ph.D., University of Chicago; M.S., University of Nebraska; B.S., Doane College.

At the time of his death, Tyler was a visiting scholar at the School of Education at Stanford University and had stayed active well into his 80s, advising teachers and administrators across the country on how to set objectives that would encourage the best teaching and learning within their schools. Tyler held faculty positions at the University of North Carolina, The Ohio State University, and the University of Chicago, where he was also Dean of the Division of the Social Sciences. He was a visiting scholar at the University of Massachusetts–Amherst; an advisor on evaluation and curriculum in Ghana, Indonesia, Ireland, Israel, and Sweden; and held 22 honorary doctoral degrees. From 1953 to 1967, he was Founding Director of the Center for Advanced Study in the Behavioral Sciences at Stanford. In 1969, he became President of the System Development Foundation in San Francisco, which supported research in the information sciences.

Tyler's influence on the discipline of education, including curriculum, instruction, and evaluation, is remarkable. During the early part of the 1900s, testing as a way in which to measure constructs such as intelligence or achievement was spreading rapidly. Testing as the sole approach to evaluating educational programs was threatening the way high school programs were being developed and delivered. Tyler questioned the appropriateness of such tests for the purpose of program or pupil evaluation. In 1934, he became Director of Evaluation of the Eight-Year Study sponsored by the Progressive Education Association. This longitudinal study, which compared the experiences of students in a variety of high school programs, is credited for widely influencing changes in curriculum development and educational evaluation methods; both were seen as integral parts of the cycle of teaching and learning. The basic principle Tyler developed is that there are a variety of ways to evaluate pupil progress and achievement, and the evaluation approach should be appropriate to the behavior or outcome to be evaluated. This meant determining the purpose of these programs right at the start. It was during this study that Tyler first conceptualized the objectives-based approach to educational evaluation, an approach that continues to influence curriculum development and evaluation today.

Tyler published more than 700 articles and 16 books, but he is best known for *Basic Principles of Curriculum and Instruction,* first published in 1949. In this book, he lays out the four basic principles of objectives-based evaluation: (a) defining appropriate learning objectives, (b) establishing useful learning experiences, (c) organizing learning experiences so that they have the maximum cumulative effect, and (d) evaluating the curriculum and revising those aspects that did not prove to be effective.

Tyler was an adviser on education to six U.S. presidents. He served on an impressive range of committees, including the National Council for the Education of Disadvantaged Children and the Science Research Associates, and he was appointed to the Task Force on Older Americans under President Lyndon Johnson. He was the first President of the National Academy of Education. In the 1960s, he was asked by the Carnegie Corporation to chair the committee that eventually developed and initiated the National Assessment of Educational Progress (NAEP). Tyler helped set guidelines for the expenditure of federal funds and contributed to the policies established in the Elementary and Secondary Education Act of 1965. His work was, and remains, influential.

UNDERSTANDING

Understanding is a kind of knowledge that comes through living in a situation with participants of that situation and gaining a practical working knowledge of what they are experiencing. It cannot be obtained through objective means alone but involves inquirers participating with those studied and examination of the inquirer's own responses to the experience as well as those of other participants. In evaluation, understanding is viewed as necessary for an evaluator who seeks to account for values underlying participants' behaviors, as well as meanings participants associate with those behaviors in their cultural context.

—*David D. Williams*

See also VERSTEHEN

UNIQUE-CASE ANALYSIS

A framework used within a case study evaluation approach, *unique-case analysis* assumes that each case has unique attributes and that much can be learned by concentrating on a single case. Using unique-case analysis, an evaluator would first capture and respect the details of each individual case being studied and analyze the data collected from each case within its own context. A cross-case analysis might follow, depending on the framework of the evaluation and the quality of the individual case studies.

—*Leslie K. Goodyear*

Further Reading

Stake, R. (2000). Case studies. In N. K. Denzin & Y. S. Lincoln (Eds.), *The handbook of qualitative research* (pp. 435-454). Thousand Oaks, CA: Sage.

UNITED STATES AGENCY OF INTERNATIONAL DEVELOPMENT (USAID)

USAID is the U.S. government agency that provides assistance to foreign countries in agriculture, human services, health, and economic development. U.S. foreign aid has always had the twofold purpose of furthering America's foreign policy interests in expanding democracy and free markets and improving the lives of the citizens of the developing world. USAID was created in 1961 during the Kennedy administration to administer economic assistance programs. The substantial investment of aid in foreign countries has meant that USAID has contributed to the development of evaluation practice in developing nations and for development projects.

UNOBTRUSIVE MEASURES

Unobtrusive measures are those measures used to collect data that are found naturally in field settings and that can be used without participants' awareness or alteration in the natural course of events. Questionnaires, interviews, and direct observation are intrusive in the sense that the participants realize they are being questioned or watched. A major difficulty with subjects' awareness that they are participants is that their behavior may be affected by this knowledge. The major types of unobtrusive measures include physical traces (such as worn floors), books, computers, documents, letters, and observations in which the subject is unaware of being researched.

—*Marco A. Muñoz*

Further Reading

Webb, E. J., Campbell, D. T., Schwartz, R., & Sechrest, L. B. (1999). *Unobtrusive measures.* Thousand Oaks, CA: Sage.

■ URBAN INSTITUTE

In 1968, U.S. President Lyndon B. Johnson established a blue-ribbon commission of government officials and civil leaders to charter a nonprofit, nonpartisan research institute to study America's cities and urban populations. Today, the Urban Institute continues to examine a wide range of social, economic, and governance problems facing the nation. It provides information and analysis to public and private decision makers and strives to raise citizen understanding of the issues and trade-offs in public policy making. Project funding comes from government agencies, foundations, and multilateral institutions such as the World Bank.

Current Urban Institute policy research covers a broad range of topics and related subtopics, including adolescent and youth development, governing, children, health and health care, cities and metropolitan regions, housing, crime and justice, immigration, data, international issues, the labor market, education, race, ethnicity, gender, the elderly, tax policy, families and parenting, and welfare reform and safety net issues. Headquartered in Washington, DC, a multidisciplinary staff of about 400 works in its 10 policy centers and cross-center programs.

—*Jeffrey G. Tucker*

■ UTILITY TESTS

Utility tests offer a set of criteria for judging evaluations that parallels the more traditional validity tests for experimental research. Just as validity tests look for and attempt to counteract threats to validity, utility tests look for and attempt to counteract threats to

utility. In a classic article that introduced the idea of utility tests, Weiss and Bucuvalas examined the criteria that decision makers employ in judging evaluation and policy research. They found that decision makers employ both *truth tests* and *utility tests.* Truth tests are a layperson's equivalent of a researcher's validity tests. Utility tests involve additional criteria that are conceptualized from the point of view of intended users:

- *Relevance.* Does the evaluation relate to my needs and interests as a real-world decision maker?
- *Understandability.* Can I make sense of the findings, or are they presented with so much research jargon that an ordinary person cannot really understand them?
- *Conclusiveness.* Was some conclusion reached or judgment made that has program or policy implications, or are there so many qualifications attached to the findings that they are essentially inconclusive?
- *Actionability.* Can I do something with the findings? Do they provide concrete direction and reasonable recommendations?
- *Political viability.* Does the evaluation speak to real-world conditions and take into account political realities, or is it an "ivory tower" report?
- *Fairness.* Can I trust the findings? Is the evaluator credible, the report balanced?
- *Utility.* Overall, is the evaluation significant enough for me, as a busy decision maker, to spend time on? Is it useful to me?

Although evaluation users place a high premium on utility tests, some controversy exists within the profession about whether evaluations should be judged by utility. Those opposed argue that methodological rigor and validity should be primary. They worry that too much attention to utility will lead to weak designs. Tension can occur between "truth tests" and "utility tests," but the evidence shows that those who commission evaluations want both. In response, the evaluation profession has adopted both utility and accuracy standards as criteria of excellence.

Involving intended users in the evaluation process has been one major approach to reducing threats to utility, as in utilization-focused evaluation. Some evaluators worry that methodological rigor may be sacrificed if nonscientists collaborate in making methods decisions. On the whole, the evidence supports the view that high-quality involvement of intended users will result in high-quality, useful evaluations.

Decision makers want data that are useful *and* accurate. Validity and utility are interdependent. Threats to utility are as important to counter as threats to validity. Skilled evaluation facilitators can help nonscientists understand methodological issues so that they can judge for themselves the trade-offs involved in choosing among design options to guard against threats to both validity and utility.

—Michael Quinn Patton

Further Reading

Patton, M. Q. (1997). *Utilization-focused evaluation.* Thousand Oaks, CA: Sage.

Weiss, C. H., & Bucuvalas, M. (1980). Truth tests and utility tests: Decision makers' frame of reference for social science research. *American Sociological Review, 45,* 302-313.

UTILIZATION-FOCUSED EVALUATION

Utilization-focused evaluation begins with the premise that evaluations should be judged by their utility and actual use; therefore, evaluators should facilitate the evaluation process and design any evaluation with careful consideration for how everything that is done, *from beginning to end,* will affect use. Utilization-focused evaluation is concerned with how real people in the real world apply evaluation findings and experience the evaluation process. The goal of utilization-focused evaluation is intended use (of the evaluation results) by intended users.

In any given evaluation, there are many potential stakeholders and an array of possible uses for the evaluation's findings. Utilization-focused evaluation requires moving from the passive notion of informing an audience to the active concept of working with intended users to meet their evaluative information needs. This means identifying specific primary intended users and their explicit commitments to concrete, specific uses. The evaluator facilitates judgment and decision making by intended users rather than acting solely as a distant, independent judge. Utilization-focused evaluation operates from the premise that evaluation use is too important to be merely hoped for or assumed. Use must be planned for and facilitated.

The utilization-focused evaluator develops a working relationship with intended users to help them determine what kind of evaluation they need. This requires negotiation in which the evaluator offers a menu of possibilities. Utilization-focused evaluation does not depend on or advocate any particular evaluation content, model, method, theory, or even use. Rather, it is a process for helping primary intended users select the most appropriate content, model, methods, theory, and uses for their particular situation. As the entries in this encyclopedia demonstrate, many options are now available in the feast that has become the field of evaluation. In considering the rich and varied menu of evaluation, utilization-focused evaluation can include any evaluative purpose, any kind of data, any kind of design, and any kind of focus. Utilization-focused evaluation is a process for making decisions about these issues in collaboration with an identified group of primary users, focusing on their intended uses of evaluation.

A psychology of use undergirds and informs utilization-focused evaluation. Research on use shows that intended users are more likely to use evaluations if they understand and feel ownership of the evaluation process and findings; they are more likely to understand and feel ownership if they have been actively involved; and by actively involving primary intended users, the evaluator is training users in use, preparing the groundwork for use, and reinforcing the intended utility of the evaluation every step along the way.

THE PERSONAL FACTOR

Clearly and explicitly identifying people who can benefit from an evaluation is so important that evaluators have adopted a special term for potential evaluation users: *stakeholders.* Evaluation stakeholders are people who have a stake—a vested interest—in evaluation findings. In any evaluation, there are multiple possible stakeholders: program funders, staff, administrators, and clients or program participants. Others with a direct, or even indirect, interest in program effectiveness may be considered stakeholders, including journalists and members of the general public or, more specifically, taxpayers, in the case of public programs. However, stakeholders typically have diverse and often competing interests. No evaluation can answer all potential questions equally well. This means that some process is necessary for narrowing the range of possible questions. In utilization-focused evaluation, this process begins by narrowing the list of potential stakeholders to a much shorter, more specific group of primary intended users.

It is not sufficient to identify an agency or organization as a recipient of the evaluation report. Organizations are an impersonal collection of hierarchical positions. People, not organizations, use evaluation information—thus the importance of the personal factor.

The personal factor is the presence of an identifiable individual or group of people who personally care about the evaluation and the findings it generates. Research on use has shown that if a person or group is actively involved with and interested in an evaluation, evaluation results are more likely to be used. The personal factor represents the leadership, interest, enthusiasm, determination, commitment, assertiveness, and caring of specific, individual people. These are people who actively seek information to make judgments and reduce decision uncertainties. They want to increase their ability to predict the outcomes of programmatic activity and thereby enhance their own discretion as decision makers, policy makers, consumers, program participants, funders, or whatever roles they play. These are the primary users of evaluation.

THE STEPS IN A UTILIZATION-FOCUSED EVALUATION PROCESS

First, intended users of the evaluation are identified. These intended users are brought together or organized in some fashion, if possible (e.g., an evaluation task force of primary stakeholders), to work with the evaluator and share in making major decisions about the evaluation.

Second, the evaluator and intended users commit to the intended uses of the evaluation and determine the focus of the evaluation (for example, formative, summative, or knowledge generating). Prioritizing evaluation questions will often include consideration of the relative importance of focusing on the attainment of goals, program implementation, or the program's theory of action (logic model). The menu of evaluation possibilities is vast, so many different types of evaluations may need to be discussed. The evaluator works with intended users to determine priority uses with attention to political and ethical considerations.

The third overall stage of the process involves methods, measurement, and design decisions. Primary intended users are involved in making methods decisions so that they will fully understand the strengths and weaknesses of the findings they will use. A variety of options may be considered: qualitative and quantitative data; naturalistic, experimental, and quasiexperimental designs; purposeful and probabilistic sampling approaches; greater and lesser emphasis on generalizations; and alternative ways of dealing with potential threats to validity, reliability, and utility. More specifically, the discussion at this stage will include attention to issues of methodological appropriateness, believability of the data, understandability, accuracy, balance, practicality, propriety, and cost. As always, the overriding concern will be utility. Will the results obtained from these methods be useful—and actually used?

Once data have been collected and organized for analysis, the fourth stage of the utilization-focused process begins. Intended users are actively and directly involved in interpreting findings, making judgments based on the data, and generating recommendations. Specific strategies for use can then be formalized in the light of actual findings, and the evaluator can facilitate following through on actual use.

Finally, decisions about dissemination of the evaluation report can be made beyond whatever initial commitments were made earlier in planning for intended use. This reinforces the distinction between intended use by intended users (planned utilization) versus more general dissemination for broad public accountability (where both hoped-for and unintended uses may occur).

Although in principle there is a straightforward, one-step-at-a-time logic to the unfolding of a utilization- focused evaluation, in reality the process is seldom simple or linear. For example, the evaluator may find that new users become important or new questions emerge in the midst of methods decisions. Nor is there necessarily a clear and clean distinction between the processes of focusing evaluation questions and making methods decisions; questions inform methods, and methodological preferences can inform questions.

Every evaluation situation is unique. A successful evaluation (one that is useful, practical, ethical, and accurate) emerges from the special characteristics and conditions of a particular situation—a mixture of people, politics, history, context, resources, constraints, values, needs, interests, and chance. The phrase "active-reactive-adaptive" describes the nature of the consultative interactions that go on between utilization-focused evaluators and intended users. Utilization-focused evaluators are active in identifying intended users and focusing useful questions. They are reactive in listening to intended users and responding to what they learn about the particular situation in which the evaluation unfolds. They are adaptive in altering evaluation questions and designs in the light of their increased understanding of the situation and changing conditions. Active-reactive-adaptive evaluators do not impose cookbook designs. They are genuinely immersed in the challenges of each new setting and authentically responsive to the intended users of each new evaluation.

Being active-reactive-adaptive explicitly recognizes the importance of the individual evaluator's experience, orientation, and contribution by placing the mandate to be "active" first in this consulting triangle. Arriving at the final evaluation design is a negotiated process that allows the values and capabilities of the evaluator to intermingle with those of intended users.

THE ACHILLES HEEL OF UTILIZATION-FOCUSED EVALUATION

The Achilles heel of utilization-focused evaluation, its point of greatest vulnerability, is turnover of primary intended users. The process depends on the active engagement of intended users, so losing users along the way to job transitions, reorganizations, reassignments, and elections can undermine eventual use. Replacement users who join the evaluation late in the process seldom come in with the same agenda as those who were present at the beginning. The best antidote involves working with a task force of multiple intended users so that the departure of one or two is less critical. Still, when substantial turnover of primary intended users occurs, it may be necessary to reignite the process by renegotiating the design and use commitments with the new arrivals on the scene. When new intended users replace those who depart, new relationships must be built. That may mean delays in original timelines, but such delays pay off in eventual use if evaluators attend to the foundation of understandings and relationships on which utilization-focused evaluation is built.

PREMISES AND LESSONS

Here are some practical lessons about and premises of utilization-focused evaluation.

1. Not All Information Is Useful. To be power laden, information must be relevant and in a form that is understandable to users.

2. Not All People Are Information Users. Individuals vary in their aptitude for engaging evaluative information and processes. Differential socialization, education, and experience magnify such differences. In the political practice of evaluation, this means that information is most powerful in the hands of people who know how to use it and are open to using it. The challenge of use is one of matching: getting the right information to the right people.

3. Users Can Be Trained. Evaluators working with intended users have some responsibility to *train* those users in evaluation processes and the uses of information. Training stakeholders in evaluation methods and processes attends to both short-term and long-term evaluation uses. Making decision makers more sophisticated about evaluation can contribute to greater use of evaluation over time. A utilization-focused evaluator looks for opportunities and strategies for creating and training information users.

4. Information Targeted at Use Is More Likely to Hit the Target. It is difficult to know, before a decision is made, precisely what information will be most valuable. Utilization-focused evaluation aims to increase the probability of gathering appropriate and relevant information by focusing on real issues with real timelines, aimed at real decisions.

5. Only Credible Information Is Ultimately Powerful. The characteristics of both an evaluation and an evaluator affect use, and one of the most important characteristics of each is credibility. The more politicized the context in which an evaluation is conducted and the more visible an evaluation will be in that politicized environment, the more important to credibility will be an independent assessment of evaluation quality to establish credibility.

6. Utilization-Focused Evaluators Need Special Skills. To keep an evaluation from being caught up in destructive group processes or power politics, a utilization-focused evaluator needs to be politically savvy and skillful in group facilitation. By recognizing the inherently political nature of evaluation, evaluators can enter the political fray with some sophistication and skill.

7. Attend to Use Throughout the Process. Strategizing about use is ongoing and continuous from the very beginning of the evaluation. Use is not something one becomes interested in at the end of an evaluation. By the end of the evaluation, the potential for use has been largely determined. From the moment stakeholders and evaluators begin interacting and start to conceptualize the evaluation, decisions are being made that will affect use in major ways.

8. Seek High-Quality Engagement. High-quality participation by intended users is the goal, not high-quantity participation. The quantity of group interaction time can be inversely related to the quality of the process. Evaluators conducting utilization-focused evaluations must be skilled group facilitators.

9. Distinguish Use From Dissemination. Use is different from reporting and dissemination. Reporting and dissemination may be means to facilitate use, but they should not be confused with such intended uses as making decisions, improving programs, changing thinking, and generating knowledge.

10. Distinguish Use From Completing a Report. From a utilization-focused perspective, completing a final report does not conclude an evaluation. Follow-through is needed to help intended users understand and apply a report's findings. This may mean budgeting for an evaluator's involvement beyond the report so that the evaluator can facilitate utilization.

11. Evaluators Need Solid Ethical Grounding. How can evaluators maintain their integrity if they become involved in close, collaborative relationships with stakeholders? How does the evaluator take politics into account without becoming a political tool of only one partisan interest? Evaluators can find themselves on the proverbial horns of a dilemma: Getting too close to decision makers may jeopardize scientific credibility; remaining distant may undermine use. The ethics of building close relationships concern the integrity, neutrality, and corruptibility of the evaluator. These concerns center on the fundamental ethical question: Who does an evaluation— and an evaluator— serve?

Evaluators need to be deliberative and intentional about their own moral groundings and attend thoughtfully to concerns about whose interests are represented in the questions asked and who will have access to the findings. In every evaluation, an evaluator's reputation, credibility, and beliefs are on the line. A utilization-focused evaluator is not passive, simply accepting and buying into whatever an intended user initially desires. The active-reactive-adaptive process connotes an obligation on the part of the evaluator to represent the standards and principles of the profession as well as his or her own sense of morality and integrity, plus attending to and respecting the beliefs and concerns of other, primary users.

A second issue concerns how the interests of various stakeholder groups are represented in a utilization-focused process. The preferred solution is to work to get participants in affected groups representing themselves as part of the evaluation-negotiating process. Thus, where the interests of disadvantaged people are at stake, ways of hearing from or involving them directly should be explored; disadvantaged persons should not just be represented in a potentially patronizing manner by the advantaged. Whether and how to do this is part of what the evaluator negotiates.

11. Use Should Be Planned and Calculated, Including the Costs of Achieving Use. Serious attention to use involves financial and time costs that are far from trivial. These costs should be made explicit in evaluation proposals and budgets so that utilization follow-through is not neglected for lack of resources. The benefit of these costs is greater use.

—*Michael Quinn Patton*

Further Reading

Patton, M. Q. (1997). *Utilization-focused evaluation.* Thousand Oaks, CA: Sage.

Evaluation Practice Around the World

Afghanistan

Seeds Against Malnutrition in Afghanistan: An Experience in Participative Performance Evaluation Training

Following political changes in Afghanistan, French medical NGO Aide Médicale Internationale (AMI) felt the need to reassess its interventions in a country where it had been present for more than two decades. Through a participative and consensual process with actors in the field and in France (using the Delphi technique with 33 persons, who were contacted by e-mail), the following evaluation question was defined: Which criteria can be used to evaluate program performance?

To allow for a better appropriation of the evaluation results, we combined two original participative approaches—we focused on the needs of those using the results and we allowed for maximum involvement of stakeholders. Three training and action workshops were carried out over 3 days in Mazar-e-sharif, Gulbahar, and Kabul (three regions where AMI is involved) with 77 people from local communities, the Ministry of Health, and AMI medical and non-medical staff. The aim of those workshops was to make participants aware of the basic concepts of program evaluation and to teach them a logical model that would help them to determine what to expect from projects in their local context. The AMI logical performance model served as a tool for sharing a common vision of projects by identifying the chain of results from output to impact.

This method, which aims at creating useful and usable indicators of performance through training sessions, may have appeared somewhat laborious at the time. However, it emphasized the importance of using a participative method. It would have been easier and faster to implement WHO indicators in AMI programs in Afghanistan, but it would have been unnatural, and nobody would actually have used that method of performance evaluation. This approach had already been used, with a partially similar organization, in Québec, but it was necessary to adapt examples and exercises to the Afghan public, all the more so since the group members had very diverse backgrounds (which we take pride in), and there were some illiterate members. Having doctors and farmers work on the same project is not customary, in Afghanistan or anywhere else! It was therefore necessary to adapt training tools both before and during the workshops to take into account the various reactions of the participants to the examples. For instance, it was very useful to illustrate the concepts of the

logical model through concrete examples inspired by everyday life, such as the example of seeds (inputs) to obtain apple trees (outputs) then apples (outcomes) used to feed children and reduce malnutrition (impact). To illustrate the concepts of objectivity and subjectivity, we used the example of a judge who had to hear a case of excessive use of a field by a neighbor who happened to be the judge's brother. Numerous role-playing sessions, simulation games, and practical exercises were used to alternate with useful but austere theoretical and conceptual sessions.

The ethical dimension, whether for evaluation or simply for intervention, was very new to all stakeholders. Much to my surprise, when I explained the concept, the moderator-interpreter (who was also a medical doctor) turned to me and asked me what I meant by "ethics." There is a long way to go in that respect.

These workshops led to the creation of a list of indicators related to the concerns of local actors. To that list, we added generic indicators usually used for this type of program and indicators used in AMI. Through the two AMI local experts, a first selection of significant and useful indicators was carried out, using criteria of quality and relevance. This work constitutes an answer to the need for tools to facilitate continuous feedback and periodic production of reports evidencing the results.

The process is not finalized yet, but we believe this approach (collective workshops and permanent support through our local experts) will lead to the creation of tools for project evaluation.

Performance evaluation of health programs is difficult, particularly when it aims at making sure that NGO activities intended to help the poorest populations in the world have a significant impact on the health and well-being of the destitute. However, rather than evaluating impact, it is more realistic to focus on outcome (change for the beneficiaries of programs) rather than on the activities carried out (output: consultation, training, etc.), To achieve this, it remains indispensable that all stakeholders involved in the implementation of a development (or an emergency) program participate in the definition of expected outcomes. For that reason, the participative approach used during this mission in Afghanistan seemed relevant to us, and verbal and formal feedback on the workshops was extremely enthusiastic.

This work is difficult, because the evaluator has to understand that he is only an expert in the "container" (as opposed to the contents). He needs to share his knowledge and act as an animator and facilitator, whereas local actors are experts in the content and need to be involved in the evaluation, from the choice of evaluation questions to the analysis and interpretation of data. The viability and usefulness of such an evaluation mechanism for projects depends on the approach used. Active (and not fictitious) participation of stakeholders (from communities to the Ministry of Health) in the process is difficult yet must not be seen as a constraint but as a crucial viability and usefulness factor.

—*Valéry Ridde*

Further Reading

Johnson, H., & Fafard, A. (2002). *L'évaluation, mieux la comprendre et l'entreprendre* [Evaluation: Better understanding and operationalization] (Project of the Régie régionale de la Santé et des Services sociaux Chaudière-Appalaches). Québec, Canada: Johnson and Roy.

Ridde, V. (2001, November 12). *L'approche participative et l'influence sur la prise de décision dans un contexte international d'aide d'urgence: Une évaluation en Afghanistan* [The participative approach and its influence on decision making in the international context of emergency aid: An evaluation in Afghanistan]. Paper presented at the 10th Annual Meeting of the Société Québécoise en Évaluation de Programme, Montréal, Canada.

World Health Organization. (1996). *Catalogue of health indicators: A selection of important health indicators recommended by WHO programmes* (WHO/HST/SCI/96.8). Geneva, Switzerland: Author.

◼◼ UTILIZATION OF EVALUATION

Evaluation utilization (or evaluation use) refers to the way that evaluations and information from evaluations affect the programs on which evaluations are conducted. Were progressive changes made in a program as a consequence of an evaluation? Did an evaluation generate a new understanding of or a modification of beliefs about the program or aspects of the program?

The concern for evaluation utilization initially developed in the United States during the 1960s. There were many reasons for this, including the enormous growth in demand in these years for evaluations to be conducted. Major social programs were initiated that often mandated end-of-year evaluation reports. The subsequent rush to evaluate attracted many researchers who lacked awareness of the distinctions between research and evaluation and who failed to understand properly the contexts in which evaluations were to take place. The result was a multitude of evaluation reports that lacked relevance to program personnel. This was particularly true for evaluations conducted at the local program level, such as those in schools, school districts, mental health clinics, social welfare agencies, and the like. Thus, many evaluation reports sat on the shelf, fulfilling the requirement of evaluation but generally disregarded.

Although prior to the 1960s some conceptualization had been done on aspects of knowledge and research use, there had not been much interest in extending this to a consideration of evaluation use. The distinction between research and evaluation is an important one: *Research* refers to generalizable knowledge and thus potentially may be used very broadly and in a variety of contexts. Research may also have influence many years after it is completed. *Evaluation* refers to the activity of examining the process and the impact of a specific program at a specific time. Thus, evaluation use is restricted to the program under examination and, roughly, the time frame during which the evaluation is implemented. With an evaluation, program personnel are known, the specific context is understood, and the evaluator has a role in helping to define the particular areas to be evaluated. Further, evaluators can, through their actions, seek to define an evaluative role, relationships, and procedures that may enhance utilization. Consequently, use is potentially more achievable for evaluation than for research.

RESEARCH ON UTILIZATION

The concern expressed by Carol Weiss in 1972 for greater understanding of evaluation utilization ushered in a period in which great attention was paid to conducting the necessary research. In addition to Weiss, important studies were conducted by Michael

Patton, Marvin Alkin and colleagues, Jean King and colleagues, Robert Braskamp, Robert Brown, and Diane Newman and others. This research identified factors associated with the likelihood of greater evaluation utilization. These factors can be categorized into three groupings: characteristics of users, context, and the evaluation itself.

In considering the first of these, researchers found a number of characteristics and attitudes of potential users of which evaluators should be aware. These included users' expectations for the evaluation, their prior experience and current disposition toward evaluation, and their perception of the risks they faced in having the evaluation performed.

The context in which an evaluation takes place is also important in framing potential utilization. Characteristics of the project or program, including its age or maturity, may set bounds for willingness to innovate and, consequently, willingness to make use of evaluation information. Intraorganizational features, such as relationships between the project and the levels of bureaucracy within the larger organization can also have impact. Factors external to the program or organization, such as community climate or the role of external funding agencies, can also exert influence.

Researchers studying evaluation utilization also focused on aspects of the evaluation itself that influenced potential evaluation use. Clearly, the way in which the evaluation is conducted may enhance the possibility of use taking place. Aspects of evaluation that researchers identified include the procedures used (methods and type of evaluation model), information dialogue (the amount and quality of interaction between evaluators and potential users), the nature of the evaluation information (its relevance and specificity), and evaluation reporting (the frequency and timing of the information and the style and format of written and oral presentations).

Perhaps the most influential of the evaluation factors identified by researchers is the evaluator. The expertise and credibility of the evaluator are important determinants of whether program personnel and other potential users heed the results of an evaluation. Perhaps of greater importance than the evaluator's expertise and credibilty are his or her personal characteristics, such as personality and style. Ability to develop rapport with users and to involve users in the evaluation is key if utilization is to occur. The evaluator must be politically sensitive to the context. Of greatest importance, however, is the evaluator's commitment to wanting use to occur. When evaluators view their efforts as important and are committed to use taking place, it is more likely to occur.

CONCEPTIONS OF USE

Initial discussions of the concept of use occurred in the knowledge utilization literature. Studies by researchers from the Center for Research on Utilization of Scientific Knowledge at the University of Michigan examined the ways in which social science knowledge influenced federal decision-making processes. An early distinction was made between "knowledge for action" and "knowledge for understanding." The former was referred to as *instrumental use,* indicating instances where respondents in the study could document the specific way in which the social science knowledge had been used for decision-making or problem-solving purposes. Knowledge for understanding was referred to as *conceptual use,* indicating instances in which the knowledge about an issue influenced a policy maker's thinking although the information was not put to a specific, documentable use. These distinctions between instrumental and conceptual knowledge utilization have become part of the evaluation utilization literature.

Subsequently, the notion of additional types of evaluation utilization have emerged. One of these refers to instances in which the evaluation is conducted either to support publicly a decision that has already been made or for the symbolic prominence of having an evaluation conducted. The first we refer to as *legitimative utilization* because no instrumental actions or changes in thinking emanate from the evaluation; rather, the use justifies or legitimates a prior action. The second we refer to as *symbolic use* because the evaluation is not being conducted to evaluate a program but rather to imply or symbolize something that is part of the agenda of someone associated with the program or evaluation. An administrator, for example, might have an evaluation conducted to enhance his or her own reputation or to put off detractors by demonstrating that a process is in place to do something about a problem.

In recent years, a number of evaluation theorists (Jennifer Greene, Jean King, and Michael Patton) have introduced the notion of *process use.* These theorists and others came to recognize that the evaluation process itself could have impact; that is, it could lead to utilization. They observed that the act of conducting an evaluation and the interactions between the evaluator and various stakeholders can lead to changes in the individuals or in the organization. Thus it is not the findings of the evaluation that contribute to use but the process itself.

Further consideration of process use has led to the conclusion that the process could be used either instrumentally or conceptually. That is, the process might lead to decisions or program actions taking place or to changes in thinking and understanding about oneself, the program, or the organization. Thus a distinction may be made between *findings use* and *process use,* each being employed instrumentally or conceptually. The symbolic use and the legitimative use described earlier fall into these two categories: Legitimative use, because it depends on the findings of the evaluation to rationalize an earlier decision, is within the findings use category; symbolic use, which depends only on the process being conducted, is process use.

EVALUATION INFLUENCE

Some evaluation writers have introduced the term *evaluation influence.* They contend that the designation *evaluation utilization* is too limiting. They believe that evaluations have impact in many different ways, in many different places, and at many different times. However, evaluation use typically refers to the impact of the evaluation (findings or process) within the context of the program being evaluated, within some reasonable time frame. Evaluation influence refers to the impact on an external program, which may or may not be related to the program evaluated or to the impact of the evaluation at some future time. An important distinction between evaluation influence and evaluation use is that evaluators who are concerned with evaluation use can actively pursue a course of action to potentially enhance utilization by recognizing the evaluation factors and attempting to be responsive to them, but evaluation influence is more difficult to predict or to control. Therefore, evaluation influence and evaluation use can be differentiated based on the awareness of users and evaluators that intended use has occurred.

MISUSE

There are instances where evaluation findings are taken out of context or misinterpreted by users for their own advantage. Thus a program director might excerpt a portion of the evaluation findings, omitting the caveats to present a more positive result than the

findings support. Such instances are labeled *evaluation misuse.* The opposite of *use* is *nonuse; misuse* represents the manner of use. Misuse is an ethical issue on the part of stakeholders and other recipients of evaluation information. Misuse may be intentional or unintentional, depending on stakeholders' and other recipients' knowledge and understanding of the evaluation findings and procedures. Based on these considerations, there are different degrees of misuse.

MODIFICATION OF EVALUATION THEORIES AND TEXTS

The research on evaluation utilization has had substantial impact on evaluation thinking. The concern for fostering evaluation utilization has led evaluation theorists to consider what prescriptions they might make in indicating how to conduct an evaluation. A number of theorists considered the factors that encouraged high levels of utilization (previously discussed) and incorporated many of these features into their descriptions of how to conduct an evaluation. Indeed, *utilization-focused evaluation* is based exclusively on the notion of conducting an evaluation in a manner intended to enhance the utilization that occurs. *Participatory evaluation* focuses on the desire to enhance the potential users' engagement in the evaluation. The belief is that such participation enhances "buy-in" (the users' sense of commitment to the evaluation findings) and therefore increases the likelihood that utilization will occur. Further, stakeholder participation is viewed as leading to potentially enhanced process use, as participants acquire skills and gain insights.

Even among those evaluation textbook writers who, in their approach to evaluation, are not oriented toward increased utilization as a priority, there is a growing recognition of utilization influences and concerns. This is evidenced by sections devoted to these topics in all textbooks and by "utility" as the first of four standards of high-quality program evaluation in the *Program Evaluation Standards.*

—*Marvin C. Alkin*

Further Reading

Alkin, M. C., & Taut, S. (2002). Unbundling evaluation use. *Studies in Educational Evaluation 29*(1), 1-12.

Hofstetter, C. H., & Alkin, M. C. (2002). Evaluation use revisited. In D. Stufflebeam & T. Kellaghan (Eds.), *International handbook of educational evaluation* (pp. 197-224). Boston: Kluwer Academic.

Evaluation Practice Around the World

Greece

A Case of Political Use of Evaluation in Greece

Evaluation of the outcomes of policies and programs in Greece began to develop as a direct result of our participation to the European Union (Vergidis, 1999). However, these evaluations can be considered neither independent nor reliable. To demonstrate the political application of evaluation in Greek educational policy, we will refer to the evaluation working committee's report on the evaluation of educational reform, which was promoted by the Ministry of Education in 1997. The reform concerned mainly secondary education. The number of subjects in which students were examined rose from 4 to 14 at the entry examination (Panhellenic Exams) from lyceum to university. In addition, the professional and technical lyceums were abolished and replaced by technical and professional schools. Graduates of these schools could not participate in university entry examinations. This reform was strongly opposed by both pupils and teachers. The pupils of the lyceum occupied schools all over the country, and no teaching of lyceum pupils took place for almost 3 months.

In September 1999, the minister of education appointed an evaluation working committee to evaluate the outcomes of this educational reform. The report was submitted in January, almost 4 months later. Considering all this, this story will elaborate on the approach, the evaluation method (Commission Européenne, Fonds Structurels Communautaires, 1999a, 1999b), and the implicit perceptions held by the committee rather than on the report's final suggestions.

It is explicitly stated in the report that its goal, as put forward by the minister of education, was "the evaluation of the implementation of the educational reform programs in both primary and secondary education emphasizing the Unified Lyceum [and] the monitoring of the implemented programs." School councils and school directors of first and secondary education participated in the committee; in contrast, researchers did not participate. The chairman of the committee was a university professor of Ancient Greek literature, with no experience in social research.

An examination of the evaluation report reveals that there is no systematic collection of data concerning the evolution of the reform. The fact that the report lacks any reference to quantitative data—specifically, the number of the established day-long kindergartens and primary schools or the extent of remedial teaching and the number of vocational schools that were founded—is illustrative of the absence of anticipated outcome measures. The data used for the evaluation were not, as it seems, founded in any scientific method.

The evaluation report is characterized by the absence of theoretical framework and a scientific step-by-step procedure (European Commission, 1997). The report identifies opinions of various people that simply belong to the political, financial, journalistic, and educational world, people who by no means represent the educational world institutionally or constitute a representative or selected sample. This selected opinion "easily ascertained the unanimous positive attitude of public opinion regarding the aims of the reform and the needs dictating it."

Still, the selected sample voiced negative remarks and suggestions, which are characterized by the committee in the report as "dogmatic rejection" of the reform. Consequently, there is a basis neither for the "unanimous positive attitude of public opinion" nor for the "complete social and educational acceptance" of the educational reform, as stated by the committee, especially given the additional fact that the teachers went on strike and the pupils of the lyceums did sit-ins, which lasted several weeks, demanding the abolition of the educational reform.

Moreover, the report lacks any systematic reference to the planning of the educational reform, and there is no clarification of the general and specific aims of educational policy or of the expected outcomes, results, and impacts. This serves to emphasize the absence of any form of diagnostic evaluation. Formative evaluation was attempted without preceding diagnostic evaluation of the planning of the particular educational reform and without the existence of any monitoring mechanism of its implementation.

The unexpected results included in the report are of particular interest. One of the two unexpected results mentioned is "the unexpectedly large number of pupils [that] opted for vocational education [not out of mere preference but due to the perplexity and fear of the demanding unified lyceum] led the newly established institutions of vocational education to unnatural gigantism, which enhanced old and created new dysfunctions." In this case, the committee noted the observed turn of pupils to vocational education, this odd and unexpected result, without skepticism or further research.

The second unexpected result of the educational intervention referred as well to pupils. According to the report, "In relation to the lyceum examination system, the pupils' protests overcame [all expectations based on] the previous year...leading to the loss of valuable attention [and social control] to the totally renewed venture."

However, the evaluators characterized the educational reform as a "bold effort," a "brave step," a "brilliant idea." Furthermore, they emphasized already from the first pages of their report that "the reform dared for the first time [to establish] modern and effective regulations."

It seems that the evaluation of the committee did not examine the problems that appeared. Consequently, the committee's contribution to the improvement of educational policy remains limited and inconclusive, because usable knowledge was not produced. After 2 years, this reform was abolished by the same government (but by a new minister of education). The previous minister of education, who "took the brave step," was barely elected as a deputy in the subsequent elections. The report of the evaluation was never published.

—Dimitris Vergidis

Further Reading

Commission Européenne, Fonds Structurels Communautaires. (1999a). *Evaluer les programmes socio-économiques: Conception et conduite d'une évaluation* [Evaluating socioeconomic programs: Conception and control of an evaluation] (MEANS, Vol. 1). Luxembourg, Belgium: Office de Publications Officielles de Communautes Européennes.

Commission Européenne, Fonds Structurels Communautaires. (1999b). *Evaluer les programmes socio-économiques: Glossaire de 300 concepts et termes techniques* [Evaluating socioeconomic programs: Glossary of 300 concepts and technical terms] (MEANS, Vol. 6). Luxembourg, Belgium: Office de Publications Officielles de Communautés Européennes.

European Commission. (1997). *Evaluating EU expenditure programmes: A guide. Ex post and intermediate evaluation.* Brussels, Belgium: DG XIX.

Vergidis, D. (1999). Ekpedeftiki politiki ke axiologisi [Educational policy and evaluation]. In D. Vergidis & Th. Karalis (Eds.), *Ekpedefsi enilikon: Schediasmos, organosi ke axiologisi programmaton* [Adult education: Planning, organization, and program evaluation] (Vol. 3). Patras, Greece: Greek Open University.

■■ VALIDITY

Writing a general statement about validity in evaluation is a hazardous business. The field of evaluation is so diverse and complex and it has such an array of models, approaches, forms, and disciplinary homes that generalizing about evaluation is invariably a potentially foolhardy enterprise. Moreover, this is historically disputed territory. Validity is related to truth. They are members of the same family, so to speak. Truth, however you cut it, is an essentially contested concept with little agreement about what constitutes the right basis for truth-seeking activities. Of course, much has already been said about validity. There are various classic explications of validity from some of evaluation's most notable theorists: Donald Campbell, Thomas Cook, Lee J. Cronbach, Egon Guba, Ernest House, Yvonna Lincoln, Michael Patton, Michael Scriven, and Robert Stake, to name a few.

Much of the justification for doing evaluation is that it can at least offer approximations to the truth and help discriminate between good and bad, better and worse, desirable and less desirable courses of action. It is not surprising, therefore, that one of the defining problems of the field of evaluation remains the validation of evaluative judgments. There are three main issues that have beset discussions about validity in evaluation. The first issue has to do with the nature and importance of generalization and the ways in which evaluation can and should support social decision making. In turn, this issue depends on the assumptions made about the objects of evaluation (practices, projects, programs, and policies), how they are theorized, and the political context of evaluation. The second

issue is the extent to which nonmethodological considerations, such as fairness, social responsibility, and social consequence, should inform discussions about validity. The third issue, and seemingly the most intractable, is the extent to which it is possible to have a unified conception of validity in evaluation. Given the methodological and substantive diversity that now characterizes the transdisciplinary field of evaluation, is it possible to have common standards for and a shared discourse about validity? This issue is acutely felt in debates about whether the traditional discourse of scientific validity in quantitative research is relevant to qualitative approaches to evaluation.

The publication in 1963 of Donald Campbell and Julian Stanley's chapter "Experimental and Quasi-experimental Designs for Research on Teaching" is probably the single most significant landmark in the conceptualization of validity. This and Campbell's later work with Thomas Cook, *Quasi-Experimentation: Design and Analysis Issues for Field Settings,* published in 1979, were the touchstones for most, if not all, discussions about validity in evaluation and applied research more generally. Campbell and his colleagues introduced a nomenclature and framework for thinking about validity and constructing the research conditions needed to probe causal relationships. Central to this experimental tradition has been the development of strategies (designs) for controlling error and bias and eliminating plausible rival hypotheses or explanations.

Discussions about validity in the experimental tradition have resulted in a shared language about the threats to validity associated with different research designs and types of validity (e.g., internal validity, external validity, statistical conclusion validity, construct validity). The distinction between internal and external validity has been of particular importance in discussions about validity. Internal validity usually refers to the validity of inference from and confined to a particular study or domain of investigation. It is about the validity of statements or judgments about the case or cases under investigation. It addresses the question: Did the treatment make a difference in this experimental instance? By contrast, external validity refers to whether inferences or judgments from a study or domain of investigation apply to other populations, settings, or times. It is about whether findings generalize. In classic theories of experimental design, internal validity was taken to be the sine qua non of external validity. This was because establishing internal validity was regarded as the basic minimum for the interpretability of experiments. Thus generalization depended first and foremost on establishing that the findings of the study were true for practical and methodological purposes. The codification of various threats to validity has been central to the experimental tradition and has proved useful in the evaluation of social and educational intervention programs. Threats to validity indicate some of the prototypical rival hypotheses or alternative explanations for whether the program is in fact responsible for changes in outcomes and whether it will generalize. A list of threats to validity would often include the following:

- *History.* Events occurring between observations or testing can provide an alternative explanation of effects.
- *Maturation.* Processes (e.g., growth, becoming more experienced, fatigue) within the respondents can produce changes as a function of the passage of time.
- *Testing.* Taking a test once will have an effect on the scores of a second testing.
- *Instrumentation.* Changes in measurement protocols or observers may produce changes in the outcomes captured.
- *Statistical regression.* Changes occurring by virtue of respondents starting out in extreme positions or being selected on the basis of their extreme scores could be erroneously attributed to the treatment.
- *Selection.* Biases result from differences between the kinds of people in comparison groups.
- *Mortality.* Theis does not refer to death necessarily but to the differential loss of people from comparison groups for any reason.
- *Compensatory equalization of treatments.* There is a tendency for planned differences between comparison groups to break down under the social pressure for fairness.
- *Diffusion or imitation of treatments.* Control groups may autonomously adopt the practices or program of the experimental groups.
- *Interaction of selection and experimental treatment.* The treated population may display unrepresentative responsiveness.
- *Reactive effects of experimental arrangements.* Experimental conditions may make the setting atypical (Hawthorne effects).

A major strength of experimentalism—its focus on creating the conditions to test "causal" claims and infer the "causal" relationships between specific variables in a domain of investigation—is also its weakness, at least in the context of program and policy evaluation. The precedence given to internal validity undermines the usefulness or applicability of an evaluation. Threats to internal validity are reduced by rigorous control over the experimental conditions. Rigorous control, however, tends to limit the application of evaluative conclusions because the context of the experiment is unrepresentative of the contexts of application. Put simply, there is often a trade-off to be made between validity-enhancing and utility-enhancing evaluation designs. The experimentalist tradition places too much emphasis on establishing causal relationships between variables, thus limiting the extent to which it is possible to confidently extrapolate from an evaluative study to other implementation strategies, settings, populations, and times. This is significant. When a program or social practice is developed in a new setting, it is adapted by different people at different times for different populations. It is not the same program or practice. The difference between the original and the intended copy may be substantial or slight, but important differences there will be. The issue here is whether evaluation should strive to support formal generalization or whether it should be more concerned with the potential for wider transferability and with supporting the capacity to learn from the experience of others. A related limitation of experimentalism is lack of attention to the reasons that programs work (the so called black-box problem). Advocates of "realist" or theory-driven approaches to evaluation have argued that the prominence given to internal validity has been at the expense of developing theories about the underlying causal mechanisms that generate outcomes in particular contexts.

The question of whether validity is solely a technical matter has become a critical issue in evaluation, as it has in educational measurement. In his prescient and influential book *Evaluating With Validity,* Ernest House argued that technical considerations alone cannot fully address the problem of bias in evaluation. Rejecting the primacy of operational definitions of validity, he said that the validity of an evaluation depends on whether it is true, credible, and normatively correct. In short, validity in evaluation is not only concerned with technical standards but with fairness and social consequences. Developments in educational measurement theory have similarly stressed the importance of taking into account value implications and action outcomes when considering the validity of test scores for particular uses.

Involving stakeholders in the validation of an evaluation is one way to move beyond technical validity issues. Participant validation involves different interest groups, particularly intended users and those whose work and lives are represented in an evaluation, in commenting on matters such as the accuracy, fairness, relevance, comprehensiveness, truthfulness, and credibility of an evaluative account and its conclusions and recommendations. By its nature, participant validation poses practical constraints, notably for large-scale, systemwide evaluations. There are risks associated with disagreement and competition among stakeholders that have to be managed. Sponsors or executive decision makers, for example, may object that disseminating draft evaluation reports to others runs counter to their own proprietorial rights and is a breach of the customer-contractor relationship that typifies much commissioned evaluation. Nevertheless, participant validation has an important role to play in strengthening confidence in an evaluation and building consensus around its conclusions and recommendations. Perhaps most important, it widens the social basis of validation and helps protect against evaluation being seen as little more than a bureaucratic service to the politically powerful.

Validity is a contested concept. It is contested because there are disputes about its meaning, how it should be pursued, its relevance to evaluative inquiry, and its intelligibility in the face of postmodern, antifoundational critiques of traditional research. Whether it is because of a crisis of representation or disenchantment with science or, more mundanely, a consequence of the political economy of academic disciplines, validity has become a vexing and confusing concept.

Some want to give validity up altogether: It is too modern, too prescriptive, too concerned with demarcating the acceptable from the unacceptable; also, it is part of an epistemologically repressive or coercive regime of truth, authoritarian and distasteful. This is not a position that can be sustained by those doing evaluation, however. In practice, evaluation can fulfill its promise of being useful only if the knowledge it produces is credible, and such credibility as it can muster depends in part on claims to truth. There are other demands to change the meaning of validity and redefine its various methodological expressions, personalize and politicize its meanings, and develop new criteria for quality in evaluation: trustworthiness, goodness, credibility, authenticity, efficacy, and generative or transformational power, for example. What lies behind some of these attempts to recast validity is a belief that the traditional paradigms of social science and classical conceptions of validity have failed applied research and evaluation because they are limited and conservative, binding us to traditional values and a singular version of reality and blinding us to alternative perspectives and multiple truths. These arguments and ideas about validity have largely been explored and elaborated in the context of debates about the fundamental differences between quantitative and qualitative research. Quantitative methodologies have been associated with positivist or scientific epistemology. By contrast, qualitative methodologies have been associated with naturalistic or constructivist epistemologies. Traditional concepts of validity have been rejected by some evaluation theorists of a qualitative persuasion because of a belief that quantitative and qualitative methods of knowing belong to different and incommensurate paradigms. It is hardly surprising that these issues are unresolved. Still, the assumption that methodology is inextricably linked to coherent metaphysical paradigms is probably overstated. Similarly, the belief that qualitative and quantitative ways of knowing and validating knowledge are incompatible because they originate from different and incommensurate worldviews is, in some measure, an unsubstantiated empirical claim. The danger with paradigmatic representations of methodology is that they can easily become caricatures, unanchored from the experience and practice of evaluation. However, even if there are no fundamental reasons to conclude that qualitative and quantitative ways of knowing and validating are incommensurate, there remains a feeling that the concepts of validity associated with experimentalism are not as meaningful or productive for evaluations that draw on ethnography, case study, or naturalistic inquiry for their modus operandi. In these evaluations, the judgments of participants and users as to the quality of an evaluation are often a crucial element in the process of validation.

Evaluation is difficult to do. This is because its purpose is to inform decision making and social understanding. Evaluation is meant to be useful, and mostly this means useful in the short run, matching the timing of organizational and political decision making. Inevitably this requires striking a balance between timeliness, utility, and methodological ideals. What makes this hard is that the context of social valuation and decision making is often overtly political. Evaluation can impinge on interests and values in unpredictable ways. Political standing, reputations, and resource allocations may be at stake. Negative evaluations can be used by some at the expense of others associated with a policy, program, project, or practice. Evaluation findings are a possible resource for securing advantage, and correspondingly, they are a possible threat. Evaluation may intrude into autonomous spheres of action and semiprivate workspace, and the knowledge it produces provides opportunities for control. Evaluation is best seen as an activity that can affect the distribution of power and resources. That evaluation is deeply imbued with politics has become something of an accepted truism. Issues of territory, competition, hierarchy, reputation, and privacy impinge on the work of evaluators to a greater extent than is usual in research. The political context can undermine an evaluation, affecting the kind and quality of evidence available to it, the validity of findings, how they are received, and what can be learned. As a consequence, specific measures must be taken to foster the credibility and openness necessary for the successful conduct of evaluation. In this context, validity has an important job to do. It helps stand guarantor for the independence and impartiality needed for trust in an evaluation. It is essential in the defense against the robust criticism that can be expected when evaluators report unwelcome news.

Validity is not a property of approaches to or methods of evaluation. At its most rudimentary, validity refers to the reasons we have for believing truth claims, what Dewey called "warranted assertibility." These truth claims may take many forms: statements of fact, conclusions, representations, descriptions, accounts, theories, propositions, generalizations, inferences, interpretations, and judgments. Irrespective of their form, what is important is the warrant evaluators have for the claims they make. *Warrant* here refers to justifying conditions, reasons, and arguments. Validity speaks to why we should trust a representation of reality or an evaluative account. One way to think about validity is not so much cutting the difference between truth and its pretenders, but providing us with a sense of the limitations of knowledge claims. Despite its objective connotations, validity is important in evaluation precisely because of the socially constructed, fallible, provisional, and incomplete nature of knowledge and the personal and political propensity to act as if this were not the case.

—*Nigel Norris*

Further Reading

Bickman, L. (Ed.). (2000). *Validity and social experimentation.* Thousand Oaks, CA: Sage.

Campbell, D. T., & Stanley, J. C. (1963). Experimental and quasi-experimental designs for research on teaching. In N. L. Gage (Ed.), *Handbook of research on teaching* (pp. 171-246). Chicago: Rand McNally.

Cook, T. D., & Campbell, D. T. (1979). *Quasi-experimentation: Design and analysis issues for field settings.* Boston: Houghton Mifflin.

House, E. R. (1980). *Evaluating with validity.* Beverly Hills, CA: Sage.

■■ VALUE-FREE INQUIRY

Value-free inquiry is the belief that evaluative conclusions cannot or should not be made on the basis of scientific evidence. This view is often associated with the work of sociologist Max Weber, who asserted that a scientist should be a disinterested observer of the social world, focused on describing and understanding but not on judging or prescribing. Evaluation as a discipline and a profession does, however, focus on judging and prescribing and therefore challenges this notion of scientific inquiry. Michael Scriven has used the term *valuephobia,* or an irrational fear of evaluation, which is helpful for understanding the persistent advocacy of value-free inquiry in general and in evaluation in particular. Individual and group fears often maintain the myth of value-free inquiry.

See also VALUES

Further Reading

Scriven, M. (1991). *Evaluation thesaurus.* Newbury Park, CA: Sage.

■ VALUE JUDGMENT

A *value judgment* is a judgment of the merit, worth, or value of something. Value judgments are a critical part of evaluation, such as in weighing and synthesizing criteria or evidence and in the outcome of evaluations. In common language, value judgments are often erroneously equated with subjective, individualistic, arbitrary claims, and indeed this is the typical dictionary definition. For example, a common definition might be something like, "an assessment that reveals more about the values of the person making the assessment than about the reality of what is assessed." In philosophy, however, value judgments are a reasonable and appropriate topic for study. Theories of value ask, "What sorts of things are good?" or "What does *good* mean?" or "If we had to give the most general, catch-all description of good things, what would that description be?" Value theory and judgments can define *good* and *bad* for a community or society, and these notions of value affect the community and politics, such as when, for example, governments decide what is good and encourage it by cutting taxes on those activities, removing regulations or laws, and providing subsidies.

See also VALUES

■ VALUES

A common definition of evaluation states that it is the determination of the *value* (merit, worth, or significance) of a program, project, policy, object (e.g., a textbook), or even a person (as, for example, in personnel evaluation or performance auditing). Four important issues are involved in discussing the notion of value in light of this definition.

The first issue has to do with what "having value" means. Consider the following uses of the term *good:* "That performance of *Street Car Named Desire* was good." "John is a good person." "That program for treating drug addiction is good." In the first statement, *good* clearly refers to some kind of aesthetic value (it depends on some account of what beauty is); in the second statement, *good* refers to some notion of moral value (it depends on some account of the virtues or standards for moral behavior). In the third statement, *good* might well be a synonym for *effective,* and it points to another kind of value; namely, utility or instrumental value. Judgments of value in evaluation often involve judging both instrumental and moral value and, perhaps on some occasions, aesthetic value as well. For example, an evaluator might judge a drug treatment program to be good because it meets some well-defined interest or need or because it has instrumental value—it lends itself (or is a means) to achieving some desired purpose or end. However, this program could also be judged in terms of some standards of moral value as well. For example, the program might be effective in helping its clients overcome their addictions; however, suppose the personnel in the program treat the clients in inhumane ways. Clearly, in this situation, judgment of moral values would be necessary in rendering a decision that the program is good. Less frequently, judgments of aesthetic value may also come into play. Consider, for example, an evaluation of a recycling center in a local community. Whether it is good (has value) would most certainly involve judging instrumental value; it might also involve a judgment of moral value in considering whether workers involved with the technology are operating in a safe environment; and it could well involve aesthetic judgment in determining whether the center is in some sense an intrusion on the surrounding landscape.

The second issue is whether the common definition of evaluation noted here is acceptable—that is, whether the practice of evaluation *ought* to be concerned with making value judgments (of course, this is itself a value judgment). There is considerable disagreement here. Some evaluators argue that their responsibility is primarily scientific description and explanation. Thus, if the object in question is a drug treatment program (X), they would describe the features of X—what is done, by whom, how often, to whom, when, and so on. They would also determine the relationship between X and its desired outcomes (Y, Z), taking into account factors (e.g., B and C) that might mitigate or confound that relationship. They might also consider whether X achieves its desired outcomes efficiently (i.e., consider costs). Having done this, they would render a judgment to the effect that "X (under conditions B and C) leads to Y and Z." Judging value here is synonymous with scientific appraisal or explanation of what happened and why. A generous interpretation of this way of thinking of evaluation is that it involves judgment of the *instrumental* value of X; namely, whether X is effective and efficient in achieving its desired purpose. Other evaluators argue that this way of thinking about evaluation is at best incomplete and, at worst, not evaluation.

They claim that to judge the value of the program, the evaluator must take into account a variety of value considerations beyond utility (or beyond whether the program is effective). For example, the evaluator must judge the value of the desired purpose of the program and the conduct of the staff in view of legal and ethical considerations and must determine the basis for saying that the program has utility or instrumental value (is, for example, the criterion one of the greatest good for the greatest number?). In sum, these evaluators consider that the judgment of value extends beyond the matter of scientific appraisal of whether and how a program works. The position one adopts in this dispute depends in a significant way on how one views the third and fourth issues.

The third issue is whether value judgments are an objective or subjective matter. The subjectivist holds that value judgments are in the eye of the beholder, so to speak. These judgments are nothing more than expressions of personal preferences, tastes, emotions, or attitudes on the part of individuals. They are to be distinguished from statements that describe the world. Descriptions and explanations are based on facts. The facts of that matter are capable of being rationally debated and resolved, and hence descriptions and explanations can be judged as either true or false. Thus, the determination of the utility of the program—whether it is instrumental in achieving its intended objectives—is really the only judgment that matters, because that determination rests only on the facts of the matter. In contrast, judgments of value, because they express only some "feeling state," can never be resolved by rational means. They will be endlessly argued.

The objectivist disagrees and argues that evaluators rarely deal with statements that are purely objective fact ("the distance between point A and point B is five miles") or purely subjective preference or taste ("The wine from Italy is better than the wine from Indiana"). Rather, evaluators deal with (a) statements that are simultaneously descriptive and evaluative depending on the context (e.g., "J has a degree from Harvard") and (b) statements that appear to be descriptive but whose meaning involves a value basis (e.g., "J is more intelligent than L, X is a good program"). Objectivists argue that value judgments are rationally defensible and disputes over whether such statements are true and objective are resolvable. Thus there are such things as moral disagreement, moral deliberation, and moral decision.

The fourth issue concerns who has responsibility for making value judgments in evaluation. There are two schools of thought here. One holds that the evaluator should only describe and report the various value positions at stake in what is being evaluated and make descriptive statements to the effect that "if you value A, then B is the case." Here, it is the primary responsibility of stakeholders, not the evaluator, to make the judgment of value. Evaluators who assume that their primary task is one of scientific appraisal and explanation typically take this position. Likewise, evaluators who subscribe to the view that value judgments are subjective would be likely to take this position as well. Another school of thought, aligned with the objectivist view of values, argues that it is the evaluator's responsibility to render a judgment of value by taking into account all relevant values bearing on the merit, worth, or significance of what is being evaluated. These evaluators aim to take into account and synthesize various sources of value, such as needs assessments, professional standards for a practice, legal and regulatory considerations, program objectives, and relevant comparisons. Within this school of thought, there is disagreement on just how this synthesis and judgment is to be made. Different procedures are defended, including clinical inference, an all-things-considered synthesis that provides the most coherent and defensible account of value, a heuristic qualitative weight and sum procedure, and the use of nondeductive reasoning to develop an argument scheme.

—*Thomas A. Schwandt*

Further Reading

Fournier, D. M. (Ed.). (1995). Reasoning in evaluation: Inferential leaps and links. *New Directions for Evaluation, 68.*

House, E. R., & Howe, K. (1999). *Values in evaluation and social research.* Thousand Oaks, CA: Sage.

Schwandt, T. A. (1997). The landscape of values in evaluation: Charted terrain and unexplored territory. In D. J. Rog & D. Fournier (Eds.), Progress and future directions in evaluation: Perspectives on theory, practice, and methods. *New Directions for Evaluation, 76,* 11-23.

▪▪ VANDERPLAAT, MADINE

(b. 1955, The Netherlands). Ph.D., M.A., B.A. Sociology of Education, Dalhousie University, Halifax, Nova Scotia.

VanderPlaat is Associate Professor of Sociology and Women's Studies and Chair of the Department of Sociology and Criminology at Saint Mary's University in

Halifax, Nova Scotia, and has worked extensively with Health Canada's Population and Public Health Unit.

Her work has focused on the development of evaluation approaches based on critical theory and the principles of social inclusion, particularly in the field of community-based health promotion. Her work has been influenced by a number of people, including Jürgen Habermas, Seyla Benhabib, Patti Lather, Nancy Fraser, John Forrester, Frank Fischer, Jennifer Greene, and David Fetterman.

She is a coauthor of *Sociology: Making Sense of the Social World,* an introductory sociology textbook, and has published in many evaluation journals.

■■ VERACITY

In general, *veracity* means truthfulness, accuracy, conveying or perceiving truth. Evaluators seek to base their claims accurately and truthfully on trustworthy information gathered in the light of participants' values. Evaluators idealize veracity in their work. However, many evaluators believe that what any one person calls *truth* is better viewed as that person's subjective perception of such. Perceptions are influenced by values, assumptions, inquiry methods, and many other characteristics of evaluation participants. However, although evaluators usually do not claim absolute veracity in all they perceive, claim, or report, they seek to honor veracity in the context of the values they and those they serve hold.

—*David D. Williams*

■■ *VERSTEHEN*

A German word that means "understanding," *verstehen* has been elaborated to signify interpretive understanding of the meaning of human action. The term has been explored by many philosophers and theorists of social inquiry and defined as both the unique purpose for human sciences and the method for such inquiry. The term reminds evaluators that they are seeking to understand the values and perspectives of the participants in their studies through participation with them as fellow human beings in addition to whatever other methods they use. Without such subjective reflection, evaluators cannot hope to respond to stakeholders' concerns appropriately.

—*David D. Williams*

■■ VOICE

Based on literacy and on sociolinguistic and critical perspectives in the social sciences, *voice* is a concept that relates to issues of authority, power, and representation, often in texts. The work of Bakhtin, in particular, raises questions about who is speaking, who is not speaking, who is hearing, and how. Stakeholder involvement, particularly in the context of participatory evaluation, may address issues of voice in an evaluation; that is, involving stakeholders may demonstrate an effort to include and represent many voices. Alternative forms of representation, such as poetry or drama or polyphonic texts, are often the means of giving voice to the evaluation's stakeholders.

Further Reading

Bakhtin, M. M. (1986). *Speech genres and other late essays* (C. Emerson & M. Holquist, Eds., V. W. McGee, Trans.). Austin: University of Texas Press.

WADSWORTH, YOLAND

(b. 1951, Melbourne, Australia). Ph.D., B.A., Monash University, Melbourne.

Wadsworth has contributed to evaluation theory in a number of ways, including the two approaches to evaluation called open inquiry and audit review; the concept of multireference groups (commonly referred to as stakeholders) and the metaphor of them "coming to the table" together in evaluation activity; the critical reference group perspective as a method for guiding evaluation design, questions, theoretical analyses, problem-solving formulations, and applied trial results; and moving beyond the positivist or relativist conundrums.

Her contributions to evaluation practice include pioneering the use of fourth-generation and fifth-generation evaluation, including the use of dialogic and multilogic crossover designs (e.g., exchange of evaluative material between stakeholders and the iterative generation of further evaluative material and new practice and policy); the application of participatory action research to internal evaluation, extending to the use of "whole systems" or "scaled-up" action evaluation; and building in evaluation to daily practice in health and human services, particularly including the active engagement of service users.

Influences on Wadsworth's work are the classical U.K. and U.S. urban and suburban community studies; the critical and interpretive theory of Alvin Gouldner and Anthony Giddens; and, later in her work, nonreificatory systems thinking, group analytic and type and temperament theory, social movements, and every client with whom she has ever worked.

In evaluation, she is most appreciative of Patton, Lincoln, and Guba's intellectual contributions.

Wadsworth was part of the pioneer evaluation field in the newly expanding public services during the 1970s in Australia (especially child and family health and community services and community health). She was the convener of the Melbourne Evaluation and Research Group network for a decade and author of Australia's best-selling introductory evaluation text *Everyday Evaluation on the Run* (now in its second edition). She was the 1995 recipient of the Australasian Evaluation Society's Caulley-Tulloch Prize for Pioneering Evaluation Literature (with Maggie McGuiness and Merinda Epstein) for a sequence of studies involving building in consumers' evaluative feedback to, and collaboration with, staff of acute psychiatric hospital services. In 1996, she was the recipient of the Australasian Evaluation Society's Evaluation Training and Services Award for outstanding career contribution to evaluation.

WALBERG, HERBERT J.

(b. 1937, Chicago, Illinois). Ph.D. Educational Psychology, University of Chicago; M.Ed., University of Illinois, Urbana-Champaign; B.Ed., Chicago State University.

Walberg is Research Professor of Education and Psychology at the University of Illinois at Chicago.

For four decades, Walberg has contributed to the meta-analyses of achievement effects of methods and conditions of education. He has been an advisor and evaluator for many public and private agencies in the

United States, Israel, Sweden, Japan, and other countries. Walberg is called frequently to provide expert testimony before Congress and federal district and state courts.

In his research, Walberg employs experiments and analyses of large national and international data sets to examine the factors in homes, schools, and communities that promote learning and other human accomplishments. For the U.S. Department of Education and the National Science Foundation, he carried out comparative research in Japanese and American schools. For the U.S. Department of State and the White House, he organized a radio series and a book about American education that were distributed in 74 countries.

His main intellectual influences are Milton Friedman, Gary Becker, Benjamin Bloom, Benjamin Wright, Chester Finn, Margaret Wang, Susan Paik, and Arthur Reynolds.

Walberg chaired the scientific advisory group for the Paris-based Organization for Economic Cooperation and Development project on international educational indicators. He also advised UNESCO and the governments of Israel, Japan, Sweden, and the United Kingdom on education research and policy. He currently chairs the board of Chicago's Heartland Institute, a conservative think tank.

Walberg is Coeditor of the *International Encyclopedia of Education* (currently in its fifth edition). He is Editor of booklets on "what works" practices that are distributed in hard copy to education leaders in more than 150 countries and are also available on the Internet through UNESCO. He was recently appointed Distinguished Visiting Scholar at Stanford University's Hoover Institution and is a fellow of four academic organizations, including the American Association for the Advancement of Science, American Psychological Association, and the Royal Statistical Society. Walberg is also a founding Fellow and Vice President of the International Academy of Education, headquartered in Brussels.

▉ WALKER, ROB

(b. 1943, Bedford, England). Ph.D. Science Education, Kings College, University of London; M.Phil. Sociology, University of London; B.Sc. Sociology, London School of Economics.

Walker is on the faculty at the University of East Anglia and is Director of the Centre for Applied Research in Education (CARE). He works as part of a four-person team called the Learning Technology Group, which offers advice and support on the effective use of technology in learning and teaching. He has also been on the faculty at Deakin University in Australia, the University of Keele, and London University.

He has made significant contributions to use of case study methods in research and evaluation. Walker's contributions to education and curriculum evaluation are through both his evaluation projects and his published works, which include *A Guide to Classroom Observation* (with Clem Adelman); *Changing the Curriculum* (with Barry MacDonald); *Biography, Identity and Schooling: Episodes in Educational Research* (with Ivor Goodson); and *Research as Social Change* (with Michael Schratz). He worked with Jack Easley and Bob Stake on the NSF Case Studies in Science Education, now classic examples of quality case study research. Walker has also contributed to the understanding of narrative in evaluation through his writing, as well as through his multimedia presentations of case studies, such as the UNESCO CD-ROM *Growing Up in Cities* and *Hathaway Primary School: A Multimedia Case Study*.

Walker was influenced early on by Basil Bernstein, who supervised Walker's work for his master's degree in philosophy. Bernstein encouraged him to do classroom research when not many people were doing it and also encouraged him to use film to record classroom activities, a method Walker continues to use. Walker's strongest influences, however, have been his Australian colleagues, Chris Bigum, Marie Brennan, and Stephen Kemmis, and his colleagues at CARE, Barry MacDonald, John Elliott, Jean Rudduck, and Lawrence Stenhouse.

Walker has advised and participated in the work of numerous external organizations and agencies, including government, universities, schools, publishers, museums, galleries, consumer and client groups, the police, commercial and business companies, foundations, and the media. He has been recognized for his excellence in teaching (he was the recipient of the 1991 Deakin University Foundation Award for Excellence in Teaching) and uses of multimedia (in 1996 he was a finalist for the Australian Multimedia Awards) and educational technology (in 1989, he received the Australian Society for Educational Technology Award).

WARRANTS, WARRANTABILITY. See Logic of Evaluation

WEIGHT AND SUM. See Quantitative Weight and Sum

■■ WEISS, CAROL HIRSCHON

Ph.D. Sociology, M.A. Government, Columbia University; B.A. Government, Cornell University.

Weiss is the Beatrice B. Whiting Professor at the Harvard University Graduate School of Education, where she has been since 1978. Her interests in evaluation began in the 1960s when she evaluated a domestic Peace Corps program in central Harlem. She has consulted on evaluation for dozens of agencies, including the U.S. General Accounting Office, the Department of Education, the World Bank, the Rockefeller Foundation, the National Academy of Sciences, and the Canadian International Development Research Centre. She has been Guest Scholar at the Brookings Institution, a Senior Fellow at the U.S. Department of Education, a Congressional Fellow, and a Fellow at the Center for Advanced Study in the Behavioral Sciences. She has given keynote addresses to evaluation societies around the world.

A pioneer in evaluation methods and theories, Weiss has made path-breaking contributions. They include (a) recognition that evaluation has political dimensions, (b) a broader conceptualization of what it means to "use" evaluation, and (c) development of a theory-based approach to understanding the effects of evaluation. All of these ideas have now been incorporated into mainstream evaluation thought.

When Weiss began her work in evaluation, the evaluator was seen as a neutral observer above the fray. She showed that evaluators studied programs and policies that were the consequence of political activity and that results had possible ramifications for the political fortunes of the programs. Moreover, evaluation itself had a political stance. It demonstrated that the program was important enough to deserve evaluation but also problematic enough to require it. Evaluation focuses on the relatively minor problems that can be "fixed" and ignores the basic premises on which the program is based. It tends to take for granted the whole environment in which the program works. Weiss believed that evaluators needed to become more aware of the political role they play.

Weiss' extensive research on evaluation use has shown that despite the seeming disregard of many evaluation findings, the findings in fact often influence the way that people think about a program. Over time, the new understandings can percolate into program decisions. She called the process "enlightenment."

Weiss developed some of the earliest ideas about what is now called "theory-based evaluation." In her 1972 text, she discussed (complete with diagram) the value of basing evaluation on the theory underlying the program and showed methods of doing it. She suggested that evaluators could follow the sequence of ministeps that staff assume will lead from initial inputs to desired results. When evaluation tracks the attainment of these intermediate steps, it can show not only final outcomes but also *why* the program is or is not working as planned and *where* the theory is supported or breaks down.

Among her 11 books are *Evaluation Research,* one of the first comprehensive texts, which sold hundreds of thousands of copies and has been translated into Spanish, German, and Thai, and *Evaluation* (1998), which has also been translated into Ukrainian. She sees evaluation as a means to help make programs more responsive to people's needs and make the world a more humane place.

For her work, Weiss has received many awards, including the Howard Davis Memorial Lecture Award, Knowledge Utilization Society (1991); Policy Studies Organization Award (1988); and the Alva and Gunnar Myrdal Award for Science, Evaluation Research Society (1980).

In Shadish, Cook, and Leviton's *Foundations of Evaluation,* Weiss is one of the seven people and the only woman whose work is discussed, making her in effect the "Founding Mother" of evaluation.

■■ WESTAT

Westat is an employee-owned research corporation serving agencies of the U.S. government, as well as businesses, foundations, and state and local governments. This company, located in Rockville, Maryland, and formed in 1961, is a major contract research and evaluation organization in the United States. In addition to their contributions as a statistical survey research organization, Westat contracts for custom research and program evaluation studies across a broad range of subject areas. Westat has technical expertise in survey and analytical methods, computer systems technology, biomedical science, and clinical trials.

—*Jeffrey G. Tucker*

▪ WESTED

WestEd is a nonprofit research, development, and service agency. The agency traces its history back to 1966, when Congress created a network of regional educational laboratories. In 1995, two of those original laboratories (Far West and Southwest Regional Laboratories) joined forces to form WestEd. WestEd serves Arizona, California, Nevada, and Utah, but the laboratory's work also extends throughout the rest of the United States, as well as internationally. WestEd work focuses on learning at all stages of life—from infancy to adulthood, both in school and out. WestEd's evaluation research program includes evaluation studies, program design and policy formation, and professional development and training.

WESTERN MICHIGAN UNIVERSITY EVALUATION CENTER. *See* EVALUATION CENTER

▪ WHITMORE, ELIZABETH

(b. 1939, Newton, Massachusetts). Ph.D, Cornell University; M.S.W., B.A., Boston University.

There have been two main influences in Whitmore's life as an evaluator. One has been her background in social work, both as a practitioner and as an educator. This has pushed her to continually focus on connecting practice and theory and to deepen her understanding of the effects of contextual factors on people's daily lives. It has helped her take the larger (social, political, cultural, economic) context into account when conducting evaluations. Her social work training has also reinforced the practical aspects of theory, the "So what does all this mean in terms of practice?" aspect.

The primary influence for Whitmore was her introduction to participatory action research, which she encountered in the early 1980s when she visited the Highlander Research and Education Center (in New Market, Tennessee). From her experiences at Highlander, Whitmore carried away ideas about people being the experts in their own lives and the democratization of knowledge creation and incorporated them into her own evaluation practices. At Cornell University, she was taught a variety of evaluation models, the vast majority being quantitative and based in fairly conventional social science theory. At that time, the stakeholder model was brand new and was seen as an exciting innovation in the field. Whitmore, being J. Greene's first graduate student at Cornell, claims that Greene's "mentoring was (and is) tremendously valuable for me. Our discussions about the role of empowerment in evaluation and the complexities of actually practicing participatory evaluation played a crucial role in helping me to clarify my thinking." It seemed quite natural to apply her learning from Highlander to ideas of stakeholder evaluation. Her contributions in this area helped to create and advance the field of participatory evaluation.

She is Editor of the Participatory Evaluation issue of *New Directions in Evaluation* (Vol. 80, Winter 1998). Over the years, she has conducted a number of evaluations using participatory evaluation. She has also been active in discussions of feminism in evaluation and was one of those involved in initiating the Feminist TIG at AEA.

▪ WHOLEY, JOSEPH S.

Ph.D. Philosophy, M. A. Mathematics, Harvard University; B. A. Mathematics, Catholic University.

Wholey is Professor of Public Policy and Planning at the University of Southern California. A leading authority in performance measurement and program evaluation, Wholey is Senior Advisor for Evaluation Methodology at the U.S. General Accounting Office. He is a former Deputy Assistant Secretary, U.S. Department of Health Measurement and Human Services; Director of Program Evaluation Studies for the Urban Institute; and President of the Evaluation Research Society. He also chaired the Virginia Board of Social Services, the Washington Metropolitan Area Transit Authority, Hospice of Northern Virginia, the Arlington County Board, and the Arlington Partnership for

Affordable Housing. Wholey is a member of the National Academy of Public Administration.

In addition to his work on performance measurement, Wholey is one of the evaluation theorists exploring and explicating the idea of evaluability assessment. Recently he headed a review of the Government Performance and Results Act to be used by federal programs to help them improve the effectiveness of their services. His work has contributed to developing information for agencies that will encourage greater internal use of outcome information by making program improvements.

He is the author of *Organizational Excellence; Evaluation and Effective Public Management; Evaluation: Promise and Performance; Zero-Based Budgeting and Program Evaluation;* and *Evaluation and Effective Public Management* and coauthor of the *Handbook of Practical Program Evaluation, Improving Government Performance, Performance and Credibility,* and the federal evaluation policy.

▓ WILDAVSKY, AARON B.

(b. 1930, Brooklyn, New York; d. 1993, Oakland, California). Ph.D. Yale University; B.A. Brooklyn College.

At the time of his death, Wildavsky was the Class of 1940 Professor of Political Science and Public Policy and a member of the staff of the Survey Research Center at the University of California at Berkeley, where he had taught since 1962. He had also been Chair of the Political Science Department and founding Dean of the Graduate School of Public Policy. Previously, he had taught at Oberlin College and was briefly President of the Russell Sage Foundation. He held honorary degrees from Brooklyn College, Yale University, and the University of Bologna. He served as the President of the American Political Science Association and was a Fellow of the American Academy of Arts and Sciences, the National Academy of Public Administration, and the Center for Advanced Study in the Behavioral Sciences.

Wildavsky was the author or coauthor of more than 39 books and a great many articles and reviews. His works spanned many disciplines, including the budgetary process; policy analysis; political culture; foreign affairs; public administration; comparative government; presidential elections; and the crafts of

teaching, research, and administration in political science. Many of his books have greatly influenced the field of political science, especially *The Subfield of Implementation* (with Jeffrey Pressman) and *The Private Government of Public Money* (with Hugh Heclo). The American Society of Public Administration named his book *Politics of the Budgetary Process* the third most influential work in public administration in the last 50 years. He has received many prizes and awards from a variety of organizations, including the 1981 Paul F. Lazarsfeld Award from the American Evaluation Association.

▓ WORLD BANK

The World Bank's mission is to fight poverty and improve the living standards of people in the developing world. It is a development bank that provides loans, policy advice, technical assistance, and knowledge-sharing services to low and middle income countries to reduce poverty. In 2003, the World Bank provided $18.5 billion and worked in more than 100 developing countries, which provided support for education, health, debt relief, biodiversity, infrastructure (such as water, transportation, power), and conflict resolution.

The Operations Evaluation Department is an independent unit within the World Bank that was created in 1970 by then World Bank President Robert McNamara. The unit reports directly to the bank's Board of Executive Directors, assessing what works and what does not, how a borrower plans to run and maintain a project, and the lasting contribution of the bank to a country's overall development. The goals of this department's evaluations are to learn from experience, to provide an objective basis for assessing the results of the bank's work, and to provide accountability in the achievement of its objectives. As with many large funding agencies, this internal evaluation examines both programs of funding (for the World Bank, this means looking at assistance programs at the country level) and particular funded projects. The department's evaluation tools are project reviews, country assistance evaluations, sector and thematic reviews, and process reviews.

Agencies such as the World Bank have a substantial presence throughout the developing world, and therefore their strategies for evaluation have had substantial influence on not only their primary mission but on the nature of evaluation in those same countries.

Further Reading

Picciotto, R. (2002). Evaluation in the World Bank: Antecedents, methods, and instruments. In J. Furubo, R. C. Rist, & R. Sandahl (Eds.), *International atlas of evaluation.* New Brunswick, NJ: Transaction.

WORLD CONSERVATION UNION (IUCN)

The World Conservation Union (IUCN) includes 140 member countries including more than 70 states, 100 government agencies, and 750 NGOs. Since 1948, the databases, assessments, guidelines, and case studies prepared by IUCN's global membership, commissions, and secretariat are among the world's most respected and frequently cited sources of information and reference on the environment. In the 1990s, the IUCN developed its monitoring and evaluation initiative to provide evaluation support to regional and global managers at project, program, senior management, and governance levels. Its aim is to improve skills, knowledge, learning, and institutional capacities in monitoring and evaluating the relevance, effectiveness, accountability, and efficiency of IUCN's program.

Further Reading

IUCN, the World Conservation Union. (2003). *About IUCN.* Retrieved June 24, 2004, from http://www.iucn.org/about/index.htm

WORTH

Worth is an outcome of an evaluation and refers to the value of the evaluand in a particular context, as opposed to the evaluand's intrinsic value, which is its *merit.* Worth and merit are not dependent on each other, and an evaluand (e.g., a doctor) may have merit (she is a highly skilled cardiologist) but have little worth (the hospital needs an anesthesiologist). The opposite is also the case (the hospital has found an anesthesiologist but not a very good one). The worth of an evaluand requires a thorough understanding of the particular context as well as the qualities and attributes of the evaluand.

WORTHEN, BLAINE R.

(b. 1936, Utah). Ph.D. Educational Psychology and Research, The Ohio State University; M.S., B.S., University of Utah.

Worthen is Professor of Psychology at Utah State University and previously held faculty positions at The Ohio State University and the University of Colorado. A career evaluator, he was Director of Research and Evaluation at Northwest Regional Laboratory (with responsibility for directing federally mandated evaluations in 17 states) and Director of the Western Institute of Research and Evaluation (an evaluation-contracting organization that has conducted over 350 evaluations for local, state, and national clients, such as the W. K. Kellogg Foundation and the U.S. Air Force).

Worthen has contributed significantly to conceptions of evaluation that have emerged in the past 40 years. He was the senior author, in 1973, of one of the first comprehensive evaluation texts, *Educational Evaluation: Theory and Practice* (with James R. Sanders). This text was the first to review and analyze seminal evaluation thinking. Its sequel in 1987, *Educational Evaluation: Alternative Approaches and Practical Guidelines* (with James R. Sanders), summarizes and categorizes all of the extant evaluation theories and models into a conceptual structure. The expanded 1997 edition of this text, *Program Evaluation: Alternative Approaches and Practical Guidelines* (with James R. Sanders and Jody L. Fitzpatrick), extends program evaluation to all fields, and the fourth edition includes more recent, inclusive advocacy and empowerment evaluation theories. In these texts, Worthen has promoted an eclectic multimethod approach to evaluation, foreshadowing more recent proposals for mixed-methods evaluations. Primary influences on his conception of evaluation include Egon Guba and Michael Scriven.

Also the author of numerous professional articles and texts on various practical and applied evaluation issues, Worthen was the senior author of *Evaluating Educational and Social Programs* (with Karl R. White, 1987) and *Measurement and Evaluation in the Schools* (with Walter R. Borg and Karl R. White, 1993). Many evaluation practitioners have adopted his simple steps for designing and conducting evaluations. As Editor of the *American Journal of Evaluation* and *Evaluation Practice,* Worthen has contributed to many important dialogs about issues confronting the evaluation profession, including recent debates about certification of evaluators.

In 1997, he received the American Evaluation Association's Myrdal Award for Outstanding Evaluation Practitioner. He had previously received the American Educational Research Association's Best Evaluation Study award.

Throughout his career, Worthen has been actively involved in preparing future evaluators. In that role, he directed Utah State University's Research and Evaluation Methodology doctoral program (one of four evaluation training programs NSF selected to train evaluators for NSF projects). He also mentored the recipient of AEA's Guttentag Award in 2000 for Most Outstanding Young Evaluator. He has directed more than 200 evaluation workshops and seminars for national professional associations and the Evaluators' Institute.

Worthen's top priorities are his family and his faith, and his favorite pastimes are art, writing poetry, and reading C. S. Lewis and Neal A. Maxwell.

⊞ WYE, CHRISTOPHER G.

(b. 1942, Washington, DC). Ph.D., M.A., Kent State University; B.A., Parsons College.

Wye is Founder and Director of the Center for Improving Government Performance at the National Academy of Public Administration, which offers technical assistance and consulting services regarding strategic planning, performance measurement, and performance-based management. As a recognized expert on performance-based management, Wye spent 20 years in the Senior Executive Service of the federal government, leading policy, evaluation, monitoring, and management functions. Since he joined the National Academy in 1991, he has established not only the Center for Improving Government Performance but the Performance Consortium, a group of more than 30 federal agencies that have joined under the academy's auspices to support effective implementation of the Government Performance and Results Act. The Performance Consortium provides a venue for peer-to-peer exchange of good practices through an annual program of workshops, discussion forums, conferences, and practice papers.

Wye's career-long interests have been policy analysis, program evaluation, and performance measurement. He has a concentrated focus on short-term, low-cost methodologies employed within existing time frames and budgets and designed specifically to facilitate utilization.

He has authored numerous articles and edited collections. Wye was cochair of an American Evaluation Association review of evaluation in the federal government in the mid-1980s and one of the principal architects of the American Evaluation Association's Guiding Principles for Evaluators. Wye served on the Board of Directors of the American Evaluation Association and is a University Fellow of Kent State University and a National Endowment of the Humanities Fellow.

He received the American Evaluation Association's Gunnar Myrdal Award for Government Service (1989), the Louis Pelzer Award from the *Journal of American History* for his 1972 article "The New Deal and the Negro Community: Toward a Broader Conceptualization," and the Presidential Rank Award for Senior Executive Service to the U.S. Government.

Author Index

Subject Index

Entry titles and corresponding page numbers are in **bold.**